Grappling Glory

Celebrating a Century of Minnesota Wrestling & Rassling

by
Ross Bernstein

NODIN PRESS

"Grappling Glory: Celebrating a Century of Minnesota Wrestling & Rassling"
by Ross Bernstein

WWW.BERNSTEINBOOKS.COM

ISBN#: 1-932472-31-2

Published by Nodin Press • 530 North Third Street • Minneapolis, MN 55401 • (612) 333-6300

Printed in Minnesota by Bang Printing , Brainerd
Proofread by Joel Rippel

PHOTO CREDITS:

Photos by Mike Lano, wrealano@aol.com: 11, 148 (Norris), 151 (Goldylocks), 155 (Lynn), 156 (Nord), 161 (Lane), 162 (Madusa),
165 (Holly & Koloff), 167 (Beverlies), 169: (Flair), 171 (Norton), 172 & 187 (Waltman), 174 (Benjamin), 182 (Szopinski)
Photos by Brian Bukantis: 11, 125, 127-134, 136-139, 145-148, 151-152, 155, 157-159, 162, 166-169, 175-178, 182-183, 186
Minnesota Historical Society: 122, 123, 125-127, 131, 143, 161, 174
Minnesota State High School League: 14, 16-40
University of Minnesota: 6, 8 12-13, 64-74, 109, 114-115, 143, 188-193
The Guillotine: 48, 53, 62, 95
Tim Cortes: 4
University of Michigan: 47
Iowa State University: 62
University of Minnesota-Duluth: 101
Bemidji State University: 102
St. Cloud State University: 79
Winona State University: 103
Minnesota State University. Mankato: 75-78
University of Minnesota Morris: 99-100, 120-121
Minnesota State University, Moorhead: 96-98
Southwest State: 99
Augsburg College (Don Stoner): 50, 83-90
Concordia College: 90
St. John's University: 92, 94
St. Thomas University: 95, 108, 111
John Vraa: 106
Brad Rheingans: 110, 132, 187
Adnon Al-Kaissy: 135, 172-173
Joe Laurinaitis: 180
Jeremy Borash: 183
George Schire: 184
Elizabeth Crouch: 59
USA Wrestling: 99, 112
*Photos from the respective individuals themselves: 46-61

*(*Some photos were acquired from various university and sports related web-sites, thanks to you for your help in acquiring those!)*

ACKNOWLEDGEMENTS:

I would really like to thank all of the people that were kind enough to help me in writing this book. In addition to the countless pro,
college and university sports information directors who I hounded throughout this project I would like to sincerely thank all of the more
than 100 gracious people who allowed me to interview them. In addition, I would particularly like to thank my publisher, and friend,
Norton Stillman. Thank you for your continued support.

Tim Cortes	Paul Allan	Sarah Burhau	Brian Bukantis	Dick Black	John Wodele
Jesse Ventura	Anne Abicht	Gordon Slaybau	Mike Lano	Scot Davis	Ron Malcolm
Verne Gagne	Bob Nygaard	John Toren	Jim Beshey	Jim Jackson	Don Dravis
J Robinson	Troy Andre	Doug Reese	Jeff Beshey	Joe Burns	Elizabeth Crouch
George Schire	Brian Curtis	Gary Abbott	Eddie Sharkey	Bill Irwin	Julie Arthur-Sherman
Joel Rippel	Larry Scott	Jeremy Borash	Todd Okerlund	Dan Chandler	Kay Brausen
Randy Johnson	Kelly Loft	Larry Hennig	Gene Okerlund	The Koslowskis	Norman Borlaug
Don Stoner	Mike Herzberg	Joe Laurinaitis	Alan Rice	Brandon Paulson	Stan Kowalski
Jim Cella	Jen Walter	Adnon Al-Kaissy	Jack Eustice	John Grygelco	Wally Johnson
Mike Hemmesch	Ann Johnson	Brad Rheingans	Spencer Yohe	Bill Sutter	Todd Rendahl
Don Nadeau	Howard Voigt	Greg Gagne	Don Meyers	Robb Norman	*H.J. Pieser
Gene McGivern	John Vraa	Buck Zumhofe	Jim Short	Dee Woodard	

For Sara and Campbell, the two loves of my life...

COVER PAINTING BY TIM CORTES

I would especially like to express my gratitude to renowned sports artist Tim Cortes for allowing me the privilege of showcasing his newest masterpiece on the cover of my new book. I couldn't be more pleased with the final product and simply can'tthank him enough for all of his hard work. If you would like to purchase a signed, limited edition print of it, please check out his web-site or contact his studio in Duluth for details.

One of the nation's premier photo realism artists, Tim Cortes uses colored pencils as his preferred medium. Hundreds of his collectible lithographs have been sold throughout North America and his clients are a venerable who's-who of American sports. From Shaquille O'Neal to Mark McGwire and from Wayne Gretzky to Troy Aikman, Cortes has been commissioned to create countless commemorative works of art over the past two decades.

Cortes' paintings have also been featured in numerous venus around the world, including: the US Hockey Hall of Fame, Franklin Mint, Kelly Russell Studios and Beckett's Magazine, as well as on trading cards, pro sports teams' game-day programs, and in various publications. Known for his impeccable detail, Cortes has dedicated his life to the pursuit of celebrating the life and times of many of the world's most famous athletes and the sporting events in which they play.

Cortes grew up in Duluth, where he later starred as a hockey goaltender at Duluth East High School. After a brief stint in the United States Hockey League, Cortes went on to play between the pipes for two seasons in the mid-1980s for the University of Minnesota's Golden Gophers. Cortes then decided to pursue his passion of art and sports full-time, and enrolled at the prestigious Minneapolis College of Art and Design. He has been painting ever since!

Presently, Tim lives in Duluth with his wife Kathy and their two children. He continues to play senior hockey and also gives back by coaching both youth football and hockey. In addition, in 2002 Tim was named as the goalie coach for the University of Minnesota-Duluth Women's Hockey program. In 2003 Tim even got to meet President George W. Bush when his three-time NCAA National Champion Lady Bulldogs made their third straight trip to the White House to be honored. *Hey, this guy really gets around!*

TIM CORTES STUDIO

Tim Cortes has created literally hundreds of different pieces of sports art over his illustrious 20-year career in the business, and tries to keep his print edition sizes low to ensure sellouts and collectability. His latest success, personalized sporting prints, has proven to be extremely popular among his dedicated clientele. From parents, to fans, to the athletes themselves, the concept of putting your own child's name, painted right on the piece itself, is truly all the rage.

From *"Game Winner,"* which enables the clients' NAME and NUMBER to be remarqued onto the back of a young goal-scorers hockey jersey; to *"Prized Possessions,"* which features a collection of hockey equipment with the last name of the client remarqued onto the front of the hockey helmet, to *"Local Legend,"* which features a vintage golf bag and clubs with the NAME and chosen COURSE remarqued onto a brass member's tag — they are sure to make the ultimate gift for the sports fan in your life.

If you would like to purchase a signed, limited edition print of any of Tim's works of art, please check out his web-site or contact his studio in Duluth — where you too can own a piece of sports history.

**TIM CORTES STUDIO
921 NORTH 40TH AVENUE EAST
DULUTH, MN 55804
(218) 525-4953**

WWW.TIMCORTESART.COM
MITCORTES@AOL.COM

"Local Legend"

"The Old Ball Game"

"Prized Possessions"

TABLE OF CONTENTS

INTRODUCTION

Welcome to "Grappling Glory," my newest book celebrating a century of both Minnesota's rich amateur wrestling history, as well as its colorful professional wrestling history. While these two surely make from some strange bedfellows, I can assure you that each has its own place in the book: amateur in the first half and professional in at the latter. I had to be careful in marrying two completely different entities for the project, always being sure to acknowledge that amateur wrestling is a sport, while professional wrestling is a form of sports-entertainment. There are many common denominators between the two, however, in that they both require athleticism, hard work and a lot of self-confidence to succeed. Both have also produced a whole bunch of extraordinary people over the years, and that is what this book is all about — celebrating those who have made Minnesota proud.

As a kid, raised in the southern Minnesota town of Fairmont, I, like so many others, grew up watching professional wrestling on TV — Verne Gagne's "All-Star Wrestling" to be specific. It was on like every 20 minutes, or so it seemed, and it was just inevitable that you would wind up watching it every now and then. When you flipped through the channels and saw Da Crusher pounding on some poor bastard, it was like the sirens calling you in. I mean you simply had to watch, it was nearly impossible not to. Now, I wasn't a huge fan by any stretch, but I did enjoy watching guys like Nick Bockwinkel beat the crap out of bums like Jerry Blackwell from time to time — and hey, who didn't? It was a total escape from reality, just pure, harmless entertainment at its best. Pro wrestling was all about good versus evil with over-the-top storylines that kept you coming back for more. And, the biggest thing about pro wrestling that made us all scratch our heads was the age old question, *"was it fake"*.

Back in the '70s, when I was a little kid, I for sure knew that Santa, the Easter bunny and the tooth fairy were all just a figment of my imagination, way before I ever dared mention the *"f"* word. That was taboo, you just didn't do it. Sure, it looked kind of *"not real,"* but who was I to say for sure. Later, when it was revealed by the powers-that-be, that it had all been a well orchestrated hoax with predetermined outcomes for all those years, it was a big let down. I didn't want to know that any more than I wanted to know how the magician saws the lady in half. So, when they *"outed"* themselves, surely there was going to be a mass-exodus of loyal fans never to be heard from again, right? Wrong. In fact, after it happened in the mid-1980s, the popularity of the business exploded — with television numbers that were off the charts.

And, with the genie out of the preverbal bottle, so to speak, pro wrestling evolved from the old-school characters of yesteryear to a new era of hulking athletes, capable of flying across the ring in a bedazzling symphonic soap opera of which we had never seen the likes of before. Still kickin' it old-school, however, was our very own American Wrestling Association (AWA), which was headquartered right here in Minneapolis, and had a cast of characters which performed throughout its "territory." As a result of its success over the years, the Gopher State had become a hot-bed for many of the industries' biggest stars. Guys like Hulk Hogan, the Road Warriors and even Jesse Ventura all got their start here, as did a legion of others who grew up with it and then made it a career.

But, when the business evolved from old-school to new-school, one man, Vince McMahon, the owner of the powerful World Wrestling Entertainment promotion, slowly took over. It was, in many aspects, life imitating art, in that a big New York bully was about to wreak havoc on our local boys who had done good. As a result, the AWA, along with nearly every other smaller regional promotion around the country, was driven out of business. The AWA hung in there like a champ for as long as she could, but finally turned out the lights in 1991 —

making it truly one of the saddest days on record for pro wrestling fans in the Land of 10,000 Lakes. Much of the book chronicles this epic battle, as well as the triumphs and tribulations of one man, Verne Gagne — the godfather of Minnesota wrestling.

Now, as for amateur wrestling, I was a big fan of that as a kid too. In fact, I wrestled up through junior high school, but had to quit after I broke my shoulder on a poorly executed fireman's carry. Oh well, I stuck with hockey after that, but certainly didn't miss sleeping in a garbage bag or spitting in a cup all day to try and make weight. *Those were the days!* But hey, my buddies and I still used to love going to the high school state tournament every year, watching all the action and just taking in the sights and sounds. Wrestling was huge in my home town and guys like my buddy, Joe Burns, whose dad was a legendary local wrestling coach, epitomized how much the sport was beloved down there. Joe, who has some of the best cauliflowered ears you will ever see, even had a dog named Mat. Get it, *"Mat Burns...",* how appropriate is that for a wrestling family? I love stuff like that!

Anyway, being from southern Minnesota we knew of the sport's illustrious history, much in the same way kids from the Iron Range know about hockey. And, while the Eveleths, Roseaus and International Falls of the world could claim the role of the underdog David, competing against the goliaths out on the ice at the state hockey tourney, so too could the Blue Earths, Goodhues and Owatonnas out on the mat. That was OUR deal.

In fact, one of the most interesting things I found in spending the last year researching the book, was why wrestling was indeed so popular in the small towns throughout southern Minnesota. For the answer, you have to head south, past Interstate 90, until you are deep into the heart of Iowa, where wrestling was and still is, like religion. They got hooked on the sport years before we did and really deserve much of the credit for getting it going up here. In fact, a great number of wrestlers who competed collegiately in Iowa, wound up getting their first teaching and coaching jobs throughout southern Minnesota during the 1930s, '40s and '50s. As a result, they introduced wrestling programs to a whole new generation of kids who would get hooked the same way that they did. You see, as coaches, they needed to find hard working kids who were tough and extremely self disciplined. Well, as luck would have it, the rural farming communities of southern Minnesota were just what the doctor ordered.

Having grown up in a farming community, I can tell you first hand that farm kids are not like the other kids. Nope. They are way harder working and way more responsible than I ever was. In fact, I was amazed at how much those guys did before I was ever even up in the morning — doing chores, feeding animals and working in the fields. On a family farm everybody pitches in, and that is just the way it is. Doing stuff like that all day will make you physically strong too, which is always a bonus when it came to a sport like wrestling. Families also had a lot of kids to help out, which is why a lot of the famous brother dynasties hail from down south as well. Plus, the beauty of wrestling was the fact that it didn't matter how big you were. Hey, to play football or basketball you need to either be big or tall, or you will eventually wind up on the sidelines. Well, in wrestling, the 98-pounder is just as valuable to his team as

The Pride of Fairmont..."Balc"

is the heavyweight, and there were plenty of small farm kids who were tough as hell too.

Other factors included economics, and the fact that it didn't cost very much to start a program. And, in small towns there was not a lot else to do, so everybody supported the team and rallied behind it as a source of community pride. Add that to the fact that they had no hockey to compete with numbers-wise (that didn't come to the region until years later), and it was a recipe for success. Coaches started youth programs and with that, presto, they had their own feeder systems leading right into their high school programs. Furthermore, I would add too that in wrestling, unlike most sports, there is not a lot of politics involved with who starts and who is benched. In wrestling, the kid who beats out every other kid in his weight class wrestles on the varsity. Period. So, in that regard, it is one of the most fair sports around, and certainly appealing for many a-typical kids who were not necessarily interested in playing traditional sports such as football or basketball.

You know, a great story to illustrate my theory involves a family which was synonymous with wrestling in Fairmont, the Balcoms. They were these huge farm kids who all worked on their dad's farm implement business and were just stronger than hell. Jeff was a year older than me and we played football together. He was a great guy and after winning the 1986 state high school championship as a heavyweight, even went on to wrestle for the Gophers. The dude was huge. It was either something in the well water on that side of town, or it was from lifting all of those tractors. Either way, he was stronger than an ox. Anyway, one of my favorite high school stories involves one of Balc's older brothers, who, incredibly, was probably even bigger and stronger than old Balc himself.

Well, one day, as the story allegedly goes, he was in his last class of the day at good ol' Fairmont High. It was in the Fall, harvest time, and like most country kids, he had to work on the farm after school. Anyway, as the teacher was writing on the chalkboard, a couple of gnarly dudes apparantly lit off a fire-cracker in class. Bang! But, when the teacher turned around and sternly asked who did it, of course no one said a word. While the teacher was pretty sure he knew, he told the class that they were not going to be dismissed until someone came forward to claim responsibility. Sure enough, the final bell rang, and sure enough, they all sat in their seats as the entire student body began leaving the building. Finally, after about 15 minutes, big Balc stood up and calmly walked over to the two guilty culprits. There, he picked them each up out of their chairs by the backs of their necks and said, *"He lit it, he threw it, and I'm goin' home to take out the damn crops!"*

You know, rural, blue collar farm kids are the best, and even though I was a *"city kid,"* I would like to believe that deep down, I am one of them. At least I hope so.

Anyway, back to my theory. As I was saying, Iowa transplants such as Rummy Macias, at Minnesota State University, Mankato, began coaching and having great success. As a result,

other wrestling coaches were fostered, and the concept of *"success breeds success"* was charging along full steam ahead. While this has gone wonderfully for our state over the years, another central theme in the book deals with the state-of-the-state of college wrestling today as well. While the Gophers are one of the premier programs in the country, and our youth and high school programs are considered to be amongst the best in the business as well, sadly, we are losing many of our small college programs. Economics and politics are issues that are discussed in depth in the book, with the basic message always being the same: how do we improve wrestling for the kids and ensure the sports' longterm existence. It is a very passionate subject that gets discussed at great length throughout the book.

Well, there you have it. From youth, to high school, to college, to freestyle and Greco Roman Olympic competition, Minnesota has seen it all. So many wonderful people have been a part of this sport and have done so much to give back to the next generation — which is what it is all about. Wrestling is a sport with roots that run back tens of thousands of years, to ancient civilizations, where men battled one another in what is considered to be the oldest sport known to man.

Today, meanwhile, wrestling has evolved into both an amazing amateur sport, complete with the most intense one-on-one battles that can be found in athletics; as well as an incredible form of entertainment, which has brought joy to millions of families in the form of professional rassling. Both are awesome in their own way, and yes, while they are two completely different animals, don't tell that to grappling legends such as Verne Gagne, Brad Rheingans or Brock Lesnar — all of whom have made the transition from the mat to the squared circle, gaining fame and fortune along the way.

All in all, the book came together beautifully, and I couldn't be happier with the finished product. I am truly honored to be able to bring so many wonderful people to life in it and honor both their legacies as well as their memories. While some of their stories are riveting, others are downright hilarious. And really, the book is as diverse as the people featured in it. That is what makes it so much fun. So, sit back, relax, and enjoy. I hope you have half as much fun reading about these amazing people as I did putting it all together. It was truly an experience of a lifetime.

CAVEAT EMPTOR!

(kâ´ve ât´ emp´tôr)

Hey, this is Latin for "Buyer Beware..."

I feel that it is necessary to issue a caveat of sorts for my new book, and in so doing, explain the parameters as to what it is all about. You know, I will be working on my 30th book this year, and it seems like every time I write a book like this, I get a whole boat-load of e-mail and letters from people telling me that they were appalled because I forgot to include so-and-so, or that they were shocked because their favorite *(fill in appropriate choice: player, coach, brother, father, sister, fourth cousin, gardener, etc.)* wasn't in there. With that, I want to formally proclaim right here and now that this book is not a complete history of both amateur and professional wrestling. Period.

Rather, it is a celebration of many of our state's greatest wrestlers, from both sides of the fence — from high school state champs to world heavyweight champs. There are so many outstanding men and women deserving of being in a book like this, and for those who I left out, I sincerely apologize. A book which would include all of them would probably take about 10 years to write and would come in at around 10,000 pages. That wouldn't be a book... it would be a major home appliance. Ouch!

Technically speaking, I should also mention that I did not list the names on all of the photo captions for the high school tournament teams in the index, it was too tedious a task. In addition, many of the records listed only last names, which made it even more difficult to record the history accurately. As for Catholic league history, I apologize to you as well, there was no information readily available for me to go with and rather than do bits and pieces, I left it out to focus on the public school side of things. On the pro side, the information was solid, but sometimes sketchy — I did the best that I could and I hope I got it right.

Overall, I chose to highlight a good sampling of local heroes, both native Minnesotans as well as the transplants, at the youth, high school, college and professional levels. Some were obvious choices while others might have been a reach. All of them, however, had a very unique and interesting story to tell, and all of them have touched the lives of countless people along the way. In all, I interviewed more than 100 people for the book, trying to include as many personal opinions and stories as possible.

When it was all said and done, the book came out very fun and informative in nature. I really tried to make it a true blend of history as well as a good discussion of current events, and hopefully I succeeded in my mission. While I am very proud of the finished product, I can assure you that I will not be winning any Pulitzer's any time soon. This is supposed to be a fun book to enjoy reading about history and sharing memories — nothing more, nothing less. You know, my books have oftentimes been referred to as the ultimate *"bathroom-books,"* which, as a sports author, you pretty much have to take as a complement I suppose!

Hey, it is not about the wins and losses, it is about the journey, and I hope your journey in reading my book was as enjoyable as mine was in bringing it all together. Thank you.

FOREWORD BY JESSE VENTURA

One of the most charismatic and colorful characters ever to hail from the great state of Minnesota, Jesse Ventura has lived a life most of us could only dream of. One of the most recognizable personalities in the worlds of sports-entertainment, politics and show business, he is, in a word, a legend. From the grappling ring to the political ring, he has seemingly done it all, and with a style all his own. So, who better to talk about the wonderful world of professional wrestling in the Land of 10,000 Lakes than our very own, Jesse Ventura…

Born, on July 15, 1951, James George Janos grew up in the blue-collar middle class South Minneapolis Longfellow neighborhood. His father, George, the son of a Slovakian immigrant, was a World War II hero who worked as a laborer for the Minneapolis street maintenance department. His mother, Bernice, who also served in World War II, was a nurse anesthetist. Janos enjoyed spending time with his family as a kid and quickly developed a love of sports. He would go on to star as a defensive end for the Roosevelt High School Teddies football team and was also the captain of the swimming team as well. In 1968 Janos' Teddies won the Minneapolis Conference and the Twin Cities Championship over rival St. Paul Central, it was as far as a team could go in those days before the advent of the state football playoffs. In high school, Janos was THE man, complete with a hot-rod GTO and plenty of pretty girls by his side.

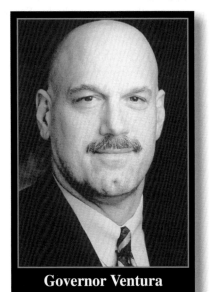

Governor Ventura

After graduating from high school in 1969, Janos decided to follow his older brother into the Navy to serve in Vietnam. There, he joined the special forces and was trained as a SEAL. As a member of the elite commando fighting group, he endured rigorous mental and physical training. An already tough S.O.B. suddenly got a lot tougher. In all, he would serve for six years in the Navy, four on active duty and two in the reserves, receiving an honorable discharge in 1973.

After a few months of chilling out in southern California, Janos returned home to Minnesota and attended North Hennepin Community College on the G.I. bill. There, he played football and also took a semester of wrestling — a phys-ed class which covered the basics of amateur grappling. You see, at the same time, he had been kicking around the idea of getting into pro wrestling. Janos loved to watch it as a kid and figured it might be worth a shot. An avid bodybuilder, the six-foot-five, 250-pound Janos, who was named "best physique" in his school yearbook, came out of the military looking buffed. So, he hooked up with local trainer Eddie Sharkey, who agreed to show him the ropes at his 7th Street Gym in downtown Minneapolis. The rest, they say, is history.

"I was a fan of pro wrestling as a youngster, like so many kids were during that era of the late '50s and early '60s," said Ventura. "I remember always watching it Saturday nights from 6:00 to 7:00 on TV, and then, if I was lucky, we would all pile into the car and head down to the old Auditorium to see the action live and in person. It was wonderful. The wrestlers were larger than life to me. Later, it shifted to Sunday mornings, where it aired the hour before the Vikings came on — which was the perfect lead-in. Those were the days, I remember them fondly.

"Later, when I went into the Navy, I kind of lost track of it. Then, I didn't become a fan again until I came home on leave one time just before I got out in 1973. I came home just before being discharged so that way I didn't have to cut my hair! Anyway, I came home and I remember turning on the TV and seeing

'Superstar' Billy Graham. I was hooked again, just like that. He was the guy who inspired me to wrestle, I just loved his style. Well, one night I had nothing to do so I went down to the Auditorium by myself to catch the show. There was one seat left in the front row and I took it. I will never forget seeing Billy (Graham) perform that night, he was amazing. It was the first time I ever saw him in person and it was at that point that I really started to think seriously about getting into the business. I just said to myself, 'I want to do what he does…', and I went for it.

"As far as getting started, that is an interesting story too. I had originally actually applied to Verne Gagne's wrestling school, but for whatever the reason he wasn't running a training camp that year. He wrote me a nice letter back though saying that my credentials, as a Navy Seal and all of that, were very good, and that I was welcome to attend his next camp. Well, I was very aggressive at the time and I wanted to get into the business right then and there. Well, I remembered seeing a little ad in the Minneapolis paper that said 'Pro Wrestling School: 7th Street Gym…'. So, a couple of college buddies of mine from North Hennepin, where I was going to school and playing football at the time as a 23-year-old freshman, went down there to check it out. We were all barbell nuts, always in the weight room together, and thought it would be fun.

"We got there and it was great. It was down on 7th and Hennepin, which was famous at the time for all the boxers and wrestlers who trained there. Scott Ledoux was just a young kid starting out back then and I would always see him down there too. So, I met with Eddie Sharkey and he agreed to train me for $500 bucks, which included a full-membership to the gym as well — which was also worth $100 bucks. That was big money back in those days. Eddie told me that he would train me to the point where I would be capable to go out anywhere in the country and have a match. So, I jumped in and trained with him for a couple hours a night, seven nights a week, for seven straight months.

"Eddie was a classic, a real throwback. He ran around with some real characters too. I remember my buddies and I used to take supplements for bodybuilding, not steroids or anything, just protein shakes and vitamins and that kind of thing. Well, Eddie used to sell us that stuff, usually from the trunk of his car, and let's just say that he could beat the prices in the stores dramatically, if you know what I mean. We never asked too many questions. He was great though, and those were fun times.

"Well, finally, when Eddie felt that I was ready, he sent out some pictures of me to a few different promoters that he knew. At that point, because I knew that I was going to be a villain, I needed to change my name — for safety reasons. That gave me a really unique opportunity. I mean we all go through life with names which are given to us by our parents. Well, I got to rename myself and I just always loved the name Jesse. It had a neat ring to it, a flamboyant sound, like 'Jesse James,' and I just thought it was neat. As far as Ventura, that was another story. When I first started out, my persona was going to be like a California surf-bum. I had been stationed in San Diego as a frogman back in the Service, and I knew every grain of sand on every beach up and down the southern California coastline. I ran in it, crawled in it and lived in it when I was out there, so it only made sense to me to go with something like that. So, one day I picked up a map of California and just started matching the name Jesse to the towns on the map. When I hit Ventura, bing!, the light bulb went off, and that was it. From that moment on I was Jesse Ventura. Anyway, a promoter from Kansas

City called shortly thereafter, and that was how I started my professional wrestling career."

Ventura made his ring debut in 1975 in the NWA's Central States territory, a smaller "training ground" promotion out of Missouri. It would be just a matter of time before he would take the world of wrestling by storm, emerging as a major force in the Central States and then heading to Portland's Pacific Northwest Wrestling territory after that. There, he twice wore the Pacific Northwest Heavyweight title belt and also captured five PNW Tag Team championships as well.

"One of the funniest stories of my career happened when I was out in Portland and wound up wrestling Jimmy 'Superfly' Snuka, in a 'Loser-Leaves-Town' match," he said. "That was a standard ploy the promoters would do back then when a guy was ready to move on to any one of the other 26 territories to wrestle. Whenever someone was leaving they would build up a big match to where the loser had to pack up and get out of Dodge, literally, and the fans loved it. Well, the night after I beat him a bunch of huge Fijians showed up at my place and they thought it was all legit. They didn't know it was all part of the act and they wanted to beat the #$%@ out of me! Apparently, Fijian blood runs pretty deep. They were pissed that I had beaten their guy and that he was now going to have to leave town. I survived, but that was something else, let me tell ya."

By 1978, Ventura had paid his dues and was ready to hit the big time. So, he moved home to Minnesota, where he joined Verne Gagne's American Wrestling Association (AWA). There, he gained a lot of national television exposure and emerged as one of the industries' biggest rising stars. With his over-the-top attitude and flashy outfits, which included dark shades and feather boas, the fans loved him. He was also a great athlete, and with his ripped biceps, he gained instant credibility with the veteran grapplers. And, with his "Body Breaker" finishing move, he was a force in the ring. He would eventually partner with manager Bobby "The Brain" Heenan and before long was wrestling the top names in the business.

That next year Jesse "The Body" Ventura, as he was now known as, teamed up with another young star-in-the-making, Adrian Adonis, and together they made up the "East-West Connection," winning the AWA World Tag team title on July 20, 1980. The two were billed as the top heel, or bad-guy, draw in the territory and were packing houses wherever they went. A year later, however, Ventura decided to leave the AWA for the greener pastures of Vince McMahon's World Wrestling Federation (WWF).

"As for leaving and moving on to work for Vince, that was a very unique time in the business," said Ventura. "At that point and time in my career I had been wrestling for 10 years and I was really frustrated. So, for me it was a last hurrah. I thought, you know what, Vince has this idea and if it fails we are going to get blackballed and none of us would ever work again — because they (the other promoters) made that very clear. But, for me, at that point in my career, I figured that if I didn't work again that was OK. The grind of it all had certainly taken its toll at that point, so I figured why not give it a shot? There was not going to be any gray area with it either, it was going to be a big success or a big failure. But that was a risk I was willing to take at the time. I have always felt that you will never be successful in life unless you are willing to take a gamble. I was up for a new challenge and in hindsight it was a great move. There were some money issues too, but needless to say, we were successful at a level they never comprehended.

"In my opinion the reason why the AWA ultimately went out of business years later was because Verne Gagne didn't know, tactically, how to fight a war. And even though they were not fighting with weapons, make no mistake about it, it was a war. The big mistake Verne made was not securing his own territory before invading his opponents'. You have to protect your backyard first and foremost, and I don't think he did that. The fact that he chose to expand at that time, told me that his ego got in the way of him. When Vince came in here, to Minnesota, Verne responded by going into New York. Well, it killed him. He didn't have the manpower,

he didn't have the staff and he just wasn't prepared to do it. It drained his bank account. To me it was a gross miscalculation on his part. He should have simply continued to run his territory as it was and solidify what he had, rather than expand the war when he clearly wasn't prepared to do it."

In 1983, Ventura twice defeated Memphis legend Jerry "The King" Lawler for the Southern Heavyweight title. He would later tangle in a series of memorable matches with Andre the Giant and Hulk Hogan, which generated even more fan interest for him along the way. Finally, in 1984, Ventura got a big push and was all set to battle Hulk Hogan for the WWF World Heavyweight Championship. But, just before the event, Jesse developed a nearly lethal blood clot and was rushed to a hospital in San Diego. The years of constant punishment and pounding on his body had finally caught up with him. Fearing the worst, he decided to retire from active competition, rather than risk permanent injury. It was a major blow for one of the business' top personalities who was clearly at the top of his game.

"You know, the traveling in this business was so tough and it got to be a real grind," he said. "My frequent flyer mileage on Northwest Airlines was in the millions. The only good part about that was the fact that every Christmas I just gave out free tickets to everybody. Seriously though, it was hard on me and my family. I remember flying 28 days one August alone, and that was just crazy. In fact, that was right before I got sick, and I am sure that all of that travel had something to do with my pulmonary embolism."

Not ready to hang it up completely, however, Ventura spun the incident, claiming it was "due to being exposed to Agent Orange in Vietnam." With that, he entered the next phase of his professional career, becoming a color commentator for the WWF. As a heel announcer, Ventura's personality shined brightly. Whether it was with Gorilla Monsoon doing WWF Pay Per Views, the NBC Saturday Night Main Event Show, or doing ringside announcing with Mean Gene Okerlund, he was a huge hit. With his "call it like I see it" brash attitude, his distinctive deep voice, and his dry sense of humor, the fans loved to hate him — which made his popularity soar even higher. And, he never fully retired from the ring either, still finding time to compete in occasional six-man tag team matches, which weren't as physically demanding or dangerous.

"I suffered a pulmonary embolism the night before I was supposed to wrestle Hulk Hogan," he said. "We were all set to travel around the world battling one another, but I wound up spending a week in the intensive care unit out in a San Diego hospital instead. I can't tell you how much money that cost me, not being able to tour with him. But, I am a believer that things happen for a reason and it opened the door for other things, which were very positive for me. I faced a real dilemma at that point, being in the prime of my career, and then suddenly being told that I couldn't compete anymore. Like all athletes, you never think that it could end so abruptly, but it did. You start to think about what you are going to do from there. I mean you can't walk in to a company, like Control Data, apply for a job and put down 'professional wrestler' as your previous work experience. You wouldn't get very far. It was tough, I mean there ain't no pension in wrestling, le me tell ya. Anyway, because of that injury I wound up becoming an announcer, which led me to far greater things than I think I would have ever achieved by just being a wrestler.

"Anyway, I wound up calling my old friend Tom Ryther, the sportscaster from Channel 11," said Ventura. "I asked him about getting into the business and he set me up with his boss, who brought me over and gave me the opportunity to go out and actually do a real story. So, I went out and got Cyndi Lauper and we did a piece where she died my hair. It was great. Well, Vince McMahon actually saw it and wound up calling me right after that to get me on board. It was fate.

"Announcing was great. I had a lot of fun, especially with guys like Gene Okerlund. He was the best there was in the business and a real class guy. You know, Gene and I were great together. If there were ever two people who truly meshed, it was us. There was no oil and water there at all. He was the straight man of the act, and the perfect foil for someone like me. We needed each other to make it work. Both of us were great, but together we were even greater. Gene was just a real professional and was always up for trying anything, which always made it interesting. You know, I actually gave 'Mean Gene' his name too, and I was very proud of that. I used to call him 'Mean Gene the Hot Air Machine,' but that got to be too long, so it wound up being just 'Mean Gene.' Incidentally, I actually grew up listening to Gene on the radio too, back when he was 'Gene Leader,' the DJ at KDWB and WDGY back in the '60s, and his big thing was 'Follow your Leader…'. He has come a long way since then, that is for sure.

"We just had great chemistry together. I remember jumping on him one time about his son, Todd, who was playing high school hockey for Burnsville at the time, and they were just about to start playing in the state tournament that weekend. It was so perfect. We were doing pre-interviews for our show on Tuesday and those weren't going to play until Sunday morning, later that week. Anyway, I had no idea how Burnsville was going to do, but I speculated that they were going to do pretty well. So, I accused Todd of being a big hot dog out on the ice and just really laid into him about this and that on the interview. You know, to give Gene a hard time. Well, Todd ended up being the leading scorer in the state tournament and it fit just perfect. Me, the villain, riding Gene about his son not passing to any of his teammates and taking all the glory for himself, like father like son. Then, it aired that Sunday and it was just a riot!"

Meanwhile, with all of the television exposure he was receiving, it was only natural that Ventura find his way back to Hollywood. His big-screen debut came in 1986, when he co-starred as a tough commando in the sci-fi action flic, "Predator," alongside Arnold Schwarzeneggar. (His infamous line "I ain't got time to bleed" came from this movie.) The next year he did the futuristic action film, "The Running Man," which also starred Schwarzeneggar, and he would later appear in the blockbuster "Batman and Robin" as well. By the end of the 1980's, Ventura was a household name.

At about the same time, Ventura was having problems with WWF management over some financial issues and as a result, he was "let go." Jesse got the last laugh though, all the way to the bank.

"It's funny, when I sued McMahon in federal court it was Verne (Gagne) of all people, who was my star witness," laughed Ventura. "The WWF was pooh-poohing me, saying that announcers didn't mean anything. That was their tactic against me, that announcers were meaningless and that I could have been replaced by anybody. They proclaimed that the actual wrestling was what sold their product, but old Verne got up on the stand and said that wasn't true. He said it took a combination of many different things to sell it, just like professional football. Then he actually gave me what I considered to be a great compliment when he said, 'Jesse Ventura is to pro wrestling, what John Madden is to pro football.' I mean when the jury heard that it was all over. That put it into a context that they could relate to. Verne had a lot of credibility as an amateur and pro wrestler, and of course as a promoter, so that really helped my case. I will never forget asking him to testify on my behalf, after everything we had gone through. His famous quote to me was 'I hate Vince more than you, I'll do it…' How great is that!"

So, after giving Hollywood another shot, Ventura came back to wrestling, this time as a color commentator with Ted Turner's rival WCW, doing pay-per-views and Saturday night shows. Meanwhile, it was during this time that Ventura realized that he had the power to really make a difference. Inspired, he ran and won the mayoral election back in his hometown of Brooklyn Park. He finally got out of wrestling for good a few years later, to focus on politics and other business ventures. He would serve as mayor from 1991-95, championing crime reduction as one of his main platforms.

From there, Ventura became a successful radio talk show host in the Twin Cities on KFAN sports radio. In addition, he also

served as a commentator for the NFL's Tampa Bay Bucs and later with the Minnesota Vikings.

"When I got into announcing football games, that was a lot of fun too," he said. "It was fun for me because, again, it was conquering another thing that I was told I couldn't do. Football, to me, was easy because I had a good understanding of it, and I enjoyed it. So, that was a pretty smooth transition for me to go from wrestling to pro football."

It was on the radio, however, where Ventura could truly express his opinions on just about everything. The daily open forum which allowed "common people" to discuss the issues on his show was a huge hit. During that time, Ventura also kept it real by serving as a volunteer football coach at nearby Champlin Park High School as well.

Finally, after becoming so fed up with the "system," Ventura decided to do the unthinkable — he ran for governor. And, while many scoffed at his idea, he truly "Shocked the World" when he became the 38th governor of Minnesota on November 3, 1998. After running a low-budget grass-roots campaign, complete with his own line of action figures, Ventura, running on the Reform ticket, beat out two firmly established political figures in Attorney General Skip Humphrey and St. Paul Mayor Norm Coleman. Ventura's broad appeal, particularly to young voters, was the difference as he sparked a renewed interest in making government work better. With that, Ventura and his wife, Terry, along with their two children, Tyrell and Jade, became Minnesota's first family.

Ventura's victory was world-wide news and he even appeared on the cover of Time magazine. Over the next four years his common sense attitude proved both refreshing as well as controversial. The extremely opinionated Ventura always spoke his mind and literally changed politics as we know it. From the "Tonight Show" to "Hardball" to "Playboy," Ventura was everywhere during his tenure as governor, and the media "jackals" simply couldn't get enough of him.

He also did some controversial things during that time as well, including refereeing a pay-per-view wrestling match between "Stone Cold Steve Austin," "Triple H" and "Mankind" at the 1999 Summer Slam, which was held at Target Center in Minneapolis. He even later served as a color commentator for Vince McMahon's racy upstart XFL football league on NBC as well.

"Ironically, what is so hilarious about that whole thing is that Vince and I are closer friends today than we ever were when I was wrestling," said Ventura. "We get along great now, probably because it is a distant relationship, rather than a direct one. You know, it is funny. Over the years I wrestled against all the top names in the business and sold out major arenas across the country, yet, the biggest pay-off I ever received in my career was when I got back in the ring as a freaking referee!"

In addition, Ventura found time to pen two best-selling books, and even saw a network television movie made about his life. When it was all said and done, however, he decided not to run for a second term. He wanted to leave the game on his own terms, and that is exactly what he did.

"I still believe that one of the biggest problem in our nation today is career politicians," said Ventura. "I mean I could have been reelected as mayor, but I chose to do one term. I could have been reelected as governor, but again, I chose to do one term. I left being governor on my own terms and I am fine with that. The media could never understand how I could walk away from all that power, but I had my reasons, and I was not about to tell them. That, of course, really drove them nuts.

"You know, I would have to say that the biggest downside to my life right now is my relationship with the local media. Simply put, I will never speak to the Minnesota press ever again. They are terrible. I have been attacked by the media, personally, as have my children, so I have now made it a personal policy of mine not talk to them ever again. And they hate that. It drives them crazy.

"I learned a valuable lesson when I was governor and that was when you reach a certain level of notoriety, you can never, ever have a relationship, or do any interviews where you live. You have to keep that as your sanctuary, or you will not survive. I think Prince is brilliant that way. My view is that I am not going to give them any stories to earn them a living any more. Those days are over and I will not give them that satisfaction. I even have a few friends who have radio shows here, but I have told them that I won't come on their programs either. I am sorry. Because if I do, the other media, which is desperate to get a quote from me, will lift what I say and make stories out of it for their own personal agendas. It has happened before and it will happen again. So, in hindsight, seeing what me and my family have gone through, I wish that I would have taken that approach much earlier in my career. I still do plenty of national interviews, but nothing around here. I just can't trust them. I have been burned way too many times and won't go through that again. I will always put my family first, before any political aspirations, or anything.

"What angers me about it so much, and maybe it's my ego a little bit too, is that I am a local boy whose made good and all they want to do is slam me. I mean look at someone like Josh Hartnett, the young actor, they treat him like he is a saint: *'Young local kid from south Minneapolis makes it in Hollywood…'*. Well, hey, I am a local kid from south Minneapolis who made it in Hollywood and then made it all the way to governor. Yet, they view me with disdain and they trash me whenever they can. So, that is tough, but what are you going to do?"

After his tenure at the State Capital, Ventura returned to the private sector, where he went on to briefly host his own talk-show on the cable television network MSNBC, and later even taught as a Visiting Fellow at Harvard University, where he spoke on the virtues of third-party politics.

As for the business that made him a household name? Ventura acknowledges that it has changed quite a bit since his days in the ring, but he has not completely ruled out the possibility of a comeback.

"You know," he said, "people always ask if I will ever get in the ring again and my answer is always the same. If Vince puts the decimal point in the same spot, he can call me tomorrow! You never know, but I will say this, it was a pounding on your body. Some guys my age are still at it though, and God bless em'. Last Spring when I was inducted into the WWE Hall of Fame, I was talking with Ric Flair. He was a fantastic bump-man, and could always take a hit with the best of them. So, we got to talking and started doing some figuring. We figured that he probably takes at least three back drops in any one given match — that is where a guy throws you in the ropes, bends over, and then on your way back he catapults you up about six or seven feet in the air and you land flat on your back on the mat. OK, if you figure he wrestled 300 times a year, times three per match, for 30 years — that is over 27,000 back drops. I would challenge any reporter to take that kind of pounding and still call it fake. Now, was it choreographed? Certainly. You know, I love to refer to wrestling as ballet with violence. It is very artistic, like live theater, you just have to open your mind a little bit.

"As far as wrestling today being somewhat risqué? In my opinion, I think all of that is dictated by the different generations. Vince has always gone where the public leads him. He will push the envelope until the public tells him he has pushed it too far, then he will gradually reverse himself. That is his style and he has been very successful at what he does. In fact, if you have watched it lately, you will see that it features a lot more 'holds' now and they are going back to the old style a little bit. I think they are doing that because of all the injuries. The action is so intense now, with so much acrobatic stuff, that guys are just getting too beat up. He

works those guys hard, real hard. It will be interesting to see how that plays out though. I think that the crowds tuning in and attending the matches are very educated on what is going on in the ring now and they don't have the patience to see guys 'selling' holds for long periods of time like in the old days. They love the action, and that has been what has gotten them this far.

"You know, in my opinion, wrestling today, or at least the last five years or so, is a lot like the style that has been predominant in Mexico for the last 30 years. We used to laugh at it, yet here it is up here. One of my favorite stories ever in Mexican wrestling involved a match between a guy and the invisible man. How classic is that? It even sold out. They had a guy under the ring pulling strings to make the ropes move and then the wrestler just basically beat the hell out of himself for a while. The invisible man even won. Unbelievable. So, the point is that interesting storylines, and even 'fantasy' plot lines, work. The fans want more action and more stories, not the old cauliflowered eared style of days gone by. Today it is all about hype, about show business, and that is why it has been so successful."

On his life both inside and outside of the squared circle, Ventura is both optimistic and proud of his achievements.

"You know I am proud of the success that I have had both in and out of the ring," he said. "At the various stages of my life when I was focusing on so many different careers, they were all

The Body...

equally important to me. I mean I am extremely proud of my six years as a Navy Seal; I am proud of my 11 years in the ring; I am proud of the five years of broadcasting that I did; and beyond that I am extremely proud of the movies; the books; being a mayor and then the governor — I am proud of all of those things. I am also proud of being a father and husband too, because that is the most important thing in my life.

"Would I do it all over again? Sure, but there are some things I would have done differently. For instance, instead of renting apartments at every territory I went into, I would have bought a big mobile home for my wife and I. That would have been the way to go. No flying, no rent, just you and the open road. But, overall, I am very proud of my wrestling career. I never hid from it. I am glad that others within the business are not doing so today either, because I think it is a terrific business. Wrestlers should be looked upon as the athletes

that they are, and be respected for what they do, instead of being ridiculed by the media — just because their from of entertainment has predetermined outcomes. Hey, so does a Broadway play."

Today, Ventura is enjoying life with his first lady, Terry, at their home in Dellwood. He is taking each day on his own terms and is also keeping his options wide open for whatever opportunities may come his way down the road.

"I am just having a terrific time right now," he said. "I took up fishing again and I even lost 40 pounds when I was out at Harvard. So, I am back in shape and my waistline is under 40 inches for the first time in a long time. I am feeling pretty good. You know, I am just taking it all in and will see where it leads me. And, hey, even though my back feels like its 83, I am a young 53, so I have a lot of miles left on these tires."

From "Jesse the Body" to "Jesse the Mind," Jesse Ventura did it all. A man driven by the will to succeed, he has proven to be a hard-working, determined, yet unlikely hero we can all root for. Who knows, maybe one day soon we will be calling him "Mr. President," after all, he has hinted about running for the oval office in 2008. Stay tuned… do you suppose they allow feathered boas in the White House?

THE HIGH SCHOOL TOURNEY

Minnesota has a long and storied prep wrestling history with roots that run all the way down to… Iowa? That's right, and the genesis of how it all came to be is as amazing as the old state tourney herself. Interestingly, our high school wrestling success can be traced back to a single, one credit chemistry lab class, back in 1935 at the University of Minnesota. It was that class which caused a big conflict in the schedule of a young Gopher grappler by the name of Norman Borlaug. Borlaug, who graduated from Cresco High School in 1932, came to Minneapolis to wrestle and play baseball for the Gophers. Borlaug really wanted to play baseball, but because his chem lab was at the same time as baseball practice, he had to focus solely on wrestling.

Luckily for us, Borlaug would pour his heart and soul into growing the sport of wrestling in Minnesota, a state which at the time had no sanctioned state tournament whatsoever. At first, Borlaug learned the ropes from then Gopher coach Brian McKusick, a part-time University employee who had twice as many losses on his resume as he did wins. Borlaug could see that while there were many good athletes on the team at that time, the lack of a full-time coach who could recruit the top kids from the area had really taken a toll. In addition, he realized that without a successful high school program, like the one he had just come from down in Iowa, there could be no chance of his Gophers ever amounting to anything.

So, Borlaug talked to some University officials about the possibility of raising the funds necessary to hire a full-time coach. They reluctantly agreed. With that, he called up his old high school coach back at Cresco, a guy by the name of Dave Bartelma, and literally recruited him to come to Minnesota to take over. Bartelma, who was also the principal at Cresco, had just led his kids to five consecutive Northwest Iowa district championships along with a pair of state high school championships as well. Needless to say, he had himself a pretty good gig down there. But, he was willing to roll the dice, so he said yes. It would be a decision that would forever change the landscape of amateur wrestling in the state of Minnesota.

Bart, as he was affectionately known, took over in Gold Country in 1935, inheriting a team which had a grand total of just nine wins over the previous five seasons. Knowing that he was going to need a feeder-system, he immediately set out to lobby the Minnesota State High School League about the possibility of creating an annual state tournament. The league, which was already dealing with budget cutbacks following the Great Depression, was not keen on adding a new sport to their curriculum which had very little following at that point.

So, Bart set out to educate the masses. There were scattered wrestling programs here and there, but it was all basically club level at best. He knew that he had to popularize the sport, so he barnstormed throughout the state with his Gopher wrestlers by his side and put on wrestling clinics for kids, parents and potential coaches throughout from Goodhue to Grand Rapids. He spoke at assembly programs, board meetings and did whatever he could to gain his sport more notoriety. It was not always easy though, and he had to deal with a lot of adversity along the way. One of his biggest hurdles early on was convincing local mothers that amateur wrestling was nothing like professional wrestling — which was all that many of them knew of the sport at that point. Bart assured the mothers that "King Kong" Kashey, nor anybody else for that matter, would be body-slamming their little Jimmy or Johnny.

Norman Borlaug

Finally, in 1937, Bart convinced not the MSHSL, but rather the University of Minnesota, to agree to stage what would be considered as the first ever state high school wrestling tournament. Gopher Athletic Director Frank McCormick was a strong advocate of the University's wrestling program and saw the potential for creating a high school event which could only benefit his program in the future. With that, Bart sent out invitations and then set out to deal with the logistics of hosting the event, which was to be held at the U of M's Field House. For starters, he rounded up all of his Gopher wrestlers to serve as officials for the matches, and even rallied the students from his physical education classes to serve as runners, scorekeepers and timers. Everybody pitched in.

With that, it was announced that eight schools would be participating in the inaugural state tourney: Minneapolis Marshall, Minneapolis Washburn, Minneapolis Edison, St. Paul Central, University High School, Braham, Milroy, Osakis Minneapolis West and Hastings. From there, Bart laid down the ground rules, which were literally new and unique to each team that participated. The inexperienced young grapplers had only vague ideas regarding the "official" rules, seeing as they had very little formal coaching up to that point. Bart explained that the regulations "prohibited the use of the twisting hammerlock, the over-scissors, the strangle hold, full nelson, toe hold, body slam, bending or twisting fingers to break holds, or for punishment purposes, or any hold which is utilized for punishment pur-poses only. There was also to be striking, kicking, gouging, hair pulling, butting, elbowing, strangling, or any other maneuvers which endanger life or limb."

Furthermore, there were no re-strictions as to the number of wrestlers a school could enter either, and Minneapolis Marshall took full advantage of that loophole by entering 13 kids into just nine weight divisions: 95-pound, 105-pound, 115-pound, 125-pound, 135-pound, 145-pound, 155-pound, 165-pound and heavyweight, or unlimited. By no surprise, Marshall went on to win the tournament by scoring 40 points, while Osakis and Minneapolis West tied for runner-up honors with 23 points each.

Marshall was dominant, winning five of the nine individual weight categories, with four of those five earned by falls. Captain Jimmy Van Gorden, 95 pounds, kicked off the festivities by sticking Bob Welch of Milroy in just 50 seconds. Al Ledding was next at 105 pounds, followed by Ed Harlan at 115. Frank LeDuc then won the 145 pound crown, while Martin Furlong took the title at 165. The other four titles went as follows: Ray Kaufman (Mpls. West) 125 pounds; Max Hawkins (Osakis) 135 pounds; Ivan Johnson (Osakis) 155 pounds; and Leonard "Butch" Levy (Mpls. West) heavyweight. While the inexperienced contestants were often left clueless as to just how the officials were going to score their matches, it all seemed to work out. And, despite the fact that some of the spectators were confused if not bewildered over what took place, overall it was deemed as a big success. (The tourney paid instant dividends too when Butch Levy later announced his intentions to wrestle for the Gophers that next year. Levy, who would later emerge as an NCAA national champion as a heavyweight, also starred on the gridiron for the Maroon and Gold as well.)

Seeing the success of the tourney, the MSHSL then agreed to sanction the tournament from there on out. Said Bartelma of his hard work finally paying off: "It was indeed gratifying to know that high school wrestling had been initiated and that coaches were satisfied enough to urge that the tournament become an annual affair."

While the MSHSL took over from there, Bartelma then focused his efforts to the other side of the coin, creating an outlet for his graduating Gopher seniors to participate in so that they too could stay involved and even get into coaching at the high school level. With that, Bart initiated the Northwest Athletic Union wrestling tournament, which was first held at the Pillsbury Settlement House and later at the U of M's Farm Campus. AAU wrestling was all the rage during this era and gave kids opportunities to continue to participate in the sport.

(Bartelma started the Minnesota AAU wrestling program in 1938, only to see it terminated when he left the University in 1951 to become chairman of the Physical Education Dept. at the University of Colorado. Some 13 years later, however, a pair of former Gophers, Alan Rice and Verne Gagne started it back up as the Minnesota Amateur Wrestling Club. One of the most prominent clubs of its kind in the country, the Gopher Wrestling Club, as it was later renamed, would specialize in developing top Greco-Roman wrestlers from around the area, incredibly producing at least one wrestler on every U.S. world championship or Olympic team for more than 40 straight years.)

Meanwhile, Bartelma knew that he had to recruit coaches to get into the sport and he was brilliant in convincing many high school football coaches that wrestling would be a wonderful way to keep their top stars in outstanding game-shape during the off-season. He had a vision for taking the kids full circle and it would pay off down the road, big time. Ultimately, as his Gopher teams got better over the years, interest in the sport grew, and with that more kids went out for wrestling. It was a masterfully orchestrated plan. As the years went by, many of Bart's protégés went on to teach and coach, among them included: Stan Hanson, who went to Minneapolis Marshall, Joe Pazandak, who went to Minneapolis West, and John Malton, who coached at Minneapolis Edison. Eventually, other high school tourney alumni would do the same, including Mark Woodward of Osakis and later Robbinsdale, Sky Wilcox at Mound and later Austin, and Kermit Anderson who started out at Litchfield and then went to Mounds View.

To fill in the gaps, Bart even served as a "mission," going back to his native Iowa, where wrestling was extremely popular and didn't have to compete with hockey for kids during the winter, and recruited even more coaches. Among his finds were LuVerne Klar, Keith Young, Fred Stoeker, Gene Lybbert and Dick Black. Others would include Garth Lappin, who, in just nine years at Anoka, won two titles, placed third, fourth twice and fifth. Not bad! Perhaps his greatest catch, however, was Rummy Macias, who would serve as the head coach at Mankato State University. Rummy became a legend in southern Minnesota and developed more high school coaches than maybe anyone in the country during his tenure.

Long considered to be the "Father of Minnesota Wrestling," David Bartelma's vast wrestling knowledge combined with his contagious enthusiasm were the just the right ingredients to get it all started. Oh, and as for whatever happened to Norman Borlaug? Well, after reaching the conference semifinals in 1937, he went on to receive his master's and doctorate from the U of M in the field of plant pathology. (He also coached the Gopher freshman team during that time as well.) It would lead him down a path of studying genetics and agricultural technology, and after discovering a high-yielding disease-resistant form of wheat, he was

David Bartelma

awarded the Nobel Peace Prize. In fact, it has been estimated that he has saved more lives than any other person who ever lived on planet Earth. Not bad — it just goes to show what wrestling can do for a kid!

From those humble beginnings, so began our illustrious state tourney. She grew exponentially from there, and by 1941 it became necessary to have four regional tournaments. Marshall was the state's first power, winning the first four titles. Leading the way for Marshall was Jim Van Gorden, who, from 1937-40, won four straight titles at 95, 105, 125 & 145 pounds. Marshall was co-champs in 1940 alongside Robbinsdale, which then took over as the new kids on the block and went on to win six straight state titles of their own. They were an official dynasty, led by a kid named Verne Gagne, who won back to back heavyweight titles in 1942 and 1943. Gagne, of course, would later go on to win a pair of national championships at the University of Minnesota as well, while also doing double duty as a star lineman out on the gridiron.

During the World War II era, wrestling experienced a plateau in growth as most young coaches and many college aged kids were sent overseas. After that, however, the sport grew like crazy. By 1948 there were 35 teams competing and that total increased to 55 by 1954. Austin became the first outstate team to win a crown in 1948, signaling a shift in power perhaps from the Twin Cities to Southern Minnesota, where the sport was growing like wildfire throughout the small towns.

The next grappling powers of this era were Anoka, which won titles in 1949 and '50. The star of the Tornadoes was Dick Mueller, who won three state titles from 1949-51 and later went on to win a national championship for the Gophers. It is interesting to note that while Mueller was one of the state's best ever, he was widely considered to be weak from the standing position, while outstanding from the "down" position. A reason for this might have been because of the marginal facilities back in those days. You see, Anoka's workout area in their high school gym was extremely long and narrow, running along-side the basketball floor, and as a result, little practice could be held from the standing position.

Wayzata, which won three straight from 1951-53, was next, followed by tiny Blue Earth, which won three titles from 1956-58. Blue Earth's 1957 squad, meanwhile, will go down as one of the best of all-time, scoring a then record 65 points and even having all five of its qualifiers win state titles.

One of the most memorable state tourneys came in 1955, when Anoka's Dick Board won a referee's decision over Blue Earth's Don Dravis for the 127 pound title, thus giving the Tornadoes the championship in thrilling style. Helping out Dick to win the team title was his brother, Bob, who also took home the hardware at 120 pounds.

The state tourney's popularity was booming and suddenly found itself cramped for space at the University of Minnesota. So, in 1955 she moved south, where she set an attendance record of 3,123 at Mankato State Teachers College. By 1960 the crowds were standing room only, so to accommodate the growing number of fans, the tournament was moved to Gustavus Adolphus College. She remained in St. Peter for two years and then headed back to a new facility in Mankato, where, in 1966 the attendance figure reached a whopping 17,638. Hopkins was the team to beat of this era, winning a trio of state titles in 1963, 1967 and 1968.

By now, kids of all shapes and sizes

Verne Gagne

were enjoying the fact that wrestling required a full team effort, from the 98-pounder to the heavyweight. And, in addition to big kids and little kids giving it a shot, other kids with special circumstances also made history. Among them were a couple of inspiring champions who had to overcome physical handicaps to attain their goals. John Ross, who was blind, won the 133 pound title in 1953 for Minneapolis Marshall. Then, in 1959, Jerry Byers of Mankato won a pair of state titles at 95 pounds in spite of having only one foot. High school wrestling was all about heart, not about disabilities, and more and more kids were realizing that.

Another thrilling tourney came in 1964, when LuVerne Klar's Mankato squad finally got the monkey off his back after finishing as the runner-up on six previous occasions. That year Mankato was neck and neck with state power, Robbinsdale, which had nine contestants entered in the meet, compared to Mankato's five. They were tied at 34 points apiece after the first three rounds on Friday, and both schools qualified three wrestlers for the finals. The Robins had two entries in the consolation bracket, however, compared to Mankato's one, giving them the advantage. Well, as the drama unfolded it all came down to the wire with Mankato edging the Robins 44-43, thanks to Gary Rudenick, who somehow pinned Redwood Falls' three-time state champ Howard Leopold for the extra point.

At the end of the decade there were 275 teams participating in wrestling statewide. That same year the tournament was moved to St. Cloud, where it remained for two years, before being moved back yet again to the University of Minnesota — where nearly 25,000 fans came out to see the action. Finally, in 1970, the tournament was moved to St. Paul, where she set up shop in the plush new St. Paul Civic Center. There, the tourney got a makeover of sorts as well, moving to a new format which saw a two class dual team and individual competition

By the early 1970s wrestling was starting to move north. With the exception of Litchfield, Hibbing, and St. Cloud, nearly all the schools in the tourney up to this point were either from the Twin Cities or from Southern Minnesota. Wrestling had struggled to move into hockey country, but slowly but surely it was making its way westward and north, with schools such as Alexandria, Brainerd, Grand Rapids, Park Center and Olivia jumping onboard. It wasn't long before the local vernacular was replacing such terms as slap-shots, wristers and five-holes with new ones such as whizzers, cradles and full-nelsons.

In 1973 there were 338 schools participating in high school wrestling. Why was the sport growing in such popularity? Much of the credit should be given to the outstanding leadership which came from several key individuals who helped to grow the sport at the grass-roots level. Men such as Sky Wilcox of Austin, Harry Bachaus of Mound, Kermit Anderson of Litchfield and Mark Woodward of Robbinsdale were among those who did more than their fair share. And when they stepped aside, the next wave jumped right in, including: Klar, Prunty, Black, Kiffmeyer, Grygelko, Meyers, Board, Malcolm and many others.

It is also interesting to note that in the early days of the tournament there was no "team championship." In fact, teams which won titles did so based on individual tournaments and were declared champs based on rankings. Later, in the 1970s, the dual meet state tournament system came into effect which is what we see today. To better describe that genesis is the man who made it all come to fruition, Don Meyers.

"You know, one of the things that I am most proud of over my career was helping to create the 'team concept,' " said Meyers, who coached at Fridley High School for more than a decade. "One of the dilemmas with wrestling back in the 50s and 60s was the fact that as teams advanced into the district tourna-

ments, some kids got eliminated from their teams, and then even more got eliminated at the regions. As a result, just a few kids might have wound up on a team that went to the state tournament. In fact, in those days teams actually won tournaments with only three wrestlers representing the entire team. What it was doing was killing fan interest because they could no longer follow their hometown wrestlers. So, Ron Malcolm and I went to the High School League and got the ball rolling with regards to changing the system. We laid out a plan to change it and they agreed to implement it on an experimental basis. As a result, Minnesota became the first state in the nation to determine a high school wrestling championship under the team concept. Since then most of the other states followed at the high school level and even the colleges came around too and adopted a national dual tournament. While it was initially not well received by the coaches, the acceptance by the fans was overwhelming. Track and field also later followed suit with their 'true-team concept' as well. It changed the rules for the better and I was very honored to have played the lead role in getting that done."

Into the 80's and 90's wrestling continued to grow and expand. Small, outstate schools such as Staples and Canby would emerge as teams-to-beat, while Brainerd finally showed up on the radar to become northern Minnesota's first titlist. And of course, you can't talk about Minnesota wrestling without talking about the emergence of Apple Valley, which has become not only a superpower in Minnesota, where they have won an incredible 13 state titles since 1983, but also nationally, where they have been consistently ranked amongst the top programs in the country. In fact, Apple Valley's success has allowed them to even compete against the best of the best, a move which some insiders aren't too big on.

You see, high school wrestling is ever expanding, as evidenced by the fact that there is now a Final Four every year, an event sponsored by the National High School Coaches Association. The group brings together the four best high school wrestling teams in the country — at least according to the NHSCA rankings, and puts them together in a head-to-head tournament format. Included in the 2004 event was powerhouse Apple Valley, which was ranked No. 2 going in but ultimately lost out early on. The Final Four wasn't without its share of controversy though. In fact, the National Federation of State High School Associations (NFHS), says "such events run contrary to the purpose of high school sports and give prep sports the feel of their college or professional counterparts." Still, the NFHS does not wield the power to stop such independent organizations as well as their sponsors from organizing such events.

Well, our little tourney is all grown up now and even plays host to some 65,000 rabid fans who now make the annual trek to the Xcel Energy Center in St. Paul to watch it all go down. And what a time it is over there, taking in the sights and the sounds, and just being around other wrestling people. If you are a wrestling person, then you understand that statement perfectly well; if you are not a wrestling person, then no explanation is necessary. To those who love this great sport, nothing can compare. The lessons and values of hard work and determination which our kids learn out on the matt are things they will undoubtedly take with them for a lifetime. Hey, getting more and more kids the opportunity to compete so that they can have fun and create some memories which will last a lifetime — that is what this sport is all about. Then, if kids want to try to take it to the next level, and compete at either a junior college, division III, II or I school, more power to them. We should support them all and encourage them to also give back to the sport which gave them so much. If they do that, then old Bart's master plan back in 1937 will keep going, and his legacy will live for the next generation of kids.

Butch Levy

ALL-TIME TEAM STATE CHAMPS

1937	Mpls. Marshall	1983	Apple Valley (Class AA)	
1938	Mpls. Marshall	1983	Staples (Class A)	
1939	Mpls. Marshall	1984	Bloomington Kennedy (Class AA)	
1940	Mpls. Marshall & Robbinsdale	1984	Staples (Class A)	
1941	Robbinsdale, Mpls. Vocational & Wayzata	1985	Apple Valley (Class AA)	
1942	Robbinsdale	1985	Staples (Class A)	
1943	Robbinsdale	1986	Apple Valley (Class AA)	
1944	Robbinsdale	1986	Canby (Class A)	
1945	Robbinsdale	1987	Paynesville (Class A)	
1946	Robbinsdale	1987	Simley (Class AA)	
1947	Mound	1988	Canby (Class A)	
1948	Austin	1988	Simley (Class AA)	
1949	Anoka	1989	Simley (Class AA)	
1950	Anoka	1989	St. James & Foley (Class A)	
1951	Faribault & Wayzata	1990	Anoka (Class AA)	
1952	Wayzata	1990	Paynesville (Class A)	
1953	Blue Earth & Wayzata	1991	Apple Valley (Class AA)	
1954	Owatonna	1991	Paynesville (Class A)	
1955	Anoka	1992	Frazee (Class A)	
1956	Blue Earth	1992	Simley (Class AA)	
1957	Blue Earth	1993	Foley (Class A)	
1958	Blue Earth	1993	Forest Lake (Class AA)	
1959	Anoka	1994	Apple Valley (Class AA)	
1960	Alexander Ramsey	1994	Canby & Foley (Class A)	
1961	Robbinsdale	1995	Apple Valley (Class AA)	
1962	Owatonna	1995	Canby (Class A)	
1963	Hopkins	1996	Hastings (Class AA)	
1964	Mankato	1996	St. Michael Albertville (Class A)	
1965	Cooper	1996	Wheaton/H-N (Class B)	
1966	Albert Lea	1997	Apple Valley (Class AAA)	
1967	Fridley & Hopkins	1997	Hayfield (Class A)	
1968	Hopkins	1997	St. Michael Albertville (Class AA)	
1969	Cooper (New Hope)	1998	Dassel-Cokato (Class AA)	
1970	Caledonia	1998	Owatonna (Class AAA)	
1971	Albert Lea	1998	St. James (Class A)	
1972	St. James	1999	Apple Valley (Class AAA)	
1973	Fridley	1999	Frazee (Class A)	
1974	Minnetonka	1999	Jackson County Central (Class AA)	
1975	Fridley	2000	Apple Valley (Class AAA)	
1976	Albert Lea (Class AA)	2000	Jackson County Central (Class AA)	
1976	Canby (Class A)	2000	Paynesville (Class A)	
1977	Anoka (Class AA)	2001	Apple Valley (Class AAA)	
1977	Canby (Class A)	2001	Blue Earth Area (Class AA)	
1978	Anoka (Class AA)	2001	Goodhue (Class A)	
1978	Staples (Class A)	2002	Apple Valley (Class AAA)	
1979	Canby (Class A)	2002	Blue Earth Area (Class AA)	
1979	Fridley (Class AA)	2002	Frazee & Medford (Class A)	
1980	Bloomington Kennedy (Class AA)	2003	Apple Valley (Class AAA)	
1980	Goodhue & Staples (Class A)	2003	BOLD (Class A)	
1981	Albert Lea (Class AA)	2003	Litchfield (Class AA)	
1981	Staples (Class A)	2004	Apple Valley (Class AAA)	
1982	Brainerd (Class AA)	2004	Pierz (Class A)	
1982	Staples (Class A)	2004	St. Michael Albertville (Class AA)	

STATE CHAMPS: 1937-2004

(Source: MSHSL & The Guillotine)

1937 Team Champion: Mpls. Marshall
1937 Individual Champions:
95 - Van Gorden, Mpls. Marshall
105 - Ledding, Mpls. Marshall
115 - Harlan, Mpls. Marshall
125 - Kaufman, Mpls. Marshall
135 - Hawkins, Osakis
145 - DeLuc, Mpls. Marshall
155 - Johnson, Osakis
165 - Furlong, Mpls. Marshall
Hwt - Levy, Mpls. West

1937: Minneapolis Marshall

1938 Team Champion: Mpls. Marshall
1938 Individual Champions:
85 - Brakke, Milroy
95 - Rooney, Robbinsdale
105 - Van Gorden, Mpls. Marshall
115 - Swarts, Osakis
125 - Taychek, Mpls. Marshall
135 - Cecere, Mpls. Marshall
145 - DeLuc, Mpls. Marshall
155 - Johnson, Osakis
165 - Hatfield, St. Paul Central
Hwt - Levy, Mpls. West

1938: Minneapolis Marshall

1939 Team Champion: Mpls. Marshall
1939 Individual Champions:
85 - Hammes, Robbinsdale
95 - Barber, Mpls. Marshall
105 - Hastings, St. Louis Park
115 - Crofoot, St. Louis Park
125 - Van Gorden, Mpls. Marshall
135 - O'Neill, Mpls. Marshall
145 - Widstrom, Mpls. Marshall
155 - Fay, Mpls. Marshall
165 - Johnson, Mpls. Marshall
Hwt - Bowen, Mpls. Washburn

1939: Minneapolis Marshall

1940 Team Champions: Mpls Marshall & Robbinsdale (Co-Champs)
1940 Individual Champions:
85 - Hughes, Mpls. Marshall
95 - Humphrey, Robbinsdale
105 - Barber, Mpls. Marshall
115 - D. Lunman, Mpls. Marshall
125 - F. Crofoot, St. Louis Park
135 - Mato, Mpls. Marshall
145 - J. Van Gorden, Mpls. Marshall
155 - Berg, Mpls. Edison
165 - E. Priebe, Robbinsdale
Hwt - A. Smith, Redwood Falls

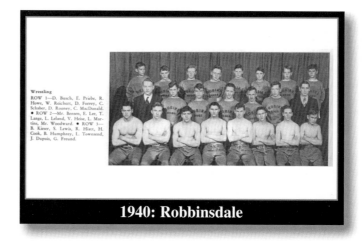

1940: Robbinsdale

1941 Team Champions: Robbinsdale, Mpls. Vocational & Wayzata (Co-Champs)
1941 Individual Champions:
85 - Pasicznyk, Mpls. Vocational
95 - Rand, Mpls. Vocational
105 - Humphrey, Robbinsdale
115 - D. Rooney, Robbinsdale
125 - F. Crofoot, St. Louis Park
135 - Hughes, Wayzata
145 - C. Hensel, Wayzata
155 - J. Jordan, Wayzata
165 - R. Howe, Robbinsdale
Hwt - K. Knutson, Austin

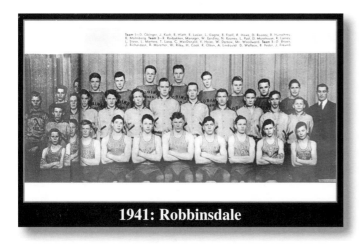

1941: Robbinsdale

1942 Team Champions: Robbinsdale
1942 Individual Champions:
85 - Obinger, Robbinsdale
95 - Tucker, Litchfield
105 - Steve Zarby, Mpls. Vocational
115 - Humphrey, Robbinsdale
125 - Widdowson, Mpls. Roosevelt
135 - Kuch, Robbinsdale
145 - Larson, St. Louis Park
155 - Hadley, Mpls. Vocational
165 - Gagne, Robbinsdale
Hwt - Cook, Robbinsdale

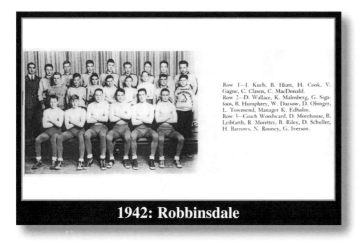

1942: Robbinsdale

1943 Team Champions: Robbinsdale
1943 Individual Champions:
85 - Sigafoos, Robbinsdale
95 - Dick Pierson, Robbinsdale
105 - Freund, Robbinsdale
115 - Finnemore, Mpls. Henry
125 - Leuer, Wayzata

1943: Robbinsdale

135 - Widdowson, Mpls. Roosevelt
145 - Toarangean, Mound
155 - C. Westlund, Robbinsdale
165 - Ahlberg, Mound
Hwt - V. Gagne, Robbinsdale

1944: Robbinsdale

1944 Team Champions: Robbinsdale
1944 Individual Champions:
103 - Forshier, St. Louis Park
112 - Dick Pierson, Robbinsdale
120 - Brantley, Austin
127 - Tucker, Litchtield
135 - Freund, Robbinsdale
138 - Leuer, Wayzata
145 - Geyen, Mound
154 - Palmer, Mound
165 - Roles, Robbinsdale
Hwt - Ahlberg, Mound

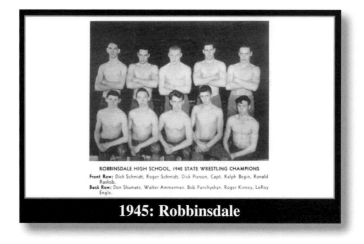

1945: Robbinsdale

1945 Team Champions: Robbinsdale
1945 Individual Champions:
103 - Jordan, Wayzata
112 - Nonnemacher, New Ulm
120 - Dick Pierson, Robbinsdale
127 - Dykhoff, Wayzata
135 - Rice, University High
138 - Shumate, Robbinsdale
145 - Roskob, Wayzata
154 - Goyen, Mound
165 - Gillis, Rochester
Hwt - Mattson, Mpls. Vocational

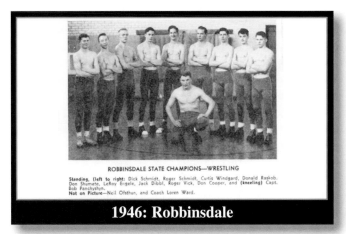

ROBBINSDALE STATE CHAMPIONS—WRESTLING

Standing, (left to right): Dick Schmidt, Roger Schmidt, Curtis Windgard, Donald Raskob, Don Shumate, LeRoy Engele, Jack Dibbl, Roger Vick, Don Cooper, and (kneeling) Capt. Bob Panchyshyn
Not on Picture—Neil Ofsthun, and Coach Loren Ward.

1946: Robbinsdale

1946 Team Champions: Robbinsdale
1946 Individual Champions:
103 - Ofsthun, Robbinsdale
112 - Cates, Litchfield
120 - W. Bearl, Anoka
127 - Sandgren, Austin
135 - M. Sweet, University High
138 - A. Rice, University High
145 - D. Shumate, Robbinsdale
154 - C. Windgard, Robbinsdale
165 - R. Panchyshyn, Robbinsdale
Hwt - Engel, Robbinsdale

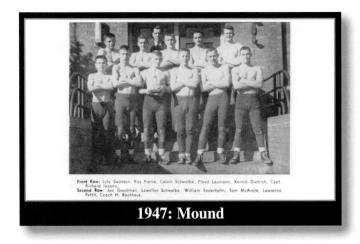

Front Row: Lyle Swanson, Roy Pierce, Calvin Schwalbe, Floyd Laumann, Kermit Dietrich, Capt. Richard Iacono.
Second Row: Joe Goodman, Lewellyn Schwalbe, William Soderholm, Tom McArdle, Lawrence Pettit, Coach H. Bockhaus.

1947: Mound

1947 Team Champions: Mound
1947 Individual Champions:
95 - Shroyer, Austin
103 - Folkert, Rochester
112 - Schwalbe, Mound
120 - W. Roles, Robbinsdale
127 - D. Cates, Litchfield
135 - R. Lacono, Mound
138 - W. Pearson, Mpls. Roosevelt
145 - L. Schwalbe, Mound
154 - M. Jensen, Albert Lea
165 - H. Dilley, Litchfield
Hwt - John Lund, Austin

1948 Team Champions: Austin
1948 Individual Champions:
95 - Hyland, Austin
103 - Chas Ofsthun, Robbinsdale
112 - J. Bengston, Owatonna
120 - V. Westlund, Anoka
127 - W. Bearl, Anoka
135 - J. Weimerskirsch, Litchfield

138 - W. Hardy, Austin
145 - D. Cooper, Robbinsdale
154 - D. Corrigan, Litchfield
165 - W. Friederich, Austin
Hwt - J. Dorfman, University High

AUSTIN WRESTLING TEAM

Back Row, (left to right): Sky Wilcox, Coach; Gomer, Johnson, L. Hyland, Snater, Goslee, Ray Lemmerman, Asst. Coach.
Front Row: Stern, Manager; R. Hyland, Barnett, McGee, Frederick, Hardy, Hoff, Fell, Manager.

1948: Austin

1949 Team Champions: Anoka
1949 Individual Champions:
95 - Hendrickson, Owatonna
103 - Chas Ofsthun, Robbinsdale
112 - Dick Mueller, Anoka
120 - O. Christenson, Litchfield
127 - W. Oglund, Mound
135 - F Laumann, Mound
138 - R. Vick, Robbinsdale
145 - J. Pierson, Robbinsdale
154 - R. Lindberg, Anoka
165 - C. Dilley, Rochester
Hwt - J. Hevsberg, Mpls. Marshall

ANOKA

Front Row, (left to right): James Elmer, Richard Mueller, Frank Lindberg, Vernon Westlund, Warren Schultz, and Dewey Bearl.
Back Row: Mark Klonowski, Coach; Robert Bomberger, Robert Duerr, David Herbold, Thomas Granfield, Richard Davis, and Kenneth Dehn.

1949: Anoka

1950 Team Champions: Anoka
1950 Individual Champions:
95 - Moore, Wayzata
103 - Kermit Zelke, Winona
112 - Chas Ofsthun, Robbinsdale
120 - Dick Mueller, Anoka
127 - L. Swanson, Mound
135 - R. Davis, Anoka
138 - O. LaTourelle, Blue Earth
145 - J. Mann, Robbinsdale
154 - R. Lindberg, Anoka
165 - R. Peterson, Mpls. Marshall
Hwt - C. Radechel, Winona

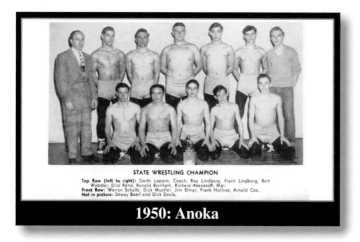

STATE WRESTLING CHAMPION
Top Row (left to right): Garth Lappin, Coach, Roy Lindberg, Frank Lindberg, Bert Webster, Dick Rand, Ronald Burnham, Richard Atanasoff, Mgr.
Front Row: Warren Schultz, Dick Mueller, Jim Elmer, Frank Holmes, Arnold Cox.
Not in picture: Dewey Bearl and Dick Davis.

1950: Anoka

1951 Team Champions: Faribault & Wayzata
1951 Individual Champions:
95 - Kelley, Albert Lea
103 - Bearl, Anoka
112 - R. Moore, Wayzata
120 - Dick Mueller, Anoka
127 - C. McIntosh, Wayzata
135 - C. Blegen, Faribault
138 - R. Malcolm, Blue Earth
145 - F. Lindberg, Anoka
154 - V. Kispert, Faribault
165 - K. Leuer, Wayzata
Hwt - P. Voldmun, Albert Lea

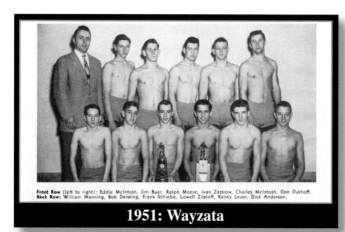

Front Row (left to right): Eddie McIntosh, Jim Baer, Ralph Moore, Ivan Zastrow, Charles McIntosh, Don Dykhoff.
Back Row: William Manning, Bob Deisting, Frank Schiebe, Lowell Zitsloff, Kenny Leuer, Dick Anderson.

1951: Wayzata

Front Row (left to right): Ray Wayne, Jerry Valentyn, Francis Headline, Roger Jarvis, Clyde Craig.
Back Row: Richard Post (Mgr.), Don Duchene, Cletus Blegen, Jerry King, Ruben Prinzing, Vaughn Kispert, Glenn Gerdes (Coach).

1951: Faribault

1952 Team Champions: Wayzata
1952 Individual Champions:
95 - Coffee, Mound
103 - Kark, Blue Earth
112 - R. Moore, Wayzata
120 - Kermit Zelke, Winona
127 - I. Zastrow, Wayzata

135 - J. Langenfeld, Hastings
138 - O. Meyers, University High
145 - C. Bengston, Owatonna
154 - R. Wayne, Faribault
165 - K. Leuer, Wayzata
Hwt - R. Kubes, Northfield

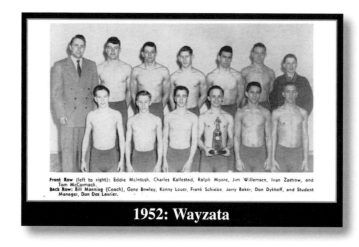

Front Row (left to right): Eddie McIntosh, Charles Kallestad, Ralph Moore, Jim Willemsen, Ivan Zastrow, and Tom McCormack.
Back Row: Bill Manning (Coach), Gene Bowley, Kenny Leuer, Frank Schiebe, Jerry Baker, Don Dykhoff, and Student Manager, Don Des Laurier.

1952: Wayzata

1953 Team Champions: Blue Earth & Wayzata (Co-Champs)
1953 Individual Champions:
95 - Coffee, Mound
103 - Kriewall, Blue Earth
112 - Arnie DeLeon, Blue Earth
120 - J. Ross, Mpls. Marshall
127 - Kermit Zelke, Winona
135 - I. Zastrow, Wayzata
138 - Koehnen, Mound
145 - F. Weber, Blue Earth
154 - O. Dyhkoff, Wayzata
165 - J. Dale, Anoka
Hwt - Greene, Faribault

Front Row (left to right): Rollo Ehrich, Emil Kark, Arnold DeLeon, Roger Kriewall, John Breen, James Reifsteck, and Fred Weber.
Back Row: Coach Keith Young, Ronald Paschke, Donald Mensing, Richard Hannamen, and Richard More. (Not in picture: Darrel Sohn, Larry Prescott, and Manager Kenneth Heilig).

1953: Blue Earth

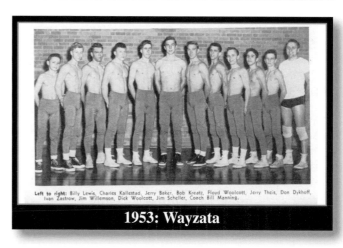

Left to right: Billy Lewis, Charles Kallestad, Jerry Baker, Bob Kreatz, Floyd Woolcott, Jerry Theis, Don Dykhoff, Ivan Zastrow, Jim Willemson, Dick Woolcott, Jim Scheller, Coach Bill Manning.

1953: Wayzata

Standing (left to right): Jerome Jacobsen, Harold Maile, Roy Minter, Ronald Baker (Co-Capt.), Fred Stoeker (Coach), James Peterson (Co-Capt.), Ronald Slezak, Richard Wolesky, Sam Bengston.
Kneeling (left to right): Eugene Stoltman, Ronald Jacobsen, Arthur Nott.

1954: Owatonna

Row 1: David Frank, Bradley Hooper, Gary Olsen, Gerald Fuller, Alfred DeLeon.
Row 2: Monte Peterson, Edward Bleess, John Breen, David Sohn.
Row 3: Coach Gene Lybbert, James Reifsteck, John Murphy, Ronald Weise, Albert Russ.

1956: Blue Earth

1954 Team Champions: Owatonna
1954 Individual Champions:
95 - Downey, Mankato
103 - Meyers, Rochester
112 - Shoemaker, Anoka
120 - Arnie DeLeon, Blue Earth
127 - Olson, Faribault
135 - Wadekamper, Faribault
138 - Bengston, Owatonna
145 - B. Koehnen, Mound
154 - Baker, Owatonna
165 - Minter, Owatonna
Hwt - Larry Hennig, Robbinsdale

135 - C. Coffee, Mound
138 - D. Sohn, Blue Earth
145 - J. Reifsteck, Blue Earth
154 - J. Kuelbs, Redwood Falls
165 - W. Koehwen, Mound
Hwt - A. Russ, Blue Earth

Front Row: Coach Garth Lappin, Mgr. Paul Sutterer.
Back Row: Don Larsen, Bill Horbal, Stan Wilson, Alfred Scott, Dick Board, Bob Board, James Einst, Henry Bi, Tom Walters.
Missing on picture—James Mead, Elwin Brown, Joe Kline.

1955: Anoka

Front Row, left to right: Alfred DeLeon, Gary Olsen, Bradley Hooper, David Frank, Richard Krumm.
Second Row: John Murphy, Harlan Schwab, Glendon Sohn, Monte Peterson, Claire Krukenberg.
Back Row: Albert Russ, Richard Frisbie, Coach Gene Lybbert.

1957: Blue Earth

1957 Team Champions: Blue Earth
1957 Individual Champions:
95 - Harlan Leopold, Redwood Falls
103 - Naylon, Mankato
112 - B. Hooper, Blue Earth
120 - L. Ward, Mankato
127 - Al DeLeon, Blue Earth
135 - J. Kelley, Robbinsdale
138 - M. Peterson, Blue Earth
145 - D. Ostrom, Rochester
154 - H. Schlieff, Rochester
165 - John Murphy, Blue Earth
175 - Stan Christ, Mankato
Hwt - A. Russ, Blue Earth

1955 Team Champions: Anoka
1955 Individual Champions:
95 - Stoltman, Owatonna
103 - Al DeLeon, Blue Earth
112 - J. Kline, Anoka
120 - B. Board, Anoka
127 - D. Board, Anoka
135 - J. Reifsteck, Blue Earth
138 - Peterson, Blue Earth
145 - B. Eckstrom, Wayzata
154 - J. Paddock, Litchfield
165 - L. Glynn, Rochester
Hwt - L. Christ, Mankato

1956 Team Champions: Blue Earth
1956 Individual Champions:
95 - Schmidt, Wayzata
103 - Noff, Owatonna
112 - J. Kline, Anoka
120 - B. Wilson, Anoka
127 - J. Kelley, Robbinsdale

Front Row: Charles Quaday, Dale Wiederholt, Ronald Nelson, Bradley Hooper, Gary Olsen, Alfred DeLeon.
Back Row: Frederick Bleess, Monte Peterson, Donald Engelby, Glendon Sohn, Richard Frisbie, and Coach Gene Lybbert.

1958: Blue Earth

1958 Team Champions: Blue Earth
1958 Individual Champions:
95 - Gary Erdman, Mound
103 - Sorbrook, Crosby-Ironton
112 - O. Stottler, Princeton
120 - B. Hooper, Blue Earth
127 - L. Ward, Mankato
135 - Al DeLeon, Blue Earth
138 - J. Graham, Mpls. Roosevelt
145 - M. Peterson, Blue Earth
154 - G. Weihrauch, St. Cloud
165 - J. Hook, Robbinsdale
175 - Stan Christ, Mankato
Hwt - B. DeCent, Crosby-Ironton

Front Row: Edward Wilson, Rodney Wilson, Ralph Bieven, Bruce Adams, Grant Nelson, Bill Owen.
Back Row: Ron Malcolm, Coach, Chris Wagner, Dale Meyers, Bill Mathews, Allan Duerr, Ken Kost, Gary Nelson, Student Manager.

1959: Anoka

1959 Team Champions: Anoka
1959 Individual Champions:
95 - Byers, Mankato
103 - Gary Erdman, Mound
112 - B. Adams, Anoka
120 - R. Bleess, Blue Earth
127 - R. Wilson, Anoka
135 - D. Frank, Blue Earth
138 - K. Kost, Anoka
145 - D. Schuster, Owatonna
154 - D. Christ, Mankato
165 - J. Hook, Robbinsdale
175 - C. Wagner, Anoka
Hwt - Stan Christ, Mankato

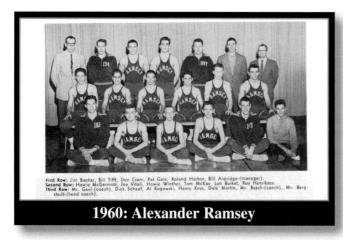

First Row: Jim Backer, Bill Tifft, Don Cram, Pat Gale, Roland Horton, Bill Aldridge-(manager).
Second Row: Howie McDermott, Joe Vitali, Howie Winther, Tom McKay, Len Burket, Roy Henriksen.
Third Row: Mr. Gaul-(coach), Dick Schaaf, Al Rogowski, Henry Keys, Dale Martin, Mr. Busch-(coach), Mr. Bergstedt-(head coach).

1960: Alexander Ramsey

1960 Team Champions: Alexander Ramsey
1960 Individual Champions:
95 - Byers, Mankato
103 - Gary Erdman, Mound
112 - C. Quaday, Blue Earth

120 - R. Bleess, Blue Earth
127 - H. Winther, Alexander Ramsey
135 - L. Kennedy, Albert Lea
138 - L. Lyden, Mounds View
145 - J. Olson, White Bear Lake
154 - D. Christ, Mankato
165 - R. Hendrickson, Alexander Ramsey
175 - M. Rognlie, Mpls. Washburn
Hwt - L. Schroht, Owatonna

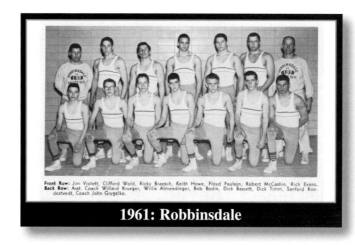

Front Row: Jim Violett, Clifford Wold, Ricky Braesch, Keith Howe, Floyd Paulson, Robert McCashin, Rich Evans.
Back Row: Asst. Coach Willard Krueger, Willis Almendinger, Bob Bodin, Dick Bassett, Dick Timm, Sanford Rondestvedt, Coach John Grygelko.

1961: Robbinsdale

1961 Team Champions: Robbinsdale
1961 Individual Champions:
95 - Howard Leopold, Redwood Falls
103 - Ron Ankeny, Blue Earth
112 - J. Johnson, Grand Rapids
120 - B. Henry, Owatonna
127 - R. Lorenz, Worthington
135 - Harlan Leopold, Redwood Falls
138 - J. Carlson, Glenwood
145 - J. Olson, White Bear Lake
154 - A. Firchau, St. James
165 - R. Basset, Robbinsdale
175 - N. Mattson, Grand Rapids
Hwt - J. Brooke, Albert Lea

Seated: Bob Henry, Jerry Brown.
Standing: Dick Black, Coach; Helmer Lembke, Dale Nelson, Gene Wilken, Brian Hage, Bob Sahf, David VonWald, Stan Schuster, Jim Wolfe, Doug Ebeling, Jerry Kading, John Tuthll.

1962: Owatonna

1962 Team Champions: Owatonna
1962 Individual Champions:
95 - Hazewinkel, Anoka
103 - Keraten, Mounds View
112 - Howard Leopold, Redwood Falls
120 - Ron Ankeny, Blue Earth
127 - B. Henry, Owatonna
135 - T. True, Austin
138 - L. Severson, Northfield
145 - Don Hasselius, Aitkin
154 - J. Beier, Grand Rapids

165 - J. Beier, Grand Rapids
175 - J. Ray, Windom
Hwt - Gary Hoehn, Hopkins

1963 Team Champions: Hopkins
1963 Individual Champions:
95 - Ogdie, Bloomington
103 - Entield, Northfield
112 - J. Anderson, Fridley
120 - M. Callahan, Albert Lea
127 - Howard Leopold, Redwood Falls
135 - Ron Ankeny, Blue Earth
138 - T Anderson, St. James
145 - B. Wendel, Windom
154 - S. Guggisberg, Fairfax
165 - F. Kallstrom, Browns Valley
175 - M. Ryback, Anoka
Hwt - Gary Hoehn, Hopkins

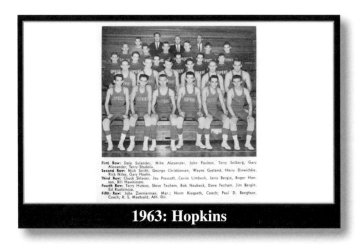
First Row: Dale Sulander, Mike Alexander, John Paulson, Terry Solberg, Gary Alexander, Terry Stodola.
Second Row: Nick Smith, George Christiansen, Wayne Gysland, Harry Dinwiddie, Rick Niles, Gary Hoehn.
Third Row: Chuck Sklader, Jay Prescott, Carrie Limbeck, Jerry Bergin, Roger Hanson, Bill Hawkinson.
Fourth Row: Terry Hutson, Steve Techam, Bob Neubeck, Dave Techam, Jim Bergin, Ed Ruotsinoja.
Fifth Row: John Zimmerman, Mgr.; Norm Kragseth, Coach; Paul D. Bengtson, Coach; R. S. Maetbald, Ath. Dir.

1963: Hopkins

1964   Team Champions: Mankato
1964   Individual Champions:
95 - Sulander, Hopkins
103 - Randy, Hastings
112 - G. Neist, Albert Lea
120 - M. Howe, Robbinsdale
127 - J. Labalestra, Alexander Ramsey
135 - O. Rudenick, Mankato
138 - J. Riesselman, Park Cottage Grove
145 - C. Bownick, Robbinsdale
154 - G. Bradshaw, Robbinsdale
165 - J. Taylor, Thief River Falls
175 - J. Hinz, St. Paul Park
Hwt - D. Beech, Mounds View

Left to Right: Dean Otto, Barry Bertrand, John Street, Jim Ewoldsen, Steve Byers, Gary Rudenick, Dan Droog, Lowell Willock, Mark Anderson, Bruce Krider, Doug Nelson, Jan Willard, Luverne Klar, Coach.

1964: Mankato

1965 Team Champions: Cooper
1965 Individual Champions:
95 - Ruedy, Hastings
103 - Taylor, Cooper
112 - K. Stauch, Albert Lea
120 - F Nicols, Crosby-Ironton
127 - H. Simm, Owatonna
135 - J. Labalestra, Alexander Ramsey
138 - P. Straub, Le Sueur
145 - P. Collier, Spring Lake Park
154 - M. Maas, Fridley
165 - G. Bradshaw, Cooper
175 - D. Stamp, Brainerd
Hwt - M. Mortenson, Grand Rapids

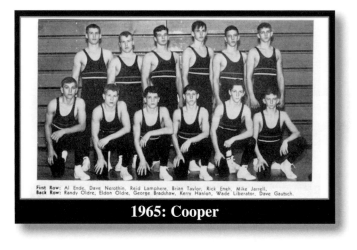
First Row: Al Ende, Dave Nerothin, Reid Lamphere, Brian Taylor, Rick Engh, Mike Jarrell.
Back Row: Randy Oldre, Eldon Oldre, George Bradshaw, Kerry Hanlon, Wade Liberator, Dave Gautsch.

1965: Cooper

1966   Team Champions: Albert Lea
1966   Individual Champions:
95 - Saric, Hopkins
103 - Allen, Albert Lea
112 - M. Tello, Spring Lake Park
120 - P. Sullivan, Robbinsdale
127 - J. McPherson, Stillwater
135 - R. Holland, Fridley
138 - T. Riesselman, St. Paul Park
145 - S. Rice, LeRoy
154 - J. Lee, Bemidji
165 - K. Anderson, St. Francis
175 - G. Elzen, Faribault
Hwt - T. Tripp, Osseo

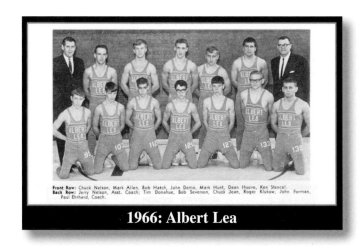
Front Row: Chuck Nelson, Mark Allen, Bob Hatch, John Demo, Mark Hunt, Dean Hoeve, Ken Stencel.
Back Row: Jerry Nelson, Asst. Coach; Tim Donahue, Bob Severson, Chuck Jean, Roger Klukow, John Forman, Paul Ehrhard, Coach.

1966: Albert Lea

1967   Team Champions: Fridley & Hopkins (Co-Champs)
1967   Individual Champions:
95 - Ross, Robbinsdale
103 - Saric, Hopkins
112 - M. Tello, Spring Lake Park

120 - J. Sorvic, Hopkins
127 - R. Lamphere, Cooper
135 - S. Perala, Windom
138 - S. Carlson, Fridley
145 - J. Johnson, Janesville
154 - C. Palmer, Fridley
165 - C. Jean, Albert Lea
175 - R. Brekke, Faribault
Hwt - T. Tripp, Osseo

154 - S. Carlson, Fridley
165 - K. Anderson, St. Francis
175 - B. Backlund, Princeton
Hwt - C. Scheuer, St. Cloud Tech

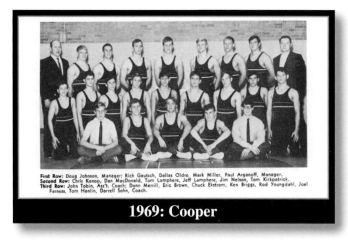
1969: Cooper

First Row: Doug Johnson, Manager; Rich Gautsch, Dallas Oldre, Mark Miller, Paul Arganoff, Manager.
Second Row: Chris Konop, Dan MacDonald, Tom Lamphere, Jeff Lamphere, Jim Nelson, Tom Kirkpatrick.
Third Row: John Tobin, Ass't. Coach; Donn Merrill, Eric Brown, Chuck Ekstrom, Ken Briggs, Rod Youngdahl, Joel Farness, Tom Hanlin, Darrell Sohn, Coach.

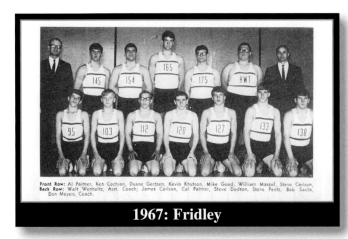
1967: Fridley

Front Row: Al Palmer, Ken Cochian, Duane Gertzen, Kevin Knutson, Mike Good, William Massof, Steve Carlson.
Back Row: Walt Wenholtz, Asst. Coach; James Carlson, Cal Palmer, Steve Dodson, Steve Pentz, Bob Sachs, Don Meyers, Coach.

1969   Team Champions: Cooper
1969   Individual Champions:
95 - Thompson, Prior Lake
103 - Stellmach, Marshall
112 - J. Lamphere, Cooper
120 - O. Demarais, Foley
127 - M. Hickman, Buffalo
135 - R. Gautsch, Cooper
138 - D. Richards, Ellendale
145 - R. Enger, St. James
154 - R. Lee, Bemidji
165 - R. Johnson, St. Louis Park
175 - J. Farness, Cooper
Hwt - C. Scheuer, St. Cloud Tech

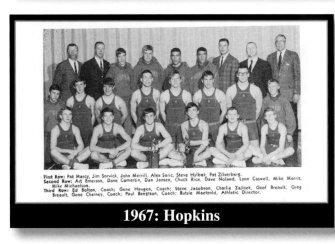
1967: Hopkins

First Row: Pat Marcy, Jim Sorvick, John Merrill, Alex Saric, Steve Hylbak, Pat Zilverberg.
Second Row: Art Emerson, Dave Comartin, Dan Jansen, Chuck Rice, Dave Noland, Lynn Caswell, Mike Morris, Mike Michaelson.
Third Row: Ed Bolton, Coach; Gene Haugen, Coach; Steve Jacobson, Charlie Zajicek, Geof Breault, Greg Breault, Gene Cherney, Coach; Paul Bengtson, Coach; Butsie Maetzold, Athletic Director.

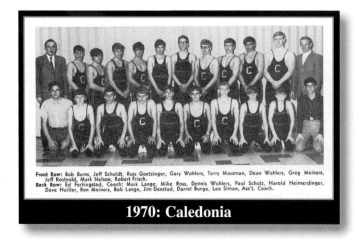
1970: Caledonia

Front Row: Bob Burns, Jeff Schuldt, Russ Goetzinger, Gary Wohlers, Terry Massman, Dean Wohlers, Greg Meiners, Jeff Rostvold, Mark Nelson, Robert Frisch.
Back Row: Ed Ferkingstad, Coach; Mark Lange, Mike Ross, Dennis Wohlers, Paul Schutz, Harold Heimerdinger, Dave Heiller, Ron Meiners, Bob Lange, Jim Denstad, Darrel Bunge, Leo Simon, Ass't. Coach.

1968   Team Champions: Hopkins
1968   Individual Champions:
95 - Swanson, St. Francis
103 - Hendrickson, Northfield
112 - 5. Hylbak, Hopkins
120 - J. Sorvic, Hopkins
127 - P. Saxe, Forest Lake
135 - P Marcy, Hopkins
138 - J. McPherson, Stillwater
145 - C. Plate, Grand Rapids

1970   Team Champions: Caledonia
1970   Individual Champions:
95 - Malchow, Anoka
103 - Knight, Hopkins
112 - T. Svendson, Coon Rapids
120 - J. Lamphere, Cooper
127 - R. Livingood, Olivia
135 - L. Silverberg, Hopkins
138 - M. Lange, Caledonia
145 - D. Sheriff, Alexandria
154 - D. Cummings, LeRoy
165 - Tom Jean, Albert Lea
175 - B. Rheingans, Appleton
Hwt - M. Steidl, Alexandria

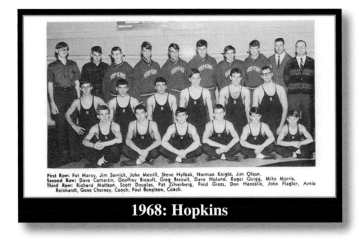
1968: Hopkins

First Row: Pat Marcy, Jim Sorvick, John Merrill, Steve Hylbak, Norman Knight, Jim Olson.
Second Row: Dave Comartin, Geoffrey Breault, Greg Breault, Dave Noland, Roger Quigg, Mike Morris.
Third Row: Richard Mattson, Scott Douglas, Pat Zilverberg, Fred Gross, Don Hanzalik, John Flagler, Arnie Reinhardt, Gene Cherney, Coach; Paul Bengtson, Coach.

1971   Team Champions: Albert Lea
1971   Individual Champions:
95 - Loeding, Austin
103 - Costello, Park Rapids
112 - T. Hughes, Spring Valley
120 - W. Hartzberg, Armstrong
127 - O. Winslow, Hayfield
133 - L. Benson, Staples
138 - L. Zilverberg, Hopkins Lindbergh
145 - L. Goodnature, Albert Lea
154 - M. Hughes, Wayzata
165 - Tom Jean, Albert Lea
175 - B. Rheingans, Appleton
Hwt - O. Blaske, Osseo

1971: Albert Lea

1972   Team Champions: St. James
1972   Individual Champions:
98 - MacArthur, Osseo
105 - Costello, Park Rapids
115 - B. Dale, Robbinsdale
119 - R. Clark, Dover-Eyota
126 - G Thompson, Staples
132 - J. Patton, Spring Lake Park
138 - D. Doerieg, Olivia
145 - B. Schmidt, Renvilie
155 - M. Lange, Caledonia
167 - Tom Jean, Albert Lea
180 - T Wilmes, Osseo
Hwt - O. Blaske, Osseo

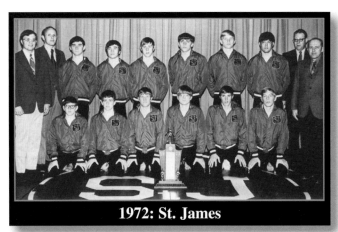

1972: St. James

1973   Team Champions: Fridley
1973   Individual Champions:
98 - Kish, Anoka
105 - M. McArthor, Osseo
112 - O. Thayer, Fridley

119 - J. Eustice, Janesville
126 - H. Pellinen, Hutchinson
132 - B. Schandle, Burnsville
138 - K. Fladeboe, Willmar
145 - G. Hummel, Crosby-Ironton
155 - J. Lunde, Albert Lea
167 - S. Barnum, Moorhead
180 - G. Holmberg, Buffalo
Hwt - G. Pederson, Bloomington Jefferson

1973: Fridley

1974 Team Champions: Minnetonka
1974 Individual Champions:
98 - Dickinson, Fridley
105 - K. Kish, Anoka
112 - M. Anderson, Barnesville
119 - K. Minkel, Olivia
126 - B. Sauter, Prior Lake
132 - S. Egesdahl, Minnetonka
138 - B. Schandle, Burnsville
145 - J. Huls, Holdingford
155 - Kevin Lindbergh, Fertile
167 - J. Berthiaume, Cooper
180 - B. Link, Caledonia
Hwt - B. Bennett, North St. Paul

1974: Minnetonka

1975 Team Champions: Fridley
1975 Individual Champions:
98 - Jordan, Elk River
105 - Grimes, Bemidji
112 - G. Shaw, Faribault
119 - F. Full, Canby
126 - L. Kihlstadius, Albert Lea
132 - O. Zilverberg, Hopkins Lindbergh
138 - B. Craven, Prior Lake
145 - B. Johnson, Prior Lake

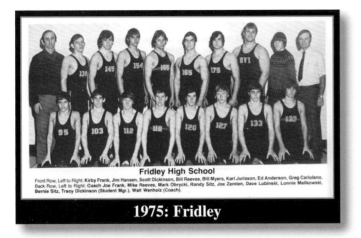

Fridley High School
Front Row, Left to Right: Kirby Frank, Jim Hansen, Scott Dickinson, Bill Reeves, Bill Myers, Karl Jurisson, Ed Anderson, Greg Cariolano. Back Row, Left to Right: Coach Joe Frank, Mike Reeves, Mark Obrycki, Randy Sitz, Joe Zemien, Dave Lubinski, Lonnie Malikowski, Bernie Sitz, Tracy Dickinson (Student Mgr.), Walt Wenholz (Coach).

1975: Fridley

155 - Bill Babcock, St. Peter
167 - K. Berres, Parkers Prairie
180 - P. Kozlowski, Pipestone
Hwt - S. Tobin, Moorhead

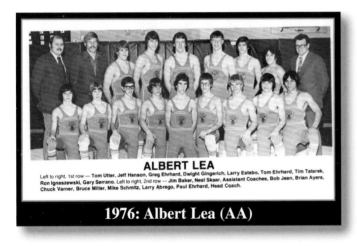

ALBERT LEA
Left to right, 1st row — Tom Utter, Jeff Hanson, Greg Ehrhard, Dwight Gingerich, Larry Estebo, Tom Ehrhard, Tim Tatarek, Ron Ignaszewski, Gary Serrano. Left to right, 2nd row — Jim Baker, Neal Skaar, Assistant Coaches, Bob Jean, Brian Ayers, Chuck Varner, Bruce Miller, Mike Schmitz, Larry Abrego, Paul Ehrhard, Head Coach.

1976: Albert Lea (AA)

1976 Team Champions: Albert Lea (AA) & Canby (A)
1976 Individual Champions:
Class AA
98 - Barron, Mpls. Central
105 - Fraley, Forest Lake
112 - Myers, Fridley
119 - Wasmund, Worthington
126 - Saba, Spring Lake Park
132 - Seawell, Mpls. Edison
138 - Scott Benner, Robbinsdale
145 - S. Madigan, Mankato West
155 - M. Obrycki, Fridley
167 - K. Keckeisen, Mankato West
180 - J. Hohertz, Minnetonka
Hwt - G. Ganyo, St. Louis Park

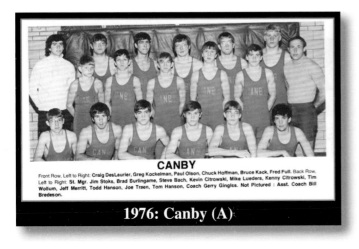

CANBY
Front Row, Left to Right: Craig DesLaurier, Greg Kockelman, Paul Olson, Chuck Hoffman, Bruce Kack, Fred Full. Back Row, Left to Right: St. Mgr. Jim Stoks, Brad Burlingame, Steve Bach, Kevin Citrowski, Mike Lueders, Kenny Citrowski, Tim Wollum, Jeff Merritt, Todd Hanson, Joe Traen, Tom Hanson, Coach Gerry Gingles. Not Pictured : Asst. Coach Bill Bredeson.

1976: Canby (A)

Class A
98 - Sowers, Staples
105 - Merritt, Canby
112 - Carr, Battle Lake
119 - T. Kriewall, Blue Earth
126 - F. Full, Canby
132 - Zimmer, Wabasso
138 - J. Johnson, Staples
145 - P Lippert, Olivia
155 - D. Peterson, Luverne
167 - R. Knutson, Stewartville
180 - G. Berg, Gaylord
Hwt - S. Werner, Norwood-Young America

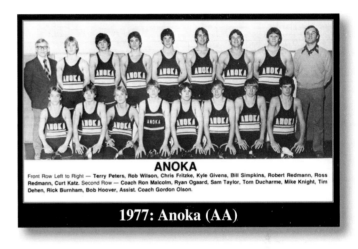

ANOKA
Front Row Left to Right — Terry Peters, Rob Wilson, Chris Fritzke, Kyle Givens, Bill Simpkins, Robert Redmann, Ross Redmann, Curt Katz. Second Row — Coach Ron Malcolm, Ryan Ogaard, Sam Taylor, Tom Ducharme, Mike Knight, Tim Dehen, Rick Burnham, Bob Hoover, Assist. Coach Gordon Olson.

1977: Anoka (AA)

1977 Team Champions: Anoka (AA) & Canby (A)
1977 Individual Champions:
Class AA
98 - Barron, Mpls. Central
105 - V. Martinez, Osseo
112 - Schmidt, Forest Lake
119 - Rose, Burnsville
126 - Wasmund, Worthington
132 - J. Martinez, Osseo
138 - Bonk, Buffalo
145 - Moore, Forest Lake
155 - Tesch, Mounds View
167 - Mitchell, Spring Lake Park
180 - Eisinger, Orono
Hwt - Miller, Stillwater

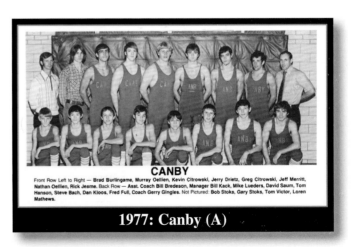

CANBY
Front Row Left to Right — Brad Burlingame, Murray Oellien, Kevin Citrowski, Jerry Drietz, Greg Citrowski, Jeff Merritt, Nathan Oellien, Rick Jesme. Back Row — Asst. Coach Bill Bredeson, Manager Bill Kack, Mike Lueders, David Saum, Tom Hanson, Steve Bach, Dan Kloos, Fred Full, Coach Gerry Gingles. Not Pictured: Bob Stoks, Gary Stoks, Tom Victor, Loren Mathews.

1977: Canby (A)

Class A
98 - Anderberg, Braham
105 - Hackle, Appleton
112 - Merritt, Canby
119 - Carr, Battle Lake

126 - Dahlheimer, St. Michael-Albertville
132 - Anderson, Barnesville
138 - Knutson, New Richmond
145 - Sommers, Gaylord
155 - Mistic, Blackduck
167 - Minsink, Clarkfield
180 - Johnson, Goodhue
Hwt - Hansen, Canby

1978 Team Champions: Anoka (AA) & Staples (A)
1978 Individual Champions:
Class AA
98 - Clem, St. Francis
105 - Mooney, Robbinsdale
112 - Vic Martinez, Osseo
119 - Gary LeFebvre, Elk River
126 - Robert Redmann, Anoka
132 - Bruce Arvold, Alexandria
138 - Jim Tredeau, Simley
145 - Jim Mead, Blaine
155 - Tim Houg, Moorhead
167 - Jerry Tesch, Mounds View
185 - Pat Faber, Mpls. Edison
Hwt - Tom Brutscher, Little Falls

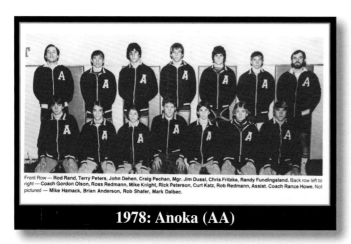

Front Row — Rod Rand, Terry Peters, John Dehen, Craig Pechan, Mgr. Jim Dussl, Chris Fritzke, Randy Fundingsland. Back row left to right — Coach Gordon Olson, Ross Redmann, Mike Knight, Rick Peterson, Curt Katz, Rob Redmann, Assist. Coach Rance Howe. Not pictured — Mike Hamack, Brian Anderson, Rob Shafer, Mark Dalbec.

1978: Anoka (AA)

Class A
98 - Werner, Perham
105 - Pat Halloran, Glencoe
112 - Marc Novacek, Greenbush
119 - Joe Berry, Waubun
126 - Steve Carr, Battle Lake
132 - Dave Sikora, Staples
138 - Mike Keogh, Waubun
145 - Mark Aho, Frazee
155 - John Lundberg, New London-Spicer
167 - Les Mistic, Blackduck

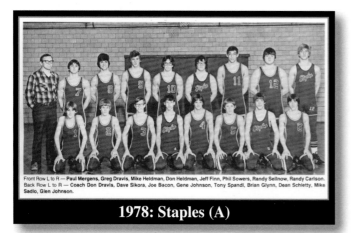

Front Row L to R — Paul Mergens, Greg Dravis, Mike Heldman, Don Heldman, Jeff Finn, Phil Sowers, Randy Sellnow, Randy Carlson. Back Row L to R — Coach Don Dravis, Dave Sikora, Joe Bacon, Gene Johnson, Tony Spandl, Brian Glynn, Dean Schletty, Mike Sadlo, Glen Johnson.

1978: Staples (A)

185 - Don Dahl, Dover-Eyota
Hwt - Tom Hanson, Canby

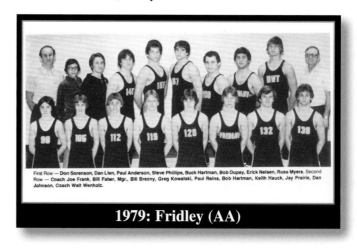

First Row — Don Sorenson, Dan Lien, Paul Anderson, Steve Phillips, Buck Hartman, Bob Dupay, Erick Nelsen, Russ Myers. Second Row — Coach Joe Frank, Bill Faber, Mgr., Bill Brezny, Greg Kowalski, Paul Rains, Bob Hartman, Keith Hauck, Jay Prairie, Dan Johnson, Coach Walt Wenholz.

1979: Fridley (AA)

1979 Team Champions: Fridley (AA) & Canby (A)
1979 Individual Champions:
Class AA
98 - Guse, Austin
105 - Clew, St. Francis
112 - Grimes, Bemidji
119 - Arne, Orono
126 - Bigelbach, F. B. Kellogg
132 - Carr, Moorhead
138 - Ross Redmann, Anoka
145 - Mead, Blaine
155 - Hoffman, New Ulm
167 - Tofto, Bloomington Kennedy
185 - Mueller, Woodbury
Hwt - Vavrosky, Bloomington Kennedy

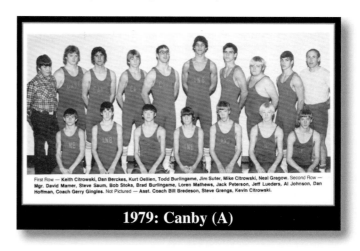

First Row — Keith Citrowski, Dan Berckes, Kurt Oellien, Todd Burlingame, Jim Suter, Mike Citrowski, Neal Gragow. Second Row — Mgr. David Mamer, Steve Saum, Bob Stoks, Brad Burlingame, Loren Mathews, Jack Peterson, Jeff Lueders, Al Johnson, Dan Hoffman, Coach Gerry Gingles. Not Pictured — Asst. Coach Bill Bredeson, Steve Grengs, Kevin Citrowski.

1979: Canby (A)

Class A
98 - Pfaffinger, Blue Earth
105 - S. Werner, Perham
112 - Barrett, Annandale
119 - Fuchs, Paynesville
126 - Finley, Chatfield
132 - Quiram, Waterville-Elysian
138 - Squibb, Bird Island-Lake Lillian
145 - Cubbelde, Pipestone
155 - Engler, Diiworth
167 - Hammers, Perham
185 - Jessen, New Richland-Hartland
Hwt - Held, Waubun

1980 Team Champions: Bloomington Kennedy (AA) & Goodhue & Staples (A)
1980 Individual Champions:

Back Row, L. to R.: Jim Hoeve, John Morgan, Mike Luzar, Jim Luzar, Gary Heusbourg, Jim Johnson, Todd Arens. **Front Row, L. to R.:** Scott Sturgeon, Troy Pladsen, Tim Evavold, Mike Lembeck, Greg Allen, John Pribble, Chris Lembeck. **Not Pictured:** Blake Bonjean.

1980: Bloomington Kenney (AA)

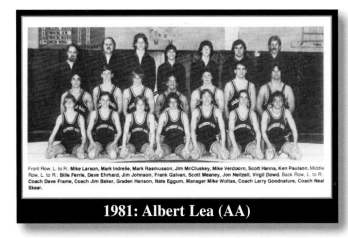

Front Row, L. to R.: Mike Larson, Mark Indrelie, Mark Rasmusson, Jim McCluskey, Mike Verdoorn, Scott Hanna, Ken Paulson. **Middle Row, L. to R.:** Bille Ferrie, Dave Ehrhard, Jim Johnson, Frank Galvan, Scott Meaney, Jon Neitzell, Virgil Dowd. **Back Row, L. to R.:** Coach Dave Frame, Coach Jim Baker, Graden Hanson, Nate Eggum, Manager Mike Woltas, Coach Larry Goodnature, Coach Neal Skaar.

1981: Albert Lea (AA)

Class AA
98 - Gliva, Rosemount
105 - Gene, Austin
112 - Anderson, Fridley
119 - Bergerson, Wayzata
126 - Habisch, Buffalo
132 - Dehen, Anoka
138 - Langlais, Apple Valley
145 - Arens, Bloomington Kennedy
155 - Arvold, Alexandria
167 - Seeger, Minnetonka
185 - Hicks, Hastings
Hwt - Graeber, Armstrong

138 - Wiklund, Bloomington Kennedy
145 - Hall, Coon Rapids
155 - Morgan, Bloomington Kennedy
167 - Dyer, St. Paul Johnson
185 - Schwab, Forest Lake
Hwt - Luzar, Richfield

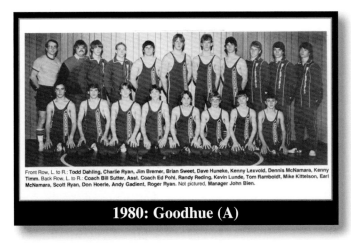

Front Row, L. to R.: Todd Dahling, Charlie Ryan, Jim Bremer, Brian Sweet, Dave Huneke, Kenny Lexvold, Dennis McNamara, Kenny Timm. **Back Row, L. to R.:** Coach Bill Sutter, Asst. Coach Ed Pohl, Randy Reding, Kevin Lunde, Tom Ramboldt, Mike Kittelson, Earl McNamara, Scott Ryan, Don Hoerle, Andy Gadient, Roger Ryan. **Not pictured, Manager John Bien.**

1980: Goodhue (A)

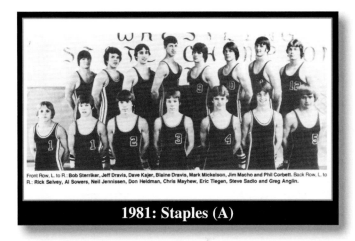

Front Row, L. to R.: Bob Sterriker, Jeff Dravis, Dave Kajer, Blaine Dravis, Mark Mickelson, Jim Macho and Phil Corbett. **Back Row, L. to R.:** Rick Selvey, Al Sowers, Neil Jennissen, Don Heldman, Chris Mayhew, Eric Tiegen, Steve Sadio and Greg Anglin.

1981: Staples (A)

Class A
98 - D. Goeb, Monticello
105 - D. Werner, Perham
112 - Mergens, Staples
119 - Wetz, Morris
126 - Kriewall, Blue Earth
132 - Woitalla, Albany
138 - Studer, Sherburn
145 - Christensen, Frazee
155 - Haag, Lewiston
167 - Gross, Blackduck
185 - Blanshan, Waconia
Hwt - Jenson, Foley

1981 Team Champions: Albert Lea (AA) & Staples (A)
1981 Individual Champions:
Class AA
98 - Jorgenson, Elk River
105 - Indrelie, Albert Lea
112 - Whelan, Brainerd
119 - Roehrick, Faribault
126 - Hanna, Albert Lea
132 - Clemens, Cooper

Class A
98 - Rick Goeb, Monticello
105 - D. Goch, Monticello
112 - Lexvold, Goodhue
119 - Braaten, Glenwood/Villard
126 - Evan, Wells-Easton
132 - Heiling, Redwood Falls
138 - Barrett, Annandale
145 - Heldman, Staples
155 - Zanda, Browervilie
167 - Wolf, Adrian
185 - Meyer, Luverne
Hwt - Baumgartner, Olivia

1982 Team Champions: Brainerd (AA) & Staples (A)
1982 Individual Champions:
Class AA
98 - Lembeck, Bloomington Kennedy
105 - Rick Goeb, Anoka
112 - Cashman, Blaine
119 - Gliva, Rosemount
126 - Pritchett, Apple Valley
132 - Roehrick, Faribault
138 - Rabine, Park Center
145 - McGrath, Anoka
155 - Sanders, Buffalo
167 - Nielsen, Spring Lake Park
185 - Peterson, Cambridge
Hwt - Luzar, Richfield

1982: Brainerd (AA)

Front Row, L. to R.: Ron Koering, Bob Waytashek, Matt Whelan, Jim Caughey, Ken Anderson, Kevin Koep. Back Row, L. to R.: Coach Bruce Thompson, Joe Frazer, Scott Grater, Craig Bergren, Pat Ostrowski, Bruce Olson, Asst. Coach Bob Whelan. (Not Pictured: Jon Norman, Rick Ashbrook, Brent Baloun, Todd Nichols.)

Class A
98 - Bob Sterriker, Staples
105 - O. Werner, Perham
112 - Miller, Renvilie-Sacred Heart
119 - B. Dravis, Staples
126 - Corbett, Staples
132 - Hand, Sherburn
138 - Salo, New York Mills
145 - Weller, New York Mills
155 - Schuster, Delavan
167 - Theede, Lewiston
185 - Payne, Hancock/Cyrus
Hwt - Becker, Adrian

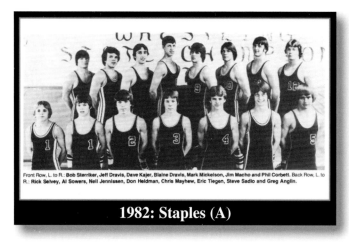

1982: Staples (A)

Front Row, L. to R.: Bob Sterriker, Jeff Dravis, Dave Kajer, Blaine Dravis, Mark Mickelson, Jim Macho and Phil Corbett. Back Row, L. to R.: Rick Selvey, Al Sowers, Neil Jennissen, Don Heldman, Chris Mayhew, Eric Tiegen, Steve Sadlo and Greg Anglin.

1983 Team Champions: Apple Valley (AA) & Staples (A)
1983 Individual Champions:
Class AA
98 - Mullenberg, Faribault
105 - R. Habiach, Buffalo

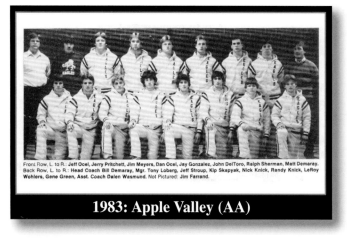

1983: Apple Valley (AA)

Front Row, L. to R.: Jeff Ocel, Jerry Pritchett, Jim Meyers, Dan Ocel, Jay Gonzalez, John DelToro, Ralph Sherman, Matt Demaray. Back Row, L. to R.: Head Coach Bill Demaray, Mgr. Tony Loberg, Jeff Stroup, Kip Skapyak, Nick Knick, Randy Knick, LeRoy Wohlers, Gene Green, Asst. Coach Dalen Wasmund. Not Pictured: Jim Farrand.

112 - Jorgenson, Rosemount
119 - Rick Goeb, Anoka
126 - Bonjean, Bloomington Kennedy
132 - Caughey, Brainerd
138 - Koffski, Coon Rapids
145 - Green, Apple Valley
155 - Rogers, Worthington
167 - Sande, St. Paul Central
185 - Nielsen, Spring Lake Park
Hwt - Hanson, Faribault

Class A
98 - Bob Sterriker, Staples
105 - Mark Krier, Plainview
112 - Anderson, Maple Lake
119 - Miller, Renville-Sacred Heart
126 - Cyr, Oklee/Plummer
132 - Thier, Adrian
138 - McNamera, Goodhue
145 - Kastner, Elbow Lake-Wendell
155 - Christianson, Canby
167 - Palmer, Royalton
185 - Shepersky, Menahga
Hwt - Williamson, Appleton

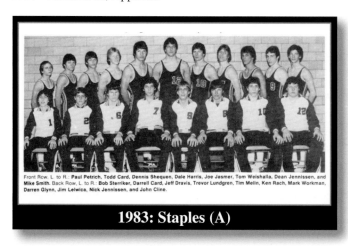

1983: Staples (A)

Front Row, L. to R.: Paul Petrich, Todd Card, Dennis Shequen, Dale Harris, Joe Jasmer, Tom Weishalla, Dean Jennissen, and Mike Smith. Back Row, L. to R.: Bob Sterriker, Darrell Card, Jeff Dravis, Trevor Lundgren, Tim Melin, Ken Rach, Mark Workman, Darren Glynn, Jim Lelwica, Nick Jennissen, and John Cline.

1984 Team Champs: Bloomington Kennedy (AA) & Staples (A)
1984 Individual Champions:
Class AA
98 - Calliguri, Hibbing
105 - Collins, Bloomington Kennedy
112 - Matt Demaray, Apple Valley
119 - Pawlitschek, St. Paul Como Park
126 - Lembeck, Bloomington Kennedy
132 - Caughey, Brainerd
138 - Fink, Park Cottage Grove
145 - Warner, Hibbing

1984: Bloomington Kennedy (AA)

Front Row, L. to R.: Ben Schad, Dan Shand, Steve Breyette, Gordy Morgan, Marty Morgan, Jon Sharratt, Dan Collins. Back Row, L. to R.: Tom Breuning, Chris Lembeck, Dave Meier, Landan Hagert, Mike Wilson, Jeff Johnson, Jeff Helgeson. Not Pictured: Mike Walsh.

155 - Tousignant, Faribault
167 - Meier, Bloomington Kennedy
185 - Sterner, Marshall
Hwt - Ullom, Faribault

Class A
98 - Buringa, Plainview
105 - Werner, Perham
112 - Mark Krier, Plainview
119 - Tougas, Oklee/Plummer
126 - Miller, Renville-Sacred Heart
132 - Engler, Fulda
138 - Dorn, Adrian
145 - McDonald, Watertown-Mayer
155 - Mikel, Medford
167 - Kvien, Roseau
185 - Palmer, Royalton
Hwt - Kevin Mettler, Mankato Loyola

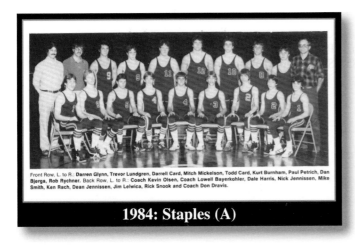

Front Row, L. to R.: Darren Glynn, Trevor Lundgren, Darrell Card, Mitch Mickelson, Todd Card, Kurt Burnham, Paul Petrich, Dan Bjerga, Rob Rychner. Back Row, L. to R.: Coach Kevin Olsen, Coach Lowell Bayerkohler, Dale Harris, Nick Jennissen, Mike Smith, Ken Rach, Dean Jennissen, Jim Lelwica, Rick Snook and Coach Don Dravis.

1984: Staples (A)

1985 Team Champions: Apple Valley (AA) & Staples (A)
1985 Individual Champions:
Class AA
98 - Darren Droegemueller, Osseo
105 - Calliguri, Hibbing
112 - Dave Droegemueller, Osseo
119 - Houg, Albert Lee
126 - Matt Demaray, Apple Valley
132 - Bergeron, Wayzata
138 - Short, Simley
145 - Needham, Apple Valley
155 - Morgan, Bloomington Kennedy
167 - Farrell, Osseo
185 - Dillemuth, Albert Lea
Hwt - Hagert, Bloomington Kennedy

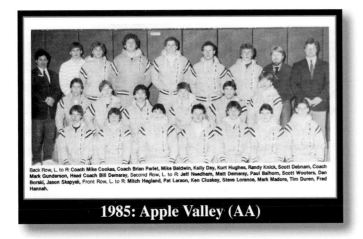

Back Row, L. to R: Coach Mike Cookas, Coach Brian Parlet, Mike Baldwin, Kelly Day, Kurt Hughes, Randy Knick, Scott Debnam, Coach Mark Gunderson, Head Coach Bill Demaray. Second Row, L. to R: Jeff Needham, Matt Demaray, Paul Balhorn, Scott Wooters, Dan Borski, Jason Skapyak, Front Row, L. to R: Mitch Hegland, Pat Larson, Ken Cluskey, Steve Lorence, Mark Madore, Tim Duren, Fred Hannah.

1985: Apple Valley (AA)

Class A
98 - Schmitz, Brooten
105 - Morgan, Battle Lake/Underwood
112 - Kuznik, Crookston
119 - Mark Krier, Plainview
126 - Miller, Renville-Sacred Heart
132 - Becker, St. Michael-Albertville
138 - Dorn, Adrian
145 - Weber, Madison
155 - Massop, Mapleton/Amboy-Good Thunder
167 - Storm, Walker-Hackensack
185 - Koenig, Butterfield-Odin
Hwt - Math, Aitkin

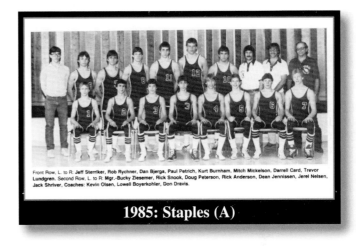

Front Row, L. to R: Jeff Sterriker, Rob Rychner, Dan Bjerga, Paul Petrich, Kurt Burnham, Mitch Mickelson, Darrell Card, Trevor Lundgren. Second Row, L. to R: Mgr.-Bucky Ziesemer, Rick Snook, Doug Peterson, Rick Anderson, Dean Jennissen, Jerel Nelsen, Jack Shriver, Coaches: Kevin Olsen, Lowell Boyerkohler, Don Dravis.

1985: Staples (A)

1986 Team Champions: Apple Valley (AA) & Canby (A)
1986 Individual Champions:
Class AA
98 - Clem, St. Francis
105 - Hegland, Apple Valley
112 - Lemair, Prior Lake
119 - D. Droegemueller, Osseo
126 - Beatty, Rosemount
132 - Matt Demaray, Apple Valley
138 - Bergeron, Wayzata
145 - Miley, Anoka
155 - Duval, Park Cottage Grove
167 - Nelson, Elk River
185 - Short, Simley
Hwt - Balcom, Fairmont

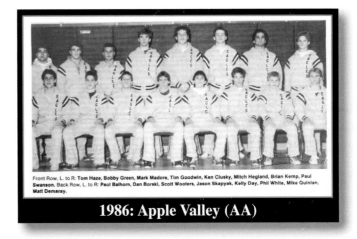

Front Row, L. to R: Tom Haze, Bobby Green, Mark Madore, Tim Goodwin, Ken Clusky, Mitch Hegland, Brian Kemp, Paul Swanson. Back Row, L. to R: Paul Balhorn, Dan Borski, Scott Wooters, Jason Skapyak, Kelly Day, Phil White, Mike Quinlan, Matt Demaray.

1986: Apple Valley (AA)

Class A
98 - Bergeron, Oklee/Plummer
105 - Douglas, Hayfield
112 - Tangen, St. James
119 - Kuznik, Crookston

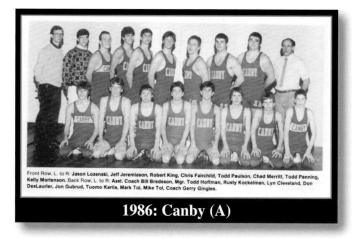

First Row, L. to R: Jason Lozenski, Jeff Jeremiason, Robert King, Chris Fairchild, Todd Paulson, Chad Merritt, Todd Panning, Kelly Mortenson. Back Row, L. to R: Asst. Coach Bill Bredeson, Mgr. Todd Hoffman, Rusty Kockelman, Lyn Cleveland, Don DesLaurier, Jon Gubrud, Tuomo Karila, Mark Tol, Mike Tol, Coach Gerry Gingles.

1986: Canby (A)

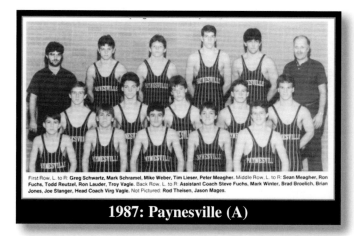

First Row, L. to R: Greg Schwartz, Mark Schramel, Mike Weber, Tim Lieser, Peter Meagher. Middle Row, L. to R: Sean Meagher, Ron Fuchs, Todd Reutzel, Ron Lauder, Troy Vagle. Back Row, L. to R: Assistant Coach Steve Fuchs, Mark Winter, Brad Broelich, Brian Jones, Joe Stanger, Head Coach Virg Vagle. Not Pictured: Rod Theisen, Jason Mages.

1987: Paynesville (A)

126 - Corey Olson, Hayfield
132 - Wurm, Maple Lake
138 - Otterness, Cannon Falls/Randolph
145 - Bullerman, Adrian
155 - Karila, Canby
167 - Ochsendorf, Dawson-Boyd
185 - Nelson, Grand Meodow/LeRoy-Ostronder
Hwt - Garvick, Paynseville

167 - Fouquette, Maple Lake
185 - Gibson, Chokio-Alberta/Clinton/Graceville
Hwt - Nelson, Grand Meodow/LeRoy-Ostrander

1988 Team Champions: Simley (AA) & Canby (A)
1988 Individual Champions:
Class AA
98 - McDowell, Grand Rapids
105 - Scanlon, Minnetonka
112 - Martin, Mpls. Roosevelt
119 - Duren, Apple Valley
126 - Thompson, Hibbing
132 - Droegemueller, Osseo
138 - Short, Simley
145 - Jones, Mpls. Roosevelt
155 - Harrison, Simey
167 - Olsen, New Prague
185 - Schultz, Albert Lea
Hwt - Tim Tekautz, Hibbing

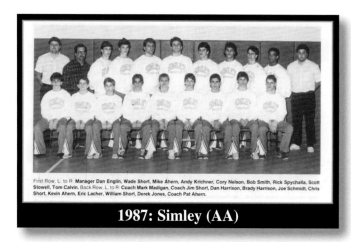

First Row, L. to R: Manager Dan Englin, Wade Short, Mike Ahern, Andy Krichner, Cory Nelson, Bob Smith, Rick Spychalla, Scott Stowell, Tom Calvin. Back Row, L. to R: Coach Mark Madigan, Coach Jim Short, Dan Harrison, Brady Harrison, Joe Schmidt, Chris Short, Kevin Ahern, Eric Lacher, William Short, Derek Jones, Coach Pat Ahern.

1987: Simley (AA)

1987 Team Champions: Simley (AA) & Paynesville (A)
1987 Individual Champions:
Class AA
98 - Martin, Mpls. Roosevelt
105 - Bisek, New Prague
112 - Menne, Forest Lake
119 - Todd Enger, Rochester Mayo
126 - Barrett, Columbia Heights
132 - Seeger, Grand Rapids
138 - Jones, Simley
145 - Tousignant, Faribault
155 - Kirpach, St. Francis
167 - Skapyak, Apple Valley
185 - Short, Simley
Hwt - Ziebol, Richfield

Class A
98 - Jeff Sterriker, Staples
105 - Bergeron, Oklee/Plummer
112 - Bennett, Clarissa
119 - Mike Morgan, Battle Lake/Underwood
126 - Block, LeCenter
132 - Anderson, Maple Lake
138 - Lorenson, Greenbush
145 - Corey Olson, Hayfield
155 - Darren Cain, Arlington-Green Isle

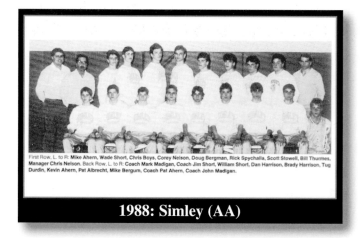

First Row, L. to R: Mike Ahern, Wade Short, Chris Boys, Corey Nelson, Doug Bergman, Rick Spychalla, Scott Stowell, Bill Thurmes, Manager Chris Nelson. Back Row, L. to R: Coach Mark Madigan, Coach Jim Short, William Short, Dan Harrison, Brady Harrison, Tug Durdin, Kevin Ahern, Pat Albrecht, Mike Bergum, Coach Pat Ahern, Coach John Madigan.

1988: Simley (AA)

Class A
98 - Peterson, Elgin-Milville
105 - Jay Walz, Brownton
112 - Merritt, Canby
119 - Eustice, Janesville
126 - Ripplinger, St. Michael-Albertville
132 - Dandurand, Clarkfield
138 - Goodhart, Beardsley/Browns Valley
145 - Vymola, Norwood-Young America
155 - Corey Olson, Hayfield, Dodge Center
167 - Darren Cain, Arlington-Green Isle/Gaylord
185 - Gibson, Chokio-Alberta/Clinton/Graceville
Hwt - Dietchlor, Park Rapids

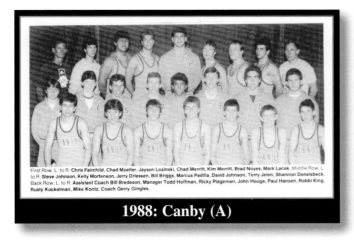

First Row, L. to R: Chris Fairchild, Chad Moeller, Jayson Lozinski, Chad Merritt, Kim Merritt, Brad Noyes, Mark Lacek. Middle Row, L. to R: Steve Johnson, Kelly Mortenson, Jerry Driessen, Bill Briggs, Marcus Padilla, David Johnson, Terry Jelen, Shannon Denelsbeck. Back Row, L. to R: Assistant Coach Bill Bredeson, Manager Todd Hoffman, Ricky Plageman, John Houge, Paul Hansen, Robbi King, Rusty Kockelman, Mike Kontz, Coach Gerry Gingles.

1988: Canby (A)

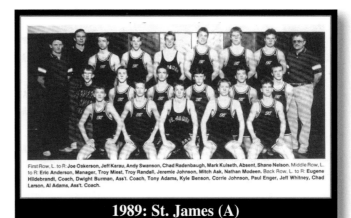

First Row, L. to R: Joe Oskerson, Jeff Karau, Andy Swanson, Chad Radenbaugh, Mark Kulseth, Absent, Shane Nelson. Middle Row, L. to R: Eric Anderson, Manager, Troy Miest, Troy Randall, Jeremie Johnson, Mitch Ask, Nathan Modeen. Back Row, L. to R: Eugene Hildebrandt, Coach, Dwight Burman, Ass't. Coach, Tony Adams, Kyle Benson, Corrie Johnson, Paul Enger, Jeff Whitney, Chad Larson, Al Adams, Ass't. Coach.

1989: St. James (A)

1989 Team Champions: Simley (AA) & St. James (A) & Foley (A) (Co-Champs)
1989 Individual Champions:
Class AA
103 - Patton, St. Francis
112 - Fornicoia, Richfield
119 - Phillips, Anoka
125 - Hoialmen, Winona
130 - Miller, Rochester John Marshall
135 - Springer, Anoka
140 - Carlson, Willmar
145 - Kroells, Elk River
152 - Willy Short, Simley
160 - Pribyl, Monticello
171 - Schmitz, New Prague
189 - Sharratt, Bloomington Kennedy
Hwt - Tim Tekautz, Hibbing

1990 Team Champions: Anoka (AA) & Paynesville (A)
1990 Individual Champions:
Class AA
103 - Brandon Paulson, Anoka
112 - Brian Miley, Anoka
119 - Brian Asleson, Apple Valley
125 - Erin Dougherty, Totino Grace
130 - Jason Birr, Buffalo
135 - Troy Haglund, Willmar
140 - Wade Short, Simley
145 - Chad Carlson, Willmar
152 - Tom Olson, Buffalo
160 - Jason Olson, Hibbing
171 - Travis Herndon, Apple Valley
189 - Joel Sharratt, Bloomington Kennedy
Hwt - Billy Pierce, Minneapolis Roosevelt

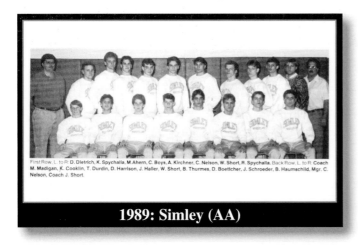

First Row, L. to R: D. Dietrich, K. Spychalla, M. Ahern, C. Boys, A. Kirchner, C. Nelson, W. Short, R. Spychalla. Back Row, L. to R: Coach M. Madigan, K. Cooklin, T. Durdin, D. Harrison, J. Haller, W. Short, B. Thurmes, D. Boettcher, J. Schroeder, B. Haumschild, Mgr. C. Nelson, Coach J. Short.

1989: Simley (AA)

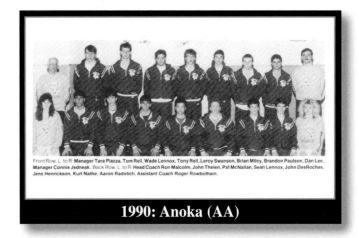

Front Row, L. to R: Manager Tara Piazza, Tom Reil, Wade Lennox, Tony Reil, Leroy Swanson, Brian Miley, Brandon Paulson, Dan Lee, Manager Connie Jedneak. Back Row, L. to R: Head Coach Ron Malcolm, John Thelen, Pat McNallan, Sean Lennox, John DesRoches, Jens Henrickson, Kurt Nathe, Aaron Radotich, Assistant Coach Roger Rowbotham.

1990: Anoka (AA)

Class A
103 - Meine, Crookston
112 - Hansen, Madison
119 - Becker, St. Michael-Albertville
125 - Bogart, Belgrade-Brooten-Elrosa
130 - VanCura, Heron Lake-Okabena-Lakefield
135 - Block, LeCenter
140 - Mack, New York Mills
145 - Kurtz, Norwood-Young America
152 - Thoreson, St. Charles
160 - Lange, Martin County West
171 - Nelson, Stewartville
189 - Loeffler, St. Clair
Hwt - Steve King, St. Clair

Class A
103 - Lenny Meine, Crookston
112 - Dennis Bly, Stewartville
119 - Jeremy LaVigne, Foley
125 - Tim Halbakken, Dover-Eyota
130 - Eddy Dehmer, St. Michnel-Albertville
135 - Chad Gage, Heron Lake-Okabena-Lakefield
140 - Kevin Newgard, Milaca
145 - Darrin Heldman, Staples-Motley
152 - Todd Lange, Martin County West
160 - Scott Wilts, Kerkhoven-Murdock Sunburg
171 - Chad Nelson, Stewartville
189 - Brad Loeffler, St. Clair
Hwt - Shawn Ehrich, Blue Earth Area

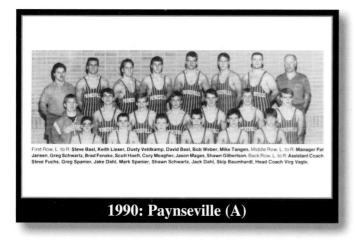

First Row, L. to R: Steve Bast, Keith Lieser, Dusty Veldkamp, David Bast, Bob Weber, Mike Tangen. Middle Row, L. to R: Manager Pat Jansen, Greg Schwartz, Brad Fenske, Scott Hoeft, Cory Meagher, Jason Mages, Shawn Gilbertson. Back Row, L. to R: Assistant Coach Steve Fuchs, Greg Spanier, Jake Dahl, Mark Spanier, Shawn Schwartz, Jack Dahl, Skip Baumhardt, Head Coach Virg Vagle.

1990: Paynseville (A)

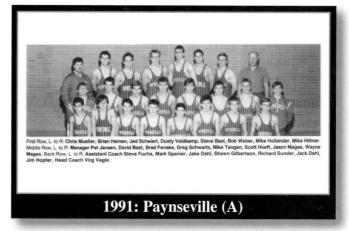

First Row, L. to R: Chris Mueller, Brian Heinen, Jed Scheierl, Dusty Veldkamp, Steve Bast, Bob Weber, Mike Hollander, Mike Hiltner. Middle Row, L. to R: Manager Pat Jansen, David Bast, Brad Fenske, Greg Schwartz, Mike Tangen, Scott Hoeft, Jason Mages, Wayne Mages. Back Row, L. to R: Assistant Coach Steve Fuchs, Mark Spanier, Jake Dahl, Shawn Gilbertson, Richard Sunder, Jack Dahl, Jim Hopfer, Head Coach Virg Vagle.

1991: Paynseville (A)

1991 Team Champions: Apple Valley (AA) & Paynesville (A)
1991 Individual Champions:
Class AA
103 - Dan Dietrich, Simley
112 - Brandon Paulson, Anoka
119 - Jason Reitmeier, Worthington
125 - Mark Wellstone, Apple Valley
130 - Erin Dougherty, Totino Grace
135 - Jason Birr, Buffalo
140 - Ryan Cummings, Osseo
145 - Scott Peterson, Alexandria
152 - Wade Short, Simley
160 - Travis Herndon, Apple Valley
171 - Walter Binger, Cambridge
189 - Tony Kenning, St. Cloud Tech
Hwt - Billy Pierce, Mpls. Roosevelt

1992 Team Champions: Simley (AA) & Frazee (A)
1992 Individual Champions:
Class AA
103 - Ty Friederichs, Osseo
112 - Brandon Paulson, Anoka
119 - Brandon Howe, Totino Grace
125 - Andy Reigstad, Willmar
130 - Jason Reitmeler, Worthington
135 - Jason Cuperus, Worthington
140 - Jason Melcher, St. Francis
145 - Carl Carlson, Willmar
152 - Mike Dowdell, Totino Grace
160 - Dave Mendenhall, Albert Lea
171 - Walter Binger, Cambridge
189 - Greg Karsten, Owotonna
Hwt - KarI Jones, Apple Valley

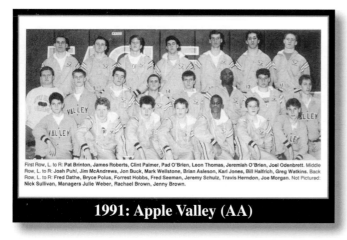

First Row, L. to R: Pat Brinton, James Roberts, Clint Palmer, Pad O'Brien, Leon Thomas, Jeremiah O'Brien, Joel Odenbrett. Middle Row, L. to R: Josh Puhl, Jim McAndrews, Jon Buck, Mark Wellstone, Brian Asleson, Karl Jones, Bill Halfrich, Greg Watkins. Back Row, L. to R: Fred Dathe, Bryce Polus, Forrest Hobbs, Fred Seeman, Jeremy Schulz, Travis Herndon, Joe Morgan. Not Pictured: Nick Sullivan, Managers Julie Weber, Rachael Brown, Jenny Brown.

1991: Apple Valley (AA)

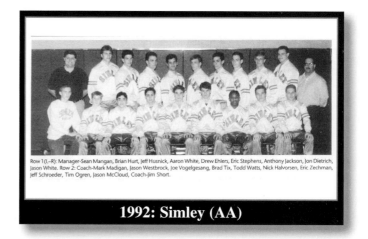

Row 1(L–R): Manager-Sean Mangan, Brian Hurt, Jeff Husnick, Aaron White, Drew Ehlers, Eric Stephens, Anthony Jackson, Jon Dietrich, Jason White. Row 2: Coach-Mark Madigan, Jason Westbrock, Joe Vogelgesang, Brad Tix, Todd Watts, Nick Halvorsen, Eric Zechman, Jeff Schroeder, Tim Ogren, Jason McCloud, Coach-Jim Short.

1992: Simley (AA)

Class A
103 - Brian Heimerl, Lester Prairie/Holy Trinity, Winsted
112 - Mike McDougall, Lake Crystal-Wellcome Memorial
119 - Tim Jansma, Heron Lake-Okabena-Lakefield
125 - Josh Heckman, Wells-Easton/South Central
130 - Eddy Dehmer, St. Michael-Albertville
135 - Jeff Bullerman, Wells-Easton/South Central
140 - Greg Schwartz, Paynesville
145 - Shane Nelson, St. James
152 - Reese Kuck, Deer River/Northland, Remer
160 - Brian Sutter, Goodhue
171 - Chad Nelson, Stewartville
189 - Josh Tietje, Fairmont
Hwt - Shawn Ehrich, Blue Earth Area

Class A
103 - B. J. Mariotti, St. Michael-Albertville
112 - Aaron Gudahl, Blue Earth Area
119 - Bill Soine, Montevideo
125 - Chad Kraft, Heron Lake-Okabena-Lakefield
130 - Tim Jansma, Heron Lake-Okabena-Lakefield
135 - Gordy Thompson, Staples Area
140 - Brad Fenske, Paynesville
145 - Jose Trevino, St. Paul Humboldt
152 - Scott Hoeft, Paynesville
160 - Jeff Egeland, Sauk Centre
171 - Tanner Young, St. Charles
189 - Link Steffen, Granite Falls-Clarkfield
Hwt - Dieken Swalla, MACCRAY, Clara City

1992: Frazee (A)

Row 1 (L–R): Nick Riewer, Scott Schermerhorn, Steve Wilkowski, Tim Wokasch, Adam Tate, Chad Mitchell, Tom Wacker, Allen Hamm. Row 2: Assistant Coach-Marty Aho, Hans Wothe, Tim Trieglaff, Mike Rux, Ryan Osterman, Mark Hendrickson, Nathan Matejka, Tyler Trieglaff, Jeff Zitzow, Head Coach-Clay Nagel, Manager-Theresa Ehnert.

1993 Team Champions: Forest Lake (AA) & Foley (A)
1993 Individual Champions:
Class AA
103 - Brad Fisher, Austin
112 - Ty Friederichs, Osseo
119 - Henry Gerten, Rosemount
125 - Brandon Howe, Totino Grace
130 - Brice Thornburg, Forest Lake
135 - Jason Davids, Forest Lake
140 - Jason Cuperus, Worthington
145 - Troy Marr, Forest Lake
152 - Brett Svendsen, Elk River
160 - Justin Hahn, Forest Lake
171 - Brent Hoffman, Totino Grace
189 - Jeremy Goeden, Grand Rapids
Hwt - Jason DeVries, Forest Lake

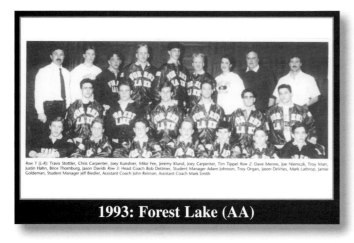

Row 1 (L-R): Travis Stottler, Chris Carpenter, Joey Kunshier, Mike Fee, Jeremy Klund, Joey Carpenter, Tim Tippel Row 2: Dave Menne, Joe Niemczk, Troy Marr, Justin Hahn, Brice Thornburg, Jason Davids Row 3: Head Coach Bob Dettmer, Student Manager Adam Johnson, Troy Organ, Jason DeVries, Mark Lathrop, Jamie Goldeman, Student Manager Jeff Biedler, Assistant Coach John Reiman, Assistant Coach Mark Smith

1993: Forest Lake (AA)

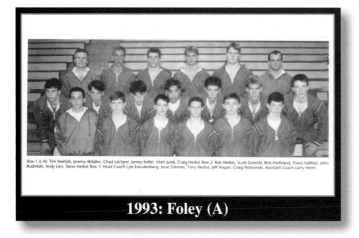

Row 1 (L-R): Tim Wertish, Jeremy Ahlalter, Chad LaVigne, Jamey Keller, Matt Jurek, Craig Herbst Row 2: Rob Herbst, Scott Gorecki, Rick Herbrand, Travis Haffner, John Rudnitski, Andy Lien, Steve Herbst Row 3: Head Coach Lyle Freudenberg, Jesse Zimmer, Tony Herbst, Jeff Hogan, Craig Piotrowski, Assistant Coach Larry Herm

1993: Foley (A)

Class A
103 - Jon Fitzgerald, Martin County West, Sherburn
112 - Brian Heimerl, Lester Prairie/Holy Trinity, Winsted
119 - Darrin Allen, Chatfield
125 - Kipp Williamson, Hayfield
130 - Jesse Curtis, Perham
135 - Rawdon Hawkinson, Watertown-Mayer
140 - Chad Kraft, Heron Lake-Okabena-Lakefield
145 - Jay Stephan, Piainview/Elgin-Millville
152 - Jim Peterson, Dover-Eyota
160 - Chris Steele, Hayfield
171 - Chris Lowrie, Zumbrota-Mazeppa
189 - Link Steffen, Granite Falls-Clarkfield
Hwt - Dieken Swalla, MACCRAY, Clara City

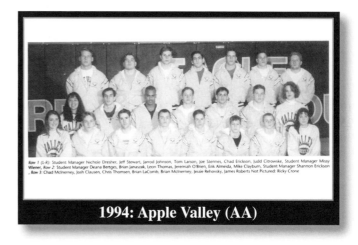

Row 1 (L-R): Student Manager Nichole Dresher, Jeff Stewart, Jarrod Johnson, Tom Larson, Joe Stennes, Chad Erickson, Judd Citrowske, Student Manager Missy Wiener, Row 2: Student Manager Deana Bertges, Brian Janaszak, Leon Thomas, Jeremiah O'Brien, Erik Almeida, Mike Clayburn, Student Manager Shannon Erickson , Row 3: Chad McInerney, Josh Clausen, Chris Thomsen, Brian LaComb, Brian McInerney, Jessie Rehovsky, James Roberts Not Pictured: Ricky Crone

1994: Apple Valley (AA)

1994 Team Champions: Apple Valley (AA) & Canby (A) & Foley (A) (Co-Champs)
1994 Individual Champions:
Class AA
103 - Chad Erikson, Apple Valley
112 - Tony Dionosopoulos, Simley, Inver Grove Heights
119 - Ty Friederichs, Osseo
125 - Barrett Golyer, Saint Francis
130 - Josh Friedt, Rochester John Marshall
135 - Nate Vilnow, Willmar
140 - Pat Smith, Osseo
145 - Troy Marr, Forest Lake
152 - Ray Wilhelm, Stillwater Area
160 - Chad Dollansky, Saint Francis
171 - Jeff Schroeder, Simley, lnver Grove Heights
189 - Jeremy Schubert, Owatonna
Hwt - Ben Bauer, Faribault

Class A
103 - Jon Fitzgerald, Martin County West, Sherburn
112 - Pat McNamara, Scott West (Belle Plaine/Jordon)

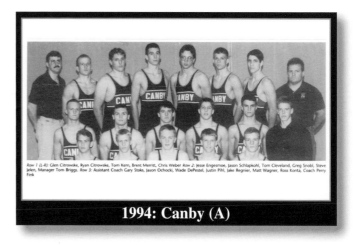

Row 1 (L-R): Glen Citrowske, Ryan Citrowske, Tom Kern, Brent Merritt, Chris Weber Row 2: Jesse Engesmoe, Jason Schlapkohl, Tom Cleveland, Greg Snobl, Steve Jelen, Manager Tom Briggs. Row 3: Assistant Coach Gary Stoks, Jason Ochocki, Wade DePestel, Justin Pihl, Jake Regnier, Matt Wagner, Ross Konta, Coach Perry Fink

1994: Canby (A)

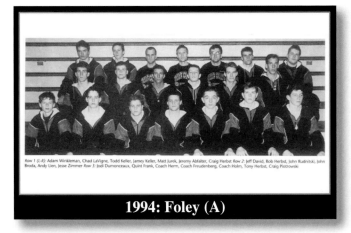

1994: Foley (A)

Row 1 (L-R): Adam Winkleman, Chad LaVigne, Todd Keller, Jamey Keller, Matt Jurek, Jeremy Ablalter, Craig Herbst Row 2: Jeff David, Rob Herbst, John Rudnitski, John Broda, Andy Lien, Jesse Zimmer Row 3: Jodi Dumonceaux, Quint Frank, Coach Herm, Coach Freudenberg, Coach Holm, Tony Herbst, Craig Piotrowski

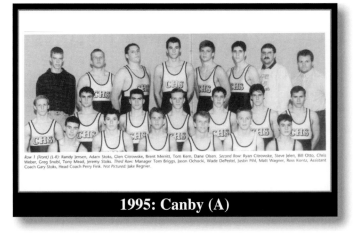

1995: Canby (A)

Row 1 (Front) (L-R): Randy Jensen, Adam Stoks, Glen Citrowske, Brent Merritt, Tom Kern, Dane Olsen. Second Row: Ryan Citrowske, Steve Jelen, Bill Otto, Chris Weber, Greg Snobl, Tony Mead, Jeremy Stoks. Third Row: Manager Tom Briggs, Jason Ochocki, Wade DePestel, Justin Pihl, Matt Wagner, Ross Kontz, Assistant Coach Gary Stoks, Head Coach Perry Fink. Not Pictured: Jake Regnier.

119 - Jamie Keller, Foley
125 - Brad Pike, Hayfield
130 - Jeremy Arndt, Wheaton/Herman-Norcross
135 - Dan Doncombe, Saint Michael-Albertville
140 - Wayne Mooney, Badger/Greenbush-Middle River
145 - Chad Kraft, Heron Lake-Okabena-Lakefield
152 - Matt Skattum, Luverne/Hills-Beaver Creek
160 - Chris Steele, Hayfield
171 - Chad Kranz, Montevideo
189 - Cory Czepa, Fulda/Murray County Central, Slayton
Hwt - Roger Pederson, Pipestone-Jasper

140 - Dana Paulson, Roseau
145 - John Weldon, Scott West (Belle Plaine/Jordan)
152 - Tim Kinsella, Litchfield
160 - Shane Colberg, Dassel-Cokato
171 - Ryan Marx, Plainview/Elgin-Millville
189 - Jeff Ziermann, Waconia
Hwt - Simon Kern, Badger/Greenbush-Middle River

1996 Team Champions: Hastings (AA), St. Michael Albertville (A) & Wheaton/Herman-Norcross (B)
1996 Individual Champions:
Class AA
103 - Judd Citrowske, Apple Valley
112 - Ben Peake, Mounds View
119 - Eric Schmiesing, Saint Cloud Tech
125 - Kelly McConville, Osseo
130 - Chad Erikson, Apple Valley
135 - Luke Becker, Cambridge
140 - Josh Cagle, Faribault (cooperative)
145 - Aron Attig, Albert Lea
152 - Jeff Stewart, Apple Valley
160 - Mike Cuperus, Worthington
171 - Joel Goeden, Grand Rapids
189 - Greg Schreder, St. Cloud Tech
Hwt - Ben Bauer, Faribault (cooperative)

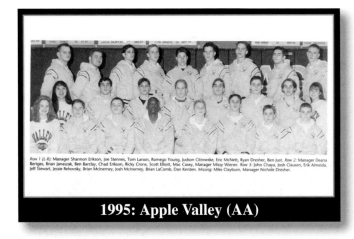

1995: Apple Valley (AA)

Row 1 (L-R): Manager Shannon Erikson, Joe Stennes, Tom Larson, Romeyo Young, Judson Citrowske, Eric McNett, Ryan Dresher, Ben Just. Row 2: Manager Deana Bertges, Brian Janauzak, Ben Barclay, Chad Erikson, Ricky Crone, Scott Elliott, Mac Casey, Manager Missy Wiener. Row 3: John Chaya, Josh Clausen, Erik Almeida, Jeff Stewart, Jessie Rehovsky, Brian McInerney, Josh McInerney, Brian LaComb, Dan Kersten. Missing: Mike Clayburn, Manager Nichole Dresher.

1995 Team Champions: Apple Valley (AA) & Canby (A)
1995 Individual Champions:
Class AA
103 - Victor Dionisopolous, Simley, Inver Grove Heights
112 - Nick Jacob, Mound-Westonka
119 - Chad Erickson, Apple Valley
125 - Ty Friederichs, Osseo
130 - Josh Cagle, Faribault
135 - Dwight Ballou, Little Falls
140 - Dan Dellwo, Chisago Lakes Area, Lindstrom
145 - Anthony Jackson, Simley, Inver Grove Heights
152 - Amir Alexander, Minnetonka
160 - Aaron Craig, Faribault
171 - Joel Goeden, Grand Rapids
189 - Josh Clausen, Apple Valley
Hwt - Mike Law, Stillwater Area

Class A
103 - Jon Fitzgerald, Martin County West, Sherburn
112 - Pat Harty, Hayfield
119 - Pat McNamara, Scott West (Belle Plaine/Jordan)
125 - Jamey Keller, Foley
130 - Ben Zimmer, Atwater-Cosmos-Grove City
135 - Brad Pike, Hayfield

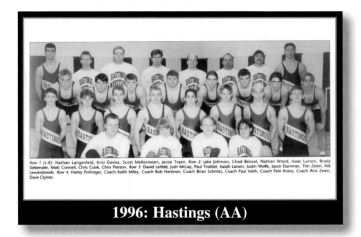

1996: Hastings (AA)

Row 1 (L-R): Nathan Langenfeld, Krisi Davies, Scott Mellesmoen, Jessie Traen. Row 2: Jake Johnson, Chad Beissel, Nathan Wood, Isaac Larson, Brady Siebenaler, Matt Connell, Chris Cook, Chris Pierson. Row 3: David Leifeld, Josh McLay, Paul Trottier, Isaiah Larson, Justin Wolfe, Jason Dummer, Tim Zeien, Nik Lewandowski. Row 4: Harley Pottinger, Coach Keith Miley, Coach Bob Hartman, Coach Brian Schmitz, Coach Paul Vaith, Coach Pete Kranz, Coach Rick Zeien, Dave Clymer.

Class A
103 - Luke Eustice, Blue Earth Area
112 - Nick Slack, Scott West (Belle Plaine/Jordan)
119 - Nick Jacob, Mound Westonka
125 - Eric Kramer, Staples-Motley
130 - Pat McNamara, Scott West (Belle Plaine/Jordan)
135 - Anthony Mollins, Perham
140 - Dana Paulson, Roseau
145 - Lance Wurm, Annandale/Maple Lake
152 - Dana Gostomczik, Janesville-Waldorf-Pemberton

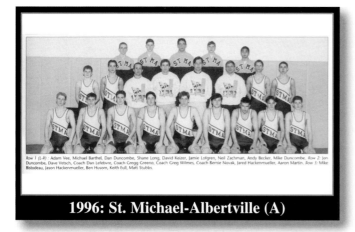

1996: St. Michael-Albertville (A)

1997: Apple Valley (AAA)

160 - Steve Saxland, Pipestone-Jasper
171 - Matt Fiedler, Sauk Centre
189 - Ryan Rettke, Morris Area/Hancock
Hwt - Lee Hiltner, Paynesville Area

Class AA
103 - Ty Eustice, Blue Earth Area
112 - Matt Strawser, Wadena-Deer Creek
119 - Chad Morrow, Kasson-Mantorville
125 - Mark Carlson, Staples-Motley
130 - Trent Hatlevig, Caledenia/Spring Grove
135 - Jason Bartels, Annandale/Maple Lake
140 - Jacob Volkmann, Battle Lake/Underwood/Henning
145 - Mike Fiedler, Sauk Centre
152 - Lance Wurm, Annandale/Maple Lake
160 - Mark Newman, Mora
171 - Tony Gansen, Scott West
189 - Jake Tieje, Fairmont Area/Martin Luther, Northrop
Hwt - Justin Staebler, Perham

1996: Wheaton/Herman-Norcross (B)

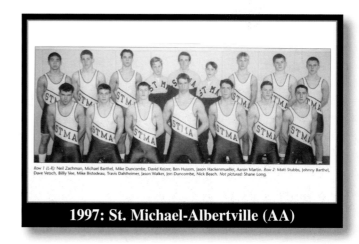

1997: St. Michael-Albertville (AA)

Class B
103 - Kris Fier, Minneota
112 - Darin Bertram, Wheaton/Herman-Norcross
119 - Ben Johnson, Kenyon-Wanamingo
125 - John Wegman, Saint Charles
130 - Peter Mursu, New York Mills
135 - Chad Stoneburg, Wheaton/Herman-Norcross
140 - Brad Pike, Hayfield
145 - Justin Baker, Kerkhovon-Murdock-Sunburg
152 - Dan Duncombe, St Michael-Albertville
160 - Paul Fabian, Wheaton/Herman-Norcross
171 - Owen Elzen, Dover-Eyota
189 - Nick Severson, Hayfield
Hwt - Ben Meyer, Pine Island

1997 Team Champions: Apple Valley (AAA) St. Michael Albertville (AA) & Hayfield (A)
1997 Individual Champions:
Class AAA
103 - Erik Hoffman, Mankato West
112 - Nick Ledin, Eden Prairie
119 - Julio Alaniz, Mankato West
125 - Kelly McConville, Osseo
130 - Chad Erikson, Apple Valley
135 - Brad Fisher, Austin/Austin Pacelli
140 - Jake Skalicky, Simley
145 - Luke Becker, Cambridge-Isanti
152 - Jacob Clark, South Saint Paul
160 - Jeff Stewart, Apple Valley
171 - Mike Cuperus, Worthington
189 - Cory Forar, Prior Lake
Hwt - Isaiah Larson, Hastings

Class A
103 - Matt Nagel, Frazee
112 - Darin Bertram, Wheaton/Herman-Norcross
119 - Marv Sims, Big Lake/Zion Christian
125 - Mike Weller, New York Mills
130 - Trevor Houn, Montgomery-Lonsdale
135 - Pat Harty, Hayfield
140 - Tony Thoma, Hayfield
145 - Klaus Alberts, Hayfield
152 - Dana Gostomczik, Janesvillle-Waldorf-Pemberton
160 - Dan Routh, New Richland-Hartland-Ellendale-Geneva
171 - Joel Howard, Badger/Greenbush-Middle River
189 - Owen Elzen, Dover-Eyota
Hwt - Mark Anderson, Rockford

1998 Team Champions: Owatonna (AAA), Dassel-Cokato (AA) & St. James (A)
1998 Individual Champions:
Class AAA
103 - Peter Zangl, New Ulm/New Ulm Cathedral
112 - Nick Ledin, Eden Prairie

1998: Owatonna (AAA)

Row 1 (L-R): Derek Johnson, Casey Kaplan, Wade Prestegard, Jeremy Wilson, Josh Sorenson, Jacob Hovden. Row 2: John Dulaney, Adam Balzer, Jeremy Jirele, Cory Urban, Chet Macht, Matt Reich, Ben Wilson, Dave Nelson. Row 3: Activities Director Gary Ridge, Joe Butler, Eli Ross, Jason Schubert, Kevin Rasmussen, Clint Seykora, Mike Kramer, James Herzog. Row 4: Statistician Keith Stark, Assistant Coach Larry Hovden, Assistant Coach Toby Erler, Assistant Coach Jeff Becker, Head Coach Scot Davis, Assistant Coach Jeremy Schubert, Assistant Coach Matt Kretlow, Assistant Coach Jack West.

119 - Dave Redinius, Eden Prairie
125 - Tony Fratzke, Hutchinson
130 - Marcus LeVesseur, Minneapolis Roosevelt
135 - Lance Martin, Elk River
140 - Mitch Marr, Forest Lake
145 - Josh McLay, Hastings
152 - Luke Becker, Cambridge-Isanti
160 - Jacob Clark, South Saint Paul
171 - Jason Waln, Elk River
189 - Jason HoIm, Northfield
Hwt - Pete Campion, Fergus Falls/Hillcrest Lutheran

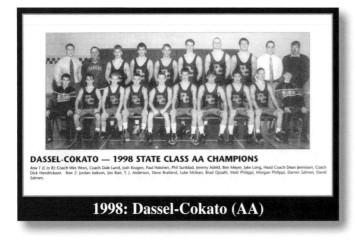

DASSEL-COKATO — 1998 STATE CLASS AA CHAMPIONS

Row 1 (L to R): Coach Wes Wren, Coach Dale Lund, Josh Krugen, Paul Halonen, Phil Sunblad, Jeremy Asfeld, Ben Meyer, Jake Long, Head Coach Dean Jennisen, Coach Dick Hendrickson. Row 2: Jordan Isakson, Jon Barr, T. J. Anderson, Steve Bratland, Luke Mclean, Brad Opsahl, Matt Philippi, Morgan Philippi, Darren Salmen, David Salmen.

1998: Dassel-Cokato (AA)

Class AA
103 - Scott Shepersky, Litchfield
112 - Luke Eustice, Blue Earth Area
119 - Matt Strawser, Wadena- Deer Creek
125 - Josh Roberts, Scott West (Belle Plaine/Jordan)
130 - Trent Hatlevig, Caledonia/Spring Grove
135 - Mark Carlson, Staples-Motley
140 - Nate Baker, Jackson County Central
145 - Nate Hanson, Jackson County Central
152 - Todd Fuller, Annandale/Maple Lake
160 - Nick Slack, Scott West (Belle Plaine/Jordan)
171 - Mike Duncombe, St. Michael-Albertville
189 - Jason Brueske, Wadena-Deer Creek
Hwt - Justin Staebler, Perham

Class A
103 - Derek Zieske, BDRSH, Renvilie
112 - Darin Bertram, Wheaton/Herman-Norcross
119 - Corey Buenger, Chatfield
125 - Matt Nagel, Frazee
130 - Jerod Boynton, Saint Charles/Saint Charles Christian
135 - Marshall Rach, Bertha-Hewitt/Verndale
140 - Trent Gunsolus, Janesville-Waldorf-Pemberton
145 - Jacob Volkmann, Battle Lake/Underwood/Henning
152 - Jeff Adams, Janesvillle-Waldorf-Pemberton

SAINT JAMES — 1998 STATE CLASS A CHAMPIONS

Row 1 (L to R): Eric Hultgren, Tony Feuchtenberger, Danon Anderson, Juan Fernandez, Dustin Kulseth, Ryan Sturm, Derrick Madison, Tyler Olson. Row 2: Head Coach Eugene Hildebrandt, Adam Johnson, Adam Koch, Ryan Rentz, Brian Holmgren, Brandon Siem, Landon Siem, Brad Steele, Assistant Coach Dwight Burman, Assistant Coach Roger Lomu.

1998: St. James (A)

160 - Dana Gostomczik, Janesvillle-Waldorf-Pemberton
171 - Joel Schrimpf, Goodhue
189 - Robert Kendall, Hinckley-Finlayson
Hwt - Brad Steele, Saint James

1999 Team Champions: Apple Valley (AAA), Jackson County Central (AA) & Frazee (A)
1999 Individual Champions:
Class AAA
103 - Derek Johnson, Owatonna
112 - Desmond Radunz, Henry Sibley, Mendota Heights
119 - Matt Shankey, Apple Valley
125 - Chris McAlpine, Elk River Area
130 - Ryan LeBeau, Prior Lake
135 - Clint Martin, Elk River Area
140 - Marcus LeVesseur, Minneapolis Roosevelt
145 - Mike Wichman, Hutchinson
152 - Josh McLay, Hastings
160 - Bryan Cowdin, Worthington/Sioux Valley
171 - Jeremy Johnson, Faribault/Bethlehem Academy
189 - Jordan Holm, Northfield
Hwt - Joe Mayberry, Bemidji

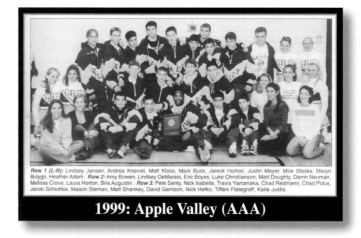

Row 1 (L-R): Lindsey Jansen, Andrea Kneivel, Matt Kloos, Mark Buck, Jareck Horton, Justin Meyer, Moe Staska, Maryn Bulygo, Heather Adam. Row 2: Amy Bowen, Lindsey DeMarais, Eric Boyes, Luke Christianson, Matt Doughty, Darrin Neuman, Melissa Crove, Laura Horton, Bria Augustin. Row 3: Pete Senty, Nick Isabella, Travis Yamanaka, Chad Redmann, Chad Polus, Jacob Schlottke, Mason Steman, Matt Shankey, David Garrison, Nick Hefko, Tiffani Flategraff, Katie Justis.

1999: Apple Valley (AAA)

Class AA
103 - Jeff Pfaffinger, Blue Earth Area
112 - Kelly Pederson, Big Lake
119 - Jeff Ollestad, Mora
125 - Luke Eustice, Blue Earth Area
130 - Jamie Carlson, Staples-Motley
135 - Ty Eustice, Blue Earth Area
140 - Jeff Thompson, Staples-Motley
145 - Mark Carlson, Staples-Motley
152 - Nate Baker, Jackson County Central
160 - Mike Fiedler, Sauk Centre
171 - Ryan Bruns, Marshall/Marshall Area Christian
189 - Kent Crowley, Fulda/Murray County Central, Slayton
Hwt - Bryce Vancura, Jackson County Central

1999: Jackson County Central (AA)

Row 1 (L-R): Kollin Leopold, Brett Hussong, Kyle Arndt, Marc Harwood, Steve Majerus, Derek Harwood. Row 2: Nick Weets, Ben Caven-Johnson, Dusty Wilking, Nate Baker, Andy Nesseth, Kayle Pauling, Assistant Coach Kevin Elder. Row 3: Head Coach Randy Baker, Jacob Drahota, Dru Wilking, Jeremiah Knabe, Blake Hendricks, Travis Ahrens, Bryce Vancura, Assistant Coach Todd Card.

2000: Apple Valley (AAA)

Row 1 (L-R): Ben Rosichan, Kurt Leavitt, Dennis McCarthy, Andre Durand, Tyrone Meyer, Bennett Isabella, Jeff Patzke, Shane Crandall. Row 2: Omar Longoria, Dan Warnemuende, Chris O'Neill, Lon Welsh, Seth Sovde, Brandon Hughson, Luke Mayer, Eric Dunivent, Joe Staska. Row 3: Charlie Falck, Lucas Christianson, Neil Wasmund, Mike Buck, Coach Craig Borey, Coach Pete Buesgens, Coach Brad Schafer, Head Coach Jim Jackson, Coach Tom O'Neill, Coach Dave Gomis, Coach Mark Wellstone, Dave Garrison, Travis Yamanaka, Jacob Schlottke. Row 4: Matt Shankey, John Dorma, Matt Doughty, Chad Polus, Brad Bruns, Chad Redmann, Mason Stedman, Paul Ristvedt, Nick Putman, Pete Senty, Nick Christianson, Mike Holtgren. Not Pictured: Matt McQuiston, Sam Chea, John Polga-Hecimovich, Nick Hefko, Manager Melissa Crone, Manager Laura Lien, Coach Bill Demaray, Coach Andy Wilkins, Coach Ben Just, Coach Jason Skapyak.

Class A

103 - Eric Sanders, Wabasha-Kellogg
112 - John Schermerhorn, Frazee
119 - Matt Jones, Lake Crystal-Wellcome Memorial
125 - Jason Foss, Royalton
130 - Kyle Dillon, BOLD, Olivia
135 - Matt Nagel, Frazee
140 - Matt Aho, Frazee
145 - Peter Miller, LeCenter
152 - Jacob Volkmann, Battle Lake/Underwood/Henning
160 - Miah Campbell, Lake Crystal-Wellcome Memorial
171 - Joe Moon, NRHEG, New Richland
189 - Justin Berg, NRHEG, New Richland
Hwt - Mike Schuch, Jasesville-Waldorf-Pemberton

119 - Jeff Pfaffinger, Blue Earth Area
125 - Austin Scarset, Redrock Central/Westbrook-Walnut Grove
130 - Steve Majerus, Jackson County Central
135 - Aaron Erickson, Minnewaska Area
140 - Shawn Williams, Brooklyn Center
145 - Ty Eustice, Blue Earth Area
152 - Dusty Wilking, Jackson County Central
160 - Nate Baker, Jackson County Central
171 - Alex Serie, Luverne/Ellsworth/Hills-Beaver Creek
189 - Jon Duncombe, St. Michael-Albertville
Hwt - Jake Helmin, Foley

Row 1 (L-R): Manager Becky Zwick, Joe Weigscheid, Joe Dretsch, Todd Larson, Tyson Sonnenberg, Jeremy Mayfield, Manager Lisa Ulschmid. Row 2: Gabe Dretsch, Adam Aho, Jason Ulschmid, Matt Nagel, Matt Aho, Jeremiah Ulschmid, John Schermerhorn, Trisha Quittschrieber. Row 3: Coach Clay Nagel, Clint Smith, Nick Courneya, Tim Nelson, Nick Woodard, Nate Woodard, Aaron Chirpich, Bryan Janke, Assistant Coach Marty Aho.

1999: Frazee (A)

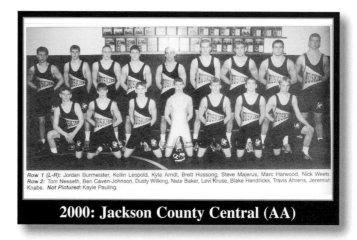

Row 1 (L-R): Jordan Burmeister, Kollin Leopold, Kyle Arndt, Brett Hussong, Steve Majerus, Marc Harwood, Nick Weets. Row 2: Tom Nesseth, Ben Caven-Johnson, Dusty Wilking, Nate Baker, Levi Kruse, Blake Hendricks, Travis Ahrens, Jeremiah Knabe. Not Pictured: Kayle Pauling.

2000: Jackson County Central (AA)

2000 Team Champions: Apple Valley (AAA), Jackson County Central (AA) & Paynesville Area (A)
2000 Individual Champions:
Class AAA
103 - Jesreal Keith, Virginia Area Co-op
112 - Mark Buck, Apple Valley
119 - Derek Johnson, Owatonna
125 - Matt Shankey, Apple Valley
130 - Chris McAlpine, Elk River Area
135 - Jamell Tidwell, Bloomington Kennedy
140 - Mike Verdeja, Simley
145 - Marcus LeVesseur, Minneapolis Roosevelt
152 - Paul Carlson, St. Francis
160 - Josh McLay, Hastings
171 - Brad Tupa, Faribault
189 - Jordan Holm, Northfield
Hwt - Chad Redmann, Apple Valley

Class AA
103 - Anthony Elg, Windom Area/Butterfield-Odin/Mountain Lake
112 - Mark Twardy, Litchfield

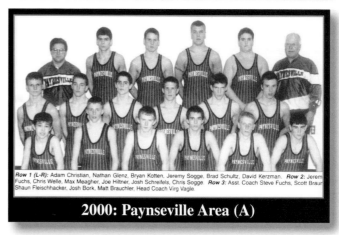

Row 1 (L-R): Adam Christian, Nathan Glenz, Bryan Kotten, Jeremy Sogge, Brad Schultz, David Kerzman. Row 2: Jerem Fuchs, Chris Welle, Max Meagher, Joe Hiltner, Josh Schreifels, Chris Sogge. Row 3: Asst. Coach Steve Fuchs, Scott Braur, Shaun Fleischhacker, Josh Bork, Matt Brauchler, Head Coach Virg Vagle.

2000: Paynseville Area (A)

Class A
103 - Eric Sanders, Wabasha-Kellogg
112 - John Schermerhorn, Frazee
119 - Aaron Kloss, Pierz
125 - David Kerzman, Paynesville Area
130 - Blaine Kuhlman, Medford
135 - Dustin Speltz, Lewiston-Altura
140 - Thad Pike, Hayfield
145 - Brian Miller, LeCenter

152 - Matt Nagel, Frazee
160 - Chris Young, Pierz
171 - Joe Moon, New Richland-Hartland-Ellendale-Geneva
189 - Johnny Frank, Wabasso
Hwt - Scott Revier, BOLD

2001: Apple Valley (AAA)

Row 1 (L-R): John Dorma, Shane Crandall, Bennett Isabella, Charlie Falck, Jeff Patzke, Sam Chea, Neil Wasmund, Bryce Wasmund. Row 2: Nick Christianson, Jarrod Yamanaka, John McCormick, Kyle Sovde, Tyrone Meyer, Mitch Cookas, Brandon Hughson, Tom LaCombe, Kurt Leavitt. Row 3: Manager Katie Kaszynski, Manager Melissa Crone, Manager Stephanie Wehrenberg, Coach Dalen Wasmund, Coach Tom O'Neill, Coach Brad Schafer, Head Coach Jim Jackson, Coach Mark Wellstone, Coach Andy Wilkins, Coach Pete Buesgens, Manager Laura Lien, Manager Maggie Louris, Manager Heather Hershiberger. Row 4: Jason White, Seth Sovde, Mike Holtgren, Lon Welsh, Chris O'Neill, Brad Bruns, Dan Warnemunde, Trevor Laws, Jacob Schlottke, Pete Senty. Not pictured: Coach Karl Jones, Coach Joe Vennewitz, Coach Jason Skapyak.

2001 Team Champions: Apple Valley (AAA), Blue Earth Area (AA) & Goodhue (A)
2001 Individual Champions:
Class AAA
103 - Charlie Falck, Apple Valley
112 - Neil Wasmund, Apple Valley
119 - Quincy Osborn, Grand Rapids
125 - Jafari Vanier, Bloomington Kennedy
130 - Jesse Marohn, Brainerd/Pillager
135 - Jamell Tidwell, Bloomington Kennedy
140 - Jacob Schlottke, Apple Valley
145 - Travis Fuhol, Cambridge-Isanti
152 - Marcus LeVesseur, Bloomington Kennedy
160 - Evan Amundson, Alexandria
171 - Bryan Cowdin, Worthington/SV-RL-B
189 - Adam Fokken, Eastview
275 - Max Lossen, Winona/Winona Cotter
Class AA
103 - Jared Evans, Blue Earth Area
112 - Leland Brincefield, Wadena-Deer Creek
119 - Logan Brincefield, Wadena-Deer Creek
125 - Jeff Pfaffinger, Blue Earth Area
130 - Ryan King, GMLOK
135 - Mike Weyer, Milaca/Faith Christian
140 - Marc Harwood, Jackson County Central
145 - Ty Eustice, Blue Earth Area
152 - Jeremy Larson, Fillmore Central
160 - Kelly Flaherty, Big Lake
171 - Ryan Flaherty, Big Lake
189 - Tim Kraemer, Rocori

275 - Josh Bresnahan, Pequot Lakes/Pine River-Backus

Class A
103 - Gabriel Mooney, Greenbush-Middle River/Badger
112 - Eric Sanders, Wabasha Kellogg
119 - Pat Salonek, Howard Lake-Waverly-Winsted
125 - Zac Roth, LakeCrystal-Wellcome Memorial
130 - David Kerzman, Paynesville Area
135 - Brent Reinhard, Medford
140 - Mitch Kuhlman, Medford
145 - Danon Anderson, Saint James
152 - Matt Nagel, Frazee
160 - Tony Schlaak, NewRichland/Heartland/Elendal/Geneva
171 - Tyler Bullerman, Adrian
189 - John Wheelock, Janesville-Waldorf-Pemberton
275 - Ryan Rosin, Nicollet

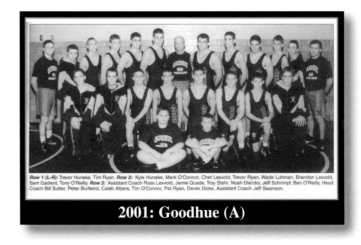
2001: Goodhue (A)

Row 1 (L-R): Trevor Huneke, Tim Ryan. Row 2: Kyle Huneke, Mark O'Connor, Chet Lexvold, Trevor Ryan, Wade Luhman, Brandon Lexvold, Sam Gadient, Tony O'Reilly. Row 3: Assistant Coach Ross Lexvold, Jamie Quade, Troy Stehr, Noah Diercks, Jeff Schrimpf, Ben O'Reilly, Head Coach Bill Sutter, Peter Burfeind, Caleb Albers, Tim O'Connor, Pat Ryan, Derek Dicke, Assistant Coach Jeff Swanson.

2002 Team Champions: Apple Valley (AAA), Blue Earth Area (AA), Medford (B) & Frazee (A) (Co-Champs)
2002 Individual Champions:
Class AAA
103 - Josh Hansen, Albert Lea/Glenville-Emmons
112 - Charlie Falck, Apple Valley
119 - Neil Wasmund, Apple Valley
125 - Quincy Osborn, Grand Rapids
130 - David Sadder, Totino-Grace
135 - Thomas McAlpine, Elk River Area
140 - Andy Pickar, Brainerd
145 - Dustin Dahlblom, Stillwater Area
152 - Jacob Schlottke, Apple Valley
160 - George Lynaugh, Simley
171 - Jared Massey, Centennial
189 - Justin Walsh, Alexandria
275 - Trevor Laws, Apple Valley

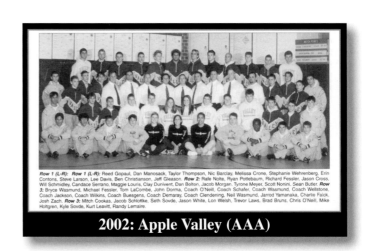
2001: Blue Earth Area (AA)

Row 1 (L-R): Sheena Wallace, Brie Lewis, Angie Olson, Danielle Schuster, Janica Smith. Row 2: Jared Evans, Ty Eustice, Travis Olson, Jeff Pfaffinger, Jake Ankey, Taylor Teems. Row 3: Head Coach Jack Eustice, Manager Ben Hoyt, Matt Bartley, Blake Murphy, Tony Boehm, Josh Hougen, Assistant Coach David Pfaffinger. Row 4: Eric Sonnek, David Mensing, Dan Ristau, Bart Oelke, Travis Krinkie, Jim Grant, Josh Malwitz, Jay Frederickson, Assistant Coach Randy Wirtjes.

2002: Apple Valley (AAA)

Row 1 (L-R): Row 1 (L-R): Reed Gopaul, Dan Manosack, Taylor Thompson, Nic Barclay, Melissa Crone, Stephanie Wehrenberg, Erin Cortons, Steve Larson, Lee Davis, Ben Christianson, Jeff Gleason. Row 2: Rafe Nolte, Ryan Pottebaum, Richard Fessler, Jason Cross, Will Schmidley, Candace Serrano, Maggie Louris, Clay Dunivent, Dan Bolton, Jacob Morgan, Tyrone Meyer, Scott Nonini, Sean Butler. Row 3: Bryce Wasmund, Michael Fessler, Tom LaCombe, John Dorma, Coach O'Neill, Coach Schafer, Coach Wasmund, Coach Wellstone, Coach Jackson, Coach Wilkins, Coach Buesgens, Coach Demaray, Coach Clendening, Neil Wasmund, Jarrod Yamanaka, Charlie Falck, Josh Zach. Row 3: Mitch Cookas, Jacob Schlottke, Seth Sovde, Jason White, Lon Welsh, Trevor Laws, Brad Bruns, Chris O'Neill, Mike Holtgren, Kyle Sovde, Kurt Leavitt, Randy Lemaire.

Class AA

103 - Tyler Safratowich, Park Rapids Area
112 - Brandon Dick, St. Michael-Albertville
119 - Jared Evans, Blue Earth Area
125 - Jeff Pfaffinger, Blue Earth Area
130 - Jeff Cooley, Red Rock Central/Westbrook-Walnut Grove
135 - Ryan King, Grand Meadow/LeRoy-Ostrander/Kingsland
140 - Jason Rhoten, Kasson-Mantorville
145 - David Whipps, Scott West
152 - Marc Harwood, Jackson County Central
160 - Travis Krinkie, Blue Earth Area
171 - Ethan Vogt, Sauk Centre
189 - Marty Engen, Paynesville Area
275 - Ben Janike, Waseca

Row 1 (L-R): Mouse King, Ashley Mohn, Melanee Laplant, Sheena Wagner, Becky Anderson, Alissa Sandberg, Stephanie Bruhn. Row 2: Kelly Janke, Dan Mayfield, Andy Quittschelber, Brenton Newling, Darren Oswald, Jake Sailer, Ben Anderson, Kerry Lockrem. Row 3: Kristie Hass, Jackie Hockett, Scott Perrine, Joe Roberts, John King, Issac Ratz, Elezabeth Buhr, Cheerleading Advisor Theres Newling. Row 4: Coach Clay Nagel, Coach Dennis Schermerhorn, Darin Drewes, Justin Olson, Dan Stenger, Gabe Dretsch, Adam Aho, Coach Marty Aho, Coach Matt Aho.

2002: Frazee (A)

Row 1 (L-R): Becky Siegling, Stats, Kurt Sohn, Ben Hoyt, Trevor Ruser, Eric Esser, Matt Bakken, Josh Hougen, Co-Head Coach Dave Pfaffinger. Row 2: Manager Jim Grant, Eric Nagel, Taylor Teems, Jared Evans, Jeff Pfaffinger, Jake Ankeny, Todd Rasmussen, Manager Bart Oelke. Row 3: Co-Head Coach Randy Wirtjes, Tony Boehn, Josh Malwitz, Travis Krinkie, Zac Campbell, Jay Frederickson, Eric Sonnek, Assistant Coach Tim Blagg.

2002: Blue Earth Area (AA)

Class A

103 - Gabriel Mooney, Greenbush-Middle River/Badger
112 - Eric Sanders, Wabasha-Kellogg
119 - Darren Oswald, Frazee
125 - Shane Masching, Hayfield
130 - Joeb Oyster, Bertha-Hewitt/Verndale
135 - Craig Luberts, Pierz
140 - Shawn Plumley, BOLD
145 - Mitch Kuhlman, Medford
152 - Cory Harnitz, Lake Crystal-Wellcome Memorial
160 - Tony Jenson, Greenbush-Middle River/Badger
171 - Tyler Bullerman, Adrian
189 - Corey Feltmann, Norwood-Young America
275 - Kory Andersen, St. James

Row 1 (L-R): Manager Cassie Neumann, Stats Anna Brady. Row 2: Scott Balzer, Dusty Kavitz, Greg Brendemuehl, Chad Mitek, Matt Barta, Danny Simmons, Brent Reinhard. Row 3: Assistant Coach Nick Neumann, Nick Yule, Brent Glende, Steve Maas, Bob Hanson, Jeremy Kaplan, Brent Yule, Mitch Kuhlman, Head Coach Dennis Whitman. Not pictured: Paul Karow, Chris Rutherford, Mitch Elzen, Kelly Markham, David Schroht.

2002: Medford (A)

2003 Team Champions: Apple Valley (AAA), Litchfield (AA) & BOLD-Olivia (A)
2003 Individual Champions:
Class AAA

103 - Zach Bigboy, Bloomington Kennedy
112 - Jayson Ness, Bloomington Kennedy

119 - Charlie Falck, Apple Valley
125 - Richard Fessler, Apple Valley
130 - T.J. Parlin, Austin
135 - Jestin Hulegaard, Anoka
140 - Andy Merkins, Hutchinson
145 - Dustin Dahlblom, Stillwater Area
152 - Andy Pickar, Brainerd
160 - Kyle Anderson, Simley
171 - George Lynaugh, Simley
189 - Jared Massey, Centennial
215 - Kyle Massey, Centennial
275 - Jon May, Hutchinson

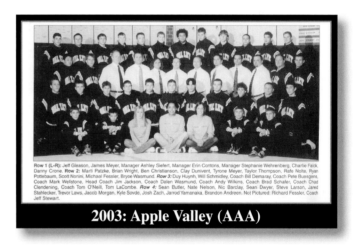

Row 1 (L-R): Jeff Gleason, James Meyer, Manager Ashley Siefert, Manager Erin Contons, Manager Stephanie Wehrenberg, Charlie Falck, Danny Crone. Row 2: Marti Patzke, Brian Wright, Ben Christianson, Clay Dunivent, Tyrone Meyer, Taylor Thompson, Rafe Nolte, Ryan Pottebaum, Scott Nonini, Michael Fessler, Bryce Wasmund. Row 3: Duy Huynh, Will Schmidley, Coach Bill Demaray, Coach Pete Busegens, Coach Mark Wellstone, Head Coach Jim Jackson, Coach Dalen Wasmund, Coach Andy Wilkins, Coach Brad Schafer, Coach Chad Clendening, Coach Tom O'Neill, Tom LaCombe. Row 4: Sean Butler, Nate Nelson, Nic Barclay, Sean Dwyer, Steve Larson, Jared Stahlecker, Trevor Laws, Jacob Morgan, Kyle Sovde, Josh Zach, Jarrod Yamanaka, Brandon Andreen. Not Pictured: Richard Fessler, Coach Jeff Stewart.

2003: Apple Valley (AAA)

Class AA

103 - Travis Elg, Windom Area/Butterfield-Odin/Mountain Lake
112 - Tyler Safratowich, Park Rapids Area
119 - Nick Kulseth, Windom Area/Butterfield-Odin/Mountain Lake
125 - Tony Noyes, New London-Spicer
130 - Jeff Cooley, Red Rock Central/Westbrook-Walnut Grove
135 - Mike Folie, Waseca

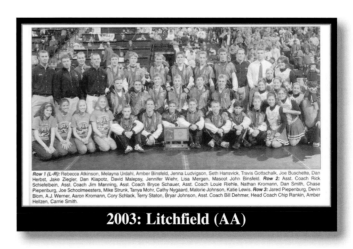

Row 1 (L-R): Rebecca Atkinson, Melayna Urdahl, Amber Binsfeld, Jenna Ludvigson, Seth Hansvick, Travis Gottschalk, Joe Buschette, Dan Herbst, Jake Ziegler, Dan Klapotz, David Malepsy, Jennifer Wiehr, Lisa Mergen, Mascot John Binsfeld. Row 2: Coach Rick Schietelbein, Asst. Coach Jim Manning, Asst. Coach Bryce Schauer, Asst. Coach Louie Riehle, Nathan Kromann, Dan Smith, Chase Piepenburg, Joe Schoolmeesters, Mike Strunk, Tanya Mohr, Cathy Nygaard, Malorie Johnson, Katie Lewis. Row 3: Jared Piepenburg, Devin Blom, A.J. Werner, Aaron Kromann, Cory Schlack, Terry Staton, Bryar Johnson, Asst. Coach Bill Dehmer, Head Coach Chip Rankin, Amber Helizen, Carrie Smith.

2003: Litchfield (AA)

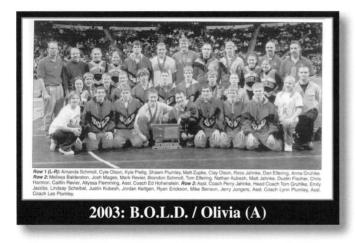

Row 1 (L-R): Amanda Schmoll, Cyle Olson, Kyle Pietig, Shawn Plumley, Matt Zupke, Clay Olson, Ross Jahnke, Dan Elfering, Anna Gruhlke. Row 2: Melissa Balderston, Josh Mages, Mark Revier, Brandon Schmoll, Tom Elfering, Nathan Kubesh, Matt Jahnke, Dustin Fischer, Chris Harmon, Caitlin Revier, Allyssa Flemming, Asst. Coach Ed Hohenstein. Row 3: Asst. Coach Perry Jahnke, Head Coach Tom Gruhlke, Emily Jacobs, Lindsay Scheibel, Justin Kubesh, Jordan Keltgen, Ryan Erickson, Mike Benson, Jerry Jungers, Asst. Coach Lynn Plumley, Asst. Coach Les Plumley.

2003: B.O.L.D. / Olivia (A)

140 - Peter Hayes, Wadena-Deer Creek
145 - Jeremy Anderson, Thief River Falls
152 - Nathan Matousek, Glencoe-Silver Lake
160 - Andy Przekwas, Roseau
171 - Jacob Bryce, Minnewaska Area
189 - Jeremy Pederson, Becker
215 - Kevan Meiners, Caledonia/Houston/Spring Grove
275 - Jeff Lucas, Scott West

Class A
103 - Zachary Sanders, Wabasha-Kellogg
112 - Gabriel Mooney, Greenbush-Middle River/Badger
119 - Eric Sanders, Wabasha-Kellogg
125 - Shane Masching, Hayfield
130 - Kelly Janke, Frazee
135 - Andy Quittschreiber, Frazee
140 - Craig Luberts, Pierz
145 - Shawn Plumley, BOLD
152 - Mitch Kuhlman, Medford
160 - Gabe Dretsch, Frazee
171 - Tom Libbesmeier, Kimball Area
189 - Craig Myhre, Minneota
215 - Casey Finck, Bertha-Hewitt/Verndale
275 - Justin Olson, Frazee

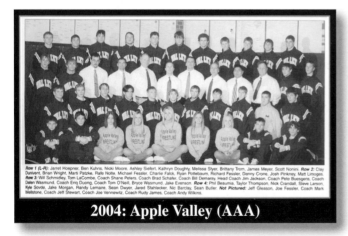

Row 1 (L-R): Jarret Hoepner, Ben Kuhns, Nicki Moore, Ashley Siefert, Kathryn Doughty, Melissa Styer, Brittany Trom, James Meyer, Scott Nonini. Row 2: Clay Dunivent, Brian Wright, Marti Patzke, Rafe Nolte, Michael Fessler, Charlie Falck, Ryan Pottebaum, Richard Fessler, Danny Crone, Josh Pinkney, Matt Limogds. Row 3: Will Schmidley, Tom LaCombe, Coach Shane Peters, Coach Brad Schafer, Head Coach Jim Jackson, Coach Pete Buesgens, Coach Dalen Wasmund, Coach Enq Duong, Coach Tom O'Neill, Bryce Wasmund, Jake Evenson. Row 4: Phil Beaumia, Taylor Thompson, Nick Crandall, Steve Larson, Kyle Sovde, Jake Morgan, Randy Lemaire, Sean Dwyer, Jared Stahlecker, Nic Barclay, Sean Butler. Not Pictured: Jeff Gleason, Joe Fessler, Coach Mark Wellstone, Coach Jeff Stewart, Coach Joe Vennewitz, Coach Rudy James, Coach Andy Wilkins.

2004: Apple Valley (AAA)

2004 Team Champions: Apple Valley (Class AAA), St. Michael Albertville (Class AA) & Pierz (Class A)
2004 Individual Champions:
Class AAA
103 - Alex Meger, Owatonna
112 - Zack Bigboy, Bloomington Kennedy
119 - Charlie Falck, Apple Valley
125 - Richard Fessler, Apple Valley
130 - T.J. Parlin, Austin
135 - Adam Elseth, Albert Lea Area
140 - Michael Fessler, Apple Valley

145 - Mitch Millner, Simley
152 - Mike Quamme, Northfield
160 - Mike Felling, Hutchinson
171 - Josh Zabel, Rochester Mayo
189 - Ousley Early, Saint Paul Johnson
215 - Mike Maresh, Champlin Park
275 - Kyle Massey, Champlin Park

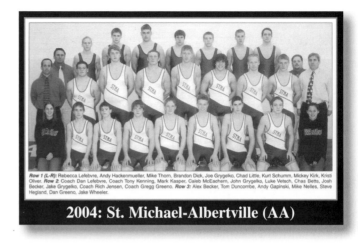

Row 1 (L-R): Rebecca Lefebvre, Andy Hackenmueller, Mike Thorn, Brandon Dick, Joe Grygelko, Chad Little, Kurt Schumm, Mickey Kirk, Kristi Oliver. Row 2: Coach Dan Lefebvre, Coach Tony Kenning, Mark Kasper, Caleb McEachern, John Grygelko, Luke Vetsch, Chas Betts, Josh Becker, Jake Grygelko, Coach Rich Jensen, Coach Gregg Greeno. Row 3: Alex Becker, Tom Duncombe, Andy Gapinski, Mike Nelles, Steve Hegland, Dan Greeno, Jake Wheeler.

2004: St. Michael-Albertville (AA)

Class AA
103 - Derek Pesta, Long Prairie-Grey Eagle
112 - Mike Thorn, Saint Michael-Albertville
119 - Travis Elg, Windom Area/MountainLake/Butterfield-Odin
125 - Nick Kulseth, Windom Area/MountainLake/Butterfield-Odin
130 - Tyler Safratowich, Park Rapids Area
135 - Cory Feehan, Rockford
140 - Stephen Pilgram, Annandale/Maple Lake
145 - Kurt Haakinson, Sauk Centre
152 - Nate Matousek, Glencoe-Silver Lake
160 - Chas Betts, Saint Michael-Albertville
171 - Mitch Vedders, Milaca/Faith Christian
189 - Tom Nesseth, Jackson County Central
215 - Jason Finley, Lake City
275 - Jesse Kahn, Plainview/Elgin Millville

Class A
103 - Zach Sanders, Wabasha Kellogg
112 - Kirk Anderson, Barnesville
119 - Joe Grasser, LeCenter/Cleveland
125 - Gabriel Mooney, Badger/Greenbush-Middle River
130 - Shane Masching, Hayfield
135 - Kelly Janke, Frazee
140 - Craig Luberts, Pierz
145 - Cory Schunk, Wabasso
152 - Adam Aho, Frazee
160 - Joe Bunne, Grand Meadow/Leroy Ostrander/Kingsland
171 - Justin LaGosh, Zumbrota Mazzeppa
189 - Cory Harnitz, LC-WM/Mankato Loyola
215 - Dusty Faber, Martin County West
275 - Jared Schwanz, St. James

Row 1 (L-R): Kaley Jensen, Mark Lust, Hank Virnig, Kyle Bednar, Nathan Janson, Scott Janson, Jon Andres, Darren Stangl, Chuck Boser, Zach Solinger, Kelsey Fuhrman. Row 2: Warren Gall, Nick Gruber, Tony Andres, Craig Luberts, Kyle Girtz, Nathan Britz, Joe Hyatt. Row 3: Mark Jensen, Mark Andres, Tim Young, Cody Luberts, Matt Mrnak, Jesse Zajac, Tyler Stumpf, Scott Saehr, Simon Waltman, Shawn Janson.

2004: Pierz (A)

HIGH SCHOOL COACHES 200-WINS CLUB

NAME	SCHOOL	RECORD
1. Bill Sutter	Goodhue	670-132-8
2. Virg Vagle	Paynesville	661-148-6
3. Scot Davis	Owatonna, Hutchinson, Bird Island-Lk Lillian, Belcourt (ND)	650-106-4
4. Gary Hindt	Wabasso	501-150-6
5. Ron Malcolm	Anoka, Worthington	464-119-5
6. Ken Droegemueller	Osseo, Worthington	440-145-4
7. Greg Greeno	St. Michael-Albertville	438-75-2
8. Lyle Freudenberg	Foley	421-87-3
9. Bill Demaray	Apple Valley, Richfield	407-70-4
10. Don Dravis	Staples	401-51-4
11. Rick Kelvington	Olivia, BOLD	379-120-10
12. Jim Short	Simley	374-160-6
13. Bob Board	Coon Rapids	372-122-3
14. Richard Chakolis	Minneapolis North	370-134-1
15. Luverne Klar	Mankato, Mankato West	358-169-12
16. Clay Nagel	Frazee, Beach	353-73-2
17. Gary Rettke	Spring Lake Park	339-236
18. Gerry Gingles	Canby	338-73-9
19. Jim Carr	Adrian	333-124-5
20. Dick Pullen	Monticello, St. Mich.-Alb.	333-175-7
21. Doug Dahl	Greenbush-Middle River	332-139-10
22. John Delozier	Rocori Bertha-Hewitt	331-136-8
23. Dick Black	Owatonna, Britt (IA)	326-123-6
24. Randy Zimmer	Milaca	324-71-7
25. Steve Techam	Bertha-Hewitt/Verndale	323-141-8
26. Eugene Hildebrandt	St. James	317-77-2
27. Robert Dettmer	Forest Lake	316-126-2
28. Mike Niemczyk	Janesville-Waldorf-Pemb.	315-233-7
29. Jim Jackson	Apple Valley	313-13-3
30. Steve Johnson	Nicollet, Ogilvie	313-186-6
31. Charlie Coffee	Bloomington	310-268-5
32. Kevin Gross	Wheaton/Herman-Norc.	308-88-5
33. Steve Bechtold	Blackduck/CassLake-Bena, Blackduck, St. John's Prep	306-200-5
34. Jeff Gallagher	Montevideo, Windom	305-233-3
35. Paul Cyr	NewRichland-Hartland-Ellendale-Geneva	297-192-11
36. Don Krusemark	Mankato West, Byron, Amboy-Good Thunder	292-186-3
37. Bruce Bartels	Annandale/Maple Lake, Annandale	286-238-10
38. Darrel Dammann	Mayer Luth./Norwood YA	283-155-6
39. Chuck Prunty	Austin	282-131-3
40. Paul Vaith	Hastings	271-72-1
41. Dave Schulte	LaCrescent	270-120-7
42. Bob Thorson	Fertile-Beltrami	270-132-6
43. Noel Bailey	Aitkin, Sauk Rapids	269-149-7
44. Dave Erickson	Hayfield	268-118-4
45. Mike Mazzitelli	Dover-Eyota	267-190-5
46. Gary Wolf	Yellow Medicine, East Clarkfield, Elbow Lake	265-138-2
47. Jack Eustice	Blue Earth Area	263-87-4
48. Bill Farmer	Shakopee	259-295-7
49. Mel Cain	Sibley East, Arlington-Green Isle, Dodge Center	255-288-5
50. Horace Mayo	Minneapolis Southwest	252-167-7
51. Neil Jennissen	Cambridge-Isanti	251-78-2
52. John Grygelko	Robbinsdale	250-40
53. Everett Sykora	Browerville	246-219-7
54. Ray Miller	BDRSH, Sacred Heart, Renville-Sacred Heart	243-259-8
55. Dennis Kaatz	Wadena-Deer Creek	235-62
56. Bob Ryan	St. Paul Humboldt	235-131-6
57. Ken Ebert	Cannon Falls	235-135-3
58. Terry Sworsky	St. Francis	232-94-5
59. Darrell Sohn	Fairfax, St. James, Robbinsdale Cooper, Armstrong	230-120-3
60. Dick Fox	Scott West, Belle Plaine	228-65-1
61. Rich Saxlund	Pipestone, Leroy-Ostrander	228-244-9
62. Harlan Steen	Raymond, MACCRAY	227-169-3
63. Jay Johnson	Eden Valley-Watkins	227-184-7
64. Joe Frank	Fridley	226-31-1
65. Paul Ehrhard	Albert Lea, Kasson-Mant.	224-34-6
66. Jeff Lamphere	Minnetonka, Wayzata, Frazee	223-153-4
67. Neal Skaar	Albert Lea	222-49-5
68. Ron Sanders	Wabasha-Kellogg	219-184-6
69. John Halverson	Lester Prairie/Holy Trinity	218-193-6
70. Doug Svihel	Totino-Grace	216-91-3
71. Jerry Kral Morgan	River Valley, Cedar Mtn	215-75-5
72. Kevin Jensen	LeCenter	215-111-3
73. Jim Nunn	Minnetonka, Brklyn Ctr, Prior Lake, Blake/Breck, De La Salle	215-174-2
74. Joe Rajkowski	Braham Area	212-230-5
75. Larry Goodnature	Albert Lea, Hutchinson	210-87
76. Jeff Bakke	EGF, Sacred Heart East Grand Forks, George (IA)	210-290-8
77. Wayne Johnson	Detroit Lakes, Hibbing	206-85-1
78. Dick Shiels	Faribault	205-66-4
79. Rodd Olson	Crookston	205-150-1
80. Clyde Lundholm	New Richland-Hartland	204-82-7
81. Leo Simon	Caledonia, Goodhue	201-59-48
82. Keith Young	Blue Earth, Cedar Fls (IA)	200-99-12

Source:: The Guillotine

ALL-TIME HIGH SCHOOL DREAM TEAM (1937-1997)

George Sigafoos	Robbinsdale	85 lbs	Mark Lange	Caledonia	140 lbs
Mike McArthur	Osseo	98 lbs	Chad Kraft	HLOL	145 lbs
Charles Ofsthun	Robbinsdale	103 lbs	Corey Olson	Hayfield	152 lbs
Howard Leopold	Redwood Falls	112 lbs	Tom Jean	Albert Lea	165 lbs
Dick Mueller	Anoka	119 lbs	Brad Rheingans	Appleton	175 lbs
Al DeLeon	Blue Earth	125 lbs	Stan Christ	Mankato	180 lbs
Steve Carr	Moorhead/Battle Lk	130 lbs	Verne Gagne	Robbinsdale	Hwt
Larry Zilverberg	Hopkins	135 lbs			

(Sponsored by Minnesota/USA Wrestling)

THE HIGH SCHOOL RECORDBOOK

Source: The Guillotine

STATE TOURNAMENT RECORDS

Team Championships (individual points): 8 - Robbinsdale

Dual Meet Championships: 13 - Apple Valley

Consecutive Dual Meet Championships: 6 - Staples, 1980-85; Apple Valley, 1999-04

Dual Meet Appearances: 23 - Canby 1975-2000; Apple Valley, 1980-2004

Dual Meet Finals Appearances: 18 - Apple Valley

Consecutive Dual Meet Appearances: 22 - Apple Valley, 1983-2004

Individual State Champions (1938-2004): 50 – Robbinsdale & Blue Earth Area

Individual State Participants: 266 - Anoka, 1938-2004

TEAM RECORDS

Dual Meet Wins (1 season): 49 - Owatonna, 2001-02 (49-5)
Consecutive Dual Meet Wins: 83 - Caledonia, 1967-74
Team Falls (1 season): 296 - Centennial, 2002-03
Team Points (1 season): 3,178.0 - Owatonna, 2002-03
Individual Wins (1 season): 611 - Owatonna, 2002-03 (611-248)
Takedowns (1 season): 2126 - Apple Valley, 1999-00
Nearfalls (1 season): 584 - Apple Valley, 2002-03 (387 3 pt./197 2 pt.)
Varsity Wrestlers Used (1 season): 51 - Owatonna, 1999-2000

INDIVIDUAL RECORDS

Five Time State Champs:
Matt Nagel, Frazee, 1997-2001
Eric Sanders, Wabasha-Kellogg 1999-03

Four Time State Champs:
Steve Carr, Battle Lake, 1976-78, Moorhead, 1979
Chad Erikson, Apple Valley, 1994-97
Charlie Falck, Apple Valley, 2001-04
Ty Friederichs, Osseo, 1992-95
Marcus LeVesseur, Mpls Roosevelt, 1998-00, Bloom. Kennedy, 2001
John Miller, Renville-Sacred Heart, 1982-85
Ty Eustice, Blue Earth Area, 1997, 1999-2001
Gabriel Mooney, Greenbush-Middle River/Badger, 2001-04
Jeff Pfaffinger, Blue Earth Area, 1999-02
Jim Van Gordon, Mpls. Marshall, 1937-40

State Titles by Brothers:
7 titles - Sanders brothers, Wabasha-Kellogg, Eric 1999 (103), 2000 (103), 2001 (112), 2002 (112), 2003 (119); Zachary 2003 (103), 2004 (103)

7 titles - Eustice brothers, Blue Earth Area, Luke 1996 (103), 1998 (112), 1999 (125); Ty 1997 (103), 1999 (135), 2000 (145), 2001 (145)

7 titles - Short brothers, Simley, John 1985 (138); Chris 1986 (185), 1987 (185); Willy 1988 (138), 1989 (152); Wade 1990 (138), 1991 (152)

Career Wins by Brothers:
1. 699 - Wurm brothers, Maple Lake/Annandale: Lloyd -171, Loren - 105, Len - 142, LeRoy - 89, Lance - 192
2. 663 - Merritt brothers, Canby: Alan - 55, Doug - 64, Bob - 54, Jeff - 107, Todd - 113, Chad - 143, Kim - 127
3. 623 - Duncombe Brothers, St. Michael-Albertville: Dan - 200, Jon - 178, Mike - 131, Mitch - 57, Paul - 53, Tom - 4
4. 552 - Short Brothers, Simley: John - 97, Chris - 124, Will - 168, Wade - 163
5. 503 - Dorn brothers, Adrian: Pat - 161, Randy - 129, Rick - 114, Mark - 99

Career Wins: 233 - Mitch Kuhlman, Medford, 1997-03

Career Falls: 159 - Kyle Massey, Champlin Park & Centennial, 2000-04

Career Team Points: 1447.5 - Matt Nagel, Frazee, 1996-01

Consecutive Wins:
1. 141 - Marcus LeVesseur, Bloomington Kennedy, 1995-01
2. 133 - Gabriel Mooney, Greenbush-Mid. River/Badger, 2000-04
3. 129 - Steve Carr, Battle Lake, Moorhead, 1976-79
4. 103 - Jeff Pfaffinger, Blue Earth Area, 1997-02

Wins in a Season:
49 - George Lynaugh, Simley, 2002-03 (49-0)
49 - Jon May, Hutchinson, 2002-03 (49-0)
49 - Mike Thorn, St. Michael-Albertville, 2003-04 (49-0)
49 - Mike Meger, Owatonna, 2002-03 (49-1)
49 - Michael Fessler, Apple Valley, 2002-03 (49-2)
49 - Charlie Falck, Apple Valley, 2003-04 (49-2)

Falls in a Season: 40 - Kyle Massey, Centennial, 2002-03

Takedowns in a Season: 446 - Jacob Schlottke, Apple Valley, 2001-02

Career Takedowns: 1,342 - Jacob Schlottke, Apple Valley, 1997-02

Win Percentage: 97.60% - Jamey Keller, Foley, 1992-95, (163-4)

Fastest Fall: 4 seconds - Nathan Bipes, McLeod.West, 1997 & Tamir Khalil, Spring Lake Park, 1998

DID YOU KNOW?

According to a study by a group of national insurance companies, wrestling is currently ranked as the third most popular sport among high school boys in the U.S. And, it is safer then football with regards to the number of serious injuries as well.

ALL-TIME COACHING RECORDS

Source: The Guillotine

Career Wins:
1. Bill Sutter, Goodhue, 670-132-8
2. Virg Vagle, Paynesville, 2004, 661-148-6
3. Scot Davis, Owatonna, Hutchinson, Bird Island-Lake Lillian, Belcourt (ND), 650-106-4
4. Gary Hindt, Wabasso, 501-150-6
5. Ron Malcolm, Anoka, Worthington, 464-119-5

Win Percentage:
1. 95.1% - Jim Jackson, Apple Valley, 313-13-3, 1995-2004
2. 87.9% - Don Dravis, Staples, 401-51-4, 1964-1995
3. 87.6% - Joe Frank, Fridley, 226-31-1, 1969 -1985
4. 86.2% - John Grygelko, Robbinsdale, 250-40-0
5. 85.5% - Scot Davis, Owatonna, Hutchinson, Bird Island-Lake Lillian, Belcourt (ND), 650-106-4, 1977-2004

Team State Championships Coached:
7 - Don Dravis, Staples (1978, '80, '81, '82, '83, '84, '85)
7 - Jim Jackson, Apple Valley (1997, '99, '00, '01, '02, '03, '04)
6 - Bill Demaray, Apple Valley (1983, '85, '86, '91, '94, '95)
5 - Gerry Gingles, Canby (1976, '77, '79, '86, '88)

Individual State Championships Coached:
21 - Ron Malcolm, Anoka, Worthington
21 - Jim Jackson, Apple Valley
18 - Bill Demaray, Apple Valley
17 - Randy Baker, Jackson County Central

16 - Jack Eustice, Blue Earth Area
16 - Ken Droegemueller, Osseo
16 - Jim Short, Simley
16 - Garth Lappin, Anoka
16 - Clay Nagel, Frazee
15 - Paul Ehrhard, Albert Lea, Kasson-Mantorville
14 - Don Dravis, Staples
14 - John Grygelko, Robbinsdale
12 - Bob Dettmer, Forest Lake

Individual State Placewinners Coached:
90 - John Grygelko, Robbinsdale
64 - Don Dravis, Staples
64 - Clay Nagel, Frazee
62 - Ken Droegemueller, Osseo
62 - Jim Jackson, Apple Valley
58 - Ron Malcolm, Anoka, Worthington
57 - Bob Dettmer, Forest Lake
56 - Jim Short, Simley
51 - Scot Davis, Owatonna

All-Time Individual State Champions by School
1. Blue Earth Area   50
1. Robbinsdale   50
3. Anoka   40
4. Apple Valley   39
5. Albert Lea   25

TOP 25 CAREER WINS

NAME	SCHOOL	GRAD	RECORD
1. Mitch Kuhlman	Medford	2003	233-11-0
2. Adam Aho	Frazee	2004	225-36-0
3. Eric Sanders	Wabasha-Kellogg	2003	223-27-0
4. Marcus LeVesseur	Kennedy, Roosevelt	2001	218-12-0
5. Matt Nagel	Frazee	2001	217-18-0
6. Jesse Jensen	Brooklyn Center	2001	214-27-0
7. Charlie Falck	Apple Valley	2004	213-11-0
8. Luke Becker	Cambridge-Isanti	1998	210-18-0
9. Matt Kraft	HLOL/Jackson	1997	209-24-0
10. Brandon Dick	St. Michael-Alb.	2004	206-18-0
11. Clay Hoeck	Milaca	2004	206-40-0
12. Chad Stender	Browerville	1991	204-12-0
13. Nate Baker	Jackson Cty Ctrl	2000	204-12-0
14. Wayne Mooney	Greenbush	1995	204-30-0
15. Kyle Massey	Champ. Park, Cent.	2004	203-35-0
16. Craig Luberts	Pierz	2004	201-16-0
17. Jared Oyster	Bertha-Hewitt/Verndale	2004	201-26-0
18. Dan Duncombe	St. Michael-Alb.	1996	200-20-0
19. Nate Matousek	Glencoe-Silver Lk	2005	198-13-0
20. Matt Gadient	Goodhue	1997	198-43-1
21. Chad Kraft	HLOL	1994	195-14-1
22. Jacob Schlottke	Apple Valley	2002	194-13-0
23. Dustin Dahlblom	Stillwater	2003	193-47-0
24. Chad Erikson	Apple Valley	1997	192-16-0
25. Lance Wurm	Annandale/Maple Lake	1997	192-24-1

MR. MINNESOTA WRESTLER

The Minnesota Wrestling Coaches Association annually presents the Mr. Minnesota High School Wrestler award to the senior that best exemplifies the highest ideals of high school wrestling in Minnesota. Judging is based on past performances, citizenship, academics, leadership, and adherence to MSHSL rules.

YR	NAME	HIGH SCHOOL
1990	Chad Carlson	Willmar
1991	Chad Nelson	Stewartville
1992	Brandon Paulson	Anoka
1993	Brandon Howe	Totino Grace
1994	Chad Kraft	Heron Lk-Okabena-Lakefield
1995	Jon Fitzgerald	Martin County West
1996	Dan Duncombe	St. Michael-Albertville
1997	Chad Erickson	AppleValley
1998	Luke Becker	Cambridge-Isanti
1999	Jacob Volkmann	Battle Lake-Underwood-Henning
2000	Nate Baker	Jackson County Central
2001	Marcus LeVesseur	Bloomington Kennedy
2002	Jeff Pfaffinger	Blue Earth Area
2003	Eric Sanders	Wabasha-Kellogg
2004	Jeff Pfaffinger	Blue Earth Area

MWCA COACH OF THE YEAR

YR	COACH	SCHOOL
1968	Don Meyers	Fridley
1969	Paul (Don) Bengston	Hopkins
1970	Darrell Sohn	Robbinsdale Cooper
1971	Paul Ehrhard	Albert Lea
1972	Paul Krueger	Saint James
1973	Joe Frank	Fridley
1974	Ray Christenson	Minnetonka
1975	Luverne KIar	Mankato
1976	Ron Malcolm	Anoka
1977	Gerry Gingles	Canby
1978	Don Dravis	Staples
1979	Ray Christenson	Minnetonka
1980	Bill Memaray - AA	Apple Valley
	Bill Sutter - A	Goodhue
1981	Mike Hanlon - AA	Elk River
	Buzz Cummins - A	Waterville
1982	Dick Shiels - AA	Faribault
	Buzz Cummins - A	Waterville
1983	Bill Farmer-AA	Shakopee
	Bill Sutter - A	Goodhue
1984	David Arens - AA	Bloomington Kennedy
	Lyle Freudenberg - A	Foley
1985	Dick Black-AA	Owatonna
	Jim Campbell - A	Plainview
1986	Terry Sworsky-AA	St. Francis
	Mike Niemczyk - A	Janesville
1987	Jim Short - AA	Simley
	Virg Vagle - A	Paynesville
1988	Bob Ryan -AA	St. Paul Humboldt
	Noel Bailey - A	Aitkin
1989	Bill Schmidt - AA	Winona
	Eugene Hildebrandt - A	Saint James
1990	Chuck Prunty - AA	Austin
	Dennis Kuisle - A	Stewartville
1991	Gerald Bakke -AA	Butfalo
	Kevin Jensen - A	LeCenter
1992	Jeff Williamson - AA	Worthington (co-coach)
	Dale Solt - AA	Worthington (co-coach)
	Jim Slinkard - A	New Prague
1993	Dave Henry - AA	Faribault
	Randy Baker - A	Heron Lake-Okabena-Lakefield
1994	Neil Jennissen - AA	Cambridge
	Bill Sutter - A	Goodhue
1995	Tim Tousignant - AA	Faribault
	Perry Fink – A	Canby
1996	Paul Vaith - AA	Hastings
	Greg Greeno - A	St. Michael-Albertville
	Mike Niemczyk - B	Janesville-Wald.-Pemberton
1997	Bob Board - AAA	Coon Rapids
	Jack Eustice - AA	Blue Earth Area
	John Leiwica - A	Kimball Area
1998	Jim Short-AA	Simley
	Steve Bechtold - AA	Blackduck/Cass Lake-Bena (co-coach)
	Jerry Cleveland - AA	Blackduck/Cass Lake-Bena (co-coach)
	Eugene Hildebrandt - A	St. James
1999	Ken Droegemueller - AAA	Osseo
	Jeff Mergen - AA	Rocori, Cold Spring
	Clay Nagel - A	Frazee
2000	Russ Holland - AAA	Park Center
	Randy Zimmer - AA	Milaca/Faith Christian School
	Dennis Whitman - A	Medford
2001	Chad Johnson - AAA	Centennial
	Dennis Kaatz - AA	Wadena-Deer Creek
	Steve Techam - A	Bertha-HewiflNerndale
2002	Brian Ihrke - AAA	Henry Sibley, Mendota Hts
	Randy Wirtjes - AA	Blue Earth Area (co-coach)
	Dave Pfaffinger - AA	Blue Earth Area (co-coach)
	Tom Gruhlke - A	BOLD, Olivia
2003	John Peterson - AAA	Elk River
	Larry Berg - A	Pine Island
	Brad Novak - AA	Becker
2004	Jim Jackson - AAA	Apple Valley
	Greg Greeno- AA	St. Michael-Albertville
	Gary Hindt - A	Wabasso

Minnesota Wrestling Coaches Association

NATIONAL WRESTLING HALL OF FAME: MINNESOTA INDUCTEES

On April 26, 2003, the Minnesota Chapter of the National Wrestling Hall of Fame and Museum unveiled its new hall of fame. Six individuals were inducted into the charter class that year, with five receiving the prestigious "Lifetime of Service to Wrestling Award," which is given in recognition of years of dedication to the development of leadership and citizenship in young people through the sport of wrestling. Honored for their countless hours of service to the sport they love, they will be permanently recognized at the National Wrestling Hall of Fame and Museum in Stillwater, Oklahoma.

Inaugural Class of 2003
Don Dravis
Rummy Macias
Ron Malcolm
Don Meyers
Roy Minter
Verne Gagne *(Outstanding American Award)*

Class of 2004
Dick Black
Bob Dettmer
John Grygelko
Skip Nalan
Jim Short
DeWaine Silker
John Ross *(Medal of Courage Award)*

BARTELMA HALL OF FAME INDUCTEES

The David Bartelma Hall of Fame is sponsored by the Minnesota Wrestling Coaches Association (MWCA Selection Committee: Steve Ricard [Chair], Bob Board, Mike Bredeck, James Campbell, Buzz Cummins, Bob Dettmer, Ken Droegemueller, David Erickson, George Graff, Don Meyers, Dennis Roos, Darrell Sohn, Bill Sutter and Spencer Yohe.)

NAME	INDUCTED FOR	YEAR
Paul Becker	Coach	------
Dave Bartelma	Athlete/Coach	1969
Paul Bengston	Coach	1969
Dr. Norman Borlaug	Athlete	1969
Mark Woodward	Coach	1969
Vern Gagne	Athlete	1970
Don Meyers	Coach	1970
Sue Meyers	Contributor	1970
Dick Black	Coach	1971
Luverne KIar	Coach	1971
Mike Tatone	Official	1971
Howard Peterson	Coach	1972
Alan Rice	Athlete	1972
Conrad Emerson	Coach	1973
John Grygelko	Coach	1973
Garth Lappin	Coach	1973
John Matlon	Coach	1973
Dr. Bill Manning	Coach	1973
Bob Board	Coach	1973
Alan Hendrickson	Coach	1973
Paul Krueger	Coach	1973
Rummy Macius	Coach	1973
Dee Cause	Contributor	1974
JackCause	Coach	1974
Charlie Peterson	Coach	1974
Darrell Sohn	Coach	1974
Ken Bergstedt	Coach	1975
Skip Nalan	Coach	1975
Virg Sales	Coach	1975
David Sohn	Coach	1976
Glen Swenson	Coach	1976
Frank Heulskamp	Contributor	1977
Wally Johnson	Coach	1977
Jim Kiffmeyer	Coach	1978
BobRyan	Coach	1978
Jack Bengston	Coach	1979
Roy Minter	Coach	1979
Chuck Prunty	Coach	1979
Ray Christenson	Coach	1980
Ehler Hendrickson	Coach	1980
Chuck Lunder	Coach	1980
Jim Nelson	Coach	1980
Gene Olson	Coach	1980
John Philo	Coach	1980
Brad Rheingans	Athlete	1980
Harry Schlieff	Coach	1980
Dick Shiels	Coach	1980
Fritz Soule	Coach	1980
Pete Veidman	Coach	1980
Bill Wasnick	Coach	1980
Chet Anderson	Coach	1981
Kermit Anderson	Coach	1981
Don Dravis	Coach	1981
Finn Grinaker	Coach	1981
Ron Malcolm	Coach	1981
Sky Wilcox	Coach	1981
Robert Dettmer	Athlete	1986
Dean Fox	Coach	1986
Clyde Ridenor	Coach	1986
Fr. William Wey	Contributor	1986
Richard Maher	Coach	1987
Horace Mayo	Coach	1987
James Van Gorden	Athlete	1987
Jim Bartels	Contributor	1988
Konnie Bartels	Contributor	1988
Burt Block, Jr	Contributor	1988
Paul Ehrhard	Coach	1988
John Fremling	Coach	1988
DeWaine Silker	Contributor	1988
Bill Sutter	Coach	1988
Jim Campbell	Wrestler	1989
Lyle Clem	Wrestler	1989
Ken Droegemueller	Coach	1989
Marlyn Hyland	Coach	1989
Charles Jean	Wrestler	1989
James Kamman	Wrestler	1989
James Martinez	Wrestler	1989
Kermit Selke	Wrestler	1989
Terry Sworsky	Coach	1989
Steve Carr	Wrestler	1990
Bill Demaray	Coach	1990
Gerry Cingles	Coach	1990
Dick Mueller	Coach	1990
Jim Short	Coach	1990
Virg Vagle	Coach	1990
Spencer Yohe	Contributor	1990
David Arens	Coach	1991
Buzz Cummins	Coach	1991
Howard Leopold	Coach	1991
Dennis Roos	Coach	1991
Earl Stottler	Coach	1991
Dan Chandler	Athlete	1992
John DeLozier	Coach	1992
Tom Jean	Athlete	1992
Richard Kelvington	Coach	1992
Larry Mollins	Coach	1992
Leo Simon	Coach	1992
Walt Wenholz	Coach/Contributor	1992
Noel Bailey	Coach	1993
James Carr	Coach	1993
Roger Gorham	Contributor	1993
Wayne Johnson	Coach	1993
Richard Pullen	Coach	1993
Charlie Coffee	Athlete	1994
Douglas Dahl	Coach	1994
Joe Frank	Coach	1994
Dale Hanson	Athlete	1994
Gary Hindt	Coach	1994
Gary Rettke	Coach	1994
Jeri Beshey	Contributor	1995
Jim Beshey	Contributor	1995
David Erickson	Coach	1995
Evan Johnson	Athlete	1995
Lewis Kennedy	Athlete	1995
Mike Niemczyk	Coach	1995
Mike Bredeck	Coach	1996
Ron Gadberry	Coach	1996
Bill Hubbard	Coach	1996
Mark Lange	Athlete	1996
Mike Rybak	Athlete	1996
Richard Chakolis	Coach	1997
David Hazewinkel	Athlete	1997
Jim Hazewinkel	Athlete	1997
Larry Zilverberg	Athlete	1997
Barry Bennett	Athlete	1998
Scot Davis	Coach	1998
Matt Demaray	Athlete	1998
Neal Skaar	Coach	1998
Dan Zilverberg	Athlete	1998
Gerry Bakke	Coach	1999
Richard Ericksrud	Coach	1999
Mike Langlais	Athlete	1999
Mike McArthur	Athlete	1999
Jim Slifta	Coach	1999
Charles Bishop	Coach	2000
Kenneth Leuer	Athlete	2000
Mike Mazzitelli	Coach	2000
Milroy Tollin	Coach	2000
William Brunner	Contributor	2000
Kenneth Ebert	Coach	2000
Woody Ferry	Contributor	2000
Reid Lamphere	Athlete	2000
Marty Morgan	Athlete	2001
Jack Willhite	Coach	2001
Doug Dufty	Contributor	2002
Jack Eustice	Coach	2002
George Graff	Contributor	2002
Gregg Greeno	Coach	2002
Ken Schmoker	Coach	2002
Bill Bredeson	Contributor	2003
Eugene Hildebrandt	Coach	2003
Byron Olson	Contributor	2003
Harlan Leopold	Athlete	2003
Bob Thorson	Coach	2003
Dale Lund	Contributor	2004
Gordy Morgan	Athlete	2004
John Morgan	Athlete	2004
J Robinson	Coach	2004
Jeff Swenson	Coach	2004

(2004 MWCA Lifetime Achievement Winners: Bruce Bartels, Annandale-Maple Lake; Larry Stroh, Annandale-Maple Lake; Virg Vagle, Paynesville; and John Zurell, Delano.)

SPENCER YOHE

Spencer Yohe has become synonymous with amateur wrestling in Minnesota and has dedicated his life to the sport he has become synonymous with. Yohe grew up on a farm in the southern Minnesota town of Caledonia, graduating from Caledonia High School in 1968. From there, he went on to get his teaching and coaching degree from Winona State University in 1972. With that, Yohe got his first job in the small town of Houston, and two years later he moved on to teach and coach in the Hancock public school system, where he has remained ever since, teaching and coaching everything from wrestling to volleyball to football to track and field. He was the school's head wrestling coach, however, from 1974-86, and led his squad to five district titles. Overall, Yohe garnered some 15 Coach of the Year honors at the high school level and his career record reads: 132-47-2 in wrestling, and 125-18 in volleyball.

In 1984 Yohe started his own business called Minnesota Mat Refinishing Company, which refurbishes wrestling mats around the United States, and is still going strong. In addition to running his own company, Yohe also served as an assistant wrestling coach at the University of Minnesota Morris from 1986-92. Following that, he became the head wrestling coach/Recruiting Coordinator for Minnesota State University Moorhead from 1992-2002, where he emerged as one of the top recruiters in Division II wrestling. There, he coached 25 Collegiate All-Americans, one NCAA II National Champion and 20 Academic All-Americans.

"Recruiting Nate Hendrickson to come to Moorhead and then to see him become the school's first national champion in over 30 years, that was really special," said Yohe. "Things like that are just the icing on the cake in this business."

From there, Yohe became very involved with helping the high school league. In addition, he also recently took over as the head coach of the Morris Area/Hancock wrestling program. He presently resides in Hancock, where, in addition to teaching physical education, he continues to give back to the sport he so dearly loves in any way he can.

Among Yohe's many awards and accolades, he is a member of the Minnesota Wrestling Coaches Association, Minnesota Coaches Association, National Wrestling Coaches Association, National High School Wrestling Coaches Association, as well as the MEA/NEA/HEA. He also serves as the Minnesota Chapter President for The National Wrestling Hall of Fame. He is also a member of six Hall of Fames: National Association of Intercollegiate Athletics, Minnesota Dave Bartelma Wrestling Coaches Association, Wrestling USA Magazine Hall of Fame, Charter Member of the Caledonia High School Wrestling Hall of Fame, Hancock/Cyrus High School Wrestling Hall of Fame, and Winona State University Alumni "Wall of Fame." Additionally, in 2002 Yohe was presented Winona State University's Highest Honor, the Presidential Medallion. That same year he was named as the Minnesota Wrestling Media Man of the Year, and has also found time to serve as the Minnesota State Editor for Wrestling USA Magazine for the past 28 years as well.

Furthermore, Yohe has served as Team Leader/Coach of eight NMA National & Minnesota Cultural Exchange Wrestling Squads that toured and competed in 19 different countries throughout the World. In addition, he has served as the Camp Director of the Greg Schwartz Memorial Wrestling Camp in Morris since 1992. The most popular commuter wrestling camp in Minnesota, it has awarded nearly three dozen scholarships over the past 12 years.

One of the best storytellers in the business, Spencer is simply a classic. He is one of those behind-the-scenes guys who has truly made a difference over the past three-plus decades for literally thousands of young people throughout the state of Minnesota, and he is still going strong.

"I wasn't as great a wrestler as were my contributions over the years," joked Yohe of his early days out on the mat. "But I fell in love with the sport and have made it my life's work. You know, I just love to see kids succeed. When they improve and get better, that just makes me feel good. I enjoy working with people and I think that I have touched a lot of lives in a positive way over the years. To get kids headed in the right direction both on the mat as well as in life is what it is all about. To make a difference in kids lives is very rewarding. To see the eyes on these kids when they get their first varsity win, things like that are priceless.

"I think I have also been able to motivate young people over the years, but I have also been blessed with some pretty darn good athletes as well. And, I have had some great assistants too, because a head coach is only as strong as his assistants. I have always tried to work a lot with the parents too, because you can't have a successful program without their support. You know, when it is all said and done for me I would just like to be remembered as someone who was good not only for the sport of wrestling, but also good for young people.

"You know, I have also been lucky that the big guy upstairs has watched over me as well," said Yohe. "I have gone through two cancer scares back in the early 90s, which included 20 chemotherapy sessions, and I am still here today. So, I am doing something right I suppose. I just can't say enough about how much I love this sport. I have had so many great times, met so many great people and have just had so much fun. That is what it is all about."

DON DRAVIS

Don Dravis grew up in Blue Earth learning the ropes from coaches Keith Young, who won three national championships as a wrestler at Iowa Teachers College, and also Gene Liebert, who also won a national title at Iowa Teachers as well. With coaches like that, it was no wonder Dravis went on to achieve great success of his own — finishing second and fourth in the state tourney during his junior and senior years at 133 pounds. Dravis graduated from Blue Earth High School in 1955 and went on to wrestle at Mankato State University. There, he studied under legendary coach Rummy Macias and wound up finishing third in the NAIA Finals.

He got his teaching degree and then headed straight to Staples, where he started teaching industrial arts and coaching wrestling in 1960. Over the next 34 years, Dravis would become a coaching legend in his own right, posting a 401-51-4 career record at the school and winning a record seven state titles along the way: (1978, '80, '81, '82, '83, '84, '85). In addition, Dravis coached 14 individual state champs along with 64 individual state place-winners as well. A two-time National Coach of the Year, Dravis was the 1978 Minnesota Coach of the Year as well. He was also enshrined into the David Bartelma Hall of Fame in 1981.

"It was just really exciting to be a part of it all," said Dravis. "I loved the competition of coaching kids and just being around them, it was wonderful. Once you build up a winning tradition, everything just kind of takes over. I mean kids want to be on a winning team and if they see you going to the state tournament all the time and having all that success, they want to be a part of that. So, once we had that, it was the ultimate recruiting tool. We never wanted to recruit kids away from other sports, but kids gravitated towards us because of those reasons.

"You know, I think that coaches go through phases where they have the most success when they have their own kids going through their programs. We also worked hard to develop a youth program in town too, so that those kids could come up through the pipeline. That was great, because it gave us a chance to get to know those kids early on and get to know their families too, which was so important. Plus, with the large families, all of the boys would come out for the team and it became a real family event. Another thing we did was every Summer we took the entire team up to Leech Lake for a week, to bond together and build chemistry.

"I would also attribute some of our success to the fact that most of our kids are country kids and because the farming is so poor up here, those kids have to work really hard out in the fields and what not. Therefore, they were physically stronger than a lot of town kids. You know, I just tried to get my kids to work harder than anybody else and get them to get into better condition. That was so important. I just figured that if one of our kids was in a close match then we could win it in the last 30 seconds. So, we ran an awful lot. We even ran before school, which for us was not a real big deal because most of those kids had already been up for hours working out on the farm. Rural kids just have a different work ethic than most kids and they are very disciplined people. Their families relied on them to do certain things and they had responsibilities which went above and beyond normal teenage kids.

"Overall, I guess I would like to be remembered as someone who was fair, but was always very competitive. I liked to push the envelope, so to speak, as far as taking things right up to the line, but not crossing the line. In fact, there are a few rules that we have in the high school league which I am the cause of. So, I have always challenged the system to make it better, but my heart has always been in the right place. If that is a part of my legacy, than so be it. I love this sport and am just so grateful to have spent so much of my life working in it alongside so many wonderful people."

SKIP NALAN

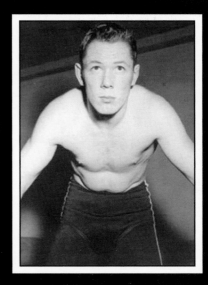

Norvard "Skip" Nalan grew up loving the sport of wrestling and went on to become a three-time Big 10 champion and two-time NCAA Champion at the University of Michigan. He then got into to teaching and coaching, which is what made him synonymous with the northern Minnesota city of Grand Rapids. There, Nalan was wrestling royalty, having coached at the high school for more than a quarter century, winning numerous Region Eight titles and once finishing as state runners-up. Nalan, who also served as an official at various levels of the sport, was one of wrestling's most respected individuals. Sadly, he passed away in the Fall of 1989.

JIM JACKSON

Jim Jackson is synonymous with Apple Valley wrestling. A coaching prodigy, Jackson graduated from Oelwein (Iowa) High School and went on to wrestle collegiately at Luther College, where he captained the team and emerged as a three-time NCAA Division III national qualifier. From there, Jackson moved to Minnesota, where, in 1980, he got his first teaching job at Scott Highlands Middle School in Apple Valley.

"One of the advantages of teaching at the middle school level is that I can get to know the kids at this age and get them interested in wrestling," said Jackson. "Plus, you can find a few diamonds in the rough down there as well and get kids who maybe weren't interested in your sport. You don't try to recruit kids away from other sports, you encourage them try new things.

For the next five years he coached junior high wrestling while also serving as a volunteer assistant at Apple Valley High School. Finally, in 1991, after serving for several years as the team's freshman coach, followed by a stint as a varsity assistant, he was named as the co-head coach alongside Bill Demaray. Together they captured three state titles. Later, in 1996, Jackson got his big break when he was named as the team's head coach. He had officially arrived.

"I worked my way up the ladder to get here," said Jackson. "It was a long trip, but I appreciate it that much more having to go through all of that. My progression is all about hard work. Nobody just said 'here is the program,' I had to work long and hard to get where I am at and I am very proud of that. We have a unique relationship, Bill (Demaray) and I. When he quit he was just burned out with a lot of different things. So, when I took over, I asked him to come back as my freshman coach. He did that for four years and then, after sitting out a year, he came back as my assistant varsity coach. He is a great guy and we are very good friends. I mean to have a guy like that on your staff is amazing, I mean he won six state championships as coach. Bill started the program and he was really the mastermind behind the dynasty. He implemented his vision and was able to recruit a lot of parents, coaches, administrators and community supporters to get behind the program. Those were the building blocks for the program and it has just grown from there. Obviously, there have been a lot of great athletes along the way and when they can see that winning tradition, that just keeps it all going."

Over the next eight years Jackson would continue to build on Demaray's success, and make history of his own. During that time he has won seven state team championships (1997, '99, '00, '01, '02, '03, '04), and coached 21 individual state champs as well as 62 state place-winners. Under Jackson Apple Valley has gained a lot of national prominence as well. In 2000 the Eagles wrestled for the national championship in Cleveland, and in 2002 they made it all the way to the final four in Oklahoma.

"Anytime a person or a business is successful, there are a lot of things that have to happen," said Jackson. "For us, it has been about defining our system and then implementing it. We have been fortunate in that we have had good support from our administration and that has allowed us to bring in good coaches. From there, we develop good athletes into good wrestlers. We just go out there and set goals, work hard and always try to improve. We think that we work harder than anybody in the country. I don't know if we do, but our kids believe that we do and that is all that matters."

The team's winning percentage under Jackson is a gaudy 95% and his overall record stands an unbelievable 313-13-3. Among his many coaching honors and accolades, Jackson was named as the 2001 and 2002 National Coach of the Year by the National Wrestling Coaches Association, and in 2001 he was named as the Minnesota Wrestling Man of the Year. Jim, who presently teaches at physical education at Falcon Ridge Middle School in Apple Valley, and his wife June reside in Lakeville with their daughter, Taylor Anne.

"I think the state-of-the-state of wrestling in Minnesota today is solid," said Jackson. "If you look at the numbers, the sport is actually growing. The programs might be lower, but that is because of consolidation. It is very strong right now. In fact, there are more kids who wrestle than play hockey in Minnesota. There are more programs, and there are more kids who wrestle. Then, you look at the state tournament, and we draw really well. Sure, we don't get as many as hockey, but we have more than 60,000 fans to come out that that is right up there nationally among the biggest and best. The event itself, however, is second to none. It is such a great time being there and the people who are there really want to be there to support the kids.

With the numbers his program puts up, it is no wonder Jackson is always seemingly under the microscope.

"With regards to 'open enrollment,' I want to clarify that our school district does not have it," said Jackson. "We do, however, have 'inter-open enrollment' throughout District 196, between Apple Valley, Eagan, Eastview and Rosemount, if the numbers justify so. People think that we recruit kids here, but we don't. The bottom line is that I have never recruited one wrestler in my life, ever. Here's what happens though. Because we are a nationally ranked program, we have a solid reputation. So, if families move here from out-state somewhere, and they want their kids to wrestle in a top program, a lot of times they will come here. But, they go to a lot of other places too. So, yes, we have people moving into our community all the time, but I don't call those kids transfers. It is a touchy situation with a lot of people but it all comes down to hard work and building a program that your community can be proud of. Every sport deals with this issue and all of the top programs have to deal with these things from time to time."

While Jackson is happy that his program is on top of the world, he knows that only hard work and dedication will keep it there.

"I have a real passion and drive to coach." said Jackson. "That passion is infectious too because if kids see you working hard, then they want to work hard too. I work really hard and put in long hours at this, and that is a big reason for my success I think. You have to be willing to go the extra mile in this business to get ahead. Then, you have to have a vision and be able to set realistic goals for the future. I am even looking five years down the road right now to see who my athletes are going to be. You have to be able to replace your top talent if you want to stay on top and that means working hard with the younger kids so that they can step up and take their place. It is a process and it takes a plan. You know, I just love wrestling, it is my life besides my family. Wrestling teaches kids and people to be very humble. There is a lot of humility in this sport, I mean there is always somebody who can beat you. There is also really no place to hide in wrestling either. The life lessons and the discipline and it takes to be a wrestler will help you later in life too."

As for his legacy, Jackson is a proven winner who keeps it all in perspective.

"I would hope to be remembered as someone who had passion, was a hard worker, was fair and was caring," said Jackson. "I am proud of the fact that we as a staff work very hard to help kids to become good citizens after high school. That is the most important thing about this job, bar none. It is also about making a difference and about being a good person. I mean it is real easy to coach a good kid, a 4.0 student and great athlete. The kids who are off the path a little bit that need your help, those are the kids I really enjoy working with. If they make a mistake along the way, they pay the consequences and we move on. If they make another mistake, I help them again. I never want to give up on anybody and I take a lot of pride in helping kids reach their goals. My fondest memories over are from the time I have spent working with so many great kids and coaches. That is what it is all about.

"We have a great tradition here and I am just proud to be associated with Minnesota wrestling. I am just a little cog in a big machine here in Apple Valley and it takes a lot of people to make this all happen. It takes a lot of people to run the show, but it takes a special person to drive the show. I really believe that is part of it, but I have also surrounded myself with great people. I mean I have six varsity assistants, great parental support, great administrative support and we have great fans who support us. I can't thank the fans and supporters of Apple Valley wrestling enough. I am humble, appreciative and grateful for their support and in many ways it is because of them that we enjoy so much success."

RON MALCOLM

Ron Malcolm grew up in Blue Earth and went on to win the 1951 state title at 138 pounds for the Bucs under Coach Conrad Emerson. Malcolm then went on to wrestle at the University of Minnesota, where he got his teaching degree. His first job came in Worthington, where he taught physical education and started the school's high school wrestling program. He quickly made an impact with the Trojans and in his second year two of his kids finished third and fourth, respectively, at the state meet. Malcolm stayed in Worthington for just two years before moving on to teach and coach at Anoka High School. There, Malcolm would become a legend.

Over the next 34 years, Malcolm guided his Tornadoes to three state championships, produced a record 21 individual state champions, 58 individual state place winners and saw four of his wrestlers compete in a total of eight Olympic games. He also racked up more career wins than any other Minnesota high school wrestling coach at the time of his retirement in 1992. In fact, he still presently ranks fifth in state history with an impressive 464-119-5 career record. Among Malcolm's many honors and accolades, he was named as the Coach of the Year in 1976, and in 1981 he was inducted into the Dave Bartelma Hall of Fame.

"It was a lot of fun," said Malcolm of his lifetime in wrestling. "It was very rewarding too, to see so many kids achieve success and follow their dreams. To have the opportunity to watch them develop was also very satisfying. I am also very proud of the fact that I had four kids go on to compete in the Olympics, which I am not aware of any other coach being able to say. Dan Chandler competed on three teams from 1976-84; Brandon Paulson was on the 1996 team; and the Hazewinkel twins — Jim and Dave, were both on the 1968 and 1972 teams. I was so proud of those kids and would say that my biggest thrill came when I got to watch each of them participate at the Olympics. I traveled to Mexico City, Los Angeles and Atlanta to watch each of them compete and nothing will ever compare to that, it was amazing. To know that I might have had a small part of their success is something I really treasure."

"I would say that my biggest contribution to Minnesota wrestling was the fact that I started the ball rolling to adopt the team concept," added Malcolm. "You see, in 1964 I had a team that didn't have a close dual meet all year long, they were outstanding. But, because there was just one class of wrestling in the state at the time, each kid eventually got eliminated through the districts and regions. As a result, we didn't qualify for the state tournament. We were really disappointed about that, because we had such a good team. So, I started campaigning for change. I explained to the board how ridiculous I thought it was that we won together as a team all year long but then all of a sudden we got into the tournament and we didn't have a team anymore. Well, it took me 10 years, but they finally changed it. My good friend Don Meyers, who coached at Fridley, was also very influential in making that happen as well, he is someone who has also spent a great deal of time working to make the system better. As a result, the team concept provides for individual success as well as team success, which is so important I think. I was real proud of that and would hope that would be a part of my legacy as a coach."

JOHN GRYGELKO

John Grygelko grew up in south Minneapolis loving sports and loving hunting. In fact, he even used to hunt ducks along the Mississippi River right near Fort Snelling back in the day. He went on to graduate from Roosevelt High School in the late 1940s. He only wrestled one year in high school, however, because he was a football star and his coach did not want him to cut any weight. From there, Grygelko went on to earn his teaching and coaching degree from the University of Minnesota, where he wrestled for the Gophers as well.

His first job came shortly thereafter as a teacher and wrestling coach at Robbinsdale High School. The Robins, which were the state's first great wrestling dynasty, had won seven straight sate titles from 1940-46. The program had slipped a bit by the time Grygelko showed up, however, as evidenced by the fact that only about a dozen kids showed up to his first practice in 1952. He would make up for that in a hurry though and in 1961 he had put the team back on top of the charts, winning his first state title. His Robins' success continued to soar from there.

In 1973, Grygelko gave up his coaching duties at Robbinsdale to become the head coach at Augsburg. He would remain at the school as a teacher however. At Augsburg, Grygelko would spend the next eight years building the foundation for one of the most successful collegiate wrestling programs in the nation. The highlight of his days with the Auggies came a few years after his arrival, when he led the team to an NAIA national runner-up finish in 1975. He would ultimately step down as the head coach of the Auggies in 1980, retiring with an impressive 98-12-1 record at the school. He then returned to coach at Robbinsdale, which would later merge schools through consolidation.

Grygelko's illustrious high school coaching career record would wind up at an impressive 250-40, which ranks fourth all-time in state history with an 86.2% winning percentage. Over his illustrious high school coaching career, Grygelko has coached 14 individual state champs as well as a record 90 individual state place winners. In 1973 Grygelko, a former coach of the year winner, was inducted into the Dave Bartelma Hall of Fame. In addition, he was also later inducted into the Minnesota chapter of the National Wrestling Hall of Fame as well. Today Grygelko resides in Bemidji. and stays involved with the sport he loves by following his grandsons, three of whom competed in the state tournament for St. Michael High School in 2004.

"Wrestling is just a wonderful sport," said Grygelko. "It doesn't matter how good you are, there is always somebody who can come along and beat you. It takes such discipline and determination to be successful in this sport and that is why I have always enjoyed it. If you work hard at it, you will be rewarded. It was easy as a coach too, from the standpoint that you didn't have all the politics about who started and who got benched. I mean in wrestling, whichever kid won in practice got to compete on the varsity. Kids could always challenge one another for a spot too, so it was always pretty fair.

"Another thing about wrestling is the fact that kids compete in it for the love of the sport, not for the glory. There is not a lot of glory in wrestling, just a lot of hard work, dedication and satisfaction of knowing that you were better than that guy across from you. Guys are totally on their own out there, there are no substitutions, no time-outs, no nothing. It is such a tough sport and that is why I think it is so cool. Wrestlers are the most humble, modest, hard working people around, and I am proud to be associated with people like that."

Considered to be on the state's true pioneers of the sport, John Grygelko is truly a Minnesota grappling legend.

"You know, I really enjoyed my time as a coach here in Minnesota," he added. "To be a part of such a wonderful tradition was very rewarding. And, to have been able to have been a part of so many kids lives really means a lot to me. There were so many great people who I was able to get to know along the way and that is what I will always remember, the people and the memories. I mean from Larry Hennig, my first state champion, to winning our first state tournament in '61, it was a marvelous time."

Some of Minnesota's Many Amateur Wrestling Clubs:

Aitkin Wrestling Club (Aitkin)
Animal House Wrestling Club (Waseca)
Anoka Youth Wrestling Club (Ramsey)
Apple Valley Wrestling Club (Apple Valley)
Blue Knights Wrestling Club (Eagan)
Chaska Stallions Wrestling Club (Chaska)
Dark Horses Wrestling Club (Glencoe)
Flat Earth Wrestling Club (Jackson)
Gold Rush Wrestling Club(Isanti)
Hi Flyers Wrestling Club (St. Michael)
Iron Wrestling Inc. (New Brighton)
Just Us Wrestling Club (Worthington)
Lakes Area Wrestling Club (Frazee)
Minneapolis Amateur Wrestling Club

Minneapolis Lions Wrestling Club
Minnesota Bulldogs Wrestling Club
Minnesota Storm Wrestling Club
Moorhead Militia Wrestling Club
New Ulm Rolling Thunder Wrestling Club
Northern Elite Wrestling Club
Northside Wrestling Club
Owatonna Wrestling Association
Prairie Lakes Wrestling Club (Fergus Falls)
Rogers Youth Wrestling Club (Otsego)
S. St Paul Wrestling Club
Sisu/Inferno Wrestling Club (Burnsville)
South Metro Blue Knights Wrestling Club
St. Francis Gladiators Wrestling Club
Wayzata Youth Wrestling Club (Corcoran)
Wolfpack Wrestling Club Maple (Grove)
Wrestling Mall School of Champions

SCOT DAVIS

Scot Davis grew up in Bloomington and wrestled at Bloomington Kennedy High School. From there, he went on to compete at Augsburg, where he emerged as an NAIA All-American for the Auggies. His first taste of coaching came while he was in college, with the Bloomington Amateur Wrestling Club and later at a nearby junior high school. Davis went on to get his teaching degree and wound up getting his first job at Belcourt High School in North Dakota. From there, he came to Bird Island-Lake Lillian, followed by a stint at Hutchinson. He even tried his hand in the college ranks, coaching briefly at the University of Wisconsin-Superior in 1985 — even earning NAIA Coach of the Year honors, but missed the action at the high school level. He began coaching at Owatonna High School in 1987 and has been there ever since, making history along the way.

"My kids always come first," said Davis, "I mean they are the ones doing all the work. But what I have been able to do as a coach is to get a lot of good people involved in promoting the sport. Just surrounding myself with good people has been the biggest key to my success. I have some outstanding assistant coaches here and that has been wonderful for our program too. We also put a lot of time into our youth feeder programs as well, which has paid off for us over the years. If you don't put in the time down there, then you can't expect the talent to be there at the high school level and you can't sustain success long term.

"Another thing we do is we wrestle a lot of kids, and to accommodate that we wrestle in a lot meets. We just want to give more kids an opportunity to compete, which is something we are proud of here. A kid can only wrestle 36 varsity matches a year prior to post-season competition, so we are forced to use more kids if you have more meets. In 1998, the year we won the title, we used 51 different kids on the varsity. By giving them the opportunity to compete on the varsity, and letter, that makes everyone happy and is a real win-win for all of us."

Davis has posted a 650-106-4 career record over his illustrious coaching career and currently ranks No. 3 all-time for career wins behind Virg Vagle and Bill Sutter. By 2005 he will be the winningest coach in state history, however, and at just 53 years of age, 1,000 wins is not out of the question at all. Davis led his Owatonna team to the 1998 state title and has also coached a total of eight individual state champs during that time, along with 51 place-winners as well. His teams have been consistently ranked amongst the best in the state and his 1996 squad, which went 34-1-1, was even ranked in the top-20 in the nation.

Among his many coaching honors and accolades, in 1998 he was named as the "National Coach of the Year" by the National High School Coaches Association. He is also is a past Minnesota Coach of the Year recipient and was inducted into David Bartelma Hall of Fame in 1998 as well. In addition, Davis is very involved on the administrative side of the sport and is a past president of Minnesota Wrestling Coaches Association. He has reinvented his position as head coach and has taken it to an entirely new level, all for the purpose of growing his sport.

"We do a lot of other things too, to promote our program. For instance, Wrestling USA Magazine has a national publication contest and our newsletter was ranked No. 1 in their national contest, which was great for us. Our team poster came in second and our media guide is always ranked either one or two as well. We also do trading cards of the kids, which were ranked No. 1 too. We also have a really good web-site, owatonnawrestling.com, which has been a lot of fun. So all of those things really show how much we care about the entire program and it also puts us closer to our community — which is so important. Sure, I teach technique and emphasize hard work, but it is the little things that really make your program successful and get people involved. If they are enthused about your program then that just carries over into everything else.

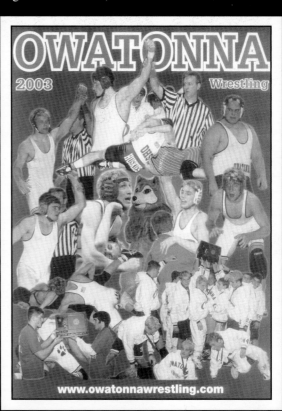

"You know, it is all about the kids. I think back to one kid in particular back at Bird Island-Lake Lillian, Rick Squibb, who had a career record of 126-6-1, with five of his six losses coming at the state tournament. When he finally won a state title as a senior, that was one of the greatest moments in my coaching career. What a great kid, he just worked so hard and was so determined. That is what it is all about.

"I would also add that it is not about wins and losses. It is about making a difference in kids lives. If all you cared about were wins and losses, then you would burn our pretty quickly. To see your kids become productive citizens later in life is so rewarding. I think too that wrestling teaches kids so many good values, particularly hard work, and that is great to see. Kids have to learn how to accept defeat in this sport too, which teaches humility. You have to be tough to be a successful wrestler and that is why a certain type of kid gravitates towards it. It is not for everybody, but for those who excel at it, they are hooked for life. That is me, I love it and feel very fortunate to have made my career doing what I enjoy."

THE SHORT FAMILY

(L to R) Chris, Calvin (Adopted Son) John, Jim, Harry Schlieff (Jim's High School Coach), Pat, Wade & Will

Jim Short grew up in the New Brighton area and went on to graduate from Mounds View High School in 1965. Short, who had been a hockey player up until junior high school, learned to wrestle from his older brother.

"He was trying to lose weight at the time for a match, so I became his workout partner. We threw the mattresses off of my mom's bed and had at it right there. He was tough, but that was how I learned."

As a senior, Short would finish as the runner-up at the 133 pound division at the state high school wrestling tournament. From there, Short went on to wrestle at St. Cloud State, where he also received a degree in mathematics. At that point, Short got his first job at Simley High School, and incredibly, he has been there ever since — teaching and coaching his way into the history books. When he got there though, there was actually no wrestling program. So, he started one.

"It was a long process," said Short. "I definitely had to work hard to make it happen. I remember, we started with 13 kids and none of them had ever wrestled before. You see, hockey and basketball had been pretty well established at the school by then, so wrestling basically got the leftovers. But, we did manage to win a meet that year. We steadily improved and became an average team through the late-1970s. Then, when our kids programs that we started early on got going, that is when we got really good. My own kids were a part of that too, so that was very rewarding to see that. They got all of their friends to come out for wrestling and they all came up through the ranks together. It was tough though, early on we were in the same region, one, as Albert Lea, Owatonna and Apple Valley, which all had great programs. We finally got transferred into region three in 1987 and that played a big role in our program finally getting over the hump."

Over the ensuing years, Short would turn Simley into a wrestling power. His program's first great wrestler was Jim Trudeau, a state champ at 138 pounds in 1978 who went on to become a two-time Big Ten champion at Minnesota. A huge part of Simley's success, however, was predicated on the fact that Short's own sons: John, Chris, Will and Wade were such unbelievable wrestlers. From 1985-91, the Shorts owned prep wrestling in Minnesota and their achievements are simply mind boggling. Over that span they collectively won a record total of seven state titles: John 1985 (138); Chris 1986 (185), 1987 (185); Willy 1988 (138), 1989 (152); Wade 1990 (138), 1991 (152). In fact, the Short brothers presently rank fourth for all-time career wins by brothers with 552 : John - 97, Chris - 124, Will - 168, Wade – 163. (Chris even had one stretch where he won 66 consecutive matches and recorded 60 consecutive pins in the process!)

"It is hard to even explain," said Short of his kids' success. "You know, as a parent, you have goals for your kids early on, but you never really expect them to attain all of them. So, then when they do, it is really special. It was really exciting to be a part of and so gratifying. They all went on to wrestle in college too, which was also just incredible. Two of them were All-Americans collegiately as well. I mean all of them got scholarships too, which can't even be put into words. Having four boys and trying to send them all to college on a teachers' salary was going to be tough, so that was just another benefit that the sport of wrestling provided our family. I should also say that the kids did other things besides wrestling too, which is very important. John played soccer and was a school record-setting pole vaulter, and the three all played football and tennis."

In all, Short would go on to lead his program to four AA state team championships and three runner-up finishes. He also coached 16 state champs along with 56 individual state place-winners over his illustrious after 27 year career as well.. Presently, he ranks 12th all-time for career wins in Minnesota with an impressive 374-160-6 record. Short, who taught algebra, statistics and computer programming for 17 years at Simley, retired from coaching in 1998 to become the school's athletic director — a position he still holds to this day. His son Will, who graduated in 1989, is now the wrestling coach at Simley.

"We just loved everything about the sport," said Short of his family. "We were always talking about it, reading about it and watching it. If the Olympics or something like that were on TV, well, then we had to try out those new moves right then and there on the floor. We did a lot of that. With four kids, I can assure you that most of our furniture got broken and re-broken pretty much non-stop. Our couches had two-by-fours for frames on them because they had been busted so many times. You see, my wife worked at nights as a dance teacher, so the kids and I would all be home together. It was trouble, big trouble. We had matches going non-stop, it was great. Our main living room, we just finally got rid of all the furniture in there altogether, and let them go at it in there. We finally got some new stuff a few years back here, when the last one left the house — my wife was pretty happy to get her house back, let me tell ya!"

Among Short's many honors and accolades, he is a member of the Dave Bartelma Wrestling Hall of Fame and was also named Man of the Year by the Minnesota chapter of USA Wrestling. In addition, the Minnesota Wrestling High School Coaches Association twice named him their high school wrestling coach of the year and he was even named as the 2004 Class AA Athletic Administrator of the Year as well. Over the years, Jim has also served the schools and students of the Minnesota State High School League as a member of numerous boards and committees. In addition, he has been a member of several task forces that created a new community aquatic center and ice arena, and was also instrumental in the organization and creation of two new athletic conferences. Short has started five new sports at Simley: girls soccer, girls hockey, boys and girls golf, and boys swimming.

Short has supported wrestling at the youth levels too. In 1992, he was the head coach of a USA Wrestling-sponsored event that paired a U.S. team with a Cuban team. He is also very active with Minnesota/USA Wrestling as well as the Ninth Grade League.

"I think the sport is in real good shape," said Short on the state-of-the-state of wrestling in Minnesota today. "At the high school level I don't think it has ever been better. In fact, there are schools adding wrestling programs right now, like Mahtomedi for instance. The numbers are great. I think our kids can compete with anybody on the national level and that doesn't even factor in Greco, which we have dominated over the years. In freestyle we are a top five state too, so we are right up there, no question. Overall, yeah, I would say that Minnesota is a top five state nationally as far as talent and reputation, right along with Iowa, Pennsylvania and Okalahoma. Our kids get a ton of division one scholarships too, and they go all over the country to compete. Our state is recruited heavily nowadays and that is great to see. Nationally we are really well respected. I mean we have the largest state tournament in the country and it draws the most spectators of any state in the union — nearly 65,000.

"Now, at the next level, a lot of small colleges around here are struggling right now because of their budget numbers, but hopefully that will get worked out. You know, I am a big Title IX proponent. It wasn't developed to cut male sports, it was created to give more kids more opportunities. Well, they have a lot of work to do to make it all work out and it is a long process. We have to figure out more ways to generate more revenue, which is the key to all sports being successful."

"You know, wrestling is just a great sport," added Short. "There's a place for every size and shape kid. Whether you weigh 103 pounds or 275, you can compete on an equal basis, and even handicapped kids can do very well. Plus when you get out on that mat, it's all up to you. I've always enjoyed the discipline of wrestling and the dedication and hard work that's required. We've had kids who have put the time in and worked hard, dedicated themselves and gotten in great shape and learned some techniques and become state champs. If you get a really tough mental attitude, you can go a long way."

Jim and his wife Pat, who were high school sweethearts (she was a wrestling cheerleader), have spent a lifetime in wrestling. It is Pat, ironically enough though, who has made it to the big-time.

"You know, my wife and I could see early on that this was going to be a lifestyle," said Short. "We've done everything pretty much as a family. I have always said that the family that plays together, stays together. You know, one time I told her that she either had to get involved or she would become a widow, because there is just so much traveling. Well, she did, and she wound up loving it. We went everywhere with the kids and we had a ball over the years. Eventually, she got really involved, probably even more involved in USA Amateur Wrestling that me. In fact, one of my dream was always to be a part of an Olympic team, and for my kids too. That was always the pinnacle for us. Well, it never came true for any of us men, but believe it or not, it did for her. That's right. In the 1996 Olympics down in Atlanta, Pat was the head pairer, or match-maker, so she actually seeded and ran the entire tournament. It was a huge job, I was really proud of her. So, now, she always makes sure to let us all know who the Olympian of the family is!"

One thing is for sure, the Short family is most definitely Long on wrestling talent.

JACK GAUSE

Jack Gause is one of the most decorated wrestling officials in the United States. For nearly 30 years, Gause served as a coach in Minnesota and even started the wrestling program at St. Cloud State University in 1949. From there, he got into officiating both domestically as well as internationally, where few Americans had been before. Gause got his first taste of the big-time during the 1967 Pan American Games, where he wound up refereeing a match in which one of the wrestlers severely bit his opponent. Gause, knowing that the two wrestlers were from rival countries in the midst of political turmoil, did the right thing by disqualifying the instigator — a call which later resulted in him receiving a lifetime ban from competition. He instantly earned the respect of his peers that day, and spent the rest of his career continuing to try do what he felt was best for the sport.

A tireless behind-the-scenes worker, Gause assisted some 160 referees in obtaining their international licenses so that the major competitions would not be limited to just a privileged few. Gause was also the first National Officials Chairman to make sure that national championships, from the youth to the senior levels, had the same consistent interpretation of the rules. In addition to coordinating countless clinics around the world, Gause also invented the point system for ranking referees and even hosted the first FILA Officials and Coaches Clinic ever to be held in the U.S. For more than 20 years, Gause officiated at nearly every World, Pan Am and World Cup Championship, including the 1976 Olympics in Montreal. Gause would also serve as the 1978 Team Leader for the U.S. Team at the World Championships and was later honored with FILA's most prestigious award, the Gold Star. Furthermore, Gause authored legislation here in Minnesota which was later adapted nation-wide, that provided for public employees to have 90 days of paid leave absence if a member of an international team. Gause, who coordinated countless clinics to provide uniform rules and a point system to rank officials.

Among his many awards and accolades, Jack and his wife Dee were both inducted into the Minnesota Wrestling Hall of Fame in 1974. Later, in 2001, Gause was honored by the National Wrestling Hall of Fame for his outstanding service with their prestigious Lifetime Achievement for Officials.

THE EUSTICE FAMILY

The Eustices are considered wrestling royalty in Blue Earth and the patriarch of the Eustice family is Jack, whose sons, Luke and Ty, are among the state's best ever. Jack grew up in Janesville and went on to become a five-time conference champion and a four time individual qualifier at the state tournament. He placed fourth as a junior and went on to capture the 119 pound state title in 1973.

Following high school Jack continued his wrestling career at Mankato State University, where he emerged as a four time All American under legendary coach Rummy Macias. As a senior, he won the 1976 NCAA Division II National Championship at 134 pounds, capping an amazing career tally of 126-21 on the mat — a record which still stands today. After completing his teaching degree, Jack got his first teaching and coaching job at Blue Earth High School. There, he took over the reigns from Dick Maher and continued to make history, guiding six teams to the state tournament over his illustrious career. His Bucs finished 6th in 1980, 5th in 1990, 3rd in 1991, 2nd in 1997, 4th in 1998 and his 2001 team won the Class AA state championship. In addition, Jack has also coached eight individual state champions who won a total of 16 titles, including seven by his two sons, Luke and Ty. Wanting to go out on top, Jack retired following his first state title in 2001. He had more important things to do, like watch his kids compete down at the University of Iowa.

"It was a big thrill to finally win," said Jack. "We had been up there several times before, but to finally take it was special. It means so much to the community here in Blue Earth and that is what it is all about. The kids had a great time and I was really proud of them, they worked really hard that year and it all came together for us."

With an impressive career coaching record is 263-87-4, Jack has been honored for his accomplishments by his fellow coaches by being named Region/Section Coach of the Year six times and was named Minnesota Class AA Coach of the Year in 1997 as well. Jack has also served as President of the MWCA and was also a member of the state wrestling advisory board to the MSHSL as well. Among Jack's other honors and accolades, he was inducted into the Mankato State University Hall of Fame in 1994. He was also selected as a member of MSU's "All Century Team" as well as the North Central Conference's "All Time Wrestling Team."

"You know, Blue Earth just has an amazing wrestling tradition," said Jack. "I mean we won four titles back in the mid-1950s. A lot of that success goes back to Keith Young, who coached the 1953 team. As a wrestler, he was a legend down in Iowa. He won three national championships down at Iowa Teachers College, which is Northern Iowa now, and was really good. I mean he is in the Iowa Hall of Fame, the National Wrestling Hall of Fame, and was just way ahead of his time with regards to coaching high school kids. Then, the next coach after Young was Gene Liebert, and he coached for just four years here, but won three titles and had like 15 or 16 individual state champs. Gene left to get into the insurance business and Keith went back to Iowa to coach.

"So, those guys really put us on the map and guys like me have just been filling in for them all these years later. I remember meeting those guys for the first time down at the Nationals at UNI in 1997. We got to talking and I asked them about the secrets of their success. Well, they took me aside and explained to me what they did back then, it was really interesting. He said 'back in our day we did inside singles and stand-ups, and the more inside singles the better...'. Gene, who was in his 70s, actually got down on the floor and demonstrated some moves for me, it was great. They were just really charismatic guys, super motivators and had excellent technique, and that is why they were so successful."

Jack, who retired from coaching in 2001, and his wife, Mona, presently reside in Blue Earth. They are the proud parents of two extraordinary sons, Luke and Ty, to of the best wrestlers to have ever come out of Minnesota. After graduating from Blue Earth High School, both brothers went on to accept full-ride scholarships to the University of Iowa, where they have continued to excel. Their records speak for themselves.

Luke was a three-time state champ at Blue Earth High School, bringing home the hardware in 1996 (103), 1998 (112) and 1999 (125). A runner-up at the state meet as a sophomore, Luke also lettered twice in football and once in golf, and was even an academic all-state selection as a senior as well. In addition, in 1999 Luke was honored nationally by the Wrestling Hall of Fame with the prestigious Dave Schultz High School Excellence Award. Presented annually to a high school senior, the award is based equally on outstanding wrestling success, scholastic achievement and citizenship or community service.

At Iowa, Luke earned all-American honors in 2001-02, his sophomore year, placing second at the NCAA Championships at 125 pounds, while also placing second at the Big Ten Championships. As a junior, Luke placed fifth at Big Ten Championships, and as a senior finished as the Big Ten runner-up. His career record with the Hawks stands at an impressive 86-26-6.

Ty, meanwhile, was a four-time state champ and five-time conference champ at Blue Earth Area High School, bringing home the hardware in 1997 (103), 1999 (135), 2000 (145) and 2001 (145). As a senior, Ty, who set a state record for career takedowns (907), also won the Junior Freestyle title at the Western Regionals. A two-time academic all-state selection, Ty also lettered in football and golf as well. At Iowa, Ty red shirted his first year and then posted a 30-10 overall record in 2002-03 en route to finishing as the runner-up at the Big Ten Championships. Ty placed third at the Big Tens in 2003-04 at 149 pounds and is projected to do even better in 2005.

"Luke and Ty grew up watching Iowa public television down here and just always wanted to be Hawkeye's," said Jack. "They have such an amazing program and I was really happy that they were able to go there and be successful. They were recruited by Minnesota as well, and that is a tremendous program too, but they had their hearts set on being Hawkeyes and that is where they wanted to go. It was neat for them to be together down there too. They lived together and they are real close as brothers, so that is nice to see. They help each other train and stay on track with school as well, which, as a parent, is great to see. We went to all their home meets and made a lot of trips to see them too, so that has been just a wonderful experience for my wife and I."

With Luke and Ty having achieved so much success, Jack is one proud papa. He keeps it all in perspective though and continues to help grow the sport he loves in whatever ways he can.

"I have always told my high school kids that if they take what they learn from wrestling and apply it towards their own lives, they will be successful in whatever they do," said Jack. "I mean hard work, perseverance, attitude and determination are qualities necessary for anything in life. You know, it takes a lot to be a wrestler, both from the kids themselves, as well as from their parents. It is a big commitment, with all the practicing and travel, and that is why the wrestling community is so close knit. It can be a year round thing for a lot of families and that takes a lot of dedication from everyone. Overall though, wrestling has been wonderful to me and my family and I can't say enough great things about it. It is the greatest sport in the world and I am just very proud to have been able to have coached in such a great community in front of so many great people."

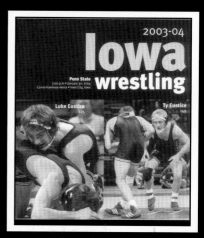

KEN DROEGEMUELLER

Ken Droegemueller grew up in the southern Minnesota town of Windom and went on to wrestle at Windom High School, graduating in 1957. There, he placed second in the region tournament three years in a row, but never made it to state — because back in those days you had to win the region tournament to advance to state tourney. From there, Droegemueller went on to wrestle at Mankato State for the legendary Rummy Macias, where he twice placed in the NCAA Division II Tournament, fourth at 137 pounds and second at 130 pounds, earning All-American honors those years as well. He graduated in 1965 and from there headed to Northfield to begin a teaching and coaching career which would span nearly four decades.

At Northfield, Droegemueller began as a junior high and assistant coach to Howie Peterson — who started the first Minnesota Wrestling News newsletter back in the 60s. Three years later, Droegemueller got the job as the head coach at Worthington High School, replacing Roy Mintor. He would spend a total of nine years with the Trojans, amassing an outstanding 121-24-2 record, including eight conference titles, nine district or sub--region titles and three regional first place finishes. In addition to producing 10 state individual place winners and two state champions, one of his teams placed third in the state tourney as well.

In 1977, Droegemueller took over as the head wrestling coach at Osseo High School. Over the next 22 years he would compiled an impressive 318-119-2 record, and long the way he would capture nine conference and 16 region/section titles. In all, he would coach 134 state entrants, 52 state place-winners and 14 state champions, six of whom became high school All-Americans. Incredibly, in his 31 years as a head coach, there was just one year in which he didn't have either a team or individual in the top six in the state. And, although he never won the "big one," he made the trip to the big dance on some 18 occasions.

Among Droegemueller's best athletes at Osseo were his two sons, Darren and Dave, who each won a pair of state titles from 1985 to 1988. Both kids would go on to wrestle at the University of Nebraska, where they made their daddy proud. While Darren received a "medical," following an injury, Dave, who later went on to become the head coach at Wayzata High School, placed second in the Big 8 Conference as a senior and qualified for the NCAA Tournament three different times. (Incidentally, Droegemueller's daughter, Deanne, was a two-time All-American gymnast at Oregon State as well.)

Droegemueller finally retired from teaching and coaching in 1999 with an overall career record of 440-145-4, good for sixth in state history. In all, he coached 16 state champs and 62 state place winners as well. Among his many honors and accolades, in 1999 he was named as the Minnesota Coach of the Year, and in 1989 he was inducted into the David Bartelma Hall of Fame. Additionally, Droegemueller also served as the regional representative as well as the secretary and president of the Minnesota Wrestling Coaches Association.

One of the sport's true good guys, Ken Droegemueller contributed a great deal to the sport he loved and left an indelible impression on the wrestlers he coached along the way.

"Wrestling was my life," said Droegemueller. "You know my goal was never to make the kids state champions, it was get them to perform up to their potential — wherever that took them. I had a lot of kids go on to wrestle in college and that was very rewarding to think that I may have played a small role in them going on to get their educations and compete at the next level.

"I had both my knees replaced not too long ago, but am still involved in the sport and still enjoy it a great deal. I help out at the state tournament every year and I also go to the nationals every year too. I also go down to Florida every year to help out my old college coach, Rummy Macias, who is 82 and still coaching down there. He is just amazing, and I really enjoy going down to help him out with his camp for a couple weeks every year.

"You know, it was a great time," he added. "I just loved being a part of it. To make a difference in kids' lives is very rewarding and that is what it is all about. We had some great times over the years and I am proud of the fact that I was able to be a part of so many success stories."

DON MEYERS

Don Meyers grew up in St. Anthony Village, just outside of Northeast Minneapolis, and went on to wrestle at University High School. There, he won the state title in 1952 at 138 pounds, graduating that same year. From there, Meyers went on to wrestle at the University of Minnesota under legendary coach Wally Johnson. He would go on to get his teaching degree from the U of M, and in 1958 began teaching and coaching wrestling at Fridley High School. He would remain at Fridley for the next decade, growing the school's wrestling program. In 1966 he led his team to a runner-up finish at the state tournament and in 1967 they won their first ever state championship. Meyers, who also as the school's athletic director, left the program that next year to become a principle at a nearby junior high school. He would eventually serve as a principle at the high school level as well.

In all, Meyers would spend 42 years in the Fridley school system, later serving as an official, State High School League rules interpreter and state tournament director. In addition to being very instrumental in starting the state officials and state coaches associations, he also served a term on the National High School Federation Wrestling Rules Committee as well. He also served as the meet manager and site-manager for the High School League from 1974-99. In 1968 Meyers was honored by being named as the Minnesota Wrestling Coach of the Year and in 1970 he was also enshrined into the David Bartelma Hall of Fame. Presently, Don and his wife reside in Blaine.

Considered by many to be the No. 1 contributor to high school wrestling in Minnesota, Don Meyers has done it all, and is still going strong — always trying to improve and better the sport which he so dearly loves.

"You know, I was so fortunate to have spent a lifetime in wrestling," said Meyers, who is retired but still serves as the executive secretary of the North Suburban Conference. "When I graduated from college, high school wrestling was really growing and I just got in at a great time to really be able to make a difference. From putting together a bibliography of wrestling resources way back when nothing like that ever existed; to starting an officials association; to creating a state tournament committee; to hosting a Saturday morning breakfast for the athletes, which still goes on to this day; to having a social for husbands and wives; to coordinating the logistics for lodging at the state tournament down at the old Leamington Hotel, complete with busing over to Williams Arena; to helping coordinate the Hall of Fame; to getting all of the plaques and awards for everything; to opening the lines of communication and dialogue so that we were all on the same page — I was just so lucky to have been a part of so many really meaningful things which have affected the sport of wrestling.

"It is wonderful to see the legacy of all that hard work still going on today, because we have one of the best wrestling programs here of any state in the country. So, I am very proud to have been a part of that. Wrestling just did so much for me and gave me so many opportunities. I used to always say to my assistant coaches that I hope that just one kid, just one, will benefit as much from wrestling as I have. If so, then I will have done OK. This sport is all about the kids and we can never lose sight of that. They learn so many values in wrestling — hard work, dedication — and they carry those things forward with them for the rest of their lives. It is a wonderful thing."

"You know, another thing that I am proud of was helping to create the 'team concept,' " Meyers added. "One of the dilemmas with wrestling back in the 50s and 60s was the fact that as teams advanced into the district tournaments, some kids got eliminated from their teams, and then even more got eliminated at the regions. As a result, just a few kids might have wound up on a team that went to the state tournament. In fact, in those days teams actually won tournaments with only three wrestlers representing the entire team. What it was doing was killing fan interest because they could no longer follow their hometown wrestlers. So, Ron Malcolm and I went to the High School League and got the ball rolling with regards to changing the system. We laid out a plan to change it and they agreed to implement it on an experimental basis. As a result, Minnesota became the first state in the nation to determine a high school wrestling championship under the team concept. Since then most of the other states followed at the high school level and even the colleges came around too and adopted a national dual tournament. While it was initially not well received by the coaches, the acceptance by the fans was overwhelming. Track and field also later followed suit with their 'true-team concept' as well. It changed the rules for the better and I was very honored to have played the lead role in getting that done."

"As far as the state-of-the state of wrestling today, I would say it is declining. I think it is bad. We used to have a very vibrant community and junior college system here with regards to wrestling and that has completely changed over the years, which is really too bad. I hate to be negative towards Title IX, but that has played a part in it. I am all for opportunities for women, don't get me wrong, I have two girls of my own, but wrestling has suffered because of it, maybe more so than any other sport. So, that worries me and I hope that we can figure out a way to get it all worked out so that we don't keep losing our programs. Because if we keep losing them, there won't be anywhere for our high school kids to go, and then there will be a trickle down affect which could start to be seen with the numbers down there. Other than that, I think the sport is great. The high school programs are wonderful and programs like Augsburg and the Gophers are among the very best in the country. So, things are good, but we have to keep working to maintain that level of excellence."

VIRG VAGLE

Virg Vagle grew up in Lake Bronson, way up in the northwest corner of the state, and attended high school in Fargo. There, Vagle played football, baseball, basketball and track — their was no wrestling program for him to participate in. Vagle then went on to Augsburg, where he played football, graduating from college in 1965. At that time, wrestling was just getting started in many high schools across the state. So, when he got his first job in Paynesville, he became the assistant coach on the newly created wrestling team. One year later, Vagle took over as the head coach — and he has been there ever since, making history along the way.

Since then, Vagle has become a high school coaching legend. In fact, Vagle ranks No. 2 in all-time in career wins in Minnesota with an amazing 661-148-6 record. In addition, he won four state championships and made numerous trips to the state tournament along the way. Vagle, who retired in 2004, was named as the Minnesota Coach of the Year in 1987 and in 1990 he was inducted into the David Bartelma Hall of Fame. A true Paynesville legend, Vagle is simply one of the best of the best and a true Minnesota wrestling coaching legend.

HOW WOULD YOU DESCRIBE YOUR COACHING STYLE? "I try to put a lot of energy into what I do and I try to get the kids to do the same. There is a lot of dedication on both sides as well as a commitment, and that is important. I have always felt that there is no free ride in our program as well. Everybody needs to work hard to accomplish their goals and we have tried to instill that attitude into our kids over the years. We have also tried to make it a lot of fun for them, which is very important too."

HOW DO YOU MOTIVATE YOUR PLAYERS? "We just try to really get involved with the kids and try to make wrestling an important aspect of their life. Maybe not the most important aspect, but certainly one of the most. We encourage them to work very hard and to try to get them to put a lot into it. We also encourage the team concept and have had a lot of success with our kids buying into that. Then, we just go to work and try to accomplish as much as we can."

LOOKING BACK WHAT ARE YOU MOST PROUD OF IN YOUR CAREER? "Watching young kids mature and grow up in a positive environment is very rewarding. To see them have a little more quality in their lives than they might have had otherwise, that is something I take a lot of pride in. Then, being able to establish a program here at Paynseville that has maintained a high level of competition over such a long period of time, that is great too. It wasn't that we were just up there in the rankings for two or three years either, we have consistently maintained a strong program in the state for a lot of years. We have just had a lot of great kids come through here and that is what has made us so successful."

HOW DO YOU BUILD TEAM UNITY & CHEMISTRY? "This has been a real key for us here at Paynesville through the years. You know, a lot of schools that have wrestling programs think of the sport as an individual one, whereas here we really look at it as a team sport. Our kids look at it that way too, and that has really helped us to be successful. From there, we have built the friendships, the camaraderie and the winning attitude amongst the players and coaches."

WHAT MOTIVATES YOU? "I have just always loved athletics. I loved it as a kid and I love it as an adult. I love the competition too. But it is more than that. I mean you know you are going to win and you know you are going to lose too, so it is watching the kids grow up and see them succeed. To see those kids with a few rough edges that maybe mature and grow a little bit more than they would've otherwise, without athletics in their life, is the biggest motivating factor for me. To see that happen makes me stick with it. Believe me, if it was just about wins and losses, I would've burned out years ago."

WHAT ADVICE WOULD YOU HAVE FOR YOUNG COACHES STARTING OUT TODAY? "Don't expect to win all the time. You have to see yourself through the tough times. The thrill of victory is great, but the only way you are going to last for an extended period of time in this business is to know how to handle the ups and the downs. Handling the downs is the most important thing you can do. That is how you get your kids to stay motivated and focused so that your team can rise above it all and be successful."

WHAT ARE THE KEY INGREDIENTS TO CREATING A CHAMPIONSHIP TEAM? "Well, you have to have some talent for starters. Then, you have to have some luck and you have to have some dedicated kids. The kids also have to have the mental and physical dedication to make it through the difficult times and to be successful. Then, you need to have camaraderie and chemistry too, that is also very important."

WHAT'S THE SECRET TO YOUR SUCCESS? "There is no secret. We have just been fortunate along the way. We have tried to see ourselves through the tough times and then get right back on track. We have not let the tough times derail us and we have also really enjoyed the good times too. That is very important. That is a big motivator for you as well as for your kids."

WHAT WOULD YOU WANT TO SAY TO YOUR FANS, BOOSTERS, AND ALUMNI WHO HAVE SUPPORTED YOU ALL THESE YEARS? "Without them we never would have had that amount of success that we have had, so thanks. Any success or credit that I have gotten over the years I want to share with all of them. They, the whole community, the athletes, the fans, the parents, the supporters, have helped earn any honors that I have gotten along the way. I hope they have enjoyed it as much as I have and I honestly think that they have."

HOW DO YOU WANT YOUR COACHING EPITAPH TO READ? "He gave to the sport and to the young people that he had a chance to coach. He treated them fair and tried to motivate them to be a little bit better people than what they would have been without athletics in their lives."

AL FRANKEN...?

Yeah, that's right! Minnesota's very own Al Franken is a Grammy-winning actor and comedian, Emmy Award-winning television writer and producer and New York Times best-selling author. Franken was born in New York City, but spent the first several years of his life living in Albert Lea, where his father opened a quilting factory. When the business closed, however, his family moved to St. Louis Park, where he grew up and graduated from high school in 1969. While there, Franken was an A student and also competed on the Oriole's wrestling team as well. He didn't win any state titles or anything like that, but he apparently held his own out on the matt — gaining invaluable experience which would undoubtedly prove invaluable as he grappled his way through the perils of show business and politics.

From there, Franken went on to attend Harvard, where he got into theater and also performing stand-up comedy. In 1975, Franken was part of the original writing staff that created NBC's hit show, Saturday Night Live, and performed on the show on and off from 1980-95. One of his favorite characters that he played on SNL was the lovable Stuart Smalley, who became the subject of Franken's first book, "I'm Good Enough, I'm Smart Enough and Doggone It, People Like Me," which was published in 1992. He then later starred in the 1995 movie, "Stuart Saves His Family," which received "two thumbs up" from Siskel and Ebert. Franken's second book, "Rush Limbaugh is a Big Fat Idiot and Other Observations," was a No. 1 New York Times bestseller, and his latest book, "Lies and the Lying Liars Who Tell Them: A Fair and Balanced Look at the Right," has received a lot of critical acclaim.

Aside from all of his television projects, Franken recently launched his own radio show in 2004 as well called, "The O'Franken Factor," and airs across the country on America's first liberal network, Air America. In addition, Al recently announced that he may run for Norm Coleman's U.S. Senate seat from Minnesota in 2008, joking *"I will be the only New York Jew in the race who was actually raised in Minnesota..."* Presently, Al and his wife of 28 years, Franni, live in New York City and have two children, Joe and Thomasin.

THE CLASH

Considered by many to be the toughest dual meet invitational tournament in the country, the Clash is an annual weekend extravaganza which plays host to more than 20 top high school wrestling teams from eight states including: California, Utah, Nebraska, Iowa, Illinois, Wisconsin, Oklahoma and Minnesota. The winner of the National High School Wrestling Duals, which it is often referred to as, is awarded the Governor's Cup, a traveling Trophy which is then presented to that team's respective Governor. In 2003 the Clash was held in Rochester, with prep power Apple Valley bringing home the hardware and then proudly presenting it to Governor Pawlenty.

DICK BLACK

Dick Black grew up in Iowa and went on to star as a wrestler in Fort Dodge, winning a state championship in 1940. After going on to wrestle at Northern Iowa University, Black got his first teaching and coaching jobs at Carroll (IA) and Britt (IA) High Schools during the late 1940s and into the early 1950s. In 1955, Black headed north of the border, to Owatonna, where he would go on to serve as the school's wrestling coach for the next 30 years, accumulating a record of 281-116-4 along the way. In 1962 his "Indians" captured the state championship and established themselves as one of the top programs in the area. In addition to coaching numerous individual state champs, Black would guide his teams to 11 District titles, six Region (section) titles and two Big Nine Conference titles. He would eventually hang it up in 1985 with an impressive career record of 327-132-4.

Among Black's many awards and accolades, he was named as the Minnesota Coach of the Year in 1985. In addition, he was inducted into the Dave Bartelma Hall of Fame in 1981 and is also a member of both the Iowa Wrestling Hall of Fame as well as the Owatonna High School Athletic Hall of Fame. Furthermore, in 2004, Black was inducted into the Minnesota chapter of the National Wrestling Hall of Fame.

"Coaching has been wonderful to me," said Black. "I am just grateful to have had the opportunity to have met so many great people along the way. Wrestling teaches kids a lot about life and if I helped some of them to become better people, then it was all worth it. Owatonna is such a wonderful community and the people here really enjoy wrestling, so I was just glad to have been a part of that great tradition."

JOHN ROSS

John Ross grew up in Minneapolis and became completely blind at the age of seven, but refused to let that handicap slow him down. He played football, baseball, basketball and even hockey (as a goalie believe it or not), as a kid, but his favorite sport was wrestling. Ross went on to become the first and only blind state wrestling champion in state history, accomplishing the feat in 1953 as a member of Marshall University High School in Minneapolis. With his trusty companion guide dog, Major, cheering him on from the sidelines, Ross captured the 120 pound title in grand fashion. Ross, who also played high school football as a guard on the defensive line, then went on to wrestle at the University of Minnesota under coach Wally Johnson, making even more history along the way.

Incredibly, during the ensuing years, Ross would even earn his living as a water skier. His blindness never hindered his ability to have fun. He once drove a car; he loved to play golf; was a champion dart thrower; and even enjoyed surfboarding with his guide dog. The guy was incredible! He would later go on to teach and coach at Comfrey High School as well. From there, he would go on to become an award-winning novelist and as the Director of the Braille Sports Foundation, even invented the wildly successful "Beep Baseball," for the blind.

In addition, he founded the "Feeling Sports" monthly magazine, and later wrote a book of the same name which won critical acclaim as well, chronicling his many exploits during his amazing life — among them included his being chosen to conduct what would prove to be the last ever interview with Babe Ruth. Sadly, he passed away shortly after the book was released in 1998. He was later honored by the National Wrestling Hall of Fame by being awarded their coveted "Medal of Courage Award." John Ross achieved so much in his lifetime and inspired countless others through his sheer determination and courage.

DEWAINE SILKER

DeWaine Silker served as a high school wrestling official in Minnesota for more than four decades. A former wrestler at Iowa State Teachers College, Silker and also served as a MSHSL Rules Interpreter for over a decade as well. The Rochester Community College professor ran the Region I Tournament at the Mayo Civic Center for years and also founded the John Philo Scholarship, which provides wrestlers from southeastern Minnesota with college scholarships.

Dave Schultz High School ExcellenceAward

The Dave Schultz High School Excellence Award, presented annually to a high school senior, is based equally on outstanding wrestling success, scholastic achievement and citizenship or community service. Winners are chosen at the state and regional levels with the national winner being named at the Wrestling Hall of Fame's Honors Weekend each summer.

Minnesota Winners
2003 Eric Sanders, Wabasha-Kellogg
2002 Jeff Pfaffinger, Blue Earth Area
2001 Marcus LeVesseur, Bloomington Kennedy
2000 Nate Baker, Jackson County Central
1999 Luke Eustice, Blue Earth Area
1998 Luke Becker, Cambridge-Isanti
1997 Chad Erikson, Apple Valley

BILL & MATT DEMARAY

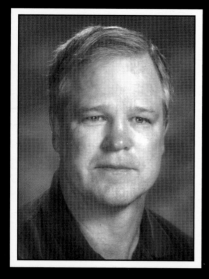

One of the most potent one-two father son punches in Minnesota wrestling history would have to be the Bill and Matt Demaray. The Apple Valley father and son combo are among the very best of the best, and here is their story:

Bill Demaray has spent the better part of three decades devoted to the sport of wrestling. Demaray grew up in Casselton, N.D., and graduated from Casselton High School in 1968. From there, Demaray went on to attend North Dakota State University, where he got his teaching degree and was a two-time NCAA wrestling champion. Demaray's first teaching job was in Fargo, for one year at an elementary school, followed by a year at Fargo South High School. From there, he moved to Minnesota, where he spent the next two year teaching physical education and coaching wrestling and football at Richfield High School. In 1976 Demaray moved on to Apple Valley High School, where he started the school's wrestling program and also served as an assistant on two state title football teams as well.

It was on the mat, however, where Demaray would shine. Over the next 20 years he would go on to lead his teams to six state titles, compiling an amazing record of 407-70-4 along the way — complete with 18 individual champions and 45 place winners. Three of those titles went to his son, Matt, who was one of the program's best ever. In 1995 Bill took a year off and then came back to serve as a co-head coach with his long-time assistant, Jim Jackson. That next year the two flip-flopped, with Jackson taking over and Demaray becoming his assistant. Together they have been simply awesome, winning another six titles for good measure. In fact, over the past 27 years, Apple Valley has posted an astounding 668-74-7 (89.2%) overall team record. During that span the Eagles have made 22 appearances won 12 state championships, finished second six times and third twice. They have completely dominated their conferences as well, winning 22 crowns and going 199-4-1 (97.7%) over that same span.

A member of the North Dakota State University and Minnesota Wrestling Coaches Halls of Fames, Coach Demaray is a high school wrestling legend. Bill and his wife, Sharon, have two sons, Chad and Matt, who both were captains of Eagle wrestling teams as well. Apple Valley High School has become synonymous with high school wrestling in Minnesota and the patriarch of that program would have to be Bill Demaray.

HOW WOULD YOU DESCRIBE YOUR COACHING STYLE? "I think that success is achieved through learning and that learning is the key to success. So, everything needs to be structured around the kids and the people involved in your program, all learning and working together. Through that they enjoy whatever it is you are working towards."

HOW DO YOU MOTIVATE YOUR PLAYERS? "You have to look at each individual. Everybody is different so I try to motivate each person by understanding where they are at as people. From there I try to put them in a position where you can compliment their positives and eliminate their negatives by dealing with them in a one-on-one environment."

LOOKING BACK WHAT ARE YOU MOST PROUD OF IN YOUR CAREER? "The opportunity that I have to work with kids and maybe make a contribution towards their lives is very rewarding. To be able to provide them with great experiences and help them learn, that is real positive for me."

HOW DO YOU BUILD TEAM UNITY & CHEMISTRY? "You build chemistry by developing an attitude where they set a goal and are working towards that goal. Once they make a commitment to that and can see that they are achieving success through the learning process, that just builds on itself. Then, when you have successful people learning and enjoying what they are doing with other people who are doing the same thing, you have a positive attitude — which translates into chemistry."

WHAT MOTIVATES YOU? "I have been blessed with so many positive things in my life that, for me, I really enjoying giving back to people and sharing whatever I have through my experiences with them. I am just motivated by helping people and am grateful to have that opportunity."

WHAT ADVICE WOULD YOU HAVE FOR YOUNG COACHES STARTING OUT TODAY? "They have to really think through why they are there. If they want to be successful and they want to help people, then they need to not worry so much about winning and losing. Instead, they should be more concerned with developing an environment where kids can learn. Once you have that, then success will follow quickly. If kids are learning then they are having fun, and if they are having fun, then they will be successful."

FAVORITE LOCKER ROOM SIGN? "I will study and get ready and maybe my chance will come." — Abraham Lincoln

WHAT'S THE BIGGEST THING YOU'VE LEARNED FROM COACHING THAT YOU'VE BEEN ABLE TO APPLY TO YOUR EVERYDAY LIFE? "I have learned over time that everybody is different and that what can motivate one person might not necessarily motivate another. So, you need to address individual needs. I think that can not only be applied to coaching but also in dealing with people in whatever profession you are in. You just need to treat people with respect and understand that people are different. Once you do that, then you will be successful in whatever you do. If you only worry about wins, then your career will be short-lived."

WHAT ARE THE KEY INGREDIENTS TO CREATING A CHAMPIONSHIP TEAM? "First you have to have a sound philosophy. You have to show people that you care and are committed to what you are doing. If they know you care, then you can encourage them as well as criticize them in a positive way to try to get them to improve. You have to develop positive relationships. There are no shortcuts in success, you have to be willing to work hard and have a strong work ethic. Now, to have a successful program, you have to have continued success at a high level over a period of time. To have a successful team, you have to have a philosophy as to why you are there. Are you there to win X number of games, or are you there to develop an atmosphere of learning where kids are going to get better and have fun? I have always believed that through the learning process you will enjoy what you are doing and also be successful."

WHAT'S THE SECRET TO YOUR SUCCESS? "I think I am a caring person and I have always had a strong work ethic."

WHAT WOULD YOU WANT TO SAY TO YOUR FANS, BOOSTERS, AND ALUMNI WHO HAVE SUPPORTED YOU ALL THESE YEARS? "I would just say thanks. I have been really blessed and I appreciate all the support that I have received as a coach and as a person. It has been so enjoyable working with young people and helping them to get better in whatever they do."

HOW DO YOU WANT YOUR COACHING EPITAPH TO READ? "I would want to be remembered as a person who cared and was very proud to help other people."

Matt...

One of the most accomplished wrestlers in Minnesota high school history would have to be Matt Demaray. Matt grew up with the sport of wrestling and learned the tricks of the trade from the best, his old man, Bill. As an eighth grader he finished as a state runner-up, but from there he dominated. He would go on to win three straight state titles over the next three years, ultimately losing to Simley standout Derek Jones in the 1987 state tourney semifinals. Despite having to compete with a severe hip injury, he came back to finish third and rounded out his illustrious career as one of the state's best ever.

From there, Matt went on to wrestle at the University of Wisconsin, where he won a pair of Big 10 titles along with a pair of back-to-back NCAA Division I titles to boot. He also won the coveted Big Ten Medal of Honor in 1992 as well. After graduating with a degree in Industrial Engineering that same year, Matt went on to become just the second Minnesota wrestler ever to win a National Open Freestyle Tournament in 1992 — a feat he repeated in 1993, 1994 and 1995 as well. Then, despite having surgery to repair several ruptured discs in his back, he narrowly missed making the 1996 U.S. Olympic squad.

During that time, Matt served as an assistant with the Badger wrestling program while also obtaining his MBA from the Kellogg School of Northwestern University. Matt and his wife Michelle, a former Eagle wrestling cheerleader at Apple Valley, have two daughters and presently reside in Chicago, where Matt works a Senior Investment Analyst.

One of the most accomplish-ed, yet humble guys around, Matt keeps it all in perspective: "My success came through two principles: No. 1 work hard, understand what the best in the country are doing, and No. 2 work smart. This basically translates into getting bet-ter every single day. There's a saying: "Nothing great comes easy!"

BILL SUTTER

Bill Sutter grew up in Mankato and wrestled under legendary coach Laverne Klar at Mankato High School. He went on to attend Mankato State University for one year, but left school early to get a job. He later got his teaching degree and got his first job teaching and coaching wrestling in the small southeastern Minnesota town of Goodhue in 1969. Incredibly, he has been there ever since.

Over the past 35 years, Sutter has emerged as the all-time winningest coach in Minnesota high school wrestling history with an amazing 670-132-8 career record. In addition, he has led two of his teams to state championships and has fostered six individual state champs as well. One of those champs was his son, Brian, who won it all back in 1991. With just over 500 souls in the entire town, it is remarkable to think that he has achieved so much with so little. Sutter retired from teaching in 2001, but still remains as the team's head wrestling coach. Among his many honors and accolades, Sutter is a two time coach of the year and was also inducted into the Dave Bartelma Hall of Fame in 1988 as well.

"Being the winningest coach in state history just means that I have had a lot of great kids through the years," said Sutter. "I was just fortunate enough to send them out there and watch them all to their best. We have really good, hard working kids here and I am proud to be a part of such a great community with such good people. There are a lot of second generation kids who come through the program and that is really neat to see too. We also have a strong youth program here as well and that is a big part of our success.

"The wrestling team is a big source of community pride down here and that means a great deal to me. I just believe in my kids and then they believe in me. Everything just kind of works out from there. Wrestling is the toughest sport that there is and it takes a special person to excel at it. The kids just work so hard for me though and I appreciate that so much. We have a different mentality in small towns that way I think. A lot of the kids come from farming backgrounds and those are some of the most hard working, disciplined kids that there are. I am just glad to have had the opportunity to have been around so many great people over the years, without their support it never would have happened.

"As for the record, I salute Scot Davis over at Owatonna, he will surpass me in 2005. Those guys can schedule 45-50 duals a year and we just don't have the resources to do that kind of thing. So, I am a one-year wonder as far as holding that honor, but will gladly hand it over to Scot, he is a great coach. Any accolades that I have ever gotten over my career are because of the kids, period. I couldn't say it any other way. You know, I have been at Goodhue for 35 years now and I am still enjoying myself, and that is what it is all about."

CHUCK JEAN

Chuck Jean grew up in Albert Lea and went on to become one of Minnesota's greatest all-time grapplers. He has also garnered a reputation for being one of the sport's all-time greatest characters as well. Jean, who won a state title for the Tigers in 1967, went on to become a two-time NCAA champion for Iowa State at 177 pounds in 1969 and 1970, and later won a pair of NAIA national title for Adams State(Colo.) in 1972 and 1973 as well. His story is as fascinating as he is.

"We've had an Olympian in Gary Neist," said Albert Lea High School coach Larry Goodnature in a 1997 Star Tribune article by Patrick Reusse. "Tom Jean was a three-time state champion. We've had a lot of great wrestlers. But Charlie is always the one who sticks out."

"Charlie," meanwhile, is Chuck Jean, the oldest of four tough Albert Lea brothers. And, despite all of the success he achieved on the matt, his most famous match occurred well outside of any gymnasiums. In fact, it came in 1970 in Iowa's Boone State Park, against a 300-pound, 14-year-old, 10-point buck named "Sammy," who was penned up in there.

According to Reusse, Jean accepted a dare from his buddy for a 12-pack that he couldn't take him down. He agreed and with that, jumped the fence.

"Sammy and I stared at each other and then he charged," said Jean in Reusse's article. "He stuck his antlers right into my chest and the Bowie knife went flying. There was a feeding trough and he carried me 15, 20 feet and slammed me into the trough. I got a lock on his neck and threw him to the ground. All this time, he was kicking me. His hooves turned the backs of my legs into raw meat. I had a pocket knife with a small blade on me. I got that out. It took 10 minutes of war before I finished him."

Jean then somehow dragged the dead buck over the fence and back to his buddies car. A few days later, they had a kegger and shishkabobbed old Sammy. According to Jean, Sammy, whom he had mounted, wound up in a Missouri bowling alley.

"Stories about that damn deer have followed me wherever I have gone," laughed Jean. "You know, it was just a spur of the moment dumb thing that I did over a 12-pack. I just jumped in there and we had at it. He tore me up pretty good but I stayed low and took him. Then, I locked his horns into the chain link fence and then swung him over the top. He was a heavy son of a gun too. He was tasty though, I can tell you that."

Jean would go on to become a two-time national champ for the Cyclones, which had also won a pair of national team titles during that span as well.

"Dan Gable was my work-out partner at Iowa State," said Jean. "We were good friends and I was close with his family too. He was so tough, I mean really tough. I could hang with him for about 30 seconds or so and then it was all over. He was the best wrestler I ever saw, bar none."

Later, after his sophomore year, jean got into some trouble when an anti-war riot with strong racial overtones erupted on campus. Being a star athlete in the wrong place at the wrong time, he wound up right smack dab in the middle of it all and the media was all over it. So, he ended up leaving school over the incident and enrolling at Mankato State University. Three weeks later, however, he left to enlist in the Army. He would spend nearly two years in the Army, and even competed on the Army wrestling team out in Virginia. There, he won a couple of silver medals at the inter-service championships and also competed in the AAU Nationals as well in both freestyle and Greco.

From there, Jean decided to attend a small NAIA college in Alamosa, Colo., Adams State. You see, one of his best friends' brother was the head coach there, so he packed up and moved to Colorado to compete for the Grizzlies. He would dominate at the school, leading his team to a pair of national team titles, as well as a pair of individual titles along the way.

Afterwards, Jean opted to stick around the Rockies and buy himself a bar. Jean, whose his wife was tragically killed in an automobile accident, later remarried and moved back to Albert Lea, where he worked with his father as a roofer while also serving as an assistant wrestling coach back at Albert Lea High School. In 2002, however, Jean moved back to Colorado to work in construction and remains there today with his family.

The legend of Chuck's matt antics are alive and well and can usually be found on various wrestling web-site chat-rooms, where is stories are continually circulated as modern day folklore. One even talks of the time he cut some 33 pounds in just three days to make weight against the 167-pounder from Mason City Community College, who had commented publicly that he could beat Jean if he were at that weight. He somehow got down there and, after torturing with him out on the matt for a while to the tune of a 17-1 margin, he stuck him right before the final whistle just for good measure.

"I didn't eat or drink for three days," laughed Jean, who is also member of the prestigious David Bartelma Hall of Fame. "I just ran and worked out non-stop. Hell, my fingers were all knotted up from cramps and stuff, it was awful. I remember after weighing in I ran over to a water fountain to get a drink and the water just ran right out of my forearms because there was no salt in there to hold it in. It was crazy. This guy said some things about me, knowing there would be no way I would ever wrestle him. Well, when I got wind of it I weighed 200 pounds, and I got down to 167 to kick his ass. That was something else, let me tell ya!"

Chuck Jean is truly a one of a kind, and one of the most colorful characters in Minnesota wrestling history.

"Growing up in Albert Lea was great," said Jean. "I had three brothers who wrestled and there were some battles in the basement over the years when we were kids. There was some broken furniture and a few holes in the walls, but it was all fun. It got me tough too, which came in handy out on the mat.

"The thing I am most proud of though, is the fact that I won four individual national championships on four national championship teams. We won together and that is what it was all about. I just loved wrestling though, it taught me a lot about hard work and about life. Those were great times, I miss them. Who knows, a coaching job just opened up down the road here and I half tempted to walk over there right now and do it. Once wrestling gets in you, you can't get rid of it… it's an awesome thing."

THE GUILLOTINE

Covering amateur wrestling in Minnesota for more than three decades, The Guillotine has long been considered to be the bible of grappling in the Gopher State. The newspaper was first started in 1971 by former St. James High School wrestling coach Paul Krueger, who wanted to publish something which covered nothing but Minnesota amateur wrestling. So, he and his wife Connie, along with their friends Bill and Sue Mohr, started writing, editing and printing the paper right out of their home. It grew from there and eventually became one of the region's most respected publications.

Krueger, who grew up in Albert Lea and went on to wrestle collegiately at Luther, later became the head wrestling coach at Truman High School in 1957. Six years later he moved up the road to St. James, where he created a dynasty. From 1963-75, his Saints made it to three state tournaments, winning one in 1972 while finishing second twice in 1969 and 1973, en route to compiling an impressive 131-15-1 overall record. Synonymous with amateur wrestling in Southern Minnesota, Krueger sadly passed away on Feb. 17, 1994, at the age of 59. Among his many teaching and coaching accolades, he is a member of the Minnesota State High School League Hall of Fame as well as a charter member of the David Bartelma Wrestling Hall of Fame.

Kruger, who retired from active coaching in 1973 to serve as the school's athletic director, continued to publish the Guillotine for several more years before selling the publication to Jim Bartels and partner Pat Schmidt. The newspaper continued to flourish under the new management, and in 1986 it was later sold to Jim and Jeri Beshey of Glencoe, where it continues to thrive and is considered the best of its kind in the nation.

Jim and Jeri Beshey grew up in Iowa, where they both went on to graduate from Britt High School. They then each went on to receive teaching degrees at Mankato State, with Jim's first job coming in Brownton, Minn., where he also served as the high school wrestling coach. Jim coached at Brownton from 1968-72, posting a solid record of 56-28-1, and even winning a District 12 title along the way. From there, Jim took a job teaching and coaching at Glencoe High School in 1974. There, he posted a 104-73-6 record on the matt, including a sixth place team finish at the 1977 State High School Tournament. One of his athletes, Pat Halloran, was a state champ in 1978 as well. During the 1980s Jim was named as the president of the Minnesota Wrestling Coaches Association, and was very influential in establishing the "Minnesota Iowa Classic," among other things. After retiring from coaching in 1986, the Besheys purchased The Guillotine from Jim Bartels, one of his former wrestlers.

The Besheys, who have been named to the Bartelma Wrestling Hall of Fame for their contributions to the sport of wrestling, have made it a family-affair. They have two sons, Mark and Jeff, and a daughter, Dawn. Both boys wrestled in high school, while Dawn was a cheerleader-turned statistician for Glencoe-Silver Lake as well. A family business to the core, the Besheys have dedicated themselves to the sport they love.

A past recipient of the National Wrestling Media Association's State Wrestling Publication of the Year, the Guillotine is a must-read for any grappling fan. In addition, the publication's web-site, which is run by son Jeff, is simply second to none. Complete with stats, records and information about youth, high school, college, Greco Roman, freestyle or Olympic wrestling, it is really one-stop shopping for wrestling fans of all ages. In addition to information on over 100 open tournaments throughout the year, the site also features very current high school and college schedules and results, wrestling camps, feature articles and wrestler profiles as well. Mark, meanwhile, has been doing photography for the paper for several years as well.

"The main goal of The Guillotine is to promote the sport of wrestling and record the history of the sport," said Jim. "We tend to dwell on the positive aspects of the sport as well. We just feel very fortunate to be able to do something we love to be a part of and to give back. That is what it is all about. Beyond that, it is great to be able to work with the state high school league, Minnesota USA Wrestling as well as the coaches association, and to keep our readers informed about the sport of wrestling throughout the state. We have such a wonderful wrestling tradition here and it is great to just be a part of that. It is also a business, and we treat it as such, but it is very rewarding nonetheless. Our subscribers are very loyal and we appreciate their support. We are planning on being around for a long, long time to be able to continue what we are doing."

Considered by those in the know to be the best of its kind in the nation, The Guillotine IS Minnesota wrestling.

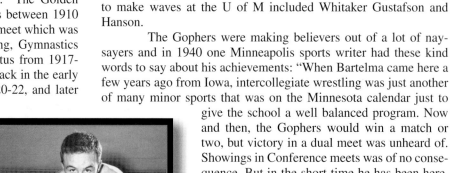

COLLEGE WRESTLING

The History of Gopher Wrestling

The University of Minnesota's illustrious wrestling history began in Gold Country some 95 years ago, back in 1910. The Golden Gophers went on to capture three conference titles between 1910 and 1913, by virtue of winning an annual an open meet which was sanctioned by the Western Intercollegiate Wrestling, Gymnastics and Fencing Association. After taking a brief hiatus from 1917-1919, for World War I, the Gophers came roaring back in the early 1920s, first under Coach Frank Gilman, from 1920-22, and later under Blain McKusick, who guided the squad from 1922-35. During this era team champions were determined by dual meet records, while individual champions were determined in a closed meet format. Steve Easter became the program's first Big Ten individual champ when he won the crown at 135 pounds in 1926, and was followed by heavyweight Ed George, who claimed one of his own just three years later. The team went through its share of ups and downs over the next decade, struggling a in both dual-meet action as well as in conference play.

Dick Mueller

By the mid-1930s, Minnesota was amongst the better teams in the Big Ten. The conference began using a point system to determine its champion and the Gophers would come close on several occasions during this era. In all, Minnesota scored four top-five Big Ten finishes in the 30s, including back-to-back third-place showings in 1936 and 1937 as well. Two Gophers also won individual conference titles, including John Whitaker (175) and Cliff Gustafson (Hwt). The 1937 campaign also saw the Gophers' first NCAA champion get crowned when Whitaker brought home the hardware that same year. As a team, they also earned its highest finish ever at the NCAA Championships, which were held in Terre Haute, Ind., that year, where they placed third in the nation.

One of the big reasons the Gophers started doing so well right about then was due to the fact that a new coach had come in for the 1936 season, Dave Bartelma. Bart, as he was affectionately known, has long been considered to be the "Father of Minnesota Wrestling," and is credited for starting the first ever state high school tournament in the Land of 10,000 Lakes. An outstanding high school coach from Cresco, Iowa, Bart knew that he had to start building a feeder-system for his Gophers and did so in 1937, when he hosted the inaugural prep tourney at the U of M's Field House. Amateur wrestling grew from there, and with that, so too grew the Gophers.

Minnesota came in sixth in 1938 behind Heavyweight Clifton Gustafson, who finished No. 2 in the country that year, and improved to fourth in '39, when the NCAA Tournament was held in Lancaster, Pa. There, the Gophers were led by 128-pounder, Dale Hanson, who brought home the program's second national championship. The Maroon and Gold won their first ever Big Ten team title in 1941, winning by a point over Iowa and

Gopher Practice circa 1925

Indiana, and then went on to place third in the Nationals out in Bethlehem, Pa. The star of the show that year was former state high school champ, Butch Levy, who brought home the top prize in the Heavyweight division that year. Other grads of Bart's prep tourney to make waves at the U of M included Whitaker Gustafson and Hanson.

The Gophers were making believers out of a lot of naysayers and in 1940 one Minneapolis sports writer had these kind words to say about his achievements: "When Bartelma came here a few years ago from Iowa, intercollegiate wrestling was just another of many minor sports that was on the Minnesota calendar just to give the school a well balanced program. Now and then, the Gophers would win a match or two, but victory in a dual meet was unheard of. Showings in Conference meets was of no consequence. But in the short time he has been here, Bartelma single handed, has made Minnesota students wrestling minded. He did a grand organization job, starting from scratch and building up. Now he's excelling as a coach. His grunters haven't lost a dual meet this year. The squad's record is so outstanding that those who know say that it's only a question of time when Minnesota will dominate the Big Ten in grappling."

The World War II years were tough on college athletic programs and the U of M was no exception. Bartelma, along with so many others, were called to duty overseas during this era and the team's performance suffered. Filling in during that time at the helm were Stanley Hanson and Clarence Osell. Bart returned to the bench in the mid '40s, however, just in time to welcome a two-time state champ from Robbinsdale High School by the name of Verne Gagne. Gagne took Gold Country by storm and wasted little time in rewriting the record books. Gagne, who also starred as a platooning end on the football team, went on to become the only Minnesota wrestler and one of only nine in conference history to win four Big Ten titles, which he did in 1944, 1947, 1948 and 1949. (He too had to leave school in 1945 to serve in the Armed Forces.) In addition, Gagne also became the program's first two-time national champion, when, after finishing third in 1947, he went back-to-back in both 1948 and 1949, at 191 and heavyweight, respectively. Gagne, who also won an AAU title and was also a member of the 1948 U.S. Olympic Greco Roman team, spent the next four decades as one of the most famous professional wrestlers in history.

Another All-American from this era was a kid from St. Paul by the name of Alan Rice, who captured a pair of Big Ten titles in 1948 and 1949. Rice, would go on to compete for more than a decade on the national and international stage in both the Greco Roman and freestyle disciplines, participating in the 1954 Pan American Games in Mexico City, the 1955 World Championships in Tokyo, and the 1956 Olympic Games in Melbourne, where he placed fifth in the Greco — the highest finish for an American at that time. He would go on to claim national

DR. NORMAN BORLAUG

Norman Borlaug is a legend. Not because of wrestling though, but for things much, much more meaningful. Like the fact that it has been estimated that he has saved more lives than any other person who ever lived. How's that for a line on the old resume? Borlaug's story is an amazing journey which begins in 1914, near the tiny northeastern Iowa town of Cresco, just 10 miles from the Minnesota border. There, Borlaug was raised on a farm and learned the values of hard work and determination — principles which would one day make him one of the most important people in the history... of well, people.

Borlaug grew up loving sports and competed in football, baseball and wrestling. After graduating from Cresco High School in 1932, he went on to attend the University of Minnesota, where, in addition to studying forestry, he competed on the Gopher baseball and wrestling teams. Interestingly, Borlaug was all set to attend the University of Iowa, where the wrestling coach had promised him a roster spot, as well as a good campus job.

"Shortly before I was to leave for Iowa, George Champlin, a football player for the University of Minnesota who lived in Cresco, drove up," said Borlaug. "He said, 'My dad said you should be at the University of Minnesota. I'm going to early football practice tomorrow. Come and ride along. You can hitchhike back if you don't like it there.' I went and never came back."

While he had to drop baseball after his freshman year because of a conflict with a chemistry lab, he excelled as a 145-pounder on the mat, even reaching the conference semifinals in 1937, his senior year. From there, Borlaug became a pioneer in Minnesota wrestling. You see, Borlaug saw the need to develop youth programs in the state, so he recruited his old high school coach, Dave Bartelma, to move to the Twin Cities and take over as the Gopher's first full-time wrestling coach. He agreed. He also organized what would become the first ever state high school tournament as well. Borlaug was instrumental in helping Bartelma get it going and even refereed the first regional and state tournaments back in 1938. He even traveled with Bartelma, conducting wrestling clinics for kids, parents and potential coaches throughout the state.

Borlaug would later receive his master's degree from the U of M in 1939 and doctorate in 1942, in the field of plant pathology. During that time, in addition to working for the U.S. Forestry Service, he refereed at high school meets in the area and also served as the Gophers freshman wrestling coach. By now, Borlaug had also gotten married to his wife, Margaret, whose brother was also a Gopher legend in his own right — George Gibson. (Gibson, who was an All-American lineman on the Gopher Football team, went on to play for the NFL's Minneapolis Red Jackets and later became a world renowned oil geologist. He also coached both football as well as wrestling at Carleton College earlier in his career as well. Sadly, Gibson died in August of 2004 at the age of 100.)

Borlaug then ventured south of the border, to work as a microbiologist in Mexico studying genetics, plant breeding, plant pathology, entomology, agronomy, soil science and cereal technology. Some 20 years later he discovered a high-yielding disease-resistant form of wheat. With that, Borlaug became one of the world's foremost humanitarians, with a new mission of setting out to feed hungry throughout the third world. As a result, he has spent the last half century traveling the world, touting the virtues of the "green revolution," and truly making a difference.

In fact, in 1970 he was awarded the Nobel Peace Prize for his immense strides in agriculture which produced food for underfed, undernourished nations. Specifically, Dr. Borlaug developed high-yielding varieties of wheat, which produced eight or nine bushels to the acre where only one had grown before. His success with wheat contributed to the development of a new "miracle rice" in the Orient with the same life-saving effects. His efforts literally saved millions of people from death by starvation.

Today, Borlaug is considered to be the world's foremost agronomist. His honors and accolades are far too many to list, but among the bigger ones he has been awarded 31 honorary doctoral degrees from universities in 13 countries. In addition to his Nobel Prize, Borlaug also received the National Academy of Science's prestigious Public Welfare Medal in 2002. Furthermore, he was presented the Aztec Eagle by the government of Mexico in 1970, America's Presidential Medal of Freedom in 1977 and the Presidential World Without Hunger Award in 1985. He is also a member of the National Agricultural Hall of Fame and has served on the President's Commission on World Hunger as well as the President's Council of Advisors on Science and Technology. In the Spring of 2004 the Minnesota Senate even made October 16th "Norman Borlaug World Food Prize Day."

As for wrestling accolades, he was inducted into the National Collegiate Hall of Fame in 1992, and in 1994 he was inducted into the University of Minnesota National M Club Lifetime Achievement Hall of Fame. Additionally, in 1992 Borlaug was honored as an "Outstanding American" by the National Wrestling Hall of Fame for his contributions to the sport and in 2004 Borlaug had a homecoming of sorts when he was inducted into the Iowa Wrestling Hall of Fame, which is located in his hometown of Cresco.

"Wrestling taught me the willingness to never give up," said Borlaug. "The lessons I learned from my time on the mat have helped me deal with adversity all over the world."

Borlaug, 91, presently resides in both Mexico City, where he has worked for 60 years, and also in Texas, where he remains active in his efforts and contributions to feeding the hungry. Nowadays, however, he primarily wears three hats: He is a Distinguished Professor of International Agriculture at Texas A&M in College Station; president of the Sasakawa Africa Association, which is working to increase farm production in Africa; and senior consultant to the director general of the International Maize and Wheat Center in Mexico. He also continues to travel the world, lecturing nine months of the year, speaking out against hunger and bureaucracy.

Through it all, however, Borlaug still shows his true colors proudly as evidenced by the fact that Gopher wrestling posters adorn the walls of his office. The sport of wrestling has truly taught Dr. Borlaug how to grapple with hunger — and he is still trying to pin that foe more than 70 years later.

"Some people say I've saved more lives than any other person in the world, but I take that with moderation," Borlaug would later say. "A lot of people have been saved, but my main contribution has been teaching. It was the teamwork of all these young scientists I've worked with that made the difference."

Borlaug is optimistic about the future, but realistic about the present.

"Millions of people still are undernourished in the world today," he said in a recent article entitled "Bread and Peace, by Vicki Stavig." "Predictions are that the world population will reach about 8.3 billion by 2025. In order to feed those people, I calculate that we will need one billion more tons of grain. That means more tons per hectare are needed. There is much work that still needs to be done."

"Hunger and peace are interrelated," he added. "Have you ever been hungry—hungry for three or four days? One needs to have that experience. When people are hungry, it disrupts everything. If you were hungry and your children were starving, you would breach the laws pretty easily. You would steal for those children. When you have poverty, hunger, and misery, it's easy to plant terrorism and all other kinds of 'isms.' The world has shrunk. We can't ignore these problems."

The good doctor also still finds time to follow his Gophers as well, something that has always been near and dear to his heart. "I still follow the Gophers as much as I can," said Borlaug. "Coach Robinson and his entire coaching staff have done a wonderful job with that program over the years and I am real proud of that. For him to lead the team to two national championships the way he did was just remarkable. Whenever I am back in Minnesota I always try to stop in and see J and the team, it is always such a thrill. It was a real honor to be a member of the Gopher wrestling team and the lessons I learned there have been with me ever since.

"You learn a great deal about hard work and discipline being a wrestler and I just think it is the greatest sport in the world. Competitive athletics has given me so much over the years and I have never forgotten that. I even helped get little league baseball going for kids here in Mexico too. They are what it is all about, kids, and that is what has been most rewarding for me in my career, helping children in any way that I can. So, if I had to say what I would like my legacy to be, it would be that I helped children."

AAU championships in both freestyle and Greco as well.

(Rice would later start the Minnesota Amateur Wrestling Club, now the Gopher Wrestling Club. There, he coached the team for what would amount to the next 25 years, winning 16 national championships along the way. One of the most prominent clubs of its kind in the country, it specializes in developing top Greco-Roman wrestlers from around the area. In fact, it is so good that it has even produced at least one wrestler on every U.S. world championship or Olympic team for more than 40 straight years, a record that no other club can boast. In 1976, seven of the 10 roster spots on the U.S. Greco roster were held by Minnesotans. Rice's continued efforts helped shape the 2000 U.S. Greco-Roman Olympic team, which claimed gold, silver and bronze in Sydney.) Later, in 1972, Rice also served as head coach of the U.S. Greco-Roman team which competed at the Olympic Games in Munich. One of the wrestlers on that team was a tough kid by the name of J Robinson, who would later go on to become the head coach of the Golden Gophers.)

Meanwhile, in 1952 Bart left to take an administrative position at the University of Colorado. His replacement would be Wally Johnson, who wrestled for the Gophers back in the early '40s. Led by Dick Mueller, who, in addition to winning three Big Ten titles (1953, 1957-58), also won a national championship at the 123-pound division in 1953, Johnson's boys finished a strong third in the conference in his rookie season at the helm. From there, Johnson would create a legacy of his own in Gold Country, winning a pair of Big Ten crowns in 1957, in Evanston, Ill., and in 1959 in Iowa City. Among some of the other Gopher stars of the '50s were Edward Anderson and Charles Ofsthun, who each earned All-American honors in 1954 at the 123 and 115-pound categories.

By the late '50s Minnesota was the best in the conference. Leading the charge during this period were a trio of All-Americans in Bill Wright and Charles Coffee, at

Pat Neu

177 and 137, respectively, in 1959, as well as Bill Koehen, who finished fourth in the country at 167 pounds in 1960. Lew Kennedy and Lee Gross each won a pair of Big Ten titles from 1963-65 and from 1964-67 the Gophers finished third in the Big Ten for four seasons straight. They were steady, but not stellar through the late '60s and into the early '70s though.

The first big star of the mid-1970s was Larry Zilverberg, who won three straight conference crowns from 1974-76. Mike McArthur won a pair of his own at 118 pounds from 1976-77. In addition, those same two years saw a duo of Gopher grapplers bring home National Championships: Evan Johnson at 190 pounds in 1976, followed by Pat Neu at 134 pounds in 1977. In 1976, Johnson was named NCAA Coach of the Year after leading them to back-to-back runner-up finishes in the Big Ten and fourth-place and seventh-place NCAA showings in 1976 and 1977, respectively.

Larry Zilverberg's brother Dan hit the scene in the late '70s and went on to win a pair of Big Ten titles of his own in 1979 and '80 at 158. Jim Trudeau and Ed Giese kept it going from there, each winning titles into the early and mid-1980s as well. Giese would also garner All-American honors in 1986 and became Minnesota's career leader with 159 wins. That same year Johnson stepped down from coaching. During his 34 seasons at the helm of Minnesota's program, he coached 28 individual Big Ten champions and wound up with a 292-209-11 career record.

His replacement would be J Robinson, who would usher in a new era of Golden Gopher wrestling and make a lot of history along the way. Originally from San Diego, Robinson wrestled collegiately at Oklahoma State and then, after competing internationally on two World teams, Robinson represented his country in the 1972 Olympic Games as a member of Team U.S.A. After serving in Vietnam, Robinson went on to serve as an assistant coach at the University of Iowa from 1976-85, helping to lead the Hawks to seven NCAA and eight Big Ten crowns.

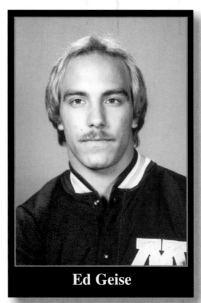

Ed Geise

WALLY JOHNSON

Wallace "Wally" Johnson grew up in Detroit Lakes during the 1930s loving sports. He played football and boxed in high school, but ironically did not wrestle because the state did not adopt the sport until the year after his graduation in 1937. Johnson then went on to become a multi-sport athlete at the University of Minnesota, where he was a member of an national champion football team and twice the Gopher's middleweight boxing champion. In addition, Johnson took up wrestling at the U, where he ultimately was named as the team captain.

From there, Johnson would go on to spread the gospel, teaching and founding wrestling programs at Luther College in Iowa in 1947, as well as at South Dakota State University in 1949. In 1952, Johnson came home to serve as the head coach of the Gopher Wrestling team. He took over from Dave Bartelma, long considered to be the "Father of Minnesota Wrestling," for his contributions with regards to starting the high school tournament. Johnson learned a lot from Bartelma, and knew that a solid high school program would mean plenty of top-notch recruits for his Gophers. So, he spent countless hours over the years putting on free clinics to Minnesota youngsters and bringing in top instructors to teach them about the sport.

From 1952-86 Johnson's career record in Gold Country was an impressive 392-209-11 (.650%). Combining Johnson's 34 years with the Gophers, along with his five seasons at Luther and SDSU, his career total swells to 427 wins. In addition to capturing a pair of Big 10 Championships in 1957 and 1959, he also coached 35 individual titlists, four NCAA champs and more than 40 All Americans as well. With the Gophers, Johnson coached 28 individual Big Ten champions, including three-time winners Dick Mueller (1953, 1957-58) and Larry Zilverberg (1974-76). At the national level, Johnson led 25 different wrestlers to 31 All-America honors. Three of his wrestlers won NCAA individual titles, including Mueller in 1953 at 123, Evan Johnson in 1976 at 190 and Pat Neu in 1977 at 134.

Four decades and more than 600 dual meets later, Johnson, who also served as the freshman football coach Murray Warmath, retired in 1986 to enjoy the fruits of his labor. Since then, he has enjoyed watching his successor, J Robinson, transform Minnesota into a national power. Johnson was tough, but fair out on the mat. He instilled a hard work ethic into his wrestlers, and earned their respect by leading by example. He always insisted his kids chose academics over athletics as well, a evidenced by the fact that nearly every one of his wrestlers graduated from school. A man of great foresight, he was the consummate builder of a sport which had no roots when he began. As one of the founding fathers of USA Wrestling, he would also serve as the organization's first president — guiding it through its tough initial years. He also contributed immensely to the growth of the Greco-Roman discipline, by opening the doors of his wrestling room to Alan Rice's Minnesota Wrestling Club and helping it develop into the nation's top program.

Among his many honors and accolades, in 1976, he was named NCAA Coach of the Year and in 1977 he was enshrined into the Dave Bartelma Minnesota Wrestling Hall of Fame. Furthermore, Johnson was later honored in 1985 as a Distinguished Member of the National Wrestling Hall of Fame, recognizing his lifetime of leadership and dedication to the well being of athletes of all ages.

"The first thing I did was get good students," said Johnson. "I think close to 99% of my wrestlers went on to graduate and I am more proud of that than I am anything else. You know, there were no shortcuts in coaching, just hard work. You can't worry about the other guy, if you take care of yourself and work hard all your life then you will be successful in whatever you do. I really enjoyed my years at the University, it was a wonderful experience. I came in contact with so many great people and was able to make a difference in many young people's lives. It is fantastic to see what that program has become and I am very proud of everything they have done over there. It is also great to see how far our high school program has come too, because I take great pride in helping to get that going as well. It is just great to see how far it has all come from my days back in the 1930s, when we didn't even have a wrestling program at my high school. Kids today have a lot of opportunities that we couldn't have even dreamed of, and that is just great to see."

In his first season, the Gophers finished the year without winning a Big Ten dual match. That, however, was about to change in a big, big way. Steadily, J followed his plan for building and recruiting a solid program from the ground up. In 1991, current Minnesota Head Assistant Coach Marty Morgan, after winning a pair of conference crowns, captured a national title, during an amazing 39-0 senior season.

In 1993 the Gophers moved into their new home, the newly renovated Sports Pavilion, formerly Mariucci Arena. There, they made history right out of the gates by upsetting top-ranked Oklahoma State, 23-16, to claim their first-ever No. 1 national ranking in front of more than 5,000 screaming fans. The team would continue to host events at the Pavilion as well as in Williams Arena next door, for their bigger matches against the Iowas and Iowa States, to accommodate more fans.

Then, in 1996 the 66th NCAA National Tournament was held at the University of Minnesota. Iowa won it all that year in front of thousands of adoring fans who had made the trek north. Robinson knew that his team was close, but needed to get over that hump in order to achieve that same level of success. In 1997 the Gophers finished third in the nation and went on to finish second in 1998 as well. They were getting and the Gophers could taste it. Later, in 1998 and 1999, Tim Hartung won back-to-back national titles at 197 pounds, becoming the first Gopher to do so since Verne Gagne a half century earlier.

Finally, in 1999, after tremendous recruiting and a lot of hard work, his Gophers went undefeated in conference duals and won the Big Ten crown. With that, they snapped Iowa's 25-year conference title win streak, said to be the longest such streak for any school in any sport. It was also the first Big Ten crown Minnesota had won in 40 years. After winning the 1999 conference title, Minnesota went on to finish second at the NCAAs for the second straight season, this time coming in just behind perennial national power Iowa.

The 2000 season was all about one guy, Brock Lesnar, a hulking heavyweight who went on to win the national championship in grand fashion. The media ate this guy up and as a result the Gophers got more exposure than at any other time in history.

Evan Johnson

Lesnar, who would go on to make millions as a professional wrestler, was one of Gold Countries' most popular and colorful all-time figures. The team would finish third that season, but was poised to finally get over the hump once and for all.

Then, in 2001, Robinson made history by leading the Gophers to their first ever NCAA National Championship with 10 All-Americans by his side the first time in NCAA history that every weight class produced an all-American.

"In 1999 we had a team that should've won," said Robinson. "We deserved to win and we did everything right, but we were just unlucky to lose the coin toss in overtime. Chad Kraft, who was a national finalist the year before, lost the coin flip in double overtime and wound up on the

bottom, and we lost the national title. It was that close. That was very hard on all of us. I even made peace with God after that thinking I was never going to win it. But, we finished third in 2000 and then roared back in 2001 to finally take it all. So, anytime you think about your first national championship it is pretty special."

When the Gophers won their first ever NCAA crown in 2001, they brought home the hardware from arguably the toughest venues in all of sports, Iowa's Carver-Hawkeye Arena — the "Lion's Den." It was a storybook ending to a fairytale season, complete with injuries, drama and hard work.

The Gophers broke several school and national records

Dave Zuniga

GOPHER ALL-BIG TEN CHAMPS

YR	NAME	WEIGHT		YR	NAME	WEIGHT
2004	Damion Hahn	197		1977	Evan Johnson	190
2003	Jared Lawrence	149			Mike McArthur	118
	Luke Becker	157		1976	Mike McArthur	118
	Damion Hahn	197			Larry Zilverberg	167
2002	Leroy Vega	125		1975	Larry Zilverberg	158
	Ryan Lewis	133		1974	Larry Zilverberg	158
	Luke Becker	157		1973	John Panning	177
	Damion Hahn	184		1970	Jim Axtell	158
	Owen Elzen	197		1966	Bob Henry	147
2001	Jared Lawrence	149		1965	Lee Gross	157
	Garrett Lowney	Hwt		1964	Lee Gross	157
2000	Brandon Eggum	184			Lew Kennedy	137
	Brock Lesnar	Hwt		1963	Lew Kennedy	130
1999	Brandon Eggum	184			Lonnie Rubis	147
	Tim Hartung	197		1961	Ron Andrews	123
	Brock Lesnar	Hwt		1959	Bill Wright	177
1998	Tim Hartung	190		1958	Dick Mueller	123
1997	Tim Hartung	190		1957	Dick Mueller	123
1994	Brad Gibson	177		1953	Dick Mueller	123
1993	Billy Pierce	Hwt			Willis Wood	Hwt
1991	Marty Morgan	177		1952	Jack Dorfman	Hwt
1990	Marty Morgan	177		1949	Alan Rice	136
	Chuck Heise	142			Verne Gagne	Hwt
	Dave Zuniga	134		1948	Verne Gagne	191
1989	Dave Dean	177			Garth Lappin	121
	Gordy Morgan	158			Alan Rice	128
1988	Keith Nix	118		1947	Verne Gagne	Hwt
1987	Dave Dean	190		1945	Richard Nelson	145
1986	Ed Giese	118		1944	Verne Gagne	Hwt
1984	Ed Giese	118		1941	Alphonse Janesko	145
1983	Jim Trudeau	167		1940	Dale Hanson	128
1981	Jim Trudeau	158		1939	Dale Hanson	128
	Dalen Wasmund	134		1937	John Whitaker	175
	Gary Lefebvre	126			Cliff Gustafson	Hwt
1980	Dan Zilverberg	158		1936	Caifron Johnson	165
1979	Dan Zilverberg	158		1929	Ed George	Hwt
	Jim Martinez	134		1926	Steve Easter	135

along the way to this historic team crown as all 10 members of the squad made significant contributions along the way. Prior to the national tournament, the Gophers breezed through the 2000-2001 season, going 19-1 in dual meets and winning team titles at the Midlands Championships, the National Duals and Big Ten Championships. Overall, Minnesota outscored its opponents in dual meets on the season by the whopping margin of 573-170.

Along the way the team recorded several lopsided victories, including blow-outs over Northern Iowa (36-3), Hofstra (33-3), Princeton (45-0), Seton Hall (37-2), Nebraska (30-9), Michigan (29-6), Purdue (31-6), Michigan State (32-3), Penn State (37-3) and Wisconsin (33-6). In addition, Minnesota also garnered wins over North Dakota State, Boise State, Indiana and Illinois. They even beat Iowa twice, a feat which a few years ago would be unheard of. The lone blem-ish on the team's record was a 25-12 loss to Oklahoma State in an early-season home dual meet which had several of the Gophers' top stars out of the lineup. The Maroon and Gold rebounded to win 14-straight dual meets to end the regular season though, including a 20-12 revenge victory over those same Oklahoma State Cowboys in the title meet of the National Duals.

All season long different members of the squad stepped up big-time as the team persevered through some tough times. When Owen Elzen went down with a knee injury, true freshman Eli Ross came in and got it done. When Elzen returned, torn ACL and all, he sucked it up and posted a 30-3 overall record, and captured third place at both the Big Tens and NCAAs. It was leadership by example and a real team effort.

Minnesota then dominated the conference's dual meet title with an amazing 8-0 campaign in Big Ten competitions. Then, at the Big Ten Championships, sophomore Jared Lawrence (149 lbs.) and redshirt freshman Garrett Lowney (Hwt.) won individual titles to lead Minnesota to a 24-point team victory over both Illinois and Iowa. With all 10 wrestlers placing in the top seven at the conference tourney, Minnesota amazingly advanced its entire lineup to the national tournament in Iowa City.

There, the Gophers wrestled as a team and got the job done. In fact, not one Gopher grappler became a finalist — marking the first time in the 71-year history of the national tournament that the winning team won the team title without one. The U of M got a full-team effort to garner an NCAA-record 10 All-Americans and 138.5 points to capture the school's first ever wrestling crown. (Iowa finished second in the team race with 125.5 points, followed by Oklahoma State with 115.5 points, Oklahoma with 93.5 points and Illinois with 89.0 points.) With the team title, the Gophers unseated the six-time defending champs from Iowa, as well as the perennial national powers from Oklahoma State. Amazingly, it was the University of Minnesota's first NCAA title in any sport since 1979, when Herbie Brooks' Gopher Hockey team went all the way.

It was regarded by many as one of the greatest team efforts in college wrestling history as the team clinched the title in the wrestle-

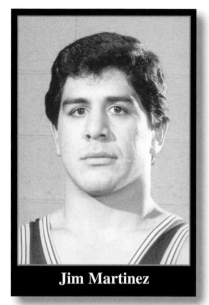
Jim Martinez

Larry Zilverberg

Dan Zilverberg

backs, without a single individual finalist. When Garrett Lowney won his third-place match to ice the trophy the Gopher faithful erupted in celebration.

"To win this way was the best way that we could have won," said Coach Robinson. "To have 10 All-Americans and nobody in the finals, and to do it in Carver-Hawkeye Arena, it's a special thing."

All 10 Gopher finished in the top eight, earning All-American status. Three finished in third place (Leroy Vega, Owen Elzen, Garrett Lowney), three in fourth (Luke Becker, Brad Pike, Jacob Volkmann), one in fifth (Damion Hahn), one in sixth (Jared Lawrence) and two in eighth (Brett Lawrence, Chad Erikson).

With the big win the boys in Maroon and Gold signified the proverbial "passing of the torch" from the Hawkeyes to the Gophers. How sweet it was.

"I had written down three goals for the 2001 season," said Robinson of that dream season. "The first was to beat Iowa, in Iowa City, one of the toughest venues to compete at in the entire sports world. I mean Iowa had multiple national championships over the years and was like 136-5 or something ridiculous in duals at Carver Hawkeye Arena. So, our chances to win were very remote. But, we went down there and somehow pulled it off. It was amazing. The second was to have 10 All-Americans and the third was to win the Big 10 as well as the national championship. Those were our team goals and I knew that they were going to be tough. I knew we couldn't win with individuals but I knew that collectively, as a team, we could do it. That became our rallying cry for the year and really drove us that season. I remember too that we also spent a ton of time training for the third day of the national tournament, which was notoriously the toughest day. It is the day when guys are just beat up and tired and want to go home. For many, their dreams have been broken and they know they don't have a chance to be an individual champion."

"Then, amazingly, it all came down to that third day. We had six guys in the semifinals that night and incredibly, they all got beat. To top it all off, Garrett Lowney, our heavyweight who was a bronze medallist in the Olympics, wound up losing a coin flip in overtime and lost the match. So, we had no finalists. But we went back and regrouped and came out that third day determined. We had a lot of leadership on that squad with guys like Hartung, Kraft, Eggum and Morgan, and we knew we still had a chance. We calculated the points and figured it out. We were still in it and we knew that this was going to be our day. This is what we had trained for and we were going to do it. I can still remember going to weigh-in with Hartung out in the van with the radio blared to the tune of 'Who Let the Dogs Out?' and that was just a great memory of how that day started. It went back and forth that day and it came down to the finals when Owen Elzen, Damion Hahn and Garrett Lowney all pinned their guys within like three minutes of each other to seal it. When it was over it took us a while to realize what had happened. We won, and it was an amazing experience to see it all come together like that."

GOPHER ALL-AMERICANS

2004
1st - Damion Hahn, 197
4th - Jacob Volkmann, 165
4th - Cole Konrad, Hwt

2003
8th - Bobbe Lowe, 125
2nd - Ryan Lewis, 133
2nd - Jared Lawrence, 149
4th - Luke Becker, 157
3rd - Jacob Volkmann, 165
1st - Damion Hahn, 197

2002
1st - Luke Becker, 157
4th - Owen Elzen, 197
7th - Chad Erikson, 141
2nd - Ryan Lewis, 133
5th - Garrett Lowney, Hwt
5th - Damion Hahn, 197
1st - Jared Lawrence, 149

2001
3rd - Owen Elzen, 197
4th - Luke Becker, 157
4th - Brad Pike, 165
4th - Jacob Volkmann, 174
8th - Chad Erikson, 141
5th - Damion Hahn, 197
3rd - Garrett Lowney, Hwt
8th - Brett Lawrence, 133
6th - Jared Lawrence, 149
3rd - Leroy Vega, 125

2000
6th - Luke Becker, 157
7th - Brad Pike, 165
6th - Jared Lawrence, 149
5th - Leroy Vega, 125
1st - Brock Lesnar, Hwt
3rd – Brandon Eggum, 184

1999
5th - Chad Kraft, 157
7th - Troy Marr, 149
5th - Leroy Vega, 125
2nd - Brock Lesnar, Hwt
7th – Troy Marr, 149
2nd – Brandon Eggum, 177
1st - Tim Hartung, 197
5th - Chad Kraft, 157

1998
2nd - Chad Kraft, 150
4th - Jason Davids, 142

7th - Brandon Paulson, 118
5th - Brandon Eggum, 177
1st – Tim Hartung, 190
3rd – Shelton Benjamin, Hwt

1997
3rd - Jason Davids, 142
3rd - Chad Kraft, 150
8th – Pat Connors, 126
3rd – Tim Hartung, 190
5th – Shelton Benjamin, Hwt

1996
5th - Jason Davids, 142
5th - Chad Kraft, 150
6th - Billy Pierce, Hwt

1995
4th – Brett Colombini, 177
6th - Billy Pierce, Hwt
6th – Tim Harris, 126

1994
3rd - Brad Gibson, 177
6th – Brett Colombini, 167

1993
5th - Billy Pierce, Hwt
8th – Tim Harris, 134
6th - Brad Gibson, 177
3rd – Willie Short, 150

1992
7th – Mike Marzetta, 158

1991
1st - Marty Morgan, 177
7th – Dave Zuniga, 134

1990
2nd - Marty Morgan, 177
2nd - Dave Zuniga, 134

1989
3rd - Chris Short, 190
6th - Marty Morgan, 167
8th - Gordy Morgan, 158
3rd – Dave Dean, 177

1988
7th - Rod Sande, 167
2nd - Keith Nix, 118

1987
2nd - Dave Dean, 177

1986
3rd Ed Giese, 118

1983
6th - Jim Trudeau, 167

1982
3rd – Jim Martinez, 142

1981
4th - Dalen Wasmund, 134
6th - Gary Lefebvre, 126

1980
5th - Dan Zilverberg, 158

1979
2nd - Dan Zilverberg, 158
3rd - Jim Martinez, 134

1977
1st - Pat Neu, 134
2nd - Mike McArthur, 118
2nd - Evan Johnson, 190

1976
1st - Evan Johnson, 190
3rd - Mike McArthur, 118
6th - Larry Zilverberg, 167

1975
3rd - Larry Zilverberg, 158

1974
2nd - Larry Zilverberg, 158

1972
2nd - John Panning, 177
6th - Jeff Lamphere, 126

1970
4th - James Axtel, 158

1969
4th - Reid Lamphere, 130

1967
2nd - James Anderson, 115

1964
4th – Larry Lloyd, 115

1963
2nd - Lonnie Rubis, 147
4th - Lew Kennedy, 130

1962
4th - Lew Kennedy, 130
4th - James Reifsteck, 157

1960
4th - William Koehen, 167

1959
4th - Charles Coffee, 137
3rd – Bill Wright, 177

1957
3rd - Richard Mueller, 123

1954
2nd - Charles Ofsthun, 115
4th - Edward Anderson, 123

1953
1st - Richard Mueller, 123

1949
1st - Verne Gagne, Hwt
4th - Alan Rice, 128
4th – Garth Lapin, 121

1948
1st - Verne Gagne, 191

1947
3rd - Verne Gagne, Hwt
3rd - Garth Lapin, 121

1941
1st - Leonard Levy, Hwt
4th – Alphonse Janesko

1940
2nd – Dale Hanson, 128

1939
1st – Dale Hanson, 128
3rd – O.W. Culbertson, 136

1938
2nd - Clifton Gustafson, Hwt

1937
1st - John Whitaker, 175
3rd - Clifton Gustafson, Hwt

1936
4th - Caifson Johnson, 158

THE MORGANS

MARTY

The Morgan brothers, John, Marty and Gordy, are among the best ever to hail from the state of Minnesota and have gone on to become icons in Gold Country as well. The brothers grew up amongst 12 siblings in Bloomington and went on to graduate from Bloomington Kennedy High School in 1981, 1985 and 1986, respectively.

John, a 1981 state champion at Bloomington Kennedy, went on to become a four-time All-American at North Dakota State University, serving as a team captain his junior and senior seasons. Internationally, John was a three-time Greco-Roman U.S. National Champion in 1989, 1991 and 1992, and also earned a pair of silvers and a bronze in the World Cup Wrestling Championships from 1988-1990. He even represented the U.S. at the 1988 Summer Olympics, placing 7th in Seoul, and was an alternate on the 1992 U.S. Greco-Roman Olympic team as well.

Gordy was a state champ for the Eagles in 1985, and then went on to wrestle at the University of Minnesota. There, he was a Big Ten Champion in 1989, earning Division I All-American honors that year as well. Gordy was also an outstanding international competitor, emerging as a three-time U.S. Greco-Roman National Champion in 1991, 1993 and 1994. In addition, he earned a silver medal in the World Cup Championships in 1991, and also placed 4th in 1989, 1990 and 1994. From there, Gordy went on to represent Team U.S.A. at the 1996 Olympics in at Atlanta, where he placed 9th in the world.

GORDY

Marty, meanwhile, was also a prep star with the Eagles and began his collegiate career at North Dakota State University, where he won an NCAA Division II national championship as a true freshman. He then transferred to Minnesota and went on to become a three-time NCAA All-American, two-time NCAA finalist and NCAA Division I champion as a senior. In his junior season with the Gophers, Marty pinned 21 opponents to set a school record that still stands today. Then, his 39-0 senior season was capped off with the prestigious Big Ten Medal of Honor, recognizing excellence in both academics and athletics. Marty continued to wrestle after college and won two Greco-Roman national titles and placed twice in both the National Freestyles as well as the National Freestyle Open. He also participated on a pair of World Championship teams and one World Cup team as well. Marty also finished third at the 1992 U.S. Olympic Trials at 198 pounds and captured second at the 1996 Olympic Trials at 180.

From there, Marty went on to become Gopher Coach J Robinson's top assistant and recruiting coordinator, a position he has now held for more than a decade. A big reason as to why the Gophers are so good year in and year out is because of his ability to recruit the top kids from around the nation.

"The biggest thing for me is that I believe in what I sell," said Marty, who was named as the NWCA Assistant Coach of the Year in 1999. "Our team and our coaches are all committed and believe in our program. When recruits come to visit, they see that commitment and that is the easiest sell."

Without question Bloomington's first family of wrestling, the Morgans have certainly made Minnesota proud.

Then, in 2002, his Gophers went 19-0 in duels, won another Big Ten title, and did it again — making it back-to-back National Championships, thus creating a dynasty in the process. This time they did it out at Albany, NY, and it was just as sweet the second time around. Under Robinson's direction that season, juniors Jared Lawrence and Luke Becker became his third and fourth NCAA champions. And, Leroy Vega, Ryan Lewis, Luke Becker, Damion Hahn and Owen Elzen added to Minnesota's strong Big Ten history with individual titles of their own.

"It was a little different to win that second one," said Robinson. "We came in ranked No. 1 and were in the drivers seat, and everyone wanted to knock us off. But we persevered and made it two in a row and that was special in its own way. We proved to everyone that we belong here and it really validated that we were for real. It was also important for us as a team for everyone to know that we weren't just a one-hit wonder. It was a real statement for our program and it felt really good. It was a different kind of satisfaction, but a tremendous satisfaction nevertheless."

Robinson's Gophers came close to making it three in a row in 2003 as well, winning their third Big 10 title, but came up just short to Oklahoma State in the NCAA Finals to finish as national runner's up. Damion Hahn won his first of what would be two straight national championships that season, emerging as one of Gold Countries' all-time fan favorites.

Robinson enters the 2004-05 season with an impressive 268-92-3 overall record, including an awesome 136-22-0 mark over the last seven seasons. He is as close to wrestling royalty as it gets in Minnesota and has single-handedly turned the Gopher Wrestling program into one of the nation's elite. Robinson is a phenomenal motivator, an amazing recruiter and is considered as a true player's coach. One of the most modest people you will ever meet, Robinson attributes much of his success to his coaching staff of Marty Morgan, Mark Schwab and Joe Russell. Most importantly, however, Robinson is a winner and the numbers speak for themselves.

During his tenure at Minnesota, more than three dozen wrestlers have earned more than five dozen All-America honors. In addition, he has also coached seven NCAA individual titleists as well: Marty Morgan (1991), Tim Hartung (1998 & 1999), Brock Lesnar (2000), Luke Becker (2002), Jared Lawrence (2002), and Damion Hahn (2003 & 2004). Robinson has also coached more than two dozen Big Ten Champions and has led his teams to top-six conference finishes in 17 of his 18 seasons, including five straight from 1999-2004.

Additionally, Robinson has coached at the national and international levels as well. In fact, he served as an assistant coach on four consecutive U.S. Olympic squads from 1976 to 1988, and then as the head coach for the U.S. at the 1983 Pan American

TIM HARTUNG

Tim Hartung grew up in Wisconsin and went on to graduate from Durand High School, where he won a state championship in 1994. Hartung, who also starred in football and baseball, then went on to wrestle at the University of Minnesota. There, Hartung emerged as one of the best in the history of the storied Gopher program. Hartung capped off an illustrious career in 1999, winning his second consecutive NCAA title at 197 pounds, finishing 39-0 on the season. The three-time Big Ten champion was named Big Ten Wrestler of the Year in 1999 and also received the prestigious Big Ten Medal of Honor that year as well. Hartung went on to graduate with a degree in kinesiology and later earned a masters degree in sports administration. From there, he spent the next four seasons as an assistant coach with the program, while still continuing to wrestle internationally. In 2004 he served as an alternate on the U.S. Olympic team which competed in Athens. When he returned he accepted the second assistant coaching position with the Iowa wrestling team behind head coach Jim Zalesky. One of the Maroon and Gold's best ever, he will surely be missed. It is just a matter of time, however, before he becomes the head coach of a major program as well.

DAMION HAHN

Damion Hahn grew up in New Jersey and went on to become a three-time state champion at his high school in Lakewood. From there, Hahn came to Gold Country, where he rewrote the record books. Hahn captured his second-straight NCAA Championship at 197 pounds in 2004 and became just the third wrestler in school history to win two national titles. He also became the fourth four-time All-American and fifth three-time Big Ten Champion in school history as well. More importantly, he helped guide Minnesota to back-to-back NCAA Championships and three straight Big Ten Championships along the way. In 2004 the Big Ten Conference named Hahn its Jesse Owens Male Athlete of the Year. He was just the fourth Gopher ever to receive the prestigious award in school history. Hahn graduated in 2004 with a degree in sports administration and plans on attending graduate school at Minnesota to earn a master's degree in kinesiology. He is also training at the school in hopes of making the U.S. team for the 2008 Summer Olympics in China.

BRANDON EGGUM

Brandon Eggum grew up in Sidney, Mont. as a prep sensation. He went on to attend the University of Minnesota and made a lot of history out on the mat along the way. Eggum won a pair of Big Ten titles in 1999 and 2000 Big at 184 pounds and then went on to place third at the 2000 NCAA Championships. The three time All-American finished his career in Gold Country with an impressive 115-23 overall record, including a 61-11 mark in dual meets. Eggum, who ranks ninth in all-time career victories, also received the coveted Big Ten Medal of Honor in 2000 as well. From there, Eggum graduated with a degree in economics and took over as an assistant with the Gopher wrestling staff, serving as the team's strength coordinator.

Jared Lawrence

Shelton Benjamin

William Pierce

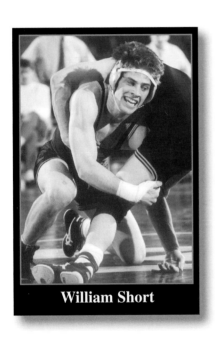

William Short

Leroy Vega

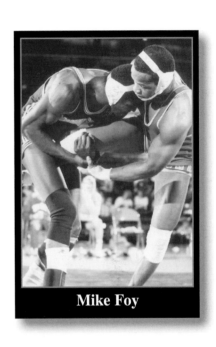

Mike Foy

Brandon Eggum

Brock Lesnar

Brandon Paulson

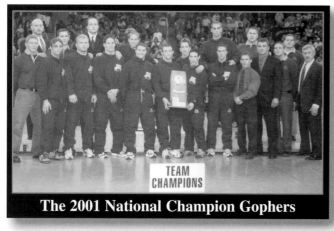

The 2001 National Champion Gophers

Luke Becker

Jacob Volkmann

Chad Kraft

Games. Among his many awards and honors, Robinson was named as the 1998 and 2001 Dan Gable National Coach of the Year, and the 2001 National Wrestling Coaches Association Coach of the Year. Furthermore, the five-time Big Ten Coach of the Year was awarded the 2001 Amateur Wrestling News Man of the Year award for his work and support of wrestling at all levels as well.

A brilliant tactician and teacher, Robinson's teams are consistently nationally ranked because he knows how to recruit and attract the top talent from around the world to his program. Since taking over Minnesota's wrestling program 18 years ago, he has built one of the strongest and most respected programs in the nation and has emerged as one of the elite college coaches in the nation — for any sport.

"One of the nicest things about winning a national title is that you can share your achievements with the entire state," said Robinson. "The feeling of joy of being No. 1 is a great thing and I am just really happy that I was able to bring that to the people. We did it together and it is all of ours to share and that is a great thing. So being a Gopher is a great, great thing for me. I have a lot of pride to be a part of this program and apart of this university. Being a part of building this tradition has just been a wonderful experience. I also want to add, however, that I am just a part of the process. When we won that first national championship we had NCAA champion watches made and we then sent one to everyone who had coached in the program from years past. We all were a part of that

J Robinson

and we wanted to let everyone share in the achievement. A lot of people believed and gave huge parts of themselves to get where we are today. It wasn't just one guy. So, I am just the keeper of the flame for a while until it starts to grow and burn. Then, I will need to pass that torch to the next guys, like Marty Morgan and Mark Schwab, who are ready to make that flame even bigger and brighter. It's a great family and I am honored to be a part of it."

In addition to their two national championships in 2001 and 2002, the Gophers have won the Big Ten team championship nine times, most recently in 2003, their third team title in four years. Minnesota has also notched runner-up finishes in the Big Ten nine times as well. In fact, the team has placed in the top five in the Big Ten in 23 of the last 28 seasons and has also produced 71 individual champs along the way.

The Gopher Wrestling program is among the very elite in the nation, right up there in the same breath as Iowa and Oklahoma State. They have made Minnesota proud with their national success and also with their ability to produce top notch kids who have gone on to make a difference both on and off the mat. That is what it is all about, and that is why they are destined for even more greatness down the road.

GOPHER NCAA CHAMPS

YR	NAME	WT
2004	Damion Hahn	197
2003	Damion Hahn	197
2002	Jared Lawrence	149
2002	Luke Becker	157
2000	Brock Lesnar	Hwt
1999	Tim Hartung	197
1998	Tim Hartung	190
1991	Marty Morgan	177
1977	Pat Neu	134
1976	Evan Johnson	190
1953	Dick Mueller	123
1949	Verne Gagne	Hwt
1948	Verne Gagne	191
1941	Leonard Levy	Hwt
1939	Dale Hanson	128
1937	John Whitaker	175

Minnesota State University, Mankato

When you think of MSU wrestling, one name immediately comes to mind, Rummy Macias. And why not? Rummy single-handedly put the program on the map and turned it into one of the top Division II programs in the country.

Rometo "Rummy" Macias grew up in Davenport, Iowa, and went on to wrestle at the University of Iowa, graduating in 1948. In 1950 Macias came to Minnesota State University, Mankato, where he would inaugurate the school's wrestling program. Macias understood the value of having a solid feeder program, so worked tirelessly to promote the sport on the amateur and prep levels throughout the area. He traveled to area high schools, spoke to school boards and even put on demonstrations to encourage them to add wrestling programs. He, more than anyone else, is the reason that wrestling is to southern Minnesota as hockey is to the north. Seemingly every small town from Worthington to Winona had a program during those days, with plenty of Cinderella stories along the way, including the likes of Caledonia, St. James

Troy Szydel (MSU)

and Blue Earth, which all went on to take home the hardware at the state tournament.

As a result of his hard work, many of his former wrestlers would go on to become high school teachers and wrestling coaches themselves. In fact, arguably no other coach in state history can claim to have produced half as many coaches as he did over the years. Perhaps that, more than anything else, will be his lasting legacy. At MSU, Rummy recruited kids from not only the surrounding areas, but also from his native Iowa, where wrestling was like religion. Because of that, his Mavericks dominated the small college scene for nearly four decades.

Macias simply dominated his competition during his tenure at Mankato and created a dynasty in the process. From 1950-88, he would guide his Mavs to a total of seven NCAA College Division Championships, 12 Division II Collegiate Championships, two NCAA Division I Collegiate Championships, and two NAIA Collegiate Championships. In addition, Macias would lead his Mavs to three national titles (NAIA championships in 1958 and 1959 and a NCAA College Division title in 1965), eight Northern Intercollegiate Conference championships, and one North Central Conference title.

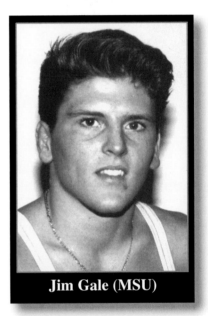
Jim Gale (MSU)

During the team's back-to-back title run in 1958 and 1959, the Mavs boasted no less than six NCAA D-II National Champs, including: Roy Minter, Jack Anderson, Jack Thamert, Dick Kubes, Maynard Nelson and Lowell Glynn. In addition, Macias had 93 of his wrestlers attain all-America status; 19 were national individual champions; 62 captured NIC individual championships and 12 won NCC individual titles.

When his tenure in Mankato finally came to an end, Macias had garnered an impressive 317-219-11 (.590) career

Tony Kenning (MSU)

MINNESOTA STATE UNIVERSITY, MANKATO: RECORD BOOK

MSU National Championship Teams
1958 - NAIA Division I
1959 - NAIA Division I
1965 - NCAA College Division

All-Time Records

Quickest Fall:	4 Seconds, Brad Henry, 1994
Consecutive Wins:	34, Gary Franke, 1970-71
Dual Victories:	24, Ross Johnson, 1997
Career Victories:	126, Jack Eustice, 1973-77
Career Falls:	84, Matt Petsinger, 1997-01
Most Falls (Season)	26, Matt Petsinger, 2000-01
Most Season Points:	124, Troy Szydel, 1997-98
Career Points:	272, Jack Eustice, 1974-77

National Champions

Roy Minter	1958
Jack Anderson	1958
Jack Thamert	1958
Dick Kubes	1958
Maynard Nelson	1959
Lowell Glynn	1959
Howard Gangstead	1964, 1965
Bob Soulek	1966, 1967
Bob Wendel	1967
Larry Amundson	1968
Ken Stockdale	1971
Gary Christianson	1975
Jack Eustice	1976
Brent Hagen	1977
Scott Madigan	1979
Craig Jordan	1980
Jim Gale	1993
Justin Smith	1994
Tony Kenning	1995, 1996
Troy Szydel	1998
Matt Petsinger	2001

RUMMY MACIAS

Rometo "Rummy" Macias grew up in Davenport, Iowa, and went on to wrestle at the University of Iowa, graduating in 1948. In 1950 Macias came to Minnesota State University, Mankato, where he would inaugurate the school's wrestling program. Nearly four decades later, Macias would leave MSU as a wrestling coaching legend. Macias simply dominated the wrestling competition in Minnesota during his tenure at Mankato and created a dynasty in the process. From 1950-88 Macias would lead MSU to three national titles (NAIA championships in 1958 and 1959 and a NCAA College Division title in 1965), eight Northern Intercollegiate Conference championships, and one North Central Conference title. In addition, Macias had 93 of his wrestlers attain all-America status; 19 were national individual champions; 62 captured NIC individual championships and 12 won NCC individual titles.

Macias also served two stints as MSU's golf coach, winning four NCC team titles and one NIC title along the way. In addition, Macias served as an assistant coach with the MSU football program as well. Among his many coaching honors and accolades, Macias has been inducted into seven Halls of Fame: MSU, NCC, NIC, NAIA, Amateur Wrestling, Minnesota Wrestling Coaches, Iowa Wrestling and the NCAA Division II Wrestling Association. Furthermore, he won several conference and national coach of the year awards, as well as an NCC Golf Coach of the Year too. He was even honored by the National Wrestling Hall of Fame in Stillwater, Okla., with a Lifetime Service Award in recognition of his dedication to the development of leadership and citizenship in young people through the sport of wrestling.

Upon retiring from coaching at Mankato in 1988, Macias moved to Florida, where he lives in Singer Island with his wife, Ruth. There, in addition to teaching golf at a local country club, Macias also serves as the wrestling coach at nearby Cardinal Newman High School. Now in his '80s, Rummy is still going strong. He even runs a wrestling camp down there every year as well, with plenty of his old protégés from back home coming down to help out. That's Rummy, always giving back, and always helping kids. Synonymous with the sport of wrestling in Minnesota, Rummy Macias is without question a true grappling legend.

LOOKING BACK WHAT ARE YOU MOST PROUD OF IN YOUR CAREER? "That I came to Mankato State with a lot of happiness and determination and I left happy. I was able to carry on a good camaraderie with all my colleagues, faculty and co-workers, and can honestly say that I never had one enemy or a person that I held a grudge against."

HOW WOULD YOU DESCRIBE YOUR COACHING STYLE? "I taught from a scientific standpoint and really emphasized mechanics, physics and leverage. Really, athletics are nothing more than angles, inertia, momentum and inert gravity. So, I think you have to understand the mechanical nuances of a human being and then teach from there. There is no forceful motion involved, it's all scientific. The ones that coach the forceful way are short-lived. That was my feeling."

HOW DID YOU MOTIVATE YOUR WRESTLERS? "It was just a do or die type of attitude that I had. I set the examples myself and was very strict on the way I coached. I always felt that if you could succeed in wrestling then you could succeed in everyday life, and that has been proven hundreds of times by individuals who I have coached. In other words, we showed them how to live, how to be dedicated and we taught by example for them to become better citizens. As a result, they learned self esteem, confidence, character and really everything an individual needs to know to be successful in everyday life. That was my philosophy."

WHAT WAS THE KEY TO RECRUITING? "You had to show your recruits that you could compete against the best. For me though, I had the jump on everybody. You see, I was just in the right place at the right time in being one of the early settlers of wrestling in the state. Coming up from Iowa I was able to stimulate the individuals in Southern Minnesota and get them excited about wrestling. Before long that area became a hotbed for wrestling talent and we tapped into that from the beginning. We got our program up and running and without scholarships we were still able to compete against the best. We just got them to believe and were able to convince them that they could do anything. Before long, all of our kids were out recruiting and telling other kids about our program. I promised them good competition and success after graduation. I was able to land a lot of big recruits that way and we had a very successful program for a number of years as a result."

HOW DID YOU BUILD TEAM UNITY & CHEMISTRY? "Wrestling is probably the number one sport for camaraderie. Oftentimes, after an individual wrestles, win or lose, the two wrestlers become friends. That is unique in sports. Wrestling is different because you are out there all alone and there is nobody to help you. We stuck together as a team though and really supported one another. Sure, we did things off the mat together too, and that all goes into building chemistry. But mostly, it comes from the kids themselves, that is the key — to get good kids who like each other and enjoy competing as a team together."

WHAT MOTIVATED YOU? "As a youngster I had goals in life and I was determined to reach the top by hard work. So, when I achieved a lot of that success as a young man at Iowa, I was able to carry a lot of that over into my coaching. I have always worked hard and have been motivated by success. I am also motivated by seeing my kids do well both on and off the mat."

WHAT ADVICE WOULD YOU HAVE FOR YOUNG COACHES STARTING OUT TODAY? "Honesty, integrity, hard work and leading by example to show your kids what it takes to become a champion. I also think it comes down to personality. Today you have to be a people person, a promoter and a salesman in order to be successful. You also have to be a good listener too. And try not to use the word 'I' so much, use 'we' instead."

record. He would retire as the patriarch of one of college wrestling's premier institutions and as a true legend of the sport.

In 1989 the torch was passed to Gary Rushing, who would guide the Mavs to a modest 40-43-4 (.460) record from 1988-93. Rushing would eventually step down to assume a full-time instructor position with the University. As a result, Jim Makovsky, who had spent the last four seasons as the head coach of Valley City State University, was brought in and he has been going strong ever since.

Now entering his 11th season at the helm of the Minnesota State wrestling program, Makovsky has posted a solid record of 117-50-2 with the Mavs. Coach Makovsky has tutored seven national champions in his career along with 37 All-Americans including, two-time heavyweight national champion Tony Kenning, three-time All-American and national champ Troy Szydel, and most recently, four-time All-American and national champion Matt Petsinger, now an assistant coach with the team. Makovsky has led his squad to the NCAA Division II Collegiate Championships on four occasions as well, from 1994-96 and again in 1998.

One of the highlights of the program's history came in 2000, when the Rummy Macias Wrestling Complex was christened within the Taylor Center — providing the school's legion of loyal fans a posh new setting to root on their Mavs. Another exciting thing happened to the program in 2004 when it was announced that the NCAA Division II Wrestling Championships, would be held at MSU that year. It would be the third time that the school has hosted the event, with the other two coming in 1966 and 1968.

In 2003 the Mavs finished with a dual record of 8-4, took home fifth-place in the NCC and a 15th place finish at the NCAA Division II tournament. With yet another solid recruiting class, the squad is poised for even more success in the rugged North Central Conference, widely recognized as the toughest conference in the nation. Rummy's legacy lives on under Coach Makovsky, as he continues to make the city of Mankato very proud indeed.

Gary Rushing

Matt Petsinger

Jason Rhoten

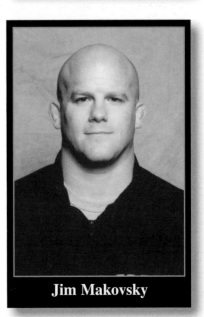
Jim Makovsky

MINNESOTA STATE UNIVERSITY, MANKATO ALL-AMERICANS

Four-Time All-Americans
Roy Minter	'56, '57, '58, '58
Al Blanshan	'58, '59, '59, '69
Jack Eustice	'74, '75, '76, '77
Jim Gale	'91, '92, '93, '94
Matt Petsinger	'98, '99, '00, '01

Three-Time All-Americans
Jack Anderson	'57, '58, '58
Jack Thamert	'58, '59, '59
Howard Gangstead	'64, '64, '65
Bob Wendel	'65, '66, '67
Larry Amundson	'66, '68, '68
Larry Goodnature	'73, '74, '76
Kurt Kuehl	'74, '75, '76
Scott Madigan	'78, '79, '80
Troy Szydel	'97, '98, '99

Two-Time All-Americans
Maunuel Macias	'52, '53
Al DeLeon	'61, '62
Ken Droegmueller	'63, '64
Mike McNamara	'64, '65
Bob Soulek	'66, '67
Al Ogdie	'66, '67
Brian Hage	'70, '71
Mike Medchill	'71, '72
Dennis Piero	'71, '72
Brad Thompson	'73, '74
Gary Christianson	'74, '75
Joel Thoreson	'91, '94
Gregg Nelson	'93, '94
Justin Smith	'94, '95
Tony Kenning	'95, '96
Ross Johnson	'96, '97
Shawn Ange	'98, '99
Ryan Rettke	'99, '00
Matt Gadient	'00, '01
Lester Berrios	'01 '02
Tony Fratzke	'02 '03

One-Time All-Americans
Ken Pridhoda ('51)
Don Dravis ('58)

John Kelly ('58)
Jerry Sharp ('58)
Dick Kubes ('58)
Clyde Lundholm ('58)
Maynard Nelson ('59)
Lowell Glynn ('59)
Jerry Slattery ('59)
Dave Frame ('59)
Bill Lewis ('59)
Dick Zeyen ('63)
Al Russ ('64)
Mike Pierro ('65)
John Alexis ('65)
Gary Storm ('65
Doug Eberling ('65)
Jim Riesselman ('66)
Jim Soulek ('67)
Tom Sowles ('67)
Mike Howe ('67)
Scott Evans ('68)
Don Ryland ('68)
Dale Richter ('70)
Steve Johnson ('71)
Ken Stockdale ('71)
Rick Brua ('73)
Dave Cummings ('73)
Dave Keller ('75)
Brent Hagen ('77)
Joe Johnson ('78)
Craig Jordan ('80)
Joel Loose ('81)
Joe Juliar ('87)
Jason Math ('89)
Jerold Stauffacher ('94)
Paul Pagel ('94)
Brad Henry ('94)
Justin Kipp ('96)
Marc Schulze ('96)
Travis Shives ('99)
Hannon Hisek ('01)
Cory Beckman ('02)
Jake Emerick ('03)
Jason Rhoten ('04)

The Taylor Center

NCAA 2004 DIVISION II WRESTLING CHAMPIONSHIPS MANKATO, MINNESOTA

St. Cloud State University

Jack Gause is credited with starting the sport at St. Cloud State in 1949. He, along with Jim Kiffmeyer and Gordie Weihrauch, all served as student coaches that inaugural season, with Jim and Gordie taking over for the next couple of years after that. Gause, of course, would go on to become a Hall of Fame official, refereeing at several Olympic Games in the future. From there, SCSU chugged along, finishing no higher than third from 1955-63, under the tutelage of coaches Glen Gerdes, Kirk Kirchner, Joel Mastropaolo and Willis Woods. Woods would go on to coach the Huskies into the early 60s, never finishing lower than third as well. Ken Cox took over in 1963, garnering the school's first NIC title in 1963. The school also finished third at the national championships that year as well. Cox, of course, would be blessed in having the Hazewinkel twins on his roster during that time as well, arguably the school's best ever. Cox would then hand the ball over to John Oxton, who would become SCSU's first long tenured coach. Oxton's tenure would begin in 1967 and go for the next 20 years, seeing plenty of success along the way. Oxton, whose teams won NIC titles in 1974, 1975, 1977 and 1978, would step down in 1987 with a very solid 167-120-9 career record. Bob Boeck and Rick Goeb would handle the coaching duties for the next five seasons until giving way to Steve Grimit, who was given the job in 1993.

Now entering his 11th season with the Huskies, Grimit, who had previously served as the head wrestling coach at Valparaiso University in Indiana, has posted a modest 62-73 record over the past decade. Grimit, who was a NCAA Division I national qualifier at Illinois State University, has coached one NCAA champion (Gene Hanemann in 1995 at 158 lbs.), several NCC champs and nearly a dozen All-America wrestlers during his tenure in St. Cloud. One of his brightest stars is Jon Duncombe, who won a pair of state titles at St. Michael Albertville High School. At SCSU, Duncombe has emerged as a two-time Division II All-American, a conference champion, and even placed second as a 174-pounder at the 2003 Division II National Championships for the Huskies. Grimit guided his Huskies to a ninth place finish at the NCAA Division II championships that year, and is poised to continue leading SCSU to bigger and better things down the road.

Gene Hanneman

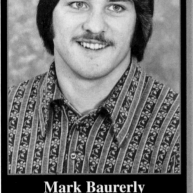
Mark Baurerly

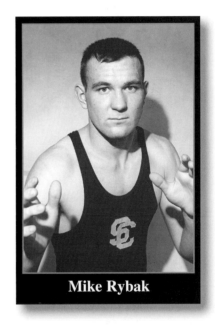
Mike Rybak

THE HAZEWINKELS

Jim and Dave Hazewinkel grew up in Anoka and went to graduate from Anoka High School, where they learned the tricks of the trade from legendary coach Ron Malcolm. Both went on to attend St. Cloud State University, where they literally rewrote the record books. Even though they were identical twins, Dave carried slightly less bulk and could wrestle at 115 pounds, while Jim mostly wrestled at 123 pounds. Jim went on to win four NAIA national titles from 1963-67 and finished as a two-time All-American in both 1965 and 1967. Dave, meanwhile, was a two-time NAIA national runner-up in 1965 and 1966 and finished as a two-time All-American in those same years as well. Jim was also an NIC conference champ in 1965 and 1967, while Dave claimed a trio of crowns in 1964-66.

From there, both brothers went on to compete in the 1968 and 1972 Olympics in Mexico City and Munich, respectively. The only time the two were ever matched against each other in competition came at the 1964 U.S. Greco-Roman Olympic trials, where it ended in a draw. Apparently, the crowd was so impressed that the two were given a five minute standing ovation. The two would go on to give back to the sport in the ensuing years as well. In fact, Dave's son Sam, a three-time Florida state champion and two-time junior national champion, currently wrestles at the University of Oklahoma.

ST. CLOUD STATE RECORD BOOK

Most Team Points in One Dual Meet Season
Jim Hazewinkel (111)   1966-67

Best Dual-Meet Season Record
John Barrett (17-0)   1982-83

Most Takedowns in One Season
Gene Hanemann (110)   1994-95

Most Pins in One Dual-Meet Season
Jim Hazewinkel (14)   1966-67

Longest Winning Streak in One Season.
Bruce Thompson (30)   1972-73

Most Dual-Meet Wins in One Season
Bruce Thompson (18)   1972-73

Longest Dual-Meet Winning Streak
Jim Hazewinkel (56)   1964-65

Most Wins in One Season
Gene Hanneman, Andy Reigstad & Dustin Darveaux
                        1994-95, 1993-94, 2001-02

Most Career Wins
Andy Reigstad (126)   1993-97

Most Tournament Championships
Dave & Jim Hazewinkel (5)   1963-64/1963-64,1966-67

Most Career Conference Championships
Mike Ryback (4-NIC)   1965-68

Most Career NCC Championships
John Barrett (3)   1983, 1984, 1986

Most Career National Championships
Jim Hazewinkel (4-NAIA)   1963-64-65-67

SCSU Olympians
1968   Dave Hazewinkel, 125.5 lbs., Jim Hazewinkel, 136.5 lbs.
1972   Dave Hazewinkel, 125.5 lbs., Jim Hazewinkel, 136.5 lbs.
1976   Bruce Thompson, 114.5 lbs.
1980   Bruce Thompson, 114.5 lbs.

NAIA National Champions
1958   Dick Anderson
1961   Monte Simner
1963   Jim Hazewinkel, Grant Nelson, Gary Smith
1964   Jim Hazewinkel, Gary Smith
1965   Dave Hazewinkel (runner-up), Jim Hazewinkel
1966   Dave Hazewinkel (runner-up)
1967   Jim Hazewinkel, Mike Rybak
1968   Mike Rybak (runner-up)

NCAA Division II Champions
1995   Gene Hanemann (158 lbs.)

NCC All-Time Wrestling Team
John Barrett, 158 lbs. (as elected in 1997)

NCC Stan Marshall Award Winner
1999   Ryan Marx

ALL-AMERICANS
1958	Dick Anderson (NAIA)
1961	Monte Simner (NAIA Champion)
1963	Jim Hazewinkel (NAIA)
1963	Grant Nelson (NAIA)
1963	Gary Smith (NAIA)
1964	Jim Hazewinkel (NAIA)
1964	Gary Smith (NAIA)
1965	Dave Hazewinkel (NAIA)
1965	Jim Hazewinkel (NAIA)
1966	Dave Hazewinkel (NAIA)
1967	Jim Hazewinkel (NAIA)
1967	Mike Rybak (NAIA)
1968	Mike Rybak (NAIA)
1972	Bruce Thompson (NCAA II)
1973	Bruce Thompson (NCAA II)
1973	Mark Bauerly (NCAA II)
1974	Mike Dahlheimer (NCAA II)
1975	Mike Dahlheimer (NCAA II)
1975	Doug Gruber (NCAA II)
1975	Jerry Schmitz (NCAA II)
1975	Steve Wenker (NCAA II)
1976	Jerry Schmitz (NCAA II)
1976	Chuck Siefert (NCAA II)
1976	Rick Clark (NCAA II)
1977	Rick Clark (NCAA II)
1977	Ron Weller (NCAA II)
1978	Jim Harstad (NCAA II)
1978	Jerry Huls (NCAA II)
1979	Andy Jirik (NAIA)
1979	Phil Herbold (NCAA II)
1979	Rolf Turner (NCAA II)
1981	Phil Herbold (NCAA II)
1981	Dave Bonk (NCAA II)
1982	Phil Herbold (NCAA II)
1983	Phil Herbold (NCAA II/4th @ 177 lbs.)
1983	John Barrett (NCAA II/2nd @ 158 lbs.)
1983	Gary Rucinski (NCAA II/5th @ 142 lbs.)
1983	Mike McGrath (NCAA II/8th @ 150 lbs.)
1984	John Barrett (NCAA II/2nd @ 158 lbs.)
1984	Noel Nemitz (NCAA II/4th at 190 lbs.)
1986	Ed Christensen (NCAA II)
1986	John Barrett (NCAA II)
1986	Paul Anderson (NCAA II)
1987	Paul Anderson (NCAA II/7th @ 126 lbs.)
1987	Ed Christensen (NCAA II/6th @ HWT)
1987	Nate Toedter (NCAA II/7th @ 190 lbs.)
1988	Nate Toedter (NCAA II)
1989	Nate Toedter (NCAA II)
1989	Rich Douglas (NCAA II)
1990	Rich Douglas (NCAA II)
1991	Rich Douglas (NCAA II)
1992	Rob Rychner (NCAA II)
1995	Gene Hanemann (NCAA II/1st @ 158 lbs.)
1996	Andy Reigstad (NCAA II/2nd @ 150 lbs.)
1997	Andy Reigstad (NCAA II/2nd @ 150 lbs.)
1999	Klaus Alberts (NCAA II/3rd @ 165 lbs.)
1999	Ryan Marx (NCAA II/5th @ 197 lbs.)
2000	Aaron Sanders (NCAA II/7th @ 133 lbs.)
2001	Dustin Darveaux (NCAA II/7th @ HWT)
2001	Luke Wren (NCAA II/5th @ 197 lbs.)
2001	Paul Arens (NCAA II/5th @ 165 lbs.)
2002	Dustin Darveaux (NCAA II/4th @ HWT)
2002	Jon Duncombe (NCAA II/4th @ 174 lbs.)
2003	Jon Duncombe (NCAA II/2nd @ 174 lbs.)
2003	Dustin Darveaux (NCAA II/2nd @ HWT)
2003	Matt Neumueller (NCAA II/3rd @ 165)

MIAC RECORD BOOK

Source: Concordia College Cobber Web-Site

MIAC Titles Won (1947-2003)

	No.	Last Title
Augsburg	31	2002-03
St. John's	14	1973-74
Macalester	5	1959-60
Gustavus	3	1966-67
St. Thomas	2	1985-86
Concordia	1	1963-64
St. Olaf	1	1950-51

All-Time MIAC Team Champions

Year	Champion
1947-48	Macalester
1948-49	Macalester
1949-50	Macalester
1950-51	St. Olaf
1951-52	St. John's
1952-53	St. John's
1953-54	St. John's
1954-55	St. John's
1955-56	St. John's
1956-57	St. John's
1957-58	St. John's
1958-59	Macalester & St. John's
1959-60	Macalester
1960-61	Augsburg
1961-62	St. John's
1962-63	St. John's
1963-64	Concordia
1964-65	Gustavus
1965-66	Gustavus
1966-67	Gustavus
1967-68	Augsburg
1968-69	Augsburg
1969-70	Augsburg
1970-71	St. John's
1971-72	St. John's
1972-73	St. John's
1973-74	St. John's
1974-75	Augsburg
1975-76	Augsburg
1976-77	Augsburg
1977-78	Augsburg
1978-79	Augsburg
1979-80	Augsburg
1980-81	St. Thomas
1981-82	Augsburg
1982-83	Augsburg
1983-84	Augsburg
1984-85	Augsburg
1985-86	St. Thomas
1986-87	Augsburg
1987-88	Augsburg
1988-89	Augsburg
1989-90	Augsburg
1990-91	Augsburg
1991-92	Augsburg
1992-93	Augsburg
1993-94	Augsburg
1994-95	Augsburg
1995-96	Augsburg
1996-97	Augsburg
1997-98	Augsburg
1998-99	Augsburg
1999-00	Augsburg
2000-01	Augsburg
2001-02	Augsburg
2002-03	Augsburg

Four-time Individual Champs

John Beatty, Augsburg, 126-142, 1987-90
Darin Bertram, Augsburg, 125, 1999-2002
Curt Burckhardt, Macalester, 191-Hwt, 1959-62
Doug Dufty, Concordia, 130-137, 1964-67
Chester Grauberger, Augsburg, Hwt., 1988-91
Nick Lewandowski, Augsburg, 177-184, 1998-2001
Mollie McLeod, Concordia, Hwt, 1980-83
Kevin Schiltz, Augsburg, 190-Hwt, 1989-93
Nick Slack, Augsburg, 165-174, 1999-2002
Ade Sponberg, Gustavus, 177-Hwt, 1955-58

All-Time Individual Champions

125 Pounds
1999	Darin Bertram, AUG
2000	Darin Bertram, AUG
2001	Darin Bertram, AUG
2002	Darin Bertram, AUG

133 Pounds
1999	John Marchette, AUG
2000	John Marchette, AUG
2001	Bryan Miller, AUG
2002	John Marchette, AUG

141 Pounds
1999	Brad Fisher, AUG
2000	Brian Jones, AUG
2001	Brad Fisher, AUG
2002	Brad Fisher, AUG

149 Pounds
1999	Josh Cagle, AUG
2000	Josh Cagle, AUG
2001	Tony Quance, AUG
2002	Jamel Tidwell, AUG

157 Pounds
1999	Justin Baker, AUG
2000	Justin Baker, AUG
2001	Jeremy Jirele, AUG
2002	Jeremy Jirele, AUG

165 Pounds
1999	Nick Slack, AUG
2000	Jeremy Abfalter, SJU
2001	Tony Abbot, AUG
2002	Tony Abbott, AUG

174 Pounds
1999	Jim Peterson, AUG
2000	Nick Slack, AUG
2001	Nick Slack, AUG
2002	Nick Slack, AUG

184 Pounds
1999	Nick Lewandowski, AUG
2000	Nick Lewandowski, AUG
2001	Nick Lewandowski, AUG
2002	Ricky Crone, AUG

197 Pounds
1999	Josh Clausen, AUG
2000	Josh Clausen, AUG
2001	Brandon Novak, SJU
2002	Kevin Rasmussen, AUG

Heavyweight
1999	Ben Bauer, AUG
2000	Ben Bauer, AUG
2001	Ben Bauer, AUG
2002	Mike Flanagan, AUG

PAST MIAC CHAMPIONS
Minnesota Intercollegiate Athletic Conference Records
Source: Concordia College Cobber Web-Site

Past Weight Classes (1949-1998)

115 Pounds
1969   Gary Svendson (SJU)

118 Pounds
1970   Gary Svendson (SJU)
1971   Terry Elfering (SJU)
1972   Terry Elfering (SJU)
1973   Terry Elfering (SJU)
1974   Jay Huffman (SJU)
1975   Murray Herstein (AUG)
1976   Murray Herstein (AUG)
1977   Gerlach (UST)
1978   Murray Herstein (AUG)
1979   Mooney (UST)
1980   Mooney (UST)
1981   Rich Barron (AUG)
1982   Steve Gliva (AUG)
1983   Delozier (UST)
1984   Rotzein (UST)
1985   Steve Gliva (AUG)
1986   Dave Barthel (SJU)
1987   Dave Barthel (SJU)
1988   Jason O'Brien (UST)
1989   Jason O'Brien (UST)
1990   Mitch Hegland (AUG)
1991   Jason O'Brien (UST)
1992   Nick Fornica (AUG)
1993   Nick Fornica (AUG)
1995   Jim Hoard (AUG)
1996   Henry Gerten (AUG)
1997   Henry Gerten (AUG)
1998   Henry Gerten (AUG)

126 Pounds
1970   Bishop (CON)
1971   Tom Svendson (SJU)
1972   Bishop (CON)
1973   Bishop (CON)
1974   Lamphere (UMD)
1975   Lamphere (UMD)
1976   Solerud (UMD)
1977   Christen (UST)
1978   Scott Whirley (AUG)
1979   Gerlach (UST)
1980   James (GAC)
1981   Anderberg (GAC)
1982   Stan D'Andrea (AUG)
1983   Stan D'Andrea (AUG)
1984   Steve Gliva (AUG)
1985   Zink (UST)
1986   Keith Gliva (AUG)
1987   John Beatty (AUG)
1988   Goebel (GAC)
1989   Menne (UST)
1990   Joe Hoialmen (AUG)
1991   Jeff Board (AUG)
1992   Mike Pfeffer (AUG)
1993   Jeff Board (AUG)
1994   Jesse Armbruster (AUG)
1995   Jesse Armbruster (AUG)
1996   Joel O'Brien (UST)
1997   Joel O'Brien (UST)
1998   Brian Jones (AUG)

130 Pounds
1949   Takkinen (MAC)
1951   Nelson (GAC)
1952   Fred Grant (SJU)
1953   Fred Grant (SJU)
1954   Louis Adderly (SJU)
1955   Kerr (UST)
1956   Kerr (UST)
1957   Kerr (UST)
1958   Kuass (GAC)
1959   Tom Brudos (SJU)
1960   NA
1961   Don Miller (AUG)
1962   Don Miller (AUG)
1963   Don Miller (AUG)
1964   Doug Dufty (CON)
1965   Doug Dufty (CON)
1966   Budd (CON)

1967   Doug Dufty (CON)
1968   Mike Good (AUG)
1969   Mike Good (AUG)

134 Pounds
1970   Mike Good (AUG)
1971   Gary Svendson (SJU)
1972   Ron Johnson (AUG)
1973   Tom Svendson (SJU)
1974   Tom Svendson (SJU)
1975   Charlie Blixt (AUG)
1976   Campbell (UMD)
1977   Sauter (SOC)
1978   Sauter (SOC)
1979   Skahan (UST)
1980   Stephenson (SMC)
1981   Scott Whirley (AUG)
1982   Scott Whirley (AUG)
1983   Bob Adams (AUG)
1984   Roehrick (SOC)
1985   Corbett (UST)
1986   Roehrick (SOC)
1987   Roehrick (SOC)
1988   John Beatty (AUG)
1989   John Beatty (AUG)
1990   Rich Elliot (UST)
1991   Rich Elliot (UST)
1992   Joe Hoialmen (AUG)
1993   Joe Hoialmen (AUG)
1994   Andy O'Brien (UST)
1995   Joel O'Brien (UST)
1996   Jesse Armbruster (AUG)
1997   Jamie Larkin (AUG)
1998   Jamie Larkin (AUG)

137 Pounds
1949   Snyder (MAC)
1951   Jim McKeown (SJU)
1952   Jim McKeown (SJU)
1953   Jim McKeown (SJU)
1954   Nelson (GAC)
1955   Don Flynn (SJU)
1956   Don Flynn (SJU)
1957   Leopold (CON)
1958   Blancher (MAC)
1959   Jerry Dalseth (SJU)
1960   Henrt (UST)
1961   Leopold (CON)
1962   Gilland (MAC)
1963   Leopold (CON)
1964   Johnson (GAC)
1965   Leopold (CON)
1966   Dufty (CON)
1967   Pat Beyer (SJU)
1968   Garrison (UMD)
1969   Colison (MAC)

142 pounds
1970   Ron Johnson (AUG)
1971   Ron Johnson (AUG)
1972   Joe Hayes (SJU)
1973   Joe Hayes (SJU)
1974   Kennedy (AUG)
1975   Kennedy (AUG)
1976   Tom Strohmayer (AUG)
1977   Rory Jordan (AUG)
1978   Rory Jordan (AUG)
1979   Bob Arvold (AUG)
1980   Rick Halvorson (AUG)
1981   Kelley (UST)
1982   Bob Adams (AUG)
1983   Neil (CON)
1984   Neil (CON)
1985   Neil (CON)
1986   Wickman (AUG)
1987   Wickman (AUG)
1988   Schaffer (AUG)
1989   Enger (UST)
1990   John Beatty (AUG)
1991   Scott Fernholz (SJU)
1992   Scott Fernholz (SJU)
1993   Kevin Fiedler (UST)
1994   Shane Nelson (AUG)
1995   Dan Tschudi (SJU)

1996   Wade Johnson (AUG)
1997   Wade Johnson (AUG)
1998   Josh Cagle (AUG)

145 pounds
1966   Leopold (CON)
1967   Nerothin (GAC)
1968   Innes (AUG)
1969   Uankoff (CON)

147 pounds
1948   John Weimerskirch (SJU)
1949   John Weimerskirch (SJU)
1951   John Weimerskirch (SJU)
1952   John Weimerskirch (SJU)
1953   McAndrews (UST)
1954   Otto Weber (SJU)
1955   Hiler (MAC)
1956   Mike Gibbs (SJU)
1957   Lawrence Betzler (SJU)
1958   Lawrence Betzler (SJU)
1959   Lawrence Betzler (SJU)
1960   Theis (UST)
1961   Mannilon (UST)
1962   Fritz (SJU)
1963   Johnson (GAC)
1964   Leopold (CON)
1965   Leopold (CON)

150 Pounds
1970   Pat Marcy (AUG)
1971   Pat Marcy (AUG)
1972   Mark Mattison (AUG)
1973   Bill Schmidt (AUG)
1974   Bill Schmidt (AUG)
1975   Bill Schmidt (AUG)
1976   John Shmshack (SJU)
1977   Benson (AUG)
1978   Jensen (CON)
1979   Brian Arvold (AUG)
1980   Bob Arvold (AUG)
1981   Bob Arvold (AUG)
1982   Bob Arvold (AUG)
1983   Shea Kennedy (AUG)
1984   Donner (CON)
1985   Tim Koffski (AUG)
1986   Tim Koffski (AUG)
1987   Fogarty (UST)
1988   Fogarty (UST)
1989   Don Wickmann (AUG)
1990   Tim Tousignant (AUG)
1991   Tim Tousignant (AUG)
1992   Todd English (UST)
1993   Rick Habeck (AUG)
1994   Stuart Nutting (AUG)
1995   Kevin Fiedler (UST)
1996   Shane Nelson (AUG)
1997   Dan Tschudi (SJU)
1998   Wade Johnson (AUG)

152 Pounds
1966   Frisch (GUS)
1967   Frisch (GUS)
1968   Nerothin (GUS)
1969   Nerothin (GUS)

157 Pounds
1949   Norman McDonnel (SJU)
1951   Frank (GUS)
1952   Wentworth (SOC)
1953   Hiler (MAC)
1954   DeVaughn Nelson (SJU)
1955   DeVaughn Nelson (SJU)
1956   Lawrence Betzler (SJU)
1957   Nellermoe (CON)
1958   James Kuelbs (SJU)
1960   Pat Murtaugh (SJU)
1961   Duerr (AUG)
1962   Pfeffer (CON)
1963   Clark (CON)
1964   Clark (CON)
1965   Evans (GUS)

PAST MIAC CHAMPIONS
Minnesota Intercollegiate Athletic Conference Records
Source: Concordia College Cobber Web-Site

158 Pounds
1970 Mark Mattison (AUG)
1971 Dennis Legatt (SJU)
1972 Pat Marcy (AUG)
1973 Pulkrabeck (SJU)
1974 Larry Osterhaus (SJU)
1975 Johnson (UMD)
1976 Smith (CON)
1977 McNamer (UST)
1978 McNamer (UST)
1979 DeVetter (UST)
1980 Stoks (UST)
1981 Stoks (UST)
1982 Shea Kennedy (AUG)
1983 Studer (UST)
1984 Shea Kennedy (AUG)
1985 Donner (CON)
1986 Forystek (STO)
1987 Mossop (UST)
1988 Berg (UST)
1989 Matt Kretlow (AUG)
1990 Matt Kretlow (AUG)
1991 Kevin Ahern (UST)
1992 Gary Kroells (AUG)
1993 Gary Kroells (AUG)
1994 Jason Scherber (SJU)
1995 Rich Schneckenberger (SJU)
1996 Wade Pehrson (AUG)
1997 Matt Ryan (SJU)
1998 Jesse Bakalyar (AUG)

160 Pounds
1966 Evans (GUS)
1967 Evans (GUS)
1968 Larry Stewart (AUG)
1969 Larry Stewart (AUG)

167 Pounds
1949 Larson (MAC)
1951 Maurer (SOC)
1952 Mezzenga (UST)
1953 Mezzenga (UST)
1954 Tom Kemply (SJU)
1955 Jim Tachney (SJU)
1956 DeVaughn Nelson (SJU)
1957 John O'Fallon (SJU)
1958 Wilson (MAC)
1959 Chuck Daggett (AUG)
1960 Jim Keulbs (SJU)
1961 Zeug (UST)
1962 Chris Wagner (AUG)
1963 Chris Wagner (AUG)
1964 Don Schriefels (SJU)
1965 Lillemoe (CON)
1966 Dale Miller (AUG)
1967 Dale Miller (AUG)
1968 Jon 'Rick' Snow (AUG)
1969 Bishop (CON)
1970 Bishop (CON)
1971 Jerry Workman (SJU)
1972 Olson (CON)
1973 John Burgeson (AUG)
1974 Robby Meyer (AUG)
1975 Mike Holleback (AUG)
1976 Lindberg (CON)
1977 Jeff Swenson (AUG)
1978 Jeff Swenson (AUG)
1979 Jeff Swenson (AUG)
1980 Borden (HAM)
1981 Borden (HAM)
1982 Jim Goodman (SJU)
1983 Jeff Schlieff (AUG)
1984 Jeff Schlieff (AUG)
1985 John Schletty (SJU)
1986 Raedeke (CON)
1987 McNamara (UST)
1988 Wondrasen (AUG)
1989 Massop (UST)
1990 Kurt Habeck (AUG)
1991 Matt Kretlow (AUG)
1992 Steve Larson (CON)
1993 Randy Eastman (AUG)
1994 Randy Eastman (AUG)

1995 Jason Scheber (SJU)
1996 Cliff Casteel (AUG)
1997 John Newman (SJU)
1998 John Newman (SJU)

177 Pounds
1949 Ted Burggraff (SJU)
1950 N/A
1951 George Prybyl (SJU)
1952 Olson (SOC)
1953 Leo Kemper (SJU)
1954 Jim Tachney (SJU)
1955 Sponberg (GAC)
1958 Fujan (UST)
1959 Stebbins (MAC)
1960 Chris Wagner (AUG)
1961 Osmundson (GAC)
1962 Osmundson (GAC)
1963 Zeug (UST)
1964 Zeug (UST)
1965 Don Schreifels (SJU)
1966 Sager (GAC)
1967 Sager (GAC)
1968 Miller (AUG)
1969 Helleckson (MAC)
1970 Henery Wollmering (SJU)
1971 Anderson (AUG)
1972 Jim Mastro (AUG)
1973 Al Bielat (SJU)
1974 Olsen (CON)
1975 Jeff Blixt (AUG)
1976 Jeff Blixt (AUG)
1977 Jeff Blixt (AUG)
1978 Cary Wenzell (AUG)
1979 Winkels (UST)
1980 Winkels (UST)
1981 Winkels (UST)
1982 Mikel (GAC)
1983 Bruce Arvold (AUG)
1984 Bruce Arvold (AUG)
1985 Kemp (BC)
1986 Larson (CON)
1987 Larson (CON)
1988 Larson (CON)
1989 Don Thein (UST)
1990 Don Thein (UST)
1991 Kurt Habek (AUG)
1992 Bill Gabler (AUG)
1993 Gary Thompson (AUG)
1994 John Moore (AUG)
1995 Cliff Casteel (AUG)
1996 John Moore (AUG)
1997 Nathan Reiff (CON)
1998 Nik Lewandowski (AUG)

190 Pounds
1970 Froehle (UMD)
1971 Tom Miller (SJU)
1972 Gehrke (GAC)
1973 Kim Anderson (AUG)
1974 Jerry Workman (SJU)
1975 Moore (UST)
1976 Jim Pappas (AUG)
1977 Durbahn (HAM)
1978 Tom Clawson (AUG)
1979 Anderson (SOC)
1980 Nelson (UST)
1981 Nelson (UST)
1982 Nelson (UST)
1983 Morlock (CON)
1984 VanSickle (UST)
1985 Morlock (CON)
1986 Morlock (CON)
1987 Pieper (GAC)
1988 Pieper (GAC
1989 Kevin Schiltz (AUG)
1990 Kevin Schiltz (AUG)
1991 Kevin Schiltz (AUG)
1992 Kevin Pavelko (CON)
1993 Marty Alger (AUG)
1994 Chris Grothe (SJU)
1995 Chris Grothe (SJU)
1996 Dan Lewandowski (AUG)

1997 Dan Lewandowski (AUG)
1998 Brandon Novak (SJU)

191 Pounds
1955 Tweit (CON)
1956 Tweit (CON)
1957 Tweit (CON)
1958 Gurtek (UST)
1959 Burckhardt (MAC)
1960 Burckhardt (MAC)
1961 Ben Pulkrabek (SJU)
1962 Burckhardt (MAC)
1963 Rettke (GAC)
1964 Rettke (GAC)
1965 Maury Nieland (SJU)
1966 Dinwiddie (GAC)
1967 Daryl Miller (AUG)
1968 Stamp (CON)
1969 Daryl Miller (AUG)

Heavyweight
1949 Stark (MAC)
1950 N/A
1951 Pichner (SOC)
1952 Clem Schoenbauer (SJU)
1953 Bob Foster (SJU)
1954 Leo Kemper (SJU)
1955 Keinholz (GAC)
1956 Ade Sponberg (GAC)
1957 Keinholz (GAC)
1958 Ade Sponberg (GAC)
1959 Gurtek (UST)
1960 Gurtek (UST)
1961 Burckhardt (MAC)
1962 Ben Pulkrabek (SJU)
1963 Offut (CON)
1964 Ken Casperson (AUG)
1965 Mays (GAC)
1966 Stamp (CON)
1967 Mays (GAC)
1968 Mays (GAC)
1969 Favorite (UST)
1970 Favorite (UST)
1971 Hashley (CON)
1972 Hashley (CON)
1973 Hashley (CON)
1974 Greg Miller (SJU)
1975 Greg Miller (SJU)
1976 Bennett (CON)
1977 Bennett (CON)
1978 Bennett (CON)
1979 Hodge (BC)
1980 McLeod (CON)
1981 McLeod (CON)
1982 McLeod (CON)
1983 McLeod (CON)
1984 Mike Chmelik (AUG)
1985 Mike Chmelik (AUG)
1986 Carlson (SOC)
1987 Carlson (SOC)
1988 Chester Grauberger (AUG)
1989 C. Grauberger (AUG)
1990 C. Grauberger (AUG)
1991 C. Grauberger (AUG)
1992 Bret Sharp (AUG)
1993 Kevin Schlitz (AUG)
1994 Eric Betterman (AUG)
1995 Eric Betterman (AUG)
1996 John Pena (AUG)
1997 John Pena (AUG)
1998 John Pena (AUG)

Augsburg College Wrestling History

Arguably the preeminent Division III college wrestling program in the United States, Augsburg College stands in a class all by themselves. While the Minneapolis institution has solid programs for many other sports, it is without question that the sport of wrestling has put it on the map. A true dynasty, the Auggies have certainly made Minnesota grappling fans very proud indeed.

According to Augsburg's Sports Information Coordinator, Don Stoner, the Auggie's rich wrestling tradition all got started 56 years ago, back in 1948, when the student newspaper, the Echo, posted this: "If you like to lie around on the floor and grunt, come over to the gym this coming Tuesday for a meeting of all wrestling aspirants…" Ten wrestlers showed up and with that, the sport went from club to varsity status. The squad went on to beat the University of Minnesota's Farm team later that year, and so began history.

The program's first coach would be a young man from Dawson, Minn., by the name of Edor Nelson. Nelson, who played football, basketball and baseball at Augsburg, graduating with honors in 1938, came back to teach and coach at his alma mater after spending the past decade teaching in high school while also serving

in the armed services for five and a half years during World War II. Nelson, who would later be considered the "father of Augsburg wrestling," guided the Auggies from their inception to 1963, slowly building the program from the ground up. The team won its first ever Minnesota Intercollegiate Athletic Conference (MIAC) title in 1961 and quickly emerged as one of the conference's top guns.

Nelson handed over the reigns to Oscar Blegen in 1963 so that he could focus on coaching football and baseball. Blegen, meanwhile, coached the team from

John Beatty

AUGSBURG COLLEGE RECORD BOOK

National Champions

Pat Marcy (150 pounds, NAIA, 1972)
Jeff Swenson (167, NAIA, 1979)
Scott Whirley (126, NAIA, 1979)
Bob Adams (134, NCAA-III, 1983)
Bruce Arvold (167, NAIA, 1983)
Steve Gliva (118, NCAA-III, 1984)
Shea Kennedy (150, NCAA-III, 1984)
John Beatty (134, NCAA-III, 1988; 142, NCAA-III, 1990)
Chet Grauberger (HWT, NCAA-III, 1991)
Gary Kroells (158, NCAA-III, 1992; 158, NCAA-III, 1993)
Nick Fornicoia (118, NCAA-III, 1993)
Joe Hoialmen (134, NCAA-III, 1993)
Jesse Armbruster (126, NCAA-III, 1995)
Tom Layte (150, NCAA-III, 1995)
Dan Lewandowski (190, NCAA-III, 1996; 190, NCAA-III, 1997)
Henry Gerten (118, NCAA-III, 1997; 118, NCAA-III, 1998)
Jim Peterson (167, NCAA-III, 1998)
John Marchette (133, NCAA-III, 1999)
Josh Cagle (149, NCAA-III, 2000)
Nick Slack (174, NCAA-III, 2000)
Josh Clausen (197, NCAA-III, 2000)
Ben Bauer (HWT, NCAA-III, 2000; HWT, NCAA-III, 2001)
Darin Bertram (125, NCAA-III, 2001)
Nik Lewandowski (184, NCAA-III, 2001)
Tony Abbott (165, NCAA-III, 2002)
Marcus LeVesseur (157, NCAA-III, 2003; 157, NCAA-III, 2004)
Matt Shankey (125, NCAA-III, 2004)
Mark Matzek (133, NCAA-III, 2004)
Joe Moon (174, NCAA-III, 2004)

All-Americans

5-time — Steve Gliva ('81, '82, '83, '84, '85).

4-time — John Beatty ('87, '88, '89, '90); Tom Hall (82-'83, '84, '85); Nik Lewandowski ('98, '99, '00, '01).

3-time — Jesse Armbruster ('94, '95, '96); Bruce Arvold ('82, '83, '84); Darin Bertram ('99, '00, '01)*; Josh Cagle ('98, '99, '00); Randy Eastman ('93, '94, '95); Brad Fisher ('99, '01, '02); Nick Fornicoia ('91, '92, '93); Henry Gerten ('96, '97,' 98); Chet Grauberger ('89, '90, '91); Joe Hoialmen ('90,'91, '93); Brian Jones ('97,' 98, '00); Shea Kennedy ('82, '83, '84); Matt Kretlow ('88,'89, '91); Dan Lewandowski ('95,'96,'97); John Pena ('96, '97, '98); Jim Peterson ('97, '98, '99); Kevin Schiltz ('89, '90, '93); Bill Schmidt ('73, '74, '75); Nick Slack ('00, '01, '02); Jeff Swenson ('77, '78, '79); Scott Whirley ('79, '81, '82).

2-time — Tony Abbott ('01, '02); Bob Adams ('82,'83); Brian Arvold ('79,'80); Jesse Bakalyar ('97, '98); Ben Bauer ('00, '01); Eric Bettermann ('94, '95); Charlie Blixt ('74, '75); Cliff Casteel ('94, '96); Greg Chmelik ('84, '85); Josh Clausen ('99, '00); Ricky Crone ('02, '03); Bill Gabler ('91, '92); Mike Good ('69, '71); Mitch Hegland ('89, '90); Ron Johnson ('71, '72); Wade Johnson ('97,'98); Gary Kroells ('92, '93); Marcus LeVesseur ('03, '04)*; John Marchette ('99, '00); Mark Matzek ('03, '04)*; Joe Moon ('03, '04); Kevin Rasmussen ('01, '02); Jamell Tidwell ('03, '04)*.

1-time —Bob Arvold ('82); Rich Barron ('81); Jeff Blixt ('77); Greg Brendemuehl ('03)*; Joe Cullen ('04)*; Dustin Dahlblom ('04)*; Stan D'Andrea ('83); Scott Davis ('73); Mike Flanagan ('02); Keith Gliva ('86); Kurt Habeck ('91); Rick Habeck ('92); Justin Hahn ('97); Rick Halvorson ('80); Murray Herstein ('75); Dave Janaszak ('94); Dean Kennedy ('75); Tom Layte ('95); Pat Marcy ('72); Bryan Miller ('01); Daryl Miller ('69); Stuart Nutting ('94); Wade Pehrson ('96); Mike Pfeffer ('92); Jeff Schlieff ('86); Matt Shankey ('04)*; Bret Sharp ('92); Mark Simmonds ('04)*; Jack Solem ('74); Jeff Stoks ('81); Gary Thompson ('93); Tim Tousignant ('91); Ryan Valek ('04)*; Shane Wevley ('98); Donny Wichmann ('89); Dave Wygant ('77).

(* denotes active wrestlers in 2003-04; Note: Tom Hall, Steve Gliva, Bruce Arvold, Bob Adams were NAIA and NCAA III All-Americans in the same year)

HENRY GERTEN

Henry Gerten grew up in Rosemount and went on to capture the 119-pound state title in 1993 at Rosemount High School. From there, Gerten wrestled at the University of Wisconsin for one year, before transferring to Augsburg. There, he dominated, becoming just the fourth Auggie grappler to win two individual NCAA Division III national titles. A three-time MIAC champion and three-time All-American, Gerten finished his illustrious three-year career with a record of 104-7, the best all-time winning percentage in school history, and even went 44-0 –during his senior campaign — the first Auggie ever to accomplish such a feat. Gerten, who even beat the 1996 Olympic bronze medallist from Cuba during a meet that year, went on to graduate with honors with a degree in elementary education and later received a Master's degree from Saint Mary's University as well. From there, Gerten, of the greenhouse family fame, went on to coach the Team Minnesota Elite 15 and 16-year-old wrestlers for seven years. In addition to currently serving as the head coach for Team Minnesota/USA (Cadets), Henry also serves as the head coach of the Dakota County Technical College Blue Knight.

1963-66, until stepping aside to make way for Ron Pfeffer, who wasted little time in making a name for himself, winning an MIAC title in his second season. And he didn't stop there, winning two more to make it three in a row from 1968-71. Pfeffer left after that season and was replaced by Mike Good, who coached the Auggies for just one season before passing the torch to John Grygelko, who came to the College after an extremely successful stint as the head coach at Robbinsdale High School.

In all, Grygelko would spend eight years building the foundation for one of the most successful collegiate wrestling programs in the nation. He won six straight MIAC crowns from 1975-80 and established his Auggies as the team to beat not only in the

Brian Arvold

conference but also on the national scene in the NAIA as well. Perhaps the highlight of his days with the Auggies came in 1975, when he led his boys to an NAIA national runner-up finish. In addition, Augsburg finished seventh in 1971, fifth in 1974, seventh in 1977 and third in 1979, under his tutelage. Grygelko would ultimately step down as the head coach of the Auggies in 1980 to return to high school coaching, retiring with an impressive 98-12-1 record.

From there, former Auggie All-American Jeff Swenson took over the program's head coaching duties and he has been there ever since, making a lot of history along the way. Considered by many to be the preeminent Division III college wrestling coach in the country, Swenson jumped in and started making waves at the school, and hasn't looked back since. Swenson led the Auggies to an MIAC title in his first year behind the wheel and incredibly, he would 21 out of the next 22. How's that for dominance?

The '90s were defined as the "Augsburg decade" in small-college wrestling. The Auggies ruled the national scene, finishing no lower than second in eight of the nine Division III national championships held during that span, and capturing five national

championships along the way in 1991, 1993, 1995, 1997 and 1998. Then, at the 1999 MIAC championships, Swenson's boys took all 10 individual conference titles — the first time such a feat had ever happened in the 50-plus years of the MIAC meet.

Augsburg continued its small-college domination into the new millennium, becoming the first college in NCAA Division III history to win three straight national championships, claiming titles in 2000, 2001 and 2002. In 2003 and 2004, Augsburg finished second to rival Wartburg (Iowa), one of the schools' primary arch nemesis over the past 20 years. In fact, since 1990, Augsburg has finished either first or sec-

Brian Jones

ond in 15 of the 16 Division III national championship tournaments, with a lone fourth-place finish in 1994. Incredibly, no other NCAA wrestling school in ANY division can make such a similar claim.

Even when they finishing second they still find a way to make history. Such was the case in 2004, when the Auggies tied a Division III record with four individual national titlists, claimed nine All-Americans and produced the most points ever for a runner-up at the national tournament, 140.5. In fact, Augsburg's point total that year was more than all but three winning championship point-totals in Division III history!

Since the program's inception back in the late '40s, it has produced 162 All-Americans — a record 126 in Division III and 36 in

Darin Bertram

JEFF SWENSON

Jeff Swenson is an Auggie Wrestling coaching legend. Period. Swenson grew up in South Minneapolis loving sports and in 1975 came to Augsburg to wrestle and play football. On the mat, Swenson produced a 102-17 record, earning NAIA All-American honors three times (1977-79) and winning the national title at 167 pounds in 1979. On the gridiron, Swenson was a dominant linebacker, earning four letters for the Auggies and leading the team in the tough MIAC. For his efforts, Swenson earned the school's senior Honor Athlete award. From there, Swenson, who earned degrees in health and physical education, and later got his master's degree in health from the University of Minnesota in 1982, became an assistant coach with both the Auggie wrestling and football teams.

In 1980 Swenson served one year as an assistant under Auggie wrestling coach John Grygelko, and then assumed the head coaching duties in 1981. Since then, Swenson has gone on to build a small college wrestling dynasty. Under Swenson, Augsburg has won a record eight NCAA Division III wrestling national championships in the last 14 years. Augsburg has had top-two national finishes in 15 of the last 16 years, top-four finishes the last 16 seasons in a row and top-20 national finishes every year since 1971. Augsburg has also captured 20 MIAC team championships and eight national team titles as well. In addition, he has produced 133 All-Americans, including 32 individual national champions along the way.

Now entering his 23rd season with Augsburg (Swenson left Augsburg to coach at Rosemount High School from 1985-86), Swenson's collegiate coaching record stands at an unbelievable 292-38, and is among the best in the nation.

Swenson also has some outstanding assistant coaches with him during his journey to the top as well including, Scott Whirley and Don Wichmann. Whirley was a three-time All-American at Augsburg, who won the national championship at 126 pounds in 1979 and three MIAC titles along the way. Wichmann, meanwhile, was an All-American in 1989 and a three-time MIAC champion as well. They have been the top assistants at the program for 13 and 18 years, respectively.

Swenson is just as proud of his team's success in the classroom as he is of their success on the wrestling mat. Augsburg has had 80 Scholar All-Americans (awarded by the National Wrestling Coaches Association) and in 1998-99, earned the Division III academic national championship with a team grade-point average of 3.48. Augsburg is the only school in Division III wrestling to be in the top 10 both academically and on the mat every year of the six the NWCA has awarded an academic national championship in Division III.

Among his many coaching accolades, including numerous conference coach of the year awards, in 2001 Swenson was named Lutheran College National Coach of the Year (all sports) from Lutheran Brotherhood, and in 2002, he earned National College Coach of the Year honors (all divisions) from Wrestling USA Magazine. In addition, in 1999 Swenson was inducted into the Augsburg Athletic Hall of Fame, and in 2004 he was inducted into the Minnesota Wrestling Coaches Association/David Bartelma Wrestling Hall of Fame.

In addition to serving as the Men's Wrestling Head Coach, Swenson also serves as the Interim Assistant Dean for Athletics and Recreation at Augsburg as well. In this role, he supervises the men's and women's intercollegiate athletic departments, the athletic facilities department, and the college's intramural athletic program. Showing no signs of slowing down, Swenson is still going strong and continues to set the standard in Division III wrestling. He is simply one of the best of the very best at what he does, and continues to make Minnesota proud.

LOOKING BACK WHAT ARE YOU MOST PROUD OF IN YOUR CAREER? "I would say I am most proud of our alumni and what they are doing now. I am real proud of the fact that I have been able to have the opportunity to be a part of their lives. I hope I have made a difference in their lives in a positive way, and they have become better people because of that. Now, 25 years later, it is just mind boggling to think about all of our alumni who are out there doing great things in the world."

HOW WOULD YOU DESCRIBE YOUR COACHING STYLE? "I would say that I am an organized, systematic, demanding motivator."

HOW DO YOU MOTIVATE YOUR PLAYERS? "I try to motivate our student athletes with a logical approach. I try to read people and have had good success with that. The key is learning what motivates each individual because you can't motivate everyone the same way. While we attempt to treat everybody fairly, quite honestly we don't treat everybody the same because everybody is different. One thing we do that I am very proud of, however, is that we include our entire team in everything we do. For instance, every year after Christmas we take a very expensive trip to Florida and we include the entire roster of around 35 guys. We include our entire team in all of our competitions as well, so that almost everybody can get a full schedule of matches. We always talk about 35 guys going in the same direction, and 35 guys helping one another for the good of the team. All 35 guys will earn varsity letters, all 35 guys will get national championship rings and all 35 guys will be in the team picture at nationals — even though only one guy represents us in each weight class. That is how we motivate our kids to be team players and to push themselves to be the best they can be."

WHAT ARE THE CHARACTERISTICS OF LEADERS? "That is a real tough question, because I think every leader has their own characteristics. Take my four captains for this upcoming season: the first one is outgoing, friendly, very organized and is a real take the bull by the horn type; the second is very quiet and doesn't say boo, works out extremely hard, and he leads by example; the third one is fabulous in the wrestling room, he has a magnetic personality, has knowledge beyond his years and the kids really respond to him, but he needs to learn how to be a good leader off the mat; then the fourth captain needs to develop more self confidence to be the great leader that he can be, but as a former valedictorian he leads in the classroom. So, leaders come in all shapes and sizes and have many different characteristics. That's why we usually have several captains instead of just one each season, because that way we just get that much more leadership."

WHAT IS THE KEY TO RECRUITING? "Being proud of the product that you are selling and having a successful product. You have to remember that you are providing a service for families."

HOW DO YOU BUILD TEAM UNITY & CHEMISTRY? "We talk a lot about accepting everybody for who we are and about finding the positives in individuals as opposed to the negatives. We talk about how everybody has something unique to offer and contribute to our team and that is what team chemistry is. Then, it goes back to including all 35 guys in nearly everything we do. We build team unity by being together and by encouraging each other to be our best."

WHAT MOTIVATES YOU? "I think what motivates me is knowing that I have made a difference in my kids' lives; knowing that I have made their lives better; knowing that I had something to do with them graduating from college and then getting a job; and knowing that through a great wrestling experience that they have become a better person."

WHAT IS THE KEY TO GOOD TIME MANAGEMENT? "I think planning ahead is the key. I put together 'to-do' lists every night and just try to stay on top of everything as best I can. Beyond that I make up job descriptions for everything, and emphasize good communication between everybody. Things will get done if you tell people how to do them and when to do them. One of the things I learned from Dan Gable (Iowa's legendary wrestling coach) is to plan in reverse. Everything we do, including our wrestling schedules, I do in reverse order. So, last year I started out by planning a trip to the national tournament on March 6th and just worked my way back. You also have to also visualize to be successful, and I do that."

WHAT ADVICE WOULD YOU HAVE FOR YOUNG COACHES STARTING OUT TODAY? "Make sure you can live a balanced life and make sure you don't try to do too much. I would also say that no high school wrestling coach should ever coach a Spring sport. You just get spread too thin. Overall, I just think that wrestlers are real needy athletes and they need your attention year-round."

FAVORITE LOCKER ROOM SIGN? "My favorite saying is 'One percent improvement every day' which means that this year we can get 132 % better from October 21st to March 6th. Then, in our wrestling room we have a sign that reads: 'To be a champion: practice like a champion, handle academics like a champion and behave socially like a champion.' Beyond that, we have a saying: 'The pursuit of excellence while building men,' and that saying is on the backs of our tee-shirts as well."

WHAT'S THE BIGGEST THING YOU'VE LEARNED FROM COACHING THAT YOU'VE BEEN ABLE TO APPLY TO YOUR EVERYDAY LIFE? "To do things at the highest possible level and never give anything less than 100%."

WHAT ARE THE KEY INGREDIENTS TO CREATING A CHAMPIONSHIP TEAM? "Good leadership with the coaches and good leadership with your captains. Then, it is developing a work ethic amongst your team and being able to have the student athletes to incorporate those things."

WHAT'S THE SECRET TO YOUR SUCCESS? "I think it is focusing on the journey and not the destination. We just want to focus on improving all the time, no matter what we do. We go over our evaluation sheets from the year before several times throughout the season and then try to work on making things better for the next year. Whether it is an academic plan, a weight training plan, a cardiovascular training plan, or a practice plan — we document it and evaluate it. You know, another thing is that we don't talk about winning at all in our practice room. The kids have goals to be national champs and to beat this guy or that guy in a dual, and I don't think you can prevent that. I mean the internet has made it all but impossible to shelter athletes from knowing about their opponents. But, our program is not win oriented, it is goal oriented and improvement oriented. When you have that, winning takes care of itself."

WHAT WOULD YOU WANT TO SAY TO YOUR FANS, BOOSTERS, AND ALUMNI WHO HAVE SUPPORTED YOU ALL THESE YEARS? "I would just say thanks for supporting us and for being there for us. We couldn't have done it without you. We have just great fans at Augsburg. We always have the largest crowd at nationals and we appreciate that so much. The Augsburg Wrestling program is not about me, it is about the kids. You know, as successful as our program has been, people don't always know who the head coach at Augsburg is, and I am flattered to hear that. In fact, I consider that to be one of the greatest compliments that we could receive, because it means that this hasn't been about me, it is always about the kids and the program."

HOW DO YOU WANT YOUR COACHING EPITAPH TO READ — HOW DO YOU WANT TO BE REMEMBERED AS A COACH? "He made a positive difference and made the lives of his student athletes better."

NAIA competition. In addition, Augsburg wrestlers have earned 35 individual national titles — a record 31 in Division III and four in NAIA competition.

On the local scene, while the MIAC ended wrestling championship competition in the late '90s, the Auggies managed to win the last 16 MIAC team championships in a row, and 26 of the final 28. Augsburg also won all 14 MIAC Team Duals tournaments held, outscoring conference opponents by a whopping 3,266-145 margin. And, the Auggies even had an 18-season, 88-match winning streak against MIAC opponents as well. Furthermore, since 1979, Augsburg has gone 210-17 against all of its NCAA Division III opponents.

The program is just as solid off the mat as well, boasting some 80 National Wrestling Coaches Association Scholar All-Americans over the past 21 seasons, the most of any college in any division in the nation. In fact, Augsburg is the only school in NCAA Division III wrestling to finish in the top 10 both in competition on the mat and in the academic team competition in each of the seven years that the NWCA has awarded an academic team national championship. Aside from winning the academic national title in the 1998-99 season, the program has had team grade-point averages of 3.30 or better every year of the NWCA team GPA listing.

Under Jeff Swenson, Augsburg College continues to amaze and impress. What he has done at the school is nothing short of incredible. As for the future? In 2004 local grappling legend Alan Rice gave a $1 million gift to Augsburg as part of the college's "Access to Excellence" capital campaign. Rice dedicated the gift to

Ben Bauer

MARCUS LeVESSEUR

Marcus LeVesseur grew up in South Minneapolis and went on to become a four-time state champ, earning a trio of titles at Minneapolis Roosevelt High School from 1998-2000, and a fourth at Bloomington Kennedy High School in 2001. He capped his illustrious prep career with a 218-12 record, including a state-record 141 straight victories down the stretch. From there, LeVesseur enrolled at the University of Minnesota, but did not compete as a Gopher and decided instead to transfer to Augsburg after one semester. There, he has been dominant, winning two NCAA Division III national titles at 157 pounds while compiling a perfect 84-0 record along the way. So good is LeVesseur, that he beat out five Division I wrestlers to claim the USA Wrestling University National Freestyle title in 2004 to represent the United States at the world championships in Lodz, Poland, where he placed 10th.

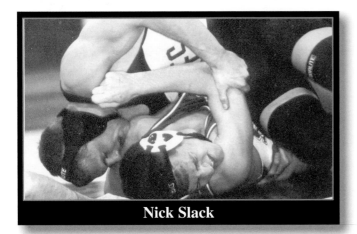

Jim Peterson

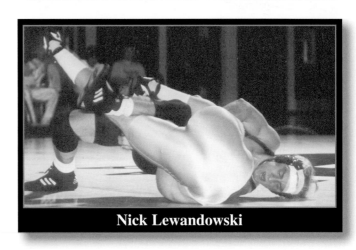

Joe Moon

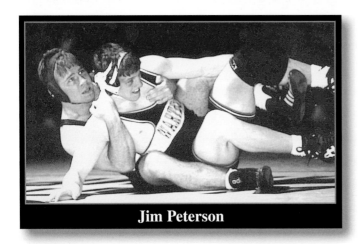

Nick Slack

Nick Lewandowski

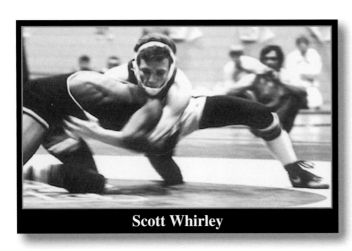

Scott Whirley

Daryl Miller

EDOR NELSON

Edor Nelson was born and raised in Dawson and graduated from Dawson High School in 1933, where he played football, baseball, basketball and track. Nelson went to Augsburg that next year and played football, basketball and baseball, graduating with honors in 1938. From there, Nelson got his first teaching and coaching job in Lamberton, where he stayed for three years. After that he went into the armed services for five and a half years during World War II, later working under General Patton, and even serving as a prisoner of war for six months in a German prison camp. When he returned home in 1946 he went back to Augsburg and began teaching and coaching several sports, including football, basketball and baseball, as well as wrestling and hockey — both of which he is credited with starting at the school. (He also got his master's degree from the University of Minnesota in 1947 as well.)

Nelson would go on to become a fixture at Augsburg. In all, he coached football at the school for 23 years (1947-69), finishing with a 58-118-10 record, the most wins in school history. He also coached baseball for 33 seasons (1946-79), earning MIAC titles seven times (1947, 48, 59, 61, 63, 73 and 75). Nelson was an associate professor in Augsburg's health and physical education department for 32 years as well, retiring in 1978. Among Nelson's many coaching accolades, he was inducted into the Minnesota Football Hall of Fame in 1973 and was also named MIAC Baseball Coach of the Year in 1975 as well. Then, in 2001, Augsburg honored Edor by re-dedicating their outdoor athletic field in his name as the "Edor Nelson Field." Today Edor is retired and living in Minneapolis. He still follows Auggie athletics, and also roots for his son, who coaches high school football in Eagan as well. A true Augsburg legend, Edor Nelson is old-school, and proud of it.

HOW WOULD YOU DESCRIBE YOUR COACHING STYLE? "I believed that the kids came first and I based all of my coaching on that philosophy. I adapted my style to the players I had and just got them to work as hard as they could. We had some good years at Augsburg and we had some great kids along the way. I also believed that education came first and sports were secondary. We liked to win of course, but we had our priorities straight."

HOW DID YOU MOTIVATE YOUR PLAYERS? "I always told them that what they were doing was preparation for life. I reinforced to them that sports was a stepping stone for their careers. I told them that they were not going to play sports all their life and that they were going to have to get a job and work later on. So, they should learn as much as they could and try as hard as they could so that they could better be prepared for life after college. I would ask them what they wanted to do with their lives and then we would sit down and set goals together. Then, we would analyze those goals periodically to see how they were doing."

WHO WERE YOUR COACHING MENTORS? "My high school coach, Art Agge. He was a St. Olaf graduate and a great basketball player. He took me under his wing and I learned a lot from him. He was a great guy and I wanted to be like him."

LOOKING BACK WHAT ARE YOU MOST PROUD OF IN YOUR CAREER? "I would say the results that came about later in life with many of my players is what I am most proud of. The success that they had was just wonderful to see. I think almost every one of them turned out to be a good citizen and that makes me very proud."

WHAT WAS THE KEY TO RECRUITING? "Sell them on a good education. I used to tell them that they were coming to college for a purpose and Augsburg offered a very fine education. The parents always went along with that too."

HOW DID YOU BUILD TEAM UNITY & CHEMISTRY? "I used to set a lot of team goals as well as individual goals for my kids. I think most of my kids got along for the most part and that carried over to the athletic field. We spent a lot of time together off the field and that helped to build unity together too. I used to tell my kids to make every minute count and that would translate into success both on and off the field."

WHAT MOTIVATED YOU? "My interest in kids. I was interested in developing good citizens, that was my biggest motivation. I wanted them to be successful in life."

WHAT ADVICE WOULD YOU HAVE FOR YOUNG COACHES STARTING OUT TODAY? "Remember that the kids are the most important thing. Treat them all fairly and remember that you are working with the development of youth. Beyond that, keep it all in perspective and don't get carried away with things. Life is too short for that."

WHAT'S THE BIGGEST THING YOU'VE LEARNED FROM COACHING THAT YOU'VE BEEN ABLE TO APPLY TO YOUR EVERYDAY LIFE? "I think it has given me an interest and perspective in many other things. I have a great interest in being patriotic, I have a great interest in the community as a whole and I have a great interest in just living a good life."

WHAT ARE THE KEY INGREDIENTS TO CREATING A CHAMPIONSHIP TEAM? "Loyalty, teamwork and cooperation are the biggest things. Sure, you need to have some talent, but you can't get very far without the other things."

ON HOW SPORTS HAVE CHANGED: "You know, sometimes I think some of the parents have gotten too carried away. Too often they care only about their own kids and they forget about why the kids are there. Some of them need to be more realistic in what sports really means. I think sports have kind of gotten out hand a little bit. It used to be more down to earth. I think that sports are just a part of life and they are not as important as everyone wants to make them out to be. Sometimes the fans are out of hand and that is sad to see too. I think back to my days in the armed services, that was life and death and really important. Sports is just supposed to be fun while you get your education. We need to remember that I think."

WHAT'S THE SECRET TO YOUR SUCCESS? "I suppose my family. They encouraged me a great deal and that meant a lot to me. Also, I was genuinely interested in the development of young people and I cared about the kids I worked with."

WHAT WOULD YOU WANT TO SAY TO YOUR FANS, BOOSTERS, AND ALUMNI WHO HAVE SUPPORTED YOU ALL THESE YEARS? "I think they should all be very proud of what these kids have done for the University, the community and for our country. Thanks to everyone who helped make that possible and for their support."

HOW DO YOU WANT YOUR COACHING EPITAPH TO READ — HOW DO YOU WANT TO BE REMEMBERED AS A COACH? "I would like to be remembered as someone who had his players best interests at heart. I wanted my kids to go on and become successful in life. I also did something to help make this a better country and a better community, and that is how I would like to be thought of."

the creation of a Greco-Roman wrestling training center as a part of the Si Melby Hall expansion on campus. The training center will attract both youth and adult wrestlers to train in the Greco-Roman discipline year round and will also enable the school to attract world-class athletes to train in its facilities.

As for future problems for the coach and his overachieving program? That's easy. They are eventually going to need some more real estate over in Si Melby Hall to house all of their medals and national championship trophies. Stay tuned!

1998 National Champs

Concordia College

The father of Concordia wrestling is Finn Grinaker, who graduated from Concordia in 1948, where he played football, basketball, track and golf. From there, the Halstad native would go on to coach at the college for nearly four decades. Grinaker founded the wrestling program at Concordia at Concordia in 1953 and went on to guide the program for the next 29 years. Along the way, Grinaker's Cobbers won an MIAC title in 1964, doing wonders for the growth of the sport in the northern half of the state.

The heydays for the program came in the mid to late '60s, when stars such as Harlan and Howard Leopold, Doug Dufty, and Dennis Stamp, all achieved great success. Harlan Leopold was a was a three-time MIAC champion and four-time NAIA All-American; Howard Leopold was a three-time MIAC champion who went on to coach for more than 30 years at Mound High School; Dufty was a four-time MIAC champion who went on to coach at the University of Minnesota, Morris; and Stamp was a four-time MIAC Champion who even went on to wrestle professionally in Verne Gagne's American Wrestling Association.

BARRY BENNETT

Barry Bennett came to Concordia from North St. Paul and went on to win three national titles in the heavyweight division, including 74 matches in a row, and earned a place in the NAIA Wrestling Hall of Fame. As a, All-American defensive tackle on the Cobber football team, Bennett later went on to play for 10 seasons in the NFL with the New Orleans Saints and New York Jets.

When it was all said and done, Grinaker had inspired 18 All-Americans and touched countless lives along the way. He retired in 1988 as a real Concordia coaching icon. Doug Perry later took over the program in 1991 and has been there ever since. Perry, who coached at Worthington High School for 17 years prior to coming to Moorhead, was a 1965 Concordia graduate as well. During his tenure with the Cobbers, Perry has coached one All-American, three Academic All-Americans, three MIAC Champions and 22 MIAC All-Conference athletes along the way. Perry, who also serves as an assistant football coach at the school, was honored in 2002 by being named as the MIAC Coach of the Year.

Harlan Leopold

FINN GRINAKER

Long considered as the father of Concordia wrestling, Finn Grinaker graduated from Concordia in 1948, where he played football, basketball track and golf. From there, the Halstad native would go on to coach at the college for nearly four decades. Grinaker founded the wrestling program at Concordia in 1953 and went on to guide the program for the next 29 years. In addition to producing 18 All-Americans, Grinaker's Cobbers won an MIAC title in 1964. He was also a head coach in basketball for two years, head golf coach for 20 years and an assistant football coach for 39 years under coaches Christiansen and Christopherson as well.

One of the most respected coaches and professors in Concordia's history, Grinaker became the backbone of the physical education department through his farsighted curriculum, innovations and dedication to excellence in his teaching. He retired in 1988 as a real Concordia coaching icon.

CONCORDIA RECORD BOOK

Cobber Four-Time MIAC Champions
Doug Dufty   1964-65-66-67
Malcolm McLeod   1980-81-82-83

Cobber Three-Time MIAC Champions
Al Tweit   1955-56-57
Harlan Leopold   1963-64-65
Fred Hashley   1971-72-73
Terry Bishop   1970-72-73
Barry Bennett   1976-77-78
Jeff Neil   1983-84-85
Paul Morlock   1983-85-86
Brett Larson   1986-87-88

Cobber Two-Time MIAC Champions
Roger Leopold   1957-1961
Howard Leopold   1965-1966
Charles Bishop   1969-1970
Dennis Stamp   1966-1968
Dennis Olson   1972-1974
Paul Donner   1983-1984

Cobber One-Time All-Americans
1962	Harlan Leopold	3rd NAIA
1963	Harlan Leopold	3rd NAIA
1964	Harlan Leopold	3rd NAIA
1965	Harlan Leopold	4th NAIA
1965	Doug Dufty	2nd NAIA
1966	Howard Leopold	2nd NAIA
1968	Dennis Stamp	6th NAIA
1976	Barry Bennett	1st NAIA
1976	Kevin Lindberg	5th NAIA
1977	Barry Bennett	1st NAIA
1978	Mark Jensen	2nd NCAA III
1978	Barry Bennett	1st NCAA III
1979	Mark Jensen	5th NCAA III
1980	Malcolm McLeod	6th NCAA III
1981	Malcolm McLeod	7th NCAA III
1982	Malcolm McLeod	4th NCAA III
1983	Malcolm McLeod	2nd NCAA III
1983	Malcolm McLeod	5th NAIA
1988	Brett Larson	4th NCAA III
1990	Chip Halverson	4th NCAA III
1999	Nathan Reiff	7th NCAA III

Career Wins
Steve Larson   124-63-2
Mike Northcutt   103-39-2
Mark Jensen   102-26-1
Paul Morlock   101-29-2
Mollie McLeod   101-29-1

Cobber MIAC Wrestling Champions
126 Pounds
1970   Terry Bishop
1972   Terry Bishop
1973   Terry Bishop

130 Pounds
1964   Doug Dufty
1965   Doug Dufty
1966   Paul Budd
1967   Doug Dufty

137 Pounds
1957   Roger Leopold
1961   Roger Leopold
1963   Harlan Leopold
1965   Harlan Leopold
1966   Doug Dufty

142 pounds
1983   Jeff Neil
1984   Jeff Neil
1985   Jeff Neil

145 pounds
1966   Howard Leopold
1969   Uankoff

147 pounds
1964   Harlan Leopold
1965   Howard Leopold

150 Pounds
1978   Mark Jensen
1984   Paul Donner

157 Pounds
1957   Nellermoe
1962   Pfeffer
1963   Clark
1964   Clark

158 Pounds
1976   Smith
1985   Paul Donner

167 Pounds
1965   Lillemoe
1969   Charles Bishop
1970   Charles Bishop
1972   Dennis Olson
1976   Lindberg
1986   Tom Raedeke
1992   Steve Larson

177 Pounds
1974   Dennis Olson
1986   Brett Larson
1987   Brett Larson
1988   Brett Larson
1997   Nathan Reiff

190 Pounds
1985   Paul Morlock
1986   Paul Morlock
1992   Kevin Pavelko

191 Pounds
1955   Al Tweit
1956   Al Tweit
1957   Al Tweit
1968   Dennis Stamp

Heavyweight
1963   Ron Offut
1966   Dennis Stamp
1971   Fred Hashley
1972   Fred Hashley
1973   Fred Hashley
1976   Barry Bennett
1977   Barry Bennett
1978   Barry Bennett
1980   Malcolm McLeod
1981   Malcolm McLeod
1982   Malcolm McLeod
1983   Malcolm McLeod

Source: Cobber Sports Web-Site

St. John's University

St. John's has had a long and storied wrestling program which began back in 1941. Following the war years the program resumed its schedule under a series of player/coaches, including John Condon, Norman McDonnell, Jack Hayneman, John Weimerskirch, Jim McKeown, Jerry Miller, Jim Tacheny, DeVaughn Nelson, Larry Betzler, Mike O'Fallon and Jim Kuelbs, until Bob Dumonceaux took over in 1960 as the first non-student coach. Dumonceaux coached on and off for five seasons in Collegeville, until passing the torch to Terry Haws.

Haws, who had previously coached wrestling at St. James High School (1948-58) and at St Cloud Cathedral High School (1958-67), also coached football and golf at St. John's as well. Haws guided the Johnnies for seven seasons until his tragic death in 1973. Sadly, Haws died of a massive heart attack while the team was competing in Cleveland, Ohio, for the National Catholic Championships. He was just 49 years old.

During his tenure as coach at St. John's, Haws compiled an impressive 65-9-2 dual record, won three MIAC conference titles (1971, '72, '73), two National Catholic Titles (1971, '72), produced 16 MIAC Conference Champions, 11 National Catholic Champions, 6 NAIA All-Americans and 1 NAIA National Champion. At the time of his death, Haws held the nation's longest dual meet streak of 51 consecutive victories, which currently ranks third among all wrestling programs in Division I, II or III.

In 1973 Roger Ludwig came in and was asked to take over a program which had been devastated by the loss of its leader. Ludwig would forge ahead, however, posting a solid 24-9 record in his sophomore campaign. Greg Miller took over the reigns of the program in 1975, leading the Johnnies for four modest seasons, until passing the torch to Jim Lind. Lind posted a 16-22 record for the next two seasons and later stepped aside in 1981 to make way for former Johnny grappler, John Elton. Elton grabbed the wheel and took off, and he has been going strong ever since.

Elton would coach at St. John's for the next 23 seasons, achieving tremendous success along the way. In 1981, Elton posted a modest 4-5-1 record. Since that season, SJU has never dropped below .500 and it has won 10 or more dual meets 18 times. In 2004, SJU finished with a 12-4 dual record and finished third at the NCAA Great Lakes Regional, with three wrestlers advancing to the NCAA Championships. At the national level, SJU has qualified athletes to the NCAA Division III tournament in 19 of the past 20 seasons, including 19 NCAA All-Americans and 29 Scholar All-Americans.

Elton retired following the 2004 season with an impressive 273-100-5 dual meet record. In addition, his teams have posted an impressive .729 winning percentage during his tenure as well. For his efforts, Elton has been named MIAC Coach-of-the-Year in 1984, 1993, 1995 and 1997. At the national level, SJU has qualified athletes to the NCAA Division III tournament in 18 of the past 19 seasons, including 18 NCAA All-Americans and 26 Scholar All-Americans.

John Newman

Brandon Novak

TERRY HAWS

Terry Haws was born in the small southern Minnesota town of Tracy and grew up loving sports. He would go on to become a coaching icon over his illustrious career, first establishing and building wrestling programs at St. James High School (1948-58) and St Cloud Cathedral High School (1958-67), before coming to St. John's University. In addition to wrestling, Haws coached football and golf at SJU as well. It was on the mat, however, where he was dominant.

During his tenure in Collegeville, Haws compiled an impressive 65-9-2 dual record, won three MIAC conference titles (1971, '72, '73), two National Catholic Titles (1971, '72), produced 16 MIAC Conference Champions, 11 National Catholic Champions, 6 NAIA All-Americans and 1 NAIA National Champion. Sadly, he died of a massive heart attack while the team was competing in Cleveland, Ohio, for the National Catholic Championships. He was just 49 years old. At the time of his death, he held the nation's longest dual meet streak of 51 consecutive victories, which currently ranks third among all wrestling programs Division I, II, III. Haws' coaching career, both collegiate and high school, spanned 26 years.

He was one of the founding fathers of the sport, and at the time of his death (February 2, 1973), he had coached wrestling longer than any other coach in the history of Minnesota.

Well liked and greatly respected by his peers, Haws, was intense on the mat, but a great guy off of it. One funny story about the former coach came a year before Haws died, when he suffered a heart attack during a meet against Augsburg. He later spent a month in the St. Cloud hospital, where he lost more than 60 pounds in recovery. In the midst of it all his wife asked him who he would want his pallbearers to be at his funeral if he didn't pull through. Haws, very weak and tired, immediately perked up and responded, "The Augsburg wrestlers, they were the ones who almost killed me!"

With a legacy still going strong in the lives of those he touched, Haws was survived by his wife and nine children.

ST. JOHN'S RECORD BOOK

Saint John's M.I.A.C. Champions (1948-2003)

Year	Name	Weight
1948	John Weimerskirch	147
1949	John Weimerskirch	147
	Norman McDonnel	157
	Ted Burgraff	177
1951	Jim McKeown	137
	John Weimerskirch	147*
	George Pribyl	177
1952	Fred Grant	130
	Jim McKeown	137
	John Weimerskirch	147
	Clem Schoenbauer	Hwt
1953	Jerry Miller	123
	Fred Grant	130
	Jim McKeown*	137
	Leo Kemper	177
	Bob Foster	Hwt
1954	Louis Adderly	130
	Otto "Sy" Weber	147
	DeVaughn Nelson	157
	Tom Kemply	167
	Jim Tachney	177
	Leo Kemper	Hwt
1955	Don Flynn	137
	DeVaughn Nelson	157
	Jim Tachney	177
1956	Don Flynn	137
	Mike Gibbs	147
	Lawrence Betzler	157
	Devaughn Nelson	167
1957	John O'Fallon	167
1958	Gary Sauer	123
	Lawrence Betzler	147
1959	Gary Sauer	123
	Tom Brudos	130
	Jerry Dalseth	137
	Lawrence Betzler	147
1960	Pat Murtaugh	157
	Jim Kuelbs*	167
1961	Ben Pulkrabek	191
1962	Tony Leifeld	123
	John Fruth	130
	John Fritz	147
	Ben Pulkrabek	Hwt
1964	Don Schreifels	177
1965	Don Schreifels	177
	Maury Neifeld	191
1967	Bob Westby	123
	Pat Beyer	137
1969	Gary Svendsen	115
1970	Gary Svendsen	118
	Henery Wollmering	134
1971	Terry Elfering	118
	Tom Svendsen	126
	Gary Svendsen	134
	Denis Legatt	158
	Jerry Workman	167
	Tom Miller	190
1972	Terry Elfering	118
	Joe Hayes	142
1973	Terry Elfering	118
	Tom Svendsen	134
	Joe Hayes	142
	Dave Pulkrabek	158
	Al Bielat	177
1974	Jay Huffman	118
	Tom Svendsen	134
	Larry Osterhaus	158
	Jerry Workman	190
	Greg Miller	Hwt
1975	Greg Miller	Hwt
1976	John Shimshack	150
1982	Jim Goodman	167
1985	John Schletty	167
1986	Dave Barthel	118
1987	Dave Barthel	118
1991	Scott Fernholz	142
1992	Scott Fernholz	142
1994	Jason Scherber	158
	Chris Grothe	190
1995	Dan Tschudi	142
	Rich Schneckenberger	158
	Jason Scherber*	167
	Chris Grothe	190
1997	Dan Tschudi	150
	Matt Ryan*	158
	John Newman	167
1998	John Newman*	167
	Brandon Novak	190
2000	Jeremy Abfalter	165
2001	Brandon Novak*	197

MIAC Outstanding Wrestler

Most Career Victories

#	Name	Record	Years
1.	Matt Ryan	143-48-0	1993-97
2.	Rich Schneckenberger	140-30-0	1990-95
3.	Dan Tschudi	126-30-0	1993-97
4.	Jason Scherber	124-37-0	1991-95
5.	Andy Lien	116-26-0	1994-98
6.	Scott Fernholz	114-42-1	1989-92
7.	John Newman	101-28-0	1995-99
8.	Brandon Novak	101-15-0	1997-01
9.	Chris Boys	100-46-0	1991-95
10.	Chuck Chmielewski	91-47-0	1984-88
	Chuck Griffith	91-55-0	1999-03

Match Career Points

#	Name	Points	Years
1.	Rich Schneckenberger	1,358 pts.	1990-95
2.	Dan Tschudi	1,253 pts.	1993-97
3.	Matt Ryan	1,078 pts.	1993-97
4.	Chuck Chmielewski	1,058 pts.	1984-88
5.	Jason Scherber	972 pts.	1991-95
6.	Mike Timm	955 pts.	1997-00
7.	Brandon Novak	910 pts.	1997-01
8.	John Newman	898 pts.	1995-99
9.	Jose Del Moral	864 pts.	1987-91
10.	Andy Lien	837 pts.	1994-98

JOHN ELTON

John Elton grew up in the Twin Cities and graduated from Bloomington Lincoln High School in 1976. There, Elton placed second at the Minnesota State High School Wrestling Tournament as a 145-pounder. As a collegiate wrestler, Elton was a four-year standout for the Johnnies and captured a National Catholic Championship during his senior season. Elton also qualified for the NCAA tournament at 150-pounds in 1979 and 1980 as well as at the NAIA tournament in 1977 and 1978. Elton would go on to graduate with honors from St. John's in 1980 and then got into coaching. He would take over at his alma mater that next year and make history along the way.

Elton would coach at St. John's for the next 23 seasons, achieving tremendous success along the way. In 1981, Elton posted a modest 4-5-1 record. Since that season, SJU has never dropped below .500 and it has won 10 or more dual meets 18 times. In 2004, SJU finished with a 12-4 dual record and finished third at the NCAA Great Lakes Regional, with three wrestlers advancing to the NCAA Championships. At the national level, SJU has qualified athletes to the NCAA Division III tournament in 19 of the past 20 seasons, including 19 NCAA All-Americans and 29 Scholar All-Americans. Elton retired following the 2004 season with an impressive 273-100-5 dual meet record. In addition, his teams have posted an impressive .729 winning percentage during his tenure as well. For his efforts, Elton has been named MIAC Coach-of-the-Year in 1984, 1993, 1995 and 1997. At the national level, SJU has qualified athletes to the NCAA Division III tournament in 18 of the past 19 seasons, including 18 NCAA All-Americans and 26 Scholar All-Americans.

Although Elton stepped down as the program's head coach in 2004, he will remain involved as an assistant coach. In addition, he will also remain employed at St. John's, working in the position of Master Gardener. John and his wife Joan presently reside in St. Cloud and have two children.

St. Olaf

St. Olaf College began its wrestling program back in the late 1940s, when the Minnesota Intercollegiate Athletic Conference came into existence. The program fared well early on, winning what would prove to be its only MIAC crown in 1951. In addition, the Oles have had one NCAA Division II individual champion over the years, Dave Schmidt, who won the 177-pound division back in 1964. Countless others would achieve success with the program as both individuals and as members of outstanding teams.

Head Coach Ken Pratt has been with the Oles for 14 years and joined the St. Olaf staff after working with the legendary Rummy Macias at Mankato State for two years as an assistant. Pratt, who wrestled collegiately at Cornell College, in Mt. Vernon, IA., won three Midwest Conference championships for the Rams, and was a three time national qualifier. With the Oles, Pratt has made solid strides and was awarded for his efforts by being named as the MIAC Coach of the Year in 1996 season. He has also done a lot of work with Minnesota USA Wrestling, serving the organization's Cultural Exchange Director, and also the team leader for the 1997 Minnesota Storm Cultural Exchange Team which traveled to Sweden.

Pratt's top assistant in Northfield is Pete Sandberg, who competed at Winona State from 1966-70 and finished 6th in the NAIA nationals, 3rd in the Midlands and wrestled in two NCAA Division I Championships. Sandberg's previous coaching experience came at Winona State, Buena Vista College, Rosemount High School, and with several clubs as well. Sandberg has also served as a director of Minnesota USA Wrestling and as cultural exchange director, even leading Minnesota teams on trips to France, Russia and South Africa.

In 2003 the Oles finished sixth out of the 16 teams in the NCAA regional. They were led by first year wrestlers Jason Moore, who was the champion at 165, Skipp Sandberg, who placed sixth at 174, Ryan Jacobson, who finished fifth at 133, and Tony Rezac, who finished fifth at 141. The Oles were paced by two-time national qualifier and NCAA postgraduate scholarship recipient Alex Morf. who finished fifth at 149 as well.

Furthermore, it was recently announced that the 2005 NCAA Division III Wrestling Championship will be on the campus of St. Olaf in Northfield. The competition will be held in the St. Olaf Tostrud Center Fieldhouse, with the connecting Skoglund Fieldhouse as the site with workout and warm-up mats throughout the championship.

"We are excited about all of this, but especially being able to help showcase the great Division III wrestling in the upper Midwest," said Sandberg. "Minnesota wrestling fans will really enjoy getting to see wrestling powerhouse, Augsburg College, as they always hit their peak for this meet. St. Olaf, Saint John's, and Concordia all have quality athletes who will be in the hunt for qualifying spots in 2005. With the addition of the Wisconsin and Iowa Conferences, it should be a great couple of days of wrestling."

St. Thomas

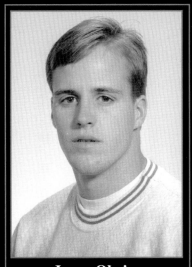

Tim Krieger

St. Thomas, like so many other schools, was forced to eliminate its intercollegiate wrestling program in April of 2001 as part of several university-wide budget cuts. The program had a rich history, however, going all the way back to the inception of the MIAC. Perhaps the biggest highlights of the Tommy program came in 1981 and 1986, when they managed to dethrone powerhouse Augsburg to win their only two MIAC team titles. They would later achieve success on the national level when they finished third at the 1991 NCAA D-III championships with just three wrestlers, nonetheless. One of them, Jason O'Brien, who competed at 118 pounds, became the Tommies' first wrestler to win an individual national championship. Incidentally, Jason's brothers, Andy and Joel, also wrestled for STU, with Joel emerging as a two-time NCAA runner-up in both 1996 and 1997.

The program was later blessed to have a couple of elite level coaches as well, including three-time U.S. Olympic Greco-Roman wrestler Dan Chandler, who later went on to become the U.S. Olympic Greco-Roman head coach in 2000 and an assistant in both 1992 and 2004. Then, in the mid-1990s, former Iowa State All-American Tim Krieger, who won a pair of NCAA titles with the Cyclones, took over.

Jason Obrien

Coach Dan Chandler

BUCKY MAUGHAN

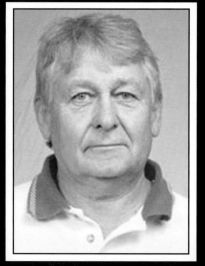

Arthur "Bucky" Maughan grew up in Canonsburg, PA, where he was the state high school champion and owned a string of 70 consecutive prep victories. From there, he went on to wrestle at Indiana University, but later transferred to Moorhead State University, where he competed in the 115-pound category. There, Maughan became the only Dragon to ever win a Division I individual National Championship, when he did so in 1963 by pinning Gil Sanchez of Colorado State University in the finals of the 115-pound class. Maughan also won a pair of NAIA national championship at 123 pounds as well.

Maughan then went on to coach at North Dakota State University in 1964, where he would become a legend. In fact, he is still going strong. Maughan, only the second wrestling coach in the school's history, has gone on to guide the Bison to a 394-112-11 record over the past 39 years, including four NCAA Division II National Championships (1988, 1998, 2000 and 2001) along the way. In addition, the Bison have captured five second-place national finishes (1972, 1982, 1983, 1992, 2002) and six third-place finishes (1973, 1984, 1987, 1989, 1993, 1995) as well. In all, Maughan's teams have finished in the top 10 of the nation 31 times. That includes a string of 15 straight years that was ended in 1996 as the Bison finished 13th. NDSU has also recorded 26 finishes in the top five.

The NDSU wrestling program has taken giant strides under Maughan and has recorded 35 consecutive winning seasons during his tenure. The Bison have also won a total of 16 NCC titles during his tenure, including nine straight from 1982-1990 — the second longest championship streak in any sport in the North Central Conference history.

Among his many coaching honors and accolades, Maughan is member of the Dragon, NAIA, NSIC and Division II Wrestling Halls of Fame. Furthermore, in 2003 he was inducted into the National Wrestling Hall of Fame in Stillwater, Okla. Maughan is also a past member of the executive committee of the National Wrestling Coaches Association and is a past president of the NCAA Division II Coaches Association as well.

Maughan and his wife, Leota, have two sons, Jack and Bret. Both followed in their father's athletic footsteps. Jack was a two-time Division II All-American wrestler for the Bison and is currently the head coach at Northern Colorado. Bret was a two-time All-American and national runner-up at 118 pounds for the Bison in 1991 and is currently an assistant to his father.

Minnesota State University, Moorhead

Minnesota State University, Moorhead has had a rich wrestling heritage over the years, and first gained national prominence back in the 1960s. Head Coach Bill Garland led his Dragons to six NCAA Division I tournaments as well as six NAIA Collegiate Championships during that magical decade. In fact, the Dragons reached the pinnacle of college wrestling in 1964, when they won the National Association of Intercollegiate Athletics (NAIA) National Championship at Spearfish, SD. Undefeated in dual meet competition, Moorhead State captured three individual titles by Jim Dreitzler at 130, Frank Mosier at 167, and heavyweight Bob Billberg. Bucky Maughan, meanwhile, who had become the first, and only, division one champ in school history by winning the 115 pound title at the 1963 NCAA Division I National Championships, wound up in second in 1964. For his efforts, Bill Garland was named as the NAIA's National Wrestling Coach of the Year.

Billberg was one of the greats of this era. In addition to winning the NAIA crown in 1963, he also went on to qualify for the NCAA Division I National Championships as well, finishing second to Joe James of Oklahoma State University, in a match that was televised on ABC Wide World of Sports. Earlier, Billberg stunned defending national champion Jim Nance of Syracuse University, 2-1, in the semifinals, ending Nance's string of 78 consecutive victories. Billberg, who would go on to become enshrined into the NAIA Hall of Fame, later added another NCAA I runner-up finish in 1966 as a senior.

As a result of MSU's outstanding success, the entire Northern Intercollegiate Conference benefited, and with that the other member schools began recruiting higher quality kids. The program would go through a lot of ups and downs through the ensuing years but remained solid. Then, in 1988, the program got a new coach by the name of John Sterner, who had wrestled collegiately at South Dakota State University and had been coaching high school wrestling in South Dakota for more than 20 years. Sterner hit the ground running at MSU and his teams would go on to capture six consecutive Northern Sun Intercollegiate Conference championships during a remarkable run from 1995-2000, and made a lot of noise on the regional and national levels during that time as well. In 1997 MSU placed 11th at the NCAA II nationals. Then, in 1999 MSU earned its sixth straight NSIC title — also placing third in the North Central regional tournament, and sending five wrestlers to the 2000 NCAA Division II Championships.

In 15 years of

Bill Garland

Bob Billberg & Maughan

MSU-MOORHEAD RECORD BOOK

NATIONAL CHAMPIONS

NCAA DIVISION I
1963 - Bucky Maughan (115)

NCAA DIVISION II
1997 - Nate Hendrickson (167)

NAIA
1962, 1963	Bucky Maughan (123)
1964, 1966	Bob Billberg (HWT)
1966, 1967	Rick Stuyvesant (137)
1964, 1967	Frank Mosier (167)
1961	Earl Stottler (123)
1964	Jim Dreitzler (134)

NSIC
2002 - Scott Larson (141), Josh Jansen (157), Luke Duffy (165), Mike Richards (174)
2001 - Scott Larson (141), Mike Richards (165), Travis Nagel (174)
2000 - Tom Grafstrom (125), Scott Larson (133), Pete Dickenson (149), Travis Nagel (174), Erik Johnson (184)
1999 - Tom Grafstrom (125), Scott Larson (133), Dwight Ballou (141), Pete Dickenson (149), Jason Thompson (157), Jeff Deibel (165), Travis Nagel (174), Erik Johnson (184)
1998 - Tom Grafstrom (118), Brad Weigandt (126), Dwight Ballou (141), Tom Ritchie (150), Nate Hendrickson (167), Chad Churchill (HWT)
1997 - Rob Wagner (126), Nate Hendrickson (167), Tyler Trieglaff (190)
1996 - Mike Manger (126), Nate Hendrickson (158), Thad Handrick (167), Tyler Trieglaff (190)
1995 - Jason Sjostrom (134), Nate Hendrickson (158), Thad Handrick (167), Keenan Spiess (177), Tyler Trieglaff (190)
1994 - Joey Andreason (126), Jason Sjostrom (134), Bobby Olson (190)
1993 - Bobby Olson (190)
1992 - Thad Handrick (158)
1991 - Jason Sjostrom (134), Bill Welder (150)
1990 - Jayme Paquin (134), Bill Welder (150), Steve Ricard (167)
1986 - Al Foltz (142)
1985 - Greg Lofteness (167), Daryl Tysdal (HWT)
1984 - Daryl Tysdal (HWT)
1983 - Joe Gaughan (134)
1977 - Rhett Hilzendeger (126), Jim Jones (158)
1975 - Tom Lenihan (126)
1974 - Lyle Freudenberg (150)
1973 - Steve Borders (134), Bob Bowlsby (167)
1972 - Al Goeden (177)
1970 - John Sigfrid (177)
1969 - John Morley (115), Bill Germann (130), Bob Hall (152), Bill Henderson (191)
1968 - Bill Germann (130), Mike Fitzgerald (137), Rick Stuyvesant (145), Bob Hall (152)
1967 - Bill Germann (130), Rick Stuyvesant (145), Frank Mosier (167)
1966 - Snowbound, unable to compete
1965 - Rick Stuyvesant (130), Wally Ott (137), Raphael Gonshorowski (145), Henry Conley (152), Dick Miller (167), Bob Billberg (HWT)

1964 - Raphael Gonshorowski (137), Bob Billberg (HWT)
1963 - Rick Kelvington (115), Frank Mosier (167), John Dana (HWT)
1962 - Banks Swan (115), Bucky Maughan (123)
1961 - Banks Swan (115)
1960 - Bill Cronen (167)

PLACEWINNERS
NCAA Division I
1969 - John Morley (115, 5th)
1967 - Rick Stuyvesant (137, 6th)
1966 - Bob Billberg (HWT, 2nd)
1965 - Rick Kelvington (123, 5th)
1964 - Bob Billberg (HWT, 2nd)
1963 - Bucky Maughan (115, 1st)

NCAA Division II
2001 - Travis Nagel (174, 6th)
2000 - Pete Dickinson (149, 8th)
1999 - Dwight Ballou (141, 8th), Pete Dickinson (149, 8th)
1998 - Nate Hendrickson (167, 6th)
1997 - Nate Hendrickson (167, 1st), Tyler Trieglaff (190, 7th)
1996 - Nate Hendrickson (158, 4th)
1981 - Joe Gaughan (134, 8th)
1978 - John Lind (190, 7th)
1977 - Rhett Hilzendeger (126, 3rd)
1971 - Jim Gildersleeve (158, 6th)
1970 - John Sigfrid (177, 5th)
1969 - John Morley (115, 2nd), Jim Gildersleeve (160, 4th), Mike Fitzgerald (145, 4th), Bill Henderson (191, 6th)

NAIA
1995 - Jason Sjostrom (134, 3rd), Nate Hendrickson (158, 3rd), Levi Hillmer (HWT, 8th)
1994 - Jason Sjostrom (134, 3rd), Bobby Olson (190, 4th), Joey Andreasen (126, 6th)
1993 - Bobby Olson (190, 4th), Christian Ochsendorf (HWT, 4th), Joey Andreason (134, 6th), Keenan Spiess (167, 8th)
1991 - Jack Goodhart (HWT, 6th)
1985 - Daryl Tysdal (HWT, 5th), Allan Foltz (134, 6th), Justin Birkelo (118, 7th)
1968 - Rick Stuyvesant (145, 2nd), Bill Henderson (191, 3rd)
1967 - Rick Stuyvesant (137, 1st), Frank Mosier (177, 1st), Rick Kelvington (123, 4th), Bill Germann (130, 3rd), Mike Fitzgerald (145, 4th), Bill Henderson (191, 6th)
1966 - Rick Stuyveasant (137, 1st), Bob Billberg (HWT, 1st), Bill Germann (130, 3rd), Dick Redfoot (152, 3rd), Frank Mosier (167, 4th), Raphael Gonshorowski (145, 6th)
1965 - Raphael Gonshorowski (145, 2nd), Bob Billberg (HWT, 3rd), John Morley (115, 4th), Rick Stuyvesant (137, 6th), Dick Miller (167, 6th)
1964 - Jim Dreitzler (130, 1st), Frank Mosier (167, 1st), Bob Billberg (HWT, 1st), Bucky Maughan (123, 2nd), Raphael Gonshorowski (137, 4th), Don Pate (147, 5th)
1963 - Bucky Maughan (123, 1st), Raphael Gonshorowski (130, 5th)
1962 - Bucky Maughan (123, 1st), John Dano (HWT, 3rd)
1961 - Earl Stottler (123, 1st), Banks Swan (115, 2nd)
1960 - Bill Cronen (167, 2nd)
1959 - Rufus Bankole (123, 4th), Henry Hettwer (191, 4th), Ron Wiger (HWT, 4th)

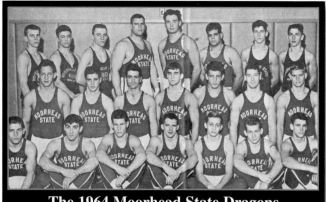
The 1964 Moorhead State Dragons

collegiate coaching, John recorded an impressive 149-96-2 career mark. In addition to his dual meet success, the Dragons flourished in post-season competition as well, dispatching 54 representatives to NAIA National Championships and 21 to NCAA Division II showdowns. The Dragons also garnered 24 All-American awards, including a national championship and nine Academic All-America recipients. In addition, John, whose twin brother Mike coached wrestling at Southwest State University from 1969-98, also spent 10 years as an assistant with the football Dragons as well.

Sterner then passed the torch to Keenan Spiess, who had spent the last four seasons as the head coach of Fargo North High School.. A native of Fargo, Spiess was named an NAIA honorable mention All-American as a sophomore and junior with the Dragons, and qualified for the national tournament again as a senior. A transfer from North Dakota State University and a tri-captain of the 1995

THE STERNER BROTHERS

The Sterner brothers are practically wrestling royalty in the Land of 10,000 Lakes. Known for their intensity and competitiveness, they have become legendary figures in the world of Minnesota wrestling. Here is their story: Mike & John Sterner, twin brothers, were born in Sheridan, Wyo., and raised in Sioux Falls, S.D. They then went on to star in football, wrestling and track, graduating from Boys Town (Neb.) High School in 1957. From there, the two wound up together at South Dakota State University, where they both played football and wrestled.

At SDSU Mike played right guard and nose tackle in football and wrestled at 177 pounds. He was named the 1961 North Central Conference Most Valuable Lineman and was a co-captain of the 1961 squad which finished 8-2 and tied the University of Northern Iowa for the NCC championship. Mike was also named as the Jackrabbits' Most Valuable Wrestler following both his junior and senior seasons.

John, meanwhile, went into the Army after high school, and then went on to join Mike at SDSU a year later. There, he lettered three times in football and wrestling, and was an All-North Central Conference selection in both sports as a senior.

From there, Mike, who is older than John by 15 minutes, first taught and coached at the Flandreau (S.D.) Indian School, then returned to South Dakota State as a graduate assistant in football and wrestling. He completed his master's degree at SDSU and then moved north, teaching and coaching three years at Hettinger, N.D. Mike then came to Southwest State University in 1969 to serve as the head wrestling coach from 1969-98. At SSU, Mike coached 47 NAIA and NCAA All-Americans, including two NAIA National Champions and one NCAA II National Champion. His Mustangs won six NIC Championships, achieved several top 10 finishes in the NAIA meet, and posted a 255-206 record during his tenure. In addition, Mike was named NIC Coach of the Year seven time and was inducted into the NAIA Hall of fame in 1991 as well. Mike also coached 17 years of Mustang football, including four as the head coach from 1973-76. Mike would later get his doctorate from BYU and serve as the chairman of SSU's Department of Health and Physical Education.

Mike and his wife, Karen, an assistant professor of education at SSU, have two children, Michelle and John. John, meanwhile, is SSU's only national champion in wrestling, winning the 190-pound division in 1989. He also played four years of football at SSU and was a key member of the 1987 team which earned the school's first NAIA Division I playoff berth as well. John would later serve as his father's assistant coach, and ultimately take over as the head coach at SSU — where he presently remains.

Brother John, meanwhile, first started out coaching as a graduate assistant back at SDSU for one year, and then began his teaching and coaching career in 1963 at Chariton (Iowa) High School. There, he led his team to a third place finish at the 1964 Iowa State High School Wrestling Tournament. John later coached St. Mary's High School in New England, N.D, to the 1969 North Dakota State Class B Championship, and was honored as North Dakota State Class B Coach of the Year that season as well. John would build a stellar five-year prep dual meet record of 71-7-0 at the school. John later moved to Stevens High School in Rapid City, S.D, that next year to serve as the school's head football coach. Three years later he joined the South Dakota Tech staff and served as wrestling coach for four seasons, posting a 24-8-0 mark, before the sport was discontinued. In 1978 John accepted a teaching and coaching position in the public school system in Rapid City. Ten years later, he came to MSU Moorhead, where he took over the Dragon Wrestling team in 1988.

John hit the ground running at MSU and his teams would go on to capture six consecutive Northern Sun Intercollegiate Conference championships during a remarkable run from 1995-2000, and made a lot of noise on the regional and national levels during that time as well. In 1997 MSU placed 11th at the NCAA II nationals. Then, in 1999 MSU earned their sixth straight NSIC title — also placing third in the North Central regional tournament, and sending five wrestlers to the 2000 NCAA Division II Championships. In 15 years of collegiate coaching, John recorded an impressive 149-96-2 career mark. In addition to his dual meet success, the Dragons flourished in post-season competition as well, dispatching 54 representatives to NAIA National Championships and 21 to NCAA Division II showdowns. The Dragons also garnered 24 All-American awards, including a national championship and nine Academic All-America recipients. In addition, John also spent 10 years as an assistant with the football Dragons as well. John and his wife JoAnn have one daughter, Kay.

squad, Spiess claimed the NSIC 167-pound crown in 1995 as well. While the NSIC no longer offers a team championship in wrestling, the Dragons will compete in the NCAA Division II regional and national tournaments. In all, MSU Moorhead has produced 12 individual national champions, including 167-pound Nate Hendrickson, the NCAA Division II National Wrestler of the Year in 1997. After two tantalizing near misses, Hendrickson, a Menahga native who grew up on a dairy farm as one of 12 kids, found the third trip to the national wrestling tournament to be the charm when he captured the NCAA Division II 167-pound title in 1997. Hendrickson's heroics lifted Moorhead State to 11th place on the final team standings, MSU's loftiest finish at an NCAA Division II national tourney since a fifth place showing back in 1969. Hendrickson secured All-American honors for a third straight year as a junior and became the first Dragon to win a national title since Frank Mosier in 1967.

Perhaps Bucky Maughan, who had a front row seat to watch Hendrickson's historic 9-1 victory over Jerod Quincy of Central Missouri State in the championship match, said it best: "I'm very happy for him. He looked great in the finals, and I told him he made a real believer out of me. I'm happy to see him lead MSU back to respectability on the national level. That's what you need, a star, and others will follow."

Southwest Minnesota State University

When you think of Southwest Minnesota State University wrestling, one name immediately comes to mind, Sterner. Why? Because for the last 35 years there has been a Sterner serving as the program's head coach. And, while Coach Mike retired in 1998, his son John was right there to take the torch and keep it burning brightly.

Mike Sterner came to Southwest State University in 1969 after graduating from South Dakota State University, where he both wrestled and played football. From there, he taught and coached at the high school level, before heading to SMSU in Marshall. There, Mike would build up the wrestling program and turn it into one of Minnesota's finest. Over his illustrious 30 year career at SMSU, Mike coached 47 NAIA and NCAA All-Americans, including two NAIA National Champions and one NCAA II National Champion. His Mustangs won six NIC Conference Championships, achieved several top 10 finishes in the NAIA meet, and posted a 255-206 record during his tenure. SMSU also finished 7th in 1989, 8th in 1986, 9th in 1991 and 10th in 1984 at the NAJA national championships under his watch as well.

A few of the stars of that era was Bill McDonald, SMSU's only four-time All-American (1986-89); Leon Bullerman, who captured the NAIA national title at the 158-pound class in 1991; and Coach Sterner's son, John, who also won an NAIA national title, his coming in the 190 pound division in 1989. When it was time to step down, Mike, who also coached 17 years of Mustang football, passed the torch to his son, John. (Incidentally, John was named for Mike's identical twin brother of the same name who just happened to be the wrestling coach at UM-Morris.) The seven-time NIC Coach of the Year and NAIA Hall of famer couldn't have been prouder.

John Sterner

John, meanwhile, who also played four years of football at SMSU, was anxious to dive in and hit the ground running. He had previously served as his father's assistant coach for several years and was ready to make a name for himself. With that, he took over in 1998 and found immediate success when 190-pounder Link Steffen became the program's first NCAA Division II national champion that same year. From there, John recruited hard and worked even harder. His efforts paid off three years later when he led his Mustangs to the NSIC championship in 2001. He had officially arrived. John continues to keep his father's legacy alive and is poised for even bigger and better things down the road.

University of Minnesota, Morris

The University of Minnesota, Morris wrestling program was, like so many other small college programs of late, sadly put to sleep in 2004. The school had a very proud history and tradition, however, dating back to the 1960s, when they won their first two Pioneer Conference titles in 1964 and 1965. Douglas Dufty, a Fergus Falls native, who won four MIAC titles at Concordia College, then took over as Morris' head wrestling coach at in 1969. Under Dufty the team went on to capture a trio of Northern Intercollegiate Conference titles from 1979-81. The team qualified for the NCAA Division III Championships five times from 1979-82 and in 1980 had its best finish ever, placing fourth in the Finals.

Dufty was a two time NIC Coach of the Year and NCAA Division III National Coach of the Year in 1981 as well. During his 11-year tenure, his teams posted 100 dual wins and four top 10 finishes in the NCAA Division III National Wrestling Championships. Those years produced three NCAA Division III National Champions as well as 17 NCAA All Americans, of which two went on to be members of the U.S. Olympic Wrestling teams — Dennis and Duane Koslowski. The Koslowski brothers were without question the biggest things to hit the UM-Morris campus in quite some time. The two would literally put the school on the national wrestling map by going on to become two of the most decorated wrestlers in American history. While Dennis won a pair of national championships in 1980 and 1982, Duane won one of his own in 1981. Both would go on to compete on the national and international stage, making Minnesota proud every step of the way.

The team qualified for the NCAA

The Koslowski Brothers

Bill McDonald

DOUG REESE

Doug Reese grew up in Geneva, IL, and went on to wrestle at Northern Michigan University. From there, Reese went on to win a silver medal in the 1993 Master's World Freestyle Championships in Toronto at 130 kilos. Reese later got into coaching and took over as the head coach at Morris in 1990. He would guide the team for 14 seasons, before losing his program in 2003. Reese, who taught in the Wellness, Sports Science Department at Morris, is known worldwide for his scientific approach to training, along with developing strong mental skills in his athletes. Reese has produced 25 national champions, 122 All-Americans, 31 Academic All-Americans, 16 U.S. National Team members, and 10 U.S. World Team Members.

Reese, who is also a member of the USA Wrestling national coaching staff, served for eight years on the Board of Directors of USA Wrestling, the National Governing Body of Wrestling in the United States. During his term of service, Reese was Chairperson of the Women's Wrestling Committee, and also served on the Coaches Council Executive Board, the International Exchange Committee, and the Steering Committee. Reese is also a current member of the U.S. National Freestyle Wrestling Coaching Staff. Reese has made 14 trips overseas to Europe and Latin America coaching elite U.S. teams. In addition, Reese has coached in five world championships as well as the Pan-Am Championships in the past seven years. Reese was even the fourth coach in the United States to earn Gold Level Coaching Certification from USA Wrestling.

Reese is also executive director of To The Next Level, a non-profit organization committed to helping athletes and coaches reach their true potential on and off the field of play. TTNL runs camps and clinics and is currently using Olympic Solidarity grants from the International Olympic Committee to teach sports management training, and to teach coaches how to coach affectively. Reese also served as the Assistant to the Athletic Director at UMM, and is the faculty sponsor of the Fellowship of Christian Athlete huddle on campus.

Reese was also instrumental in establishing Morris as the first college in the nation to sponsor women's wrestling as an official varsity sport. And, while it too was eliminated by school officials in 2004, Reese coached and developed a total of 113 women All-Americans at the Junior, University and Senior levels. In the process a total of 16 women had qualified to make the U.S. National Team, while 10 UM-Morris wrestlers have represented the U.S. while competing in the World Championships as well. In addition, Reese has led his women wrestlers to top place finishes in every tournament in which UM-Morris competed, including a total of seven national championships. A real pioneer in the sport, in addition to serving as the Chairperson of USA Wrestling's Women's Wrestling Committee, Reese and also served as a coach and administrator for Women's Team USA on many national and international tournaments. Winners of four University National Team Championships, it was a sad day for Minnesota wrestling when Morris turned out the lights on the Lady Cougars.

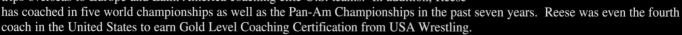

Division III Championships in 1986 and continued to have solid success throughout the decade of the '80s. In 1990 Doug Reese took over as the team's head coach and during his tenure at Morris he would produce 25 national champions, 122 All-Americans, 31 Academic All-Americans, 16 U.S. National Team members and 10 U.S. World Team Members. The team had its best ever finish at the NCAA Division II National Championships in 1999 when they took 26th that year, also finishing 18th in the NAIA as well. Leading the charge for Morris was All-American B. J. Friedrichs, who placed 6th at 177 pounds.

Reese was also instrumental in establishing Morris as the first program in Minnesota to offer women's college wrestling. And, while it too was eliminated by school officials in 2004, Reese has coached and developed a total of 113 women All-Americans at the Junior, University, and Senior level. In the process a total of 16 women had qualified to make the U.S. National Team, while 10 UM-Morris wrestlers have represented the United States while competing in the World

Dante Lewis

Championships. In addition, Reese has led his women wrestlers to top place finishes in every tournament in which UM-Morris competed, including a total of seven national championships.

UM-Morris Records

Most Points Scored in a Match - 40, Wilbur Borrero, 1978
Best Season Record - 40-3, Kevin LeClair, 1979-80; Dante Lewis, 2002-03
Longest Winning Streak - 29, Kevin LeClair, 1978-79
Most Victories in a Season - 46, Randy Rager, 1999-2000
Most Career Victories - 162, Randy Rager, 1996-2000 (Winningest Wrestler in NCAA History - tied with Randy Lewis of the University of Iowa)
100 Career Wins – (162) Randy Rager, (125) Kip Lynk, (112) Kirby Frank, (110) Tom Beyer, (106) B.J. Friedrichs, (105) Matt Bisek, (102) Paul Court
Most Conference Titles - 3, Dante Lewis (2001-03); Tom Beyer (1978-81); Jeff Merritt 1980-82)
Most All-American Titles - 3, Dennis Koslowski (1978, 1980, 1982); Tom Hanson (1979, 1980, 1982); Jim Williamson (1985, 1987, 1988)

NCAA Division III National Champions
1986 - Greg Dravis (118)
1982 - Dennis Koslowski (Hwt)
1981 - Duane Koslowski (Hwt)
1980 - Dennis Koslowski (190)
1979 - Tom Beyer (176)

University of Minnesota Duluth

Despite the fact that the University of Minnesota Duluth's wrestling program got eliminated in 1996, the grappling Bulldogs made a lot of noise in their three decades of mat action. The main man behind all but five of those 30 years was Head coach Neil Ladsten, who racked up a solid 172-141-4 career record while leading the Bulldogs to six Northern Sun Intercollegiate Conference crowns. In addition, UMD produced 19 All-Americans during that time, including 158-pounder Mike Hirschey of Glenwood, the only Bulldog to ever win a national individual title, when he did so at the 1987 NAIA Championships in West Liberty, VA.

The late 1970s and early '80s were among the best for the Dogs. From 1979-83, UMD went 41-11-0 in dual meets and was anchored by the likes of NCAA II All-Americans Jim Paddock, a 150 pounder out of St. Paul (1980), John Heisick, a 190 pounder out of Bloomington (1981), Jerry Hoy, a 118 pounder out of Apple Valley (1982) and Phil Sowers, a 150 pounder out of Staples (1983).

Of the aforementioned, Hoy certainly ranks among the most prolific wrestlers to ever throw on a UMD singlet. He posted an awesome 103-18-1 individual tally (.848%) during his tenure in the Port City and captained the Bulldogs to their first-ever NSIC championship as a senior in 1982. That same year he attained All-America honors after placing second at the NCAA Division II Championships. Hoy, a member of both the NSIC and UMD Athletic Hall of Fames, is the only Bulldog to compete in an NCAA Division I event, accomplishing that feat at the 1982 championships in Ames, IA, where he finished the year as the 13th ranked 118 pounder in all of college wrestling. (Incidentally, Hoy would go on to become an Air Force pilot and flew dozens of combat support missions as part of Desert Storm. While in the Service, Hoy won a pair of U.S. Air Force individual championships in 1986 and 1987 and captured the 1987 Armed Forces title at 125.5 pounds as well. He presently lives in Markville, where he works as a realtor.)

Other wrestlers who made their mark at UMD would include the Dravis brothers, Blaine and Jeff, a pair of NAIA All-Americans from the mid 1980s whose father, Don, was the legendary wrestling coach at Staples High School; Trevor Lundgren, another Staples grad who earned NAIA All-American honors in both 1988 and 1989; and Hopkins High School alum Ron McClure, UMD's lone four-time NSIC individual titleholder, who earned a pair of NCAA D-II All-American honors.

Jerry Hoy

Mike Hirschey

Sean Perkins & Neil Ladsten

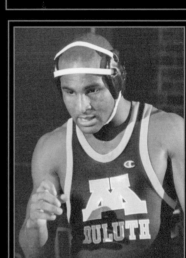

Ron McClure

BEMIDJI'S CHET ANDERSON

While Bemidji State University no longer offers wrestling, back in the day, Chet Anderson was synonymous with the program. Anderson grew up loving sports in White River, South Dakota. Anderson would become a football star at White River High School and then go on to play college football at the University of South Dakota, where he would eventually get his teaching degree. Just prior to graduating, however, Chet was called into active duty and spent five years overseas in World War II. There, he oversaw 130 men as an infantry company commander and even led his company into the occupation of Japan at the end of the war. At the onset of the war, while Chet was in Fort Ord, Calif., he played on a military football team with many players who had been playing in the NFL. He learned a great deal about the game while playing on the team, and many of those lessons would influence his coaching style years later. Anderson came home to finish college at USD after the war and from there he got his master's degree in education from the University of Minnesota.

Anderson's first teaching job, nine years after he started college, was at Anoka High School, where he coached football for four years and won a Suburban Conference title. From there, he taught two years in a parochial school in Iowa, and after that he came to Bemidji State in 1955. Anderson would teach physical education and health at BSU for 26 years, and coach everything from football to wrestling to tennis for the Beavers as well. While he had great success coaching football at BSU for 10 years, winning three conference titles from 1957-59 and posting a 43-34-5 career record, it was on the matt where Anderson became a real coaching legend. Anderson stepped aside as football coach following the 1965 season to concentrate on wrestling, where the Beavers were becoming a force among the nation's small colleges. Anderson guided the Beaver grapplers to several NAIA second-place finishes and coached four NAIA collegiate champions in 1971 (Bob Dettmer), 1975 (Bob Whelan), 1976 and 1978 (Kevin Kish — twice) as well. Dettmer, along with Pete Saxe (1970-73), were also four-time NIC Conference champs as well. His program also produced countless all-conference and all-Americans too. In all, Anderson coached wrestling at Bemidji State for 26 years and would coach wrestling for a total of 34 years before finally retiring in 1981. While Anderson was elected to the NAIA Wrestling Hall of Fame in 1975, his greatest honor, however, came in 1996, when the football stadium at Bemidji State was renamed as Chet Anderson Stadium in his honor.

HOW WOULD YOU DESCRIBE YOUR COACHING STYLE? "I think I was very honest and very organized. I would say my philosophy to the game stemmed from my desire to have my players understand how I wanted the game to be played in every way. I had a plan for each player and for where he was going and what he wanted to be. I was an officer in World War II and went through military training to become an infantry company commander, so that training really prepared me for coaching. I was very disciplined and expected the same from my kids. I wanted my teams to be very optimistic. I wanted them to leave the field at practice the night before a big game believing that they were going to win. I didn't want them to be overconfident, but I wanted them to put forth their best effort so we could win. I always wondered how you could say you were a good team if you always placed yourself as an underdog and every game you won was an upset. I was totally against the 'Gloomy Gus' approach."

HOW DID YOU BUILD TEAM UNITY & CHEMISTRY? "I think team unity comes from a loyalty to the school, a loyalty to the community and a loyalty to the team itself. So, I tried to build chemistry on my teams by being very honest and very focused on being something in life. I wanted them to have goals and then I wanted them to reach for those goals. I also wanted my team members to be friends and to bond together. That is where good team unity comes from. You just need to stress that the team comes first, no matter what, and individuals come second. Ideally, you try to build a setting which is like a family, with everyone working together towards a common goal. Captains were very important in building chemistry and I relied on them heavily."

WHAT ARE YOU MOST PROUD OF IN YOUR CAREER? "Aside from all of the great kids that I had in my programs through the years, I would say that my biggest thrill as far as on the field went was when we took the team down to South Dakota and beat my alma mater, the University of South Dakota, very soundly. That meant a great deal to me and was right up there."

WHAT MOTIVATED YOU? "My military experience was extraordinary. The dedication that you have to have is unlike anything else. You see, in the military sense, as a commanding officer you were responsible for your men and to your men. That was a 24 hour a day responsibility that truly motivated you to be the best you could be. I tried to carry that with me in life to always be strong and take care of my men."

WHAT ARE THE KEY INGREDIENTS TO CREATING A CHAMPIONSHIP TEAM? "First of all you have to have ability, and beyond that there has to be cohesiveness, friendships and loyalty. You know, I don't feel that teams really play for coaches. I feel that teams play for themselves, for their teammates, for their school and for their community. That binding of the individuals together is the main ingredient for winning I think."

WHAT'S THE SECRET TO YOUR SUCCESS? "I always felt that practice never ended on the practice field. So, after practice I would go through the locker room and compliment players and try to tell them things to work on for the future. That was important and it kept me in touch with the kids on a one-to-one basis. I also ran highly organized practices to utilize everyone's practice time to the fullest. There was no standing around for me, I wanted practice to be short, maybe an hour and a half, but very precise. I wrote out the plans on the bulletin board so every player knew what would take place that day and how much time would be spent doing each drill."

WHAT WOULD YOU WANT TO SAY TO YOUR FANS, BOOSTERS, AND ALUMNI WHO HAVE SUPPORTED YOU ALL THESE YEARS? "I always wanted the fans to see the game not in terms of wins and losses, rather I wanted them to appreciate the team effort. I hoped that they would cheer for our teams, not one individual at a time, but as a team — a whole unit. I always strived to have our teams represent our community and I wanted them to make the people very proud. So, thanks for all of their support, we appreciate it."

HOW DO YOU WANT YOUR COACHING EPITAPH TO READ — HOW DO YOU WANT TO BE REMEMBERED AS A COACH? "I would want to be remembered as somebody who was a role model. I always wanted to be a role model and I hope to be judged for that in every way. Maybe that was from my military background, but I always wanted to live a life that was exemplary and I wanted my team to respect me for that. In turn, I hope that many of them would live that way as well. I hope too that my kids knew that I was always concerned and cared for them, for their futures, and that I always considered them to be part of my family."

WINONA STATE UNIVERSITY

Jim Tanniehill

WINONA STATE WRESTLING RECORDS (1954-76)

CAREER WIN %

Jerry Wedemeier	(1958-62)	80-4-1	.947
Jim Tanniehill	(1965-67,68-70)	117-14-3	.884
John Zwolinski	(1964-67)	55-9-0	.859
Ray Wicks	(1965-68)	72-18-1	.797
Merle Sovereign	(1963-67)	50-16-1	.754

CAREER WINS

Jim Tanniehill	(1965-67, 68-70)	177
Jerry Wedemeier	(1958-62)	80
Bill Hitesman	(1968-72)	76
Ray Wicks	(1965-68)	72
Ernest Middleton	(1971-75)	61

FOUR-TIME NIC CHAMPIONS

Jerry Wedemeier	(1959-62)
Jim Tanniehill	(1966, 1967, 1969, 1970) 160, 160, 160, 158 (respectively)

NAIA CHAMPIONS

1959 First Place: Jerry Wedemeier	Heavyweight
1961 First Place: Jerry Wedemeier	Heavyweight
1962 First Place: Jerry Wedemeier	Heavyweight

Jerry Wedemeier

NAIA HALL OF FAME

Athletes

Barry Bennett, Concordia-Moorhead (Minn.), 1987
Bob Billberg, Moorhead State (Minn.), 1984
Frank Mosier, Moorhead State (Minn.), 1984
Robert "Bob" Dettmer, Bemidji State (Minn.), 1985
Mike Rybak, St. Cloud State (Minn.), 1995
Gary Smith, St. Cloud State (Minn.), 1981
Dave Hazewinkel, St. Cloud State (Minn.), 1978
James Hazewinkel, St. Cloud State (Minn.), 1975
Rick Stuyvesant, Moorhead State (Minn.), 1983
James Tanniehill, Winona State (Minn.), 1990
Jerry Wedemeier, Winona State (Minn.), 1972
Arthur Maughan, Moorhead State (Minn.), 1976
Robert Whelan, Bemidji State (Minn.), 1989

Coaches

Chester A. Anderson, Bemidji State (Minn.), 1975
Fran McCann, Winona State (Minn.), 1990
Rometo Macias, Mankato State (Minn.), 1980
Mike Sterner, Southwest State (Minn.), 1991

Meritorious Service

Bob Jones, Winona State (Minn.), 1977
Spencer Yohe, Hancock (Minn.), 1998

MINNESOTA COMMUNITY COLLEGE CONFERENCE

The Minnesota Community College Conference (MCC) is an important circuit for the development of kids wanting to play at the next level. Teams with wrestling programs, which were added to the circuits repertoire in 1969, in this conference include: Ridgewater College (Willmar), Minnesota West Community & Technical College (Worthington), Rochester Community & Technical College, Itasca Community College (Grand Rapids) and Dakota County Technical College (Apple Valley). The league, which falls under the jurisdiction of the National Junior College Athletic Association (NJCCA), gives countless kids an opportunity to get an education while still being able to play the sport they love. And, for many of those kids, it is a stepping stone along their way to competing in Division I, II or II, where scholarships are always the big prize.

MCC TEAM CHAMPIONS

Year	State Champion
2003-04	Ridgewater
2002-03	Ridgewater
2001-02	Ridgewater
2000-01	Itasca
1999-00	Itasca
1998-99	Ridgewater
1997-98	Itasca
1996-97	Ridgewater (formerly Willmar)
1995-96	Willmar
1994-95	Itasca
1993-94	Willmar
1992-93	Willmar
1991-92	Itasca
1990-91	Willmar
1989-90	Willmar
1988-89	Willmar
1987-88	Willmar
1986-87	Willmar
1985-86	Willmar & Worthington
1984-85	Willmar
1983-84	Anoka Ramsey
1982-83	Willmar
1981-82	Willmar
1980-81	Willmar
1979-80	Worthington
1978-79	Willmar
1977-78	Willmar
1976-77	Willmar
1975-76	Willmar
1974-75	Willmar
1973-74	Willmar
1972-73	Willmar
1971-72	Anoka Ramsey
1970-71	Normandale
1969-70	Fergus Falls

NJCAA WRESTLING HALL OF FAME

Coaches:
1979 John Philo, Rochester Community College
1980 Roy Minter, Willmar Community College
1983 Stanley Hotzler, Worthington Community College
1997 Mike Rybak, Itasca Comm. College (Grand Rapids)

Wrestlers:
1982 Glen Karsten, Worthington Comm. College (1962-63)
1999 Leon Bullerman, Worthington Comm. College (1988-89)
2003 Randy Wirtjes, Rochester Community College

Contributors:
1979 Joe Rockenback, Rochester Community College
Ernest Gould, Worthington Community College
1980 Bruce Traphagen, NJCAA Tournament Director
1981 Donald Rickers, Worthington Community College
William Wirtanen, Mesabi Community College
Glenn Evensen, Worthington Community College

1983 Dukes, Worthington Community College
Jim Wychor, Worthington Community College
1984 Ken Roberts, Tournament Director
1987 Bruce Lease, Worthington Community College

Rochester Community and Technical College

Led by longtime coach Chuck Siefert, an All-American grappler at St. Cloud State University, the Yellow Jackets have produced nine NJCAA All Americans as well as eight Individual National Champs over the years, including:

Name	Year	Weight
George Ceplecha	1964	123 lbs.
Don Mullenback	1965	130 lbs.
Don Mullenback	1966	130 lbs.
Jack Radabaugh	1966	137 lbs.
Jim Johnson	1966	152 lbs.
Rich Mihal	1967	160 lbs.
Darrell Hartle	1968	152 lbs.
Randy Wirtjes	1982	167 lbs.
David Miller	2001	Hwt

Itasca Community College (Grand Rapids)

All-Americans

Name	Weight	Year
Dave Vetsch	141	2000
Dave Strack	174	2000
Jason Waln	184	2000
Chris Thompson	133	2001
Mike Hanson	157	2001
Chad Kostecka	hwt	2001
Tat Romero	174	2002

Minnesota West Comm. and Technical College (Worthington)

Minnesota West Community and Technical College has garnered a lot of success over the years, producing 14 NJCAA All-Americans as well as eight Individual National Champions. In addition, behind Coach Robert Purcell, Minnesota West also made a trio of trips to the NJCAA Collegiate Championships from 2000-02, garnering six All-Americans along the way.

Name	Year	Weight
Howard Gangestad	1962	123 lbs.
Ron Lorenz	1962	137 lbs.
Ron Tuin	1962	177 lbs.
Glen Karsten	1962	hwt
Glen Karsten	1963	hwt
Leon Bullerman	1988	158 lbs.
Leon Bullerman	1989	158 lbs.
Justin Blasius	1992	177 lbs.
Nate Hanson	2000	157 lbs.
Chad Uhrig	2000	125 lbs.
Chad Uhrig	2001	125 lbs.
Ryan Stoks	2001	174 lbs.
Bryan Cowdin	2002	165 lbs.
Karl Knothe	2002	hwt

Ridgewater College (Willmar)

Ridgewater College has made great strides over the years, producing nine NJCAA All-Americans as well as three Individual National Champions. As a team, Ridgewater has made it to the NJCAA nationals on six occasions: 1966, under Coach Jerry Slattery; 1972, under Coach Roy Minter; 1994 under Coach Jack Denholm; and from 2000-02, Coach Troy Haglund led his boys to the promised land — placing eighth in 2002 with a 56 point turnout, highlighted by four All-American performances.

Dakota County Technical College

Led by former Augsburg All-American Henry Gerten, the Blue Knights qualified a pair of grapplers on to the NJCAA National meet in Rochester in 2004. In Gerten's sophomore campaign at the helm, DCTC believes it can enter the next level of competition and beyond.

ROY MINTER

Roy Minter grew up in Owatonna and went on to win a state championship in 1954. From there, Minter went on to wrestle at Mankato State University under legendary coach Rummy Macias. There, from 1955-57, he emerged as a three-time conference champion and three-time All-American as a 177 pounder. Then, as a senior in 1958, he won the NAIA National Championship at 191 pounds. After graduating with his teaching degree, Minter went on to teach and coach at Worthington High School. Minter guided the Trojans for the next 10 years and in 1968 resigned to take over as the head coach of Willmar Junior College, as it was then known as. (It would later be renamed as Willmar Community College and now it is known as Ridgewater Community College.)

Minter would become a coaching legend at Willmar, guiding the program for nearly a quarter century and ultimately retiring in 1992. There, Minter led his squad to 18 Minnesota Community College Conference (MCCC) state championships during his 24 years with the school, also producing some 50 All-Americans as well as one national individual champion during that span as well. So good dominant was Minter, that at the time of his retirement in 1993 he had won more NJCAA Matches (325) than any other coach in NJCAA history.

Minter, whose teams were consistently nationally ranked, was also one of the most popular camp clinicians of all time. Over his illustrious 35-year coaching career He also gave back to the sport he loved by tutoring many of our states' top high school wrestling coaches. Among his many coaching honors and accolades, in 1979 Minter was inducted into the Dave Bartelma Hall of Fame and in 1980 he became a member of the NJCAA Wrestling Hall of Fame. In addition, he also received the prestigious Lifetime Service to Wrestling Award from the National Wrestling Hall of Fame in Stillwater, Oklahoma.

The godfather of junior college wrestling in Minnesota, Roy presently splits time in retirement both up at his lake place in Park Rapids as well as back in Willmar, where he keeps busy doing woodworking and hanging out with his grandkids.

"You know, I speak at a lot of banquets and I always tell people that if it weren't for wrestling I would probably be either digging ditches or serving time," joked Minter. "Wrestling has just been such a wonderful part of my life and I have really been blessed to have been able to coach for as long as I did. I got hooked on the sport at a very young age and it just kind of stuck with me until I had made a career out of it."

"My success in wrestling came because I had a lot of confidence," he said. "I figured there wasn't anything I couldn't do if I set my mind to it. That was the biggest thing. Then, I had coaches like Paul Becker, Fred Stoker and Rummy Macias, who taught me so much. The biggest thing I learned from Rummy was that life is not a gift, it is achieved — meaning you get out of life what you put into it. He also taught me that if you can turn the impossible into possible, then you will succeed in whatever you do. Then, what I learned from Paul Becker, my high school coach, was that out of your beliefs are born deeds; out of your deeds you formed habits; out of your habits you build your character; and your character determines your destination. That was printed on a sign above our wrestling room door and I read that every day. To me that said that if you were willing to work hard and pay the price, then you could accomplish anything. Finally, Fred Stoker was a technician guy. He was a great wrestler, even finished as the NCAA national runner-up back in the late 40s. I learned a lot about the principles of the sport from him too, he was a hell of a guy."

"Kids today have a tremendous advantage over when I was growing up, that is for sure," Minter added. "We got our weight training by throwing bails of hay and pitching the contents of the barnyard. Now, kids start so early and are in camps and what-not by the time they are five or six years old and they have such good technique not, it is amazing. The coaches are getting kids into diet, conditioning and weight training at an early age and that is why kids today are that much better I think. But, while that is great for some kids, I worry that others will burn out by the time they are in high school. Kids who wrestle are just disciplined, hard working kids though, and that makes them unique I think."

"As far as recruiting went, I think the word got out that I treated the kids fair," said Minter. "My office door was always open too, to talk about whatever kids wanted to talk about. We didn't have any money to give them at that level, but we had a lot of fun. I was firm but fair with my kids, but I treated them as individuals. Knowing which buttons to push on which kids was a big part of being successful. I also told my kids that if they were willing to come and pay the price, then I would teach them everything they would need to know about wrestling. From there, if they did that, then I could help get them a scholarship to a four-year school. That was always an incentive for every kid. Sure, I talked to a lot of the top kids, the two-time and three-time state champs, and I told them if they can get in with the Gophers or somewhere else, great. But if they can't, I guarantee that they will want you after a year or two with me. We also went after the character guys who worked hard and came back after tough losses, sometimes those guys turned out to be our best wrestlers. You know, some of my former wrestlers are my very best friends to this day. I think that is unique for a coach too.

"Another big thing was all the wrestling camps that I put on over the years. I met a lot of kids as youth wrestlers and in turn they wanted to come wrestle for me because they knew me and knew my style. After a while everyone knew who I was in the area and that was a big part of our success through the years, no question. I also got to know all the high school coaches from within 50 miles and B.S. with those guys as often as we could. It was like therapy talking to those guys, telling war stories and discussing our problems. It was great. Those guys turned out to be my best recruiters over the years because we knew each other and trusted each other."

"As far as the state of the state of junior college wrestling," said Minter, "it has seen better days. You know, back in 1974 there were 18 schools with wrestling and now there are only five: Worthington, Rochester, Willmar, Grand Rapids and Dakota County. That is really unfortunate. I think one of the reasons for the decline is due to the fact that a lot of the coaches are not on the campus with the kids. So, unlike at the college and university level, where Title IX was a factor for dropping programs, at the community college level it was more about not having a full-time person running the show. That is just my opinion. It is tough to be competitive with a part-time coach nowadays and that is unfortunate.

"As far as at the high school level, I think it is pretty good. I will say though that one of the biggest problems we are facing is from all of the small schools consolidating. These small towns had a big sense of pride when they had their own schools, but after three or four of them combine, a lot gets lost. The numbers go down a lot of times after that too, because now instead of three or four kids each wrestling varsity at their own school, now just one of them will make it. So that is too bad too."

"There have been so many funny stories that have happened over the years," said Minter. "One of my favorites came one time years ago when we were driving home from a tournament. Well, when a wrestler cuts a lot of weight for a match and then gets some food in him, he gets really gassy. So, on this one trip I am driving and my wife, Mary Jo, was in the passenger seat. Sure enough, Wade, that was his name, cut a loud one in the back seat. So I say very stern, 'Wade, how dare you pass gas in front of my wife?' And he looks up at Mary Jo and says, 'I am so sorry Mary Jo, I didn't know it was your turn...' I laughed so hard I almost plowed into the ditch after that one!

"Another funny one came one time after a kid took some Milk of Magnesia to make weight. Well, he wound up making one hell of a mess all over the mat. It was ugly. He just took off right in the middle of the match and ran into the locker room. That poor son of a gun, doing that in front of all those people — he never lived that one down. He was too embarrassed to come back out and finish, he just forfeited and went home. Quite frankly, I would have done the same!"

"Hard work, dedication, discipline, humility and sacrifice are the most important things I learned from wrestling," said Minter. "I also learned to have respect for yourself as well as for your opponent, and then you have to have some kind of faith — whatever that may be. One of my favorite sayings along the way was the 'hard work, commitment and diligence turn dreams into reality.' I tried to live by that too.

"You know, the highlight for me is when a kid thanks me for helping him achieve his dreams and for achieving success. It was always the greatest moment at the end of a tournament to raise that kids hand and declare him as champion. Knowing that you had something to do with that is a special feeling. That's what keeps you coming back. I just hope that I had a positive influence on these kids lives. I have always tried to be a student of the game and never stop learning too. I think that is really important. I love the sport of wrestling and it is really my life. It is all I have ever wanted to do and I love it, I just love everything about it."

PAUL WELLSTONE

Paul Wellstone grew up in a tough neighborhood in East Falls Church, Virginia. As a young man, he was small in stature, but his desire and dogged determination drove him to success, in whatever he did. Too small to play football or basketball, Paul wound up on the high school wrestling team as a 98-pounder. He would climb the weight class ladder from there, competing at 103 pounds as a junior and then at 112 as a senior — even finishing as high as second place that year.

"I went out in 10th grade," said Wellstone in a 1993 state tournament program article by Bruce Brothers, "and we had a really good team. I never lost a dual meet. But, then I had the misfortune of wrestling one of (Virginia's) truly great wrestlers, and he beat me in the finals every year until my senior year. That year I went out with mononucleosis. So I never won a state championship."

From there, Wellstone went on to attend the University of North Carolina, where, as a 126-pounder, he was dominant. In fact, went undefeated for two years, winning the Atlantic Coast Conference title during his sophomore season. Incredibly, he passed on a chance to go to the NCAA Tournament that year though, because he had more pressing issues to deal with. You see, he was already married to his high school sweet heart, Sheila, at that point and they were busy raising their one year old son, David. So, Paul gave up his dream to go to work, and support his family.

Wellstone went on to graduate with a Political Science degree and later earned a Doctorate in 1969. From there, he accepted a teaching position at Carleton College, where, over the next 21 years, he would go on to become one of the universities' most highly-regarded professors. He also helped out with the school's wrestling program and even found time to coach at a nearby junior high school as well. In fact, he even got back onto the matt, serving as an official at local meets.

As the years went by, Wellston's two sons, David and Mark, got into wrestling. While David suffered several injuries, which prevented him from participating in the state tournament, Mark had great success. Mark, who finished fourth at state in 1990, wrestling for Northfield, competed for Apple Valley as a senior. The 125-pounder's finest hour then came in the finals of the 1991 state tournament when he beat Amir Abdelwaaed of Osseo with a late reversal to win 2-0, claiming the state title. His Eagles also won the team title that year as well.

"It turned out to be just a dream come true," recalled Paul, who was recently honored by the National Wrestling Hall of Fame as an "Outstanding American." "He went through and won the state championship. It couldn't have ended on a better note. When he won, I literally was jumping up and down, I was so happy. I was running up and down the halls at the Civic Center."

Mark would go on to wrestle at the University of Wisconsin but was forced to call it a career when he suffered a serious knee injury. He returned to Minnesota after that, however, and wound up teaching Spanish at St. Paul Humboldt High School. He has also served as an assistant coach with the Apple Valley folkstyle and freestyle wrestling teams for the past seven years as well.

"My dad definitely had a passion for wrestling," said Mark in a 2003 Star Tribune article. "I would come home on weekends from a tournament and the first thing I would do was call my dad and let him know how the matches went."

Paul, of course, would go on to make Minnesota proud in 1990, when he upset incumbent Rudy Boschwitz for a position in the United States Senate. There, he was known for his "grassroots" approach to getting things done. As an advocate to preserving family farm and rural community life in America, Wellstone served on numerous senate committees, including the Small Business and Veterans' Affairs Committees; the Foreign Relations Committee; and the Health, Education, Labor and Pension Committee. In addition, he worked on legislation that benefited children and provided them with quality education and health care.

During his two subsequent terms in office, Wellstone always tried to get back to see the tourney. He even drew upon his lessons from the matt to deal with those in the senate.

"Wrestling was pretty good training for politics and public life," he said. "Before debates I used to get pretty ner-vous, but then I said to myself, 'You wrestled, and you were more nervous than this before matches.' "

Tragically, on October 25, 2003, Senator Wellstone, his wife Sheila, daughter Marcia Wellstone Markuson and four others, died in a plane crash near Eveleth. The nation was shocked and saddened by the horrible news. Among those honoring the fallen hero was Mark's Apple Valley High School wrestling team, which wore green armbands at the 2003 state tournament in his honor.

"I think wrestling saved me," Wellstone prophetically recalled from the 1993 state tournament program article. "Wrestling and athletics had a huge influence on my life. In wrestling I found something that gave me confidence. I still feel a per-sonal connection to wrestling because I know what it did for me."

GRECO ROMAN & FREESTYLE

Long considered to be mankind's oldest and most basic form of recreational combat, wrestling's origins can be traced all the way back to the dawn of civilization. Carvings and drawings estimated to be between 15,000 and 20,000 years old have been found in cave dwellings throughout southern Europe, while other artifacts were later discovered throughout the Middle East and North Africa as well. The sport evolved over the centuries, however, and by the time the first Olympic Games rolled around in 708 BC, the competition included oiled bodies fighting in the palestra's of ancient Greece.

Today, there are literally hundreds of different styles of wrestling around the world, including: Glima in Iceland, Schwingen in Switzerland, Sombo in Russia and Cumberland in Britain, among others. With regards to international competition, however, there are two main forms of amateur disciplines: Greco-Roman and freestyle. Judo, a form of jacket wrestling which emphasizes throws is considered a separate sport altogether. Greco-Roman, meanwhile, concentrates on taking your opponent to the mat and exposing his back. Greco-Roman is the most popular international style worldwide. It also limits holds to the upper body and forbids attacking your opponents legs. Lastly, freestyle is similar to the American collegiate style, called folkstyle, where holds are relatively unlimited and can be applied to any part of the body. Only Greco-Roman wrestling was on the programme at the first modern Olympic Games when they resumed in Athens in 1896, freestyle was added in 1904 in St Louis and both styles have been going strong ever since. They have also been embraced in the Land of 10,000 Lakes as well. In fact, Minnesota is without question the nation's hotbed for Greco-Roman wrestling. The primary reason for that is the result of one man's vision, Alan Rice, the "Greco Godfather" of Minnesota. A true legend, perhaps no one has done

more to grow the sport of Greco-Roman wrestling in the United States than Rice, who is just as generous with his money as he is with his time and resources. He has spent a lifetime involved in competing, coaching and promoting amateur wrestling, and is one of the main reasons as to why the sport is so successful here.

Alan Rice grew up in St. Paul and went on to become a two-time state champion at University High School, graduating in 1946. From there, Rice wrestled at the University of Minnesota, where he captured a pair of Big Ten titles in both 1948 and 1949. He would go on from there, however, to compete for more than a decade on the national and international stage, participating in the 1954 Pan American Games in Mexico City, the 1955 World Championships in Tokyo, where he finished fifth in freestyle, and the 1956 Olympic Games in Melbourne, where he placed fifth in the Greco-Roman discipline — the highest finish for an American at that time. He would go on to claim national AAU championships in both freestyle and Greco as well. With accolades like that, it was no wonder that Rice would want to continue to see his sport grow and evolve.

In 1963 Rice started the Minnesota Amateur Wrestling Club (now the Minnesota Storm Wrestling Club). There, he coached the team for what would amount to the next 15 years, winning 16 national championships along the way. (One of the most prominent clubs of its kind in the country, it specializes in developing top Greco-Roman wrestlers from around the world. In fact, it is so good that it has even produced at least one wrestler on every U.S. world championship or Olympic team for more than 40 straight years, a record that no other club can boast. In 1976, six of the 10 roster spots on the U.S. Greco roster were held by Minnesotans. Later, in 1972, Rice also served as head coach of the U.S. Greco-Roman team which competed at the Olympic

MINNESOTA/USA WRESTLING

Dan Chandler

Minnesota/USA Wrestling is the Minnesota state chapter of USA/Wrestling, the National Governing Body for the sport of wrestling in the United States and, as such, is its representative to the United States Olympic Committee (USOC) and the International Wrestling Federation (FILA). Working closely with them and through them, Minnesota/USA Wrestling offers local wrestlers the best wrestling experience they can have and plenty of opportunities to compete. Anybody can wrestle or coach with MN/USA Wrestling as long as they purchase a membership card. These membership cards include a medical/accident and liability insurance program that covers adult supervised practices, competition in sanctioned events, and travel to and from the events. Membership also offers local, regional, and national events for athletes to compete in, discounts on USA Wrestling merchandise, and a subscription to USA WRESTLER, the official publication of USA Wrestling.

MN/USA Wrestling is a very active organization with over 5,000 competitors and coaches, as well as many other officials, pairers, tableworkers, and volunteers; all of whom make the organization the success that it is. There are more than 100 active wrestling clubs in towns and cities throughout Minnesota, with athletes competing in various age groups: Kids, generally 14 years and younger; Cadets, generally 15-16 year olds; Juniors, generally high school age; FILA Juniors, generally 17-20 year olds; University, generally college age; Open, generally college age and beyond; and Women, including all girls and women. These athletes compete in both freestyle and Greco-Roman wrestling and now folkstyle too. The organization also oversees the nationally renowned Minnesota Storm Wrestling Club as well.

At the youth level, Minnesota continues to make strides and is seeing more and more kids take up the sport. Minnesota hosts hundreds of tournaments and competitions every year, drawing thousands of kids from around the Midwest to compete here at various times throughout the year. Our kids always performs well at the AAU Junior Olympics competition in Des Moines too, the largest national multi-sport event held annually for youths in the country. Other events include the ASICS/Vaughan Junior & Cadet National Championships, which feature more than 2,000 young wrestlers competing in the world's largest wrestling tournament at North Dakota State University's Fargodome. All in all, the state-of-the-state of youth wrestling looks good, and will only get better.

ALAN RICE

Better known as the "Greco Godfather," Alan Rice is a legend in the world of Minnesota wrestling. Perhaps no one has done more to grow the sport of Greco-Roman wrestling in the United States than Rice, who is just as generous with his money as he is with his time and resources. He has spent a lifetime involved in competing, coaching and promoting amateur wrestling, and is one of the reasons why the sport is so successful here in the Land of 10,000 Lakes.

Alan Rice grew up in St. Paul and went on to become a two-time state champion at University High School, at 133 and 138 pounds, respectively, graduating in 1946. From there, Rice wrestled at the University of Minnesota, where he captured a pair of Big Ten titles in both 1948 and 1949. He also became Gold Country's 10th All-American with his place finish at the 1949 NCAA tournament. Upon graduating in 1950, Rice moved to New York City, where he began working in the investment business. There, he wrestled for the New York Athletic Club as well.

He would go on from there, however, to compete for more than a decade on the national and international stage, participating in the 1954 Pan American Games in Mexico City, the 1955 World Championships in Tokyo, where he finished fifth in freestyle, and the 1956 Olympic Games in Melbourne, where he placed fifth in the Greco-Roman discipline — the highest finish for an American at that time. He would go on to claim national AAU championships in both freestyle and Greco as well.

Rice moved back to Minnesota in 1959 and shortly thereafter he started the Minnesota Amateur Wrestling Club (now the Gopher Wrestling Club). There, he coached the team for what would amount to the next 25 years, winning 16 national championships along the way. (One of the most prominent clubs of its kind in the country, it specializes in developing top Greco-Roman wrestlers from around the area. In fact, it is so good that it has even produced at least one wrestler on every U.S. world championship or Olympic team for more than 40 straight years, a record that no other club can boast. In 1976, seven of the 10 roster spots on the U.S. Greco roster were held by Minnesotans. Rice's continued efforts helped shape the 2000 U.S. Greco-Roman Olympic team, which claimed gold, silver and bronze in Sydney.)

Later, in 1972, Rice also served as head coach of the U.S. Greco-Roman team which competed at the Olympic Games in Munich. One of the wrestlers on that team was a tough kid by the name of J Robinson, who would later go on to become the head coach of the Golden Gophers.

While Rice competed in both freestyle and Greco-Roman, it would be the latter that would make him a household name. Wanting to grow the sport, which had not been very popular in the U.S. at the time, he embarked on a journey which has lasted for more than a half century to do just that.

A highly successful businessman in the field of investment securities, Rice has continued to give generously to the sport he loves, helping countless kids to pursue their dreams along the way. Among his many incredible contributions over the past three decades, he has helped to raise and contribute nearly $1 million to endow the Minnesota club for continued training in both Greco-Roman and freestyle. In addition, in 2004 Rice gave a $1 million gift to Augsburg College as part of the college's "Access to Excellence" capital campaign. Rice dedicated the gift to the creation of a Greco-Roman wrestling training center as a part of the Si Melby Hall expansion on campus. The training center will attract both youth and adult wrestlers to train in the Greco-Roman discipline year round and will also enable the school to attract world-class athletes to train in its facilities.

The gift was given in memory of his wife, Gloria, who sadly passed away in 2001 at the age of 74. The two, who were married for 44 years, shared a love of amateur wrestling and worked together in establishing Minnesota as a national hotbed for amateur wrestling. And, although Alan garnered the lion's share of attention for his accomplishments in amateur wrestling, Gloria was a major behind-the-scenes contributor for the advancement of the sport as well. In addition to playing a vital role in creating the highly-successful Gopher Wrestling Club, Gloria was the first woman to learn the complicated "pairing" system used by the Europeans to determine the order in which tournament matches were to be conducted. She then went on to teach other women how it worked, thus incorporating literally thousands of wives, sisters, daughters and even grandmothers into the sport as pairers. In fact, she was even credited with helping the U.S. to earn a silver medal at the 1971 World Championships, when she alerted the officials to a questionable rules interpretation and thus, saved the day. Together, Alan and Gloria traveled the world, supporting the sport of wrestling.

"I was very blessed financially, being in the investment business," said Rice, who presently resides in St. Paul. "So, I have been fortunate in that over all my years of coaching and participating in the sport, I have never had to take any money away from it. I have always been a very proud volunteer and that means a lot to me. My goal is to use my savings of a lifetime to help children, which there is no better cause. I don't want to wait until I am gone to do so either, I want to give it now, so that I can enjoy it. I am only sorry that my loving wife can't be with me to see what a difference can be made in so many lives. She shared my passion for the sport and was quite a lady. So, to endow those programs, at the University of Minnesota and at Augsburg, in her name, means the world to me."

Among Alan's many honors and accolades, he was inducted into the National Wrestling Hall of Fame in Stillwater, Okla., as a Distinguished Member. In addition, he has been inducted into the University of Minnesota's 'M' Club Hall of Fame, the Minnesota Wrestling Hall of Fame and the Helms Foundation Hall of Fame. His decades of hard work have truly made a difference and for that, Alan Rice will forever be known as the "Godfather of Greco-Roman wrestling."

"It wasn't so much what I have done for wrestling, but what wrestling has done for me," said Rice. "I had moderate success as a wrestler, but have been so fortunate to have just been able to spend my lifetime surrounded by so many wonderful people in the sport of wrestling. It is very satisfying to me to see the results of much of my hard work over the years. We have had so many good kids from Minnesota go on to represent us over the years, internationally, and that has been great to see. I was very proud to be a member of the very first U.S. Greco-Roman team which competed in the Olympics and I have tried to give back and support the sport in any way I can since then.

"I would like to think that I had a small part in the fact that Minnesota has sent so many kids to the Olympics in Greco-Roman wrestling. That means an awful lot to me. From getting kids started early on and then watching them develop and grow is so satisfying to me. To see them enjoying themselves and working so hard is what it is all about. I have had a lot of parents tell me over the years that I have made a difference in their children's lives, and that means a great deal to me too. To see kids work hard at something and then achieve some success is great to see.

"Another reason why we have been so successful over the years is because we have been able to bring other wrestlers from around the world here to train with us," added Rice. "That experience was invaluable. There is one funny story I will never forget, it was in 1966, at the World Championship in Toledo, Ohio. The Iranian coach came to me and told me that he had a wrestler who would like to stay in America to train and study. He asked if I could help him, and I agreed, so I brought him back to Minnesota. I got him a place to stay, fed him and he helped me do some coaching in return. As a result, over the years a lot of other Iranian wrestlers would come over here and visit him and train with us at the club. It was wonderful for our guys to learn from them, because they had outstanding international experience.

"Later, in 1973, the World Championships were held in Tehran and I was the administrative head of the U.S. team. I saw many of those same young men over there and they treated my like royalty over there, it was great. Anyway, a few years later, I get a call one day from some guy over at the Minneapolis airport telling me that there was a foreign guy there who couldn't speak English, but knew two words: "Alan and Rice.' It turned out to be Kosrow Vaziri, who had heard of me and wanted to come to America to live and train. So, I went and got him and got him set up over here and he trained with us. He was an outstanding amateur wrestler and eventually became an American citizen. He later competed for the U.S. on some National Teams as well. Well, one day he came to me and asked me to introduce him to my friend, Verne Gagne. He wanted to get into professional wrestling at that point and he knew that Verne and I were good friends. Verne agreed and he went on to become the 'Iron Sheik.' He was quite a guy.

"You know, Greco used to be freestyle's little sister years ago and we have totally changed that now, and that is so great to see," Rice continued. "I mean we have sent a kid from Minnesota to either the World Championships or the Olympics every year for more than four decades now, and that is extremely gratifying to see. So, starting the Minnesota Amateur Wrestling Club was something that I am really proud of. We originally started it for kids at the University, but we later opened it up and it became world renowned. It is still going strong and is a big part as to why Minnesota has such a strong wrestling tradition to this day.

"As far as the state of the state of wrestling in Minnesota today, I would say that there are some good things and some bad," he said. "While the Gophers and Augsburg are doing extremely well and have established their programs amongst the very best in the nation, we are losing too many others. I think that there has been some misuse of the Title IX program as well. Don't get me wrong, I am all in favor of women in sports. But there are some who are using the program to make it a class warfare between feminism and attacking men's sports — one of which is wrestling. That is hurting the sport terribly I think. We have lost over 400 programs over the years and that is really too bad. I guess I just don't see how dropping men's sports helps women? Kids are the ones who are suffering, so hopefully we can get that worked out. Overall though, things are pretty good at the youth levels and the numbers are there. They are the future of the sport, so we all need to do our part to make sure that it is strong and healthy for them by the time they want to pursue their dreams at the college or international levels. That is what this is all about, helping kids to fulfill their dreams."

Games in Munich. One of the wrestlers on that team was a tough kid by the name of J Robinson, who would later go on to become the head coach of the Golden Gophers.

"The father of Greco Roman wrestling is without a doubt, Alan Rice," said former Olympian Duane Koslowski. "Alan single-handedly built up our program to the point where now it is second to none. If you go back to the late 70s, Minnesota was about in the middle of the pack with regards to producing guys who could compete on the international stage. Every now and then we would get a really good guy who would emerge, but we never had a lot of success at either the World Championships or at the Olympics. The U.S. back then, was an 'easy draw,' if you know what I mean. We were not taken very seriously by anybody back then.

"At the time, the Polish wrestlers were dominating all of those events. So, what Alan did was he drove up to

Brad Rheingans

Northeast Minneapolis, to the Polish neighborhoods, and talked to some of the community leaders up there. He told them that he wanted to bring in the Polish National Wrestling Team to train with the Minnesota wrestlers and wanted to know if they would put them up. They were all over it and Alan was able to bring in like 15 wrestlers to train with the Minnesota Greco club team for a couple of months. It was invaluable experience for the guys to learn how to wrestle that international style from the wrestlers themselves. The results of that little experiment came out at the next National Championships, where the U.S. had like eight or nine champions out of the 10 weight classes. And, a lot of those matches had two Minnesotans wrestling for first and second place as well. From that time on there have pretty much been at least two or three members of the World team who have been Minnesotan. And now, the product of all of that is the fact that as all of us have kids now, we are coaching and teaching and giving back to the next generation. Now you have guys like Dan Chandler giving back as well and it is just success breeding success. It is just great to see."

While Rice competed in both freestyle and Greco-Roman, it would be the latter that would make him a household name. Wanting to grow the sport, which had been more popular in places such as Russia, Iran and Turkey, than in the U.S. at the time, he embarked on a journey which has lasted for more than a half century to do just that. His legacy is alive and well today and in good hands with people such as Dan Chandler, who has taken the torch and made it glow even bigger and brighter.

A three-time Olympian, Chandler served as the head coach of the 2000 U.S. Olympic Greco-Roman team which com-

DAN CHANDLER

Dan Chandler grew up in Anoka and wrestled under legendary coach Ron Malcom at Anoka High School. There, Chandler made it to the state tourney as an individual, but came up just short.

"It was disappointing that we never got to win a state team tournament," he said. "We were 13-0 in dual meets in 1970 and were just dominant, but because Austin was ranked No. 1 and we never got to face off against them, we finished as No. 2 in the state that year."

Chandler graduated in 1970 and went on to wrestle at the University of Minnesota. As a junior and senior he placed third and fourth in the Big Ten Conference, respectively, and went on to compete both years in the NCAA Tournament as well. From there, Chandler would go on to become one of the greatest amateur wrestlers in state history and literally become synonymous with the sport of Greco-Roman wrestling.

As an athlete, Chandler was a member of three U.S. Olympic teams (1976, 1980 & 1984) and also competed in six World Championships, placing as high as fifth in the 1979 games. He also won medals in three Pan American Games, including golds in 1975 and 1979. In all, he has won an American record 12 Greco-Roman national championships and has garnered 12 International medals along the way.

During that span, Chandler also became a world renowned coach. His first gig was as an assistant coach at the University of Minnesota from 1975-86. He also served as the head coach at the University of St Thomas from 1987-90 as well. In 1984 Chandler retired from competition to join the USA Wrestling national coaching staff and has been with the organization ever since. Along the way, however, Chandler coached a whole bunch of U.S. Olympic and National teams, an honor which has made him a legend in grappling circles.

After coaching the 1990 and 1993 World Cup teams, Chandler served as head coach of the 1994 Pan American team, which won the team title. From there, he went on to serve as the head coach of the 1995, 1997 and 1999 U.S. Greco-Roman World teams. During that span, Chandler was a member of the 1988 U.S. Olympic Greco-Roman team's coaching staff, and later served as an assistant coach for 1992 U.S. Olympic team, which featured silver medallist Dennis Koslowski, of UM-Morris. He also served on the coaching staff of the 1996 U.S. team as well.

Finally, in 2000, Chandler was named as the head coach of the U.S. team which competed in Sydney. The U.S. had its best Olympic Greco-Roman performance that year, winning three medals and placing third in the medal count. Among those who brought home hardware that year was former Gopher, Garrett Lowney, who won a bronze. Chandler was rewarded for his efforts again in 2004 when he was named as head coach of the 2004 U.S. Olympic Greco-Roman team which competed in Athens.

"I enjoy coaching at all levels, but really like coaching kids, particularly at the junior level," said Chandler. "For instance, the Junior National Championship is the biggest junior wrestling tournament in the world and it is held every year up in Fargo, with more than 5,000 kids competing. It is awesome. Every state participates and sends a team of 15 & 16 year-olds and 17 & 18 year-olds up there. Plus, there are girls wrestling now too, which is great to see as well. I have coached there every year going back to 1985, for 20 years, and love to work this those aged kids. To see them develop and grow it amazing. You can really work with them and make a difference. They are so enthusiastic and impressionable at that age and they just want to learn. Then, to see those kids go on to wrestle in college and beyond is so exciting. So, that is a lot of fun."

Chandler, who has been named Greco-Roman Coach of the Year by USA Wrestling a record five times (1994, 1995, 1997, 1999, & 2000), presently serves as the head of "Minnesota USA Wrestling." There, he coaches athletes in the state on all age levels and is truly making a difference. In addition, he also coaches the Minnesota Storm club team, which features many of the best Greco-Roman athletes in the nation. The Storm, considered as one of the most successful club teams in the world, competes in the Senior and age-group levels.

"So many guys from our club team have gone on to do well at the Olympics and that is always such a thrill for me," said Chandler. "Guys like Brandon Paulson, who won a silver, Garrett Lowney, who took bronze, Dennis Koslowski won a couple medals, Jimmy Martinez won a medal too. Then, to be in Rulon Gardner's corner when he won the gold in 2000 was something I will never forget. That was such a huge thrill for me. What is amazing is that the U.S. has had medal winners from the Minnesota USA Wrestling club team in five of the past six Olympic Games. There are only two countries in the world which can say that, the U.S. and Russia, so that is pretty amazing. You know, training guys for the Olympics is really a thrill. The guys are so focused. I mean it is their entire life's work on the line and you want to help them achieve their dreams. It is an exciting thing to be there in that environment. For all the coaching things you can do, the Olympic Games is the ultimate."

For Chandler, who presently resides in Minneapolis with his family, it is a dream come true to have been able to spend his lifetime doing something he truly loves.

"I have always just really enjoyed being around the sport," he said. "Doing something you love to do is a lot of fun and I am very luck in that regard. Wrestler, whether competing or coaching, has never been a job, it has always been something I have loved.

"As far as the state-of-the-state of Minnesota wrestling, I would say there are good things and bad things. I think it is pretty popular right now, which is good, and the numbers have been fairly steady. I know our membership has stayed around 4,500 kids a year and I think the high school numbers are strong too. On the other side of the coin, I would say that sometimes kids are pushed too hard too young. I see a lot of parents who are really aggressive and have high expectations for their kids, which is good, but sometimes I think they can go too far. Overall, though, things are really good. Everybody seems to be doing the best that they can and we are all working towards common goals, which is to help kids. We are all also competing for funding dollars as well, which is tough all over, but things look good as far as the big picture goes.

"I think the reason Minnesota is so strong in Greco is because of Alan Rice. He started the tradition back in the 1960s and I would like to think that I have carried a lot of his ideas over into the next generation. I was able to get Minnesota USA Wrestling to sponsor a Greco program for high school kids back in the 1980s and that has just grown and grown. Now, we have a junior cadet program too, which is great to see as well. The goal behind all of it is to get kids interested in wrestling at a young age and keep them into it for as long as possible, that is what it is all about."

THE KOSLOWSKI BROTHERS

The Koslowski brothers are Greco Roman wrestling royalty in Minnesota and are among the most decorated national and international athletes in U.S. history. Dennis and Duane grew up in Doland, South Dakota, loving sports. But, while the two were very good football players early on, they were definitely late bloomers when it came to wrestling. They came on strong during their junior and senior seasons though, and wound up getting the opportunity to compete at the University of Minnesota Morris. There, they both emerged as big men on campus, both on the gridiron as well as on the mat. Without a doubt, the two put Morris on the wrestling map. In fact, Dennis was a three-time NCAA Division III All-American and wound up winning two National Championships in 1980 and 1982, while Duane was a one time All-American, winning one National Championship in 1981.

"You now, I was never one of those guys who grew up dreaming of going to the Olympics or anything like that," said big brother Dennis, who is older than Duane by a whopping 26 minutes. "I was certainly no blue-chipper coming out of high school or anything. I actually wasn't very good back then at all and I didn't even really start hitting my stride until I was in college. So, I was a real late bloomer. I was almost trying to fit into my body every year I competed it seemed like. Believe it or not, I wrestled through high school at 105, 119, 138 and 167. Then in college I started at 177, moved up to 190 and wound up as a heavyweight. That was a lot of growing! But when I finally settled down I got pretty good.

"Then, after college I wanted to continue competing. Well, Minnesota has a such a strong wrestling tradition, especially on the Greco side, and that just seemed like a logical move. I remember my first taste of international wrestling came against Brad Rheingans, who used to come up to Morris when we were there to train with us. He was really talented and I learned a lot from him over the years. I had also gotten accepted into chiropractic school after graduating from Morris in 1981, so that made it tough to continue going to school while still training. But, it all worked out and if anything, going to school just made me more disciplined with my wrestling.

"Now, to see the situation at Morris is very disappointing. For them to have to cut the program was devastating. There were some coaching issues there and it eventually caught up to them. It is really too bad."

"My brother and I were late bloomers," added Duane. "I mean physically we were not that big or strong. We weren't really great high school wrestlers either, until our senior years. We wanted to play football as well as wrestle, and there weren't a lot of opportunities to do that in South Dakota. So, we decided to go to Morris. Their head coach at the time, Doug Dufty, came out and met us face to face and basically sold us on the school. That really impressed us that he would come all that way to meet us. I mean that drive is brutal… there is a reason they say the state here is the telephone pole! Anyway, we really liked him so we signed up. Then, when we got there, we lobbied the football coach, Al Molde, to let us play there too. He agreed and we both wound up starting for three years on the line as well. It was a great time being there and if we had to do it all over again, we would do it.

"Now, to see Morris lose their wrestling program was very, very disappointing. I think the fault in it is the fact that the school's standard for what defines success had dropped so precipitously from when we were there that by the time it got so bad, they couldn't recruit kids to a losing program. So, the school basically turned around and said we're going to give it up because not enough kids were interested. Well, the fact of the matter is that if the incumbent coach who was running the program at the time failed to achieve success over an extended period of time, then the ability to recruit kids just dries up. So, it was a bad deal all the way around. Kids are attracted to a winning program and they lost that over time, so it became increasingly difficult to find quality athletes to compete there. It was really a travesty. I mean when Dennis and I were there we were consistently ranked as a top 10 team in all of Division III, and we even finished third one year. So, the base was there, but it eroded over time until it was gone."

After college, Duane got out of wrestling for what would amount to three years, when he moved back to South Dakota to work in the insurance business. Dennis, however, began competing internationally, where he struggled at first, but then came on strong. Later, when Duane saw Dennis lose a controversial decision at the 1984 U.S. Team Trials, only to see that guy go on to win a silver medal at the Olympics, he decided to move back to Minnesota and get back into it. The brothers became training partners at that point and the rest they say, is history.

Over the next 15 years or so, the two would go on to compete on the national and international stage, bringing home plenty of hardware along the way. Competing in the Greco-Roman division, Dennis went on to become a five-time World Place finisher and six-time National Champion. In addition, he won a silver medal at the 1992 Olympic Games in Barcelona, as well as a bronze at the 1998 Olympic Games in Seoul.

"I would like to be remembered as someone who was a late bloomer who hung in there and worked hard to achieve success," said Dennis. "You know, not enough is said about kids who develop late I think. I mean how many four-time state champs have we had who have gone on to have a lot of success at the Division I level? So, if I was a recruiter, I would look more at the kid who was maybe a runner-up his junior year and then a state champ his senior year. That is the kid who I would recruit. He still has some rubber on the tires, if you will, versus maybe the kid who has had a lot of success early on. That was me, I definitely fit that mold. You are just always learning, even at my last match, when I was 32 years old, I still felt that I was learning.

"I mean I was on seven U.S. National teams, won seven national titles, competed on two U.S. Olympic teams and five U.S. World teams. Even there, I didn't win any medals until my fourth international competition. But from there, I medalled in all the others. So, for me at that point I knew what it took to win. I knew how to train, how to prepare both mentally and physically and I knew that I was always going to be there in the end. I would also say that being a chiropractor also helped me because I had a great knowledge of the body and of physiology, and could apply that to how I trained and took care of my body. As a result, I was able to train right, eat right, stay healthy and avoid injuries as I got older."

"Beyond that, I am also proud of the fact that even though I came up through some pretty modest surroundings as far as coaching, facilities, training and that kind of thing, that I was still able to compete with the best in the world. Nothing was ever handed to my brother and I along the way, so we just had to work really hard for our success."

"Competing with my brother was awesome," said Dennis. "We are so close and such good friends. I couldn't have achieved half of what I achieved without him, that is for sure. Not only was he a great brother, he was also a great coach too. You know, being twins, it was tough because we had to compete at different weights in order to both have a shot at winning events. Well, he was really good about that and he was the one who kind of fell on the sword as far as gaining weight. I mean we were both ideal at 220 pounds, but he moved up to heavyweight so that we could both compete. I mean he only weighed 250 soaking wet, and he had to go up against guys a lot bigger than him. So, that was tough."

"You know, you have to always keep a positive attitude in wrestling, because some things are just out of your control," he added. "I remember one time at the 1986 World Championships in Hungary I was wrestling this guy named Thomas Gaspar, who was Hungarian. He was the reigning European champion and I had never beaten him before, he was really good. Now, one thing about international wrestling that is really tough to deal with sometimes is the fact that a lot of times the host countries of major tournaments will always try to push through at least one of their own to win a medal. It makes the locals happy, but it really sucks for everybody else. Anyway, I wound up drawing his name in the second round and I knew I was done for.

"I will never forget, I was up 1-0 with just 15 seconds left and it should have been 2-0, but I got worked by the ref on a call a few minutes earlier. Well, we came back from out of bounds to the middle of the mat and I started across the center to approach him and the ref blew the whistle. Then, he blew it again before I could touch him and proceeded to double-disqualify us — which essentially put him into the next round. It was unbelievable. I mean it was the only way they could get the guy to advance, and that was how it went down. He ultimately went on to win the World Championship too, which was tough to swallow.

"Well, the vindication for me came years later when a Hungarian patient of mine showed me an article from a Hungarian newspaper in which Gaspar, who went on to become the head of his countries' wrestling federation, was quoted. One of the questions asked him who he feared most in all of his years of wrestling, and he said it was me. He said 'wrestling Dennis Koslowski was like wrestling death itself.' That was awesome!

"Anyway, that is one of wrestling's dirty little secrets and I ran into that all over the world, but there is nothing you can do. You just have to stay positive and keep with it. There is a quote from Billy Mills, a Native American from South Dakota who won a gold medal at the 1964 Olympics in the 10,000 meters, which I have always remembered. Basically, it went something like 'Find your positive desires in life because with desire comes motivation, with motivation comes work, and with work comes success.' That always stuck with me and have never forgotten it."

Competing in the Greco-Roman division, Duane went on to become a two-time World Place finisher and four-time National Champion. In addition, he finished eighth at the 1998 Olympic Games in Seoul.

"My brother and I took a lot of pride in the fact that even though we came from a small school but were still able to compete at the highest level, the Olympics," said Duane. "I mean most of the kids who make it that far come from Big 10 or Big 8 schools, and they are driven by great coaches, such as the Dan Gables of the world, who have a lot of resources. Well, we didn't have that. We didn't have anyone pushing us when we got to that level to do all the extra little things that require a lot of discipline. As a result, my brother and I set our own regime, our own training schedule and we basically did it all on our own.

"Even when we were training at the University of Minnesota, I can tell you that 90% of the time we were the only ones there. We eventually turned that disadvantage into an advantage because we were much more self-disciplined than most of the other guys. In fact, I am sure that if you asked my brother who his coach was he would say it was me, and I would do the same for him. We were very close and we were able to really push each other to be the best we could be. The result of all of that hard work was the fact that we each emerged as the best U.S. Greco wrestlers in our weight classes for three straight years. We were both undefeated during that stretch and that is something we are both very proud of. Plus, being able to do it together made all of our success mean even that much more. So, to be able to wrestle for your country on the world's stage, that meant a great deal to us, no question."

"You know, a lot of people judge your success based on the awards you get," Duane added, "but the best thing about being fortunate enough to participate in the sport of wrestling is the reward it gives you about understanding personal accountability and overcoming adversity. Wrestling just reinforces the fact that you can do virtually any task that you point your mind to if you want it badly enough. I gained so much from wrestling and feel so blessed to have been able to spend as much time in it that I did. Success in wrestling isn't just defined by wins and losses, it is much deeper than that. The life long personal lessons you learn from this sport will be with you for the rest of your life. That is what it is all about in my mind. Wrestling is one of those sports where anybody can participate. I mean it is not like football or basketball, where you have to either be 250 pounds or six-foot-six. There are opportunities for kids of all sizes, weights and backgrounds, and that is what makes it so exciting."

"Overall, I think wrestling in Minnesota is tremendous," said Duane. "The Title IX issue has made some things interesting but overall I think the sport is very healthy. The one thing with that is that sometimes young kids who come through smaller programs and are maybe late bloomers, like Dennis and myself, may never be able to get the opportunity to enjoy competing at that next level. What I can tell you though is because of the work of people like Dan Chandler, at USA Wrestling, a lot of our kids are going on to wrestle at Division One programs all over the country. The Minnesota kids have the year round training available to them, in both Greco and freestyle, and get a lot of attention at the junior levels, so that makes them very marketable."

"I just really enjoyed the entire process, from training to learning to competing," he added. "I feel very lucky to have been able to do something I love for so long, it was a tremendous opportunity that I would like to think I made the most of. Thanks to everyone who supported us over the years, it was truly our pleasure."

Presently, Dr. Dennis works as a chiropractor and has his own practice in Minneapolis. He and his family presently reside in Minnetonka. Duane, meanwhile, recently moved to Washington D.C., in the Summer of 2004 with his family, where he works for the Pacific Life Insurance Company. Both are interested in teaching and coaching their kids, to give back to the sport which has given them so much.

BRANDON PAULSON

Brandon Paulson grew up in Anoka and began wrestling when he was just five years old. As a junior high schooler, he began competing on the national and international stage. As a cadet, he won the 1988 Cadet National doubles championship and then won the 1989 Cadet National champion in freestyle, along with the U.S. Junior Nationals as well. In 1990 he won the doubles title at the U.S. Olympic Festival and also took the Espoir Nationals championship in freestyle.

Meanwhile, Paulson went on to attend Anoka High School, where he learned the ropes from legendary coach Ron Malcolm. There, he won three state titles from 1990-92 and also participated in tennis. As a prep wrestler, Paulson made history be becoming the first high school wrestler ever to make the senior-level Team USA, when he qualified for the 1991-92 U.S. Greco-Roman National Team. That year he finished third in the World Team Trials, fourth at the Concord Cup and won the Espoir Nationals Doubles Championship. In 1992 he won the Junior Nationals and finished Fifth in the U.S. Nationals too.

In 1993 Paulson went on to attend the University of Minnesota, where, under the tutelage of coach J Robinson, he would excel. He also hit the international wrestling scene, where he would emerge as one of Minnesota's best ever. As a Gopher, he earned All-American honors in 1998, his senior year, ultimately finishing seventh in the 1998 NCAA Championships. He also received the coveted Big Ten Medal of Honor that year as well. After graduating from the U of M with a degree in Management, Paulson continued to compete for Minnesota Wrestling USA's team "Minnesota Storm," which was coached by former Olympian Dan Chandler.

During that time, he continued to compete on the national and international stage. In 1992 he emerged as the Espoir National champion and finished second in the Espoir World Championships. In 1995 he won the University Nationals championship, the U.S. Olympic Festival title, was second at the U.S. Nationals and finished second at the World Team Trials.

In 1996 he won the U.S. Olympic Team Trials and took third at the U.S. Nationals. More importantly, however, Paulson did Minnesota proud that year when he won a silver medal at the 1996 Olympics in Atlanta, competing in the Greco Roman category at 114 pounds.

"It was a huge honor to represent my country at the Olympics," said Paulson. "To win a medal is something I will never forget."

In 1999 Paulson took third at the U.S. Nationals, second in the World Team Trials and won the Winter Classic championship. The next year he took third at the Pan American Championships and came in second at the U.S. Olympic Team Trials — narrowly missing a spot on the Olympic team. Paulson vowed to make the 2004 Games, however, and worked hard over the next couple of years. From 2001-03 he won the World Team Trials championships and in 2001 he was a silver medallist at the World Championships.

In 2002 and 2003 he won the U.S. Nationals and in 2003 he came in second at Pan American Games, Dave Schultz Memorial International and Concord Cup. Then, in 2004, he laid it all on the line for one last hurrah, ultimately losing to 1996 Olympic silver medallist Dennis Hall in the finals for the right to represent the U.S.A. in Athens in the 121-pound Greco-Roman category. Wanting to do his part, Paulson went to Athens with Hall to help him train and get ready for the Olympics — that is the type of person he is.

"That was tough," said Paulson of his loss to Hall. "I wanted it so bad, but that is the way it goes sometimes. It was the last match out of a best-of-three final and it went three overtimes — which was like wrestling three straight matches. It was unbelievable. I mean it was the longest finals match in Olympic Trials history. I was just spent, mentally and physically. So much goes through your head during that time and it was hard to keep it together. I am still not completely over it, that one will be with me for a while. But you know, he and I are great friends and were training partners for a long time, so I was happy to help him afterwards in any way that I could. That is what it is all about."

With that, Paulson called it a career, and it was an amazing one at that. Brandon is the only Minnesotan to have won a national title on all four age-group levels up through the open divisions (Cadet, Junior, Espoir & University), and is among the best in the world to have ever competed in the sport.

Presently, Brandon works with his father at Paulson Construction, building custom homes. He and his wife Rochell have two daughters, Sydney and Abby, and reside in Coon Rapids.

"Wrestling has given me so much," said Paulson. "I have met so many great people, seen so many interesting things around the world and just have so many wonderful memories. The lessons that you learn in wrestling; the hard work, the determination, setting and reaching goals, it all carries over into real life. I was given the opportunity to compete at a very young age and I tried to make the most of it. My dad brought me everywhere to wrestle when I was a kid and I competed in just about every tournament that I could. As a result of that early success though, by the time I was a sophomore I was already competing against Olympic level athletes. It started from there and just kept going for me. I loved it back then and that passion carried all the way through my entire career.

"You know, now that it is all said and done, I guess I would like to be remembered as a competitor. I want to be known as a guy who always went out there, competed hard and gave it my full effort. You never got 50% from me, you always got everything I had, and I was proud of that. I always consistently gave it my best effort in every match I competed in, whether I was winning or losing, and that attitude really helped me throughout my career. I always wanted my opponent to know that he was in for a fight, whether I was ahead by six points or down by six points — I was wrestling the same way, full-out. I think I earned a lot of respect from my peers because of that too."

One of the most decorated wrestlers in Minnesota history, Paulson hopes to continue giving back to the sport he loves.

"I coached kids when I was younger and I would love to continue with that," said Paulson. "I would particularly like to work with the kids at the international level, the world class athletes. We have such a strong wrestling tradition here in Minnesota and especially on the Greco side, this has really been the place to be over the past 40 years. Alan Rice started it all and it just got passed down from there, which has been great. Now Dan Chandler is carrying the torch and because of guys like him, guys like me can compete at such a high level. He is such an awesome coach, and I was really lucky to have him in my corner for so many years. So, yeah, I want to give back the same way the other guys did and just do my part to keep it all going."

peted in Sydney, is practically wrestling royalty in Minnesota. The Sydney Olympic team won 3 medals (Gold, Silver and Bronze) including Rulon Gardner's famous victory over never before defeated Russian great Alexander Karelin. The Bronze medal was won by Minnesota Storm member Garrett Lowney. Chandler has been named Greco-Roman Coach of the Year by USA Wrestling a record five times and presently serves as the head of "Minnesota USA Wrestling." There, he coaches athletes of all age levels and is truly making a difference. In addition, he also coaches the "Minnesota Storm" club team, which features many of the best Greco-Roman athletes in the nation and has won nine team championships as well as several dozen individual titles over the years. The Storm, considered to be one of the most successful club teams in the world, competes in the Senior and age-group levels, where they consistent-ly bring home the hardware. More importantly, they give young men and women the opportunity to stay home so that they can train and compete with the best of the best, without having to move off to some far away locale. The results have been overwhelming and continue to grow year in and year out.

Incredibly, this Minnesota connection has produced wrestlers that won 5 consecutive Olympic medals for the United States since 1984. There are only two countries in the world which can say that, the U.S. and Russia, which says a lot for what has been going on right in our own backyard for all these years. Under Chandler's leadership, Minnesota will undoubtedly continue to dominate the landscape of big-time national and international competition, inspiring the next generation of future grapplers, one at a time.

JOE RUSSELL

Joe Russell grew up in Oregon and went on to graduate from Gresham High School in 1988, where he won two state high school titles, compiling a 90-1 record along the way. From there, Russell competed internationally, becoming a two-time Junior National champion, Espoir National Champion, place winner at Espoir World Championships, and two-time World School Boy Champion. Russell then came to Minnesota to wrestle for the Gophers, serving as the team captain in 1992, while also earning All-Big Ten Academic honors as well. Russell, who later attended law school at the U of M, also practices law part-time with an emphasis on sports law issues. During that time he became an assistant with the team — a position, which has evolved, and he has now held for nine years.

Russell is also the head coach of the Minnesota Storm Junior World and University teams and has led his squads to a second-place finish in the 1997, '98 and '99 University National Championships. The Storm also won the 1996, 1999 and 2000 FILA Junior National Team Championship in both freestyle and Greco-Roman. In 2002, under Russell's tutelage, the squad added another FILA Junior National Greco-Roman Team Championship as well.

In addition, in 1998, Russell served as the coach of Team USA in a world freestyle dual versus Germany. Also in 1998, he was selected as the coach for the USA Wrestling Tour de Monde team in Hungary. Russell also coached Team USA in a world freestyle dual meet versus Cuba in 1999. He coached the U.S. 17-and-under team at the Cadet World Championships in August 1999 in Denmark. For his efforts, Russell was voted the 1999 USA Wrestling Person of the Year for the University and FILA Junior Age Divisions. In the summer of 2000, Russell was selected to coach the U.S. Junior Team at the 2000 Pan American Championships in Peru. In 2001, he coached a team of USA All-Stars in the First Annual Utah Greco-Roman Challenge in Sandy, Utah. Furthermore, in 2003, he coached Team USA at the Junior Pan American Championships in Bogota, Colombia. There, a trio of Gophers — Tommy Owen, Matt Nagel and Drew Hageman, medalled for the U.S., with Hageman taking gold in both freestyle and Greco-Roman.

Incidentally, Russell's partner in crime with both the Storm as well as with the Gophers was Mark Schwab, who left the programs in the Summer of 2004 to take over as the head coach of Buena Vista University in Iowa. In addition to coaching the Storm to three Espoir National Championships in 1996, 1997 and 1999, Schwab was also an assistant coach for the U.S. Junior World team in Sydney, in 1999. Then, in the summer of 2001, Schwab served as head coach of U.S.'s Junior World Freestyle Championships team and also coached a team of 20-and-under wrestlers in Uzbekistan as well. While wrestling fans everywhere wish Mark well, Minnesota wrestling will most certainly miss his leadership and credibility.

GARRETT LOWNEY

Garrett Lowney grew up in Appleton, Wis., and went on to graduate from Freedom High School, where he emerged as a three-time Wisconsin state champion. From there, Lowney headed west, to the University of Minnesota and compete for the Golden Gophers. At the U of M, Lowney was dominant, finishing third at the NCAA Championships in 2001 and then fifth in 2002 as a heavyweight. Lowney, who also captured a Big Ten title in 2001, went on to achieve great success on the international stage in the Greco-Roman discipline. A member of Team USA since 2000, Lowney's proudest moment came at the 2000 Summer Olympic in Sydney, where he won a bronze medal. In between stints in the U.S. Nationals or World and Pan American Championships, Lowney trains in Minnesota as a member of Dan Chandler's highly regarded Minnesota Storm club team. Despite suffering severe neck injury in 2003, which left him unable to compete in the World Championships, Lowney came back to make the roster of the 2004 U.S. Olympic team which competed in Athens. As a result, Lowney continued Minnesota's long tradition of sending a wrestler to the Olympic games every year since the early 1960s.

GRECO & FREESTYLE RECORDS

All-Time U.S. Greco Roman National Champions

198 pounds
1984 - Mike Houck
1985 - Mike Houck

220 pounds
1983 - Dennis Koslowski
1986 - Dennis Koslowski
1987 - Dennis Koslowski
1988 - Dennis Koslowski
1991 - Dennis Koslowski
1992 - Dennis Koslowski

Heavyweight or 286 pounds
1985 - Dennis Koslowski
1986 - Duane Koslowski
1987 - Duane Koslowski
1988 - Duane Koslowski

Minnesota Freestyle, Greco-Roman, Junior Freestyle, Junior Greco-Roman & FILA Junior World Greco-Roman Championships

Source: wrestlinghalloffame.org

USA Cadet Freestyle Championships
1987   Joe Block (132), Steve King (167)
1988   Brandon Paulson (88), Joel Sharratt (182)
1989   Brandon Paulson (103.5), Chad Nelson (167) and
         William Pierce (HVY)
1992   Dan Devine (182.5)
1997   Josh McLay (154)
1998   Marcus LeVesseur (132)

USA Cadet Greco-Roman Championships
1986   Willy Short(138.5), Tug Durdein (HVY)
1987   Joe Block (132), Steve King (167)
1988   Brandon Paulson (88), Joel Sharratt (182.5)
1989   Brandon Howe (103.5), William Pierce (HVY)
1992   Chris Steele (167), Dan Devine (182.5)
1993   Jim Alexander (143)
1994   Tawain Hunter (103.5)
1996   Tony Larson (83.5), Jacob Clark (143)
1997   Josh McLay (154), Jareck Horton (182.5)
1998   Matt Nagel (132), Nick Zajac (167) and Jordan Holm (182.5)

USA Junior Freestyle Championships
1973   Mike McArthur (114.5)
1976   Scott Madigan (154)
1979   Jon Schoe (HVY)
1987   Chris Short (191.5)
1989   Steve King (220)
1990   Joel Sharratt (191.5)
1991   Jason Reitmeier (123), Billy Pierce (HVY)
1992   Jason Reitmeier (132)
1994   Chad Kraft (143)

USA Junior Greco-Roman Championships
1983   Blake Bonjean (132)
1986   Steve Duval (154)
1989   Brandon Paulson (98), Steve King (220)
1990   Jason Davids (98), Billy Pierce (HVY)
1991   Jason Klohs (220), Billy Pierce (HVY)
1992   Brandon Paulson (114.5)
1993   Jose Trevino (154), Jason McCloud (HVY)
1995   Josh Cagle (132)
1996   Brad Pike (143)
1997   Isaiah Larson (HVY)
1998   Jacob Clark (165)

USA FILA Junior World Greco-Roman Championships
1995   Jeremy Goeden (198)

Minnesota Storm Wrestling Club
USA Senior Greco-Roman Championships
1971   Dave Hazewinkel (125.5), Jim Hazewinkel (136.5)
1972   Dave Hazewinkel (149.5), Jim Hazewinkel (136.5)
1975   Brian Gust (125.5), Pat Marcy (149.5) and Dan Chandler (180.5)
1977   Dave Clardy (125.5), Brian Gust (136.5), Pat Marcy
         (149.5), Dan Chandler (180.5) and Brad Rheingans (220)
1978   Bruce Thompson (125.5), Brian Gust (136.5)
1982   John Hughes (149.5), James Andre (163) and Tom Press (180.5)
1983   Jim Martinez (149.5), James Andre (163) and Dennis
         Koslowski (220)
1984   Jim Martinez (149.5), Tom Press (180.5) and Mike
         Houck (198)
1985   Jim Martinez (149.5), Mike Houck (198) and Dennis
         Koslowski (HVY)
1986   Jim Martinez (149.5), Darrell Gholar (149.5), Dennis
         Koslowski (220) and Duane Koslowski (HVY)
1987   Jim Martinez (149.5), Dennis Koslowski (220) and
         Duane Koslowski (HVY)
1995   Marty Morgan (180.5)
1996   Marty Morgan (180.5)
1998   Jason Klohs (213.8)

USA University Freestyle Championships
1995   Gary Kolat (136.5)
1997   Billy Pierce (HVY)

USA University Greco-Roman Championships
1995   Brandon Paulson (114.5)
1996   Jason Klohs (198), Karl Jones (HVY)
1997   Brent Boeshans (213.8), Billy Pierce (HVY)

USA FILA Junior World Freestyle Championships
1995   Chad Kraft (149.5)

USA FILA Junior World Greco-Roman Championships
1986   Ernie McNeal (105.5), Marty Morgan (163), Chris Short
         (180.5) and Jim Richardson (HVY)
1995   Troy Marr (149.5)
1996   Tim Kinsella (163), Brandon Eggum (180.5) and Brent
         Boeshans (220)
1998   Leroy Vega (132)

GRECO & FREESTYLE RECORDS

Minnesota USA Wrestling
USA Senior Greco-Roman Championships
1992   John Morgan (180.5), Dennis Koslowski (220)
1993   Gordy Morgan (163)
1994   Gordy Morgan (163)

USA University Freestyle Championships
1993   Willy Short (163)

USA University Greco-Roman Championships
1992   Jason Klohs (220)
1994   Jason Klohs (198)

USA FILA Junior World Freestyle Championships
1992   Billy Pierce (HVY)
1993   Tolly Thompson (HVY)
1994   Henry Gerten (125.5)

USA FILA Junior World Greco-Roman Championships
1992   Brandon Paulson (114.5), Jason Klohs (220) and Billy
        Pierce (HVY)
1993   Brandon Paulson (114.5)
1994   Troy Marr (149.5)

Twin Cities Wrestling Club
USA Senior Greco-Roman Championships
1974   Brian Gust (125.5), Gary Alexander (136.5) and Pat
        Marcy (149.5)

1981   James Andre (163), Dan Chandler (180.5) and Abdul
        Raheem Ali (198)

Gopher Wrestling Club (Duluth)
USA Senior Freestyle Championships
1988   Melvin Douglas III (198)

USA Senior Greco-Roman Championships
1988   Dalen Wasmund (136.5), Darrell Gholar (180.5), Dennis
        Koslowski (220.0) and Duane Koslowski (HVY)

USA FILA Junior World Freestyle Championships
1987   Jeff Balcom (HVY)
1988   Chris Short (198)

USA FILA Junior World Greco-Roman Championships
1988   Todd Enger (149.5), Marty Morgan (180.5)

Minnesota Jets
USA FILA Junior World Freestyle Championships
1990   Brandon Paulson (105.5), Steve King (220)

USA FILA Junior World Greco-Roman Championships
1990   Steve King (220)

MINNESOTA OLYMPIANS

Alexander, Gary	1976 Greco-Roman 62 Kg, Did Not Place	
Chandler, Daniel	1976 Greco-Roman 82 Kg, Did Not Place, 1980 Greco-Roman 82 Kg, Did Not Compete 1984 Greco-Roman 82 Kg Did Not Place	
Foy, Michael	1988 Greco-Roman, Did Not Place, 1992, Did Not Place	
Gagne, Verne	1948 Greco-Roman 100 Kg Did Not Place	
Gust, Brian	1980 Greco-Roman 57 Kg, Did Not Compete	
Hazewinkel, Dave	1968 Greco Roman 125.5 Did Not Place, 1972 Did Not Place	
Hazewinkel, Jim	1968 Greco Roman 136.5 Did Not Place, 1972 Did Not Place	
Johnson, Evan	1976 Greco-Roman 90 Kg, 7th Place	
Koslowski, Dennis	1988 Greco-Roman 220 lbs, Bronze Medal	
Koslowski, Dennis	1992 Greco-Roman 220 lbs, Silver Medal	
Lowney Garrett	2000 Greco-Roman 213.75 lbs, Bronze Medal	
Lyden, Larry	1968 Greco-Roman 74 Kg, Did Not Place	
Marcy, Patrick	1976 Greco-Roman 68 Kg, Did Not Place	
Martinez, James	1984 Greco-Roman 68 Kg, Bronze Medal	
Morgan, Gordon	1996 Greco-Roman 74 Kg, 9th Place	
Morgan, John	1988 Greco-Roman 82 Kg, 7th Place	
Neist, Gary	1972 Greco-Roman 74 Kg, Did Not Place	
Paulson, Brandon	1996 Greco-Roman 52 Kg, Silver Medal	
Rheingans, Brad	1976 Greco-Roman 100 Kg, 4th Place 1980 Greco-Roman 100 Kg, Did Not Compete	
Rice, Alan	1956 Greco-Roman 62 Kg, Did Not Place	
Thompson, Bruce	1976 Greco-Roman 52 Kg, Did Not Place, 1980 Greco-Roman 52 Kg, Did Not Compete	
Zuniga, David	1996 Greco-Roman Did Not Place	

Source: www.usoc.org

GOPHERS IN INTERNATIONAL COMPETION

Gopher Olympians:
Alan Rice, 1956
Evan Johnson, 1976
Michael Foy, 1988, 1992
Dave Zuniga, 1996 (10th-Place)
Garrett Lowney, 2000 (Bronze Medallist)
Dan Chandler, 1976, 1980, 1984
Jim Martinez, 1984 (Bronze Medallist)
Gordy Morgan, 1996 (Ninth-Place)
Brandon Paulson, 1996 (Silver Medallist)

Gophers in National & International Competition
1997 FILA Junior Nationals Freestyle (2nd Place)
Ryan Lewis (2nd), Luke Becker (4th), Brad Pike (7th), Damion Hahn (4th)

1997 FILA Junior Nationals Greco-Roman (2nd Place)
Ryan Lewis (3rd), Leroy Vega (5th), Brett Lawrence (3rd), Jared Lawrence (5th), Josh Krebs (3rd), Mitch Marr (5th)

1997 U.S. Open Nationals Freestyle
Willy Short (4th)

1997 World Team Greco-Roman
David Zuniga

1998 University Nationals Freestyle
Bart Golyer (7th)

1998 University Nationals Greco-Roman (2nd Place)
Bart Golyer (4th), Ty Friederichs (4th), Brad Pike (3rd), Josh Krebs (7th), Tim Kinsella (5th), DeLaney Berger (6th), Brent Boeshans (2nd)

1998 FILA Junior Nationals Freestyle
Leroy Vega (3rd), Brett Lawrence (2nd), Chad Erikson (5th), Damion Hahn (3rd), Mike Cuperus (5th), Owen Elzen (6th)

1998 FILA Junior Nationals Greco-Roman (1st Place)
Leroy Vega (1st; 10th at world championships), Chad Erikson (7th), Mike Cuperus (2nd), Ken Howard (3rd), Owen Elzen (8th)

1998 U.S. Open Nationals Greco-Roman
Bart Gotyer (5th), David Zuniga (3rd), Jason Klohs (1st), Billy Pierce (3rd)

1998 World Team Trials Greco-Roman
Jason Klohs

1999 University Nationals Freestyle
Bart Golyer (4th), Luke Becker (8th), Brad Pike (7th)

1999 University Nationals Greco-Roman (2nd Place)
Bart Golyer (1st), Ty Friederichs (5th), Jacob Clark (3rd), Ken Howard (3rd), Garrett Lowney (1st), Shelton Benjamin (8th), Mike Flanagan (4th)

1999 FILA Junior Nationals Freestyle
Leroy Vega (1st; 5th at world championships), Ryan Lewis (3rd), Jared Lawrence (1st; 5th at world championships), Luke Becker (2nd), Jacob Clark (3rd), Damion Hahn (1st; 4th at world championships)

1999 FILA Junior Nationals Greco-Roman (1st Place)
Jared Lawrence (1st), Mitch Marr (2nd), Jacob Clark (2nd), Mike Cuperus (1st), Ben Bly (5th), Garrett Lowney (2nd; 1st FILA Junior World)

1999 U.S. Open Nationals Greco-Roman (1st Place)
Brandon Paulson (3rd), Dave Zuniga (1st), Jason Klohs (3rd), Billy Pierce (4th)

1999 World and Pan American Team
Dave Zuniga (2nd at Pan America Games), Jason Klohs (2nd at Pan American Games; 7th at world championships)

2000 University Nationals Freestyle
Ryan Lewis (1st), Damion Hahn (1st), Jared Lawrence (2nd), Matt Kraft (7th)

2000 FILA Junior Nationals Freestyle
Jared Lawrence (1st), Damion Hahn (1st), Luke Becker (3rd), Jacob Volkmann (6th), Desmond Radunz (8th)

2000 FILA Junior Nationals Greco-Roman
Tyler Marr (2nd), Drew Hageman (3rd), Desmond Radunz (4th), Josh McLay (5th), Mike Flanagan (6th), Eli Ross (6th), Jacob Volkmann (8th)

2000 FILA Junior World Championships
Jared Lawrence (3rd), Damion Hahn (8th)

2000 U.S. Open Nationals Freestyle
Tim Hartung (7th)

2000 U.S. Open Nationals Greco-Roman
Garrett Lowney (2nd), Jason Klohs (3rd), Billy Pierce (5th)

2000 Pan American Championships
Garrett Lowney (3rd)

2001 U.S. National Championships Greco-Roman
Garrett Lowney (1st), Brent Boeshans (7th)

2001 U.S. National Championships Freestyle
Brandon Eggum (4th), Tim Hartung (4th), Ryan Lewis

2001 World Team Trials Greco Roman
Garrett Lowney (1st), Brandon Paulson (1st)

2001 World Team Trials Freestyle
Brandon Eggum (2nd), Tim Hartung (6th)

2001 Junior Nationals Greco-Roman
Matt Nagel (1st)

2001 Junior Nationals Freestyle
Marcus LeVesseur (4th)

2001 World Championships Greco-Roman
Garrett Lowney (DNC), Brandon Paulson (2nd)

2001 World Championships Freestyle
Brandon Eggum (2nd)

2002 Pan American Championships Freestyle
Brandon Eggum (2nd)

2002 U.S. National Championships Freestyle
Tim Hartung (1st)

2002 U.S. National Championships Greco-Roman
Brandon Paulson (1st), Garrett Lowney (1st), Billy Pierce (2nd), Leroy Vega (8th), Brent Boeshans (8th)

2002 U.S. University Freestyle Nationals
Damion Hahn (1st)

2002 U.S. University Greco-Roman Nationals
Brett Lawrence (2nd), Eli Ross (2nd), Josh McLay (5th), Drew Hageman (7th)

2002 FILA Junior World Team Trials Freestyle
Tommy Owen (1st), Drew Hageman (4th)

2002 FILA Junior World Team Trials Greco-Roman
Matt Nagel (1st, Outstanding Wrestler), Drew Hageman (2nd), Eli Ross (2nd), Cole Konrad (5th), Tommy Owen (6th)

2002 Junior Pan American Championships Freestyle
Drew Hageman (1st), Matt Nagel (2nd), Tommy Owen (3rd)

2002 Junior Pan American Championships Greco-Roman
Drew Hageman (1st), Matt Nagel (2nd), Tommy Owen (2nd)

2002 U.S. Junior National Championships Freestyle
Cole Konrad (1st), Will Holst (5th)

2002 U.S. Junior National Championships Greco-Roman
Cole Konrad (1st), Quincy Osborn (2nd), Will Holst (7th)

2002 World Team Trials Freestyle
Tim Hartung (1st)

2002 World Team Trials Greco-Roman
Brandon Paulson (1st), Garrett Lowney (1st)

2002 World University Championships Freestyle
Damion Hahn (4th)

2002 World Championships Freestyle
Tim Hartung (DNC)

2002 World Championships Greco-Roman
Brandon Paulson (8th), Garrett Lowney (DNP)

2004 U.S. Junior Pan-Am Championships
Mack Reiter, C.P. Schlatter and Roger Kish

MINNESOTANS MAKING US PROUD...

GET TO KNOW EM'...

Gary Alexander of St. Paul won the U.S. Greco Roman wrestling championship 136.5 lbs title in 1972 and 1975. He was a member of the US Olympic Greco-Roman wrestling team in 1976.

Abdul Raheem of Minneapolis won three US Greco-Roman wrestling titles from 1977 to 1979.

R. Barber of Minneapolis won the US freestyle wrestling championship 121 lbs title in 1942.

Charles Coffee of Minneapolis won the US Greco Roman wrestling championship 138.5 lbs title in 1967.

Michael Foy of Minneapolis was a member of the US Olympic Greco-Roman wrestling team in 1988 and 1992. He won US Greco-Roman wrestling championship 198 lbs titles in 1989, 1991, 1992, 1995, and 1996.

Verne Gagne of Robbinsdale was a member of the US Olympic wrestling team in 1948 and also won a US freestyle wrestling championship title in 1949.

Brian Gust of Lakeville won the US Greco-Roman wrestling championship 125.5 lbs title in 1977, and was a member of the US Olympic Greco-Roman wrestling team in 1980.

Dale Hanson of Minneapolis won the US freestyle wrestling championship 123 lbs title in 1940.

Dave Hazewinkel of Coon Rapids won five US Greco-Roman wrestling championship 125.5 lbs titles from 1967 to 1972. He was a member of the US Olympic Greco Roman wrestling team in 1968 and 1972.

Jim Hazewinkel of Coon Rapids won three US Greco Roman wrestling championship 136.5 lbs titles from 1966 to 1969. He was a member of the US Olympic Greco Roman wrestling team in 1968 and 1972.

Michael Houck of Robbinsdale won US Greco-Roman wrestling championship 198 lbs titles in 1981, 1984, and 1985. He also won two World Greco Roman wrestling championship titles in 1984 and 1985. He was coach of the US Greco-Roman wrestling team in 1990.

Bob Johnson of Minneapolis won the US Greco-Roman heavyweight wrestling title in 1968.

Evan Johnson of Maple Plain was a member of the US Olympic Greco-Roman wrestling team in 1976.

Jason Klohs of Osseo won the US Greco ‹Roman wrestling championship 214 lbs title in 1998.

Len Levy of Minneapolis won the US freestyle heavyweight wrestling title in 1942.

Larry Lyden of Hopkins won three US Greco-Roman 171.5 lbs wrestling titles from 1968 to 1972. Lyden was a member of the US Olympic Greco-Roman wrestling team in 1968.

Pat Marcy of Minnetonka was a member of the US Olympic Greco-Roman wrestling team in 1976.

Jim Martinez of Osseo won US Greco-Roman 149.5 lbs wrestling titles in 1983, 1984, 1985, 1986, and 1987. Martinez was a member of the US Olympic Greco-Roman wrestling team in 1984.

Mike McArthur, of Osseo, was an alternate on the 1976 Olympic Freestyle team and a member of the 1979 World Cup team. He later served as an assistant coach on the 1995 World Championship team, the 1996 Olympic Freestyle team, and was the coach for the 1998 World Cup team.

Gordy Morgan of Bloomington won the US Greco-Roman 163 lbs wrestling title in 1991, 1993, and 1994. He was a member of the US Olympic Greco-Roman wrestling team in 1996.

John Morgan of Bloomington was a member of the US Olympic Greco-Roman wrestling team in 1988. He won US Greco-Roman 180.5 lbs wrestling titles in 1989, 1991, and 1992.

Marty Morgan of Bloomington won the NCAA Greco-Roman 177 lbs wrestling title in 1991 and US Greco-Roman 180.5 lbs wrestling titles in 1995 and 1996.

Gary Neist of Albert Lea was a member of the US Olympic Greco-Roman wrestling team in 1972.

Brandon Paulson on Anoka was a member of the US Olympic Greco-Roman wrestling team in 1996.

Tom Press of Minneapolis won the US Greco-Roman wrestling 180.5 lbs titles in 1982 and 1984.

Brad Rheingans of Appleton won five US Greco-Roman wrestling 220 lbs titles from 1976 to 1980. He was a member of the US Olympic Greco-Roman wrestling team in 1976 and 1980.

James Tanniehill of Minneapolis won the US Greco-Roman wrestling 163 lbs title in 1969.

Bruce Thompson of Rosemount won four US Greco-Roman wrestling 114.5 lbs titles from 1976-80. He was a member of the US Olympic Greco-Roman wrestling team in 1976 and 1980.

David Zuniga of New Brighton was a member of the US Olympic Greco-Roman wrestling team in 1996.

WOMEN'S WRESTLING

Women's wrestling in Minnesota is a work in progress that has had to overcome a lot of obstacles over its journey to equality. Like so many other things in athletics, women are usually the last to get invited to the big dance. And, while wrestling has long been considered to be the oldest sport in the history of mankind, ironically, it has only taken a few thousand years for those "kind men" to give the ladies their opportunity to cut a rug out on the mat.

While women have competed in a bevy of various contact sports, such as judo, karate, taekwondo and boxing, among others, over the years, it is amazing that wrestling would create so much controversy. Sure, the sport has grown considerably over the past 15 years, but it still faces many hurdles down the road. Much of the problem with girls wrestling, at the youth and high school levels, is that there are just not equal opportunities.

You see, wrestling has been, and will always be, about equal opportunities with regards to one criteria: weight. So, it would make sense that a 115 pound girl would be equally matched against a 115 pound boy, right? Well, in theory that is all well and good. But, because too many people simply can't get past the idea of two kids of the opposite sex wearing tight singlets and rolling around together on a mat, the girls have simply not been given their fair shake. For many, fair would be 115 pound girls wrestling 115 pound girls. But, because of the fact that schools have had to deal with so many budget cut-backs over the years, it has been extremely difficult to start and properly fund girls-only programs.

**Tabitha Ramsey
(UM-Morris)**

As a result, the girls, for the most part, have had to compete against the guys in a mixed-gender environment. And, according to the Minnesota State High School League, that is just fine. They acknowledge that even though the sport is based on weight, boys typically have more muscle mass than girls. So, they feel that they have a duty to tell parents that this may lead to an increased risk of injury.

The problem is not so much about injuries, but rather with a lot of the boys who simply don't want to wrestle the girls. Reasons vary from not wanting to hurt them, to not wanting to touch or grab them in a sexual manner. But the biggest reason has to be good ol' "boys will be boys," and simply not wanting to get humiliated by getting his butt kicked in front of hundreds of hometown fans by... yup, a girl. Their loss, right? Yeah, literally, because according to the rules, if a player refuses to wrestle it goes down as a forfeit. And it is not just the boys who refuse, oftentimes it is their coaches who don't want to subject their kids to that type of peer pressure.

A handful of female high school wrestlers in Minnesota have persevered though, and have garnered a lot of respect from both the parents as well as from their peers along the way. Among them is New Ulm's Ali Bernard, a 5-foot-7, 160-pound high school senior won the 2004 Girls Junior World Championship title in Turkey. She later captured the U.S. senior national title at 147 pounds as

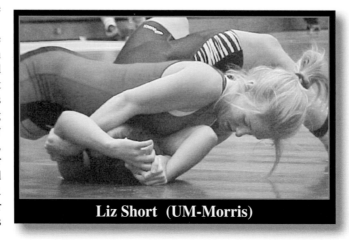

Liz Short (UM-Morris)

well. Against other women, Bernard is tough, really tough. Against the stronger guys, however, she is humbled. The four-time varsity letter-winner, who grew up grappling against her older brother, went 7-22 in her first three seasons with the Eagles, but then dominated many of her male counterparts as a senior to finish a solid 8-11.

Bernard is not exempt from the vast swings in the weight that wrestlers are forced to deal with either. In fact, she has competed anywhere from 148 to 171 pounds over her career, making the old cliché, feast or famine, a part of daily routine.

Another lady grappler is Rachael Holthaus, a 5-foot-1, 105-pound high school senior from rural Bowlus, who wrestles as a member of the Royalton High School team, where her dad coaches. Holthaus got started early and went on to win the Girls U.S. Wrestling Junior Nationals in 2003 and then took second in 2004.

"I was a shy little kid," said Holthaus in a recent Minnesota Women's Press article by Michele St. Martin. "Wrestling is a sport where you have to talk, and my parents thought it would be good for me. There were other little girls who wrestled, but they usually quit after fifth grade. By the time I was old enough to realize the thing about wrestling boys, I was so involved in wrestling that it didn't make a difference. Ignorance is bliss, I guess. And then there was a rumor that women's wrestling would become an Olympic sport, and that kept me going."

"It's their coaches and parents who have the problems," she added. "Some parents and coaches won't let the boys wrestle me. I really don't see the boys objecting. Wrestlers just want a good, challenging partner."

And speaking of the Olympics, women's wrestling was the only new sport at the 2004 Summer Games in Athens. Will the national exposure boost the popularity of the sport the same way it did girls gymnastics and soccer? Will thousands of little girls tug at their mommy's pant leg and beg them to let them wrestle? Probably not. But it is a start, and it can only grow from there. Neither Bernard or Holthaus made the U.S. team, nor did Woodbury High School graduate Jenny Wong, who was the U.S. champ at 112 pounds in 2002, the runner-up in 2001 and 2003. She finished third at nationals in 2004, and out of the running. All three are expected to have a shot at Beijing in 2008 though.

While the Olympics are the pinnacle of success for women wrestlers, there are still so many more pressing issues with regards to growing the base of the pyramid of their sport. They need to lobby hard to create more youth programs as well as high school and college programs too. At the prep level there are just a handful of states which have initiated legislation to get the girls on an equal footing. In 1997, the State of Michigan sponsored the first ever women's state high school championships and the numbers have been steadily increasing. Currently, the states of Texas and Hawaii have instituted an official state championship for girls, as well as all-girl high school wrestling teams. Michigan, California, Iowa, Massachusetts and Florida also offer separate girls programs as well.

At the collegiate level there are presently only seven colleges and universities in the U.S. which offer dedicated women's wrestling programs: Cumberland College in Williamsburg, Kentucky; Lassen College in Susanville, California; MacMurray College in Jacksonville, Illinois; Menlo College in Atherton, California; Missouri Valley College in Marshall, Missouri; Pacific University in Forest Grove, Oregon; and Neosho County Community College in Chanute, Kansas. In addition, Cal-State Bakersfield's Men's Varsity Team allows women competitors too. Beyond that, there are numerous club teams at the University of Hawaii, Cleveland State, Ursinus College (PA), as well as several throughout Canada as well.

Minnesota was at the forefront of that movement, but was dealt a drastic blow in 2004. You see, in 1993, the University of Minnesota-Morris was the first college in the nation to sponsor women's wrestling as an official varsity sport. Twelve years later, budget cuts and politics made the Lady Cougars extinct. Head women's freestyle wrestling coach Doug Reese led his ladies to top place finishes in every tournament in which UM-Morris competed in, including a total of seven national championships. Reese coached and developed a total of 113 All-Americans at the Junior, University and Senior level as well. In the process a total of 16 women had qualified to make the U.S. National Team, while 10 UM-Morris wrestlers have represented the U.S. while competing in the World Championships. Reese, one of the sports' biggest supporters, also served as the Chairperson on USA Wrestling's Women's Wrestling Committee and was a U.S. National Coach for Women's Freestyle Wrestling as well.

When Reese, who also served as the men's coach at Morris, originally proposed the idea of sponsoring women's wrestling, he was not originally taken very seriously.

"They thought I was talking about mud or Jell-O wrestling," Reese joked. "I had to explain that this was serious, Olympic style wrestling. We really had a lot to prove at the start, but once we proved the team had some serious athletes, everyone got behind us."

Furthermore, Reese was the team leader and head coach for the 1998 U.S. Women's Team which competed in the Pan Am Championships in Winnipeg, where the U.S. squad won silver. Later, in 2003, three former Lady Cougars came home with Pan Am Gold: Tina George, Sally Roberts and Sarah McMann, and all three went on to win medals at the 2003 World Championships in New York City as well. More recently, Tabitha Ramsey, a junior from Texas, was also selected to represent the U.S. at the 2004 Pan American Games in Guatemala City.

With numbers like that it hard to understand why we are losing so many of our programs. They are literally fighting for their lives out there, and there seems to be no life preserver in sight. Much of the debate surrounds Title IX legislation, which has inadvertently reduced the number of men's programs

Katie Downing (UM-Morris)

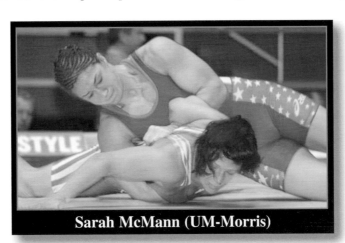
Sarah McMann (UM-Morris)

over the years. Case in point: the NCAA Division I national tournament now features less than 100 schools, down in numbers by almost 50 percent in the last decade alone.

But Title IX was created to, among other things, create more opportunities for women both in the classroom as well as on the athletic field. In fact, women's wrestling fits the NCAA's criteria for emerging sports programs to a tee. Many insiders believe that women's wrestling at the collegiate level is an ideal solution to the pitfalls of Title IX. You see, a lot of schools that support men's wrestling programs are out of compliance with Title IX, with money and scholarships always being a factor. By adding women's wrestling to an athletic program, however, an athletic department can actually save money. The equipment, the facilities and, most importantly, the coaches, are already in place — all that is needed are singlets, warm-ups and travel expenses. The fact of the matter is that while many wrestling fans were crying foul, women's ice hockey became a NCAA and Olympic sport. And, wrestling is way less expensive than hockey. So, it can be done.

As the sport continues to grow both domestically and around the world, more and more little girls will undoubtedly get the fever and want to be a part of the action. More and more nations are sponsoring teams and competitions for women and girls, ages seven to the senior open level, and that can only bode well for the sport as a whole. And, as more and more girls demand equality, more high schools will respond. It is about supply and demand, and the demand needs to get bigger and, quite frankly, louder.

USA Wrestling, the national governing body of the sport, has made great strides and has been instrumental in organizing more club teams, as well as more international freestyle programs and championships at the Cadet, Junior, University and Senior levels. In addition, USA Wrestling also offers Tour du Monde opportunities for the women, giving them the chance to experience new cultures, international travel, training and competition within completely different environments.

The bottom line is this, we all need to do more to build the sport and help it grow. Hey, nobody wants to see men's programs get cut, no way, but there has to be a way for girls and women's programs to get a shot as well. We just need to sharpen our collective pencils and get it done. Period. It is a wonderful sport for both sexes and should be enjoyed equally. The values such as self-discipline, goal setting, self-respect and hard work, that are synonymous with wrestling are not mutually exclusive to the guys, and should be afforded to those who are willing to put forth the effort. The wrestling rooms should be open to women too.

Girls have been and will continue to grapple with stereotypes and discrimination for their opportunity to compete. Hopefully that can change and one day every little girl can grow up dreaming of one day becoming anything from a Cadet medallist to an Olympic medallist, they just need someone to open the door. Hey, once you have had the opportunity to see two well conditioned female athletes competing with outstanding technical skills up close and personal, you too will be sold.

FROM WRESTLING TO RASSLING...

...BEHOLD THE GLORY OF BIG-TIME PRO GRAPPLING IN MINNESOTA

PROFESSIONAL WRESTLING

In the Beginning...

Professional wrestling has long and winding roots which have run throughout the Land of 10,000 Lakes for more than a century. It is somewhat difficult, however, to substantiate much of the history and records from the early years of this celebrated form of entertainment. Why? Well, this is due in large part to the aura and mystique of the "reality" that has shrouded the business since the dawn of time. Is it real or is it fake? That has always been the million dollar question. The answer... it would seem, is that for the most part pro wrestling has pretty much always had predetermined outcomes. Sure, there were bare-knuckle brawlers who settled scores the old fashioned way back in the day, but as time went by, it became more and more of a mixture between sports and entertainment. Perhaps legendary Texas wrestler Nike Kozak said it best: "For those who believe, no explanation is necessary; for those who don't believe; no explanation will do."

To put it into a historical perspective, let's back to 1880, when several thousand fans in New York City flooded Gilmore's Gardens (the future site of Madison Square Garden) to watch William Muldoon beat Thebaud Bauer for the World Greco-Roman Wrestling Championship. Muldoon was probably the sport's first pure professional and became a superstar, traveling the countryside after serving in the Civil War, wrestling all would-be challengers and always coming out on top. Muldoon even partnered with bare-knuckle champ John L. Sullivan to form a traveling show in which they beat the heck out of people from coast to coast.

Another star of the this era was Martin "Farmer" Burns, a 150 pound Iowa native who also traveled the country, and won an estimated 6,000 contests. Burns would be recognized as a two-time U.S. wrestling champion during this era. In May of 1905 the first ever North American World Champion was crowned when Olympian George Hackenschmidt downed Tom Jenkins. Hackenschmidt would eventually be crowned as the World "Catch-as-Catch-Can" Champion (a label which would later be recognized as the original National Wrestling Alliance's world title). The first tag team matches took place shortly thereafter and before long big crowds were turning out to watch the incredible displays of athleticism and courage. Some of these epic matches even lasted for several hours, oftentimes featuring both men lying on the mat in a dual headlock stalemate. How's that for riveting action?

Three years later, in what many felt was a prelude to what we consider modern day wrestling, Hackenschmidt clashed with Frank Gotch in Chicago's Dexter Park. There, Gotch, who trained under Farmer Burns and was an expert at submission holds, fouled Hackenschmidt relentlessly and even oiled himself down to make it nearly impossible for his opponent to grab a hold of him. Hackenschmidt eventually got so frustrated that he quit, leaving Gotch with the World title. This apparently marked the beginning

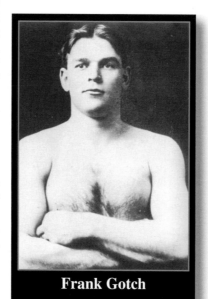

Frank Gotch

of modern-day wrestling rivalries, a hallmark of the sport to this very day. Other great characters would follow, including "The Masked Marvel" in 1916 and Ed "The Strangler" Lewis, who won the world title in 1920.

Eventually, pro wrestling grew in popularity, and with that it evolved into more of a form of entertainment. More and more of the grapplers began to assume stage names, complete with costumes, masks and outlandish personas. Promoters soon followed and with them came elaborate choreographed storylines complete with good-guys clashing with villains, bloody battles, and, most importantly, big crowds. The giant, hulking warriors sucked the fans in and the riveting drama kept them coming back and begging for more.

After the Great Depression, people were lining up to see the action, proving once and for all that pro wrestling was here to stay. Fans soon became riveted to the action, listening to the matches on their radios and reading about their heroes in the local newspapers. Droves of adoring fans came out week after week to watch their favorite stars at venues large and small. From what began in bingo halls and smoky bars eventually grew into large arenas holding upwards of 30,000 people. In the Twin Cities, the old Minneapolis and St. Paul Auditoriums were the first big arenas to host the action up close and personal.

By the 1940s there were local promoters in nearly every market, big and small, from coast to coast, organizing shows. Before long, it was commonplace for promoters to line up cards where they would have each others stars battle one another in different markets. The response to this was overwhelming. The new blood was great for business and the fans ate up the new heated rivalries when the out-of-town villains would enter the fray. Grappling legends such as Gorgeous George, one of the business' first true showmen, had paved the way for a new generation of wrestlers who were determined to grow their craft while trying to get rich and famous in the process.

Eventually, in 1947, dozens of local promoters from around the Midwest got together and decided to consolidate. They wanted to maneuver around the strict anti-trust laws of the era regarding monopolies by forming an alliance which would recognize the first real and tangible world heavyweight champion amongst the various promoters. The result was the formation of the National Wrestling Alliance (NWA), a organization which would last for more than a half century. Basically, the local market promoters of each territory throughout the U.S. and Canada paid yearly membership dues, and in return the sanctioning body would send the nationally recognized champ to tour through those markets. There, he would defend the NWA Heavyweight title belt against that promotion's local hero in a best of three falls match on cards they promoted. With the ability to unify most of the top promoters across North America with a common champion to promote, they would emerge as the most powerful entity in professional wrestling.

Grapplin' Abe

Did you know that prior to the Civil War, Abraham Lincoln was quite the wrestler back in the day? That's right, "Honest Abe" was even crowned as the Sangamon County Wrestling Champion in New Salem, Ill., in 1831 at the age of 21. The 16th President's grappling prowess is even the subject of an entire exhibit at the International Wrestling Institute and Museum in Newton, Iowa.

The problem in the early days of the alliance, however, was that many of those rival promoters, some of whom were a bit on the… shall we say, "shady and egotistical" side, started claiming that their regional champion was the world champ — leading to chaos and bitter feuds. Each promoter figured that his local stud should be recognized as the NWA's "World Champ," which was impossible. So, it was decided that a "unified" champ, decided upon by the promoters themselves, would be crowned. They agreed and with that, the two top contenders, Orville Brown and Lou Thesz, were pitted against one another. Well, a match was arranged between the two, but an untimely automobile accident ended Brown's career. As a result, Thesz was awarded the NWA World championship belt in the Winter of 1949. Thesz would go on to defend his title around the country at the various territories and in all would hold the championship belt on six different occasions over his illustrious career.

As the post-war boom of the late 1940s and early 1950s continued, wrestling's "modern era" as it was called, the business chugged along and enjoyed its place in the world of sports entertainment. While the NWA pretty much ruled the roost across the nation at this point, there were some rumblings occurring amongst the ranks. Several "splinter groups" were looking to make more money and were frustrated that their parent organization was making decisions that were not favorable to them. The winds of change were blowing. Eventually, one man came in and changed the rules forever, and his name was Verne Gagne. Here is his story...

Enter Verne Gagne & The American Wrestling Association (AWA)

Verne Gagne was born on February 26, 1926, in Corcoran, Minn., and grew up on a farm in Hamell during the Great Depression, where he attended a one-room school house. A tremendous athlete, Gagne grew up loving sports. He also grew up tough. In fact, he left home at age 14 after his mother passed away to live with relatives. He learned the value of hard work at an early age, having to get his first job as a young boy, sweeping and cleaning up at a local tavern and beauty shop before school. He would later wind up at Wayzata High School for one year, ultimately transferring and graduating from Robbinsdale High School in 1943. There, he earned all-state honors in football under coach Red Sochaki., and, even though he weighed only 185 pounds, he also won a pair of state heavyweight wrestling championships in 1942 and 1943. Robbinsdale, under the tutelage of coach Mark Woodward, was a wrestling dynasty in those days and was right in the midst of winning a record seven straight state titles from 1940-46.

From there, Gagne was recruited to play football at the University of Minnesota. But his main sport with the Gophers quickly became wrestling. After winning the Big Nine heavyweight wrestling title in 1944 as a freshman, Gagne went into the Marine Corps to serve in World War II. Stationed in California, Gagne played football for the El Toro Marine team for the next two years, while also teaching the art of hand to hand combat as well. He returned to the Gophers in 1946, however, and picked up right where he left off.

As a platooning tight end and defensive end, Gagne was outstanding on the gridiron; but on the matt, he was simply unstop-

Joe Stecher

Abe Kashey & Farmer Tobin

pable. Gagne went on to win three more conference heavyweight titles over the next three years, along with a pair of NCAA national championships — as a 191-pounder in 1948 and as a heavyweight in 1949. (The latter came against future pro wrestler, Dick Hutton, from Oklahoma, in a double overtime thriller. That match had a lot of meaning for Gagne, who had previously lost to Hutton on a controversial referee's decision in the 1947 national finals.) The three-time All-American was also a member of the 1948 Olympic Greco Roman team, and even won the 1949 AAU championship as well.

After playing in the prestigious College Football All-Star Game in Chicago against the NFL Champion Philadelphia Eagles, Gagne signed with Curly Lambeau's Green Bay Packers. (He had originally been drafted by the Chicago Bears in 1947, but because Papa Bear Halas wanted him to give up a year of eligibility and sign a contract as a junior, Gagne said no thanks.) Verne played for the Pack throughout the 1949 pre-season, but just before the first regular season game Lambeau informed him that because the Bears still owned his rights, and wouldn't release him, he couldn't legally play. So, Gagne said "to heck with football" and, luckily for us, went into the profession that would make him one of the most recognizable athletes of his day, professional wrestling.

Gagne had always been intrigued with the world of professional wrestling and used to love listening to Bronko Nagurski's wrestling matches on the radio as a kid. So, when Minneapolis promoter Tony Stecher encouraged him to give it a shot, he agreed. You see, Verne had something most pro grapplers didn't have at that time, legitimate athletic credibility. As a Gopher football and wrestling star, he was a well known commodity and very marketable to the media. And, in addition to being very articulate, he was a muscular good looking guy — the prototypical "babyface."

Verne jumped in head first and began to learn the ropes from local wrestlers Joe Pazandak and George Gordienko. He made his pro debut on May 3rd, 1949, against Abe "King Kong" Kashey in Minneapolis, winning by disqualification in a match refereed by boxing legend, Jack Dempsey. Shortly thereafter, Verne headed to Texas, where he worked for promoter Morris Sigel.

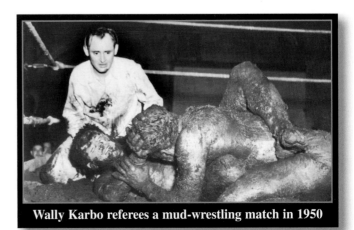

Wally Karbo referees a mud-wrestling match in 1950

Former Boxing Great Jack Dempsey Refs a 1943 Match

There, he was an instant success, capturing the Texas heavyweight title belt by defeating Leo Newman in Houston. Gagne continued his "push" by local promoters and eventually went on to obtain the NWA World Junior Heavyweight title belt in 1950, when he beat Sonny Myers in Tulsa. Gagne would defend the strap against many of that era's top draws, but never got the opportunity to seriously contend for the coveted NWA World heavyweight belt. That belonged to legendary grappler, Lou Thesz, a big-time fan-favorite and top money earner, someone the promoters were determined to keep elevated as the champ. Gagne got his shots against Thesz, but never got the green light to defeat him — which brings us back to our story, and those old winds of change...

By the early 1950s television was changing the landscape of professional wrestling. TV was a relatively new medium at this time and, believe it or not, professional wrestling was one of the first programs to be broadcast nationally throughout the United States. The two were made for each other and before long the fans at home were tuning in by the millions. The driving force behind it all at that time were the DuMont Network, which was based in Chicago, and CBS, which was out of New York. People were just so transfixed over the new invention, that they were lining up to watch whatever was on, and luckily for wrestling fans, a big chunk of what they saw was wrestling. Fans from coast to coast were instantly sucked in and mesmerized by not only the athleticism, but also the drama.

Technology in the early '50s was primitive by today's standards, but the pro wrestling ring was an ideal setting for TV. It was easy to produce and the programmers loved it. Viewers were hooked, but as they got to know the characters up close and personal, they wanted a little more — they wanted some drama and some theatrics. Said wrestler turned promoter Bruce Hart, the son of legendary grappler Stu Hart: "It was a grand time to be a wrestler. Every city had an office and the boys were paid quite well. With TV things went from back alley 'shoots' (real fights) of the early 1900s to showmanship. Every office had a wrestling cowboy, Indian, German whacko, and so on. Every city ran their own territory built around a local hero."

In 1953 Gagne won the United States title, which was still a notch below the NWA World Heavyweight title, but could be seen defending his belt every weekend on the DuMont Network.

Chief Little Bear

Before long, Verne had became a household name, thrilling fans from coast to coast with his high-flying aerial acrobatics. From Chicago to Minneapolis and from New York to Boston, Verne was on the road every week pummeling the likes of Gorgeous George, Dick the Bruiser and Killer Kowalski. Once, in 1953, Gagne was the headliner at New York's famed Madison Square Garden, where a riot nearly occurred outside when more than 5,000 rabid fans were turned away from the sell-out. With his infamous "Gagne Sleeper" finishing move, Verne held the U.S. title for more than two and a half years before losing it to Wilbur Snyder in 1956.

By now, additional programming had been created for the most coveted television time slots and wrestling was falling out of favor with the powers-that-be. They were searching for more family-friendly programming and wanted to go in a different direction. So, programming shifted to a more regional basis, where promoters had to find local television affiliates to broadcast their shows. It was a huge blow, and one that would forever change the landscape of professional wrestling.

Gagne, meanwhile, was still traveling the circuit. Over the next couple of years he would recapture a pair of U.S. titles, as well as a regional title in Omaha. He also won a handful of Minneapolis tag-team titles alongside several former Gopher football legends, including his boyhood hero, Bronco Nagurski, as well as Butch Levy and Leo Nomellini. With Verne's success, the local NWA promoter in Minnesota, Tony Stecher, wanted him to become the NWA World Champ. Thesz, of course, held the belt, and the other promoters did not want him to lose it because that might mean that they would lose money on an unknown commodity coming in and not being able to fill their seats with spectators.

Joe Pazandak

Finally, in the Summer of 1957, all hell broke loose in Chicago when contender Edouardo Carpentier apparently beat reigning champ Lou Thesz in a controversial best-of-three falls match to capture the NWA's world title. But, because one of those falls came by virtue of a "disqualification," Thesz was allowed to keep his belt. A few renegade promoters disputed the decision, however, and decided to recognize Carpentier as their new world champ. One of those promoters was Stecher, who was tired of seeing Verne never getting his shot and wanted to see some new blood. Another was Nebraska promoter Joe Dusek, who sanctioned the passing of the title from Carpentier to Gagne that next year when he beat him in a title match in Omaha — really throwing a monkey wrench into the mix.

So, with one group of promoters recognizing Thesz as the NWA champion and the other throwing their support to Gagne, it didn't take a rocket scientist to figure out something had to be done. The situation quickly worsened with the other promoters and a lot of lobbying was being done behind the scenes to unify the belt, but it never happened. Many speculated that Gagne's lack of size was the reason that he never got a shot at the NWA title versus Thesz, while others speculated that it was just good ol' politics as usual. One thing Verne did know was that he was not going to come out on top with that many of the old boys rooting against him. So, Verne, who had since lost the world title belt to the masked "Dr. X" a few months after winning it in Omaha, decided to make some history of his own.

With that, Verne got together with the Stecher family

Bill Kuusisto

(Tony Stecher had since passed and his son Dennis was running the show) and did the unthinkable — he bought out the NWA's Minneapolis territory (the Minneapolis Boxing & Wrestling Club) and in the process formed a rival circuit called the American Wrestling Alliance. (It should be noted that the name "AWA" had originally been used by Boston promoter Paul Bowser from the late 1920s through the early 1950s, and then again briefly in the mid-1950s by a pair of promoters from Chicago named Ray Fabiani and Leonard Schwartz. Gagne's reincarnation of the AWA, however, would be an entirely new and independent venture.) Gagne was now on his way to becoming one of the business' biggest players. In fact, it would be the beginning of an illustrious business and entertainment empire that would span the next four decades.

Joining Verne was Wally Karbo, a part-owner of the promotion along with the Stechers, who was also a longtime referee and promoter in the area. It would be the perfect one-two punch, with Verne starring as the champ and running the show from behind the scenes, and Wally serving as the out-front promoter. While it might have seemed somewhat unusual that Gagne was both the star attraction in the ring and also running the promotional end of the business, in reality this type of arrangement wasn't uncommon during that era. In fact, several other well known promoters would also book themselves as the top star in their own territories, including: Fritz Von Erich in Dallas, Dick the Bruiser in Indianapolis, and The Sheik in Detroit, to name a few.

(It is also interesting to note that there may be a good reason as to why the NWA didn't put up a huge fight over Gagne leaving the cartel and starting their own rival circuit. You see, according to the website www.kayfabememories.com, just a few years earlier in 1956, "...the U.S. Attorney General announced that the NWA and its member promoters had been investigated and charged with monopolization of professional wrestling by blacklisting, boycotting, coercion and other illegal tactics." Translation: perhaps the NWA didn't want to look like they were monopolizing the industry, so they didn't scream and holler when a splinter opposition group wanted to break off and do their own thing. Or, stay with me here, some conspiracy theorists have even hypothesized that the entire transaction was planned out all along to show the government that the NWA was indeed not a monopoly, and was just fine with other competitors. Who knows? That one will remain just an "alleged" theory at best.)

Anyway, because the newly created AWA didn't want any hard feelings with the old guard, they issued a "peace offering" of sorts when they issued an ultimatum to then NWA World champion Pat O'Connor to defend his championship in 90 days against their No. 1 contender, Verne Gagne, or else be stripped of it. Gagne then issued a public challenge to O'Connor to unify the belts, but his cries fell on deaf ears. How would the NWA promoters respond? As could be expected, they laughed and ignored the challenge, figuring the AWA would be out of business by years end anyway.

Boy were they wrong. With that, Gagne was awarded the AWA World championship belt on August 16, 1960, meaning there were now officially two major sanctioning bodies in the world of professional wrestling.

While the AWA steadily expanded its roots outward, eventually moving into cities such as Winnipeg, Milwaukee, Chicago, Denver and Omaha, most territories still didn't recognize Gagne as the world heavyweight champ. So, he wrestled in those locales without the belt, as a top contender. But, when he came home, or wrestled in "friendly" territories, he was the AWA world champ. It was a brilliant business strategy, because on one end he pacified his rival promoters, and on the other he built up his name recognition even more on a national basis.

"Back when we first got started out, you had to have television, or you couldn't survive," said Gagne. "I was lucky, I got into the business just as TV was getting popular, but pro wrestling was just made for TV. It was a perfect fit, no question, the numbers were huge — then and now. Our first Saturday night show, broadcast all over on the DuMont Network out of Chicago, was a big success and really got us started. I mean for two hours in prime time every Saturday night, we were it, and those were the days, let me tell ya. That network was red hot throughout the country and I was right there when it all got going, getting all that air time for the better part of eight years. It was a huge break for me, no question. As a result, when I finally decided to buy my own promotion, here in Minnesota, I had already gotten a lot of national exposure, so it was an instant success. I bought the promotion from Dennis Stecher, after his father Tony had died, and turned it completely around in less than six weeks. I was only in my twenties at that time, but it was one heck of a ride starting that thing from the ground up and getting it going. I had made a name for myself here as a wrestler, both with the Gophers and later in professional wrestling, so that gave me a lot of credibility early on too."

Pro Wrestling Takes off in the Land of 10,000 Lakes

From there, the Midwest became a hotbed for the business, with much of the new talent being discovered and trained by the locals. Among them was Gagne himself, who started to recruit and train local athletes to participate in his AWA. Gagne also had a great knowledge of the local and regional television markets. Combine that with he and Karbo's keen understanding of good ol' fashioned showmanship, and it was a recipe for success. Wrestling's popularity soared, local arenas were being filled with fans wanting to see their heroes up close and personal, and with all that came fame and fortune for many of the performers.

"I worked guys out at our farm in Chanhassen, in the old barn, where we had our training camp," said Verne. "A lot of guys used to want to get into the business and think that they could hack it, so we would bring them out to the farm. Once there, it was all over in about 15 minutes. For most of them, they couldn't get back to their cars and get out

Georgous George

Lou Plummer

Verne Gagne

of there fast enough, it was hilarious. I used to get the biggest kick out of these big guys who used to say 'ah heck, I can do this stuff, anybody can do that…', and then bring out there and put them through a routine. We used to just beat the heck out of these guys, and very few actually made it into the business. There were a lot of bruised bodies as well as bruised egos that left the old barn in those days!"

(It is interesting to note that Gagne's trainees over the years included: Greg Gagne, Jim Brunzell, Blackjack Lanza, Ricky Steamboat, Gene Anderson, Al Ragowski, Larry Heiniemi, Baron Von Raschke, Bob Remus, Ken Patera, Chris Taylor, Bob Bruggers, Playboy Buddy Rose, John Nord, Brad Rheingans, Ric Flair, Steve Olsonoski, Buck Zumhoffe, Scott Irwin, Larry Hennig, Curt Hennig, Big Van Vader, Blackjack Mulligan, Paul Ellering and Bulldog Bob Brown, among many others.)

Another reason why pro wrestling was so popular at this point was the belief that it was all "real." In reality, it was very secretively scripted by the promoters, with the wrestlers themselves knowing the predetermined outcomes of each match. Having said that, however, that did not mean that the athletes were not putting it all on the line night in and night out. They were there to put on a good show and make it appear as realistic as possible. As a result, the wrestlers worked hard to put on elaborately choreographed performances which often included severely injuring themselves and or their opponents. Blood, broken bones and even paralysis were all part of the deal and no one really knew for sure on any given night how the chips were going to fall.

As the crowds became more educated and entertained, they raised their level of expectations. Wrestling was all about good guys and bad guys, or "babyfaces" and "heels," almost mirroring society as a whole. If a political issue came up that would make national news, then an evil wrestler from a rogue terrorist nation might soon be worked into the action — bringing a sense of nationalism into the mix as well. Not everyone could be either a good guy or a bad guy though, which led to opportunities for both up-and-comers, as well as old standbys, which were called "jobbers." Jobbers were guys who didn't do much or say much, rather, their job was to make the star look good. They needed to lose on cue and do it convincingly, usually by winding up on the receiving end of that particular star's signature "finishing move." They took a pounding, for usually not a lot of money, but were an integral part of the action night in and night out.

For the wrestlers, it was often tough to keep up the persona. One old school grappler, Eddie Sharkey, would later

remark that his parents "went to their graves believing that pro wrestling was real." It was all about the mystique and while many suspected that there was something fishy going on, no one really knew for sure. That was all part of the attraction. It was also tough for the wrestlers to keep up the act out in the real world. In reality, most of the wrestlers were good friends and would often travel to matches together on long road trips. If the fans saw these arch villains together though, their cover would be blown. Sharkey spoke of one incident in particular which nearly blew it all wide open. It happened in Oklahoma when two fierce rivals, one good guy and one bad guy, were out one night together when they were involved in a car accident. When the locals found out that the two of them were in the same car all hell broke loose. Speculation ensued that perhaps the good guy may have been kidnapped. The two wrestlers had to get out of Dodge after that and move to another territory. Luckily, back in the day, wrestlers could do that sort of thing without too much trouble. Just a quick stage-name change, perhaps the addition of a mask, and poof… a new character with a brand new identity was born.

Meanwhile, the first AWA card was held on August 9, 1960, in Minneapolis, with Jack Pesek beating Jim Grabmire; Roy

Tony Stecher

Born the son of a Bohemia immigrant in 1889, Tony Stecher would go on to prominence as one of the first big-time manager and promoters. The Nebraska native, who excelled at amateur wrestling as a youth, would later relocate to Minnesota, where he would emerge as Minneapolis' top boxing and wrestling promoter during the 1930s. He tried his hand at pro wrestling, but found he was better as a businessman, so he managed his kid brother, Joe, instead. With his "leg-scissors" finishing move, Joe was one of the sports first big stars. In fact, he defeated Charlie Cutler to become the first widely recognized world heavyweight champion after the retirement of Frank Gotch in 1915. Tony would go on to become the father of Minneapolis boxing and wrestling. In fact, he was one of six founding charter members of National Wrestling Alliance and ran the Minnesota territory during the 1940s and 50s. Stecher even hosted the NWA's first convention in Minneapolis in 1948 as well. After his death, his son Dennis took over. He in turn sold the promotion, which was operated under the Minneapolis Boxing and Wrestling Club umbrella, to Verne Gagne in 1959. Gagne, of course, renamed it as the American Wrestling Association. Stecher's legacy would continue in the Land of 10,000 Lakes for the next three decades as the AWA grew and expanded before ultimately closing its doors in 1991.

Nick Bockwinkel

McClarty defeating Don Colt; and Bob Rasmussen downing George Grant. Then, for the main event, a tag-team match featuring Tiny Mills and Stan Kowalski, known as "Murder Incorporated," beat Verne Gagne and Joe Scarpello by disqualification. (Since Mills and Kowalski had been the last tag team champions of the NWA territory in Minnesota, they were billed as the first AWA tag team champs when the two promotions merged together.)

Gagne, ever the showman, was smart enough to realize that the fans enjoyed the drama of seeing their champ occasionally get beat. Then, he realized pretty quickly that they loved to rally behind the former champ and watch him rally back to win the belt back from the bad guy. They loved the storylines, the interviews and the good versus evil aspect of it all. This would be a hallmark of Gagne's professional career, and one of the reasons why he was so wildly successful. Before legions of fans from throughout the Midwest were tuning into Gagne's weekly "All Star Wrestling" show, which aired every Saturday night from the old Calhoun

Beach Hotel, in Minneapolis. Generations of kids would attend live tapings as well, giving them the opportunity to see their heroes up close and personal.

One of Gagne's first toughest challengers as AWA heavyweight champ was former Canadian Football League star, Gene Kiniski. Kiniski was a tough S.O.B. and the local fans absolutely hated him. He was the perfect ying to Gagne's yang. Verne was the All-American boy and Kiniski was a classic villain who screamed at the fans whenever he could. Their feuds were legendary, which led to some good drama over the years as they exchanged the title belt back and forth. Another favorite opponent of Gagne's early on was Bill Miller, who was better known as the masked "Mr. M." The new villain was a big hit as the locals despised him right out of the gates. He and Verne went back and forth during the early 1960s with the drama always winding down to the crowd cheering to get Verne to unmask him. No wrestler could ever do it though because instead of going for the winning pin fall, they would always get distracted by trying to get his mask off, which would ultimately lead to their demise. Mr. M would then use some sneaky, underhanded tactic like bashing his opponent over the head with a foreign object to win in dramatic fashion. The subplots were both cheesy and predictable, but the fans ate it up.

Over the next couple of years the AWA slowly but surely expanded its foothold throughout the Midwest. Omaha, in particular, was a region that was similar to Minneapolis in that they recognized their own champion. The territory was also very friendly to Gagne as he even wore the local heavyweight championship belt there for nearly a year in 1962 after defeating local stars such as Don Leo Jonathan, Fritz Von Erich and Reggie "Crusher" Lisowski.

Da Crusher

motion in the country. McMahon would emerge as a force to be reckoned with, first along the east coast, and later across the country. With that, there were now three big promotions with their respective champs being: Verne Gagne (AWA), Lou Thesz (NWA) and Bruno Sammartino (WWWF).

Other villains would arise for Gagne over the next several years, among them being Maurice "Mad Dog" Vachon, a former member of the 1948 Canadian Olympic Wrestling team. His act as a deranged, out-of-control maniac scared the heck out of the fans and proved to be a breath of fresh air for the AWA. Their battles proved to be epic, with Vachon often winning the belt and keeping it for long periods of time. This was a change of pace for the AWA, which was clearly trying to create and establish some new blood within the organization. The promotion was expanding its territory and more and more cities were leaving the NWA to come on board.

Mad Dog's popularity as the AWA's top heel was enough to get him a better gig with a rival promotion. So, in 1967 Verne needed to bring in some new blood to keep his fans interested. Enter former Syracuse football and wrestling star Dick Beyer, a mysteriously masked brute who Gagne renamed as "Dr. X." The fans loved Dr. X's shtick. From offering a whopping $10,000 to any wrestler who escaped from the clutches of his vaunted figure four leg lock, to bragging during his interviews that if any man could beat him in a best of three falls match, he would take off his mask and reveal himself. This made from some good drama. As a result, he would often lose his first fall, only to build the suspense for the second one — which he always wound up winning in dramatic fashion, along with the third. In fact, whenever he won by submission, he would always play it up by begging the referee to untangle his legs from his opponents, declaring that his figure four move was wound up so tight that not even he could release his own death grip.

Once, after illegally jumping into the ring and interfering with Gagne, even "injuring" the star during a big television match, Dr. X instantly became the AWA's most hated villain. It wasn't long before many of the promotion's other good guys were lining up to do battle with this new nemesis, including: Bill Watts, The Crusher, Dick the Bruiser, Wilbur Snyder, Igor Vodik and Chris Markoff, among others. Dr. X rose through the ranks and eventually beat Gagne that next year, only to lose it right back a few weeks later.

Dick the Bruiser

Because of the close proximity, many wrestlers who competed in Minnesota also worked in Omaha too. Eventually, in 1963, the Minneapolis and Omaha territories merged, with the Omaha territory recognizing the AWA titleholder as the consensus world heavyweight champion.

After the merger, Gagne's main arch rival became the Crusher. The two were polar opposites, and the crowd loved to hate the big beer swilling brawler from Milwaukee. They would exchange title belts off and on for the next couple of years, selling out arenas all along the way. Later, Gagne teamed up with Moose Evans to beat the Crusher and "Dick the Bruiser" for the AWA's tag team title. The crowd simply ate it up. (Incidentally, the Bruiser, along with Wilbur Snyder, would later take over as the main promoters in Indianapolis with the WWA. As a result, the promoters/wrestlers partnered by jobbing for each other in their own territories, while also sharing undercard talent as well. The move was a great boost to the growth of the AWA.)

Future tag-team foes for Gagne would include "Handsome" Harley Race and "Pretty Boy" Larry Hennig, a fellow Robbinsdale High School alum. Fans from nearly every town on the AWA circuit were lining up to see the action in person, it was just good fun family entertainment. Around that same time something big happened in the world of professional wrestling. East Coast promoter Vince McMahon Sr., like Gagne, finally got fed up with the NWA and decided to start his own rival promotion. With Bruno Sammartino as his star attraction, McMahon's World Wide Wrestling Federation (WWWF) hit the mat as the third major pro-

The AWA Rolls Into the '70s

As the decade of the '70s came rolling in, the AWA was evolving. The promotion was expanding not only throughout the Midwest and into Canada,

Mad Dog Vachon

but also across the pond to Japan, where they struck a reciprocal exchange agreement with the International Wrestling Enterprise — thus bringing Japanese stars Kobayashi and Kusatsu here to perform. With announcer Marty O'Neill calling the shots, the fans came out in droves to check them out. It was great family entertainment and the price was right.

"The '60s and '70s were very good times for the boys," recalled former wrestler turned trainer/promoter Eddie Sharkey. "Work was plentiful and the pay was good. I was blessed. I started wrestling in the carnivals, wrestling tough guys out of the crowds who bet they could last 10 minutes with you. Eventually, I got to be a main-eventer. In those days, it was rare that any guy could work regularly at home — and the AWA really was the place to be."

By now Verne was in his early 40s and feeling the grind on his old bones. So, the circuit focused more on tag team titles, saving the heavyweight title defenses for special occasions — when they knew that they could really pack the house. This gave Verne more time to travel throughout the territory and defend his belt against their local stars. The difference on this go-around, however, was that Verne wasn't afraid to show a different side to his character persona. You see, Verne had always been a babyface, or good guy, but he was now evolving and was willing to spar toe-to-toe with other babyfaces in order to show his mettle. As a result, a new rougher and tougher side of Verne was seen as he let the world know that even though he was old, he would do whatever it took to defend his title.

Tragedy struck the AWA family in the Summer of 1971 when Red Bastien and Hercules Cortez, who had just beaten Mad Dog and Butcher Vachon for the AWA tag team titles in Milwaukee, were driving back to Minneapolis from Winnipeg and their car overturned near St Cloud. Sadly, Cortez, who was driving, was killed. The show went on though, and Bastien, who was only slightly injured, returned to the ring with the Crusher as his new partner. The duo then went on to beat Hans Schmidt and Baron Von Raschke, as well as Larry Hennig and Lars Anderson, before eventually dropping the straps to Ray Stevens and Nick Bockwinkel.

Bockwinkel, a veteran of many wrestling wars over the years, would go on to become synonymous with the AWA as the promotion's most arrogant and hated heel — bar none. The drama was perfect: a smug know-it-all bully versus Gagne, the All-American hero — their feuds made for some great storylines. Between solo heavyweight title matches and tag-team contests featuring Bockwinkel and Ray "the Crippler" Stevens,

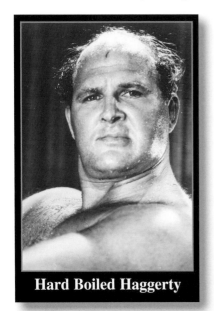

Hard Boiled Haggerty

versus Verne and British grappler Billy Robinson, it was a recipe for success. (Incidentally, Gagne and Robinson's act was so popular that they were even featured in a movie entitled "The Wrestler," which came out in 1974 starring Ed Asner as a promoter and chronicled the plight between two fictional characters played by both Verne and Billy.)

Among the AWA's new stars during this era included: Blackjack Lanza, Superstar Billy Graham, Chief Wahoo McDaniel, Baron Von Raschke and Edouardo "The Flying Frenchman" Carpentier. With the AWA growing in the Midwest and the WWWF growing out East, it was only a matter of time before the two promotions crossed paths. The first big-time import from the WWWF to the AWA was the Russian Bear, Ivan Koloff. Koloff, who had unseeded the legendary Bruno Sammartino for the WWWF title, came to the AWA with his signature bear hug finishing move. He and Gagne would spar more than a half dozen times in the early 1970s, giving Verne yet another solid villain he could draw fans in with.

In 1973 Verne's son, Greg, hit the mat. It was clear who the heir apparent was going to be as the fans fell in love with the young grappler. Before long Greg teamed up with a former Gopher football teammate of his by the name of "Jumpin" Jim Brunzell to form a tag-team duo called the "High Flyers." With their boyish good looks and All-American style they quickly rose up the ranks and became the darlings of the AWA. The dynamic duo got their first big break in front of a televised audience in August of 1974 when they took on former AWA tag team champs Ray Stevens and Nick Bockwinkel, along with their manager, Bobby "The Brain" Heenan. There, the High Flyers won by disqualification as they got pummeled after the final bell. The drama ensued when Larry Hennig came to the rescue by jumping into the ring. Hennig, who had been a bitter rival to Greg's father, Verne, was now a family ally. In fact, Verne even teamed up with Hennig after that for some tag team matches. Go figure. The soap opera rolled on and the fans ate it up.

On November 8th, 1975, Bockwinkel, with the "illegal" help of Big Bad Bobby Duncum, finally beat Verne to capture the AWA's heavyweight title. With that, Verne's seven year AWA title reign was over. This was a very significant event which ultimately gave Heenan, and his family stable of heels a clear good versus evil platform against the likes of The Crusher, Dick The Bruiser," Billy Robinson and Larry Hennig. Good always prevails over evil though, and such was the case in 1977, when The High Flyers defeated Blackjack Lanza and Bobby Duncum to become the AWA tag team champions. Greg was getting a big push from his old man, and steadily emerging as the heir apparent.

Eventually, as most had expected, the Gagne's teamed up to from perhaps the most famous father-son tag-team of all time. But, when they could still not defeat the AWA Tag Team title holding duo of Ray Stevens and Pat Patterson, Verne took drastic measures by partnering with his old nemesis Mad Dog Vachon. And, sure enough, they got the coveted AWA tag team belt back — defending it against all would-be contenders during the Summer of 1979.

By 1980, Verne had made it pretty clear that he was going to hang up the leotards and focus on the business side of the promotion. His last heavyweight bout took place in 1981 against Nick Bockwinkel in what was billed as his swan-song retirement match. With his vaunted "Gagne Sleeper," Verne, of course, won. So, by virtue of being ranked as the top contender, Bockwinkel was then awarded the AWA title. Similarly, when Verne earlier was stripped up his tag team belt alongside Mad Dog (Verne missed some bookings due to competing overseas at the time and was thus stripped of his title.), the "East-West Connection" duo of Jesse Ventura and Adrian Adonis were given the title by default as well.

It is interesting to note that back in the day, promoters used to remain loyal to just a select few heavyweight champs who they could completely trust with their belt. You see, according to Oakdale wrestling historian, George Schire, promoters were very cautious about who they put their belts on because they had to be sure that they didn't get a loose cannon out there who might get beat by some up-and-comer who wanted his 15 minutes of fame by injuring the champ in front of a live audience, or on television, and win the belt. That would have been disastrous, because all of the storylines would have to be changed in order for the promoter to explain why some jobber beat his champ. So, promoters would crown what was referred to in old-school wrestling terms as a 'hooker,' a guy like Lou Thesz, who, if he had to, could take his opponent and within seconds, break his arm or seriously hurt him if need be. He was just that good and that strong. He was a professional and lived by the code, but if another wrestler got too cute with him, he would let him have it in order to keep him in line and protect the belt. In the AWA, Nick Bockwinkel was a guy who Verne Gagne knew he could trust. So, when he put his belt on Nick, he knew that he could defend it. He also knew that he would drop it if he wanted the storyline to go that way as well. There were a lot of other big name guys who were rising stars in the AWA during this era, but simply couldn't be trusted to drop the belt when they were asked to. So, that is a big reason as to why Nick reined so long at the top.

As the new decade of the '80s was ushered in, the AWA was going strong, running events from coast to coast, as well as in Canada, Mexico, Europe and even the Middle East. By now several new stars hit the local scene to challenge Bockwinkel, including Tito Santana, Dino Bravo, Rick Martel and former Olympian Brad

Verne Gagne

Rheingans. There was also a good crop of heels as well, including the 500 pound beast, Jerry Blackwell, who, alongside Big John Studd, wreaked havoc on the AWA as tag-team partners during this era. Other bad guys who found success during this time were Sheik Adnon Al-Kaissy, who was billed as a wealthy Arabian madman. He eventually teamed up with Blackwell by offering him millions of dollars and his own harem of women. "Sheik Ayatollah Blackwell" and Al Kaissy then became all the rage, but after Al Kaissy busted his arm in a match against Mad Dog Vachon, he was replaced with former Olympic weightlifter Ken Patera — whose contract was purchased by the Sheik from Bobby Heenan. Together, the nasty duo would go on to beat Greg Gagne and Jim Brunzell for the AWA tag team title in 1983. Sound complicated? That was the point. The elaborate storylines were the hook which kept the fans interested.

The biggest star of this era, however, came in the Summer of 1981, and his name was Hulk Hogan. Hogan, who had feuded with Andre the Giant as a heel in the WWWF the year before, was pretty unpolished. But, after refining his look in Japan, he appeared in the AWA as a new babyface and quickly became a big-time fan-favorite. With huge bulging biceps and charisma coming out of his ears, the blond-haired behemoth was destined for stardom. So much so, in fact, that he was cast as "Thunder Lips" in the movie Rocky III starring Sylvester Stallone — a role which brought him as well as the AWA a lot of publicity. Hogan later traveled the territory with Blackwell, doing his "body slam challenge" at every stop along the way.

"Hulkamania" was truly running wild at that point, but when he allegedly never got the big push to be the AWA champ, he left to join Vince McMahon Jr.'s newly-renamed World Wrestling Federation (WWF), which had been making a lot of noise on the

east coast. Hogan pinned Bockwinkel several times during his tenure in Minnesota, but each decision was reversed. The climax came on April 24th, 1983, at the St. Paul Civic Center, during "Super Sunday," the AWA's first true "super-card." There, Hogan pinned Bockwinkel to win the belt, but later had the decision reversed by AWA President Stanley Blackburn, citing the fact that Bockwinkel had been illegally thrown over the top rope earlier in the match — which the ref didn't see. The 18,000+

Andre The Giant

fans in attendance almost rioted, as did the 4,000+ fans watching on closed circuit TV in the Roy Wilkins Auditorium next door, but the decision stood. Some cried foul, others just plain cried, but that was the direction the promotion wanted to go. Apparently, Hogan was upset over what percentage of royalties he was going to get from some merchandising, and it just soured from there. It was apparently a behind-the-scenes political thing that most fans weren't aware of at the time.

So, the Hulk up and left for greener pastures, and found his title belt almost immediately in Vince McMahon Jr.'s WWF. McMahon, meanwhile, had decided to capitalize on the cable television boom and took his promotion national, paying big bucks for guys willing to join forces with him. It was a big step, and one that would ultimately pay off in spades. McMahon needed new talent and wasn't afraid to go out and get it from rival promoters — at whatever the cost. He also needed a front-man to be his world champ and Hogan was going to be that man. Hogan's departure was just the beginning of a mass-defection that would eventually wipe out nearly every small market promoter in the country.

Times… They Were a Changin'

You see, Verne still did business the old fashioned way, with a handshake, and expected loyalty in return. He also still believed in principle that his philosophy of featuring a mix of seasoned veterans along with some young bucks as skilled athletes, packaged as "family entertainment," was the way to go. Verne rewarded the guys who worked hard and were dedicated. And why not, it had worked for more than two decades.

Gagne and McMahon had two very different fundamental approaches to the business. While McMahon was focusing on the entertainment side of the business, Verne was hanging on to the more traditional "athletic" approach. Wrestlers started getting bigger and more muscular, many of whom were taking steroids, and with that came more acrobatic high flying moves. McMahon's philosophy was based more on televising short, action-packed made for TV vignettes, complete with

Bobby Heenan & Nick Bockwinkel

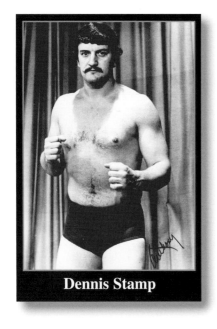

Dennis Stamp

extremely risqué and oftentimes very sexual storylines. Verne, meanwhile, was old-school and was still of the opinion that his wrestlers' matches should last much longer that long and featured back and forth "selling," "maneuvering" and "strategy," to tell the story. McMahon's style was a new, different type of show and with the dollars he was throwing around, it was about to revolutionize the entire industry. As a result, the AWA began to make some changes in order to generate more revenue. While they too had a solid television deal, they couldn't afford to become complacent. McMahon had deep pockets, was getting a lot of national television exposure and was simply determined to rule the roost.

Meanwhile, back to the ring… Now, while either Gagne or Bockwinkel had been the heavyweight champ almost exclusively up until that point in history, Nick, like Verne, was getting up there in years and needed an heir apparent. So, in the summer of 1982 Verne tried something different and brought in the relatively unknown Otto Wanz, a 350 pound Austrian to upset Bockwinkel. Although it was a short reign as champ, just six weeks before Nick won it back, it was a pretty big deal at the time because it came from way out in left field. Times were changing and drastic measures were apparently starting to be taken. (Wanz allegedly paid upwards of $50,000 in exchange for the title reign.)

Bockwinkel had since successfully gone on to defend his title against several foes, including Wahoo McDaniel, Mad Dog Vachon, Blackjack Lanza and Brad Rheingans, among others. Later, in 1984, Gagne entered into another cross-promotional agreement with Shohei "Giant" Baba's All Japan Pro Wrestling, and allegedly agreed to have Japanese star Jumbo Tsuruta beat Bockwinkel for the AWA heavyweight belt in Tokyo. Gagne had worked a lot in Japan over the years and had a good relationship with Baba. It was another money maker for the promotion, but one that didn't sit well with the fans, who weren't that familiar with the unknown Tsuruta.

By now attendance was down and several other major AWA stars had bolted for the WWF, including Jesse Ventura, Bobby Heenan and even announcer "Mean Gene" Okerlund. Gagne, perhaps leery of losing rising star Rick Martel to McMahon, had him beat Tsuruta for the AWA strap. Martel, a babyface, was solid, but not flashy. He was a seasoned veteran, however, and was a good looking French Canadian with an excellent physique.

To spice things up a little bit, on April 21st, 1985, at the St Paul Civic Center, Verne took the tights out of the attic and teamed up with Greg to defeat Nick Bockwinkel

Ken Patera & Brad Rheingans

and Mr. Saito. The crowd ate it up, but the promotion was in serious need of some star-power, like Hogan in the WWF or Ric Flair, who was the reigning NWA champ. So, they then brought in a pair of tag teams to shake things up, "The Fabulous Ones," who were hot down in Memphis, and the "Road Warriors," who were from the Twin Cities, but had been competing in Georgia. The two immediately became rivals, with two totally different good versus evil styles. While the Fabs were, well fabulous, the Warriors were face painted muscular bikers — patterned after the Mad Max character from the movie the Road Warrior. Hawk and Animal, the two Road Warriors, were instant stars and got a big push right out of the gates. They quickly got over on the defending AWA champs, Crusher and Baron Von Raschke, taking their belts in Vegas that year. From there, they dominated, beating the likes of the Blackjacks, Bruiser and Crusher, and the father son duo of Larry and Curt Hennig.

That next year, in defensive maneuver against the WWF's expansion plans, Gagne rallied the troops. Here is how it went down: Several promoters, Gagne of the AWA, Jerry Jarrett of the NWA/TNA & CWA, Ole Anderson of GCW, Jim Crockett Promotions, and a couple other smaller NWA promoters, got together to form "Pro Wrestling USA," a national federation which would co-promote big, elaborate wrestling shows that would air nationally on ESPN. While the first show took place in Memphis, others were promoted across the various member's territories. Several of them, however, were taped in the New Jersey Meadowlands, right in rival McMahon's back yard — sending him a clear message that they weren't going to be intimidated by his expansion. The Climax of the tour took place at "Superclash," where more than 21,000 fans crammed into Chicago's Comiskey Park on September 28, 1985, to watch Ric Flair battle Magnum TA for the NWA title, and Rick Martel clash with Stan Hansen for the AWA crown. The federation quickly soured, however, and a few months later the AWA got out of Dodge — taking ESPN with them.

That next year the Road Warriors finally got beat when the Freebirds interfered in their match against the underdog duo of "Gorgeous" Jimmy Garvin and "Mr. Electricity" Steve Regal. As a result, Hawk and Animal headed south, to greener pastures, where they would go on to become the most successful tag-team tandem in the history of pro wrestling. Even with the ESPN contract, they knew that they would never get the kind of money in the AWA that they would elsewhere, so they bolted.

Another interesting storyline came when Jim Brunzell departed the AWA for the WWF in June of 1985. With one half of the very popular High Flyers now gone, a new partner was needed for Greg. So, Sgt. Slaughter was brought in with the angle that he was going to "toughen" Greg up by taking him under his wing and putting him through boot camp. The two then came out in camouflaged fatigues and went on to beat the team of Bockwinkel and Stevens. When the G.I. Joe gimmick got old, Greg teamed with Curt Hennig and Scott Hall to battle Bockwinkel, Stevens and Zbyszko in a series of six man tag-team matches. As far as the heavyweight singles title at this point, it was Martel's to lose, and he did just that on December 29th, 1985, when he lost to longtime nemesis Stan "the Lariat" Hansen, in East Rutherford, New Jersey.

Attendance was way down at AWA venues by 1986 and more and more wrestlers were leaving the promotion to join the WWF or NWA, which were both offering more money to the top studs. Such was the case for Steve Regal, who, while holding one half of the AWA's tag-team belt, jumped ship for more dough. Desperate times called for desperate measures, and later that year Verne came out of retirement for what would prove to be the last time. In what was billed as his "final-final" match, Verne beat Sheik Adnon Al-Kaissy on April 20th, 1986, back home in Minneapolis, going out on top.

A different situation occurred that same year when singles champ Stan Hansen was stripped of his belt for refusing to drop the title to Nick Bockwinkel. Hansen, who had successfully defended the strap against Nick at "WrestleRock," earlier in the Metrodome, also beat the likes of Curt Hennig, Scott Hall, Jerry Blackwell and Sergeant Slaughter, among others. Hansen, however, was a longtime employee of the All Japan Pro Wrestling promotion and very committed to its promoter, Shohei Baba, who wanted him to wear the prestigious AWA championship belt on his next tour of Japan. Well, Verne apparently wanted him to drop the strap to Bockwinkel in Denver during the Summer of 1986, and when he refused, it was announced at the arena that because he didn't show up for the match, he was DQ'd. (Hansen was allegedly blackballed for several years as a result.)

Bockwinkel was then awarded the belt, and this time Verne had him pegged as an aging babyface. The AWA's top bad-guys came at old St. Nick, and he fended them all off one by one, just like old times. His first big challenger though, was a local kid by the name of Nord The Barbarian, who fought hard but could never upend the champ. Curt Hennig, meanwhile, who, along with Scott Hall had lost the tag-team title to Playboy Buddy Rose and Pretty Boy Doug Somers, started wrestling singles. He was quickly billed as the top contender to Bockwinkel, and finally got his shot at the old man near the end of that year, losing a one hour heart-breaking draw which was nationally televised on ESPN.

Hennig got his revenge that next year at "Superclash II," an all AWA affair held in San Francisco, where he knocked Bockwinkel "out cold." The drama unfolded when Nick's old arch nemesis, Larry Zbyszko, who was at ringside, secretively handed Hennig a roll of quarters, which he in turn used to whack Nick over the head. Well, afterwards, AWA President Stanley Blackburn ruled that the match was going to be reviewed over that next week, pending a meeting of the board. Apparently, what fans didn't know was that the stall tactic was really so Hennig could make up his mind as to whether or not to accept a contract he had just been offered with the WWF. Well, he ultimately chose to stay, and with that the dramatic announcement was made that Hennig was the new AWA heavyweight champion. Hennig was a rising star in the world of professional wrestling and deservedly so. A tremendous amateur athlete, he was technically sound and could carry a match. (As for Nick, he would go on to do color commentating on AWA television broadcasts.)

Meanwhile, on the tag-team side of the biz, Verne had found a real gem in the duo known as the Midnight Rockers, Shawn Michaels and Marty Janneatty, who had captured the straps from Buddy Rose and Doug Somers in a bloodbath back in 1986. The Rockers were the biggest thing to hit the AWA since the Road Warriors, and, more importantly, were putting butts back into the seats. But, like so many of the other rising stars of the era, the Rockers too took the money and ran, all the way to the WWF after dropping the belts to Boris Zukhov and Soldat Ustinov in Lake Tahoe, on May 25th, 1987.

That next year Zhukov also jumped from the AWA to the WWF, to form the "Bolsheviks," alongside Nicolai Volkoff. With that, the promotion announced that Pretty Boy Doug Somers would be joining Ustinov in a title match held in Memphis against Jerry Lawler and Bill Dundee. (The reason the match was held in Memphis was because Verne had allegedly struck a deal with long-time Memphis promoter Jerry Jarrett to share talent between the two promotions.) They lost, and a week later, Lawler and Dundee subsequently lost to Dr. D. and Hector Guerrero, who subsequently got beat that following week to the "Original Midnight Express," Dennis Condrey and Randy Rose. Then, a few months later, the Midnight Rockers, who had been recently "let go" by the WWF, returned to the AWA and promptly won back their old belts over the Midnight Express on December 27th in Las Vegas. (Incidentally, the reason that particular match was held in Vegas was because Verne had agreed to move some of the AWA's television tapings from its WTCN studios in Golden Valley to the Showboat Casino in Las Vegas.)

So, with Curt Hennig making a lot of noise as the heavyweight champ, the AWA's prospects were looking up. After grappling with a few sentimental old-timers, including an Indian Strap match with Chief Wahoo McDaniel which was seen nationally on ESPN, Hennig was pitted against Greg Gagne. It was no secret that Verne wanted Greg to be the AWA Heavyweight champ, but at this

Jesse Ventura

stage of his career, Greg was barely 200 pounds soaking wet. By now the wrestlers were getting huge, many by "artificial" means, and Greg simply did not fit that mold. Many speculated that it would be difficult for the fans just to accept Greg as the heavyweight champ when he didn't physically have the attributes needed to beat some of the industries' new behemoths. Verne had the two feuding every week on TV, however, and built up a solid rivalry. Soon, the fathers even got involved — Larry "The Axe" helping Curt, and Verne, out there making sure that Larry kept it clean for Greg. It was classic, old-school drama, and the fans appreciated it.

Anyway, while most of their bouts wound up as double disqualifications, on November 26th, Greg apparently finally got the green light and beat Hennig at a match in Minneapolis. While he was announced as the new AWA Heavyweight Champion, the ruling was later controversially overturned. Why? Many speculated that the other small regional promotions in the Midwest protested behind the scenes and lobbied to have it reversed, figuring they wouldn't be able to "sell" the idea of Greg as the champ against the much bigger, flashier opponents. For whatever the reason, the title was returned to Hennig. As a result, Verne created the AWA International TV Championship belt, a new title, separate from the AWA Heavyweight Championship strap. And, as expected, Greg became the inaugural TV champ when he beat Adrian Adonis on December 27th, 1987 in Las Vegas.

Hennig now needed a new foe and he found it in Jerry "The King" Lawler, who had gained a lot of national media attention because of his notorious feud with comedian Andy Kaufman. (In what all turned out to a giant hoax, years later, Lawler, who was actually good buddies with Kaufman in real life, got into a huge fight with the eccentric comedian on the David Letterman Show. He later proceeded to pummel him to a match, and "supposedly" even broke his neck.) Hennig and Lawler brawled in front of his hometown fans in Memphis that next year with the King coming away with the title. Shortly thereafter, Hennig, like so many stars before him, left the AWA for the WWF.

Lawler would defend the title on numerous occasions around the South, as per the agreement between Gagne and CWA promoter Jerry Jarrett to share talent. Back in Minnesota, meanwhile, the AWA tag team champion Midnight Rockers were in need of new nemesis, thanks to the fact that the Original Midnight Express and their manager Paul E. Dangerously had left for the NWA. So, Verne gave a young, charismatic kid a shot by the name of Diamond Dallas Page, a heel manager of a new duo named "Badd Company," featuring Paul

Adrian Adonis

The High Flyers

Diamond and Pat Tanaka. Shortly after their arrival they were given a big push and captured the AWA World Tag Team title on March 19th, 1988 in Las Vegas. "DDP," as he would become known, had a gimmick where, in addition to always being surrounded by beautiful babes, he was always talking on his cell phone at ringside. Eventually, when the ref wasn't looking, he would proceed to whack someone over the head with it to get his boys over the top. DDP would remain with the AWA for nine months before bolting to a rival promotion.

On the singles side of things, Greg Gagne, after defending the AWA International Television strap throughout the Summer of 1988, finally lost the title to former NWA champion Ronnie Garvin, that Fall in Memphis. Lawler, meanwhile, finally found his perfect arch rival, "The Modern Day Warrior," Kerry Von Erich — the son of legendary promoter Fritz Von Erich, who ran the Texas based WCCW. Each was beloved in his own respective hometowns of Memphis and Dallas, which translated into big gate receipts for the promoters.

With that, a trio of federations (Gagne's AWA, Jerry Jarrett's Memphis based CWA and Fritz Von Erich's Texas based WCCW) got together and announced their first ever pay-per-view special called "Super Clash III," which was going to be held on December 13th, 1988, in Chicago. After plenty of hype on ESPN, the show was booked with extremely high expectations. Finally, after a lot of feuding over who should win what, and which undercards should feature whom, the main event was set with WCWA champion Kerry Von Erich battling AWA champion Jerry Lawler. So, with three heads working as one, there would be some serious competition for the WWF, right? Wrong.

The event was, by most accounts, a huge flop. Lawler wound up using a foreign object to smash Kerry over the head and he wouldn't stop bleeding, so the referee inexplicably stopped the match with the King prevailing. Overall, the matches were solid, but the attendance was a bust, with just over one thousand fans showing up. There was even a "Lingerie Street Fight Battle Royal," on the undercard of the event, — a new trend in the biz that was

clearly a departure from the "family entertainment" angle of the past. From there, the three promoters fought over the bills and the three-way partnership was dissolved on very bad terms.

In the fall-out, the WCCW, which was hedging on a big turnout and solid TV numbers, went belly-up. There were then bought out by Jarrett, who merged it with the CWA to form the USWA. Meanwhile, the WWF was swallowing up smaller territories left and right, and Jim Crockett Promotions, which had bought out many NWA territories and also gone national, was being sold to billionaire Ted Turner, where it would be renamed as WCW. With that, wrestling now had three big powers, the WWF, the WCW and Verne' AWA, which was about to go on life-support. The business was changing so drastically, that it was very difficult even for the fans to try and keep it. It was also difficult for the wrestlers themselves, who, in the old days could work one territory for a while and then, after the storylines there all played out, could move on to another. The territory system was now gone and all the big money was in national television syndication, which required big money and big stars.

When the dust from Super Clash III finally cleared, Verne apparently stripped Lawler of his AWA heavyweight title, which was also supposed to be considered as the "Unified World title." Lawler had refused to wrestle in any AWA territories until some financial matters were cleared up, so, he was essentially fired. Lawler was so upset that he apparently kept the AWA title belt, leaving Gagne to literally create a new one. (He used the TV title in the interim.) But, because ESPN kept airing replays of the event, most fans didn't realize what was going on behind the scenes. So, the AWA had to wait a while before finally declaring a new champ. Ultimately, Gagne held a Battle Royal in St Paul during the Winter of 1989 to determine the promotion's new champion. There, Larry "The Living Legend" Zbyszko eliminated Tom Zenk to wind up as the last man standing. (Zenk, a former "Mr. Minnesota" bodybuilder, would later leave the promotion over a notorious "contract dispute.") Zbyszko, meanwhile, who was also Gagne's son-in-law, was the perfect heel who the fans loved to hate.

As for the tag-team side of the business, Badd Company was finally upset by "The Olympians," Brad Rheingans and Ken Patera. Their reign on top would be short-lived though, as a new duo was getting a big push from above, "The Destruction Crew." Local boys, Mean Mike Enos and Wayne "the Train" Bloom, along with manager Luscious Johnny Valiant, were all the rage in the Fall of 1989, and they wound up claiming the straps from Greg Gagne and Paul Diamond in an elimination match, which determined the new title holders. The belts, meanwhile, had been forfeited after Patera suffered an earlier injury.

Ironically, that would be one of Greg Gagne's final matches, as his numerous injuries finally got the best of him. So, he decided to hang em' up for good, but not before creating a "career ending injury angle," in which the 500 pound Samoan giant Kokina attacked him while he was doing a ringside interview. It was the end of an era for one of the sport's true good guys who literally grew up in the business.

By now the AWA was on its last legs. The fan base was down, the ratings on ESPN were down, and the promotion continued to hemorrhage its top talent to the WWF and WCW. (In addition to Hennig a few years ago, others defectors would include: Rick Martel, Ron Garvin, Sgt. Slaughter, Boris Zhukov, Baron Von Raschke, Kokina Maximus, Bobby Heenan, Ken Patera and Buddy Rose, among others.) In the Winter of 1990, Zbyszko had a couple of memorable matches against Mr. Saito in Japan, and then, after losing the belt, regained it that Spring in St Paul at Super Clash IV. The Destruction Crew later went out on loan to the upstart WCW, where they competed as the masked "Minnesota Wrecking Crew II," and brawled with the Steiner Brothers. They would return later that year, only to lose their AWA straps to the tag-team duo of DJ Petersen and the Trooper, in a match down in Rochester.

Finally, after a failed "Team Challenge Series," a series of gimmick matches where points were earned by wrestlers competing in a long, drawn out plot to win a $1 million prize, the American

Do You Remember the 1974 Movie, "The Wrestler?"

In 1974 the classic movie "The Wrestler" was made right here in the Twin Cities. The story was loosely based on the life of a wrestling promoter trying to keep his business afloat with an aging world champion and pressure from the mob. Ed Asner starred as the promoter while Verne Gagne was featured as the champ. In addition to a great scene where Dusty Rhodes and Dick Murdoch destroy a bar (incidentally it was Big Stan Mayslack's restaurant up in Northeast Minneapolis), a host of other local grapplers are featured in the flick including: Billy Robinson, Larry Hennig, Ken Patera, Wahoo McDaniel and a young Ric Flair. Many of the wrestling scenes were shot over at the old St. Paul Auditorium and the training camp was actually Verne's old barn at his farm near Chanhassen.

Wrestling Association sadly turned off the lights in early 1991. Things got so bad that they eventually had to film their shows in a closed studio because no fans were showing up. ESPN finally cancelled its contract and with that, the once proud organization which had truly pioneered the business of professional wrestling, was gone. It was a sad day for Minnesota wrestling fans and surely a sad day for Verne Gagne.

Verne Gagne was a showman, a throwback, an old-school legend who believed in "athleticism" over "entertainment," and finally succumbed to McMahon and his ever growing circus when the checkbook eventually ran dry. The AWA was the last successful independent outpost, and when it went goodbye, so went a lot of history. Aside from an outfit in Nashville, NWA-TNA, the business today is pretty much a monopoly controlled by McMahon — who pretty much either bought everybody out or forced them out by raiding their talent pools over the years. Hey, it worked, his WWE plays in 170 markets worldwide, has mind-boggling television ratings and has evolved into a multi-billion dollar business. Wrestling today is much, much different from the "good old days"

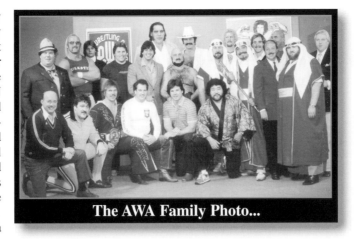

The AWA Family Photo...

back at the old Minneapolis and St. Paul Auditoriums, however. Steroids, raunchy storylines and four-letter words are all a part of the world of professional wrestling these days — a world most of the old-timers, sadly, want no part of.

Verne Gagne's legacy will be that of the greatest wrestler, amateur and professional, ever to hail from the great state of Minnesota. The reason so many wrestlers have come out of Minnesota and onto the national scene is because of Verne, and his dream of starting his own promotion nearly four decades ago. Generations of kids grew up watching All Star Wrestling, and it is as much a part of the fabric of life here in the Land of 10,000 Lakes as hot dogs and apple pie. As a result, this area features some of the most loyal and educated wrestling fans in the world. Yeah, good ol' rasslin' gave us all a lot of enjoyment over the years. We loved to watch, either in person, or on the tube, and escape from reality for 60 minutes with friends and family. It is sad that the old AWA had to go out on a whimper rather than a big bang, like it should have. Hey, it was a great ride though Verne, thanks for the memories — your legacy will live on forever.

Is it Real? Or is it...

Kayfabe: A term whose origin is derived from old "carny," or carnival, jargon for "fake." By definition, Kayfabe generally refers to the protecting of industry secrets, and also of or related to inside information about the business. Diehard wrestling fans are oftentimes referred to as "kayfabers."

The notion that pro wrestling actually had "predetermined outcomes" had always been a contentious issue between the wrestlers and promoters, and with the fans over the years. That all changed forever in the mid-1980s though, when Vince McMahon Jr., the head of the powerful World Wrestling Federation, came clean. You see, at the time, pro wrestling had always considered itself a "sport," and as such, was sanctioned by various local athletic commissions. The commissions were set up in certain states to regulate the ethics and rules of various sports, particularly boxing, with regards to gambling. They then imposed commissions on particular sports, such as pro wrestling, in order to verify their claims of validity and authenticity. They also regulated safe working conditions for the athletes; protected them from being taken advantage of by shady managers; prevented promoters from advertising outlandish claims in the media; and also implemented rules regarding personal safety for fans attending events. The states also wanted to protect themselves from frivolous lawsuits as well.

Well, McMahon eventually decided that he no longer wanted to pay the hefty fees to the commissions anymore, so he publicly declared that pro wrestling was no longer a sport, but a form of entertainment, show-biz — complete with matches that had predetermined outcomes. In layman's terms, he had just explained in detail how the magician pulled the rabbit out of his hat, and oh by the way, for you kids out there, there is no Santa Clause either. It was a bombshell. Deep down, sure, we all sort of knew, but the mystery and drama was what kept us coming back for more.

You see, up until that point, while many speculated that wrestling was fake, there was a strict honor code of silence amongst the performers which protected the industries' most sacred trade secrets. Aside from the wrestlers, refs and promoters, only a chosen few were a part of the backstage fraternity known as the inner circle. It was a code based largely on the traditions dating back to the old carnival days of the late 1800s, where no one dared question their validity... or else! Should anyone dare say the "F" word (fake), then there would be hell to pay. In fact, there were a few high profile incidents in the 1980s which made headlines on that very subject. The first came in 1984, when wrestler "Dr. D" struck ABC News 20/20 reporter John Stossel across the face after he questioned the reality of it all, causing permanent hearing damage. Stossel later sued and apparently won a large settlement. Another episode came a year later when Hulk Hogan publicly demonstrated a firm chokehold on actor Richard Belzer, who had previously called wrestling fake.

So, with the "F" word out the window, and the truth revealed, now what? Well, incredibly, instead of fans saying "Hah, I told you so, it was fake all along..." they tuned in on TV and showed up at the events in record numbers. As a result, McMahon's WWF exploded in popularity. As for the over-the-top soap opera storylines? They got even more wild and the fans couldn't get enough of it. It was a big risk, but one that paid of big time for McMahon, and for the business of professional wrestling.

And, speaking of the "F" word, it is an pretty funny story as to just how the WWE actually did gt the "F Out!" Vince McMahon Jr.'s World Wrestling Federation (WWF), THE dominant player in pro wrestling, was forced to change its name to the WWE after the World Wildlife Fund won a lengthy lawsuit over them a few years back. So, how did McMahon go about spinning that angle? He launched an ad campaign introducing the new and improved WWF, which just got the "F" out... Hey, that's not bad!

THE CAST OF CHARACTERS...

BARON VON RASCHKE

Baron Von Raschke

The Claw... enough said. Simply put, Baron Von Raschke is a Minnesota wrestling intuition. Born in Omaha, Neb., in 1940, Jim Raschke played football and wrestled at Omaha North High School, where he won the 1958 Nebraska state heavyweight wrestling championship as a senior. Heavily recruited as both a wrestler and lineman, Raschke opted to stay home and attend the University of Nebraska, where he twice earned All-American honors and even won the Big Eight Conference heavyweight title as a wrestler in 1962. That next year Raschke became just the second American ever to place in international Greco-Roman wrestling competition, when he won a bronze medal at the 1963 World Games. Raschke later made the 1964 Olympic team but could not participate due to an injury he suffered just days prior to the event.

From there, Raschke was drafted and served in the Army, where he also wrestled on the Army wrestling team. There, he won AAU national wrestling titles in freestyle and Greco-Roman in 1964 and then won a gold medal in the 1965 U.S. Military Inter-Service championships. Upon being discharged, Raschke returned home and put his Biology degree to good use by getting a job as a junior high school teacher in Omaha. It was during that time that he met local a local wrestling promoter, who in turn, introduced him to Verne Gagne. Raschke had always been intrigued by professional wrestling and thought he would give it a try. Gagne, himself an accomplished amateur wrestler, invited Raschke to come to Minnesota and begin training.

With that, he moved north, working by day as a substitute teacher, and at night learning the tricks of the trade. He first started out setting up matches and refereeing but eventually got into the ring as a grappler in 1966. He was all set, except for a good stage name. He had been training with "Mad Dog" Vachon at the time and he told Raschke that he looked like a tough German and needed a good gimmick. After passing on his first recommendation, "Baron Von Pumpkin," he settled on the name "Baron Von Raschke" and the rest, they say, is history.

"You know, when I first started out as Mad Dog's partner, we were both bald and ugly, he was short and I was tall, and the fans started booing us, so we were made out to be villains," said Raschke. "Our reputation spread from there and we just went with it. We got pretty good together and could really pack em' in when we performed together. It was just a lot of fun."

Raschke ventured out from there and won his first title in Montreal that next year, defeating Edouardo Carpentier for the IWA championship. It would be the first of many over the next several decades. As his popularity grew, the Baron decided that he needed a finishing move. Shortly thereafter the "brain claw" was born, and perhaps no other wrestler in history has become more synonymous with any one specific signature hold.

"It was an interesting transformation," said Raschke. "By

nature I am a very shy person. Even when I first got into the business I hated public speaking and my interviews, as myself, Jim Raschke, were dull and boring. But, when I became the Baron, that all changed. All those inhibitions I had, all those deep psychological restrictions that I put on myself were completely wiped out. As the Baron, I could say whatever I wanted to and I was just a totally different character."

Baron would travel throughout North America and Japan for the next several years, from Canada to Ohio to Indiana to Texas, and eventually earned the role as one of wrestling's top heels "bad guys." (Just how tough was the Baron? He once spent a Summer in Canada wrestling a grizzly bear to make ends meet!) Portrayed as an evil Nazi-like character, the Baron would goose-step around the ring and speak in a deep German accent — much to the delight of the patriotic American fans. During his television interviews he would talk about how much he loved to squeeze the blood out his opponents' skulls and that he couldn't control the claw because it simply had a life of its own. The fans at it up.

Before long the brain claw became the most feared hold in the promotion and fans everywhere began begging for an American hero to defeat the hated villain. Eventually, "Dick the Bruiser" emerged as the Baron's chief rival and their matches were epic. Later managed by Bobby "The Brain" Heenan, Raschke, would teamed up with Ernie "The Big Cat" Ladd to win the WWA Tag Team title. But, after losing the strap to Bruiser and Bruno Sammartino, the Baron decided to try his hand in another promotion.

So, Raschke came back to Minneapolis to try his hand in Verne Gagne's American Wrestling Association in early 1974. There, he teamed up with Horst Hoffman and feuded with the likes of Superstar Billy Graham and Dusty Rhodes. Three years later Raschke left the AWA for the NWA's Mid Atlantic promotion out of the Carolinas. Shortly thereafter he won the TV title over Ricky Steamboat, only to lose it a few months later to Paul Jones. Fittingly, the Baron and Jones later teamed up to win the NWA tag team title that next year and they held the belts for nearly six months before losing them to Paul Orndorff and Jimmy "Superfly" Snuka.

By 1980 Raschke was competing in Georgia Championship Wrestling. He stayed for a year and, after winning and losing the heavyweight title, returned to the Mid Atlantic area to settle some old scores. Shortly thereafter he headed back to Minnesota to seek revenge for his old partner, Mad Dog Vachon, who had been "knocked out" of the business by Jerry Blackwell. The Baron was at home in the AWA, here in Minnesota, and the fans loved him — even transforming him into a beloved "good guy." He would ultimately receive a few title shots against AWA champ Nick Bockwinkel, but it just wasn't in the cards for him to wear the belt

Finally, on May 6th, 1984, in Green Bay, the Baron and the Crusher upended Jerry Blackwell and Ken Patera for the AWA tag team title. They would hold the belts for just three months, however, before losing them to the Road Warriors. From there, Raschke traveled the world, performing and entertaining countless fans along the way. He eventually moved on to the NWA promotion down south, where he and in with Ivan and Nikita Koloff to capture the six man championship. By the late 1980s the Baron was wearing down so, he got into managing other wrestlers, including the Warlord and the Barbarian for a short time in the WWF. Eventually, when the AWA folded in 1991, Von Raschke hung up the tights, returning to the ring occasionally to do independent shows throughout Minnesota and Wisconsin.

"I enjoyed it," said Raschke of his lifetime in wrestling. "It was a lot of fun for a lot of years. I met a lot of great people and got to see the world through wrestling. It was tough moving around with my family so much over the years, but it was an adventure and we have had a good life. Sure, it was tough on the kids sometimes, but we eventually settled down here in Minnesota and have enjoyed it. My wife is from here originally, so our plans were always to get back here at some point."

Raschke also saw the business start to change towards the

end of his career, and not always for the best.

"On wrestling today, I think it is terrible," he said. "You know, it used to be kind of a family thing, where mom, dad, grandma, grandpa and the kids could come out on a Saturday and have a good time. Now, it is awful, so violent and so dirty, and some of these guys are steroid freaks too. The kids are seeing things that they shouldn't be seeing and are learning four letter words that they have no business learning. Plus, nowadays everything is scripted. I used to love doing interviews, we all did, that was where our personalities really came out, and that is how the fans really got to know us."

Upon hanging up the tights, Raschke and his wife opened a seasonal gift shop in Lake George, outside of Park Rapids. When he wasn't working at the store, however, he got back into working as a substitute teacher. They later sold the business and retired to Wabasha, where they presently reside. Raschke can still be found at local events signing autographs and telling war stories to the fans who still adore him. He would later be enshrined into the Professional Wrestling Hall of Fame in Newton, Iowa, where he was honored for his achievements both in and outside the ring. With his infamous "Dat is all da people need to know!" line, the Baron will forever be remembered as a true classic.

BARRY DARSOW

Barry Darsow

Barry Darsow grew up in Robbinsdale, where he played hockey for the Robins before graduating in 1978. It was no surprise that Darsow would want to get into wrestling, considering the fact that several of his buddies in high school were Tom Zenk, Rick Rude, Dean Peters, Curt Hennig, John Nord and Nikita Koloff — all of whom would go on to stardom as pro grapplers. With that, Darsow learned the ropes from legendary trainer Eddie Sharkey. At six-foot-two and nearly 300 pounds, Sharkey knew early on the kid was going to be a star in the world of professional wrestling. Darsow's first big role came as "Krusher Krushov," a member of the "Russians," alongside Ivan and Nikita Koloff, in the UWF. One of the trios' first big events came in 1985, when they beat the Crusher, Dick the Bruiser and Baron Von Raschke at the AWA Super Clash.

From there, Darsow went on to play the part of "Smash" in the WWF tag team powerhouse known as Demolition, alongside Ax (and later) Crush. Known as heavy metal power wrestlers, similar to the Road Warriors, Demolition was one of the biggest tag teams of the WWF at the time and held the promotion's tag-team title belts on three occasions. As entertainers the duo was tough as nails and the crowds loved their reckless seek-and-destroy attitude. With their faces covered in war paint and their bodies clad in black and chrome, Demolition used a combination of power and intimidation to annihilate their opponents. They would eventually break up after losing at Summerslam 1990, but Darsow would later re-emerge as the character, "Repo Man." In 1992 the Repo Man lost to Crush at Summerslam, which was held in England's Wembley Stadium.

Darsow would then go on to assume the WCW role of the "Blacktop Bully," and in 1995 wound up losing to Dustin Rhodes in the first ever "King of the Road" match — which took place on the flatbed of a moving tractor trailer while it was speeding down the road. During the match both men allegedly "bladed," or cut themselves in order to bleed for the camera, and as a result were dismissed from the company. Darsow later returned to WCW, wrestling under his own name. He would later re-emerge once again under the gimmick of "Hole in One" Darsow, who played the role of a semi-psychotic golfer. A very versatile and rugged athlete, Darsow will always be known as a solid multi-purpose wrestler capable of successfully transforming his persona at any time.

THE IRWIN BROTHERS

Bill Irwin

Scott Irwin

Duluth's most famous wrestling duo by a long shot would have to be the Irwin brothers, Scott and Barney William, or Bill. The tandem performed together around the world as tag-team partners for nearly a decade before Scott tragically passed away in 1987 as the result of a brain tumor.

Both Scott and Bill grew up in Duluth and graduated from Duluth Central High School in 1971 and 1973, respectively. From there, Scott went on to star as a defensive tackle for the Golden Gopher Football team from 1971-74. Bill, meanwhile, laced up the skates at nearby St. Scholastica, where his squad won an NAIA National Championship in 1975. Scott, who was a teammate of future grappler Jim Brunzell over at the U of M, decided to give pro wrestling a shot, so he signed up for Verne Gagne's training camp. Three months later, Scott was sent to the WWWF and became "Eric," a member of the Lumberjacks tag-team.

Wanting to follow in his big brothers footsteps, Bill decided to give pro wrestling a try as well. So, he moved down to Charlotte in the Fall of 1977, where Scott was performing at the time. There, he learned the ropes for the next several months, working alongside his brother and his buddies. Bill got his first gig working in Atlanta, where, as "Wild Bill" Irwin, he got some invaluable seasoning. He eventually got back together with his brother, now known as Scott "Hogg" Irwin, and together they made history.

At first the Irwins formed a tag-team duo called the "Long Riders" and later they worked under masks as the "Super Destroyers." They first started out in Texas, managed by Skandor

Akbar, and later traveled the country, performing in various promotions along the way. With their trademark Superplex finishing move, they took the wrestling world by storm as one of the hottest heel tag teams around.

"It was usually really fun being a bad guy," said Bill. "You got to be real extraverted and you were usually in control in the ring too. I mean you were there to make the fans hate you and the better you did that, the better the response you would get. Plus, bad guys usually made more money too."

Over the next several years the Irwins, both together as well as with others, would go on to capture several heavyweight championship belts, including the MSWA Tag Team, WCCW Television, NWA Texas Tag Team, NWA American Tag Team, NWA National Tag Team, NWA U.S. Tag Team, NWA Florida Tag Team, NWA Central States Tag Team, AWA Southern Tag Team, Canadian International Tag Team, GWF Tag Team and WWF Tag Team, among others.

On September 5, 1987, Scott, who had also wrestled briefly in Florida under the name of "Thor the Viking," sadly passed away. Bill, however, continued his career both as a single as well as with other tag-team partners. In the early 1990s he headed back to Texas and later worked in Japan. Then, in 1997, he did a brief stint in the powerful WWF, using a hockey player gimmick nicknamed as "The Goon."

Shortly thereafter, Bill hung up the boots for good. The grind of the business, not to mention the politics, had finally taken their toll. Presently, Bill works in the mortgage business back in Duluth. And, even though he is officially retired, he still has a ring in his back garage where he trains young wannabes every now and then, just to get his fix. He likes the fact that there are a few local kids who want to get into the business, but knows their chances of making it in today's marketplace are slim.

"Duluth has always supported pro wrestling over the years," said Bill. "Whenever the AWA would come up here, fans would show up and support it over at the old Auditorium. Harvey Solon was the big promoter in town back then and I certainly remember following it as a kid. It was never huge around here, but it was around from time to time. Aside from myself and my brother, I think Lenny Lane is really the only other guy who made it to the big-time out of Duluth. On the amateur side, however, it was basically non-existent. I don't think any of the high schools up here even had wrestling and I know that UM-Duluth dropped their program a while back too. UW-Superior has it, but I that is about it. Hey, this is hockey country and I guess that is why amateur wrestling never really took hold up here."

Looking back, Bill has great memories of his days in the ring and still follows the biz.

"Sure, there are some things I miss about not being in the business anymore," said Bill. "Like hanging around the guys and just the camaraderie that you developed, that is what I miss most. Driving from town to town with a 12-pack after a match — the little stuff like that, where you really got to know the guys. It was tough though, always being on the road. I mean you went from airports to arenas to hotels to airports pretty much non-stop, it was a real grind. The glory and fame goes away real fast and then it was just you and the guys. They become your family after a while. I think when it is all said and done you also miss performing too, I mean it was a rush to be out there in front of all those people doing your thing. I don't think you ever get it out of you completely. Once you are in this business, it is just a part of you forever."

BOB BACKLUND

Bob Backlund

Bob Backlund grew up in Princeton and went on to wrestle collegeiately at North Dakota State University, where, in addition to earned second place honors at the 1971 NCAA Championships in the 190-pound weight division, he also played football. From there, Backlund got into professional wrestling, learning the tricks of the trade from local promoter Eddie Sharkey during the early 1970s. After debuting in the Minneapolis-based American Wrestling Association, he ventured out onto the circuit to compete for a couple independent companies throughout the South. There, he won several titles including a tag team belt with the legendary Jerry Brisco and another with Steve Keirn in the Florida region of the NWA.

Finally, in 1978, he caught his big break when he got an invitation to wrestle in Vince McMahon Sr.'s WWWF. Backlund jumped at the opportunity to be involved with big-time pro wrestling and couldn't wait to head east to New York City. There, he was immediately cast as a good guy as his baby-face good looks, hard work ethic and "boy next-door" charm won over the fans right out of the gates. "The Golden Boy" as he was known, got his first taste of victory in 1978, when he beat the "Superstar" Billy Graham to win the WWWF Heavyweight Championship. It was the beginning of one of the longest belt dynasties of all time as Backlund would wear the strap proudly for nearly six straight years — defeating all challengers along the way.

Finally, in 1983, Vince McMahon Jr. had taken over the business from his father and decided it was time for a change. McMahon was paving the way for a new era of superstars including the likes of Hulk Hogan, Randy "Macho Man" Savage and Andre the Giant. Backlund, who was smaller and had more of a wholesome image, could see the writing on the wall. It all came to a head when he was defeated by the Iron Sheik's "camel clutch" at Madison Square Garden. Backlund's manager, Arnold Skaaland, threw in the towel and the rest, they say, is history. With no where to go, Bob quietly went into retirement.

Then, in a stunner, Backlund came out of retirement at the age of 43 to get back into the ring. Proving that he was still in great shape, he lasted over one hour in the 1993 Royal Rumble. He also competed in Wrestlemania that year as well, defeating the likes of Shawn Michaels, Doink the Clown and Rick Martel along the way. That next year everything changed for Backlund when he "snapped" in the ring after losing a controversial title match against Bret Hart. Applying his patented "chicken wing" submission hold, Backlund refused to let go, causing the fans to completely turn on him. It was as if he had been "turned to the dark-side" with the flick of a switch, and with that, he instantly became one of the most hated villains in WWF history. How's that for an extreme makeover!

Now a heel, Backlund played up his new found fame with a persona never before seen. Part of his shtick was to scream at the fans and tell them to sit up straight, behave themselves, don't swear, and to even carry a copy of a dictionary around with them so they could comprehend the complicated words he spoke to them. The fans grew to despise him, and it worked. In fact, the gimmick worked so well that he was given a title shot that next year at the Survivor Series and won back his old belt more than a decade later from Bret Hart.

His reign on top included another clever angle in which "Psycho Bob," as he was now occasionally referred to as, announced that he was running for President of the United States in 1996. The WWF did it up big-time and even held rallies and had buttons made up supporting their "crazy lunatic." Well, that premise eventually ran dry. So, after losing his belt that year, Backlund made another comeback of sorts, this time as the co-manager of "The Sultan," alongside his old nemesis the Iron Sheik. The act didn't catch on though and was eventually phased out. He returned briefly in 1999 as a mentor to former Olympian Kurt Angle, but that storyline was scrapped as well. With that, Backlund's improbable comeback was over and he decided to hang it up for good.

Incredibly, Backlund spent the next two years going back to school in order to take a shot at winning a seat in the U.S. Congress out of Connecticut, where he resided. Then, in the Fall of 2000, after campaigning hard and raising a lot of money, the Republican candidate went for it. When the votes were tallied he had garnered more than one third of the popular vote, but came up just short in the heavily Democratic district. It was a great run for a great person who has given back a lot to his community, and someone who has certainly made Minnesota proud.

BOB BRUGGERS

Bob Bruggers

Bob Bruggers grew up in the small town of Danube, where he starred as a four-sport athlete. In fact, he earned All-State honors four times in three different sports and went on to earn a whopping 21 varsity letters with the Hawks in basketball, football, baseball and track. After graduating in 1962, Bruggers went on to play linebacker for the University of Minnesota's Golden Gopher football team. From there, Bruggers went on to play in the AFL/NFL with the Miami Dolphins from 1966-68 and San Diego Chargers from 1968-71.

Upon hanging up his cleats in 1971, Bruggers came back to Minnesota and hooked up with Verne Gagne, who felt that he could have a solid career in pro wrestling. There, Bruggers trained alongside the likes of Ric Flair, Ken Patera, Greg Gagne and Jim Brunzell, learning the trade from a group of would-be stars out at Verne's training camp-barn in Chanhassen. So, with his "football tackle" finishing move, Bruggers jumped in and gave it his best shot. He wound up heading to the Carolinas for his first gig because of his close friendship with former NFL star Chief Wahoo McDaniel. Things were going well and that next year he teamed up with Paul Jones to win the Mid Atlantic Tag Team title.

Then, sadly, on October 4, 1975, Bruggers suffered a career-ending injury when the airplane he was flying in crashed in rural North Carolina as he was on his way to a match. With him at the time was Ric Flair, who broke his back, Johnny Valentine, who

was paralyzed from the waist down, and the pilot, who was killed. A Minnesota sports legend, Bruggers would later be inducted into the state's High School League Hall of Fame.

BRAD RHEINGANS

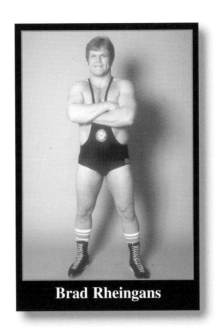

Brad Rheingans

Brad Rheingans grew up in the small western Minnesota town of Appleton, where he emerged as a three sport prep star. On the gridiron Brad was the MVP and co-captain of his 1970 high school football team, and on the track he was a two time district discus and shot-put champion. It was on the matt, however, where he really excelled — ultimately leading him to future fame and glory. As a prep wrestler Brad was a two time state high school champion, earned All American honors in 1971, and was the National Junior World Greco Roman champion that year as well.

"It meant a lot to represent my home town," said Brad. "I was a small town guy, I mean even to go to Minneapolis from Appleton was like culture shock. I remember being literally scared the first time I walked into Williams Arena, it was a big mental adjustment. But to know how much it meant back home when one of their own did well was a real motivating factor. I am very proud of my roots and it was a real honor to have won those state titles at the tournament. They had a parade for me and everything, it was pretty cool."

Rheingans then went on to star at North Dakota State University, where, from 1971-75, he rewrote the record books. He was a three-time North Central Conference champion at 177 and later 190-pounds; a four time NCAA All American; and in 1975 he won the NCAA Division II national championship at 190-pounds. In addition, Rheingans also advanced to the 1975 NCAA Division I national championships, where he ultimately finished fourth in the country. After three and a half years in Grand Forks, Brad decided to pursue a career competing against the world's top international competition.

"You know, I had really good scholarship offers from a lot of Big 8 schools, but when you are a young kid you are influenced by the people closest to you," said Brad. "Well, my high school coach was Bob Maughan, whose brother was Bucky, who coached at North Dakota State. So, because of that, I wound up going there. In retrospect, I am really glad I went to NDSU, it was great. I was originally a pharmacy major, and took a ton of math, chemistry and physics, but wound up with a degree in exercise physiology in 1979 when I went back to finish up. It was a great time up there and hey, I still got to compete at a really high level and still made it to the Olympics, so I wouldn't have changed a thing."

From there, Rheingans went on to capture the 220-pound title at the 1975 U.S. Pan American Games in Minsk, Russia. That next year he fulfilled a lifelong dream when, after winning the 1976 U.S. Olympic Trials, he became a member of the United States Greco-Roman Olympic team which competed in Montreal. There, he placed fourth, the highest finish by a U.S. team member that year.

"It was a real honor to represent my country in the Olympics," said Brad. "I finished fourth, which was pretty good, but sure, somewhat disappointing that I didn't medal. But, I had only been wrestling Greco for less than a year, so it was all new to me. I had actually beaten the guy who beat me for the bronze earlier in the tournament, but the scoring system back then was totally different. Back then they had what were called "black marks," and they didn't have the same system of advancement like they do now. Now they have a bracket system where the winners end up in the finals. Well, under the black mark system, if you pinned a guy, you got zero black marks. If you beat him on a decision, you got one black mark and the loser got three. It was goofy. Finally, if you had six black marks, you were automatically eliminated. So, for me, I only lost one match, to the Russian in the fourth round. I had beaten the Pole (Poland) in the third round, but because he had like one black mark less than me, I wound up getting fourth.

In 1979 he took bronze at the World Games and shortly thereafter earned a spot on the 1980 U.S. Olympic team. (Brad also served as an assistant coach with the Gophers during that era as well.) That team, however, did not compete at the Summer Games in Moscow because of the American boycott issued by then President Carter. Brad, who was projected to be a medal winner, was devastated.

"To have the boycott in 1980, that was really tough. You know, looking back, if our boycott from the Games would have helped Afghanistan gain peace from Russia, then I was all for it. I mean I am all for world peace, trust me. But looking back, our not participating in the Olympics didn't do a damn thing — that's what really bothers me. So, yeah, it was tough not getting another shot at a medal, but that was just the way it went. It was completely out of my control, so what are you going to do? I got to meet a lot of great people from all over the world and literally see the world through wrestling, so I am OK with it."

In all, Rheingans was a five-time national AAU Greco-Roman champion, a two-time national USWF Greco-Roman champion and a two time gold medallist at the Pan American Games. (He would also later serve as an assistant coach on the 1984 U.S. Olympic Greco-Roman wrestling team as well.)

So, with his amateur career behind him, Brad came home and decided to pursue a career in the world of professional wrestling. As an Olympian, he had big name recognition. As a result, he was thrust into the limelight as one of the "good guys" in Verne Gagne's American Wrestling Association. With his signature cradle-suplex finishing move, Brad wrestled around the world and eventually teamed up with former Olympic weightlifter, Ken Patera, to form the successful tag-team duo known as the "Olympians." The pair would go on to achieve a lot of success together, eventually winning the AWA's World Heavyweight Tag-Team title.

Brad's biggest rival through the years though, would have to have been Nick Bockwinkel, who he fought with mercilessly. In the late 80's Brad jumped ship to compete in the World Wrestling Federation, and in the early 90's he was performing almost exclusively in Japan. In all, he would wrestle professionally for nearly two decades, entertaining millions of fans along the way as one of the sports' all-time top babyfaces.

"You know, I was lucky to have people like Nick (Bockwinkel), Jerry Blackwell, Ray Stevens and Bobby Heenan show me the ropes," said Brad. "We have a really rich wrestling heritage here and a lot of that goes back to what Verne Gagne started way back when. So, I was just lucky to have been a part of it. It was just a lot of fun competing back then, traveling around, but it was a grind too. It was also a pounding, I mean have had had both knees, a hip and a shoulder all replaced. The travel was tough too, I mean I have been to Japan 87 times, that is crazy. I have logged a lot of miles over the years, I couldn't even begin to count how many. But, it was a lot of fun times over the years too, no question."

After hanging up the leotards, Brad stayed very active in the profession as a trainer and booker. In 1987 he started his own business, The World Wide School of Professional Wrestling, Inc.

Regarded by many in the industry as one of the world's premier trainers, Brad has helped to produce some of the most successful pro wrestlers in the business over the past 15 years, including: Curt Hennig, The Steiner Brothers, The Beverly Brothers, The Nasty boys, Big Van Vader, Scott Norton and, of course, Brock Lesnar, just to name a few. So popular and revered is Brad's camp that in November of 2003 it was even featured on FOX TV's popular "Best Damn Sports Show Period."

"You know, not enough guys want to pay the price nowadays," said Brad. "I mean it is such a tough business and you really have to work at it to make it. So, I really try to focus on training guys from the grass-roots level and teach them the right way. It seems to me that there are too many people who get into this business who really have no idea what they are doing. There are a lot of hot-shot type deals now where trainers or promoters will put these guys through the basics for a short period of time, show them a few moves and then call them a professional wrestler. It is crazy.

"It's like any other profession, such as medical school or law school, if you keep the entrance exams really tough, then you will get the best people moving forward while weeding out the others. You know, I have had professional football players and former elite military guys come through my camp over the years and afterwards they would tell me that it was tougher than any training camp or boot camp. So, that is a big part of it, to weed out a lot of guys from the get-go and let the cream rise to the top.

"I have also carried over a lot of my amateur training techniques into my professional career and have found that to work well too. No matter how big guys are, they have to be in shape, because that is a big part of the business nowadays. I remember when I was in the Olympics, I weighed 220 and had just 7% body fat. Those days are long gone for me, but if you want to be a world class athlete, you have to pay the price through hard work to get there.

"There are certain standards that I have always kept. Sometime it is easy to cheapen to things up and take everybody's money, but I have always been very selective with the kind of people that I have wanted to come through here. I have always tried to keep my standards pretty high and maintain a level of respect for the business and that is why I have been so successful I think. I have a pretty good idea as to what is going on in the business at all times and that really helps too, to stay on top of things. I mean I have also been a booking agent for a promotion out of Tokyo for the past 15 years and that helps to see what is going on over there as well."

Brad knows it is not just about hard work and training either. There is a whole other side of the business, the political side, which he has lived through first hand — a commodity which gives him even more credibility with the guys.

"One of the biggest thing that I have tried to pass on to my guys are the little things that I learned from the various promoters and wrestlers in the business over the past 25 years," he said. "Take a guy like Brock Lesnar. I told him that mechanically, he would have no problem learning wrestling. I told him that the biggest thing he would have to overcome were the politics of what to say, when to say it, what not to say and just how to conduct himself in and out of the ring. It is a shark tank business and you have to be real savvy about what you do. I mean for him to climb up real quick like he did was very rare. So, you have to know what to expect from these people and be able to read between the lines a little bit.

"I also told Brock to always remember that just because he made a lot of money, that it didn't mean he was a better person. Timing is of the essence in this business and Vince McMahon saw this guy who looked like he was carved out of granite and saw a lot of dollar signs. Vince also wants a guy who has the whole package and can handle the other side of this business as well. It is another world. But, I think that Brock has done a good job of keeping his mind open and listening to some of us when we offer him advice on certain things. He has had a good attitude about it since day one and that is why he has had so much success. I told him it will be hard not to get cocky, I mean he has a pile of money in the bank now and people with agendas are always wanting to 'do things for him.' I always told him to remember the fact that his character was not him, it was just something that Vince McMahon created. That's harsh, but that is the nature of this business. Brock is a great guy and we are really good friends, so I am really happy to see all of his success, he totally deserves it."

Among Brad's many honors and accolades, he was named to the Wrestling Hall of Fame in 1984, and in 1987 he was inducted into the North Dakota State University Hall of Fame as well. In addition, in 1997 he was named as part of the All-Time Minnesota High School Dream Team, and was also named to the NCAA Wrestling Hall of Fame that same year. Finally, in 2004, Brad was honored yet again, this time by being inducted into the International Wrestling Hall of Fame in Newton, IA.

Presently, Brad resides in the Twin Cities suburb of Medina, where he continues to operate his training camp. Who knows, the next Brock Lesnar may show up tomorrow, and if he does, Brad will gladly toughen him up and show him the ropes for the long journey ahead. He also has other factors motivating him to stay in the business as well, personal ones that run deep.

"Hey, I am 50 now, but I still enjoy doing what I am doing," said Brad. "But, I still feel like I am really making a difference to a lot of people and that motivates me to keep going. Another thing that is keeping me going is a long-standing promise to my old friend Curt Hennig, that I would help train his son, Joe. He is 23 now and I am working with him, so that has been a lot of fun. I mean he will be a third generation pro wrestler and that is pretty neat. So, now that Curt is gone, I feel a responsibility to keep that going, which is pretty special to be a part of. I think he will have a good shot at getting into Vince McMahon's training camp in the Ohio Valley promotion, which will be his ticket into the WWE if he can make it there. Vince always had a pretty good relationship with Curt, he even came to his funeral, so it will be interesting to see how that all plays out in the future. I am glad to be a part of it and hope he makes it like his dad did."

The pride of Appleton, Brad Rheingans is without question one of Minnesota's greatest amateur wrestlers and all-around good guys who has given back a great deal to the sport which he loves.

"You know, the biggest thing that I learned from amateur wrestling was hard work and discipline," said Brad. "I mean from spending hours upon hours in the practice room, to running, to making weight, to getting pounded on, it was all about sacrifice. Your reward came out on the matt and it was between you and the other guy standing across from you. There was nobody there to help you at that point, it is all on you to do your best. I mean it was pretty simple, the guy who worked the hardest and did the little things better, usually came out on top. I have applied those same principles to my own business and that is what keeps my humble I think. Hard work and discipline build character and I have never forgotten that. That is a big part of why I have been successful in this business. Hey, I am still having fun."

DEAN PETERS

Dean Peters grew up in Robbinsdale alongside future pro wrestlers Curt Hennig, Rick Rude and Tom Zenk. Peters, who graduated in 1976, was the captain of the gymnastics team at Robbinsdale High School, exhibiting extraordinary strength and agility for a guy who was not that big. Despite his small stature, Peters followed his buddies into the ring and made a living on his talent and smarts.

Working under the name "Brady Boone," Peters began wrestling in the mid-1980s in the NWA's Pacific Northwest Territory as the "cousin of Billy Jack Haynes." His old buddy, Tom Zenk, was the PNW Heavyweight champion at the time, so Peters came in as a tag-teamer — capturing several Tag Team titles along-

side Ricky Santana and Coco Samoa. The next stop for the acrobatic babyface was the prestigious WWF, where he took on the persona of the masked "Battle Kat." His acrobatic moves, particularly the "moonsault," were revolutionary at the time, and reserved for those select few with a gymnastics background. Peters would seemingly land on his feet no matter which way the other guy threw him and the fans ate it up. And, his back flips and handsprings from one corner to the other made him a big-time fan favorite.

Dean Peters

After a disagreement with management, however, Peters wound up going his own way, ultimately winding up in the Florida area as "Fire Cat," winning the Sun Coast tag straps alongside Jerry Flynn in the early 90's. From there, Peters, who also competed in promotions throughout Japan as well as in the GWF, began working as a referee in the WCW. Tragically, Peters died in a car accident December 15, 1998. H was returning to his home in Tampa after refereeing several matches at a TV taping in Orlando. Known for his individuality and creativity, Peters was a tremendous athlete and a man of deep faith.

BROCK LESNAR

Brock Lesnar

Brock Lesnar grew up in the tiny South Dakota dairy farming town of Webster. There was no cable TV for young Brock, so when he wasn't working on the farm, he spent most of his time hunting, riding his motorcycle, or doing his favorite pastime — lifting weights. He loved hard work and even had two hernias by the age of six because of how hard he pushed himself. As a teenager he worked on his high school wrestling coaches' farm to make some extra money. There, according to his former coach, John Schiley, "Brock would get tired of chasing down the calves to herd them together, so he would just pick them up and throw them over the fence instead."

Lesnar was not huge as a prep athlete, however. In fact, he struggled to reach 200 pounds on the football field. His passion was wrestling though, and upon graduating from Webster High School he ventured off to Bismarck (North Dakota) Junior College to grapple collegeiately. There, Brock hit the weights hard and trained like a madman. Eventually his body filled out and at six-foot-four and 285-pounds, the hulking behemoth was unstoppable. He dominated the National Junior College Athletic Association

(NJCAA), going 56-3, and also won the 1998 national championship as a heavyweight.

From there, Brock was recruited by University of Minnesota Wrestling Coach J Robinson to head south and suit up for the Gophers. He agreed, and in no time was taking big-time college wrestling to a whole new level. Fans poured into Williams Arena to see the freak of nature throw his opponents around like bales of hay. It was a spectacle never before seen in amateur wrestling history. As a junior, Brock went 24-1, won the Big Ten title, earned All American honors and made it all the way to the NCAA Finals, ultimately losing a heartbreaking 3-2 decision to the defending national champ, Stephen Neal, of Cal State-Bakersfield. He came roaring back his senior year though, tearing through every would be opponent along the way. He posted a 26-1 record (his sole loss came against Wes Hand from Iowa State), again won the Big Ten title, again earned All American honors, and this time went on to capture the 2000 NCAA heavyweight title — beating Hand in the Finals. More importantly though, Brock was a team player and he was proud of his Gophers, who placed second in the 1999 NCAA tournament, their highest ever finish.

After the season, Brock found himself being pulled in several different directions with seemingly everybody wanting a piece of him for one thing or another. There was the possibility of competing in the Olympics; there were offers to try out to be a professional football player; and of course, there were offers pouring in from the ranks of pro wrestling. So, after taking it all in, Lesnar decided to try something totally different and go with the latter. Not knowing where to turn and who to trust, Lesnar took the advice of his mentor and coach, J Robinson, who introduced him to his old college buddy, Gerald Brisco, who was a top-notch talent agent for the World Wrestling Federation (WWF). Brisco, himself a former NWA tag-team champion, signed Lesnar to a very lucrative multi-year deal. Brock was headed to the "Show."

With that, Brock started training with local trainer, Brad Rheingans, a former Olympic and professional wrestler who ran a professional wrestling training facility in the Twin Cities. From there, Brock was off to the WWF's developmental area, called Ohio Valley Wrestling, where he learned the ropes alongside dozens of other aspiring grapplers. At first he was eased into the ring as part of a tag-team duo alongside former Gopher teammate, Shelton Benjamin. Together they were billed as the "Minnesota Stretching Crew." On February 13, 2001, the duo defeated the "Disciples of Synn" for the OVW Tag Team title in Louisville, KY. They had arrived!

Well, after a year of seasoning under his belt, traveling around, doing television interviews, and learning the tricks of the trade, Brock was moved to compete in singles competition. There, he dominated and quickly made a name for himself as a top-notch athlete capable of just about anything. He was just a physical freak of nature, with a neck like a pit-bull and muscles bulging out of muscles. The fans were in awe of him and just wanted to see what kind of havoc he was going to wreak on his opponents.

Finally, after two years of hard work and proving himself worthy of a shot at the next level, Brock was introduced to the WWF's wild world of pro wrestling as "The next big thing." On March 18, 2002, Lesnar made his WWE television debut on a live edition of Raw. With "agent" Paul Heyman by his side, Brock interrupted a Hardcore Title match by pummeling Spike Dudley, Al Snow and Maven. He jumped in, started raising hell and showcased an impressive finishing move — a fireman's carry with a spinning face buster slam. He was unbeatable, toying with the likes of established stars such as the Undertaker and even Hulk Hogan. Soon, with his patented "F-5" (tornado) signature move, he became an instant fan favorite. Then, just several months after making his pro debut, Brock made history at the 2002 Summer Slam, when he beat The Rock for the WWE heavyweight championship. At just 25 years of age, Lesnar had become the youngest champion in WWE history and also the quickest man to win the title since making his debut.

Being thrust into the national limelight was no small feat.

The multi-billion dollar WWE was investing a lot of time and resources in Lesnar and he was answering the bell at every turn. Fame and fortune soon followed as Brock suddenly found himself mobbed everywhere he went. Droves of fans wanted to meet this new icon and it was a lot to take for the simple country kid from Webster. He hung in there though and took it all in stride. With a new daughter in his life at this point and tens of millions of dollars in the bank, he was enjoying life to its fullest.

Brock was finally defeated by "The Big Show," who won the title from him at the Survivor Series when Brock's former partner, Paul Heyman, turned on him and came to the aid of his opponent. The drama was all part of the show and Brock was proving to be quite the showman. He was given another shot at his old heavyweight belt later that year, however, and this time he went on to beat former Olympian Kurt Angle in the main event of Wrestlemania to reclaim the WWE championship.

Over the next several years Brock traveled the world and became a household name to a legion of pro wrestling fanatics. As the main star of one of the biggest shows on TV, the world was Brock's oyster — he simply had it all, including a $9 million annual salary; a private eight-seat, twin-engine plane with his own personal pilot; and a beautiful mansion on 47 acres in Independence, Minn. Which is why his decision in the Spring of 2004 to retire from wrestling and pursue a career in the National Football League sent shockwaves throughout the world of sports entertainment. That's right. In fact, in March of 2004, he left about $45 million of his seven-year WWE contract on the table for the slim chance to play for the NFL's league minimum, $230,000, or about $85,000 if he ended up only making a team's practice squad.

And just why would he walk away from the money, the fame and the life of a rock star? He had simply had enough. His dream was to play pro football and at 26 years of age, he figured that if he didn't do it now, he may regret it for the rest of his life — a chance he wasn't willing to take. The low-key announcement was posted on the WWE website on the night of Wrestlemania XX: "Brock Lesnar has made a personal decision to put his WWE career on hold to prepare to tryout for the National Football League this season. Brock has wrestled his entire professional career in the WWE and we are proud of his accomplishments and wish him the best in his new endeavor."

"It was interesting," Lesnar said of his celebrity in a recent Star Tribune interview. "One time, I was walking through the parking lot in Los Angeles. Some guy yells, 'Hey, Brock!' I turn around and it's Shaq. Shaquille O'Neal. He's one of my biggest fans. How cool is that? At first, it was very cool, but that all wore off after a while." He said the grind of traveling and performing 280 nights a year — often in a different city every night — made him miserable and he just missed being around his two-year-old daughter, Mya.

"I ain't afraid of anything and I ain't afraid of anybody," Lesnar added. "I've been an underdog in athletics since I was five. I got zero college offers for wrestling. Now, people say I can't play football, that it's a joke. But I say I can. I'm as good an athlete as a lot of guys in the NFL, if not better."

With that, Brock began training for what would prove to be the toughest test of his life, getting into football shape to play a game he had not played since Webster High lost to Aberdeen Roncalli in the first round of the 1995 South Dakota small-school playoffs. Could he do it? Well, the numbers don't lie. He stands six-foot-four, weighs 290 pounds, has just nine percent body fat, runs the 40-yard dash in 4.65 seconds, bench presses 475 pounds, squats 695 pounds, has a 10-foot standing broad jump and a 35-inch vertical leap. He is basically a freak of nature, complete with the speed, power and agility of an NFL running back packed into a defensive tackle's frame. Many skeptics also alleged that his 56-inch chest, 34-inch waist, 21-inch biceps and 20-inch neck couldn't possibly be "natural," but Brock has never tested positive for steroids at any point in his career and has gladly offered to "pee in any cup, any time," to set the record straight.

But, could a guy who never even played college football

make the leap to the NFL, the toughest game on earth? It was a risk Brock was willing to take, but were any teams willing to take a gamble on an unproven former wrestler with a lot of potential, but no experience? The words "project" and "raw" kept coming up with pro scouts, who were not only concerned about his lack of football instincts, but also his celebrity factor — which they felt might prove to be a distraction with both the fans as well as the players.

"He's a project. Big time," said Vikings Player Personnel Director Scott Studwell. "As much as you'd like to take a shot on a guy like him because of his athletic history, do you do it at the expense of cutting another player? Probably not. At the expense of taking reps away from a promising young player? Probably not. With Brock, it's like you're starting from scratch."

Unfortunately, just as Brock was ready to participate in some private work-outs with a couple of teams, he was injured in a motorcycle accident in which he broke his jaw, fractured his left hand, severely pulled his groin and suffered tissue damage in his lower abdomen. He recovered though, worked hard to get back into shape, and a couple months later he got his big break with his hometown Minnesota Vikings. After impressing Head Coach Mike Tice with his speed, agility and most importantly, his passion, he was given an invitation to come to the team's training camp in Mankato. There, Brock did his best to just fit in, acknowledging the fact that he had a long way to go. He came in with an open mind, however, and tried to learn as much as he could.

"He's a lot better than we thought," said Vikings Coach Mike Tice. "We didn't think he'd be able to pick it up so quickly. He showed us that he was going to have the right work ethic and the right attention to detail. We're very proud of what he has accomplished. Hopefully it will work out for him, and hopefully it will work out for him here."

As for the reality of it all? It will be tough. At 26, he's already about five years older than most NFL rookies. And, if he spends a couple years on the practice squad along with spending the off-season playing in NFL Europe or in the Canadian Football League to learn the game, he won't be ready to contribute until he's 28 — well past the prime of many players. We'll just have to wait and see. Knowing the type of competitor he is, he will probably defy the odds and make it. He could be a special teams gladiator and eventually a sack artist, just give him time — he's the real deal. Wrestling is all about leverage, quickness and about getting underneath your opponent to beat him — the very same criteria for being a solid defensive lineman.

Lesnar said his future is wide open. He won't rule out going back to pro wrestling after football, but he also said he might also get into K-1, a professional fighting circuit in Japan, as well. Who knows? For now, his dream is to put on the pads every Sunday afternoon and hopefully one day, bring home a Superbowl trophy to Minnesota. The skeptics and nay-sayers, however, will always be there.

"That's OK; I've always had to fight for everything," said Lesnar. "I wasn't the best technician in amateur wrestling. But I was strong, had great conditioning and a hard head. Nobody could break me. As long as I have that, I don't give a damn what anybody else thinks."

Stay tuned, this saga... is far from over.

BRONKO NAGURSKI

The legend of Bronko Nagurski began back in 1926, when then-Gopher Football Coach Clarence "Doc" Spears was on a recruiting trip up in northern Minnesota. One day, while driving through International Falls, he saw a hulk of a man plowing a field — without a horse. When the curious Spears stopped to ask for directions, instead of using his finger, the kid just lifted the enormous plow and

Bronko Nagurski

pointed with it! That young man wasn't Paul Bunyon... it was Bronko Nagurski.

Bronislau Nagurski was born Nov. 3, 1908, to parents Michael and Amelia Nagurski, on the Canadian side of Rainy Lake in the small border town of Rainy River, Ontario. At the age of four, his family moved to International Falls, just a slap-shot away on the other side of the US border. His nickname supposedly came about when his first-grade teacher, after not being able to understand his mother's thick Ukrainian accent, called the youngster "Bronko," and the name stuck.

As a youngster the Bronk had to run four miles each day to school and back to the family farm, where he lived with his parents and three siblings. He grew up loving all sports, but, amazingly, in his two years of prep football at International Falls High School, his sophomore and junior years, he never played on a team that won a game. In fact, he even transferred to neighboring Bemidji High School for his senior year, because he was upset when his principal canceled the team's trip to a district tournament when a couple of other players required some disciplining. There, the transfer student was ruled ineligible to play football, but he did manage to play basketball and run track however. It was hardly the kind of a prep career that would have attracted college recruiters, even in those days.

Following high school, the "Bronk" headed south, to wear the Maroon and Gold at the University of Minnesota. (In reality, he met Doc Spears while he was up north fishing, and convinced him to come to the University.) Once there, Spears' greatest dilemma quickly became deciding where to play his new star. Then he finally figured it out — he would play him everywhere. And that's exactly what he did. Bronko would go on to play tackle, fullback, defensive end, offensive end, linebacker and he even passed the ball as a quarterback from time to time as well.

He was a massive man for his time, measuring six-feet-two and weighing in at 235 pounds. He had giant hands, donned a size-19 neck and could even run a 10.3 100-yard dash. He literally became the fullback no one could tackle and the tackle no runner could escape. As a soph-

The Bronk

omore Bronko first got noticed by the national press when he forced and recovered a late-game fumble against a heavily favored Notre Dame team, which led to a game-tying Gopher touchdown. During his junior year, wearing a steel plate to protect a couple of broken vertebrae, he almost single-handedly defeated Wisconsin when, in addition to intercepting three passes and making numerous touchdown-saving tackles, he forced a fumble and ran it in for the game-winning score.

So talented was the powerful Nagurski that he would go on to earn All-America honors at three different positions. Sportswriters decided after his senior season in 1929 that he was the best Fullback and Tackle in the nation, making him the only player in college football history ever to be named a first-team consensus All-American at two different positions in the same season. Incredibly, he was even named as an End on a few other All-America teams! Over his illustrious three year career in Gold Country, the Gophers lost a total of just four games, and none of them by more than two points.

In the fall of 1930, Bronko graduated and became THE "Monster of the Midway," literally, when he signed on with the NFL's Chicago Bears for the then-pricey, Depression-era sum of $5,000. The Bronk went on to reach superstar status in the Windy City, where he would lead the team to three NFL championships during his eight-year gridiron tenure.

It was also in Chicago where the bruising fullback's exploits soon took on legendary proportions. Papa Bear Halas, the team's owner, recalled a game against Washington at Wrigley Field, where Nagurski barreled up the middle, sent two linebackers flying in different directions, trampled two defensive backs, ran through the end-zone and bounced off the goal-post, finally bulldozing into the brick wall that bordered the dugout used by the Chicago Cubs — even cracking it. "That last guy hit me awful hard..." the dazed Nagurski would say upon reaching the sidelines.

One tall tale had him falling out of bounds during a game once, and toppling a policeman's horse standing along the sideline. Another had the Bronk missing a wild tackle and shearing the fender off a Model-T Ford that was parked near the sidelines.

As a runner, Nagurski didn't bother with dazzle and finesse, and as a lineman he never bothered to learn great technique. Instead, he simply used his brute strength to overpower his opponents. In other words, he was about as subtle as a Mack Truck. When he ran, he simply tucked the ball under his arm, lowered his giant shoulders, and charged full speed ahead — ramming through anything in his way.

"I was OK, I guess," Bronko said years later. "I wasn't pretty, but I did all right. Our teams won most of the time, so that was good. I know I'd love to do it all over again. I never enjoyed anything as much as I did playing football. I felt like it was something I was born to do."

Bronko wasn't the only star running back on the team though, as future Hall of Famer Red Grange was also in the Bears' backfield as well. In fact, Bronko even took over in that same Bears backfield for another future Hall of Famer, former Duluth Eskimo great, Ernie Nevers. "Tackling Bronko was like trying to stop a freight train running downhill…" quipped Nevers.

"Halas stockpiled backs and he believed in spreading it around," Nagurski told Sports Illustrated in 1984. "Plus, he wanted to keep me fresh for defense, where I'd put in a full afternoon."

"I have said it a thousand times, Bronko Nagurski was the greatest player I ever saw, and I saw a lot of them in my lifetime," Red Grange would later say. "Running into him was like getting an electric shock. If you tried to tackle him anywhere above the ankles, you were liable to get killed."

Overall, Nagurski was a clutch player who did whatever it took to get his team a victory. He threw the winning touchdown pass in the 1932 playoff game against the Portsmouth Spartans, and that next season he led the Bears to another NFL championship when he tossed a pair of touchdown passes in Chicago's 23-21 victory over the New York Giants.

"Here's a check for $10,000, Nagurski" said G. A. Richards, owner of the Detroit Lions. "not to play for the Lions, but just to quit and get the hell out of the league. You're ruining my team!"

In 1937, Nagurski, upset about his salary being decreased throughout the 1930s from $5,000 to $4,500 in 1931, and down to $3,700 by 1932, decided to retire, and pursue a career in pro wrestling. The Bronk had gotten into wrestling a few years earlier,

but found it tough to juggle both careers. In one three-week stretch that year, he played in five Bears games and wrestled in eight different cities: Portland. Vancouver, Seattle, Phoenix, L.A., Oakland, Salt Lake City and Philadelphia. Life in the ring was not as glamorous as he had hoped, but it was a living.

"I wrestled guys like Jim Londos, Strangler Lewis and others," said Bronko. "But they weren't in their prime then. I never liked wrestling. At that time, there wasn't a lot of money in it. And it was a sport where you worked every night and traveled a lot. I had a family at the time and didn't want to be away from home. But we were just getting out of the Depression in those days and we needed the money. The promoters told me I would make a million in no time. But it didn't happen."

In the ring Bronko was tough as nails and his opponents had a tough time throwing him around. He was managed by Tony Stecher, brother and manager of former NWA World champion Joe Stecher. Nagurski made his pro wrestling debut in February of 1933, defeating Tag Tagerson in four minutes. He won his first world heavyweight title belt in 1937 when he defeated Dean Detton. Two years later he beat Lou Thesz to earn the coveted NWA World Championship and after losing it to Ray Steel in 1940, he regained it for one last time in 1941. He would lose it for good on June 5, 1941, when Sandor Szabo pulled off the major upset.

"He was a pretty big draw," said former wrestler Stu Hart of Nagurski in a 1997 interview with Slam Magazine. "He was pretty tough to bring down in wrestling. He wasn't that fancy a wrestler either. But he was good enough to be recognized as world's champion."

Then, in 1943, because of player shortages caused by World War II, the Bears issued an S.O.S. to Nagurski to return for one final season. He agreed, and fittingly, at the age of 35, even scored the game-winning touchdown of the NFL title game against the Washington Redskins. He hung em' up for good after that season though, finishing his amazing NFL career with 242 points scored on 4,301 yards rushing. The six-time All-Pro even averaged nearly five yards per carry, a remarkable feat.

"My greatest thrill in football was the day Bronko announced his retirement," said Green Bay Hall of Fame Fullback Clarke Hinkle. "There's no question he was the most bruising fullback football has ever seen. I know, because I've still got the bruises!"

After hanging up the cleats, Bronko returned to the ring, where he wrestled professionally for more than a dozen years after that, mostly in independent circuits — a career he would later call "degrading." From there, Nagurski, who had returned to International Falls with his wife Eileen to raise their six children after his professional football playing days, quietly and unassumingly, became the most famous gas station owner in town. There, he could finally live in peace and privacy, and enjoy the fruits of his labor. He loved the outdoors, and was an avid hunter and fisherman. He also loved spending time with his kids. (One of his boys, Bronko, Jr., played football at Notre Dame and then eight seasons with the Hamilton Tiger Cats of the Canadian Football League.) Nagurski even liked the cold weather. "We don't have summer," he once joked of his beloved hometown, "just a season in the middle of the year when the sledding is poor."

He would later do some endorsements, including a couple of $50 deals for promoting Wheaties and Camel Cigarettes — which included a carton of smokes a week. "I bought Kools and gave the Camels away," he later said jokingly.

Tragically, on Jan. 7, 1990, Bronko died at the age of 81. His awards and honors include being named as a charter member of the Pro Football and College Football Halls of Fame, and being elected to the Football Writers Association of America's All-Time team. In 1995 that same group also voted to have his name attached to college football's Defensive Player of the Year award, called the "Nagurski Trophy."

In 1979 his No. 72 was retired by the U of M, and Sports Illustrated later named Bronko as Minnesota's Greatest Athlete of the Century. In addition, in 1992, International Falls honored its most famous son by opening the "Bronko Nagurski Museum," the only museum in America dedicated to a single player. That same year the Gophers' practice facility was renamed as the Gibson-Nagurski Football Complex, after Bronk and his Gopher teammate, 1928 All-American Guard George Gibson. Perhaps the biggest honor came years ago though, when his old high school renamed themselves as the International Falls "Broncos" in his memory.

Legendary Notre Dame Coach Knute Rockne called him "the only football player I ever saw who could have played every position," and George Halas said he was "the greatest fullback who ever lived. He was absolutely unstoppable."

Bronko Nagurski was larger than life, and his size 22 Super Bowl ring, the biggest ever made, was proof! Perhaps no name has become more synonymous in the history of the sport than his. Nothing says leather helmets and high-top cleats louder than Bronko Nagurski. With his barrel chest and tree trunk legs, he became one of America's most colorful all-time characters and greatest sports heroes.

Perhaps Grantland Rice, once the most respected football authority in the nation, summed him up best when he was asked to select an all-time All-Star team. "That's easy. I'd pick 11 Bronko Nagurski's. I honestly don't think it would be a contest. The 11 Nagurski's would be a mop-up. It would be something close to murder and massacre. For the Bronk could star at any position on the field — with 228 pounds of authority to back him up."

He was truly a Bronko that could never be broken...

BUCK ZUMHOFE

Buck Zumhofe

Herman "Buck" Zumhofe grew up in the small Minnesota town of Norwood Young America, and went on to star in football, baseball and wrestling at Norwood Young America High School.

"You know, I am not trying to be cocky or anything, but I would have to say that I was probably the greatest athlete that Norwood has ever had, even to this day," said Buck. "I just loved sports and loved the competition."

From there, Buck got a job as a welder at a steel shop in nearby Delano. Yearning to get back into the limelight, however, he got a "signal" from a higher calling one Saturday evening as he was watching his favorite telvision show, All-Star Wrestling.

"I remember catching the show one night when I was out at a bar with all the guys from the welding shop," said Buck. "And then I heard the announcer, Marty O'Neal, say in his deep voice, 'Do you think you have what it takes to become a professional wrestler?'. Well, the guys started egging me on to call up the number on the screen and give it a shot. So, I did. I figured I could still work at the shop, but this way I could earn a little extra money on the weekends. I thought they must have some room for a guy like me, who could come in and be a 'job-guy' or an extra, who could always get beat by the famous guys. I figured why not?

"So, I got a leave of absence from my boss and I went and signed up. They said sure, and then sent me over to Verne Gagne's wrestling camp, where I got the hell beat out of me for 12 straight weeks. It was the toughest thing I ever did in my life — bar none. I mean I did thousands of push-ups, thousands of sit-ups, it was brutal. Well, when I got done, I figured I could still work back at the shop, but it turned out to be a full-time job, working 15-20 days a month. So, I quit and hit the road.

"My first year in the business, 1976, I drove around in Gagne's truck, doing nothing but setting up and taking down the rings at his matches. It was tough, tough work. Finally, after paying my dues for a year or so, Verne sent me out to Portland to get some seasoning. I wound up spending about three years on the west coast, doing matches, and after a trip to Japan, I came back Minnesota in 1980. By now I had my 'Rock 'n' Roll' outfit with the whole get-up and I thought I was looking pretty good. Verne looked at me one time though and said, 'Do you know what you need? A radio.' And that was the final piece to my puzzle, my infamous boom-box. My career took off from there as Buck "Rock 'n' Roll" Zumhofe and I went from an opening guy, middle of the road wrestler, to a main-event guy all over the country."

Buck would emerge as a mainstay in the AWA, becoming a big fan-favorite with the locals. He would go on to wrestle around the world, from Europe to the Far East to across America. All the while he built his reputation as a real party animal. He would make his grand entrance by jamming to the tunes on his trademark over-sized boom box, and even occasionally smash it over his opponents' heads.

"I stayed in the AWA through 1984 and then headed to Texas for a couple years, to work for the Von Erichs," said Buck. "I even won the World Class Tag Team title with Iceman Parsons in 1984, and things were going pretty good. At that point, however, the mid-1980s, what I call the 'Big Man Syndrome' happened, where you either had to be on steroids or be a Hulk Hogan to get anywhere. From there, guys started getting chopped, and it got ugly. Pretty soon you weren't getting booked and it got to be too tough. I eventually came back to work for Mr. Gagne and wound up retiring as his last AWA Cruiserweight Champion."

After getting out of the wrestling business in the late 80s, Buck, who was married briefly and also has four children, got into the bar business. In the late 1990's, however, he came full circle and got back into the world of professional wrestling by starting his own independent promotion.

"About five years ago I decided that I am not chasing a dream anymore, I don't care about being a big star, I don't want to be in movies, I don't wanna do nothin'," said Buck. "All I wanted to do was wrestle, which is what I loved, and somehow I wanted to make a living at it. So, I started my own promotion, R&R Wrestling, and I run small shows throughout Minnesota, the Dakotas, Iowa, Wisconsin, Michigan and even Missouri, where I get together with my old buddy Harley Race ever now and then. We got to small towns, and set up in VFW's and schools, and that sort of thing. We might get anywhere from 75-150 people to come out to see us, and that is pretty good for what we do.

"My daughter even wrestles with me now and that's a lot of fun too. She is so tough, I mean she is not one of these 'magazine' girls like McMahon has out in New York, she is a wrestler. Period. She can take guys and throw em' in a head-lock, put em' in a hip-lock, take em' down, drop-kick em', pile-drive em' and throw them in a back-breaker, she can do it all. I taught her everything she knows. In our shows she goes by 'Louisa-Lees,' and I am hopeful that she can catch a big break one day.

"It is a lot of work though, setting it all up and getting the guys to come out. We have three rings that we use for all our shows and we hit it hard. I haven't had a weekend off now in over three years. We are working every single weekend, and then some. We did 125 shows last year and are looking at close to 160 this year. I even have a giant, 'Big Chuck Holt,' who is almost seven-foot-two and 350 pounds. In fact, he is the biggest wrestler in the business today — even bigger than anybody out in New York has got. I discovered him, have him under contract and have been training him for the past six months, so that might turn out to be a big deal. And, of course, we have got 'Bad Boy Brian,' and he has been out on the 'Jerry Springer Show' a few times, which really brings out the fans too. We bill all the shows as 'The midgets, the ladies, the giant and of course, the legend of 'Rock 'n' Roll,' Buck Zumhofe.' And we make it look good too, I mean I got my two front teeth knocked out here a couple of years ago, and I can assure you there was nothing fake about that!

"We try to make it affordable as well. I mean we can come into a bar for under a thousand bucks and give them a two and a half hour show with six wrestlers. Because of that, we can compete with a band for the same price, which is what it is all about for the bar owners — having an attraction where people will come out and buy food and liquor. On top of that, I can also tell that bar owner that if they want to add another $450 bucks to the price tag, I will bring in a star headliner, like Baron Von Raschke, who will sign autographs. So, we give them a lot of options and we get a lot of business. It is a win-win situation for both of us."

As an independent promoter Buck doesn't have a web-site to let his fans know about upcoming events. The reason may surprise you.

"We stay away from that," he said "because there are so many other local guys who will try to steal your shows. I mean sometimes other promoters, if they hear you are going to be at a bar or someplace to do a show, will actually call those places and try to re-finagle a different deal with them to see if they will dump us and use them instead. That side of the business was dirty back then and believe it or not, I think it is actually worse now. I can't afford to put guys on posters and then have them not show up to a booked show, that is a big no-no. The other problem with having a web-site, because we used to have one, is that every damn retired has-been wrestler in the world winds up calling to ask if they can get booked on your cards. Beyond that, sometimes you also run into trouble when you go into a small town and the local wrestlers there want to be a part of the action, because it is there home turf. So, there are all kinds of issues that come up in this business, and you just have to keep at it and take care of it as best as you can."

With regards to big-time professional wrestling today, Buck has a much different perspective about the business he used to be a part of.

"Wrestling today is horrible," he said. "I mean these guys today in the WWE, they are given everything to say in their interviews verbatim by McMahon. Could you imagine the Crusher, Mad Dog or the Baron doing that? No way! They would eat the freakin piece of paper the words were written on before they did that. Now it is all scripted and all a big business. It is no fun and I want nothin' to do with it. And, it is not family entertainment like it used to be either. In our shows we very seldom have guys go to the floor, outside the ring, and we don't have guys getting beaten with chairs all bloody or anything like that. We just try to make it entertaining. For instance, we usually have a couple of midgets wrestle the girls, and then the girls will wrestle the giant, and that sort of thing. It is good family kind of stuff that is harmless."

Aside from making his living doing what he loves, Buck also enjoys being back out there, amongst the old-school fans who grew up watching All Star Wrestling.

"You know, the fans still remember me and still love me," said Buck, who presently resides in Cyrus. "They still chant 'Rock and Roll' when I come out and they have just always been good to me over the years, so I appreciate that. A lot of people will come up to me and tell me that they used to see me on TV and that is always neat to be able to meet them and just show them that you are just are a real person, like anybody else.

"Do I miss it? Sure, it was a blast. And while the travel was tough, I had so many great times taking road trips from town to town with the guys, drinking beer and smoking cigars in the back seats across America. It was a trip, let me tell ya. As for my legacy, that is easy. I was the first guy ever to bring music into wrestling and I am very proud of that. I still have four or five of my original boom boxes that aren't all destroyed and I am sure they will be worth a lot of money one day. And hey, I will always be the last AWA Cruiserweight Champion too, and nobody can ever take that

away from me either. You know, it is like I tell all my new guys, 'This is the greatest business in the world…'. It really is."

BUDDY WOLFF

Buddy Wolf

Les "Buddy" Wolff grew up in southern Minnesota and went on to play football and wrestle at St. Cloud State University during the early 1960s. A solid, six-foot, 220-pound all-conference lineman, Wolff excelled as a heavyweight wrestler with the Huskies and even qualified for the 1964 U.S. Olympic trials. It was a lifelong dream of his to participate in the Olympics, but he just didn't think it was going to work out. So, he opted instead to sign a semi-professional football contract. During that same time he was also teaching school part time and coaching. He had a family by now but was still looking to do something a little more exciting and lucrative. So, he hooked up with one of his old teammates on the Husky football team, Larry Heiniemi (aka: "Lars Anderson"), who introduced him to the world of professional wrestling.

He jumped in head first and for the next two decades made a living traveling the world as a pro grappler. His role was well defined, he was not the flamboyant superstar who talked trash and lived like a rock star. Rather, Wolff was usually the guy who wound up losing to those guys. He was what is referred to as in the business as a "jobber," a mainstream worker who did his part night in and night out to keep the show moving along. He kept it clean, lifted weights, didn't do drugs and steadily chugged along. He carved out a nice niche for himself and even became a favorite match partner for the likes of Verne Gagne and Dusty Rhodes along the way. Later, he was also billed as a cousin to the Andersons, allowing him to team up with his old buddy Larry.

"I made good money in Florida in the late 1970s," Wolff said in a 2002 Star Tribune article. "Dusty Rhodes and I wrestled 13 times in a row in the Tampa Bay Auditorium. Mostly sellouts. Each match went the limit. It takes a very good performance to hold their attention for an hour. And I don't talk much."

He even gained a bit of national notoriety in 1976 when he fought Muhammad Ali in a three-round wrestling/boxing exhibition match in Chicago. Ali was preparing to fight Japan's heavyweight wrestling champ and went on tour to get tuned up. The wrestling/boxing experiment was a disaster, but Wolff did manage to knock down the champ on a couple occasions by sweeping his legs out from underneath him.

By the early 1980s, Wolff, now in his 40s, had had enough. Divorced with two daughters, he moved from St. Cloud to Hackensack — a small town about an hour north of Brainerd. There, he ran a silk-screening retail operation and later opened a restaurant, which eventually did him in. He was badly in debt and needed to start over. So, from there Wolff, a self-taught inventor who had designed a few weight lifting and exercise machines, had an epiphany one night as he was driving through Brainerd. It was storming that night and he couldn't help but notice that the high winds were tearing apart the canvas banners which were hanging on the street lights. His idea, to create a banner bracket that would flex with the wind.

So, after several failed prototypes, the "Banner Saver" was born, a rod-and-bracket contraption which rotated on hinges in the direction the wind was blowing so the banner wouldn't rip. It was a brilliant idea and before long the sales started pouring in, first from nearby towns, and then from around the world. He converted the device to a lightweight aluminum design and then began mass producing them at a Bloomington factory. By the early-2000's his business was doing more than a half-million in sales. In fact, one of his biggest clients was the U.S. Olympic Committee, which ordered several thousand banners for the 2002 Winter Games in Salt Lake City. All those years later, Buddy had finally made it to the Olympics.

BUTCH LEVY

Butch Levy

Leonard "Butch" Levy grew up in Minneapolis and went on to star as a Guard on the University of Minnesota's Golden Gopher Football team from 1939-41. As an All-Conference lineman in 1941, Levy's undefeated Gophers outscored their opponents 186-38, en route to winning the NCAA National Championship. From there, the six-foot, 260-pound behemoth was selected in the fourth round (27th overall) of the 1942 NFL Draft by the Cleveland Rams. He did not play professional football until 1945, however, as he spent the next three years serving in the U.S. Navy during World War II. In 1945, Levy suited up for the Rams and helped anchor a tough offensive line which played a huge role in defeating the Washington Redskins in the NFL championship game. Butch remained with the Rams the following season when they moved to Los Angeles, finishing second in the NFL West.

In 1947, Levy moved to the newly-formed All-American Football Conference and played for the Los Angeles Dons, earning All-AAFC first team honors that next year. He retired from professional football after that season though, and turned to professional wrestling, where he would become one of the most feared wrestlers in the 1950s. Butch came home to wrestle in Verne Gagne's American Wrestling Association, quickly earning a reputation as one tough S.O.B. On April 28, 1959, Butch teamed up with Verne Gagne for a match in Minneapolis and defeated Karol Kalmikoff and Baron Gattoni to win the NWA Tag Team title. Then, after losing the title a few months later, he teamed up with fellow Gopher Football All-American, Leo Nomellini, to win back the Tag Team title belt. They promptly lost the strap yet again when Nomellini returned to play pro football later that year. Sadly, Butch passed away on February 9, 1999, at the age of 78.

CURT HENNIG

Curt Hennig

Curt Hennig was born in Minneapolis, the son of legendary pro wrestler Larry "The Axe" Hennig, and grew up in the northern Twin Cities suburb of Robbinsdale. There, Curt loved playing all sports and loved to be the center of attention. While Curt went on to finish his senior year at Saguaro High School in Scottsdale, Arizona (because his family moved), his graduating class of 1976 back at Robbinsdale High School featured a who's-who of the future professional wrestlers including, Dean Peters, Tom Zenk and Rick Rude. (John Nord, Nikita Koloff and Barry Darsow would graduate a year later.) After a stellar prep athletic career, which included playing football, wrestling and baseball, Curt went on to play football at Normandale Community College for two years. From there, he had an opportunity to play football at the University of Minnesota, but, after injuring his knee, he opted to follow his father's footsteps into the world of pro grappling.

So, he began working out and learning the ropes from his old man as well as at Verne Gagne's wrestling camp in Chanhassen. At six-foot-three and 235 pounds, he was a specimen. He first started out working as a young jobber in the business, working throughout the Midwest and later in the Pacific Northwest territory. In 1981, Curt returned home to Minnesota and joined Gagne's AWA. There, he got a nice push and emerged as one of the federation's biggest stars. He would go on to win several titles over the next several years, including the AWA Tag Team belt in 1986 alongside Scott Hall, as well as the AWA world heavyweight belt over Nick Bockwinkel that next year. He and his father also teamed up together as well, entertaining legions of loyal fans throughout the Midwest.

In 1988 Curt headed east to perform for Vince McMahon's WWF, where he assumed a new moniker, "Mr. Perfect." McMahon was skowering other wrestling promotions to find new talent, and while Hennig was not a sculpted, muscleman brawler, he did fit the bill as an extremely talented technical wrestler. As a member of the WWF, Curt, now billed as a heel, found instant superstardom. With his patented "Perfect-Plex" signature finishing move, he would go on to beat the likes of Hulk Hogan en route to winning the coveted Intercontinental title over Tito Santana in 1990. Despite a nagging back injury which would trouble him throughout his career, he emerged as a television mainstay and traveled the world as one of the sport's top draws. Along the way he would establish himself as an A-List celebrity, battling the likes of Ric Flair, Lex Luger, Randy Savage, Stone Cold Steve Austin, Bill Goldberg, Bret Hart, Triple-H and Diamond Dallas Page, among many others.

In 1997, Hennig became a member of the hated "New World Order" (NWO) and captured the WCW's U.S. Championship during his brief time with the clique. It was one of many characters he would play over his illustrious career. Later, in 1999, he teamed up with Barry Windham to win the WCW world tag-team title as well. In 2000, Hennig's contract expired, and he spent the next year wrestling independently, winning the first MEWF (Main Event Wrestling Federation) championship. Then, despite a bad knee injury, he made a comeback to the WWE at the 2002 Royal Rumble. But, after an alleged real-life scuffle with

Brock Lesnar on an overseas flight, Hennig found himself looking for work. So, he went on to wrestle for a time in the NWA-TNA, and later with Jimmy Hart's All-Stars, assuming he would make a triumphant return to the WWE later in 2003. Tragically, that would never happen.

Sadly, on February 10, 2003, Hennig was found dead of an apparent heart attack in his hotel room near Tampa, where he was set to perform that night. Just 44 years young, Hennig, who made his home in Champlin, Minn., was survived by his wife of 20 years and four children. A great athlete and father, Hennig was among the premier performers and entertainers in the business. Full of charisma, his passion for the business and for life was his calling card. He was also a free spirit who was very funny and considered by many to be the preeminent "ribber," or prankster, in the business — a quality that endeared him to many. Once even featured on Robin Leach's "Lifestyles of the Rich and Famous," television show, Curt was certainly both. Known for always giving the fans their money's worth for more than three decades, Curt Hennig was a true Minnesota wrestling legend.

CHARLIE NORRIS

Charlie Norris *(left)*

Charlie Norris grew up on the Red Lake Indian Reservation in Northern Minnesota. A tremendous athlete, Norris was actually spotted by legendary trainer Eddie Sharkey while attending a wrestling event at the American Indian Center in Minneapolis. So impressed with the young kid was Sharkey that he offered to train him for free. A big wrestling fan, he leaped at the opportunity to learn from one of the business' all-time greats. After a lot of intense training, Norris made his pro debut in 1989 and quickly gained notoriety with his "Tomahawk Chop" finishing move. Norris first started out in Sharkey's Professional Wrestling America and won the PWA Heavyweight Title in 1989 and again in 1991.

From there, Norris moved up to the big-time, World Championship Wrestling (WCW). Norris' first big match came on August 15, 1993, at the Omni in Atlanta, when he defeated Bobby Eaton. Later that same year he would go on to beat Big Sky at the Fall Brawl in Houston. He would also team up with Shockmaster and Ice Train to defeat Harlem Heat and The Equalizer in New Orleans as well. His first big defeat came a few months later when he and Stevie Ray were beaten by Cactus Jack and Vader at a Battle Bowl in Pensacola, FL. That next year Norris went through a lot of ups and downs, ultimately feeling betrayed by his employers. They allegedly wanted him to dress up as a "goofy Indian," and as a result, he filed a discrimination lawsuit against the WCW for racial stereotyping. He eventually settled the suit, but was forced to find work elsewhere. As a result, Norris would go on to wrestle around the world, from New Guinea to Japan, before settling back down to compete in the local independent circuits. He would later find success lining up lucrative shows at Indian-run casinos.

EDDIE SHARKEY

Eddie Sharkey

Eddie Sharkey is a Minnesota grappling legend. Period. And his story is as fascinating as he is. Born Eddie Shyman, Eddie Sharkey (he later changed his name when he became a pro wrestler) grew up in south Minneapolis during the late 1940s as a huge wrestling fan. Eddie's dad, Tom, was a first-generation Polish immigrant who made his living working in the liquor display business. Together, they used to go to the old Minneapolis Auditorium to watch pro wrestling. Before long Eddie was hooked. He was small though, so he got into weightlifting and eventually became the toughest kid on the block. So tough, in fact, that after too many street fights and getting into too much trouble, his parents shipped him off to a boys' reformatory school in Red Wing. There, amongst the other kids who he could relate to, Eddie felt right at home.

"That was my education," he would later recall. "I learned everything I needed to know there: hit hard, talk fast, and never forget what honor means. That was an experience I will never forget."

Eddie ultimately quit school at 15 and shortly thereafter decided to get out of town to see the world. So, he packed up and headed west to Hollywood, where he survived by doing odd jobs such as moving furniture, washing dishes, painting cars, selling watches on street corners and even working as a bouncer at a local strip club. He loved the sunny weather and he loved his freedom. He was also intrigued by Hollywood's underworld, where he met all sorts of fascinating people who were usually up to no good. In the Summers Eddie would come home to Minnesota to see his family and hang out with his buddies down on Hennepin Avenue — where he also got into his fair share of trouble. Eddie loved to scrap and he wasn't afraid of anybody.

"I think I knocked out more guys on Hennepin Avenue than anyone in the history of Hennepin Avenue," Sharkey joked. "Those were the days."

Finally, Eddie decided to channel his energy and put it to good use, at the Mill City Gym in Minneapolis. There, he took up boxing and worked as sparring partner with middleweight contender Del Flanagan. When the boxing climate soured in the Twin Cities, however, and the main promoter in the area, Tommy Anderson, passed away, Eddie decided to move on to other things. By now it was the late 50s and Eddie still had a lot of adventure left in him, so he got a job as a carnival wrestler in the traveling "Chief Little Wolf's Athletic Show." As a carnie wrestler, Eddie made up to $40 bucks on a good day — big dough for the times. There, he grappled anywhere from 10-15 times a day, working county fairs across the Midwest. Most of the time he worked as a "jobber," volunteering to come out of the crowd and, unbeknown to the locals, wind up losing to the his buddy, who was acting as the reigning champ. Other times, however, he would take on would-be challengers from the audience — which occasionally required some skill when he came across a legitimate amateur wrestler.

"Usually it was just some drunk guy who would come up there all cocky and after a few moves he'd wind up throwing up all over the place," joked Sharkey.

When he wasn't jobbing or taking on drunks, Eddie worked a novelty act wrestling a psycho baboon named "Congo the Ape."

"They had a huge picture of an ape up on the trailer, but it was a damn baboon," Sharkey exclaimed. "He was the ugliest little thing and he used to sit up on this perch like a bird. I would come at him and clothesline him right off of there and that would really piss him off. Chief Little Wolf would come over and yell at me not to hurt him. He would scream at me not to lay on him and smother him. That is all he cared about, not me, just his precious ape. That little thing was so damn fast, he would jump at me and scratch my face before I knew what hit me. I finally smartened up figured out how to beat him though. You see, I would just lie down beside him and let him play with my hair. He was happier than hell doing that and then I would just pin him. The crowd loved it. It was actually sort of boring, but you know what they say: There's a sucker born every minute. You know, my whole life has been about wrestling baboons, some were just tougher and harrier than others."

Eventually, Sharkey got tired of life on the road and looked to get into something different. He had made some friends in the professional wrestling business, and thought that might be a good fit. Among them was a guy by the name of Lenny Montana, who would later play mobster hit-man Luca Brasi in The Godfather. Montana let Sharkey in on a little secret, the outcomes were all pre-determined by the promoters. Eddie had his suspicious, but was never completely sure. That sort of thing was real hush-hush at the time and the wrestlers knew that if they talked about it in public that they would be fired, or maybe even worse than that.

"Lenny was really the one who talked me into getting the business, he had a lot of contacts and that sort of thing," said Eddie. "He told it to me like it really was."

Well, as luck would have it, Eddie got into a bar fight one night at Luigi's Café, a popular hang-out for pro grapplers in Minneapolis, where he knocked out two guys. Word quickly spread of this tough S.O.B. and shortly thereafter he was offered a fill-in spot on Verne Gagne's upstart pro wrestling circuit, the AWA. With that, Eddie made his pro debut in 1961 on a card in Fargo as a baby-face — a real stretch from his tough-guy persona. From there, Eddie traveled the country, wrestling throughout the AWA's network of affiliate territories.

In all, Eddie would wrestle professionally for the next 10 years or so. He never got a huge push to go big-time, but he was solid. He challenged Danny Hodge a few times for the World Junior Heavyweight title and later even won the NWA's U.S. Heavyweight title belt for a stint out of Missouri as well. In the ring Sharkey felt at home, he loved the drama and all of the action. Some of that action, however, spilled out into the crowds — where it was unpredictable and oftentimes downright dangerous.

"You know, the 60s were the toughest time in pro wrestling, no doubt about it," said Sharkey. "We didn't have any police protection back then like they do now. There were no barriers up either, so we had to form a "V" and fight our way through the crowd to get in and out of the ring. It was tough, fans would be all over you. Remember, they still thought it was all real back then, so if you were a villain, they hated you and some of them really wanted to hurt you. Guys would get stabbed, hell, sometimes we would come out of a match and a guys' car would be on fire. These people didn't mess around.

"So, we had a lot of big guys who were good amateur wrestlers with us back in those days, but a lot of them didn't know how to throw a punch. I mean you were not going to get some big drunk in a hammer lock out there and take him down, because the crowd would kill ya before you had the chance. I was an escort, a puncher, as we were known, for guys to get into and out of the ring. Sure, if I had to crack a few heads out there to get by, then that is what I did. The key was to just sucker-punch the biggest one and then keep walking, never running, because that would panic the crowd into a riot. There were no lawsuits back then either, so we could do whatever the hell we wanted to. Nowadays, Jeez, these idiots would own my house and car, it is an entirely different era altogether.

"Anyway, one time in Denver, after a match, we are walking back to the dressing room and a drunk fan attacks my partner, Harley Race. I look over and see that this guy has got him in a death grip around the waist. He wouldn't let go either. On top of that, there is a woman smacking him over the head with her high heel shoe. It was nuts. So I ran over and kicked the guy in the head as hard as I could. Well, he didn't let go, so I reached over to stick my finger in his eye, only it went right into an empty socket. Harley, who had just gotten his finger bitten off, had already pulled this poor S.O.B.'s eye out! We got the hell out of there fast. So, Harley is full of blood at this point and we have to go over to the hospital to have his finger put back on. Well, sure enough, there is the other guy, who came in to have his eye fixed up. They both got patched up and we all laughed about it later. Of course, we could never go back to Denver after that, but hey, that was wrestling in the 60's, it was a crazy time."

Eventually, Eddie settled down and married a female wrestler named Dixie Jordan, who also worked for the AWA, wrestling under the name Princess Littlecloud. Eddie was happy, but the grind of the business was taking its toll.

"You know, I always wanted to be a pro wrestler, ever since I was a kid," he said. "But to tell you the truth, it was actually quite disappointing when my dream finally came true. I had built it up so high in my own mind, that the reality of it all was a real let-down. I mean I thought I would be hanging around movie stars, getting free stuff and having women all over me, but it wasn't like that at all. Eventually, it just became a job, like anything else. Traveling was the worst. By car, with a few guys, it wasn't so bad. You could have a few beers and visit, it was OK. We would usually drive to places like Winnipeg, Milwaukee, Chicago and Omaha. Flying though, that was the worst. It was so boring, so monotonous and so lonely. The grind of it all was just so tough. I mean you wake up at five in the morning to catch a flight; you get into town; go straight to the arena; you wrestle; then you get out at like midnight; so you head over to your hotel and get to sleep at two in the morning; and then you get up at five in the morning the next day to do it all over again. It was brutal."

Being in the business during this era was hard for other reasons, such as always having to defend your honor wherever you went and also living a life that was full of lies and secrets.

"It was tough always protecting the business," said Sharkey. "I mean my mother and father went to their graves knowing that professional wrestling was real. Back in those days you didn't question it. We lived by a strict code of silence, we all did, or we would be shown the door. It was tough too, because a lot of people would think of you as a phony. So, we, the wrestlers, mostly hung around with each other and really didn't hang around too many other people. We did, however, hang around a lot with the old gangsters. They knew what was going on, but they didn't care. Nobody messed with those guys. We used to hang out at a places like the Chestnut Tree, on Nicollet Avenue, as well as Luigi's and the Venice Café, which were both downtown. We used to play cards and tell stories, it was something else, let me tell you. Some of these guys were loan sharks and hit-men, but it didn't matter, we loved hanging out with each other. Those were the people I grew up with, that is where I got my education. You know, I grew up on Hennepin Avenue, it was so exciting, I miss those days."

By now, the grind was taking its toll. Finally, after an alleged incident with the boss, Eddie changed his tune and decided to make a career change.

"One time I got pretty ticked at Verne (Gagne) about the way I felt he was treating my wife, who was also a wrestler," said Eddie. "So, I headed up to the sixth floor of the old Dyckman Hotel, where the AWA's offices were, and I wanted to make a statement. So, I pulled out my gun and blew the shit out of the place, something like 14 rounds I think. It was like a James Bond movie. You know, back in the 60's, almost every wrestler carried a gun. It was a totally different time. Verne wasn't there or anything, I just wanted to make a statement I suppose. I don't know if I would have actually shot him if he had been there — maybe just one bullet in the leg or something, nothing serious. Then, I walked out of there real cool, right through the lobby. Afterwards, there were no hard feelings, Verne and I made up and he even booked me after that on his cards. Verne was tough and a lot of guys had issues with him. Hey, I love Verne, but business was business and I have always said that you're not really in the wrestling business unless you've been screwed by Verne! The bottom line for me was that I was ready to get out at that point, I wasn't enjoying it like I used to."

Meanwhile, by the late 60s, Sharkey had been looking for another source of income, so he partnered up with Ron Peterson, a former wrestler turned boxing promoter. Together, they started several business ventures, including a massage parlor in downtown Minneapolis, and later the Seventh Street Gym, where they trained boxers and wrestlers. After he and Dixie had a son and a daughter, however, Eddie decided it was time to settle down. So, he sold his interest in the gym, began dabbling in antiques and military collectibles, and ultimately wound up quitting the wrestling business for what would amount to almost a decade.

Then, in 1982 Sharkey got sucked back into the squared circle through some rather unique circumstances. You see, by now he had been bartending at a tough northeast Minneapolis biker joint called Grandma B's. There, he became buddies with a few of the bouncers, local kids, former football players. Their names were Rick Rude, Barry Darsow, Joe Laurinaitis and Mike Hegstrand.

"It was a very tough bar, real tough," recalled Sharkey. "They had a crew of bouncers that was just unbelievable. These guys were so damn tough, hell, they had to be, they took on entire motorcycle gangs."

After hearing plenty of Sharkey's war stories, the four young men asked him if he would train them to become professional wrestlers. At first Eddie said no, but then he changed his mind. He figured he could make a few bucks as a trainer and also get back into the ring under his own terms. Sharkey was no stranger to recognizing and training new talent. Guys like Jesse Ventura and Bob Backlund first got into the business at his old gym.

Little did he know it at the time, but eventually these four behemoths would emerge as superstars, with the latter two, Laurinaitis and Hegstrand, becoming the hottest tag-team of the '80s — "The Road Warriors." By now wrestling had changed radically. Vince McMahon's WWF was all about huge, muscular athletes capable of doing risky, high-flying, off-the-ropes acrobatics. These guys were just what the doctor ordered and were going to cash in big-time. Eddie had stumbled onto a gold mine.

Eddie's foray into training would be the beginning of an amazing new career as one of the industries' best ever, and his clientele would read like a who's-who. Aside from the Road Warriors, "Ravishing" Rick Rude, Barry "Smash Demolition" Darsow, Jesse "The Body" Ventura and Bob Backlund, Sharkey also trained the likes of Charlie Norris, Lenny Lane, Terry "The Warlord," Szopinski, and the Steiner Brothers, to name just a few.

"It's been said that I have trained more main-event wrestlers than anyone in the world," said Sharkey, "but it was the guys that did all the work, it was never me. A couple of years ago, I tried to count 'em all, but I couldn't. I'm pretty sure I've had more world champions than anyone else. You know, I have been asked why I was such a good trainer and my initial response was that I cared. These people are not just my students, they are my friends. I loved hanging around these guys and telling war stories, going out for drinks, that was great stuff. Building camaraderie was all part of it. Then, when my guys got booked, I looked out for them and made sure they got treated right. Once we did business together, then we were like family. I am a very loyal person, that is important to me. They don't do that anymore, now it is just a business, and that is too bad. You know, back in the day we all worked. There were 25 or so territories to work in and we all made a living. None of us were getting rich, hell no, but we all had a home and a new car. Nowadays there is one show in town and that is really unfortunate."

In addition to supplying talent to promoters as far away as

Japan, Sharkey began putting on his own independent wrestling cards at bars and nightclubs throughout the area, such as Main Event in Fridley or Grumpy's in Coon Rapids, under the banner of Pro Wrestling America (PWA). According to Sharkey, the PWA stands as the longest-running indie wrestling promotion in the country. At his training camps, however, it was all business.

"The first thing we used to teach guys was how to fall so they could protect themselves," said Sharkey. "One wrong move and a guy could break his neck. So we would spend a lot of time just learning how to fall. Then, we worked them out, to harden up their bodies and toughen them up to take all the pounding. From there, we taught guys how to do interviews, how to develop their character persona and anything else they needed to know to survive in this business — even how to bleed. Yeah, some guys just loved to bleed. They would cut themselves up along their hair line, and when they started sweating, blood would come gushing out. The fans used to love that stuff."

Sharkey has trained his guys all over. For a while they were in the basement of the Calvary Baptist Church in south Minneapolis. More recently, however, they trained in the back yard of a 1940s-style St. Louis Park bungalow, the home of his partner, Terry Fox. When it got too cold, they just headed into the garage behind the house. There was no high-flying in there though, unless guys wanted to pull wooden splinters out of their foreheads after smashing into the low rafters. Despite the modest working environment, up to 30 guys at a time would shell out about $3,000 bucks to learn the ropes from the best in the biz. And, when you attend Eddie's training camps, you can participate in his shows for life. Some guys stay a few months, while others hang around for years. Some have a dream of hitting the big-time, which many have done, while others just want to escape from reality for a while and live out their childhood fantasies of becoming a superhero or villain. Both are treated the same.

Being a promoter was a tough job. In addition to getting everything lined up, he also had to collect the money and take care of his guys. One time Eddie got into it with a fellow promoter in Eau Claire, and it cost him big-time.

"I am very loyal to my guys and this promoter shorted us a hundred bucks, so I punched him," said Sharkey. "Then, just to be cute, I broke a beer bottle over his head, which was a big mistake. If I had just behaved myself, I would have gotten a simple assault charge, but instead I got a felony. Well, at the trial I tried to show the judge that that particular brand of beer bottle wasn't very thick and couldn't possibly cause very much damage. So, I took one out of my bag and smashed it over my own head right there in court. Well, he wasn't impressed, so I got six months at the Hennepin County Workhouse. I was still able to go to work everyday, but I had to sleep in jail. I even had to pay like $37 bucks a day just to stay there on top of everything else, that was tough. I learned my lesson after that one."

Later, Eddie got into refereeing, even working for Vince McMahon's WWF for a while.

"To be a referee was very, very hard work," said Eddie, "especially doing a television taping. Sometimes I would do up to 25 matches in a day, and that was tough. A good referee is really never seen too much on television, you're just supposed to stay out of the way. I mean when was the last time you heard somebody say, 'Jeez, there's a good referee tonight, let's go to the matches.' The toughest matches were with those damn midgets, because you had to chase them all around the ring, and sometimes you even got bit. It was all fun though, and miss it."

Eddie still misses the fellas, the good ol' days, and remembers them fondly.

"There were so many characters back in the day," he recalled. "They were all half-nuts, or they wouldn't be in this business. We've been accused of a lot of things, but never of being dull people. Say what you want, but we had so much fun in those days, we were laughing all the time. You know, I used to own a house here in south Minneapolis and Harley Race lived with me. Harley was so tough, our fights were classics. It was never a question of if we'd win or lose, it was how quickly we could knock the other guys out! Anyway, there was this wrestler, Jose "Bad Man" Quintero, he was crazier than a shithouse rat. Well, he came to town one time and had no place to stay, so I rented him Harley's closet — at half price, or course. Well, one time, I will never forget, Harley came home from a long road trip and he went to hang up his coat in his closet, and when he opened up the door he nearly died of a heart attack when he saw this weird looking dude with beady little eyes sitting in there! Those were the days."

Presently, Eddie resides in the Twin Cities, where he continues to train young wannabes and promotes his shows, one Wednesday a month, at such locales as First Avenue in downtown Minneapolis. Last year he even made six trips to the Philippines and another to Chile to train wrestlers, and hopefully lay down the necessary ground work in order to start his own promotion there one day.

"Hey, you gotta go where the action is, and hopefully you can make a buck," he said. "I think I will try Costa Rica next, they really love wrestling down there."

Eddie Sharkey has just about done it all in professional wrestling: grappling, training, refereeing and promoting. He is one of the people who has really made a difference in this business and is truly a living legend. He is also a grandpa now, and has had two hip replacements — a couple of things which have slowed him down just a little bit. He still keeps it all in perspective though, and would do it all again in a New York minute.

"What can I say? It has been a great ride so far," said Eddie. "Really, my life has been a big party. I am so lucky to have been doing this for so long, 40 wonderful years. It has been rewarding to have been in the business for as long as I have and to have been able to help as many people as I have. Being around all of those great people has been a real privilege. You know, if there was ever an award for being the biggest screw-up and for having the most fun in the business, then that would have to go to me. I have built a lifetime of great memories, and nobody can ever take that away. That is a real treasure."

ERIC BISCHOFF

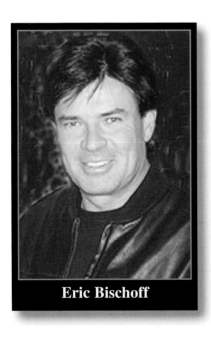

Eric Bischoff

Originally from Detroit, Eric Bischoff went on to attended the University of Minnesota, graduating with a degree in Business Administration and a minor in Radio, Television and Film. An eighth-degree black-belt martial artist, Bischoff began his career as an announcer for Verne Gagne's American Wrestling Association and eventually moved on to the WCW to work in the same capacity. He later got into management and emerged as Ted Turner's top executive. By 1995, Bischoff was luring some of the top stars of WWE to WCW and coming up with some pretty outlandish storylines to boot. As a vice president, he spawned the idea for the revolutionary New World Order (nWo) and also played a big part in WCW's Monday Nitro prime time television show, which consistently beat rival WWE's Monday Night RAW in the ratings wars.

Eventually, when Turner sold his promotion to McMahon in 2002, Bischoff came along for the ride. There, as the companies' "general manager," he continues to watch pro wrestling's television numbers as well as attendances soar. Driven by success, "Uncle Eric" oftentimes pushes the envelope with risqué storylines, but nonetheless makes for some entertaining television. A controversial character both in front of as well as behind the camera, Eric Bischoff is a real pioneer in the evolution and success of mainstream pro wrestling.

GOLDY LOCKS

Goldy Locks

Moon Shadow Goldryn (aka "Goldy Locks") grew up in a tough neighborhood in North Minneapolis. (She was named after a Cat Stevens song by her Harley-riding, music-loving hippie parents.) An interviewer/reporter for the NWA/TNA professional wrestling promotion, she is also a famous singer/songwriter solo recording artist who plays three instruments, designs her own line of clothing and sings in five different languages. Oh yeah, she occasionally mixes it up inside the ropes as well, just to keep it real!

GORDON SOLIE

Gordon Solie

Long considered "the grandfather of wrestling announcers," Gordon Solie was born Francis Jonard Labiak on January 26, 1929, in Minneapolis. When his step father adopted him as a child, however, his name was changed to Jonard Pierre Sjoblom. (Later, when he embarked on his announcing career he changed his name to Gordon Solie. Gordon was his grandmother's maiden name and Solie was his mother's maiden name.) After serving in the Air Force and working as a broadcaster with Armed Forces Radio, Solie moved to Florida in 1950. There, he worked as a disc jockey, reporter, and talk show host for a small Tampa radio station, while also announcing stock car races in the area as well. A few years later he was hired by Cowboy Luttrell as a ring announcer for $5 bucks a night. He later expanded into advertising and publicity and then got his big break in 1960 when he was hired to announce a weekly wrestling TV show in Tampa, which was syndicated throughout Florida. At first, Solie didn't know a whole lot about wrestling, but with the help of the wrestlers, he learned fast. He would oftentimes even have them put him into the various holds so he would know what every move was supposed to feel like. It was a job he took very seriously and, while other announcers sometimes treated pro wrestling as a comedy act, his deadpan announcing style and graphic commentary gave the growing form of entertainment a lot of credibility.

Solie was later hired by Ted Turner to became the voice of World Championship Wrestling from Georgia on cable Superstation WTBS during the '70s and '80s. He later went on to announce for Continental Championship Wrestling and even hosted the show "Pro Wrestling This Week," which summarized matches from the various NWA territories. (He also hosted the syndicated show, "Ring Warriors," and did play-by-play on New Japan Pro Wrestling videotapes as well.) He returned to the WCW in 1989 and stayed with the company until he retired in 1995. A few years later he was diagnosed with cancer and sadly, died, on June 28, 2000, at the age of 71.

With lines like "human chess at its finest," and "crimson mask" (for when a wrestler was bleeding heavily from his face), he became synonymous with the sport and was a real fan-favorite. Having announced an estimated 25,000 televised matches, Solie, a member of the World Championship Wrestling Hall of Fame, was the voice of classic old-school wrestling. Deeply admired and respected by those both within and outside the pro wrestling business, Gordon Solie was a true original who left a lasting legacy.

GREG GAGNE

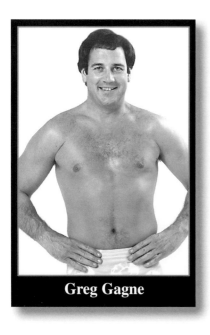

Greg Gagne

Greg Gagne grew up amidst wrestling royalty as the son of legendary grappler, Verne Gagne. Greg was born and raised in the western suburbs and went on to star as a prep athlete at Mound High School. He played football, basketball and baseball for the Mohawks, but incredibly, did not compete on the wrestling team.

"I went out for the wrestling team my junior year," said Greg, "and at 165 pounds, I pinned every single kid on the team, including the heavyweight. But the coach, for whatever reason, wanted me to cut a bunch of weight to wrestle at a much lower weight class. Well, I knew that I had a good shot of playing college football that next year and needed to keep my weight up, so I just decided to stick to basketball in the winter instead. It was too bad because I really liked it."

From there, Greg went on to play quarterback at the University of Minnesota. But, after spending a year and a half with the Gophers, the coaches decided that they wanted to turn him into a cornerback. So, he decided to transfer and accept a scholarship to the University of Wyoming. After college, Greg had a few NFL try-outs, but eventually decided to hang up the cleats in favor of the tights, and make a run at becoming a professional wrestler in his dad's legendary American Wrestling Association.

"I remember telling him that I wanted to become a wrestler," said Greg, "but instead of him saying 'great...', he said, 'what makes you think you can wrestle?', and I knew I was in for a battle right then and there. I loved to wrestle, even as a kid, I mean I grew up with it. He and I used to always wrestle when I was little too. My poor mother, it used to drive her crazy. We would go down to the basement, push all the furniture aside, and then go at it. He would hold me down, and I would get mad and frustrated, and eventually mom would have to come break it up. Sometimes we got into some heated battles, and he didn't ever let me off easy. He was old school, and so competitive, and he just wanted to make sure that I was tough."

With that, Greg came home in 1972 and started training at his father's wrestling camp, which was located on a farm by Lake Riley (next to Prince's house ironically enough), just outside Chanhassen. There, Greg and a couple of his buddies from the Gopher football team, Ric Flair and Jim Brunzell, along with former pro football player, Bob Bruggers, as well as Ken Patera and Kosrow ("The Iron Sheik") Vaziri — who had both just competed in the 1972 Olympics, in weight lifting and wrestling (for his native Iran), respectively, learned the ropes.

"We trained out in that barn for six hours a day, six days a week," said Greg. "It was so brutal, probably the hardest thing I have ever done. My dad showed me no mercy out there, I assure you. He worked us so hard, running, taking bumps, and just training like I had never trained before. He and Billy Robinson, one of his toughest wrestlers of all time, just whipped us into shape. I mean our routine started out with 1,000 free squats, then an hour of calisthenics, followed by an hour in the ring doing nothing but learning how to fall flat on the matt so that your whole body could absorb the shock. Now we were half-way through. So, from there we did an hour of holds and counter-holds, followed by another hour of one-on-one's with guys doing moves, and finally we would spend the last hour running up and down these nearby sandy bluffs. I remember Patera came in weighing 340 and left at 280, and Flair came in at about 300 and left at 250. For me though, I came in at 185 and came out at 210. All the lifting we did really bulked me up.

"Then, in the wintertime, it was so cold in that old barn that by the time you got out of the ring to take a breather, your sweat would freeze. Five minutes later, when you got body-slammed on that hard matt, you felt like a cartoon character who just got his entire body crumpled. We were in just constant pain, with matt burns and bruises everywhere. I don't think any of us had any skin on our knees, elbows or shoulders, it was just rubbed off. Eventually, after a couple months of this though, the bruises went away and your body just kind of toughened up to the punishment. It was amazing to see how much pain your body could actually take when they got done with us. So, after all of that, a six hour day of hell, we all drove back to a duplex that we lived in and lifted weights. It was insane.

"Meanwhile, we had to make some money, so my dad put us to work driving the 'ring-trucks' setting up and taking down the rings in the small towns all over. We also all got into refereeing matches too, which helped us better understand the business from a different perspective. The whole time this was going on, my dad used to always tell me that he didn't think I would make it. He would tell me I wasn't big enough, strong enough, fast enough and tough enough. That drove me, and he knew that. You know, I was fortunate in that I had worked out with Billy Robinson for about six months prior to coming into my dad's training camp, so I was in pretty good wrestling shape at the time. The other guys, though, they struggled to catch up and take it all in. We all eventually made it though, and all went on to have successful careers in the business."

From there, Greg jumped in and started learning the ropes. He first made a big splash in the ring alongside his old Gopher Football buddy, Jim Brunzell, whom he teamed up with to form one of pro wrestling's most famous babyface duos, the "High Flyers."

"I will never forget my first big tag-team match," said Greg. "It was in Denver, with Jim (Brunzell), and we were thrown in against Larry Heinimi and Buddy Wolff. For some reason, Jim and I were really big in Colorado, the fans loved us there. Anyway, we beat these guys on the first try and it shocked most of the promoters. They didn't think it was going to happen because they were the No. 1 contenders and we were just kids. Well, afterwards, Larry was really upset and we got into it in the locker room. So, that kind of set the stage for us after that. You know, our style was a little bit different and that is one of the reasons why we were so successful. We had a lot of chemistry together and we were very athletic and quick, but not necessarily really big guys — which was unique. Because we were in such phenomenal shape from our training camp days, our philosophy was to attack at a fast pace and tag each other in very quickly. We tried to continue those work-outs well after that as well, and that helped us a great deal — especially in that high altitude out in Denver."

The High Flyers started out on undercards but eventually earned main event status. Finally, on July 7th, 1977, in Winnipeg, they beat Blackjack Lanza and Bobby Duncum to capture the AWA Tag Team title. They would hold the belts for more than a year, facing off against nearly every heel team of the era. They were a new breed of wrestler, smaller, quicker and much more acrobatic than the typical big fat guys such as the Crusher and Jerry Blackwell. The fans loved it.

Jim later left the promotion and headed down to North Carolina for what would amount to two years. He returned in 1981, however, and he and Greg were reunited as tag-team partners once again. They won the belts in July of 1977 in Winnipeg from Lanza and Dumcum, and lost that title reign in September of 1978. The belts were subsequently awarded to Patterson and Stevens as the result of an injury Brunzell suffered in a charity softball game. Their second title run came in June of 1981, in Green Bay, when they defeated the East-West Connection. They then lost them in June of 1983 in Minneapolis to the Sheiks, Jerry Blackwell and Ken Patera. Eventually, in 1985, Jim left the promotion yet again, this time to compete in the WWF. By now Greg was one of pro wrestling's biggest stars. He was also a seasoned veteran and began to take a larger role in the business side of the family business. It wasn't always easy though.

"It was tough sometimes, no question," said Greg of working with his father. "There were a lot of high expectations and pressure on me all the time. When I first started I caught a lot of heat for being Verne's son. People would say 'Jeez, who is that skinny kid?'. I don't think anybody for the first five years of my career knew my name, I was just 'Verne's kid..'. So, I had to work a lot harder to convince people that I was my own man and that I deserved to be where I was. I tried to blend my father's style along with Red Bastien's and Billy Robinson's, two mentors of mine, to make my own style and it worked out for me.

"As for getting into the business side of things at that point, that was something I always wanted to do. I grew up with it and had a great understanding for what needed to be done in order to be successful with regards to scheduling and television production. Eventually it all worked out like clockwork and you could really project things well, which was key for the TV side of it all. I mean, we knew every year in the Fall that we would have Andre the Giant in town for a month to do battle royals. Then, he would take on the world champion, which would take you into Christmas. From there you did events in the winter, followed by your steel cage matches in May. Things slowed down in the Midwest during the Summer because of the weather, and then you had back to school, which was something different. So, we knew our market and we had a good plan on how to sell our product. The TV was the key. Our highest numbers for "All Star Wrestling" were something like a 27 share rating, which was about a 60% or so share of the entire audience locally. It was huge, we even outdrew the show 60 Minutes. And it wasn't just here in the Twin Cities either, the show also ran in Denver, Milwaukee, Chicago and Winnipeg, getting the same types of numbers in great time slots there as well."

Anyway, with Jumpin' Jim off to New York, Greg wound up doing more singles matches. Later, Sgt. Slaughter was brought in with the angle that he was going to toughen Greg up by taking him under his wing and put him through boot camp. The two then came out in camouflaged fatigues and went on to beat the team of Nick Bockwinkel and Ray Stevens, and later Larry Zbyszko. When the G.I. Joe gimmick got old, Greg teamed with Curt Hennig and Scott Hall to battle Bockwinkel, Stevens and Zbyszko in a series of six man tag team matches culminating at the AWA's television spectacle, "SuperClash." Among his other tag-team partners after that would be Jimmy Snuka, whom he got together with to defeat Nord the Barbarian and Bruiser Brody in a Steel Cage match at WrestleRock 1986.

In 1987 the AWA created the AWA International TV Championship belt, a new title, separate from the AWA Heavyweight Championship strap. And, as expected, Greg, with his vaunted "Gagne Sleeper" finishing hold, became the inaugural TV champ when he beat Adrian Adonis on December 27th, 1987, in Las Vegas. He later teamed up with Paul Diamond to reclaim the tag-team straps in the Fall of 1989. From there, however, Greg's long list of injuries finally caught up with him. So, he decided to hang em' up for good, but not before creating a "career ending injury angle," in which the 500-pound Samoan giant Kokina attacked him while he was doing a ringside interview. It was the end of an era for one of the sport's true good guys who literally grew up in the business.

"It got to be a grind," said Greg. "I was pretty tough, but certain injuries can be just devastating. I mean I broke a bunch of ribs, I broke my nose five times and even had my teeth knocked out, but when I got my first knee injury, I was never the same after that. I did it in a match against King Kong Brody over in Japan and wound up wrestling another two weeks on it before I had it fixed. It was brutal, when the doctor cut my knee open for surgery, the cartilage fell out in three pieces. That took eight months to heal, but it never was the same after that. I eventually had to have surgery on the other one as well, and then later on the ligaments in my ankle too. So, your body took a lot of pounding and you just had to deal with it the best that you could. We took some time off during the summers, but we still wrestled about 200 dates a year. That was pretty good, considering some promotions down south did upwards of 300-350, which was just insane.

"The worst came after Jerry Blackwell power-slammed me onto the studio floor at Channel 11. I mean, 450 pounds coming down on top of you on a concrete floor, it was all over. My back was done. Stupidly, I kept wrestling after that, but it was tough. Later, after the AWA disbanded, I had an offer to come down and wrestle with the Turner group, down in Atlanta. So, I started training again, but my back was in bad shape. The doctor told me that I had some herniated disks, and if I fell wrong I could wind up in a wheelchair. So, I called it a career right then and there. That was really hard to swallow because I think with my experience and name recognition I would have been in line for the really big money. I remember Gene Okerlund telling me that I could go out and work for McMahon in the WWF as well, but there was no way I would have ever gone to work with that guy, no way."

Greg then got into the booking and promoting side of the business. He was also in charge of the entire television production schedule as well, coordinating all the interview segments and planning a lot of the storylines for the shows. He later worked very closely with ESPN, when they partnered with them as well.

"Later in my career I started getting into the other side of the business, and that was very rewarding too. I enjoyed working on the television side as well as the promoting side. I discovered Shawn Micheals and Marty Janeatty, and hooked them together. I also got Hulk Hogan to come here too, when he was working out in New York at the time. I remember, it was back in the early 80s and we had both just wrestled in Shea Stadium. Afterwards, I saw him in the hotel lobby and we sat down to talk. Pretty soon he starts crying. So, I say 'what's the matter big man?', and he says, 'I am not going to make it in wrestling…'. 'Well, you know, I watched your match tonight,' I said, 'I think you have a lot of charisma, but you need to learn how to wrestle. Why don't you come to the AWA and we will train you?' So, he called my dad up and talked to him. I remember telling my dad that I thought this guy could be a super-star, but he needed a lot of work and was really raw. We eventually brought him in and I started working with him on the fundamentals, while my dad worked with him on his interviews.

"From there, my dad put him into a six-man tag-team along with Jim (Brunzell) and I. He was just a natural, a great athlete. But, at that time, the good veterans, like Nick Bockwinkel, Ray Stevenson or Jerry Blackwell, could really expose him. So, we kind of eased him into it. When Jim or I got control of a match, we would tag him in and have him do a couple of his things, and then when the other guy started to get back onto his feet, we would tag back in. He was a pretty quick learner, he wanted to become a much better wrestler and he had a good feel for it. Plus, he had so much charisma, that you just knew he was going to be big."

By 1991 Vince McMahon and the WWF had driven most of the smaller territories out of business, either by raiding talent, or by eating up their television time slots. Sadly, the AWA, which had hung in there like a champ right up until the end, finally had to close its doors that same year. For the Gagnes, who were pioneers of the business and did so much to put Minnesota on the professional wrestling map, it was devastating.

"You have to realize that back in the early 80s, wrestling was red-hot in all the regions throughout the nation," said Greg. "It was a network of territories built up by all these local promoters like my dad. Well, Vince McMahon was a smart guy, and he had the advantage of being out in New York, the media capital. He got connected with some investors out there and he got a lot of money behind him, that was the first thing. Then, he just set out to start acquiring other promotions, and we were one of them. I remember when my dad and I sat down and met with him to discuss it. We talked about the direction wrestling was going, we talked about the possibility of national advertising, national syndication, and we talked about the future of doing pay-per-views, which is something that was relatively new but we had already done here. Well, we didn't want to sell. But essentially what he did though, was to go around, meet with the local promoters, get their best ideas, and then implement them nationally for himself. It was unbelievable. I will never forget, after our second meeting with him, we were going to get all of the figures together to possibly work together. Well, we drove him to the airport after our meeting and as he was walking down the terminal he turned around and looked at us and said 'I don't negotiate!' That was the last time we heard from him.

"So, after that, McMahon went out and got a lot of our top talent by paying them more money, a lot more money. He even paid some guys not to show up for matches which had been booked. As a promoter, this just killed you, to promote a match and then have it cancelled at the last minute. It really hurt your credibility. And he was doing this around the country, region by region. He just eventually put everybody out of business that way. It was so frustrating, to develop young talent and then have them leave in a heartbeat for more money. After a while, it wasn't about loyalty, it was just about money. Guys wouldn't even show up for stuff. I mean Jesse Ventura didn't even show up for his last match in Winnipeg. To have sold-out arenas that you advertised and promoted, and then have main-event guys not show up for their match was absolutely devastating.

You know, we were naïve too, we never had contracts with guys, it was all based on trust with verbal agreements and handshakes. Back then a man's word was all that was necessary. That honor code was never broken until Hulk Hogan left us to go back to McMahon. That changed everything in the pro wrestling business. Once he did it, it was all over because from there everybody started doing it.

"From there, he just tried to buy up all the local TV time slots, ours included. We had to battle all of our affiliates, which ran our tapes, to keep them on board. It was really tough. I mean you work so hard for so long to build up ratings in these local markets, and then someone comes in and takes it all away. We would even send out tapes to be run on a certain week, and some stations wound up showing McMahon's stuff instead. It was incredible. Pretty soon he looked more like the AWA than we did. We counted one time, my dad and I, and we figured he took something like 38 employees from us over the years. He even stole our announcers! I remember one time we did a show in Denver and he came in and did a show of his own the night before in the same building. He would come in with a whole bunch of former AWA guys, and the fans got so confused as to what they were going to see, it was crazy. Vince McMahon had a plan, and he was determined. The guy was bright, no question about it, but I also think he was pretty shady too. He hurt a lot of people financially, who had put their whole lives into the business, and he devastated a lot of families. That is what bothers me most about him.

"Well, as this is going on, we knew that as long as we were still on ESPN, we could still break even. But, we knew that if that fell apart, then we would be done. So, we went to the Tribune Company, which had WGN-TV in Chicago, as well as a host of other affiliates around the country. Basically, we tried to work out a deal with them to become partners and keep it all going. We even spoke to Hogan, to try and get him back with a huge contract, along with some other big name guys. We worked on the deal for a long time, spent a ton of money trying to make it all go down, and later even brought in Viacom, which owned HBO, as well. It was going to be a big deal, real big. OK, we are all set, so we fly to New York to sign the paperwork, and then we get word that the workers at the Tribune's newspaper had gone on strike. They are beside themselves, they are going to lose a bunch of money, and in the end, they don't sign the contract. We were devastated. It was the final nail in the coffin for us, we finally had to throw in the towel."

Greg later went to work for the Turner Group down in Atlanta for two years, doing television production and coordinating pay-per-view events. They, like everybody else still in the business were struggling to compete with McMahon, and Greg was brought in to turn it all around.

"I went in there and got them on their way with regards to getting a prime-time program with much better ratings and time slots, ," he said. "I also got them to change their production setting — which was really schlocky at the time. So, I got down there and laid out all their pay-per-views for the next two years, something they could never have dreamed of prior to that. Then, we built the television schedules around that. I mean we were producing about eight or nine weekly shows, from the U.S. to Canada to Germany to France, as well as the pay-per-view stuff. It was a lot of work and we were hitting it hard in order to compete with McMahon. You know, I even brought Eric Bischoff with me to work down there. Well, he eventually got hired as the executive producer, which was mind-boggling to me. He wound up screwing me big-time with my contract, and eventually cut me loose. Look where he is at now, running McMahon's whole deal. Amazing. It was frustrating, so I eventually got out of the business."

"You know, after that, I wanted to parlay my experience in the television industry back into the mainstream, but it was so difficult to get people to believe in me. They just had that image of pro wrestling, and wrestlers, and I couldn't catch a break. I mean I could have brought a lot to the table for a lot of different people, but it never happened. That was unfortunate."

Greg will always be remembered as one of the all-time good guys, and is appreciative of the fans who supported him.

"I was very fortunate to have made my career doing something I loved, it was a lot of fun," said Greg. "The fans here were wonderful and I can't say enough about how much I appreciated their support. While I do miss some parts of the business, I don't miss being on the road anymore. I enjoy spending time with my family, that is what it is all about. You know, my dad instilled a very hard work ethic in me and I have tried to pass that on to my children."

Presently, Greg works in the automotive industry and also finds time to coach his kids' baseball and football teams. He and his wife Mary currently reside in the Twin Cities and have three children. Their oldest son recently graduated from Notre Dame, where he played baseball on an academic scholarship, and later signed a professional contract with the Colorado Rockies. Their daughter, meanwhile, is a senior at Northern Colorado University, where she is a star on the women's basketball team. Their third son is a freshman at Cretin and loves all sports. Incidentally, Mary's dad, Bob Graiziger, a 10-time letter-winner at the U of M, played football for the Gophers alongside Greg's dad, Verne, back in 1943. Wow! With thoroughbred athletic lineage like that, I am sure we will be hearing plenty more in the future from the Gagne kids.

JERRY LYNN

Jerry Lynn

Minneapolis native Jerry Lynn has been a mainstay in the professional wrestling business for more than 15 years. A gifted athlete, Lynn participated in gymnastics, basketball, soccer, and track prior to wrestling. Lynn first got into the biz back in 1988, after learning the ropes from former grappler turned trainer, Brad Rheingans. Lynn has wrestled all over the world and got his first taste of the big-time in 1995. Following an unsuccessful try out with the WWF, he moved over to World Championship Wrestling as the masked "Mr. J.L." There, Lynn battled Sabu at the 1995 Halloween Havoc on a WCW pay-per-view event. Despite performing well in the WCW, however, the promotion never gave him a push. So, he made his own agenda and has carved out a nice niche for himself wrestling on his own terms, when he wants and where he wants. He has been with several different promotions throughout the years, criss-crossing America, Japan, Europe and Australia.

He still occasionally gets a taste of the big-time — as was the case in 2001, when he defeated Essa Rios in his WWF ring debut in Baltimore. With his signature "Cradle Piledriver" finishing move, Lynn made his television debut that same year on an episode of "Sunday Night Heat" in Chicago, where he pinned Crash Holly for the WWF Light Heavyweight title. He moved on from there and will always be linked to his classic series of matches in the ECW against Rob Van Dam for the Television Title. The "New F'n Show" as he was known, was a big hit with the fans. From the WWF to the WCW to the TNA to the ECW to the independent circuit, Lynn is a well-traveled veteran who has made a career inside the ropes. His list of injuries tells the story of his lengthy career: he has broken both feet, both ankles, both hands, his right arm, his pelvis, and his nose, not to mention a torn abdominal and patella tendon, as well as a shoulder separation. A die-hard death metal fan, Lynn has a solid work ethic and an never-say-die attitude. The guy is a survivor more than anything else, and that is why he has hung around so long.

JIM BRUNZELL

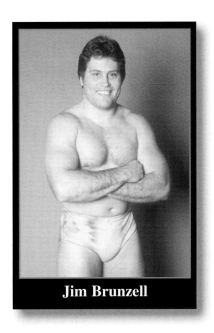

Jim Brunzell

Jim Brunzell grew up in White Bear Lake and went on to graduate from White Bear Lake High School in 1967. There, he starred as a wide receiver and kicker on the gridiron, played forward on the hard court, and even set the state high jump record on the track as well. He later went on to run track and play football at the University of Minnesota under Coach Murray Warmath from 1967-70. While there, he met a reserve quarterback by the name of Greg Gagne and the two quickly became buddies. While Greg eventually transferred to Wyoming, the two later hooked up after college. Jim, meanwhile, had gone on to play a year of semi-pro football and even had a try-out with the Washington Redskins in 1972. He didn't make it though, so he returned to the U of M to finish his degree. At that point he got a call from Greg, asking him if he wanted to give pro wrestling a shot.

He agreed, and with that, he headed over to Chanhassen, to begin training at Greg's father Verne Gagne's training camp. Joining he and Greg at the camp were a bevy of future stars, including: Ric Flair, Bob Bruggers, Ken Patera and Kosrow Vaziri, who became the Iron Sheik. Jim got pounded day in and day out at the camp, but made it out unscathed. His AWA pro wrestling debut came on December 28, 1972 in Moorhead against former Moorhead State star, Dennis Stamp, who beat him like a drum.

From there, Verne sent "Jumping" Jim down to Kansas City to get some seasoning. He spent a year in KC, wrestling up to three times a day, and wound up winning a pair of NWA World Tag-Team titles alongside Mike George. After a trip to Japan, he returned home to Minnesota, where Verne paired he and Greg up as the "High Flyers." It would be the beginning of one of the greatest babyface tag-team duos in AWA history. The two got a big push right out of the gates and instantly became big-time fan favorites. In July of 1977 they captured the AWA World Tag-Team Championship belts, and held them for more than a year.

The two faced off against nearly every heel tag-team of the era, and became a force to be reckoned with. They were a new breed of wrestler, smaller, quicker and much more acrobatic than the typical big fat guys. Finally, in 1979, Jim wanted to see what else was out there, so he headed down to North Carolina, where he won a pair of NWA Mid-Atlantic Heavyweight titles as a solo wrestler. He stayed a year and, following a brief stint in Atlanta, where he won a TV title, he came home. Jim had two young children at this point, and was eager to get back to Minnesota and the good ol' AWA.

In 1981 Jim teamed up with Nick Bockwinkel on a Japanese tour and when he returned, he and Greg reunited. Their second title run came in June of 1981, in Green Bay, when they defeated the East-West Connection. They then lost them in June of 1983 in Minneapolis to the Sheiks, Jerry Blackwell and Ken Patera. By now Hulk Hogan was in the mix and the AWA was hopping. He and many others would later leave to join Vince McMahon's WWF, however, and in the fall-out, Jim wound up leaving too. With that, he wound up in New York, where he wrestled off and on in the WWF from in 1985-93. During that time he also hooked up with Brian Blair to form the tag-team duo known as the "Killer Bees."

"Eventually, the grind of being in that world was just too much," said Jim. "I mean we worked out there. McMahon just wore people out, it was tough. I think I averaged working 27 days a month and that was just really hard on your body. You know, 5,000 matches over the years takes its toll. The injuries will catch up with you sooner or later, and that is when it gets rough. You definitely trade the fame and fortune for being treated like a piece of meat, no question. We all lived by the cliché of 'you are only as good as your last match,' because it could all go away in a hurray."

In 1993 Jim moved on to compete in WCW, followed by a stint in the WFWA, where he won the Canadian Heavyweight Championship. From there, he hit the independent circuit, emerging as the UWF Tag-Team Champion with Brian Blair in 1994. He would travel around doing the indie circuit from there on out until finally ending his career on August 13, 1999 — the day of his 50th birthday.

"I had always hoped to make it until I was 50, and after that match I said that was it, I was done," said Jim. "I had been working in the real world since 1994, but I supplemented my income by wrestling over the next six or seven years. It was fun, and neat to still be doing something athletic, which is what I really craved. It was a tough transition though. You know, one of the hardest things to deal with is making a career change after spending 25 years in one line of work. And let me tell ya, there ain't no pension in pro wrestling. We were all 'independent contractors' with no insurance, no workmen's comp, nothing, and it was up to us to invest wisely. Some did, and others, as you can see, are still trying to make ends meet by getting into the ring well into their sixties. That is too bad. There was just a lot of politics and ass-kissing in this business, and in the end, you had to know how to play their game in order to get ahead.

"Plus, you have to realize that while working as a pro wrestler had a lot of perks, it didn't really prepare you for anything after you retired. So, once you are off TV for a while, all of the fame and notoriety goes away pretty quickly. It creates a real dilemma for a lot of guys, myself included, to be fairly young and to have no resume. I mean most companies don't want to hire a 45 year old, they want a 22 year old who they don't have to pay very much. It was a tough transition, no question."

Today, Jim has a much different perspective on the business he left only six years ago.

"You know, when I got into the business it was much different than it is today," he said. "Back then, sure, we all knew it was fixed, but the best guys could choreograph it to look so real, which made it sort of like an art form if you will. What Vince McMahon has done today is totally different. Sure, there are a lot of very gifted athletes in the business now, and they do a ton of incredibly amazing and oftentimes outlandish moves — but they don't mean anything. I mean the moves appear to be so devastating, but they have no affect. Guys don't know how to register, they don't know how to sell, it is terrible. They have become a product of what Vince McMahon wants to do. He didn't necessarily want good athletes, he wanted good athletes who were characters, which he could sell. It's like Bobby Heenan used to say of it all, 'Vince McMahon has created a comic strip with real people.'

"He uses guys until they are not profitable anymore and then he chews them up and spits them out. Wait and see what happens to Brock Lesnar if he doesn't make it in pro football. Do you think Vince will want him back after he 'failed' to make it? It is crazy, all of these people's careers lie with one guy, who determines who rises and who falls. Vince creates the character and then Vince destroys the character. That is what he does. It is incredible.

"In our day, we told a story, sold moves and made it interesting. Now, it is all about hot women and foul language, which is really unfortunate. Plus, Vince's deal was all about action, he didn't want guys sitting in holds, he wanted them in and out of moves, fast, so they could get the next match on. That style was so different than that of the AWA, where you sold holds and 'built a match' with storylines. I never got along with that guy from day one. He single-handedly caused the collapse of 20-some territorial promoters and he now owns the entire business. He raided all of their top talent, including Hulk Hogan from here. I mean Hulk loved it here, he lived in Bloomington and loved working only 12 days a month. He was making good money, but couldn't turn down the offer he got from Vince. I am not saying that Verne (Gagne) wasn't entirely not at fault either. He was no saint, let me tell ya, I mean he was a very controlling, dictatorial kind of a promoter. He was a hell of a nice guy too, but business was business.

"Another by-product of McMahon's elaborate television production, was the fact that because it was so much better than anybody else's, it automatically made the fans at home watching believe that everything else was the minor leagues. McMahon even had Dick Ebersol, the president of NBC Sports, working with him and they would spend like hundreds of thousands of dollars putting together a single show. Well, everybody else was spending just a few bucks to have a guy interview somebody next to a wall. That is what the fans were used to, it was cheap, but it worked. Well, once Vince started with the glitz and the glam, it was all over for everybody else. Nobody could match that. Plus, when he went nationally, now you had fans seeing two competing shows, something that was totally new and different. So, when they compared them side by side, they could figure out pretty quickly which was the most entertaining show to watch. And, they figured that anybody who was anybody was going to be in the WWF, which is where all the big money was. That was just devastating to the other wrestlers. Eventually it became a situation of 'If you can't beat em', join em…'. So, the whole thing is pretty incredible when you stop and think about it."

Presently, Jim and his family reside in Vadnais Heights and he works in sales for a janitorial supply company in New Brighton, a position he has held for the past five years. A babyface to the end, Jumpin' Jim and his signature High Drop Kick finishing move, was always one of the good guys.

"When it is all said and done I would like to be remembered as an athlete who was well liked and had a lot of integrity," he added, "that is what it is all about."

JOHN NORD

John Nord

John Nord grew up in the Twin Cities and graduated from Robbinsdale High School in 1977. There, at six-foot-eight and more than 300 pounds, he excelled at football. Nord, like so many of his other high school buddies from Robbinsdale (Tom Zenk, Rick Rude, Dean Peters, Curt Hennig, Nikita Koloff and Barry Darsow), wanted to get into the professional wrestling business. So, he jumped in head first and started to learn the tricks of the trade.

Nord made his debut in the American Wrestling Association in 1981 as "Nord The Barbarian." By 1984

Nord had established himself as a one of the industry's young guns. He was used as a monster heel and later became a member of Sheik Adnon Al Kaissey's army, teaming frequently with the Mongolian Stomper and Boris Zhukov. Before long, Nord was given a push to challenge for the AWA throne. In fact, he even beat long-time champ Nick Bockwinkel in a series of non title matches, but came up short when the actual hardware was on the line.

In 1988 Nord headed west to the Pacific Northwest territory to tag-team with his old pal from Minnesota, Scott Norton, to form "The Lumberjacks." There, he also teamed with "The Grappler," to form "The Breakfast Club," as well. By the early 1990s, Nord was on to bigger and better things, competing in the World Wrestling Federation as first "The Viking," and then as "The Berzerker." Managed by Mr. Fuji, Berzerker always won his matches by tossing his opponents to the outside of the ring and winning via a count-out. One of his early highlights as this character came against "The Undertaker," which saw him trying to stab the giant with a sword.

Nord left the WWF in early 1993 and began competing for All Japan Pro Wrestling. After a four-year stint overseas, Nord resurfaced in World Championship Wrestling with short blonde hair and sunglasses under the name "Yukon John Nord." He briefly teamed with former high school buddy Barry Darsow in 1997 before receiving his release from WCW in 1999. From there, Nord hit the independent circuit, entertaining legions of adoring fans along the way.

KEN PATERA

Ken Patera

Ken Patera grew up in Portland, Ore., loving sports. He went on to attend Brigham Young University on a track and field scholarship, where, in the late 1960s, he won a pair of NCAA championships in both the shot-put, as well as in weightlifting. After narrowly missing out on making the 1968 U.S. Olympic team, finishing fourth by less than a quarter inch in the shot-put competition, Patera turned his attention to international power lifting. There, he went on to win four straight Senior National weight lifting titles and in 1971 he also won four gold medals at the Pan American Games in Columbia. That next year he fulfilled a dream by representing the United States at the 1972 Olympics in Munich, only to come up short due to a knee injury.

"It was a real honor to represent my country, no question," said Patera. "I will also never forget the day everything went down with the Israeli hostage crisis in the Olympic village. I was supposed to compete that day, but they cancelled all the events when it happened. I could literally see everything that was happening from my patio, it was really scary."

From there, Patera came to Minnesota, where he had relocated to back in 1970. You see, Ken's brother, Jack, was the defensive line coach with the Minnesota Vikings at the time, and encouraged him to move here to train. His brother had also previously introduced him to Verne Gagne, who encouraged him to give pro wrestling a shot. With that, he set out to learn the tricks of the traade from Verne at his infamous training camp out in Chanhassen.

"I remember when I first moved here back in 1970," said Patera. "I was training for the Olympics and wound up living in a house with Ric Flair, who had been with the Gopher Football team but I think had flunked out of school by that time. Anyway, there were parties there almost every damn night. I mean he would go out to a bar and then at closing time he would just invite everybody over to our house for an after-bar. It was nuts. So, when the Olympics were over, I got Ric to join me at Verne's camp. At first he didn't want to, but talked him into it and he finally agreed. That was a trip over there, let me tell ya. It was me, Ric, Greg Gagne, Jim Brunzell, Bob Bruggers and Kosrow Vaziri ("The Iron Sheik"). Verne put us through the ringer out there, that was for sure. But it was a good learning experience too."

Patera made his pro debut in 1973 and at first worked mostly undercards. From there, he developed a great persona which would ultimately make him one of the top all-time heels in the business. With his patented "Swinging Full Nelson" finishing move, he became one of sport's most feared and hated wrestlers.

"People didn't care if the good guy won, they just wanted to see the villain lose," Patera joked. "Being a heel was great, you got to be creative and you got to really play with the crowd, I loved it."

He eventually moved out of Minnesota and began competing out east in the WWWF, later living in Georgia, Missouri and Texas. Meanwhile, in 1977, Patera got asked to compete in the "World's Strongest Man" competition, an event that has become synonymous with him ever since.

"I was in such debt at that point in my life," said Patera. "I was an amateur athlete for so long, competing against professionals from all over the world, and eventually it just took a toll. I mean you couldn't really have a good job while you were training, so money was tight. Anyway, the promoter who was putting on the event called me and asked me to be a part of it. I was wrestling professionally at that point and had quite a bit of name recognition from being on television all the time. Plus, I had a lot of credibility as well as a reputation for being pretty strong. I was actually the first person ever to lift 500 pounds over his head. (In his prime, Patera could clean-and-press 550 pounds and bench press 625!)

"Well, I wasn't in shape to do something like that because I had been wrestling non-stop. I mean I think I had like 20 days off a year at that point, and on top of that I had just thrown my back out in a match. Well, it was the first year of the Strongest Man and he said he would make it worth my while, so I eventually agreed. I knew most of the guys who were going to be competing because they were weight lifters, and thought it would be fun to just get away with my wife out to Hollywood for a while and make some good money too. Anyway, there were 10 events and half of them required back strength, so I didn't even try to do those. I did the other five though and still wound up taking third in the whole thing. Bruce Wilhelm won it that year, and it wound up being a lot of fun. Incredibly, that was the only time I ever competed in the event, but because ESPN Classic runs that stuff all the time, people always think that I won a bunch of titles."

In 1978 Patera defeated Wahoo McDaniel to capture the Mid-Atlantic Heavyweight crown and, after losing it, he recaptured it again by beating Tony Atlas later that year. The next year he teamed up with Big John Studd to capture the Mid-Atlantic Tag-team title as well. Then, in 1980, he won the WWF Intercontinental title by defeating Pat Patterson, and shortly thereafter he beat Kevin Von Erich for the Missouri Heavyweight crown. Patera would go on to win a pair of Georgia Heavyweight titles as well, defeating both Tommy Rich and later Jack Brisco.

Ken returned to Minnesota in 1982 to wrestle in the AWA, it was a move he would never regret.

"I love living in Minnesota," said Patera. "I have been here full-time now for almost 25 years and really enjoy it. My two younger kids grew up and went to school here, and the people are great. I liked being here back when I was wrestling not only because the AWA was here, but also for the fact that there was a major hub airport here as well. With all the traveling we did, that was a big factor to get non-stop flights when you could."

In the AWA, Patera got off to a quick start, antagonizing the fans every step of the way. He had joined Sheik Adnon Al-Kaissy's stable and alongside Jerry Blackwell they created an angle whereby transforming themselves into "The Sheiks." Later that year they won the AWA Tag Team title by defeating the High Flyers, Greg Gagne and Jim Brunzell. The Sheiks kept a stronghold on the title belts for the next year or so and every time they would be in danger of getting beat, Sheik Adnon Al Kaissy would somehow interfere and wind up saving the day. The popular heel duo seemed destined for a long title reign at that point, but an incident which happened outside of the ring quickly changed everything.

On the night of April 6th, 1984, Patera and another wrestler, "Mr. Saito," went to a McDonalds in Waukesha, Wis. But, when they were allegedly denied service, Patera got upset and tossed a huge rock through the window. The two then walked back to their hotel room next door. Shortly thereafter, a couple of police officers showed up to question them. The two grapplers allegedly resisted arrest at that point, however, and in the ensuing melee, both officers were injured. Other policemen joined in from there and subdued the two, ultimately taking them to jail. They were later found guilty of battery, and as a result, wound up spending more than a year in the slammer.

With that, the two were forced to drop their belts and leave the promotion. Patera, who was very sorry about the incident and vowed to turn his life around after that, returned to the ring a short time after his release and rejoined the WWF. There, he transformed himself into a heel and created an alliance with Bobby Heenan and Big John Studd. He later began a feud with the Heenan Family, which provided some solid angles down the road. He also later teamed with Billy Jack Haynes as well.

In 1988 Ken suffered an arm injury and was out of action for nearly half a year. After a brief return to the ring, he decided to head home, to Minnesota, where he returned to the AWA to form a tag team with Brad Rheingans called the "Olympians." That next year he and Brad defeated Badd Company for the AWA Tag Team Championship belts. Patera later got injured during a match with the Destruction Crew, however, and wound up vacating the title. From there, he called it a career. The grind of it all, combined with too many injuries had simply taken their toll.

"Being on the road was good and bad," he said. "Sure, it was tough being away from your family, but when you were out with the guys it was a party every night. It was amazing back in those days, I mean the girls were there after every show. Guys would literally just pick the ones that they wanted, it was crazy. Living the lifestyle of a professional wrestler was tough too though because you never had any privacy. Fame is a weird thing and for some guys it was hard to deal with. I mean some guys wore it on their sleeves, and really enjoyed the lifestyle. For me though, it wasn't about the glory, it was about the money. That is what I cared about. Hey it was showbiz, I didn't make more out of it than it was."

In 1988 Ken opened up a health club in North St. Paul called "Patera's Fitness." He ran that for nine years until eventually got tired of it. But, instead of just closing the doors, he got all of his clients new memberships at the clubs of their choice — proving that heels too, can be really good guys. Then, in 1997, Patera opened up a wrestling training camp in Prescott, Wis., and also ran a local independent promotion called the "All Star Wrestling Alliance," putting on as many as 40 shows a year for the next couple of years. He got out of that in 2001, however, and has been selling heavy industrial equipment in the area ever since. Now in his 60s, Ken is enjoying life. He had his hip replaced in the early '90s, but still finds plenty of time to play golf and enjoy himself. He presently resides in Woodbury with the youngest of his four children.

"To the fans who supported me all those years, thanks for the opportunity," said Ken. "I certainly enjoyed your support and had a great time. If I had to do it all over again, I would do it exactly the same way, I wouldn't change a thing. I think I found success in this business because I was very easy to get along with and I worked my ass off. I just always tried to give it 110% and then I tried to have fun too. That was what it was all about."

KENNY JAY

Kenny Jay

Kenny John Benkowski was born in 1937 and raised in the small town of Holdingford, just west of St. Cloud. There, he played football at Holdingford High School and graduated in 1955. From there, Kenny went into the armed services. When he got out in 1957, he answered an ad in a Milwaukee newspaper to attend Bob Hokinson's wrestling school. Eventually, he met up with a promoter from Chicago who brought him to the Windy City. He quickly made a name for himself as a heel and before long was traveling throughout the Midwest grappling on local cards. His momentum came to a grinding halt in 1960, however, when he was drafted back into the Army. Serving in Europe, Kenny even found a way to make a few bucks when he was on leave, wrestling in Spain and Germany.

Two years later Kenny returned home to Minneapolis, where he and his brother started a successful landscaping business. In the meantime, he also hooked up with Wally Karbo and began wrestling in the newly created AWA. Needing a new nickname, he turned to his landscaping business for a bit of inspiration — hence the name Kenny "The Sodbuster" Jay. (His middle name was John, so he used the initial.)

"The truth of the matter with my name, Kenny Jay, was that I just got too damn tired of signing autographs, I mean Benkowski took a lot of work," he joked.

From there, Kenny became a mainstay, wrestling throughout the territory on a regular basis. He later toured Japan for a long stretch as well, competing in several cage matches and taking in the sites along the way. Kenny had a day job, and as a result, never got a big push from the promoters. As a result, he was given the moniker "The Very Capable" Kenny Jay by former AWA ring announcer Al DeRusha. Considered a "jobber," or "preliminary wrestler," Kenny lasted a whole lot of years in the business by putting guys over. He was always dependable, despite having to overcome severe arthritis at times as well. He did have success early on though. Perhaps his most famous win came during his early AWA tenure came at the old St. Paul Auditorium in 1965, when he teamed with Verne Gagne and the Crusher to beat Harley Race, Larry Hennig and Chris Markoff in a six-man tag. He later teamed up with George "Scrap Iron" Gadaski as a jobber tandem, usually making their opponents look good along the way.

With his signature two thumbs up salute before his matches, along with his crippling submission hold, the infamous "Sod

Grip," which entailed putting his opponent into a headlock and then ramming his thumb in the fleshy area underneath his chin, Kenny was a classic. Over the past half century he has been in the ring with just about everybody who was anybody and has seen it all, including once wrestling an ape and even a bear. In fact, in 1975 the Sodbuster even took on Mohammad Ali in an exhibition wrestling/boxing match in Chicago, lasting one and a half rounds before getting knocked out cold.

"That was something," said Kenny. "They came and picked me up in a limo and flew me to Chicago that same day for the match. Ali was getting ready to take on some big Jap wrestler and wanted a few warm-up matches, so they asked me to do it. He boxed and I wrestled, it was real fun. Verne Gagne refereed it and Dick the Bruiser was my corner man. I hung in there with him for a while, but he eventually popped me on the chin and down I went. You know, that would have been a really big feather in my cap if I could have pinned that son-of-a-gun!"

Kenny, whose son Timmy also wrestled professionally for a spell back in the 80s, was a solid performer. He was also very well liked by his fellow wrestlers as well as the fans, and remains as one of the areas most popular grapplers. Now in his late 60s, believe it or not, Kenny is still going strong, doing independent shows around rural Minnesota and competing with the likes of former grapplers, Buck Zumhofe and the Sheik. He also hosts a charity benefit show every year for cytosis, a rare blood disease which inflicts his grandson.

"This will be the eighth year we have done the show and it just keeps getting better and better every year," he said. "Last year we held it at the American Legion in Bloomington and we had a wonderful turnout with guys like Larry the Axe, the Claw, Mad Dog, Jim Brunzel, Big K, Eddie Sharkey, Dr. X, Steve-O, Nick Bockwinkel and even Bobby the Brain. That was something else. The place was just packed. We raised a whole bunch of money for my grandson and that was just awesome."

Kenny, who lives in Bloomington with his wife, has three kids, one of whom is a partner with him in his lawn care and landscaping business. So, with Kenny still bustin' sod both in and out of the ring, technically, he is still a very "capable sodbuster!"

LARRY HENNIG

Larry Hennig

Larry Hennig was born and raised in Robbinsdale and grew up loving sports. At Robbinsdale High School, Hennig went on to star on the gridiron as an all-state tackle on the football team, while also excelling as amateur wrestler, winning a state title as a heavyweight in 1954 under legendary coach John Grygelko as well.

"Winning a state title, that was special because it represented my team and my hometown," said Hennig. "Robbinsdale had a great program back then and it was a real honor to be able to wrestle for them."

From there, Hennig accepted a scholarship to the University of Minnesota to play football for the Gophers. He stayed for one year but left after that to start a family with his wife. With that, Hennig launched his own real estate company, an entity which is still going strong nearly a half century later. At the same time, he also began training under local grappler Joe Pazandak for the career which would ultimately make him a household name, professional wrestling.

Hennig got into the biz both refereeing as well as working various preliminary matches. He quickly rose up through the ranks, however, and wound up winning the AWA Tag Team Championship alongside Duke Hoffman (aka Bob Leipler). Larry was a technical wrestler and played by the rules, as a result, early on in his career he was beaten by rougher, cheaper grapplers. In 1963 Hennig headed south to wrestle in the NWA's Texas territories. There, he adopted a more physical style and wound up claiming the Texas Heavyweight Title. It was there where he also met another wrestler by the name of Harley Race.

The two quickly struck up a friendship and began training together. Then, that next year, they headed back to Minnesota, where they competed as the tag-team tandem known as "Pretty Boy" Larry Hennig and "Handsome" Harley Race. With their newly found cocky persona and rough style, they emerged as the top heel pairing in the promotion. It was good versus evil and Verne Gagne, ever the good guy, set out to prove that Hennig's transformation was a bad move. As a result, a solid rivalry ensued between the two and over the ensuing years they would grapple together throughout the AWA's territory. Gagne partnered up with several foes to defeat the two, including the likes of Wilbur Snyder, the Crusher, Cowboy Bob Ellis, Danny Hodge, Pat O'Connor, Ernie Ladd and Bill Watts, but rarely came out on top as Hennig and Race dominated the world of tag team wrestling for the better part of five years. They got several shots at the belt and finally claimed them from Dick the Bruiser and the Crusher in 1965 — becoming the youngest world tag champs in AWA history.

"Because of the television exposure that we got in those days," said Hennig, "combined with the unique personalities who were in the sport at the time, we were as popular, if not more popular than any superstar pro athlete in town — whether that meant the Vikings, Twins, North Stars or what have you. I mean we did so many interviews, every week we were on TV, and as a result the fans really got to know us intimately through that one on one exposure. So many great characters came out of that era who are still talked about today, guys like the Crusher, Mad Dog, the Baron, and on and on. That is why wrestling was so popular back then. I mean fans could watch us on TV, and then come down to the old Auditorium and see us in person, it was a great deal. They could make a night out of it and it was great family entertainment, even part of their lifestyle. It was a special time, no doubt about it."

From there, the duo set off to travel the world, wrestling in Australia, New Zealand and Japan. In Australia, Hennig and Race made history again, becoming the first World Tag Team champions in the countries' International Wrestling Alliance. That next year the pair won their AWA tag belts back from the Bruiser and the Crusher in Chicago. But, a broken leg suffered by Hennig late in 1967 ended what would prove to be their last title run. Harley left the AWA after that, ending one of the era's top drawing attractions. Throughout the early 1970s Hennig formed a new tag-team with Larry Heinimi (aka "Lars Anderson"). Together the duo wrestled as a top heel combo, but never got a big push. So, Hennig decided to take some time off and do a stint in the WWWF out East. There, he took on a new gimmick, in order to keep himself high on the cards. So, he transformed himself from "Pretty Boy" Larry Hennig to Larry "The Axe" Hennig, which was named after his signature forearm to the head axe-like finishing move. Sporting a new red beard, he returned to the AWA in 1974 and got back together with Lars Anderson, who had been tagging with Buddy Wolff.

Together, the duo began a feud with Larry's old adversary Verne Gagne's son, Greg, and his tag-team partner, Jumping Jim Brunzell — better known as the High Flyers. After months of battling, Verne finally got into the ring with the Flyers for a six man tag team match against Hennig, Heiniemi and Wolff. As expected,

LARRY HENNIG'S FAVORITE STORY ABOUT HAYSTACKS CALHOUN...

"My funniest memory in pro wrestling happened on a trip to Japan back in the early 60s," said Larry Hennig. "You know, I wrestled in Japan 28 times and back then, to get there, you had to fly from Minneapolis to Los Angles to Hawaii to Fiji to Japan, refueling at every stop along the way. It was awful, and it took more than a day to get there. Anyway, on one trip, I was with a group of guys including a young wrestler by the name of Haystacks Calhoun. Haystacks weighed at least 700 pounds, and they were going to bill him as an up and coming sumo giant over there or something. Anyway, he wore these big bib overalls in and out of the ring, because that is all that probably really fit him.

Well, this was his first overseas trip and he was real excited. He gets on the plane and they quickly realize that there is no way he is going to fit in coach, so they gave him two seats up in first class. Hell, he was happier than a clam. Now, being an old Southern boy, Haystacks' diet at the time consisted pretty much of real basic down-home country food — and a lot of it. So, when the first class meal came, things like caviar, salmon and fine wine were all new to him. Back then first class was really fancy and if you were sitting up there you could pretty much eat all you wanted.

Anyway, he started eating and he just kept on eating. He would look back at all of us and laugh at what we were eating back in coach, taunting us along. So, about an hour after our meal, we all start to hear a moaning sound coming from the front of the plane. I mean it was loud! All of that rich food, of which his country intestines had never seen before, were about to explode. Well, he gets up to go into the toilet, but guess what, he can't fit in there. He tried and tried, but could not get in there. So, now they have to escort him all the way to the back of the plane where the galley is. As he is walking back, he starts to have stomach cramps and starts passing gas, it was awful. We were all just dying at this point. Finally, he gets back there and they empty out an old mail sack for him. The stewardesses then tied it up on both sides, held up a blanket for some privacy, and let him have at it. By now we are drinking some beers and laughing hysterically as he has it coming out of both ends, and it is loud as hell. It sounded like a bull being castrated back there, it was horrible.

Finally, after I don't know how long, he is finished and they have to get him back to first class. He literally had to shift his big belly from one side to the other to get down the aisle. As he walks by one of his bib overall straps is hanging behind him and his ass is all wet from this huge shitspot on there. Then, on top of all that, picture this — there are stewardesses walking in front of him and behind him spraying atomizers all over him as he is walking by. That poor bastard had to take the walk of shame right down the middle of the airplane all the way back to his seat. It was sad, it really was, but it was also funnier than hell at the same time. All these years later, I will never forget that story about old Haystacks Calhoun."

---

they came up short, but drew a big crowd nonetheless.

From there, Larry spent the next decade wrestling throughout various promotions both here in the U.S., primarily in Florida and along the east coast, as well as overseas in Japan. He later got the thrill of his life in 1982 when he was able to team up with his son, Curt, to capture the NWA's Pacific Northwest Tag Team title in Oregon. After one too many knee injuries, however, Larry eventually retired from active duty in 1985. A five-time AWA Tag-Team champ, Larry Hennig was a Minnesota wrestling icon. And despite his bad-guy persona in the ring, he was really one of the good guys. His views on the business today are a mixed bag, however.

"Wrestling has changed so much nowadays, it is a completely different era," said Hennig. "Now it's about big money, I mean it is a billion dollar industry. Sure, there are some great athletes out there today, but it is a completely different ballgame. It is too bad to see how it evolved, but it is nothing like it was back in our day, that is for sure."

Presently, the Axe runs "Larry Hennig Realty and Auction Company," out of St. Cloud, where his oldest son, Randy, now works his partner. A very successful businessman, at one point Hennig had six real estate offices throughout the area. Today, however, he focuses his attention on his core business around St. Cloud and the Twin Cities, and also makes sure to find enough time to spend with his 18 grandchildren.

Sadly, Larry still grieves over the sudden and tragic death of his son, Curt, who died of an apparent heart attack in his hotel room near Tampa, on February 10, 2003. He was just 44 years old. Known as "Mr. Perfect," Curt was a superstar in the world of professional wrestling, and left us far too soon.

"You know, I was so proud of Curt," said Larry. "He had to work so hard for everything he got, nobody handed him a thing along the way. He went on to become one of the top wrestlers in the world and really made his mark. His personality and his physical ability were just a one of a kind and that was why he was so successful. He was such a gifted, natural athlete, he was amazing. So, to see him achieve so much success both personally as well as

professionally made me so proud. I miss him terribly.

"You know, the way the media handled the death of my son was terrible. I am still so upset about it. It was always reported that he died of an overdose of cocaine and that is not quite all true. We still don't know what happened that night in his hotel room and we believe there may have been some foul play involved. There were a bunch of things that were reported inaccurately and I want to set the record straight. I just want the truth to come out so that his legacy can be remembered accurately. You know, I am the patriarch of this family and I have got 18 grandchildren to think about. So, I am not going to leave this world without my story being told. Period."

On looking back at his career, Larry is upbeat and optimistic.

"You know, an old wrestler once told me something I will never forget: 'Nor should the battle go to the brave; nor the race to the swift; nor riches to the rich; but time and chance happens to us all.' And what that means is that you can be the strongest guy in the world; you can be the fastest guy in the world; and you can be the richest guy in the world; but time and chance happens to us all. In other words, if you are in the right place at the right time, and you are prepared to take advantage of that opportunity when it presents itself, then you will be successful. I have never forgotten that and have always been grateful to the opportunity that I had. I certainly tried to make the most of it."

Here is an excerpt of the epitaph Larry wrote about his beloved son:

IN MEMORY OF CURT FROM DAD

"No father should have to write his son's epitaph. This is the hardest day of my life. Curt and my whole family are very special. Curt, husband, father, son, friend.

"One lyric from the Harry Chapin song, 'I Wanna Be A lot Like You, Dad, I Wanna Be A lot Like You.' Curt always wanted to be a wrestler. So we started at the beginning, at the age of six. Learn the basics and work on your body, and listen and be smart. I said, 'Curt, start with those arms and listen, when those arms

*measure seventeen inches, I'll give you five thousand dollars.'
Little did I know, it would happen so soon. I had to make pay-
ments. Curt asked, 'What is pro wrestling like, Dad?" I said,
'Curt, picture a wild stormy ocean and you are in a small boat a
long way from shore. And to survive you've got to make it to the
shore on your own, and it's not easy.' Later on, that storm became
the 'Perfect Storm', but you did it, son.
"Curt you were there, you had the chance and you did it. We are
all PROUD. I love you, son and buddy." — Dad*

LENNY LANE

Lenny Lane

Lenny Lane grew up in Duluth and graduated from Duluth Denfeld High School in the early 1990s. At six-foot-two and 225 pounds, he was an outstanding athlete. Lane got into professional wrestling through promoter Eddie Sharkey, and made his debut in 1995 working his way through the independent scene. One of his first gigs was in the Northern Premier Wrestling promotion, where he was managed by Mortimer Plumtree. From there, Lane caught a break and wound up working as a jobber in WCW, wrestling and losing to many of the companies' top stars at various shows through-
out the country.

After paying his dues for a couple of years, Lane got his big break. It would not come without some major controversy though. In late June of 1999, Lane was paired up with another long-term jobber named Lodi. Together, they were billed as the "West Hollywood Blondes," and were featured as a tag-team with an over-the-top "gay" angle. The two came out wearing pink tights, sucked on lollipops and even wore pigtails in their hair. The gimmick worked for a while, but some thought it was a bit too much.

Meanwhile, a few months later, Lane upset Rey Mysterio Jr. to win the WCW Cruiserweight Title as a singles wrestler. Lane's stock was on the rise big-time and was expecting a big push from the promotion. With his "Memory Lane" finishing move, he went on to defeat Kaz Hayashi at Fall Brawl '99 to get his first WCW pay per view win, but lost shortly thereafter to Psicosis.

By now, the heat was on with regards to his shtick with Lodi on the tag-team side of the coin. The two even came out and professed that they were actually "brothers," but it was too late. Eventually, Ted Turner's WCW censors yanked the duo, citing complaints from both fans as well as GLAAD, a homosexual civil rights group.

With that, Lane and Lodi's act was pulled. The pair would continue on, however, appearing under various gimmicks over the next few months in WCW. Among them was "Standards & Practices," which had them appearing in suits, almost mocking the company's censors. They also appeared as "Lane and Rave" for a brief period as well, but neither angle got much heat from the crowd. So, in the Summer of 2000, the pair was released from the federation.

Lane went on to wrestle for the rest of the year throughout the independent scene, using his notoriety to gain prominence in various matches. He would later reappear in WCW yet again though, this time sitting in the stands, holding up a sign that said "Use Me." His well choreographed plea worked, and he got back into the ring with the Wall, beating him in the process. From there, however, he once again "let go" due to contract problems.

Lenny came back to work in the WWF late in 2000, wrestling against Sho Funaki, but no big push followed. Lane then came back to Minnesota to work the independent Steel Domain cir-
cuit, followed by stints with Beach Wrestling, the FLWA, Southwest Premier Wrestling, and many other indie federations. That next year he joined Texas Championship Wrestling and teamed up with former WCW superstar "Sugar" Shane Helms, defeating the OverBoyz to win the TCW Tag-Team Championship belts. Helms moved on to the WWF, however, and Lane was left to hit the indie circuit yet again. After a stint in WWAS, Lane went on to win the SDW World Heavyweight belt in 2002.

Incidentally, Lane would later reveal that the idea for the "West Hollywood Blondes" was a spoof of the Saturday Night Live skit, "The Ambiguous Gay Duo." The angle, which just sort of assumed a gay angle, obviously didn't go as planned though. The powers-that-be certainly didn't follow through with the idea and as a result, Lane's bright career in the business suffered. A great athlete and a solid entertainer, Lane took some big risks to follow his dream and unlike most aspiring wannabe's, he made it. And hey, he'll bounce back in due time, just watch.

LEO NOMELLINI

Leo Nomellini

Born in Lucca, Italy, Leo Nomellini grew up in a tough neighborhood outside of Chicago, where, incredibly, he never played high school foot-
ball. He was convinced to try out for the team at the University of Minnesota, however, and blossomed very quickly into one of the school's all-time greats. In 1949, the bruising defensive tackle led the Gophers to a short-lived No. 1 ranking, even anchoring a defense that allowed just 80 points all season. Nicknamed the "Lion," Nomellini would go on to earn All-American hon-
ors that same year. Described as "One of the most magnificent specimens ever to play the game," by Bernie Bierman, Leo was truly a man among boys out on the gridiron. So good of an athlete was Nomellini, that for the heck of it, his teammate Vern Gagne, himself a national heavyweight champion, convinced him to get into wrestling. He did, and believe it or not, in just one year wound up finishing second overall in the Big Ten, losing to Ohio State's Bill Miller, whom he had pinned earlier in the season.

A two-time All-American, Nomellini graduated in 1950 and went on to become the first-ever draft pick of the upstart San Francisco 49ers. There, he would go on to star for 14 seasons in the NFL as a two-way lineman, never missing a game along the way. At six-foot-three and 265 pounds, he was the third fastest player on the team, making him the true prototypical lineman of his era. In addition, the 10-time Pro Bowler became one of the few players ever to be named All-Pro both on offense and defense, winning offensive honors in 1951 and 1952, and defensive laurels in 1953, 1954, 1957 and 1959. In 1969 Nomellini was inducted into the Pro Football Hall of Fame and later was enshrined into College Football Hall of Fame as well. One of the best pass rushers the game has ever seen, Nomellini would go down as one of the all-time greats.

Later in his career, he hooked up with his old buddy Verne, and the two of them then got together to become tag-team partners in his professional wrestling promotion, the AWA. He even won the world championship in 1956, a title he held for seven months. After retiring, Nomellini worked in the insurance industry for more than 30 years. Sadly, he passed away in October of 2000 due to complications from a stroke. He was 76.

MADUSA MICELI

Madusa

Born in Milan, Italy, Debra Miceli was raised in Minneapolis. She grew up tough and learned a lot of independence moving from foster home to foster home along the way. She was determined to work hard though, and even put herself through nursing school. With a background in gymnastics and track, the athletically gifted Miceli had always been intrigued by pro wrestling, so, when she met legendary trainer Eddie Sharkey back in the early 1980s, she seized the opportunity to get into the business.

So, she quit her nursing job to learn the ropes from Sharkey and eventually began to wrestle on the independent circuit. It was far from glamorous, working five nights a week making as little as $5 a night wrestling in bars, sometimes traveling with up to 10 people in a van out on the road. It was rough but she didn't care about the money. Whe drained her savings account, lost her house and car, and almost had to file for bankruptcy. Eventually, her hard work paid off though when she was signed by the American Wrestling Association.

Debuting as Madusa Miceli, she gained national exposure in the AWA, which was televised on ESPN at the time, and began to establish herself as one of the top women wrestlers in the business. She defeated Candi Devine to win the AWA World Women's title in 1988, earning Rookie of the Year honors that year as well. She also managed Curt Hennig for a brief stint that year too. That next year she toured Japan, eventually signing a lucrative three-year contract with the All-Japan promotion — the first American woman to do so. There, she became a rock-star, and was thrust into superstardom — complete with her own action figures and even a music CD. She also got into studying several forms of martial arts over there, and even competed in legitimate kickboxing and boxing matches. (She would later appear in several martial arts movies, including Inner Sanctum II and Shoot Fighter II.)

Medusa returned home in 1992 and got reestablished by working the independent scene for a year before signing on with WCW. There, she worked as a "valet" for several wrestlers, including Rick Rude. She established herself as a big-timer in women's

pro wrestling, however, and became a fan-favorite with her "Bridging Suplex" signature finishing move. A few years later Madusa made the jump to the WWF, where she wrestled under the name of "Alundra Blayze," and eventually won a total of three title belts with the promotion. In 1996 she left WWF and came back to WCW. Then, in one of her most notorious moments on live TV, she threw the WWF women's title belt in a garbage can during her first appearance back with WCW. It was a big hit. Madusa would go on to claim the WCW women's title, and then become the first woman to win the cruiserweight title as well. In addition, she also served as a valet for Randy "Macho Man" Savage, as part of "Team Madness" along the way.

Finally, in 2000, Miceli decided that she had had enough. She had a falling out with WWF owner Vince McMahon, and had no desire to go back to work for him. So, she made a 180-degree career change and got into monster truck racing. There, driving under her same "Madusa" moniker, she has become a star in the USHRA. In 2004 she even qualified for the Master Jam World Finals, but fell short when her truck was damaged in a crash.

"I'm sure some people see the move to monster trucks as odd but it suits me," said Miceli in a recent interview in the Winnipeg Sun. "I've always been a closet gear head and always loved my Harley. Driving a monster truck came naturally to me, thank God. Besides, I have no interest in joining wrestling — that's reverted to bra-and-panty matches. Nobody has to worry about people taking off their tops and showing their breasts in monster trucking."

A true sports entertainment diva, Debra Miceli has overcome overwhelming odds to get to where she is at — and she did it on her own terms. In fact, her "killer body" is matched only by her "killer smarts" — which is exactly what it takes to operate a 1,500 horsepower, 10,000 pound machine. One of the most accomplished women's wrestlers of all time, Madusa is one of Minnesota's finest. And, in addition to driving, she is also a television commentator for various programs on the Speed Network as well. Presently, Miceli resides in Florida, where, when she is not driving her monster truck, she enjoys scuba diving, skydiving, riding her Harley Davidson motorcycles, her horses and even raising wolves.

MEAN GENE OKERLUND

Mean Gene Okerlund & Verne Gagne

Over the past three decades Mean Gene Okerlund has become synonymous with professional wrestling. Widely considered to be the dean of all announcers, his story is as fascinating as he is.

Gene Okerlund was born and raised in the small South Dakota town of Sisseton, where he grew up playing football, baseball and basketball. After graduating from high school, Gene started working in the radio business. His family owned a couple of radio stations in the area, so he was able to get a jump-start on his career at an early age. From there, Gene went on to study journalism at the University of Nebraska, and after getting married in 1963, ultimately landed his first job at an Omaha radio station in 1965.

In 1967 Okerlund made his way to the Twin Cities, where he was hired as the program director at KDWB Radio at the age of just 24. He later jumped ship to work at WDGY, and from there took a job working as a commissioned salesman at Channel 11, WTCN-TV. The station also televised Verne Gagne's weekly "All Star Wrestling" show as well, from the second floor of the Calhoun Beach Club. It was there, where Gene caught his big break.

"Well, Marty O'Neil, the legendary announcer from St. Paul, who did the AWA's telecasts, was off for a while," said Gene. "So, Verne asked me if I could fill in for him for the taping of the live show. I told him that I didn't really know anything about wrestling, but he didn't care, he said 'just describe everything that you see.' I did, and it went all right. The best part was getting paid $250 bucks for 90 minutes of work. That was easy money and I was hooked. He brought me back part-time and eventually I got the gig. I figured out pretty quickly that if you deliver convincingly, are in control, and tell a good story, it doesn't make any difference what you are doing — it usually works out."

"From there, it all just kind of clicked," he added. "The interesting thing about it was because I really didn't know much about wrestling, I sort of made up the descriptions of the moves as they happened, to explain them to the viewers at home. Some of the expressions like a "Flying Double Furnam" or a "Beal Throw," were just things I came up with on the fly. I mean what was a "Beal Throw," well it was named after a wrestler named Benny Beal. They were just little things that I did which stuck, and it grew from there."

Later, in the early 70s, Gene started broadcasting Gagne's Canadian wrestling shows as well. He would take Verne's private plane, nicknamed "Suicide One," up to Winnipeg two days a week and then return home.

"You know, I got into the professional wrestling business just at the right time," he said. "It was just taking off at that point and television was such an important part of its growth."

Meanwhile, Gene still kept his sales gig at the television station, which eventually paid off in 1978, when he got together with a couple of friends to form their own advertising agency, which eventually became "Cohen, Okerlund & Smith." As he grew the agency, which specialized in the retail sector, his broadcasting duties also increased, and he later became the main broadcaster for the entire AWA.

"Minnesota has always had a reputation for being an amateur wrestling hotbed," remarked Gene. "Because of that, and because of the old AWA, it later became a Mecca for professional wrestling too. It really became one of the main foot-holds for developing new talent. I mean from Tony Stecher to Verne Gagne to Eddie Sharkey, to the new guys like Brad Rheingans, there is a rich history there. The list goes on and on, from Hennig to Rude to Lesnar, I mean there have been a ton of Minnesotans who have gone on to make it in this business."

As the business grew, Gene's stock rose. Finally, in 1983, Vince McMahon came to him and explained his dream of creating a national cable wrestling telecast out of New York which would eventually be seen worldwide. Geno was willing to take the risk, so he left the AWA and joined the WWF, where McMahon quadrupled his salary — thus easing any sad feelings he might have had for leaving Gagne's AWA.

He maintained his residence in Burnsville, however, and continued to work at the agency, where there were now more than 40 employees. It was tough though, especially after his longtime friend and partner, Richie Cohen, passed away that year after a long bout with cancer. So, Gene brought in some new management and became the world's best delegator. While he was in New York doing wrestling interviews, he relied on his people back home to take care of the clientele. Gene had more pressing issues and was about to ride a wave of popularity that few sports/entertainment businesses ever see.

"In about 1985, right before Wrestlemania I, the popularity of it all just exploded," said Gene. "It became mainstream at that point and a lot of celebrities started to take an interest, people like Andy Warhol, Danny Devito, Joe Piscopo, Robert DeNiro, Dianne Keaton, Bob Costas, Billy Martin, Billy Joel and even Liberace, among others. It seemed like overnight wrestling became showbiz, with glitz and glamour. Guys like Hulk Hogan, the Macho Man, the Ultimate Warrior — they all became larger than life and that is what really took it to the next level. From there, the television numbers took off and the wild storylines kept em' coming back."

Gene eventually passed the advertising business over to his son Todd, in 1991, to focus on announcing full-time. By now he was one of pro wrestling's biggest stars. He was on television around the clock, interviewing the industries' top stars. He traveled the world and hosted various shows over the next decade, helping to grow the business into a multi-billion dollar industry.

"I am very lucky, I have loved every minute of being in this business," said Gene. "And, there have been enough professional challenges for me to do along the way as well. You know, some people look down the end of their nose at wrestling people, but I was enlightened probably about 20 years ago by Dick Ebersol, who is now the chairman of NBC. I worked with him a multitude of television projects as well as an assortment of other entertainment vehicles. Working with him was invaluable. He let me work on several new shows and still allowed me to work in wrestling because he knew that it would let me keep my identification with the 18-34 year old demographic."

Gene feels right at home behind the mic, and his rapport with the wrestlers is obvious. There is a mutual level of respect there, and that is something that was earned over thousands of interviews. He even got in the ring on one occasion as well, wrestling one professional match as the tag-team partner of none other than Hulk Hogan. The two matched up against Mr. Fuji and George "The Animal" Steele as Geno even scored the pin fall, much to the fans' delight. He then quickly exchanged the tights for his trusty mic.

"You know, announcing is so much fun, I love feeding off of certain people," said Gene. "For instance, Bobby Heenan, he and I could play off of each other very well. With him, I was always the 'straight-man.' Jesse Ventura, meanwhile, he was a guy who was always in control. You know, he was actually the one who gave me the name 'Mean Gene.' Jesse was such a classic. It's a great story. Whenever I would interview him he would always start out by saying some outlandish thing like 'You know, I was with the Rolling Stones last night…', and really start name-dropping, which was all part of his flamboyant act. Well, one time I was interviewing him, it must have been around 1978, and he came up and said, 'Gene, do you know who I was partying with this past week?' and I said 'Jesse, I don't have a clue.' He says, 'I have been hanging out with Tom Petty and the Heartbreakers.' I said 'fantastic, that's great.' So he says, 'You know who Tom Petty is don't you?' and I said 'of course I do, he is a famous race car driver…' So, Jesse looks at me all hurt and says, 'That's mean…Gene!' It stuck, and that is where that nickname came from."

In 1993, after nine long years in the WWF, Mean Gene jumped to World Championship Wrestling. He remained with the company for nearly a decade as the promotion's main announcer, until WCW was sold to Vince McMahon and the WWE in 2002. Over the years, Gene has also been an integral part of creating the storylines for the wrestlers to follow in the various shows, giving his creative juices yet another outlet to flow into.

"As far as it being scripted, sure, there has to be some sort of a storyline that you have to follow," he said. "Otherwise it is just a rudderless ship. I mean a film has to have a beginning and a middle and an end, and it has to have a compelling story to capture the interest of the viewers. We are the same way and I take great pride in having a part in telling our story to our millions of fans around the world."

Gene eventually branched out into several other business ventures, all of which have done extraordinarily well for him. One, in particular, was a pro wrestling-inspired line of pizza and burgers which have really taken off.

"The idea behind 'Mean Gene's Burgers' came from the fact that my nephew, Jeff Okerlund, was the chairman of the board of Orion Foods, a subsidiary of Schwann's Foods out of Marshall. They had something like 1,500 fast food franchises that generally went into convenience stores around the country. Well, they had come up with an idea for a new burger brand and figured that their demographic was very similar to that of pro wrestling's. So, we started to talk and one thing led to another. Before long we came up with 'Mean Gene's Burgers,' and the slogan 'Just Bite Me!' followed shortly thereafter. Now, today that might be passé, but in 1996 that was pretty edgy, and certainly something that the big chains couldn't touch. Kids loved it though and it just took off from there. 'Bite the Big One!' came later for 'Mean Gene's Pizza,' and we are just having a ball with the whole thing. It is great food and people really enjoy it."

While the burgers are prepackaged and sold at colleges and military installations around the world, the fresh pizzas can be found at more than 300 entertainment channels, such as bowling alleys, bars and restaurants. As a distributor and brander, Okerlund has found a tremendous niche which continues to grow and prosper.

"I just love to entertain," said Gene, "whatever it is. I loved sports growing up, so I could talk about that, but I also loved other things, like music. In fact, I was even an accomplished musician, believe it or not. I played the trumpet and piano and even made a couple of records along the way."

When Gene isn't makin' beautiful music, he can usually be found on the tube. In fact, the list of television shows and pay-per-view events that he has hosted over the years reads like a who's-who and what's-what of professional wrestling. It all started with "All Star Wrestling," which played in over 100 markets throughout the AWA, followed by "Big Time Wrestling," out of Toronto, then "Championship Wrestling," out of Winnipeg. From there, he went to New York, where he hosted "Superstars of Wrestling," and also a cable-only show called "WWF All American Wrestling." Next was "Wrestling Spotlight," followed by "Saturday Night's Main Event." More mainstream stuff came after that, starting with "Friday Night Videos," on NBC, as well as "Up all Night," on the USA Network. And let's not forget Hulk Hogan's short-lived "Rock'n Wrestling" animated cartoon series either. By 1993 Gene was in Atlanta, doing the prime-time shows "WCW Monday Nitro," on TNT and "WCW Thunder," on TBS. He later moved back to the WWE, where he did the Spike TV magazine show "WWE Confidential," and is presently doing "WWE 24/7," where he does a lot of feature vignettes.

"The business has really changed in my day, that is for sure," said Gene. "The biggest thing has to be the size of these guys now. I mean, back then it was a beer and tee-shirt crowd with big fat guys, whereas now these guys are just massive, muscular monsters. Some of them are man-made, while plenty of others are of the synthetic variety — if you know what I mean…"

"You know, for the most part, it has been a great ride," he added. "There were a lot of good times and a lot of great characters over the years. Everything from spending some wild evenings with Ric Flair and Bobby Heenan to playing cribbage with Andre the Giant. You know, Andre loved to take me out to high class French restaurants when we were out on the road, I just worshipped the ground that guy walked on. It's the little things like that you remember. There is never a dull moment in this business, that is for sure."

Presently, Gene and his wife reside in Siesta Key, Fla., near Sarasota. He continues to work for the WWE, enjoys golf and loves spending his Summers back home in Minnesota up at his lake home near Brainerd.

"I am 61 years old. I am happy, and I think I have got a pretty good life both behind me and still ahead of me. I have got a wonderful family, my wife and I just celebrated our 41st wedding anniversary, and we've got two great kids, Todd and Tor."

(Incidentally, Todd starred on the Gopher Hockey team back in the mid-1980s and, after playing on the 1988 U.S. Olympic team, spent five years in the New York Islanders organization. Additionally, Gene and Todd are currently working together, albeit indirectly, on "WWE 24/7," a video-on-demand service featuring 40 hours of classic wrestling footage purchased for a monthly fee. Todd began producing compilation shows with his partner, Joe Ciupik, several years ago for their Twin Cities based company, www.classicwrestling.com, which also features pay-per-view shows. Since then, more than 50 Classic Wrestling shows have aired, highlighting older promotions from the golden age of wrestling such as the AWA, and may others which are now defunct. The shows average up to 15,000 orders a month from a potential universe of 28 million homes, a fat statistic which has recently peaked the interest of various satellite TV providers.)

For nearly four decades, Gene Okerlund has provided literally millions of wrestling fans countless hours of entertainment. With his dead-pan humor and quick wit, Geno is a classic. From backstage interviews, to creating dramatic storylines, to directing interviews, to producing television shows, to running several successful businesses, he seemingly does it all. And, he has brought a lot of credibility to a sports-entertainment business that continues to grow and thrive, where others have simply fallen by the wayside. A great announcer, personality and pitchman… he's Meeeaan Gene!, a real Minnesota grappling legend.

MOLLY HOLLY

Molly Holly

Nora Greenwald (aka "Molly Holly") was born in 1978 and grew up in Linwood Township, near Forest Lake. Greenwald went on to graduate from Forest Lake High School, where she served as a two-time captain of the school's gymnastics team. Greenwald, whose father was a Minnesota state power lifting champion, also enjoyed lifting weights and even set a youth bench-press record as a 14-year-old. After high school, Greenwald got the bug to try professional wrestling and wound up attending an independent wrestling school outside of Tampa, Fla. There, she learned the tricks of the trade and eventually made her debut in the summer of 1997, wrestling in the Florida area as "Starla Saxton."

Just a few months later, Greenwald won the WPWF Women's Championship by beating the reigning champ, "The Wench." From there, she tried out World Championship Wrestling and wound up spending a year honing her craft throughout the independent circuit. After paying her dues, Greenwald debuted in the WCW in 1998 — appearing mostly as a jobber and losing to most of the promotion's biggest stars. Her good looks and athleticism quickly got her noticed, however, and later that Summer she went on to capture the New Dimensions Wrestling's World Ladies Title from Malia Hosaka. Greenwald was enjoying her time in the limelight and the television cameras couldn't get enough of her.

As she continued to travel around, performing in matches,

her popularity soared. Eventually, she hooked up with Randy "Macho Man" Savage and became a valet in his "Team Madness." There, she ran interference for the "Macho Man" and got a lot more national television exposure in the process. From there, she debuted on the TV show "RAW" by pinning rival Trish with her new signature finishing move, the "Molly-Go-Round." As the drama of professional wrestling continued, Greenwald's storyline included a love affair with "Spike Dudley," which ended when she left him to become "Hurricane's" bad-girl sidekick now known as, "Mighty Molly."

Mighty Molly's first bit of drama came at the pay-per-view extravaganza, "Wrestlemania X8," where she bashed the Hurricane in the back of the head with a frying pan and pinned him to become WWF Hardcore Champion. Finally, at the pinnacle of the business, Molly was now a star of women's pro wrestling. Then, after defeating Trish in a "bikini/paddle-on-a-pole" match, where she appeared in a cat suit and smashed a paddle over Trish's head, she redefined herself as anti "T & A" and proclaimed herself as the only woman in the WWF to be "pure and wholesome."

In June of 2001, Molly's two years of hard work and perseverance were finally rewarded with the WWF Woman's title when she beat Trish for the coveted belt. She lost it a few months later at "SummerSlam," however, only to win it back several months down the road over "Gail Kim." Now known as "Molly Holly," she would go on to become the WWE champ in 2002 and 2003 as well, making history along the way. A true risk-taker, Molly even had all her hair shaved off her head as a stipulation of her loss to Victoria at WrestleMania XX in front of a sold-out Madison Square Garden crowd. She continues to be a weekly mainstay on the WWE's hit show "Raw," where, in 2004, she has teamed up with Victoria and Gail Kim on numerous occasions.

An outstanding athlete and entertainer, Nora Greenwald is one of the toughest divas in the business and continues to make Minnesota proud.

NIKITA KOLOFF

Nikita Koloff

Nelson Scott Simpson was born in 1959 and grew up living in the projects of Minneapolis. His father, a military veteran, reportedly had a difficult time adjusting to life back home and decided to leave his family when Scott was just two. As a result, Scott's mother was left to raise four children as a teacher's aide in the Minneapolis school system. It was tough, but when Scott was 10 his mom had saved enough to get off of welfare and move to Robbinsdale. There, as a sixth grader, Scott stumbled across a copy of an "Iron Man" muscle magazine and was immediately hooked. He went out and bought his first weight lifting set with money he had earned as a newspaper boy, and started pumping iron. By the time he was in junior high school he could squat nearly 500 pounds and was ripped. From there, he went on to become a star two-way lineman for the Robbinsdale Robins High School football team.

After graduating from high school in 1977, Simpson played college football, first at Golden Valley Lutheran College and later, at Moorhead State University. Determined to become a professional football player, he drove himself to be the best he could be. A pair of broken legs, however, slowed him down and ultimately cost him his shot at making it in the NFL. With his dream of playing pro ball still in his mind, he returned back to the Twin Cities and continued to train, sometimes lifting weights up to eight hours a day, while bouncing at a nearby bar at night.

After badly breaking his leg yet again while busting up a bar melee, Simpson took some time off and went to Atlanta, to spend some time with his old high school football buddy, Joe Laurinaitis, who had taken up professional wrestling with Georgia Championship Wrestling as the character "Animal" of the "Road Warriors." Simpson was no stranger to pro wrestling, in fact, several of his best high school pals had also gotten into the business as well, including: Curt Hennig, Rick Rude, Tom Zenk, Dean Peters, John Nord and Barry Darsow. So, with his workers compensation paying the rent, he began going to Joe's matches. He was interested, but still had dreams of playing for his hometown Minnesota Vikings. And, at six-foot-two, 285 pounds and just 8% body fat, he was a specimen.

Simpson returned home a few months later and got a job as disc jockey at a local bar. Shortly thereafter, he got a call from Joe with news about a wrestling opportunity down in Atlanta. Ironically, he got another call a few days later that he had been invited to a tryout with the Tampa Bay Bandits in the newly-created USFL. So, he headed back down south. Once there, Joe informed him that Jim Crockett, the head of the National Wrestling Alliance in Charlotte, N.C., was searching for new wrestlers. As luck would have it, World Tag-Team champions Don Kernodle and Ivan Koloff (aka "The Russians") were looking for a third partner and Joe suggested that Simpson might make a good "nephew" to Ivan. With the Soviets set to boycott the upcoming 1984 Olympics, Joe thought they would be a hot commodity. Simpson, despite not having a minute of wrestling experience, decided to go for it, figuring that if it didn't work out he still had his try-out with the Bandits.

So, Simpson showed up at Crocket's office in Charlotte with a cleanly shaved bald head, shocking the Russian duo with his massive physique. His 34 inch waist, 54 inch chest and ripped stomach muscles were unlike anything they had ever seen before. They took one look and hired him on the spot. With that, Simpson passed on his try-out and dove into learning the tricks of the trade. In addition, he would have to take on a whole new persona, of a mean Cold War Soviet wrestler whose country was at real-life odds with his America. His character, "Nikita Koloff," a fresh-off-the-boat stone-faced Russian, was supposed to participate in the Olympic Games in Los Angeles as a superstar wrestler and track and field athlete, and was furious that he couldn't compete. He was immediately cast as a bad-guy heel and the fans would soon love to hate him — just as predicted. With that, he made his debut in the Mid-Atlantic territory in the summer of 1984. In the ring he was a monster, destroying his opponents in just seconds flat with his signature "Russian chain" finishing move. The fans were in awe.

Simpson took his new role very seriously and remained in character 24 hours a day, even going as far as learning to speak Russian in order to give his character more credibility. He never spoke English, and oftentimes even brought "Uncle Ivan" with him when he was out and about to serve as his "translator" and better sell the gimmick in real life as well. In fact, he loved playing the part, so much so, that he later legally changed his name to Nikita Koloff. Fans booed him mercilessly and he even got death threats. But with all that came superstardom. Soon, he was traveling the world as an A-list entertainer. So believable was Simpson that he was even voted by fans as the No. 1 most-hated wrestler. Not bad, for a bad guy! He was even a finalist to land a starring role in Rocky IV as Sylvester Stallone's Russian nemesis, but they went with the blonde Dolph Lundgren instead.

In 1986 Nikita did a 180-degree turn and became a good guy. The Federation decided to partner him with wrestling legend

Dusty Rhodes, whose partner, Magnum T.A., had recently been severely hurt in an automobile accident. Simpson, enjoying the life as a top-flight entertainer, accepted the new challenge by becoming a lovable Russian who now loved America. But, would the fans buy it? Well, the big announcement was one of the best kept secrets in the business up to that point, but finally came out in Nashville, when Dusty's new "mystery" partner was announced during a steel cage match against the "Horsemen," Ole Anderson and J.J. Dillon. The drama unfolded when Dusty entered the ring and was immediately attacked from behind by Ole and J.J. Then, the overflow crowd gasped when they saw Nikita slowly enter the ring. With several dramatic pauses, Nikita looked to the audience, which was sure he would join in with Ole and J.J. in giving poor Dusty an ass-whooping. But, he shocked them all by coming to Dusty's aid instead and viciously attacking the duo. The crowd went nuts and chanted "Nikita! — Nikita!" for the next 15 minutes. From that point on, instead of snarling at kids, he would sign their autographs.

Now known as "The Superpowers," Dusty "The American Dream," and Nikita "The Russian Nightmare," went on to wrestle in front of packed houses night in and night out. Then, just as things were going great, Simpson got some real-life bad news, his wife, Mandy, had been diagnosed with cancer. Scott, at the height of his career, took a sabbatical to be with her. Making matters worse, Crockett's company, World Championship Wrestling, had been bought out by Ted Turner — leaving him with a lot of uncertainty with regards to his job. Meanwhile, Mandy's condition was deteriorating and she finally lost her battle with cancer just a year later. Scott was devastated. After going through several months of hell, Simpson mustered the courage to return to the ring — this time as a different man, complete with a crew cut instead of a shaved head. After wrestling in the AWA and several independent circuits, he returned to WCW. It wasn't quite the same though.

Now in his mid-30s, Simpson was growing tired of the travel and the overall daily grind of wrestling. He also didn't like how the WCW treated its wrestlers and figured that life was too short to be unhappy. You see, about a year after Mandy's tragedy, Scott had fallen in love with one of her old friends, Victoria. The two were later married and would go on to have their first child in 1992. Wanting to spend more time with his family, Scott decided to hang em' up for good. His final match, against Big Van Vander, an enormous 500-pound beast, would not be without its share of real-life drama, however. During the "Halloween Havoc" match, Simpson took a clothes line to the back of the head and immediately knew he was hurt. In addition to discovering a hernia at the hospital that next morning, an MRI revealed that his neck was severely damaged. The doctors basically said that any more wrestling might result in permanent injury.

With that, Simpson walked away on his own terms. He did not want to stay past his prime, and he was happy to be going out on the top of his game. When it was all said and done, Simpson was a two time NWA World Tag-Team Champion, a two time NWA World Six-Man Tag-Team Champion, a NWA/UWF Unified World Television Champion and a NWA U.S. Heavyweight Champion. (He would briefly return to the ring again, however, in 2003, as part of an angle in which he first joined back up with Dusty Rhodes — only to turn on him a short time later.)

From there, Simpson found a new spiritual calling and underwent a religious conversion. In fact, today he travels the world, ministering to people about how to make their lives more complete.

"The character that I 'played' was a heartless, cold, and evil person, a man of no compassion for anyone whatsoever," writes Koloff in his biography. "This was an easy character for me to portray, as it wasn't that far from the real me. (I would later become a 'good guy' and a fan favorite). Upon my retirement in 1993, I found myself reflecting back on my life and career. Evaluating all that I had accomplished, the accolades, the fame and the fortune, I was confused as to why I still felt empty inside. The world told me that fame and fortune would make me happy, but I had all of these things and was still unfulfilled. In October of 1993, I stepped into

a church service and when an altar call was given, in an instant, I immediately knew what was missing in my life. A relationship with Jesus Christ. My life has never been the same.

"I have been privileged and honored that the Lord has opened doors all over the world for me to minister. I have spoken in churches, schools, prisons and the streets of the U.S. and the world. As I have shared my story of how God performed 'heart surgery' on me, I have witnessed thousands come to Jesus and experience God's awesome power of changing their hearts and lives forever. The Lord has not only called me to share where He's brought me. He has also birthed messages in me for the church of today."

From Russian heel, to beloved hero, Nikita Koloff was an amazing athlete and entertainer who has truly made a difference.

PAUL ELLERING

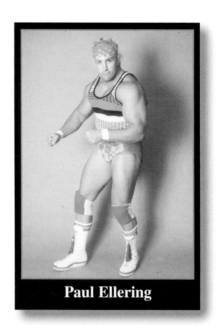

Paul Ellering

Paul Ellering grew up in the small Minnesota town of Melrose. He excelled at sports, and eventually gravitated towards weight lifting, where he emerged as national champion and later as a world record holder. Ellering got into professional wrestling first as a wrestler in the late 1970s, and then in the early '80s he formed the original "Legion of Doom," serving as the group's leader and business manager. Included in the original group were the Road Warriors, Jake "The Snake" Roberts, The Spoiler, King Kong Bundy, Buzz Sawyer and Arn Anderson. As time passed, however, and the members moved on, "Precious Paul," as he was known, focused his attention exclusively to managing the Road Warriors, while still keeping the Legion of Doom moniker for the duo. In addition to performing with the duo on television as their "manager," Ellering became a close personal friend to both Hawk and Animal, and also served as their real-life business manager as well. As the brains behind the brawn, Ellering, who occasionally got in the ring to mix things up, led the bad-ass body-building tandem to their first tag championship. From there, they went on to become the most successful tag-team partnership in professional wrestling history, winning countless belts and championships in the AWA, NWA, WCW, WWF, WWE and in Japan, along the way.

After retiring and then unretiring, Ellering eventually got out of the business for good in the late 1990s to focus on new endeavors. Among them was sled dog racing, where, in 2000, he competed in the legendary Iditarod race in Alaska as a musher. A perfectionist in whatever he does, Ellering has found success throughout his entire life. He is currently training for the 2004 race with the same dedication that earned him the title "Strongest Man in the World." In addition, Ellering runs a wrestling camp and is also a sought after motivational speaker.

"I have been involved in sports at the highest level all my adult life and found that sports are more than competition," said Ellering of his program. "It is a collection of values and associations. The powerful symbolism of sports, like the Iditarod Sled Dog Race, professional wrestling, and power lifting, can be used to inspire others to exceed. In the process of competition I always hope to create good will and character by being an example and an inspiration. With sled dogs, fitness and wrestling as my symbols, I teach goal setting [living your dreams by planning, training, and testing], the art of self-giving, and the values of a work ethic. I like to give greater meaning to adventure and challenges."

Presently, Ellering resides in Grey Eagle, Minn., with his wife and three children. There, they own a restaurant, the Historical Rock Tavern, and also a health club, where he encourages others in their quest for personal improvement.

MIKE ENOS

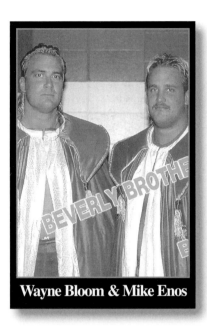

Wayne Bloom & Mike Enos

Mike Enos grew up in the Osseo area of the Twin Cities loving sports. At six-foot-three and 250 pounds, he was an out-standing athlete. Enos loved wrestling and couldn't wait to get into the business. So, after cutting his teeth around the local indie circuit, he and his buddy, Wayne Bloom, formed a tag team partnership called the "Destruction Crew," and got a gig competing in Verne Gagne's AWA during the late 1980s. The duo would eventually be given a push and wound up beating the "Olympians," Ken Patera and Brad Rheingans, and later Paul Diamond and Greg Gagne, to claim the AWA World Tag-Team Championship belts in 1989. Unfortunatley though, the Destruction Crew was not able to regain their AWA Tag Titles which they had lost, due to the fact that the AWA would go out of business that following year.

Following the collapse of the AWA, Enos and Bloom competed in the NWA/WCW, where they were put under masks and billed as the "Minnesota Wrecking Crew, Part II." As protégés of Ole Anderson and the Four Horsemen, Enos (who was billed as "The Mauler") and Bloom were put into a feud with the Steiner Brothers. After losing decisively, however, they ventured to the WWF, where they reemerged as Beau and Blake Beverly, of the "Beverly Brothers." There, the two blond-haired "brothers" became one of the most-despised tag-teams in the WWF — battling with the "Bushwhackers" and "Natural Disasters," among others. Managed by "The Genius," the duo never managed to haul in the WWF Tag-Team belts, but gained a lot of notoriety nonetheless.

In 1993 the Beverly Brothers left the WWF, roaming the various independent wrestling federations for the next several years. In 1996, Enos joined the WCW, teaming up with Dick Slater to form the tag-team "Rough & Ready." When that flopped, Enos got back together with Bloom to revive the "Minnesota Wrecking Crew," this time in the WCW. Unable to get past the likes of the Steiner Brothers, however, the pair was let go. Enos, meanwhile, then started competing in the singles bracket as "Mean Mike Enos." Enos, who wrestled both singles and also tagged with various partners, including Bobby Duncum, Jr., and fellow Minnesotan, Scott Norton, remained with the federation until 1999. He also competed in Japan during that time as well, with the NJPW.

WAYNE BLOOM

Wayne Bloom grew up in the Twin Cities and went on to graduate from Cooper High School in 1976. Bloom later got in to pro wrestling, first working with the local American Wrestling Association, and later hitting the big time in the WWF. In the AWA, Bloom formed a very successful tag-team with longtime buddy Mike Enos, who was from Osseo. Together, they were known as the "Destruction Crew." By the late 1980s the duo was performing in the WCW as protégés of Ole Anderson and the Four Horsemen. There, they became masked characters called the "New Minnesota Wrecking Crew."

After losing to the Steiner Brothers, however, they left the promotion to join the WWF. There, the two took on the persona of the "Beverly Brothers," nicknamed Beau & Blake. Wayne, who was known as "Beau Beverly," found success with his "Beau Bomb" finishing move and became a big-time fan favorite. Managed by The Genius, the two traveled the world and ultimately lost to the Natural Disasters at the 1992 Summerslam in England. They would later go back to World Championship Wrestling in the late 1990s, where, as usual, they would find success again as a tough and entertaining tag-team combo.

RIC FLAIR

Ric Flair

Ric Flair was born on February 25, 1949, in Memphis. Fred, as he was originally named by his mother, was then dropped off at the infa-mous Tennessee Children's Home Society a few weeks later. (Incidentally, the same corrupt orphanage which was later the subject of a "60 Minutes" television expose.) From there, he was adopted by Richard and Kathleen Fliehr of Edina. Back home in Minnesota, Fred was renamed Richard Morgan Fliehr. Ric, as he would later change his name to, grew up in a culture that was about as polar opposite as humanly possible with regards to what he does today. In fact, his mom was a renowned author of literature and did work for the Guthrie Theatre, where she introduced Ric to such people as Jessica Tandy, Henry Fonda and Elizabeth Taylor. His father, meanwhile, was a prominent obstetrician and gynecologist.

(Ironically, his father was not a wrestling fan but according to Ric, as a baby doctor he "delivered wrestling promoter Gary Juster, former National Wrestling Alliance Heavyweight Champion Gene Kiniski's kids [including his son Kelly, who wrestled in the WWF in the 1980s] and Superstar Billy Graham's daughter, Capella.)

"Every year for my birthday, my father would take me to the wrestling matches," wrote Ric in his 2004 autobiography enti-tled: "To Be the Man." "I loved watching the old American Wrestling Association (AWA), based in Minneapolis, and remember seeing guys like Verne Gagne, Bobo Brazil, Ray Stevens, and Red Bastien. I liked the interviews better than the matches, especially when the Crusher was on. Reggie 'Crusher' Lisowski called himself 'the man who made Milwaukee famous,' and claimed that he trained by running with a beer keg on each shoulder and dancing with fat Polish women afterward. He was a big, barrel-chested guy who called chubby girls his 'dollies,' and his opponents 'sissies' and 'turkey necks.' Sometimes he and his tag-team partner, Dick the Bruiser, seemed to get so excited after winning a match — Crusher liked to use the Bolo Punch and Stomach Claw — that they'd start slugging each other."

Ric went on to attend Golden Valley Junior High School, where, among other things, he proved to be no angel. Once, in eighth grade, he and his buddy Piper stole a car and drove some girls to a dance at the Hopkins Roller Rink. "It was something like thirty below zero and I didn't know how to work the car," he said in his book, "so when I turned on the air-conditioning instead of the heater, I completely froze the engine block."

Another time he and Piper took his dad's car over to where some girls were having a slumber party. They snuck a few out in their pajamas and eventually got busted by the cops. "The police had to contact the girls' families, and one of the fathers was so irate that he wanted to press charges," said Ric. "It was Father's Day morning when my dad arrived at the jail. 'Happy Father's Day,' I said. 'Thanks,' he grumbled, and took me home."

"Over time, my little scrapes with the law also began accumulating. I got caught riding our motorcycle around the lake (without a license) while my parents were out of town," he said. "Then I got busted trying to use a phony ID at a liquor store. It all became too much for my parents, so they decided that I'd be better off in boarding school."

So, after completing the ninth grade, Ric's parents enrolled him at the prestigious Wayland Academy in Beaver Dam, Wis., which specialized in "hard-to-handle" teenagers.

"My academics still sucked, but I lettered in three sports," he continued. "I played middle linebacker and fullback on the football team, threw the shot put, and wrestled, first at 181 pounds and then as a heavyweight. In both 1966 and 1967, I was state private school wrestling champion. Since the drinking age in Wisconsin was eighteen, it was easy to get into bars with a fake ID. It took me five years to graduate from high school, but thanks to my athletic credentials, colleges were still interested in me."

During the Summer, Ric felt the need to "get away and see the sites…"

"Every spring break, the General (his best friend) and I would hitchhike to Florida," he wrote. "I'd come home to Minnesota and tell my parents that I was going to stay with the General's family for a few days. Then, after my parents dropped me off at the train station in Minneapolis, I'd start hitching in twenty-below-zero weather until I ended up in Fort Lauderdale. When we were sixteen, we rented an apartment upstairs from a beauty salon. For the whole week, the General did the owner, while I did her daughter."

"I'm sure that if I attended school now, I'd be diagnosed with attention deficit hyperactivity disorder, ADHD," he added. "I was the epitome of the disease. I couldn't concentrate and kept getting into trouble for not listening. No one ever said that I wasn't intellectually gifted. I just couldn't slow down enough to read or study."

Ric eventually graduated and went on to attend his parents' alma mater, the University of Minnesota, in 1968. There, he played freshman football as an offensive guard. He was good enough to make the varsity, but his academics were just not up to par. He had other concerns, like girls and his new fraternity, Phi Delta Theta. There, he became pals with another football player named Mike Goldberg, who had a kid brother named Bill, who would later go on to become a megastar in the world of professional wrestling. So, after a year of non-stop partying in the Animal House, Ric wound up dropping out. The kid simply had bigger plans.

From there, Ric decided that he wanted to follow his dream and become a pro wrestler. He had been bouncing in a bar in Minneapolis when he met Olympic weightlifter and wrestler Ken Patera, who introduced him to Verne Gagne. Verne liked the kids size and loved his cocky attitude. So, he invited him to attend his training camp, where he whipped him into shape out at his old barn alongside Patera, Greg Gagne, Jim Brunzell, Bob Bruggers and Kosrow Vaziri. There, Verne beat the hell of them and got them ready for the big-time.

Finally, on December 10, 1972, "Rick Flair," as he was now known, made his debut with the AWA against George "Scrap Iron" Gadaski in Rice Lake, Wis., earning a draw. It would be the beginning of an amazing career which would span the next four decades.

Two years later, the "Nature Boy" Ric Flair (he also dropped the "k" from his first name) left the AWA and headed for the NWA's Mid Atlantic territory. There, with his boyish good looks and arrogant personality, Flair, got a big push from booker Wahoo McDaniel and wound up beating Paul Jones to win the NWA Mid Atlantic Television title. He had officially arrived. Then, in the midst of all of his new found success, his career and his life almost came to an end when the plane he was flying in, along with Johnny Valentine, Bob Bruggers and Tim Woods, crashed in rural North Carolina.

"The travel was really tough back then so I had this idea that a bunch of us could team up and use this plane, for a few hundred dollars a day," Flair later recalled. "It turns out that the plane on that day was seriously overloaded, and there was hardly any fuel either, so we couldn't turn back and then I heard this sound, it was like the engines were popping and they just died. They were gone, and we crashed. The lack of fuel probably saved my life. It was terrible. Johnny Valentine, one of the greats in wrestling, was paralyzed from the waist down and the pilot was killed."

Flair, who broke his back in three places, incredibly returned to the ring within six months and just a short time later teamed up with Greg "the Hammer" Valentine to beat Gene and Ole Anderson to win the NWA Tag Team title. Over the next five years he would go on to win five NWA United States Heavyweight titles over the likes of Bobo Brazil, Mr. Wrestling, Ricky Steamboat, Greg Valentine and Jimmy Snuka. Throughout the 1980s Flair emerged as a serious A-list entertainer. He was traveling the world and living the life of a rock star. He wrestled hard, and he partied hard. The guys hated him and the ladies loved him. His flamboyant act was just as over-the-top outside the ring as well. In fact, he even bought a limousine and hired his own chauffer to driver him around.

Over the next decade Flair, with his signature "Figure Four Leg Lock" finishing move, would win, lose, and re-claim the NWA World Heavyweight belt no less than seven times. Among his victims included: Dusty Rhodes and Harley Race (twice), Kerry von Erich, Ron Garvin and Ricky Steamboat. He would also become a member of the controversial "4-Horsemen" during this time as well, which made for some outstanding television ratings along the way.

In 1991 Flair defeated Sting to win his eighth NWA World Title. Then, when the NWA disbanded and formed World Championship Wrestling, Flair was recognized as the first WCW Heavyweight Champ. Later that year, however, Flair got into a spat with Dusty Rhodes, the top booker for WCW at that time, and wound up leaving the promotion to join with the rival World Wrestling Federation. There, under the tutelage of "manager" Bobby "The Brain" Heenan and "consultant" Curt Hennig, Flair made his presence felt in a hurry. On January 19, 1992, at the Royal Rumble in Albany, New York, Flair battled 29 other WWF superstars for more than an hour to win the WWF World Title.

Over the decade of the '90s, Flair won the WCW World Title on nine different occasions, beating the likes of Vader, Ricky Steamboat, Randy Savage, Konnan, Hulk Hogan, Jeff Jarrett and Kevin Nash. During that time, Flair traveled from coast to coast and around the world. At times he suffered serious injuries and oftentimes bloodied himself in the process, but as all good entertainers know, "the show must go on." In addition, the drama of his 4-Horsemen versus the NWO was a huge hit internationally, and the fans ate it up.

By 2001 Flair was competing in Vince McMahon's rival World Wrestling Entertainment, proving that he still indeed had it going on. Then, at Armageddon 2003, he and Batista defeated The Dudley Boyz to capture the WWE World Tag Team titles. After losing the straps later that year, the duo beat Booker T & RVD to regain them yet again. Amazingly, at 55 years of age, Ric Flair was still going strong and hanging in there with kids such as Brock Lesnar, who were half his age. And, speaking of kids, Flair's two kids, David and Reid, have also followed their old man into the ring — even tagging with him on occasion for pay-per-view spectacles.

Yup, the old timer is still at the top of his game, but knows it could all be taken away in an instant, which is why he doesn't ever take what he has for granted.

"For the last fifteen years or so, I've been told that I'm the greatest professional wrestler who ever lived," Flair said in his book. "Better than Frank Gotch or Lou Thesz, Bruno Sammartino or Verne Gagne, Gorgeous George or Hulk Hogan. Ric Flair can call himself a sixteen-time world champion. Ric Flair went on the road and wrestled every single day — twice on Saturday, twice on Sunday, every birthday, every holiday, every anniversary — for twenty straight years. I've spent more than thirty years of my life — some days good, some bad — trying to prove to myself, to my peers, and to the fans who paid anywhere from five to five hundred dollars that I could be the best at what I chose to do for a living. "When you have no equal in professional wrestling, you have no equal in the sports world. Because — despite what outsiders may think — we are not ninjas or warriors. We are a special breed who can withstand pain, exhaustion, and injury without ever coming up for air. There is no off-season in our business, and we're the toughest athletes alive.

"In the ring, I've always been at home. It's what lurks outside of it that scares me. For every legitimate punch I've ever taken to the head, every bone I've ever dislocated or every chair that's been bent across my spine, nothing can be as ruthless as the political sabotage inside the dressing room or promoter's office. While fans were saying that I could have a five-star match with anyone at any time, behind the scenes I'd be called an old piece of sh*t that didn't understand the public, couldn't read ratings, and deserved to be bankrupted along with my family.

"These weren't things I heard once or twice; it went on for years. And after a while, it almost broke me. I felt myself losing the Ric Flair strut and, in many ways, my joy for life. When I came to World Wrestling Entertainment in late 2001 after spending most of my career representing the competition, I didn't know if the wrestlers liked or respected me, or knew about my legacy. Hell, I began to wonder if I even had a legacy at all."

"To be the man, you've gotta beat the man, I'd said that so many times, taunting my opponents while I shoved my title into the camera," Flair added. "Well, I am still 'Slick Ric,' 'Secretariat in Disguise,' a kiss-stealing, wheeling, dealing, jet-flying, limousine-riding son-of-a-gun." "The bottom line is this," he concludes, "Space Mountain may be the oldest ride in the park... but it still has the longest line."

The fact that Ric Flair has been a survivor for more than 30 years in this business is nothing short of remarkable. The ultimate ring psychologist, Flair has never been the biggest wrestler, nor the most talented — but no one can question the fact that he is without a doubt the ultimate showman. Nobody sells a bump like he does and nobody has more fun. Love him or hate him, as a babyface or as a heel, Ric Flair is a one of a kind.

Presently, Flair lives in Charlotte, where he is remarried with children. He continues to wrestle and, among other things, owns a chain of "Ric Flair's Gold's Gyms" throughout North Carolina. He also recently wrote a best-selling autobiography entitled: "To Be The Man." In it he pulls no punches about the mistakes he's made in real life. His success in professional wrestling cost him his first wife and, for many years, his relationship with his old-

est children. He drank a lot and drove too fast, but he is tough and that is what has made him a survivor.

Additionally, it has long been rumored that Flair, like his old buddy Jesse Ventura, may run for governor of North Carolina as a Republican. Stay tuned on that one. With his patented "Woooooo!", Ric Flair is indeed "The Man."

DAVID FLAIR

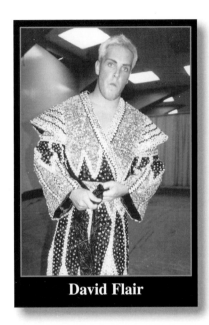

David Flair

David Flair was born and raised in Minneapolis, where he lived with his mother, ultimately graduating from Hopkins High School in the late 1990s. The son of Ric "Nature Boy" Flair, it was no surprise when David decided to follow his old man into the ring. And, while he is not quite the showman that his father is, he has quietly climbed the ladder. In fact, he has spent the last several years working in the world of professional wrestling and has even appeared in the ring with his father for the WWE as well. Whether it was shaving his father's head on a pay-per-view special or pinning WWE exec Eric Bischoff during a Nitro taping, Flair has already made a name for himself. Among his accolades in the ring, he won the WCW United States Heavyweight Champion in 1999; WCW World Tag-Team Championship alongside Crowbar in 2000; NWA World Tag-Team title with Dan Factor in 2001; NWA Georgia Tag-Team Champion with Romeo Bliss in 2001; and won the IWA Intercontinental Heavyweight Champion in 2003 as well.

RIC RUDE

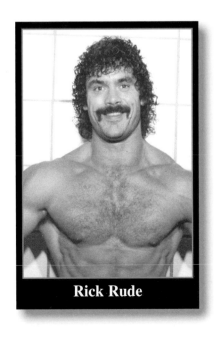

Rick Rude

Richard Erwin Rood was born in 1958 and grew up in Robbinsdale. His best friend growing up was a kid by the name of Curt Hennig, the son of local wrestling legend, Larry "The Axe" Hennig. Together, the two did a lot of hunting and fishing, and loved playing sports. Robbinsdale High School would prove to be a pro wrestling factory, having first been the original stomping grounds of Verne Gagne — one of Rick's early idols. Incredibly, along with Hennig, among Rick's high school buddies were Tom Zenk, Dean Peters,

The Robbinsdale Connection

Maybe it's the water? Robbinsdale High School has produced a boat-load of future pro wrestlers over the years starting with the living legend, Verne Gagne, who won a pair of state high school championships with the Robins back in 1942 &1943, when the team was in the midst of winning seven straight titles from 1940-46. From there, Larry "The Axe" Hennig followed suit by winning a state title of his own in 1954. By 1976 Rick Rood (aka "Ravishing Rick Rude"), Dean Peters (aka "Brady Boone") and Tom Zenk had all graduated, with Curt Hennig (aka "Mr. Perfect"), finishing his last year of high school in Arizona. In addition, over the next two years they would be joined by the likes of John Nord (aka "Nord the Barbarian"), Steve Simpson (aka "Nikita Koloff") and Barry Darsow (aka "Smash Demolition").

John Nord, Nikita Koloff and Barry Darsow — all future pro grapplers.

After graduating in 1976, Rick, went on to earn a physical education degree from Anoka Ramsey Junior College. During that time, he also worked as a bouncer at Gramma B's, a notoriously tough biker bar in Northeastern Minneapolis. There, he worked alongside Hawk and Animal of Road Warriors fame, as well as Barry Darsow. Rick quickly earned a reputation for being a really tough bad-ass. (In fact, he was so strong that he would go on to compete in the National Arm Wrestling Championships as well as various Tough Man contests, and even had a 2-0 record as an amateur boxer training under Papa Joe Daszciewicz.)

As fate would have it, a bartender at Gramma B's during that time was local wrestling trainer Eddie Sharkey, who agreed to train the burly bouncers the tricks of the trade. Sharkey saw thier potential and got them enrolled in his wrestling school. Rick, who had quit his job at the bar by this time to train full-time, was borrowing cash from his friends. He barely had enough money for gas and was sleeping in his car in order to pay for his lessons. He was determined to make it though, and he pushed ahead.

"You can talk about this and that guy being a great shooter," Sharkey would later say. "But this guy (Rude) kicked more ass than any of them. People didn't realize how tough this guy was. He'd slap guys with an open hand and it looked like their head exploded."

At Sharkey's camp Rick excelled. And, as luck would have it, Ole Anderson, who was a booker with Georgia Championship Wrestling at the time, was looking for new talent, so he brought Rick in. He was given a minor push right out of the gates with the gimmick of being the "toughest bouncer in Minneapolis." His debut match was in 1983 for a promotion in Vancouver, and from there he competed around Atlanta. His push didn't last long though and he was sent packing to the Carolinas, where he worked as jobber for Jim Crockett, and later in the Mid-South territory, where he wrestled as an undercard babyface.

From there, he hit the big time by appearing in the Memphis region for Jerry Jarrett. There, Jarrett would change his name to "Ravishing Rick Rude" and had him take on a flamboyant lady-killer personality. He would even enter the ring donning sparkly robes to the song "Smooth Operator." He also turned into a heel and was appointed a valet, Angel, who was very easy on the eyes. As he entered the ring he would yell, "Cut the music!" and berate the audience while flexing for all to see. The women would take pictures and the men would boo like hell.

With his movie star good looks and buffed bod, he was a big hit. And, with his arrogant personality and brash style, he was very hateable — which was exactly what the doctor ordered. Managed by Jimmy Hart and part of Hart's First Family, Rude went on to beat Jerry Lawler for the AWA Southern Heavyweight title. He held it for a little over a month before losing it to Tommy Rich.

A few months later he won the AWA Southern Tag Team title with partner King Kong Bundy by defeating The Fabulous Ones. He had arrived.

From there, Rude, now managed by Percy Pringle, headed to Florida, where he won the Southern Heavyweight Championship belt over Wahoo McDaniel. By late 1985 Rude was in Texas, where he took the World Class Championship Wrestling World Heavyweight crown, winning via DQ against Bruiser Brody. That next year, after wrestling on TBS TV for Jim Crockett's NWA promotion, he left abruptly to join Vince McMahon's rival WWF. He had emerged as the NWA World Tag Team Champion alongside Manny Fernandez in the NWA, but he wanted a change of scenery so he bailed.

In the WWF Rude found moderate success and was even billed as an undercard for several months. After battling with Jake "The Snake" Roberts on several occasions, however, he later joined up with manager Bobby "The Brain" Heenan, which gave him a whole new angle. After beating the Ultimate Warrior for the Intercontinental Championship at WrestleMania V, Rude was elevated to the top of most cards. But, after suffering a torn triceps and later getting into a contract dispute with McMahon over money, he ultimately quit the WWF. It was a bold move.

With that, Rude worked the independent circuit as well as in Japan until his WWF contract expired. Then, in 1991, he debuted with WCW as the masked "Halloween Phantom." There, using his "Rude Awakening" finishing move, he beat his old high school pal, Tom Zenk. A few weeks later he beat Sting to capture the U.S. title, thanks to a little outside interference from Lex Luger. He wound up vacating the title, however, after suffering a severe back injury.

By the early 1990s Rude was one of pro wrestling's top heels and biggest draws. In fact, he ended up making the finals of the coveted G-1 Tournament, and remains the first and only American to ever be booked into the finals of Japan's biggest yearly tournament. In 1994, on a Japanese tour, Rude Rude took a bad bump during a match when he caught a flying press from Sting and re-injured his neck and back. It was a serious injury and one that effectively ended Rude's career as a wrestler.

For the next three years, Rude enjoyed life and spent as much time as possible with his three children living in Tampa. Finally, in 1997, he resurfaced and signed on with ECW as a television announcer. A short while later he made up with McMahon and rejoined the WWF as a member of Degeneration X. But, the drama would continue when, after WrestleMania XIV, Rude left the WWF yet again to rejoin the WCW — following another contract dispute. There, he was pegged as a new heel announcer for the NWO and even managed his old pal, Curt Hennig, but contract problems and a television interview spat surfaced and Rude bolted. Rude actually appeared on a live "Nitro" episode as well as on a pre-taped episode of "Raw" on the same night — a big no-no between the two rival organizations.

So, he chilled out for a while and waited for his contract to expire yet again. He figured that if he could work out his Lloyds of London insurance settlement, there might be a shot at a comeback. In the meantime, however, in addition to building a new house, he was training hard to get back into the ring. Then, tragically, on April 20th, 1999, Rick died of an apparent of a heart attack in his hometown of Rome, Georgia. Survived by his wife, Michelle, and their three children, he was just 40 years old.

A consummate showman and a true icon in the business, Rick Rude was a one of a kind with his own style. An amazing entertainer and athlete, he will dearly be missed by his legions of loyal fans.

SCOTT NORTON

Scott Norton

Scott Norton grew up in the Twin Cities and went on to attend local legend Eddie Sharkey's wrestling school in the late 1970s. There, Norton trained in the basement of a south Minneapolis church alongside future wrestling stars such as "Ravishing Rick Rude," Barry Darsow (aka "Smash of Demolition") and the "Road Warriors." At six-foot-three and more than 350 pounds, Norton was a giant, and stronger than an ox. In fact, he initially made a name for himself in another type of wrestling altogether — arm wrestling, where he became a superstar. There, Norton held over 30 arm wrestling titles, including four U.S. National Championships. Norton, who has won tournaments with both his left and right arms, gained notoriety early on in his career when he appeared in the Sylvester Stallone arm wrestling movie, "Over the Top."

From there, Norton got into professional wrestling full-time. He refined his skills with local trainer Brad Rheingans and made his ring debut in 1988 versus his old buddy, Wayne Bloom, in Verne Gagne's AWA. Norton got his nickname "Flash" by winning matches so quickly. After a stint in the AWA, he headed west, to grapple in the NWA's Pacific Northwest territory and in 1990 won the PNW Heavyweight Title. There, he also teamed with fellow Minnesotan, John Nord, to form the duo known as the "Lumberjacks."

With his "Power Bomb" and "Shoulder Breaker" finishing moves, Norton was a big hit. From there, he headed overseas, to Japan, where he found stardom. He became a main attraction there with his brute strength and raw speed. In 1992, he teamed with Tony Halme to win the IWGP Tag Team Championship, defeating the Steiner Brothers. Later, after losing the belt, he teamed up with Hercules Hernandez to form the "Jurassic Powers," and together they won the belts back from the Hell Raisers in 1993.

In 1995 Norton came to WCW, where he teamed with Ice Train as a duo called "Fire & Ice," and later became one of the initial members of the New World Order. He also teamed with Marcus "Buff" Bagwell numerous times as Vicious 'N' Delicious, until Bagwell's neck was injured in 1998. He then wrestled mostly singles, where, despite having success, did not receive a big push from the powers-that-be. So, he headed back to Japan, where he had already achieved a level of notoriety. After winning the IWGP World Title, Norton came home to wrestle again in the WCW, this time as a member of the Black 'n' White. From there, he returned to Japan, winning the IWGP World Heavyweight Title yet again in 2001 — becoming just the third American to hold the coveted crown, alongside Hulk Hogan and Vader.

One of Minnesota's finest, Norton, who presently resides in Georgia, continues to entertain his fans throughout the world.

SCOTT LEDOUX

Scott Ledoux

Scott LeDoux grew up in Crosby-Ironton during the 1950s, loving sports and loving life. He played basketball in high school, but his passion was boxing. Scott got into the sport as a young-ster and went on to become one of Minnesota's most cele-brated athletes. During the late 1970s and early '80s, LeDoux was ranked among the top heavy-weight contenders in the world. During that time he was in the ring with 11 world champions (three of them were exhibitions) and brought two heavy-weight championship fights to Minnesota, one against Mike Weaver in 1978 and the other against Larry Holmes in 1980. While LeDoux didn't win any title belts, he did manage two draws, against Leon Spinks and Ken Norton.

One of the highlights of his illustrious career, however, came in 1978, when he saw his name on the marquis of New York City's famed Madison Square Garden, where he beat Pedro Soto in a 10-round decision. Over the years he fought them all, from Muhammed Ali to George Foreman to Frank Bruno.

"I have had a lot of fun over the years," said Scott. "I think I have served Minnesota well and have put us on the map many times over my career. I still get national recognition, which is good for our state — and it hasn't been because I have been in jail or any-thing else bad that you see with a lot of athletes nowadays. I have had a great life, seen the world through sports, and met so many wonderful people. You know, I have been in the ring with 11 heavy-weight champs. The good news is I have never been knocked out... the bad news is I remember everything!"

LeDoux retired from the boxing ring in the mid-1980s, and from there jumped right into the wrestling ring.

"Verne Gagne and I were friends and he asked me to be a 'special referee' in some of his matches," said Scott, who wound up wrestling about 150 pro matches over the next three and a half years. "I did, and from there it just grew and grew until I was offi-cially one of the guys. I wrestled Larry Zybysko quite a bit over the years, and he was a lot of fun to work with. My finishing move was a solid right to the chin, and that was no gimmick either! It was just a neat thing to do at the time and I enjoyed it for the most part.

"You know, the wrestling was a lot of fun, but it was the travel that really wore me down. People have no idea how much traveling is involved in that business. They schedule those guys just about every night of the week in a different town every night. I can seriously remember waking up a few times and not knowing what city I was in. It was just a blur we traveled so much. I don't miss that part of it at all. I really enjoyed being with the guys though. Most of them were really good people to hang around with. I used to travel with Curt Hennig, Scott Hall and Nick Bockwinkel quite a bit, and we had some great times on those road trips together. I had a great deal of respect for Nick, he was probably my favorite guy to be with. He had some great stories and was really a class act."

Scott's life changed drastically in 1989 when his wife, Sandy, sadly passed away. He had two young children at the time and needed to take care of his family. So, he hung up the tights for good and headed home. His view on the business would change over the next 15 years.

"Pro wrestling was a lot of fun," said Scott. "But it was not a sport, it was a form of entertainment. They do a great job at what they do, no question. I will also say that there are a lot of outstanding athletes in the business too. And when you are in that ring, you surely take your share of bumps and bruises. I remember being in battle-royals and getting thrown over the top rope and landing on the concrete below. That was not very fun at all. People think that kind of stuff is fake too, and I can assure you, it wasn't! As far as wrestling today, it is very entertaining, but way too sexual. So, it is not the family type entertainment that it used to be, but a lot of people certainly find it enjoyable."

From there, Scott got into a whole bunch of good stuff, including training local fighters from around the area. He also became very involved in civic issues and, in addition to serving on the Minnesota Racing Commission, he also served on the Minnesota Boxing Commission for more than 18 years until it was abolished as well. Later, in the '90s, Scott was in such good physical condition that he trained with Mike Tyson for a few months, and in 2001 he even got back into the ring with Lennox Lewis as part of a piece he did for ESPN. In fact, he was so good on TV that he became a regular fight commentator for ESPN and presently serves as an analyst for Friday Night Fights on ESPN2. Among Scott's other hobbies, he has also worked with several Minnesota Wild hockey enforcers, training them on the finer points of how to throw a punch.

After nearly four decades in the boxing business, however, Scott's greatest passion by far, is working with charitable organizations. In fact, he has done literally thousands of charity events over the past 20 years and is deeply involved with the Make a Wish Foundation, Special Olympics and the American Cancer Society, among others.

"For me it is all about giving back," said Scott. "I love working with charities and I love working with kids, that is just horrendous fun. It humbles me even more to realize how blessed I have been in this life."

And, if that weren't enough, in the Summer of 2004, LeDoux even stepped into the political ring, when he announced that he was running for the Anoka County Board. I guess we'll have to stay tuned to see if Scott has any "Jesse-like" political ambitions in the future! Presently, in addition to doing television commentating, Scott is also in the real estate business and resides in Andover with his second wife, Carol.

he was crowned as the PWA Light-Heavyweight champ, however, it would be the first of many belts for Waltman.

Although small, Waltman was quick and very strong, instantly becoming one of the biggest fan-favorites on the circuit. From there, he joined the upstart Global Wrestling Federation, where, in 1991, he defeated Jerry Lynn to be crowned the inaugural GWF World junior-heavyweight champion. His next step was to go overseas, to Japan and later Mexico, to gain more experience. Then, Waltman caught a break when the world of professional wrestling began to spin out of control with regards to steroid problems. The over inflated physiques which had become all the rage in the business were now revealed to be chemically enhanced by illegal drugs. As a result, a new focus was put on technical ability, skill and athleticism — all of which Waltman had in spades. After all, his charisma and tenacity more than made up for his lack of girth.

So, he came back to the States and began wrestling as "The Kamikaze Kid," "The Cannonball Kid" and eventually just "The Kid." The WWF gave him a push and when he upset superstar "Razor Ramon" on the nationally televised show "Monday Night Raw," he knew that he had arrived. His new name: "The 1-2-3 Kid," was in honor of his huge win. Waltman had gone from being a preliminary unknown to a bona fide contender overnight and just kept riding the wave from there. He eventually left the WWF in 1996 and joined WCW as a member of the New World Order. There, he was renamed "Syxx," a play on his "1-2-3 Kid" ring name (1+2+3=6 or "Syxx"). Waltman kicked off his new digs by beating Chris Jericho at Halloween Havoc, and then went on to win the WCW World cruiserweight title at Super Brawl VII, against Dean Malenko. Then, after breaking his neck during a match, Waltman was forced to take a year off.

When he came back, however, he was no longer the babyfaced good guy that he had always been. Instead, he reemerged as a bearded rebel named "X-Pac." He then joined Triple H to form the tag-team "Degeneration X." It would be the first of several gimmicks for Waltman, who, with his signature "X-Factor" finishing move, would go on to win numerous other WWF World Tag-Team, Cruiserweight and European championships over the next several years as well. From there, Waltman hit the NWA, TNA and Japanese circuits as "Syxx-Pac," because the WWE wouldn't let him use the "X-Pac" name. There, he continues to entertain his legions of fans, all the while still calling Minnesota his home.

SEAN WALTMAN

Sean Waltman

Although originally from Florida, Sean Waltman left home when he was just 17 years old to follow his dream, to become a professional wrestler. So, he packed his bags and came to Minnesota, where he learned the ropes from legendary trainer, Eddie Sharkey. Before long he was grappling as "The Lightning Kid" in the Prairie Wrestling Alliance (PWA). He made little money at first, even eating at a Catholic mission with homeless people to get by early on. In 1990

ADNON AL-KAISSY

Sheik Adnon Al-Kaissy

Born in 1939, Adnon Al-Kaissy grew up in the Iraqi city of Tikrit. Several members of his family were prominent sheiks and his uncle, a Sunni Muslim, was one of the most important religious leaders in the country at one point. One of Al-Kaissy's neighborhood acquaintances was none other than Saddam Hussein. They played sports on rival teams and grew up together. They eventually went their separate ways, with Saddam going into the military, and Al-Kaissy coming to the United States to pursue a higher education — a common practice for many Iraqi elite. An accomplished amateur wrestler in Iraq, Al-Kaissy wound up at Oklahoma State University, where he earned All-America honors wrestling on two national championship teams and even played college football — a game he had never heard of prior to coming to America. From there he got into professional wrestling, performing mostly throughout the Pacific Northwest, and during that time also earned his Masters degree in Education and Psychology from Portland State University. During the early 1960s, he even earned a trio of NWA Pacific Northwest Tag Team titles, along with a Texas Heavyweight title using the moniker "Chief Billy White Wolf."

In 1969 Al-Kaissy returned to Baghdad to visit his family, inadvertently sealing his own fate in the process. You see, by now Saddam had become a military dictator and was essentially in charge of the country. His Baath Party basically took over and pushed President Ahmed Hassan Al Bakr aside. So, when Saddam heard that Al-Kaissy was home from America, he summoned him and instructed him to wrestle for Iraq. He knew that Al-Kaissy was a local hero and wanted to use him to inspire a sense of nationalism during a time of turmoil. The choice was simple, either stay and wrestle or be shot. Of course, Al-Kaissy stayed and before long became one of the most recognizable figures throughout the entire Middle East. Al-Kaissy's athletic style of pro wrestling was new to the area and the locals loved it. They, as well as Saddam, were also totally convinced that it was real — which proved to be an interesting challenge for Al-Kaissy at times as he set up and choreographed the matches with foreign wrestlers from abroad. Saddam enjoyed watching Al-Kaissy and often told him before his matches to "be victorious… or else."

Al-Kaissy became a sort of modern day rock star. Thousands of fans followed him wherever he went and each night hundreds of admirers literally camped outside his home. His matches, which were held in Baghdad's Al Shaab soccer stadium, drew more than 200,000 fans. One match in particular,

The Iron Sheik, Sgt. Slaughter & Sheik Adnon Al-Kaissy

as part of the Iraqi military's golden anniversary celebration, featured Al-Kaissy taking on the seven-foot-four, 500 pound behemoth, "Andre the Giant." Foreign dignitaries from around the world were flown in to witness the event and more than 400,000 fans crowded inside and outside the stadium to watch the festivities. When Al-Kaissy finally won the dramatic match, the fans celebrated in typical Iraqi fashion, by wildly shooting their rifles in the air. Insanity ensued amidst the mayhem. The stories surrounding this event are simply amazing.

As a result of his success, Al-Kaissy was given riches, a new palace, women (President Al Bakr's daughter even proposed marriage to him) and also a prominent position within the Baath Party as the Director at the Ministry of Youth. Saddam was tightening his noose around the Iraqi people and was using wrestling to unite the masses in order to divert attention away from his murderous regime. Al-Kaissy, meanwhile, was stuck right in the middle of it all with no way out. As Saddam was rising in power, Al-Kaissy witnessed horrible brutality towards his fellow citizens. Widespread killings and savage torture were all part of Saddam's master plan and anyone not on board was considered an enemy. Daily executions were becoming commonplace and Al-Kaissy, who yearned for a taste of the Western culture that he had left years ago, was willing to do whatever it took to get back to the States.

After several years, Al-Kaissy's popularity became a liability to Saddam and his giant ego. Once a hero, he was now seen as a threat. Saddam's country was in crisis and a war with neigh-

boring Iran was just over the horizon. Fearful for his life, Al-Kaissy left more than $2 million in the bank and fled the country via Kuwait. Dodging snipers and assassins, he bribed his way out and never looked back. With no money and no one to turn to, he made his way to America, where he would be forced to start over. Knowing that his family would be in danger, he knew that he could never go back.

In the U.S. Al-Kaissy got back into professional wrestling and rose to stardom again during the late 1970s. At first he dressed up as his previous character from the 1960s, a Native American Indian using the moniker "Chief Billy White Wolf." He first gained notoriety wrestling in Hawaii, eventually earning the Hawaiian and WWWF Tag Team titles along the way. Eventually, in 1981, Al-Kaissy moved to Minnesota, home of promoter Verne Gagne's American Wrestling Association. There, he took on a new persona, "The Sheik," and was billed as a tough Arabian madman. With tensions running high following the Iranian hostage crisis, his notoriety as a villain grew quickly. The fans loved to hate him and he was enjoying moderate success out on the circuit. In 1987 he teamed up with Jerry Blackwell and converted him to "Sheik Ayatollah Blackwell," and together they emerged as one of the promotion's top heel tag-team title contenders..

Al-Kaissy became a mainstay in the AWA and wrestled around the country throughout the 1980s until eventually getting injured and going into semi-retirement. From there, Al-Kaissy got into managing, however, and the list of wrestlers who he managed over the years reads like a venerable who's-who of the wrestling world, including: Jerry Blackwell, Ken Patera, Sgt. Slaughter, Sheik El Domonte, Desert Fox, Masked Jungle Fighter, King Kong Brody, Nord The Barbarian, Boris Zhukov, Masked Superstar, Colonel Mustafa, Bob Orton, Mr. Hughes and Manny Fernandez, among others.

Later, following the Gulf War during the early 1990s, Al-Kaissy seized the opportunity to make a come-back. In a stroke of controversial marketing and promotional genius, Al-Kaissy, who could not compete any more as a full-fledged wrestler, changed his persona from the "Sheik" to "General Adnon," a mustached character dressed in military fatigues who looked strikingly similar to Saddam. As the "General," Al-Kaissy would serve as the ring-side manager of Sgt. Slaughter, a no-nonsense U.S. Army drill sergeant who had "fallen under Al-Kaissy's spell." The fans ate it up as the drama overseas continued to unfold. Whenever the duo hit the mat the fans shook their fists and booed mercilessly as Slaughter marched to General Adnon's orders like some sort of brainwashed hostage who had lost his soul.

The duo stayed hot for about two years with Slaughter eventually winning the WWF championship belt at the 1991 pay-per-view spectacle, Wrestlemania VII. There, he and Slaughter battled Hulk Hogan in front of millions of fans to the chants of "USA! — USA!". Things got heated after that, however, when Al-Kaissy started to wave the Iraqi flag at matches. He even presented Slaughter with a pair of special Iraqi army boots as a "gift" one time, supposedly from Saddam himself. Eventually Al-Kaissy got a real-life call from a high-level government official from Washington telling him to knock it off. They were concerned that he may ensue a riot — or even get himself shot. They did not have to tell him twice. The script was finally changed to where Sgt. Slaughter slowly reclaimed his own identity from the evil general and came to his senses just in the knick of time.

With that, Al-Kaissy, now an American citizen, settled down and returned to the quiet life of a semi-retired suburban family man here in Minnesota. He stayed in the wrestling business and eventually founded the World All-Star Wrestling Alliance, along with fellow grappler Ken Patera, promoting local shows throughout the Midwest and also developing up and coming talent for the larger circuits.

He is also a member of the local Lions Club and even organizes charity wrestling events for various causes, including the families of the victims of the Sept. 11th attacks. Following those tragic events he even offered his services to the U.S. government to work as an interpreter and to do his part to help bring the terrorists to justice. Today Al-Kaissy has two children and resides with his wife in Minnetonka.

Now in his 60s, Al-Kaissy still gets in the ring every now and then, performing as both a manager and also as "The Sheik" in small towns around Minnesota — entertaining the locals while still holding on to his passion. Most importantly, Al-Kaissy has a message about true Muslims being peace-lovers and that he is a proud American. He loves his country and thanks to the efforts of the U.S. forces, he now has the opportunity to return home and see his family one more time. He also has a dream of one day wrestling again in Al Shaab Stadium in front of thousands of now free Iraqis — knowing that he will never have to worry about Saddam, or his murderous sons, Odai and Qusai, ever again.

"It was an amazing journey, coming from Iraq to the United States," said Adnon. "I was very fortunate to have had the opportunity to wrestle and play football in college here, and then to have gotten into the professional wrestling business too. The people here are wonderful and I am very grateful that I have been able to live and work here for so many years. I like Minnesota and had a very enjoyable career here. The fans were always supportive of us and I appreciated that. There were a lot of great times and so many great memories. Those days are gone, but now it is a new chapter to see what has happened back in my native country of Iraq. For so many years it was so bad under Saddam and I can't even begin to say how happy I am that they are finally free. There is a long way to go, there are still many problems there, but it is a great start for sure. I am anxious to one day return home to see my family, I will have so many stories to tell. I can't wait."

SHELTON BENJAMIN

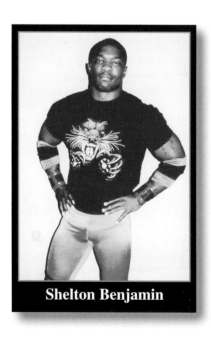

Shelton Benjamin

Shelton Benjamin grew up in Orangeburg, SC, and emerged as a two time South Carolina heavyweight state high school champion in both 1993 and 1994. At six-foot-two and 245 pounds, Benjamin was a monster. Benjamin then went on to become a Junior College national place-winner in 1995, and a JC national champion in 1996 at Lassen Community College in Susunville, CA. From there, Benjamin was recruited by the University of Minnesota, where, in 1998, he posted an outstanding 36-6 record with 12 pins to garner All-American honors.

After graduating, Benjamin became an assistant coach with the Gophers, and also served as a protégé to the team's next heavyweight, a kid by the name of Brock Lesnar. After Brock won the 2000 NCAA National Championship, the two headed to the Ohio Valley Wrestling Association to compete in the WWF's devel-opmental training program. There, the two became tag-team partners known as "The Minnesota Stretching Crew." Less than a year later the duo defeated the "Disciples of Synn" to claim the OVW Tag Team title in Louisville, KY. It would be the first of several for the two muscle-bound powerhouses. With that much success, it was only a matter of time before they were broken up and billed as singles stars.

Brock got a big push early on, however, and rose up to the ranks of the WWE sooner than expected. Benjamin, meanwhile, joined Charlie Haas in the formation of "Team Angle," a WWE tag-team managed by former Olympic wrestling star, Kurt Angle. Then, in 2003, after beating Edge and Chris Benoit, "Team Angle" defeated Los Guerreros to capture the WWE World Tag Team title. Later that same year, after defending the title several times, Benjamin and Haas had a falling out and Shelton left the "The World's Greatest Tag Team" to join Eric Bischoff's "Raw" roster. With his "Shell Shocka" signature finishing move, Benjamin then shocked the wrestling world by first upsetting Triple H in his first "Raw" match, followed by another upset over Ric Flair at Backlash 2004. He had arrived, big-time.

With poise, charisma and tremendous in-ring ability to go along with his amazing athleticism, Shelton Benjamin is clearly destined for stardom in the world of professional wrestling.

STAN MAYSLACK

Stan Mayslack

Stan Mayslack grew up in the heart of Minnesota's Polish community, Northeast Minneapolis. There, big Stan hung around the local gyms and eventually got together with Tony Stecher, Minneapolis' top boxing and wrestling promoter during the 1930s. Stan always dreamt of being a professional wrestler, and his wish finally came true when Tony put him on some local cards to see how he would do. The kid performed like a champ, and at 315 pounds, he was the real deal. With his signature "Indian Death Lock" finishing move, Stan traveled the country entertaining the locals with his own brand of rasslin'. Interestingly, Stan's next door neighbor growing up was none other than Wally Karbo, who, along with Verne Gagne, would later go on to become the main promoter of the American Wrestling Association. It was wrestling destiny.

When Stan finally decided to hang up the leotards, he got into his real passion, eating. That's right, Stan invested wisely and was able to open his own restaurant called, you guess it, "Mayslack's Polka Lounge." (It is still around to this very day up in "Nordeast" Minneapolis!) Famous for their huge juicy garlic-laced roast beef sandwiches, the legendary eatery became a mainstay for the working-class locals who used to line up outside in order to meet Stan and get one of his famous sandwiches. As Stan himself used to say, "Nobody beats Mayslack's meat...", and nobody could be Stan either — he was truly a one-of-a-kind.

STAN KOWALSKI

Stan Kowalski

Born Bert Smith, Stan "Krusher" Kowalski (he changed his name after he got into pro wrestling to that of his grandfather, a Polish immigrant) grew up in Northeast Minneapolis during the Great Depression, the youngest of six children. He loved sports and excelled as a tackle on the football team and as a heavyweight on the wrestling matt at Minneapolis North High School. He left school as a junior in 1943 to join the Navy, where he served during WWII. When he returned home a few years later he took his G.E.D. and then went on to wrestle and play football at the University of Minnesota, mostly as a second-stringer, graduating in 1950 with a degree in Journalism.

From there, Stan decided to pursue a life-long dream of becoming a professional wrestler. So, he hooked up with local promoters, Tony Stecher and Wally Karbo, and got booked onto one of their local NWA cards over in St. Paul. His first match came against big Stan Mayslack, and incredibly, nearly 7,000 more matches would follow over his illustrious 25 year career in the ring.

"Stan handled me like a little baby," joked Kowalski. "He beat me pretty good that night, but that was OK by me. I was just happy to be there. That was so much fun to get into the ring that first time, I knew right then and there that I was hooked."

After spending some time in the Twin Cities, Stan headed to Boston, where, as "Killer Kowalski," he competed for a small promotion on the east coast for about a year. There, he got booked six nights a week and learned the ropes from legendary grappler, Sandor Szabo, a six-time world champ who took him under his wing. That next year he returned home and began training with "Professor" Joe Pazandak, who taught him the virtues of "rough and dirty" wrestling. From that point on Stan turned heel, and as a "bad-guy," his career took off.

Before long, Stan hooked up with Canadian grappler, Tiny Mills, and formed the infamous tag-team duo called "Murder Incorporated." Together the pair traveled the world during the late-1950s, even embarking on a two-year world tour of Australia, Japan and India.

"We wrestled all over the place, even in a packed 80,000 seat soccer stadium in India one time," said Stan. "I remember, I had just gotten a new pair of custom boots over in Japan for $300 bucks and some new tights which cost a fortune as well. That was a lot of money back then, and I was proud as heck of those boots. Anyway, I am walking into this giant stadium all dressed up, looking good, and I see the ring where we are going to perform. Only it's not a wrestling ring, it was a mud-wrestling ring! Oh no! That was a neat time though, and Tiny was a great guy. You know, it got to the point where I could read his mind in the ring and visa versa. We were tough and the fans loved to hate us. We were the best team in the world, you can ask anybody. That was something, let me tell ya."

He and Tiny won a whole bunch of heavyweight titles during the 1950s and were THE heel tag-team duo of the era. Their arch-rival of course, was Verne Gagne, and whoever he teamed up with to battle them. It was always about good versus evil. Later,

when Gagne took over the territory and renamed it as the AWA, Stan changed his name to "Krusher Kowalski," because "Verne didn't want any killers in his promotion." As Krusher, Stan was just as popular as ever and could still pack em' in the seats — which was always the name of the game back in those days. Dressed in his signature black ensemble, Stan was cool as a cucumber in front of the cameras — always trash talking his opponents and bragging about how he was going to pound them to dust.

Stan later headed east, to wrestle in the WWWF, but always found his way home to Minnesota. He and Tiny eventually split after he got married, because he didn't want to do all the traveling anymore. As the years went by and his career progressed, Stan never forgot some of the valuable lessons that he had learned as a young kid just starting out.

"You know, I have always liked helping the young guys," said Stan. "It all comes from a lesson I learned in the ring from a six-time world champ by the name of Jim Londos. We were wrestling in a match one time up in Winnipeg and about 10 minutes into it I said to myself 'Jeez, I can beat this guy anytime I want…' So, I made a move to pin him and the next thing I know I am flat on my back with a broken nose and two black eyes. Jim just looked down at me smiling and says, 'Don't you know when an old timer is trying to help you learn?' From that day on I said to myself if I can help a young guy in any way shape or form, I will. That is why I help kids in schools and in sports to this very day."

By the end of his career, Stan was known simply as "The Big K." One of the most popular fan-favorites of all time, Stan was enjoying life, but feeling the bumps and bruises that had taken their toll over the years. The wear-and-tear of it all had become a grind. Finally, after a stint up in Calgary in 1976, Stan had an epiphany while driving home somewhere in the Dakotas.

"I will never forget it," recalled Stan. "I drove all the way home from Calgary and was just beat. So, I got home and took my gym bag and threw it down in the basement. My wife looks at me and says, 'Hey, you better go get that stuff out of there so I can wash it for your next match…' I just looked at her and said, 'You'll never have to wash it again, I quit.' I was 50 years old, I had been in the business for half my life and it just wasn't any fun anymore. It was tough to fight the young kids for the top matches, which is where the money was. I had simply had enough. "

Twenty five years, 19 world titles, 17 broken noses and more than 6,600 matches later, Big K had had enough. From there, Stan bought a couple of nightclubs, but eventually got tired of that and became a business agent for the restaurant union for the next 10 years. He officially retired in 1994, but it was at that point that he really started to get busy. His next career, as a volunteer, has practically elevated him to sainthood.

In the 20 years since retiring, Kowalski, now 78, has become synonymous with the VFW. Veterans issues are his passion and he fights for them tirelessly. Whether he is driving to Camp Ripley or the Air Force Reserve's 934th Airlift Wing to see off troops headed overseas, serving on the national POW/MIA council, or arranging for VFW posts to host dinners for the families of deployed soldiers, Stan has truly made a difference. As the District Commander, in charge of the 37 Twin Cities Metro Area VFWs, Kowalski has even recruited more than 1,000 members, with seven of them even becoming generals. He is even running for the position of state judge advocate, and may even have his eyes set on the grand daddy of them all — state commander. (Watch out Jesse!)

In addition to his work with the VFW, Stan has also become the Greater Twin Cities United Way's most prolific volunteer speaker (he gave 163 speeches last year alone), helping to generate millions of dollars a year in contributions. He also coordinates ROTC fund drives, 9/11 memorial celebrations and even finds time to help raise money for non-revenue sports at the University of Minnesota as part of their "Save Our Sports" campaign. He has also served on the Spring Lake Park School Board for the past 18 years as well.

And, if that weren't enough, Stan even bought Verne Gagne's old wrestling ring and still travels around with it to promote fundraising events for schools, charities and youth sports organizations. Despite two titanium shoulders and a titanium knee, Stan still looks like he could body-slam with the best of them. After matches he still hangs around to sign autographs and do magic tricks for the kids, just like old times.

Looking back at his amazing career, Stan is nostalgic of the old days, skeptical of the current state of affairs in pro wrestling, but thankful and appreciative to those who rooted for him.

"You know, when Vince McMahon Jr. came out and said that pro wrestling was entertainment and not a sport a few years back, us old guys were devastated," said Stan, who presently lives in Fridley with his wife Cleo. "I mean here is this young guy, kind of the P.T. Barnum of his era, and he says 'I can tell you who will win every match from here on out.' We were all out there busting our butts every night, getting beat up, and then he comes along and says we're all fake, a bunch of phonies. It really hurt us because we had built the sport up based on the fact that we told everybody it was all real. He wanted to make a circus out of it and sure enough, that is exactly what he did. Hey, he made a lot of money, but he hurt a lot of people in the process. His father, Vince Sr., was a good man and took care of the old guys. The kid though, I want nothin' to do with that guy. Nowadays wrestling isn't about wrestling, it is all entertainment. It was different back in our day. But hey, that was then and this is now. I had a wonderful career and met so many wonderful people along the way. Thanks to the people of Minnesota for supporting me over the years, it was all my pleasure."

STEVE OLSONOSKI

Steve Olsonoski

Steve Olsonoski grew up in Edina and went on to play football, hockey and baseball at Edina High School, graduating in 1971. From there, Olsonoski went to Gustavus, where he played football and baseball, and graduated with a teaching degree. He then returned to Edina in 1975, where he and taught physical education and coached for one year at a junior high school before getting laid off a year later.

At that point Olsonoski wasn't quite sure what to do, so he turned to his dad, who just happened to have played Gopher Football back in the late 1940s as a guard, alongside such legends as Leo Nomellini, Billy Bye, Clayton Tonnemaker and Bud Grant. Another one of his teammates back then was a guy by the name of Verne Gagne. The two became good friends and as a result, the Olsonoski family used to vacation every Summer with the Gagnes. Verne was practically like family. So, Steve talked to Verne and he invited him to come out to his training camp in Chanhassen.

"I will never forget that old barn, it was crazy," said Steve. "We worked so damn hard, it was tougher than anything I had ever done before. I remember the first thing that we did when we got there on day one was to get thrown out of the ring. Yeah. Verne wanted to see what you would do and how you would fall. Anyway, the first time I got thrown out I got attacked by a goose which had been nesting under the ring. It was nuts, and he kept doing it, Verne thought it was the funniest thing in the world. So, not only are you getting killed by being tossed out of the ring, but on top of that you had this goose which would come after you once you hit the ground.

"Anyway, I went through that for about three months and finally got my break in 1977 out in Portland, where they sent me to get some seasoning. I remember my first match, it was against Scrap Iron Gadaski. Well, it is just before the match and I am all nervous and I look at the card to see what time I go on, only I don't see my name. So, now I am panicked and I find the promoter to ask him if everything is all right. He says, 'Yeah, everything is OK, but we went ahead and changed your name to 'Mark Hanno,' we just didn't think you were going to draw many Pollocks out here kid…'"

Six months later Steve moved to Hawaii to work for another promotion, where he later became buddies with a flamboyant young grappler by the name of Jesse Ventura. They both returned to Portland a few months later.

"Jesse had lost a 'Loser-Leaves-Town' match in Portland against Jimmy "Superfly" Snuka just prior to his coming to Hawaii," said Steve. "Anyway, when we got back to Portland Jesse had his dramatic re-match with Superfly that first night back. Well, he winds up turning on him that night, and went heel, leaving him in a bloody mess out in the ring. So, that night he calls me up at like two in the morning and says, 'You gotta get over here, a bunch of Samoans are outside my house right now and they're really pissed!'. OK, I head over there in the middle of the night and when I get there I ask him who else is coming. He says, 'so far it's just you and me…', and I am like, 'I am outta here, good luck buddy!'. So, that was my first experience with the Governor, it was classic."

By now it was 1980 and Olsonoski had returned home to Minnesota to wrestle in the AWA. Times were changing though and Steve could see a major power-shift in the making between Vince McMahon's powerful WWF out east against all the other smaller territories everywhere else. Verne, who had an ESPN television deal and had big stars such as Hulk Hogan, was the most attractive rival of them all. Steve could see the writing on the wall.

"You know the downfall of the AWA came when Hulk Hogan left to join McMahon out in New York," said Steve. "You see, Verne started cutting a deal with his wrestlers to do tee-shirts and he was going to kick us back 25% for each one sold of that particular wrestler. Hogan, meanwhile, had an agent and demanded 50%. Well, the first week that they started selling them they sold like 8,000 Hogan tee-shirts. It was crazy. Verne now owed him something like $40 grand, but he apparantly only cut him a check for half that much, which is what he originally promised. Well, Hogan got pissed and he left for New York. From there, one by one, Hogan started recruiting guys to come out there with him.

"From there, McMahon would essentially offer guys more money along with the promise of fewer days work. Verne was stuck, what was he going to do? This guy had so much money and was willing to do whatever it took to get these guys. Then, after working for a year with him out there, McMahon would renegotiate their contracts down big-time. He knew that at that point these guys had burned their bridges with Verne, so he would lowball them for their next deal, knowing that they would basically have to take it. I mean guys were expecting a raise at that point and he totally had them by the balls. He would sit them down and basically tell them that if they didn't want the lesser deal that right then and there, that there was a guy in the next room ready to sign. And of course there was nobody there, but they didn't know that. McMahon was so smart that way and eventually he would just keep the top guys that he knew could draw well and let the others go. It was brilliant. That is why the guy is where he is at today, because he was so shrewd."

Steve remained in the AWA for a brief stint before heading south, to compete in Georgia Championship Wrestling. That next year, he beat the Mongolian Stomper to capture the NWA National Heavyweight Championship, and that same year he teamed up with Ted DiBiase to down the Fabulous Freebirds and claim the Georgia National Tag Team title. He would remain there for a few more years until breaking his hand in a match one night with Kabuki. So, he served as a television commentator for a few months while he healed up.

"They kept me around and paid me a few hundred bucks a month," he said. "They knew that when I got better a few months later that they would have that sympathy-revenge angle to work with. You know, you were never worth as much until you had something seriously go wrong with you in this business. They had to work all the angles, it was totally twisted. Anyway, they sabotaged my TV career because they didn't want me to take this other guys' job and I just didn't want to deal with it anymore. It was a lot of fun being in it for all those years, I had met a lot of great people and seen some interesting things, but I was ready."

When he finally got healthy he decided that he had simply had enough. Tired of the politics and of the grind, he hung up the tights. With that, he headed home and called it a career. At the time his father was working in the financial planning field with Billy Bye, another former Gopher Football teammate of his. They asked him to join them and he has been doing it ever since.

Presently, Steve resides in Bloomington with his wife and four boys. He works for Focus Financial and also coaches his kids youth football and baseball teams as well. "Steve-O," as he was known, wasn't always the flashiest guy in the ring, but he was an outstanding athlete and a solid technical wrestler. More importantly, he was well respected and always considered to be one of the good guys — and when you get to know him, you will realize pretty quickly that it still holds true.

THE ANDERSON FAMILY

Ole Anderson

The famous Anderson wrestling family has long been a part of professional wrestling history in Minnesota. They were tough. Period. They had no fancy gimmicks, just a rough, athletic, lumberjack-like image which seemed to resonate well with their fans. The patriarch of the dynasty was Gene Anderson, a St. Paul native who went on to become a mainstay in the old AWA back in the early 1960s. Gene, who starred in football and wrestling for the South St. Paul Packers in the early 1950s, eventually hooked up with Larry Heiniemi and Al Rogowski to make a little rassling history.

The most famous of the Andersons, however, would have to be Ole, and here is his story… Born Al Rogowski, Ole Anderson (the name he would later wrestle under) was born in St. Paul and raised on Bald Eagle Lake, near White Bear Lake. His family later moved over to Rice Street, in St. Paul, where his father owned a tavern called the Owasso Garden. Al went on to attend Alexander Ramsey High School, where he starred in wrestling, football and track. From there, he accepted a football scholarship to attend the University of Colorado. When things didn't work out there, however, he transferred to Cloud State University. After spending a few quarters there he transferred down to the University of Minnesota. He eventually transferred back to St. Cloud State, however, where he also wrestled for the Huskies as well.

From there, in 1964, Al was drafted and spent the next two

and a half years in the military, serving primarily in Germany. After getting out, he hooked up with Verne Gagne and began training to become a pro wrestler. He made his debut in 1967 as Al "Rock" Rogowski, up in Canada, and later wound up working in Omaha.

Gene Anderson

"I have a lot of respect for Verne Gagne, he has truly done it all in this business," said Al. "He was such a great help to me through the years and I am very appreciative of that. I still try to see him when I am up that way, he is just a great guy. He taught me a lot about both sides of the business, wrestling as well as promoting, and I will never forget that."

A year later Al hooked up with his old college buddy, Larry Heinimi, who had recently also gotten into the business and was working with Gene Anderson.

"I first met Larry when I was in my college fraternity doing an arm wrestling competition up at St. Cloud," said Al. "We were taking on a bunch of the football players at the time, and Larry, who was on the team, and I became friends from there. Later, when he got into pro wrestling, he teamed up with Gene Anderson, and took the name Lars Anderson. Well, when I got out of the Service,

Arn Anderson

Larry told me to come down to the Carolinas to join he and Gene, which is where they were at the time. So, after a year with Verne, I headed down there to check it out. I eventually wound up becoming an 'Anderson' as well, 'Ole,' and it just grew from there. We were billed as brothers from then on out and it was a lot of fun. The extended family of it all was interesting too because when I first started out I was also a 'cousin' to the Crusher, while the Bruiser was my 'uncle.' "

The Andersons would go on to become one of the most popular and successful family dynasties in pro wrestling history. Eventually, Ole and Gene joined as tag-team partners and became known as the "Minnesota

Larry Heiniemi

Wrestling Crew," capturing the Mid-Atlantic Tag Team title in April of 1970. From there, the duo bounced back and forth between Georgia and the Mid-Atlantic areas, while Ole also pursued a solo career as well, winning the Florida TV title and Mid-Atlantic Heavyweight titles over the next two years. He and Gene later went on to garner the first Mid-Atlantic TV Championship in 1973, followed by a Georgia Tag Team title as well.

"Minnesota was a great place to grow up," said Al, "but it was colder than a well digger's ass! Plus, the trips up there were tough. I mean you would travel up to Fort William on a Monday, drive home on an icy two-lane road, leave for Aberdeen on Tuesday, head to Peoria on Wednesday, go down to Omaha on Thursday and then wind up in Chicago for the weekend. It was really hard. I mean I remember some weeks traveling up to 2,500 miles and sometimes never even getting into a bed at night. So, once I got the taste of warm weather, that was it for me. I loved living down south, and that is where I stayed."

By the late 1970s Gene, who was much older than Ole, decided to retire. So, Ole teamed with Lars, as well as Jacques Goulet and Ernie Ladd to each win a Georgia Tag Team title. Later, in 1978, Ole, after winning the Southeast Heavyweight Championship in Alabama, partnered with Ivan Koloff. Together, they went on to capture a total of five Georgia Tag Team championships over the next two years. Ole later turned on Ivan, however, when he and Lars went incognito to become the "Masked Avengers."

That next year Ole teamed with Dusty Rhodes to take on "The Assassins" in a cage match with Gene (who came out of retirement) and Ivan Koloff as special guest referees. All hell broke loose, however, when Ole and Gene turned on Dusty and let him have it. With that, Gene came out of semi-retirement and went back to the Carolinas with Ole, where they won one more World Tag Team Championship in 1981, before Gene hung it up for good one more time.

That next year Ole teamed up with the dangerous cowboy, Stan Hansen, to win another World Tag Team Title. Later, in 1984, Ole began teaming with Thunderbolt Patterson in Georgia. They then began feuding with "Arn Anderson," who was actually Marty Lunde, and had joined the family as Ole's distant "nephew." That next year the family reunited, with Ole and Arn joining forces to turn on Patterson. With that, the bearded duo, now tabbed as the "New" Minnesota Wrecking Crew, went on to join Ric Flair and Tully Blanchard in 1986 to form the first version of the famous "Four Horsemen." The group became wildly successful over the ensuing years, complete with plenty of drama in which Ole and Arn wound up turning on each other on more than one occasion.

Eventually, after a 30-plus-year career in pro wrestling, Al decided that he wanted to spend more time with his "real" family. He ultimately hung up his boots in the late 1980s, but stayed in the business as a booker and later as a trainer. He would go on to discover a whole wealth of up and coming talent, giving a lot of kids their first shot in the big time. In fact, it was he who gave the Road Warriors their first opportunity down in Georgia Championship Wrestling. Al helped shape the industry as a booker, overseeing the offices in Charlotte (Jim Crockett Promotions), Atlanta (Georgia Championship Wrestling) and later for the Ted Turner-owned WCW.

Presently, Al is retired and living in Georgia. He still follows the sport which made him famous and also still enjoys amateur wrestling as well. In fact, his son was even a state champ a few years back as well. The two later even did some volunteer coaching together at the local high school.

Al also recently wrote his own biography, entitled "Inside Out," which has been a big hit with his legions of fans.

"It was a lot of fun putting it together," he said. "There are a lot of great stories about different wrestlers in it which makes it a lot of fun. And, it features a lot of inside information about the wrestling business too, which is the reason for the title. There are also a lot of things that I talk about that for the most part have only been privy to the wrestlers in the past. So, it is an honest assessment of what wrestling was like during the years that I wrestled, from the late 1960s into the late 1980s, and it has been very well received so far."

As for the other members of the family? While Gene sadly died of a heart attack in 1991 at the age of 58, Larry Heiniemi later went on to pursue other interests. Heiniemi, who had earlier joined up with Larry Hennig in the 1970s, later tagged with Buddy Wolff, a former gridiron teammate of his back at St. Cloud State. In fact, Wolff would later even become a member of the Anderson family, when he was pegged as a "distant cousin" at one point. After a respectable pro wrestling career in which he won a pair of NWA (Georgia) Wildside Tag Team titles, an NWA (Georgia) Tag Team title, and an NWA (Florida) Heavyweight title, Heiniemi moved on to Hawaii, where he captured a total of four Polynesian Pacific Heavyweight titles. He and Wolff later became partners in marketing several different fitness products, including an exercise devise called the tummy twister.

The Andersons have truly been an institution in the world of professional wrestling, and the Minnesota Wrecking Crew will forever go down as one of the most infamous trios in grappling history.

THE ROAD WARRIORS

The Road Warriors & Nikita Koloff

The story of wrestling's longest tenured and most successful tag-team duo is a fascinating one, and features two very different individuals: Joe Laurinaitis (aka: "Animal") and Mike Hegstrand (aka: "Hawk"). Here is their amazing story:

Joe Laurinaitis grew up in inner-city Philadelphia and moved to Minnesota when his father, who worked for Honeywell, was transferred here in the mid-1970s. Joe was a sophomore at the time and wound up graduating from Irondale High School in 1978 as a star both on the football field as well as on the baseball diamond. The power-hitting catcher even got invited to try out for the Cincinnati Reds, but his true love was on the gridiron. There, the linebacker and guard and wound up going on to play collegeiately at Golden Valley Lutheran College. At GVLC he earned All-American honors and was about to accept a full-ride scholarship to Brigham Young University, but decided instead to stick around, however, to be closer to his girlfriend, and wound up attending Moorhead State University.

(Incidentally, one of his pals on campus during his time at Golden Valley Lutheran was Timberwolves Head Coach, Flip Saunders, who was just starting out in his coaching career. Joe played basketball with him after practice from time to time and as he put it, "knocked a few heads around under the basket to toughen his guys up..." The two remained friends over the years and enjoyed bumping into each other at various sports venues throughout the country. Ironically, the two presently live across from each other near Rolling Green Golf Course in Medina and their kids are even good friends as well — small world!)

Shortly thereafter Joe got an opportunity to try out for the

USFL's New Jersey Generals, but he opted instead to pursue a career in wrestling. You see, at the time, Joe was bouncing at a tough northside nightclub called Grandma B's alongside a few of his buddies, Mike Hegstrand, Rick Rude and Barry Darsow. A bartender in the club was a guy by the name of Eddie Sharkey, a former pro wrestler who, after a lot of prodding, agreed to train the guys and show them the tricks of the trade. They trained in the basement of a south Minneapolis church in a ring that was nothing more than railroad ties, plywood and carpet, with an old wrestling mat on top.

"It was rock hard," joked Joe, "it really was the school of hard knocks!"

Joe was skeptical at first, but figured it would be fun, and, regardless of what happened, he would be able to stay in good shape to continue trying out for a pro football team. Well, as fate would have it, one night when Joe was throwing some drunk idiot out of the bar, local wrestler/promoter Ole Anderson was walking in at the same time. Anderson, who also worked as a booker for Ted Turner's Georgia Championship Wrestling, told Joe that he had a spot for him down in Atlanta, where he was working at the time. Joe jumped at the opportunity and the rest, they say, is history.

Soon after that Mike and Rick joined Joe in Georgia, and before long the Road Warriors were born when Joe and Mike decided that they would make good partners. Their friend, Paul Ellering, later joined them as their manager as well.

Mike Hegstrand, meanwhile, grew up in Chicago and later moved to Minnesota with his family. He attended Minneapolis Henry High School, where he too excelled in athletics. At six-foot-three and 245-pounds Hegstrand later got into bodybuilding. His first stint in pro wrestling was an 1,800 mile road-trip to Vancouver with Ravishing Rick Rude, where, after three matches, he got homesick, and came home. He would later travel around, until finally hooking up Joe to form the Road Warriors.

As for the name "Road Warriors," well, Joe and Mike were big fans of Mel Gibson's "Mad Max" movies and thought that would make for a good gimmick. The trademark face paint, leathers, football shoulder pads and tough, biker persona all evolved and eventually made them the most recognizable tag-team partnership in wrestling history. After spending a year in Georgia, the Road Warriors moved back home to Minnesota, where they began wrestling in Verne Gagne's AWA. Transformed from heels into good guys, Joe and Mike became instant fan-favorites.

"When we first came back I think the fans were tired of seeing old, fat guys in the ring and really liked our act," said Joe. "We were big, strong 300-pound athletic guys and we said what we were going to do, and then we did it — people appreciated and respected that."

The bodybuilding duo quickly gained a reputation for being lovable bad-asses. Seemingly every wrestling magazine on the newsstands had the Road Warriors plastered on their covers, as they quickly rose to the top. No one had seen the likes of guys that huge who could do flips, high leg drops and monster body-slams, and people were instantly drawn to them. With power moves like Hawk's "running clothesline" as well as Animal's "double gorilla press slam" and the tandem's "top-rope spike," stardom was just over the horizon.

A big part of their act was to come rushing out to ring to the music of Black Sabbath's "Iron Man" and charge their opponents before they could get ready — usually pinning them in just a few minutes flat. It was wild. This was drastically different from the old days, when the matches would take anywhere from 15-45 minutes with guys really selling moves and setting up a strategy to beat their opponent. With the popularity the sport was receiving from television, wrestling was changing from the "athletic" angle to that of "entertainment," and nobody at the time was more entertaining than the "Legion of Doom."

Finally, in the summer of 1984, the Road Warriors, who had already worn the NWA National Tag Team title belts down in Georgia, defeated the overmatched veteran tandem of Baron Von Rashke and The Crusher for the AWA World Tag Team belts. Two

promotions, two titles — they had officially arrived. They battled everyone the promoters threw at them from that point and beat them all convincingly. From there, they left the AWA and headed back down south, to compete in various promotions as well as in Japan, where they continued to enjoy great success. They would eventually own nearly every tag-team championship belt, a sign not only of success in the ring, but outside of it as well. The promoters knew who was going to make them money, and nobody could draw and sell tickets like these guys could.

"I have never seen wrestlers as completely vicious and overwhelming as these two men," said legendary ring announcer Gordon Solie in 'The Pictorial History of Wrestling.' "Besides being tremendous athletes and incredible specimens, they have developed a bent and twisted attitude, rolling roughshod over everybody."

Once Joe and Mike had a few bucks in the bank, they invested wisely. Among their early investments were a couple of weightlifting/health clubs called "The Gym" in Plymouth and the "Twin Cities Gym" in Roseville. Another great idea was one of the all-time great fads of the '90s, Zubaz. Zubaz was an idea that evolved after Joe and Mike came home from being overseas one time and were just fed up with having to sit in such small airplane seats and being so terribly uncomfortable. So, they talked to a couple of buddies of theirs, Dan Stock and Bob Truax, who were in the garment industry, and came up with these wildly colored stretchy sweat pants for big, athletic guys. They operated from a big warehouse in Brooklyn Park, where all the manufacturing was done, and before long they were selling their duds around the world. Eventually, major league sports franchises began licensing their team colors with Zubaz and before they knew it, their pants and shorts were a multi-million dollar sensation. They eventually got out of the business, but it was a "wild ride" while it lasted.

By the early '90s the Warriors were performing in the WWF as the "Legion Of Doom," and enjoying a level of popularity and success right up with the likes of superstars Hulk Hogan and The Rock. The duo of Mike and Joe would later split up and take some time off apart from one another to the tune of a couple years. Animal decided to take a break from active competition to heal some nagging back injuries, while Hawk traveled the world and later teamed up with Kensuki Sasaki to form the duo "Hell Raiders," which resulted in two IWGP tag-team titles in Japan.

Joe and Mike got back together in 1996, however, and picked up right where they left off — dominating the world of professional wrestling. From there, the duo just kept it going, entertaining millions of fans along the way. In all they would win every major title in every division of the top companies both here and in Japan, including the AWA, NWA, WCW, WWF, WWE as well as the AWF and IWF belts, and the Crockett Cup.

In May of 2003, the Road Warriors made one last swing through the WWE, losing a match to Rob Van Dam and Kane. It would be their last. Tragically, just six months later, Hegstrand died in his sleep at his home near Clearwater, Fla. He was just 46 years old. He had suffered from a heart ailment in recent years and sadly, it finally got the best of him. Ironically, Hegstrand, who lived the rock-'n'-roll-star lifestyle to the max for more than 20 years, had really settled down in the last several years prior to that. He had even found the Lord and was keeping it real.

"I was no saint," Hegstrand told the Orlando Sentinel a few years ago. "For years I put a lot of stuff in my body that I shouldn't have. Now it's just the God-made stuff. I'm eating healthy and feeling stronger."

One of the most charismatic and outrageous wrestling duos to ever lace em' up, the Road Warriors will go down as legends in the world of professional wrestling. Known for their power, strength, brutality, and sheer ruthlessness, the Road Warriors were incredible entertainers and athletes who redefined the business of professional wrestling. They were truly a one of a kind.

A CANDID CONVERSATION WITH JOE...

Animal

On Hawk: "We were together for 21 years and that says a lot. No tag-team has ever been together that long and one never will. Mike was just a great friend, a great business partner and a great person — I think about him every day. He will be dearly missed by many, many people. You know, Mike finished the race strong, because he got the forgiveness of God and got rid of all the demons in his past. Sure, he had substance abuse issues in the past, but he was clean and sober for the last eight years of his life. Most importantly, he had a heart bigger than himself."

On Success
"We experienced so much, so young, that we were just thrown in and rode the wave. It was amazing, we saw the world through wrestling. I mean a lot of guys don't even catch a break until they are in their 30s, and by then they have already been in the business for 10 years. So, we were lucky, no question. We came in with something totally different and were just in the right place at the right time. You know, we just had one of those freak gimmicks that was just so ahead of its time. It was a lot of fun."

On Life on the Road
"The wrestling business used to be a very tight-nit group, much more so than today. We used to travel together by car as well as by plane and we got to know each other like family. The road was tough too though. I have almost three million frequent flyer miles on Northwest Airlines alone! That doesn't even include the other airlines, or the private jets we had later in our career either. I am only 43, but it wouldn't surprise me if I have flown close to 10 million miles in my career. Wow, that is amazing to even say that. That was also a badge of honor as well because if you were flying that much, you were producing and in demand. Guys today, if they are hot, might work 200 days a year, whereas we were always on the road 300-350 days. I mean there were times when I woke up in the morning and had no idea where I was. The travel was just horrendous. So, for us, working out wasn't just a gimmick, we had to just stay in shape to be able to physically compete in that many matches. As for the social aspects of being on the road, that was an adventure too. You know, I was the straight one of the bunch, if you will, so a lot of times when the other guys were out drinking or whatever, I was usually the designated driver. That was just the way it was, and that was fine with me. That was just my nature, to take care of the other guys and make sure everyone got home all right. I do remember one time, however, pushing Ric Flair up to his hotel room in a luggage cart with him wearing nothing more than black socks. That was a typical night out on the weekends back in the day with old Ric. There were some wild times, no doubt about it!"

On Speaking "Carnie"
"The wrestling business has its own language, called 'carnie.' It was something learned out on the road and used in order to commu-

nicate incognito in the ring. I mean I can tell in 10 seconds if a guy is a wrestler or not, just by speaking 'carnie' to him. It is pretty funny, I could speak to another wrestler in an airport or somewhere and the guy sitting next to us would have no idea what we were saying. For example, if I wanted to say: 'Call me later tonight...', I would say "keizallmay leizay toneizay." Basically, you put the sound "eiz" in between each vowel, along with an "ay" sound at the end, and then talk real fast. It took me about a year to really fully understand it, but once I did it was like learning an entirely different foreign language. You know, the business used to be 'protected' back until the late 1980s or so, when it was proclaimed as 'entertainment' versus a sport, and we had to work really hard to keep up the illusion that it was all real. Sometimes talking in the ring is really critical, especially if a guys gets hurt. When stuff like that happens, you have to be able to trust the other guy to do the right thing. I remember one time the Warlord landed on my head, and I said 'hey man, I am screwed up here, end the match right now...' and we wrapped it up — the fans and TV guys didn't know a thing."

On Idiots
"You know, no matter where you were, out on the road or at home, you would always run into an idiot who thought he was really tough. It seemed like wherever you would go to escape from reality and just try to get away from being on the road, that one of these idiots would find you. He would come at you, full of 'liquid courage,' and try to impress his buddies or girlfriend. I would just sit back and say to myself, 'please don't pick me...' It was a lawsuit just waiting to happen and that was the last thing I wanted to do was get into a fight with some drunk meat-head in a bar. It was particularly tough for me too because I had the Mohawk, so people could recognize me when I was out. I finally started to wear a bandana just so I could get some peace and quiet when I wasn't working. It was tough. The times when it was really tough was when I came home, because when I came home I was dad. When we went out to dinner or something, I just didn't want my family to be bothered. So, out of respect to them, I would politely tell fans who would come up to me while we were out do dinner that hey, I was enjoying a meal with my family and would appreciate it if they could please come back when I was done, and I would be happy to sign an autograph for them. Minnesotans were pretty good about stuff like that, but it was a tough thing sometimes for me and my family. But, hey, that is all part of being famous I suppose and it is just something you have to deal with as best as you can."

Favorite Match
"Performing in England's Wembley Stadium in front of 90,000 people back at the 1992 SummerSlam, that certainly ranks up there. It was so loud that you couldn't even hear the roar from our Harley's as we rode in. That was so nuts. I remember Hawk rode his bike too close to me and I couldn't get off the bike on the left side. So, I had to jump off on the right side, and my calf stuck to the hot tailpipe and it burned my tights right into my leg. I was in so much pain, just jumping around. Finally, Hawk says, 'Do you have to go to the bathroom or something?' And I am like, 'No, look at my leg!' It was brutal."

On the Old AWA
"You have to give old Verne (Gagne) a lot of credit. He had a lot of success here in Minnesota and really put us on the map with pro wrestling. You know, it was too bad that things wound up the way they did with the AWA. I think that if he could have just figured out a way to have gone national with what he was doing at the time, he could've easily competed with the WWF. He had the talent, no question, but when Hulk Hogan left and then we (Road Warriors) left, it was downhill from there."

On Hanging on too Long
"You know, it is tough to see some guys still hanging on when they are way past their prime. I mean guys gotta do what they gotta do,

but I think that self respect is one thing that you have got to have in life — no matter what you are doing. And, I will also say that for the most part, the guys who did a lot of drugs, they pissed their fortunes away. It was sad to see, but that was just how it went for a lot of guys who made a bunch of money, got some fame, and then went nuts. As a result, a lot of guys were left with no choice but to hang on and do shows for peanuts way past the primes of their careers. Once you are at that point, the promoters have got you and when you have no where else to turn, that is a scary place. I have also seen a lot of guys come to the Lord several times throughout their careers as well, and you can't use that as a marketing tool to make money either. It won't work because God will take those riches away from you just as fast as you can make them. Some guys get pretty messed up being in this business for too long as well, and just can't let it go. Wrestling gets into guys, into their hearts and souls, and they can't walk away from the only thing that they know. That is just the way it is sometimes."

On the Road Warrior Alter Ego
"Sometimes my wife teases me about that. You know, in front of some people, they just don't believe you are anything but the character you play on television. So, it depends, but for the most part it is work for me and something I take a lot of pride in. For the most part it was really fun but it was scary sometimes too. For instance, I remember one time we were doing an interview for this show over in Japan and we were showing how crazy we were as these two wild bikers. So, we were slamming bottles of Tabasco sauce and eating raw chicken, and stuff like that, Hawk even ate a dozen raw eggs, shells and all — that was nuts! The funny part was that they actually believed that this was our actual daily diet. Japan was a trip for us in more ways than one. I mean, I don't think we even signed an autograph over there for the first 10 years we were there because the promoters wanted the fans to be deathly afraid of us — and they were. Sure, we did some crazy, stupid stuff, but that was all part of our act and what made us who we were as characters in the ring."

On Your Legacy
"I would want to be remembered as a good guy, a smart businessman and a good person. You know, I am really proud of what we achieved during our career together, Mike and I. We achieved something that can never be achieved again in tag-team wrestling, we are the only duo to hold five of the major titles ever in the sport of wrestling. The number of titles that we won will never be equaled in the history of the sport. Period. Because not all those companies exist today. The fact that we were that well thought of and that marketable spoke volumes. The promoters wanted us to wear their belts because we made them money. We were handsomely rewarded for being popular with the fans and that was what it was all about. That was a rush, let me tell ya. We used to live by the slogan 'Often imitated, never duplicated,' and that said a lot as well. Imitation is the highest form of flattery and we were definitely copied as models of success throughout our careers, no question. There are two entities in this business that will never exist again, the Road Warriors and Hulk Hogan. The Stone Cold Steve Austins and Rocks will come and go, but we were a monarchy. We were giants in the business and that will just never happen again. I am extremely proud of that. And, for me to be a sort of pioneer of the sport, as it was coming into what we know it as today, with the television and what have you, that also means a great deal. I take pride in knowing that I had a lot to do with building this multi-billion dollar business, and that is something I don't take for granted either. I am also proud of the fact that we were voted as the 'Tag Team of the Year' by the fans in seven of our first eight years in the business, and were also voted 'Tag Team of the Decade' and 'Tag Team of the Century' as well. That meant a lot too because we really cared about what the fans thought of us and our act. They made us and we never forgot that."

On the Future
"Well, I want to keep doing what I am doing for as long as the good Lord will let me. As long as I stay in decent shape, I can stay in the business for as long as I want. That is an awesome thing, to be able to do your own thing and make your own schedule in this business. Now, I can go to Japan every month, do the independent thing, and still have time to spend with my family. Hey, look at (Ric) Flair, look at (Hulk) Hogan, those guys are 12 years older than I am and still going strong. After that, I just want to be close to my family and spend as much time with them as I can. They have sacrificed so much for me over the years, with me being away so much, that I just can't thank them enough for their support. It has been tough being on the road the last 20 years, not always being there, but I know where my priorities are. In fact, I made a decision years ago that I wasn't going to be a part-time dad or coach. I wanted to be there for them and I have been. So, I have just sucked it up, which has meant a ton of travel. For instance, if I had a match in New York City on Saturday night, I would fly back that night or the next morning to coach my kids' game, and then fly back out that afternoon to wrestle again that night. I did that for probably 10 years, religiously, because it was that important to me. I wanted to show them that I was dedicated to what they were doing and then let my actions speak louder than my words. And hey, I was a good coach too. Heck, both my kids' football teams went undefeated for four years apiece, meaning we didn't lose a game for over eight years. That was even more fun than wrestling! Beyond that, you know, I would love to get into coaching. Ideally, if I could coach college football, that would be my dream job. I am coaching with the Minneapolis Lumberjacks (semi-pro football team) now and having a blast, but it would be fun to take that to the next level. Who knows?"

On Faith
Joe does a lot of motivational speaking as well as ministering his thoughts on life to the youth of today. In fact, he is part of a religious-based wrestling group called the Power Wrestling Alliance, run by former WWF star Ted DiBiase (aka "The Million Dollar Man"), which travels around the country doing shows and performing matches with a faith-based message. After the matches the group talks to the fans about their faith and about being accountable in life. The group does very well, oftentimes selling out arenas with fans who want to see wrestling and then talk about religion.

"It is a very special message that we are sending to kids and that means a great deal to me — especially now that Mike is gone," said Joe. "It was no secret that he liked to party and he lived a hard life, no question. I think he probably had at least 10 near-death experiences along the way, but at the end he got it right with God and that is all that matters. So, my main mission now is to help out the youth of today and to try to make a difference in their lives. You know, there comes a certain point in your life when you realize that things happen for a purpose. I think that we are all here on this earth for a reason and I think that mine was to be seen on TV by millions of people every week for the last 20 years and to make a difference. Being a Christian doesn't mean you have to be a total Bible-banger or anything like that, it just means that you believe in something and you have a relationship with God. It is about talking to kids in a language that they can understand and telling them that they have a choice in life to either go down road "A" or road "B." Each is a different path and finding which is the right path is everyone's journey that he or she needs to make. I think that I have been able to help a lot of kids make the right choices in life and that is very rewarding."

Where Are They Now?
Presently, Joe lives with his wife, Julia, and their two children, James and Jessica, in Medina. Like mom and dad, both kids are standout athletes (mom was a bodybuilder as well). James, who will be a senior in 2005 at Wayzata High School, has already verbally accepted a full-ride scholarship to play football (and maybe hockey) at the University of Minnesota. (He was also heavily recruited by Notre Dame and Michigan as well.) At six-foot-three and 230 pounds he can already bench press 300 pounds and squat

500. As a junior he led Wayzata to its first state high school hockey championship in 50 years and is among the state's top hockey recruits. Jessica, meanwhile, a freshman at Wayzata, is considered one of the best girls hockey players in the state. In addition, Joe also has another son from a previous marriage, Joseph, who is in the U.S. military, with tours of duty in Kuwait and Iraq under his belt.

As for Joe, he is wrestling both here as well as overseas, at least three weekends a month. And, despite the fact that Hawk is no longer with us, the Road Warriors are still as popular as ever. In fact, Animal recently signed a deal with the WWE to have their likeness' immortalized onto action figure dolls as part of the companies' "Legends Collection." Only 10 wrestlers were chosen for the honor and they are expected to be among the top-selling toys of the year. Joe is also working on a new book as well, entitled: "What A Rush!", which will chronicle their 20 year adventure together in the business. In addition, Joe is also going to be hosting a new show on PAX TV called "What in the World Outdoors," an extreme lifestyle magazine program which he hopes to have syndicated nationally.

TERRY SZOPINSKI

Terry Szopinski

Terry Szopinski was yet another of a long line of Minnesotans who made it big in professional wrestling. Known as "The Warlord," Szopinski was a complete monster at six-foot-five and 320 pounds. He began wrestling in the mid-1980s and probably saw his most success tagging with the Barbarian as "The Powers of Pain" in the WWF. Szopinski later wrestled in the WCW as "Super Assassin No. 2" and got a lot of attention with his "Flying Clothesline" and "Choke Slam" finishing moves. Szopinski went on to have an outstanding career in the ring, winning several belts along the way, including the NWA Central States Tag Team title with Karl Kovac in 1987; NWA's Mid Atlantic World 6-Man Tag Team title with the Barbarian and Ivan Koloff; and the WAR World 6-Man Tag Team title with Scott Putski and Bob Backlund. He began wrestling in the WWF in 1988 and continued with the company until the mid-1990s, battling nearly every major superstar along the way. Along the way the Warlord has been managed by Paul Jones, Slick, Mr. Fuji, Baron Von Raschke, Harvey Wippleman and Baby Doll.

Later, in 1996, Szopinski was forced to retire following a bad car accident involving a pizza delivery carrier, which severely limited the mobility in his neck. He was forced to take a lot of time off to recover, but eventually did make a comeback, working the independent circuit as well as over in Japan. Today, Szopinski resides in the Fort Lauderdale, Fla., area and continues to wrestle locally with both the FCW and MXPW companies.

TOM ZENK

Tom Zenk

Tom Zenk was born and raised in Golden Valley and went on to graduate from Robbinsdale High School in 1976. From there, Zenk went on to attend the University of Minnesota, where he majored in Speech Communications. While Zenk was a great athlete in high school, particularly on the soccer field, his true love was spending time in the gym, working-out. In fact, Zenk would later go on to earn the body building titles of "Mr. Minnesota," "Mr. Twin Cities" and "Mr. North Country." After that, Zenk decided to get into professional wrestling. It was a natural fit, considering the fact that several of his best high school buddies were Curt Hennig, Rick Rude, Dean Peters, John Nord, Nikita Koloff and Barry Darsow — all of whom would go on to stardom in the ring. Zenk then began training with local trainer Eddie Sharkey, to learn the tricks of the trade.

Zenk made his pro debut in 1984, beating Jimmy Doo in LaCrosse, Wis. At six-foot-one and 240 pounds, Zenk was a ripped specimen with limitless athletic potential. From there, he joined the upstart USA Pro Wrestling circuit, but moved on to participate in the AWA when the rival league folded after just a few months. Most of the wrestlers who participated in the renegade league were blackballed from competing in Gagne's AWA territory, but Zenk was just too talented to leave out. Zenk performed well in the AWA, and was even receiving national attention as "one of wrestling's brightest up-and-coming stars." He tagged with his old pal Curt Hennig from time to time, and became a babyface fan-favorite. He became frustrated though, when he never got the push he was hoping for — a push that would be reserved for Verne's son, Greg. As a result, Zenk ultimately left the promotion via a "career threatening piledriver injury," at the hands of Ray Stevens.

So, in 1985, he left to compete in the Pacific Northwest territory, where just a few months later, he and Scott Doring defeated Mike Miller and Moondog Moretti for the PNW Tag Team Title. He would later win the PNW Heavyweight singles title from Bobby Jaggers as well. From there, after working a stint in Japan, he headed north of the border to compete in Montreal alongside Rick Martel. There, he gained a lot of national exposure and finally cracked into the big-time WWF the following year.

In the WWF, Zenk competed as the "Can-Am Connection" alongside Martel. The two looked similar, both with cut, bodybuilder physiques, and were outstanding performers. Shortly after their arrival in the federation, the duo got a huge push and won the WWF World Tag Team Championship title by defeating Don Muraco and Bob Orton at Wrestlemania III. They had officially arrived. But, after some up and down matches, the duo eventually fizzled out. Zenk would ultimately leave the WWF over an alleged contract dispute and take some time off.

After spending some more time in Japan, Zenk returned to the AWA in an attempt to capture the AWA World Heavyweight Title. He came close, but couldn't get past Larry Zbyszko. Later, he would tag with Ken Patera, Wahoo McDaniel and Brad Rheingans, as well. Knowing he would not get the push he wanted in the AWA, he again left in 1989 to compete in Ted Turner's upstart WCW. With that, the "Z-Man," as he was now known, made some noise with his "Flying Dropkick" signature finishing move. There, he went on to win the WCW Television title, and later, along with Brian Pillman, wound up winning the NWA U.S. Tag Team title as well.

Zenk would later compete in Japan for the ninth time in just eight years. He bounced around a lot towards the end of his career, ultimately hanging it up on his own terms.

WALLY KARBO

Wally Karbo

The name Wally Karbo was synonymous with professional wrestling for more than 50 years. As a promoter, Karbo was a fixture on Saturday morning All-Star Wrestling since the very beginning of the old American Wrestling Association, way back in the early 1950s.

Walter Joseph Karbo was born and raised in northeast Minneapolis, the son of Polish immigrants. He went on to graduate from De La Salle High School in 1934, where he starred on the basketball team. In fact, he was even offered a scholarship to the University of Notre Dame, but money was tight, so he chose to stay home with his family. Instead, he began hanging around local gyms with his next-door neighbor and pal, Stan Mayslack. Mayslack wanted to be a wrestler, so he got together with Tony Stecher, Minneapolis' top boxing and wrestling promoter during the 1930s. Karbo loved being around the business and eventually got a job with Stecher as his assistant. Eventually he was offered a job as referee and by his mid-20s he had already refereed close to 8,000 matches. (He would referee close to 25,000 during his lifetime!)

From refereeing, Karbo soon began organizing and promoting matches. He started locally, working with Tony Stecher's National Wrestling Alliance (NWA) promotion, which was based out of Minneapolis. Throughout the 1940s and 1950s Karbo became a major player in the pro wrestling business throughout the Midwest. Stecher later passed away and his son, Dennis, took over the promotion. He eventually wanted to get out of the business though and decided to sell it to Verne Gagne, who wanted to buy in. Karbo, who had a small ownership in the company, came along for the ride.

Gagne had been wrestling professionally for a several years out of Chicago and was a pretty big star at this point. But, he was frustrated about the fact that he never got the push from the territorial owners to become the NWA's Heavyweight World Champ. So, he decided to buy the Minnesota territory from Stecher, and rename it as the American Wrestling Association in 1959. Karbo, meanwhile, was kept on as a partner and also served as the main promoter, while Gagne defended his newly created AWA title belt. From there, the business took off. The AWA's All-Star Wrestling show debuted on TV shortly thereafter, and the fans started tuning in. The AWA would be a fixture in the world of pro wrestling for more than three decades and Karbo had a lot to do with that success.

Described by those who knew him best as fair and "just one of the guys," Karbo never thought he was better than anybody else. His low-key style was perfect for the over-the-top wrestlers who were the stars of his show. He and Gagne found great success together, with each doing his part to grow the promotion. He gave countless young men the opportunity to earn a living and prove themselves in the business, giving back a lot along the way.

Karbo later sold his interest in the association in 1984. He stayed in the business though, and later emerged as the commissioner of the upstart Ladies Professional Wrestling Association. Sadly, on March 26, 1993, Karbo died of a heart attack. He was 77 years old. The entire wrestling community was shattered. Known for his civic contributions, Karbo had been honored for his work with the March of Dimes and other organizations. A good son, he also made sure to visit his 100-year-old mother at a nursing home every day as well. He also found great joy in going on fishing and hunting trips with his friends.

"Wally was sly like a fox," said former wrestler Jesse Ventura in a Star Tribune interview. "A lot of people perceived Wally as not being real brainy, but Wally Karbo knew the wrestling business better than anybody who's been in it. Wally could recognize talent and who could draw money. He enjoyed life to the fullest." "Wally WAS wrestling to Minnesota," added Ventura, who said that he grew up watching Karbo on TV since he was a little boy. "He was a legend."

JEREMY BORASH

Jeremy Borash

Jeremy Borash grew up in the Twin Cities and graduated from Minnetonka High School in 1992. From there, Borash went on to study broadcast journalism and later got into the local radio market. A die hard wrestling fan who grew up on "All Star Wrestling," Borash was determined to find an in to the wrestling biz.

After becoming the youngest Marconi Radio Award Nominee Winner in radio history at the age of 21, Borash left his Mankato, morning show to help launch the syndicated Ruth Koscielak Show, where he served as producer/sidekick to the longtime Minneapolis radio personality. After two years on the air with Koscielak, Borash was offered a host position with Ted Turner's Atlanta based World Championship Wrestling.

In March of 1999, Borash helped launch the innovatively successful "WCW Live" program on WCW.com, a web based radio program that held the title of the most listened to internet streaming media program in the world. After a year with the company, Borash was promoted to an on-air position, commentating on the WCW flagship program WCW Monday Nitro (Mondays on TNT) and WCW Thunder (Wednesdays on TBS), as well as a behind the scenes role as a head writer on both programs.

Borash is also remembered for playing Vince Russo's half-witted sidekick in 2000, nearly getting his head kicked in by Bill Goldberg while driving Russo's "Pope-Mobile" at the Cow Palace in San Francisco during a memorable WCW Monday Nitro.

When Ted Turner's WCW was purchased by the WWE, Borash helped launch the World Wrestling All-Stars with Australian concert promoter Andrew MacManus. The group went on to promote sellout tours of Europe and Australia, producing pay per view broadcasts from Sydney, Melbourne, Auckland, Glasgow, as well as a live pay per view event from the Aladdin in Las Vegas, all of which Borash served as executive producer and play-by-play announcer.

In early 2002, Borash joined longtime wrestling promoter Jerry Jarrett and son Jeff to launch Total Nonstop Action Wrestling, a weekly live wrestling pay per view event series. Borash can be seen as the company's live event host and ring announcer on camera, and serves as the company's creative video director off camera, creating and editing the video packages seen both on the company's weekly pay per view series as well as their Impact! show on Fox Sports Net.

Borash's unique presentation has landed him roles as ring announcer in motion pictures such as Chris Rock's "Head of State" from Dreamworks as well as Dove Canyon's "Sting - Moment of Truth"

Currently, TNA is the only major competitor to Vince McMahon's WWE. When WCW died, TNA was able to move in and become the first successful rival wrestling company to open its doors in nearly two decades.

"When WWE and WCW went head to head a few years ago, there were over 11 million people tuning in every Monday night," said Borash, who currently resides in downtown Nashville. "Now that WCW is gone, the WWE's numbers are at only about three million, so there are some eight million wrestling fans out there not being catered to. Those are the people we are trying to attract. Our approach is more serious and much more athletically based than the WWE as well. One unique thing we have is an octagonal ring, which allows more room for the wrestlers to operate. As a result, we get guys who can do a lot of really exciting acrobatic stuff. We also feature a lot less cheesy storylines than WWE, so we are not nearly as insulting to the fans' intelligence either. We don't go with the 'sexual' angles that the other guys do too, which we think is smart business. Right now our biggest star is Monty Brown, who used to play for the New England Patriots, but we have some veterans like Dusty Rhodes too. So, we are just trying to grow and get bigger and better. We have gained a lot of national exposure by being on FOX Sports Net too. And, despite the fact that we currently have a poor time slot, in the afternoon, it is the single highest rated program on the entire network — even beating the likes of 'The Best Damn Sports Show Period' in the ratings. So, things are looking good for us."

Jeremy has played big part of the companies' success. Praised for his audio/video work in the industry, he is also one of the main writers, bookers and choreographers for the program, putting him in on all of the behind-the-scenes action that makes the events so exciting for the viewers.

"It is so fun doing what I do," said Borash. "It is just so beyond my wildest dreams that I continually pinch myself. You know, when I was a kid I grew up watching guys like Verne Gagne, so to be a part of that world now is unbelievable. I can remember going to the Civic Center with my dad to watch the matches and was just hooked on it early on. So, to make my career in this business now is amazing."

GEORGE SCHIRE

Minnesota's Foremost Wrestling Historian

For wrestling historian George Schire, professional wrestling has been a part of his life since the mid 1950's. After he attended his first match in the old St. Paul Auditorium pitting Ivan and Karol Kalmikoff against fellow heels Mitsu Arakawa & Kinji Shibuya, he was hooked on wrestling for life.

George has a complete room in his home dedicated to and decorated with, wall to wall photos and file cabinets crammed with wrestling programs, magazines and related memorabilia that he has acquired over the last 40-plus years.

Over the years, George has been privileged to not only be first and foremost a fan, but also work in the wrestling business in various roles. He has been a fan club editor (for wrestler Ramon Torres), a writer and columnist, for magazines like Wrestling Revue, Wrestling Monthly and The Wrestling News.

George has been a ring announcer, and has done ringside commentating and play by play of matches. The later work was for Eddie Sharkey's "Pro Wrestling America" and Tony Condello's "West Four Wrestling" in Winnipeg, where George was the TV host of Condello's weekly wrestling show in the mid 1980's. In addition, Schire also worked for WCW whenever they came to either the Met Center or Roy Wilkens Auditorium as well.

George also co-hosted a weekly wrestling radio show (with Pro Wrestling Torch editor Wade Keller) on KFAN AM 1130 in the early 1990's, and before that was a frequent guest and contributor to another radio wrestling program on WWTC AM 1280 in the Twin Cities.

Schire has also worked as a manager for the STEEL DOMAIN WRESTLING promotion, where under the name of "The Authority" he played a heel manager role. At one point in time, The Authority managed both the Steel Domain Heavyweight Champion (Daryck "Old School" St. Holmes) and the Steel Domain TV champion (Gage Octane). Others that he managed for Steel Domain were "Wild Bill" Irwin and Adrian Lynch.

It is as a historian, that George is best known. Over the years, he has compiled several wrestling results (won/loss) career records that include Dick (Doctor "X") Beyer, Nick Bockwinkel, Mad Dog Vachon, Greg Gagne & Jim Brunzell, Larry Hennig & Harley Race and The Crusher & The Bruiser.

George says that he is honored to have many wrestlers as personal friends, and some of the boys like Red Bastien, Nick Bockwinkel, Baron Von Raschke, and Doctor "X" have visited his home. It is also an honor for him when many of the wrestlers call him to get information regarding their respective careers. George says that, "it isn't often that one can meet and have as friends their childhood idols."

Presently, George serves as an Executive Director for The Cauliflower Alley Club, a 40 year non-profit organization that is billed as "The Ring of Friendship," and holds annual conventions in Las Vegas. During these conventions, the legends of wrestling come together each year to share there stories and friendships of their colorful careers.

Once many years ago, when George was asked by his youngest daughter why he liked wrestling so much, George replied "because like a good friend, wrestling has always been there for me during life's ups and downs."

In real life, George has been in the banking business for the past 26 years. He has two grown daughters (Amy and Kari) and lives with his wife Lorraine of 30 years in Oakdale.

SIGNIFICANT OTHERS...

STEVE ANDERSON

Steve Anderson has been involved with professional wrestling in a rather unique way. Whether drawing editorial cartoons or writing high-profile feature articles, Anderson has worked for nearly every major wrestling publication over the past couple of decades in a senior writer role. Among them include: the Pro Wrestling Illustrated family of magazines, Total Wrestling, World of Wrestling Magazine, Extreme Championship Wrestling (ECW) Magazine, Wrestling Digest and CBS Sportsline's Wrestleline.com. In addition, Anderson has authored five books, including two with Bobby "The Brain" Heenan, entitled: "Bobby the Brain: Wrestling's Bad Boy Tells All" and "Chair Shots & Other Obstacles: Winning Life's Wrestling Matches." Anderson, who is a graduate of Concordia College and Shakopee High School, presently serves an editorial cartoonist for the Farmington Independent and the Rosemount Town Pages.

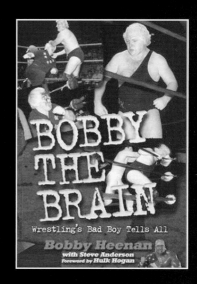

RAY WHEBBE JR.

Ray Whebbe Jr. spent a lifetime helping others. An avid wrestling fan, he was involved in the sport as a writer, announcer, booker, broadcaster, promoter, agent, television producer and referee, apparently even selling hot dogs at the matches. He just loved hanging around boxers and wrestlers and even penned a couple of wrestling history books along the way. He also loved to help those less fortunate and worked in social services much of his life. He even organized an annual rock and wrestling benefit for the homeless called, "Wrestle for Shelter." Whebbe also hosted a long-running cable access show, "The Spectator," founded a neighborhood newspaper called The Whittier Globe, wrote columns for a half-dozen other local tabloids, and even served as the editor of The Watchdog. Described as colorful and full of life by those who knew him best, Whebbe sadly died in 2000 at the age of 48, due to heart trouble.

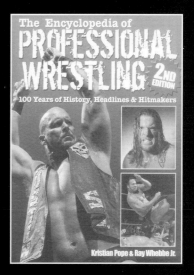

MICK KARCH

Mick Karch is best known as a ring announcer and commentator back in the old AWA. In addition to calling the action for Windy City Pro Wrestling, the IWA and the AWF, Mick has been a wrestling photographer, journalist and has even hosted his own cable television wrestling programs as well.

NORMAN KIETZER

Norman Kietzer was originally a printer from Mankato who went on to promote wrestling shows throughout southern Minnesota starting way back in the 1950s. In addition, he also published the Wrestling News Magazine, Wrestling Review as well as Wrestling Monthly, which all morphed into the Wrestling News back in the early 80s. Kietzer was one of the big players in the world of wrestling programs and literature and certainly left his mark, in more ways than one, on the industry.

THE INDIES...

It is estimated that there are more than 500 independent wrestling organizations throughout the United States today. Yup, the independent circuits, or "indies" as they are known, have always had their place in grappling's rich history, including right here in Minnesota — where they have served several purposes along the way. First, they have been and continue to be the "minor leagues" for young guys on their way up the ladder. Performing in the small venues gives them much needed ring experience to perfect their crafts, while also providing them with time both behind the microphone as well as in front of the camera to work the kinks in of their acts.

Conversely, because there are probably around 100-150 former pro wrestlers who live in the area, the indies are also a stepping stone for those aging stars who on their way back down the ladder as well. Yes, believe it or not, a lot of the "old-school" guys, like Kenny "The Sodbuster" Jay, Stan "Big K" Kowalski and Buck "Rock-n-Roll" Zumhofe are still at it, headlining local weekend cards in small towns, while still entertaining their legions of faithful fans.

Secondly, in the extremely political landscape that most pro wrestlers find themselves living and working in, the indies have always been a retreat to fall back onto when things didn't always work out up at the "Show." What this means basically is that because pro wrestler's careers are so volatile (i.e. injuries, or politics with promoters who either fire them or don't "push" them to better gigs), they at least have a place to always come back to and regroup. In fact, most states have several independent circuits, with some being more high profile than others, where guys can perform and make a few bucks.

Third, fans love to watch the indies, and are very loyal to the wrestlers who work hard for them to put on a good show. Whether indie wrestlers are performing in VFW halls, American Legions, armories, junior high school gymnasiums or even at a local tavern, they have always had a fan base which will support them. Let's face it, you can't beat good, cheap entertainment, and many indie shows are a great night out for the family, or even for a cheap date.

Lastly, the indies have become the "ultimate reality-TV show" for both young kids with big dreams, as well as for those aging baby boomers who grew up watching "All-Star Wrestling," and want to simply live vicariously through their youth. I mean besides Halloween, how often can you dress up and become a superhero, masked marvel or even a villain for an evening?

The indies have been a part of the wrestling landscape in the Gopher State for more than 100 years. It is all about supply and demand, and while there has always been a demand for a good show, the supply was always abundant thanks to the fact that this area was such a pro wrestling hotbed. We can thank Verne Gagne for that, because his American Wrestling Association, which ran from the late 1950s to the early 1990s, spurned literally thousands of wannabe's to make it big. And, while many did, traveling the world and living like rock stars, many others simply got by or had to hang it up to find a day job.

For many other former pro grapplers, however, they found great success in becoming either trainers or promoters. The most famous trainer in Minnesota wrestling history is Eddie Sharkey, who discovered and developed many of the sports' biggest stars over the last 30 years including the Road Warriors, Jesse Ventura and Curt Hennig, to name just a few. Sharkey has also run various promotions under different names over the years, such Pro Wrestling America, as well as several others which are still going strong. Sharkey is still coordinating small, independent shows around the metro area so that his "students" can perform in front of a live audience. His shows have served as a training ground for several young men who went on to hit it big including, Jerry Lynn, Charlie Norris and Sean Waltman, among others.

To promote all of this, there was a loyal media following too, such as the WWTC's Wrestling Radio Show, the annual "Wrestle for Shelter" bash, which raised money for the homeless, and former AWA announcer Mick Karch's Saturday Night Ringside Show, which was part of a successful wrestling block on Channel 23 for many years. It was quite the scene for the local die-hards who have always loyally supported their indies.

Another well known trainer is former Olympian-turned pro wrestler, Brad Rheingans, who has a training camp at his home in Hamel, in the western suburbs, where he has trained a whole new generation of stars, including the likes of the Steiner Brothers as well as Brock Lesnar. Aspiring wrestlers with dreams of performing for Vince McMahon's WWE have no problem shelling out several thousand dollars for this type of instruction, figuring it is just a necessary investment in order to get onto bigger and better things.

Other grapplers-turned promoters include Buck Zumhofe, who runs "R&R Wrestling," as well

USA Pro Wrestling

Promoters had always guarded their territories against "outsiders," who wanted to come in and take a piece of the action. One such rival indie start-up was "USA Pro Wrestling," which hit Minnesota in 1984. Led by a group of nine anonymous local investors, the group figured that there was an untapped market in smaller towns and cities which were being ignored by the established promoters. So, they leased a ring, sound and light equipment, and motor homes for touring. They hired a public relations firm, as well as TV cameramen, and even had T-shirts made — leaving no stone unturned. Finally, they rallied close to a dozen wrestlers who were not under contract locally, to perform in their traveling show, including former "Mr. Minnesota," Tom Zenk.

Their angle was to go into the towns, hype it up, and then dazzle them with an awesome sound and laser light show. They would then promote the videos from the matches as well, a relatively new concept at that time. With that, the group hit the road, setting out to embark on an ambitious eight-weekend (four times a year), 32-city tour, throughout the Midwest. Two problems quickly arose, however. First, the fans weren't familiar with the wrestlers, and secondly, the wrestlers decided that they wanted some more dough after a few weeks into the tour. As a result, the investors pulled the plug. While most of the wrestlers were blackballed for working with another promotion on AWA 'turf,' exceptions were made for Zenk, Glenn Lieske and Rick Renslow.

Eddie Sharkey

as Sheik Adnon Al-Kaissy, who used to run the World All-Star Wrestling Alliance, along with fellow grappler Ken Patera, promoting shows on various weekends throughout the area. Oftentimes, the shows will feature some old-time fan-favorites, such as Baron Von Raschke, who come out to sign autographs and occasionally dust off the old tights and get back into the ring to be a part of the action.

Another successful local outfit is Midwest Pro Wrestling, which operates as a combination training and wrestling league. MPW has a training facility in Maple Grove ("The Foundry"), where, for a few thousand bucks, grown men can live out their childhood fantasies learning the tricks of the trade, developing a character persona and grappling every Saturday night in front of about 100 spectators. From teenagers to middle-agers, aspiring grapplers at the camp are taught about ring safety, how to take a "bump," and about the unique balance of choreography and improvisation that is required to become a successful professional wrestler. "The Sheriff," "Shifty" and "Pretty Boy Delgado" are all there, working together and having a ball. Like boot camp, they run through drill after drill until it becomes like second nature. From stomping your feet in conjunction with punching your opponent in the chops, to the correct way to fall on your back, to the right way to lift someone flying through the air — it is all part of the package.

After about six months of hard core training, the new recruits spend another six months perfecting their craft in the ring. Roughly 25 or so dreamers graduate each year, with competition being fierce with regards to which people get to perform on the promotion's weekly cable-access channel. From there, they are set free, left on their own to find a gig. Some call it a career right then and there, while others try to take that next big step. That is where guys like Buck Zumhofe come in, operating shows for both the "new recruits," as well as the "aging vets." Another local promotion was an incarnation of the old AWA, which reopened in 1996 as an independent promotion called AWA Wrestling Entertainment, and hosted events throughout the state. It didn't last, as many have found, it is an ongoing series of coming and going shows — like the wrestlers themselves, most don't make it.

For the wrestlers, it is anything but glamorous at this stage of the game. Heck, if they are lucky they might make $50 bucks a night, but for many others that number may be closer to $20, or even just a few free beers after the match. In addition to spending all that money on training, many spend much, much more on elaborate costumes, props and makeup. Oh and by the way, in most instances, the wrestlers are usually there at the location setting up the ring, the lighting equipment, and even selling the tickets. So, why do they go through all of that, not to mention the serious risk of injury and humiliation, for such little money? Easy. The allure of becoming a rock star for a day combined with pure fantasy escapism. Hey, there is no boss out there telling them to work harder, no wife (or husband, yes there are plenty of women here too…), no kids, nothing — just a bunch of screaming fans rooting for a character that he or she concocted in their wildest dreams. What a rush! Most importantly, however, is the fact that these people just love pro wrestling and really want to be a part of it. That's all.

Various training camps run promotions as well, such as the Western Wrestling Association. Recently, several promotions came together this past Spring to form the

Ken Patera & Brad Rheingans

"New Steel Domain," which combined St. Paul Championship Wrestling and Midwest Pro Wrestling to launch a one hour television show on KSTC-TV called "Wrestling Legends of the 21st Century." The show, which is produced by Joe Ciupik, a former producer with the old AWA's All-Star Wrestling, is billed as "old school wrestling meets the 21st century."

"The goal is to re-establish Minnesota and the Midwest as a professional wrestling hotbed," said Ciupik, who is also the president of Digital Requests, which produces a monthly classic wrestling event for pay-per-view. "We promise a wrestling program that provides intrigue and entertainment. There will be a method to all of the madness."

Frankly, it is good to see the local groups coming together to consolidate and grow. In the old days, the big promoters fiercely guarded their territories against rival promoters, or "outsiders," and even used to threaten to blackball up and coming wrestlers who performed with them. One such independent circuit was "USA Pro Wrestling," which hit Minnesota in the winter of 1984 and was gone by that summer. Nowadays, it is an entirely different ballgame. The AWA is gone and the entire industry is basically controlled by one man, Vince McMahon, and his World Wrestling Entertainment empire. He even has his own minor league, the Ohio Valley Association, where he grooms his future stars under strict supervision.

So, the indies today have a much different focus and have much more realistic expectations as well. Sure, guys can still dream and have fun, that is what it is all about. But more importantly, the indies provide our community with great, family entertainment, while giving countless weekend warriors the opportunity to drift into "Never-Ever Land." Overall, it is just fun, and the people and businesses that comprise this niche industry realize that, and that is why they are successful.

As for the future? Well, another indie that is making some noise on the national scene is called "Real Pro Wrestling," which is unique in that it will feature former amateur wrestlers from the collegiate and Olympic ranks, competing for money. Perhaps somewhere between Ultimate Fighting and the WWE, the new pro league, which will feature its own television show, hopes to find its niche. That is what it is all about, finding something new, different and appealing to an extremely segmented sports and entertainment population that has more options than ever with regards to how they are going to spend their time and hard-earned money. It's not like the old days when there was one show in town and you had to take it or leave it. Times have changed, and so too has the landscape of professional wrestling — both big-time as well as small-time. Sure, McMahon will always be there, ruling the roost, but there are plenty of indies out there to support and enjoy as well.

Overall though, many industry insiders agree that the popularity of independent wrestling has never been higher. Much of that has to do with the success of the WWE, which has huge television numbers that rival many professional sports programs. The other reason, of course, is due to the fact that because the AWA has been out of business for nearly 15 years now, there is still plenty of demand for the locals to see live wrestling up close and personal. It is still pure entertainment, and in these tough times, people will always find time to escape from reality. Long-live the indies!

The Lightening Kid

Verne Gagne was born on February 26, 1926, in Corcoran, Minn., and grew up on a farm near Hamell during the Great Depression, where he attended a one-room school house. A tremendous athlete, he grew up loving sports. He also grew up tough, learning the value of hard work at an early age by working on his families' farm. In fact, he left home at the age of 14 after his mother had passed away to live with his relatives. Verne got his first job as a young boy, sweeping and cleaning up at a local tavern and beauty shop before school. He would later wind up at Wayzata High School for one year, ultimately transferring and graduating from Robbinsdale High School in 1943. There, he earned all-state honors in football under coach Red Sochaki., and even though he weighed only 185 pounds, he also won a pair of state heavyweight wrestling championships during his junior and senior seasons as well. Robbinsdale, under the tutelage of coach Mark Woodward, was a wrestling dynasty in those days and was right in the midst of winning a record seven straight state titles from 1940-46.

From there, Gagne was recruited to play football at the University of Minnesota, where he platooned as both a defensive end and tight end. But his main sport in Gold Country quickly became wrestling. After winning the Big Nine heavyweight wrestling title in 1944 as a freshman, he went into the Marine Corps to serve in World War II. Stationed in Santa Ana, California, Gagne played football for the El Toro Marine team for the next two years while also teaching the art of hand to hand combat to his fellow soldiers as well. He returned to the Gophers in 1946, however, and picked up right where he left off.

Gagne was outstanding out on the gridiron, but on the matt, he was simply unstoppable. There, he went on to win three more conference heavyweight titles over the next three years, including a pair of NCAA national championships — as a 191-pounder in 1948 and as a heavyweight in 1949. (The latter came against future pro wrestler, Dick Hutton, from Oklahoma, in a double overtime thriller. That match had a lot of meaning for Gagne, who had previously lost to Hutton on a controversial referee's decision in the 1947 national finals.) The three-time All-American also won the 1949 AAU Wrestling Championship as well.

"Those were the days," said Verne, "I will never forget my days at the University. I remember listening to Gopher football games on the radio, back in the 1930s, when they won all those national championships. So, to become a Gopher, that was special. I got to play alongside some great, great people including: Bud Grant, Clayton Tonnemaker, Leo Nomellini, Jim Malosky, Dick Wildung, Billy Bye, George Franck and Eve Faunce, to name just a few. Some of those guys are still my best friends to this day."

In addition, Gagne was also a member of the 1948 U.S. Olympic Greco Roman wrestling team which, incredibly, didn't get to compete at the summer games in London that year.

"The U.S. took two teams to compete, freestyle and Greco Roman," recalled Verne. "I was on the Greco Roman team, and we trained together for several months prior to heading overseas. Once we were there, the United States quickly began to dominate the first events in track and field and swimming. Then, the freestyle wrestling team competed first, doing well and even winning some medals. So, we were up next, the Greco Roman team. Well, apparently, because the powers-that-be were worried that the U.S. squad

didn't have enough international experience, particularly against the elite teams such as the Turks, they pulled the plug on us to avoid the risk of being embarrassed. It was the first Olympics after World War II and they were real concerned about how they were going to look to the rest of the world I suppose. It was awful. The night before we were set to compete, the coaches came in and told everyone the bad news. We had worked so hard to get there, we were devastated. We still got to march in the parade at Wembley Stadium afterwards, but it was really tough."

After coming home and playing in the prestigious College Football All-Star Game in Chicago, against the NFL Champion Philadelphia Eagles, Gagne signed with Curly Lambeau's Green Bay Packers. (He had originally been drafted by the Chicago Bears, but because team owner George Halas wanted him to give up a year of eligibility and sign a contract as a junior, Gagne said no thanks.) Verne played for the Pack throughout the 1949 pre-season, but just before the first regular season game, Lambeau informed him that because the Bears still owned his rights, and wouldn't release him, he couldn't legally play. So, Gagne said "to heck with football" and, luckily for us, went into the profession that would make him one of the most recognizable athletes of his day, professional wrestling.

Gagne had always been intrigued with the world of pro wrestling and used to love listening to Bronko Nagurski's wrestling matches on the radio with his grandpa as a kid. So, when Minneapolis promoter Tony Stecher encouraged him to give it a shot, he agreed. Verne had something most pro grapplers didn't have at that time, legitimate athletic credibility. As a Gopher football and wrestling star, he was a well known commodity and very marketable to the media. And, in addition to being very articulate, he was a muscular good looking guy — the prototypical "babyface."

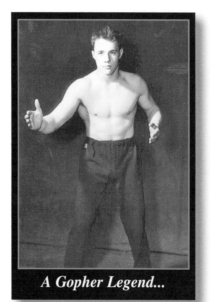

A Gopher Legend...

Verne jumped in head first and began to learn the ropes from local wrestlers Joe Pazandak and George Gordienko. He made his pro debut on May 3rd, 1949, against Abe "King Kong" Kashey in Minneapolis, winning by disqualification in a match refereed by boxing legend Jack Dempsey. Shortly thereafter, Verne headed to Texas, where he was an instant success, capturing the Texas heavyweight title belt. He continued his push by local promoters and eventually went on to obtain the National Wrestling Alliance (NWA) World Junior Heavyweight Title in 1950. His big break came when he began appearing on the old Dumont TV Network's weekly wrestling show out of Chicago. Over the next eight years he would become a household name.

Gagne would defend the strap against many of that era's top draws, but never got the opportunity to seriously contend for the coveted NWA World Heavyweight Championship belt. That belonged to legendary grappler, Lou Thesz, a big-time fan-favorite and top money earner — someone who the territorial promoters throughout the country were determined to keep elevated as the champ.

So, knowing he would probably never get his big break, Verne decided to buy his own promotion in 1960. With that, he purchased the NWA territory here in Minnesota, which had been owned and operated by the Stecher family. He renamed it as the American Wrestling Association (AWA) and hit the ground running. The rest, they say… is history! It would be the beginning of an illustrious career both in the ring as well as in the front office, where Verne owned and operated the successful promotion for more than three decades.

Over his illustrious 35-year career, Verne would hold the coveted heavyweight title belt no less than 10 times. Over that time, he traveled the world, built up a multi-million dollar business empire, and brought countless hours of joy and entertainment to families across the Midwest. Whether they attended his live pro wrestling cards held at the old Minneapolis or St. Paul Auditoriums or tuned into his legendary television show, "All Star Wrestling," the fans always got their money's worth. At its peak, the AWA ran in over 100 television markets from its Minneapolis base all the way from Chicago to Milwaukee to Winnipeg, straight through to Omaha, and on to Denver, Salt Lake City, Las Vegas and San Francisco. It was a massive territory with massive popularity, oftentimes even beating the likes of the Vikings and Twins in the local television ratings. The AWA was THE place to be during pro wrestling's heydays, and it featured a who's-who of all the top names in the business. From Andre "The Giant" to Jesse "The Body" Ventura to Ric Flair— they were all there.

Finally, in 1980, Verne made it clear that he was going to hang up the leotards and focus on the business side of the promotion. His last stint as heavyweight bout took place in 1981 against Nick Bockwinkel, in what was billed as his swan-song retirement match. With his vaunted "Gagne Sleeper," Verne, of course, won. Naturally, he came out of retirement on several occasions over the next several years though, to tag-team with his son Greg from time to time. His "final-final" match took place on April 20th, 1986, back home in Minneapolis in a win over Sheik Adnan Al-Kaissy.

He would retire as one of the most prolific professional wrestlers and promoters of all time. His AWA hung in there until 1991, when he was finally forced out of the business by rival promoter Vince McMahon, the owner of World Wrestling Entertainment. It was a sad day for wrestling fans everywhere. Verne's legacy lives on though, through our memories and through the countless number of wrestlers who he trained and gave opportunities to. Many of those athletes and entertainers are still making a living to this day doing what they love to do. They are also teaching the next generation of men and women about the importance of fundamentals and of hard work — both hallmarks of his. Nope, Verne wasn't about glitz and glam, he was a wrestler's wrestler who led by example and didn't take any crap. That's why we always rooted for him.

Verne is still a great supporter of amateur wrestling in the state, contributes wherever he can, and gives back to the sport that gave him so much. From doing fundraising for the U.S. Olympic wrestling team, to giving motivational speeches to his beloved Golden Gophers, Verne is still going strong and enjoying life. A tremendous ambassador of both amateur and professional wrestling, Verne Gagne, in a word, is a legend. So, who better to talk about the state-of-the-state of Minnesota wrestling than our very own heavyweight champ, Verne Gagne…

An Amateur Legend...

"It's good, real good," said Verne of the state-of-the-state of amateur wrestling in Minnesota today. "J Robinson has done a great job at the University of Minnesota, winning a pair of national championships; Augsburg has won a whole bunch of Division III titles and continues to dominate over there; and our high school kids seem to get better every year; so I think we are in good shape.

"But, wrestling is still a big secret, and that is a problem I think. The media just doesn't give the sport the exposure that it really deserves. I mean look at baseball, basketball, football and hockey, they get so much coverage at all levels — from high school to college to the pros. Sure, when the state tournament is going on, then they get some coverage, but it is not nearly enough. Look at the attendance for the state wrestling tournament, it is right up there with everybody else. But in a lot of ways it is still the best kept secret in town. It is a such a great sport with such great people, so I hope that it can continue to grow and gain more publicity in the future, I really do.

"I think that while we have so many great coaches at the high school and collegiate levels here in Minnesota, that they can still do more to present their sport in a way that gets them more media attention. Sure, wrestling does get some television time during the state tournament, of course, and J (Robinson) has done a great job in getting coverage over at the University with the Gophers, particularly when they compete against Iowa, their biggest rival, and that is great to see. I know it will be tough, but we need to let the rest of the world know about how wonderful this sport really is. I also think that we need to attract more people to come out and see it and experience it as well. I mean for the most part, the people who come to meets are the parents of the kids, along with some of the student body. So, we need to do a better job of making our product more marketable, so that other people will come out and support it.

"Then, when the Olympics are on TV, that is great too, but it is not nearly enough. Even there, we have had so many kids from Minnesota represent the United States in the Olympics over the past 50 years, especially in the Greco Roman division, and that is another big secret. Why? So, I am not sure if it has to come from the grass-roots levels or from higher up, or a combination of both, but we need to do a better job of selling our product to the public. As a former promoter, I can say with some confidence that we are not promoting it well enough, and I would like to see us getting the same amount of coverage that some of the other sports are getting — whether that is on TV or in the newspaper, it is important for the long-term growth of the sport.

"Now, with regards to the number of kids actually participating in wrestling, I think we are doing pretty well. It is tough to see so many college programs which have dropped their programs over the years though. That has a big trickle down affect on the kids at the high school level too, because now those kids have that many less options for themselves to wrestle at the next level — whether that is Division I, II or III, or at a junior college. So, it is important to keep as many college and university programs going as possible. I think that is one reason why programs like Augsburg are so dominant nationally, because aside from having a great tradition and great coaches, there just aren't that many top notch programs around the area. Having said that, look at the all the options that the top kids in baseball, basketball, football and hockey have. I mean those kids have probably three times as many colleges and universities to pick from than wrestlers do and I think that is unfortunate.

"As for the talent level of kids coming out of Minnesota? No question, we are right there with the best of the best and that is great to see. Our youth programs have always been strong, and they, of course, feed into the high schools. I think it all comes down to having good coaches who can turn the best athletes into wrestlers. It is tough sometimes for wrestling because the coaches have to recruit kids away from other winter sports and convince them to come out for their teams. But they seem to be doing a terrific job and we all owe them a big debt of gratitude for working so hard with our kids to make them better people.

"Now, as far as the state-of-the-state of pro wrestling

today, to be honest with you, I just don't watch it. I don't like it anymore, it is so much more different today than it was back then. A lot of the guys are on steroids today and sure, they've got the big muscular bodies that look good on TV, but there's really no wrestlers in wrestling any more. It's just a show. You know, Vince McMahon has taken it in such a different direction. Today, it has nothing to do with wrestling, it is just a product that some people like, that's all. It is so sexual in nature nowadays and not the family type entertainment of the old days. It is really too bad that this is what it has all come to, because the wrestling that I grew up with is gone. You see, McMahon came in and raided all the other promoters of their top talent. He eventually just drove everybody out and took away all of their television time. It was sad, we hung in there for a long time, but were eventually forced out with all the others. It was the end of an era, it really was.

"Part of the problem I ran into was that I couldn't make 'stars' fast enough. He kept grabbing them, and giving them more money than I could pay them, and we lost them as fast as we could create them. Looking back, I was very naive about the whole thing. I mean we had a lot of guys like Hulk Hogan, who we developed here, that left. That one, in particular, was tough. The loyalty just wasn't there. You know, back in our day we did things with a handshake. There were no contracts, nothing, and when he (McMahon) came along, that all changed.

"You know, McMahon and I were very different. I came from the school of thought where wrestling was more about athleticism, with storylines built in around athletes and competition. McMahon was never an athlete, sure he lifted a lot of weights, but that was about it. So, we had a much different approach to the business. His philosophy was based more on entertainment, with the bigger, more muscular guys, and later with the women, and the sexual angle that is so typical in the sport today. He was never afraid to take the next step, whatever it was, to get ratings. I would like to think I was better than that.

"Well, as for other topics, how about the fans? To the fans, Gosh, I would just like to say thanks, from the bottom of my heart, they were always so supportive of me through the years and I really appreciated it. You know, I loved to wrestle and I was pretty good at it, so to be able to do something you loved for so long was very special. It was just a wonderful journey. I was very lucky to spend a lifetime in this business, and then, to know that you brought joy to others in the process, well that is just icing on the cake. We were in the entertainment business and I think we did a heck of a job for all those years, and that means a lot to me too.

"I was lucky to work with some great, great people over the years. So, I would want to thank a lot of them for their contributions and hard work too. Some of these guys were just tremendous athletes, it was amazing to work with some of them. I mean for me, growing up, Bronko Nagurski was my hero, and then, to be able to be his tag-team partner later on, that was a real thrill.

"It was great too when Greg got into the business. It is always neat when your kids want to do what you are doing, and it was certainly special to have him be a part of everything that I had started. I never thought he wanted to get into it though, because he really loved football. So, when he finally came around that was wonderful. Greg was a great athlete, so he was able to pick it up pretty quickly. Of course, he grew up with it and watched it from the time he was little, so it was like second nature to him. Later, when we tag-teamed together and that kind of thing, that was really neat too. It was a lot of fun, and that was the most important thing. He was a heck of a wrestler and I was very proud of him.

"I was tough on him though. You bet. It was not easy for him, especially at the beginning when he was learning the business. I had no mercy on him, that was for sure. I worked him out at our farm in Chanhassen, in the old barn, where we had our training camp. He took a beating out there, as did all of the new recruits. It was so hot and I used to make those guys run like dogs out in the fields up and down these big hills out there. It was really tough, but it paid off for them in the long run. I just really wanted to teach them about the virtues of hard work.

"You know, I grew up tough too. I worked as a kid on the farm doing really hard work, like making hay, or thrashing or picking vegetables, and looking back, I think that was great work to do for being a wrestler. I mean you had to be really physically strong, be able to lift heavy things and just have strong hands. I developed a lot of that as a young man. It also taught me a lot about honest hard work, trust and about values — all things I have never taken for granted.

"I would also say that I learned a lot of humility as a kid too. I mean when you grow up poor, you don't really know that you are poor at the time. But, when I finally realized that, I decided right then and there that I didn't want to ever be poor ever again. So, that motivated me to be successful. It motivated me to go to college, to do well in both football and wrestling, and to be successful as a businessman. As a result, I did very well for myself and for my family. But I also never forgot where I came from, because that is still a big part of who I am.

And, Still the Champ...

"I have traveled probably millions of miles over my lifetime through wrestling and it was just a great opportunity to see the word. I mean from Japan to Europe to the Middle East, it was so interesting to see so many different people and different things. I also brought my wife, Mary, with me on a lot of trips as well and that was great too. We both loved to travel, so that was nice because being alone on trips all the time wasn't any fun. The traveling is tough on a lot of marriages in this business, so I was fortunate in that regard.

"As for my legacy? Wow, that is tough. I suppose I would want to be remembered as someone who made a difference in people's lives. I also have a wonderful family and I am proud of what I accomplished both personally and professionally. I know that our wrestling business brought a lot of joy and happiness to people over the years too, and that makes me feel very good. Again, I was just lucky to get into something that I loved to do and was good at doing. I was also very lucky to have gotten a lot of help along the way because I couldn't have done it without the help of so many great people. From my relatives, who helped raise me as a young boy, to the people who I played with at the University of Minnesota, to all of the people who touched my life in the nearly 50 years that I was in the wrestling business, to my wonderful children — I owe a lot of my success to others, and for that I am very, very grateful.

"Most importantly though, the person who I owe the most to is the woman who stuck with me through all those years, my loving wife, Mary. I would never have achieved as much as I did without her support. No way. Sadly, she passed away here a few years ago and I just can't say enough about what she meant to me. We were together since our days back in high school in Robbinsdale. I will just never forget her. She was such a great wife, companion, mother, grandma and person. We had four wonderful children together: Greg, Kathleen, Elizabeth and Donna, as well as six grandchildren, and we all really miss her.

"So, to everybody else, thanks for your support and for rooting for me over the years, I couldn't have done it without you. It was one hell of a ride I tell ya, with so many wonderful memories. Yeah, if I could do it all over again... I would do it in a heartbeat."

AFTERWORD BY J ROBINSON

J Robinson grew up in San Diego loving the sport of wrestling and went on to star for his Mount Miguel High School squad, winning two state titles and being chosen the athlete of the year, graduating in 1964. From there, Robinson went on to wrestle at Oklahoma State University and later competed internationally on two U.S. World Teams — placing fourth in 1970 and fifth in 1971 in the World tournament. He later represented his country in the 1972 Olympic Games as a member of the U.S. Olympic Team. Robinson would capture four national wrestling titles during his illustrious amateur career, two in freestyle and two in Greco-Roman.

Graduating from OSU with a Bachelor of Science degree social studies in 1969, Robinson began his coaching career with the Cowboys as a graduate assistant during his final year. He then went on to serve as a captain in the U.S. Army's First Cavalry Division, and 173rd Brigade in Vietnam from 1971-72. Upon returning home, Robinson joined the University of Iowa's wrestling staff as a graduate assistant and was later promoted to assistant in 1976. He would go on to serve as an assistant coach at Iowa from 1976-84, helping to lead the Hawks to seven NCAA and eight Big Ten crowns along the way. Robinson served as an interim head coach during the team's 1984 Big Ten and NCAA championship season as well.

Robinson was offered the head coaching position at the University of Minnesota in 1986, and he has been making history in Gold Country ever since. In his first season, the Gophers finished the year without winning a Big Ten dual match. That, however, was about to change in a big, big way. Steadily, J followed his plan for building and recruiting a solid program from the ground up. Finally, in 1999, his Gophers went undefeated in conference duels and won the Big Ten crown, breaking Iowa's 25-year conference title winning streak. Two years later, in 2001, Robinson made history by leading the Gophers to their first ever NCAA National Championship with 10 All-Americans by his side the first time in NCAA history that every weight class produced an all-American. Then, in 2002, his Gophers went 19-0 in duels and did it again — making it back-to-back National Championships and creating a dynasty in the process. Robinson's Gophers came close to making it three in a row in 2003 as well, winning their third Big 10 title, but came up just short to Oklahoma State in the NCAA Finals to finish as national runner's up.

Robinson enters the 2004-05 season with an impressive 268-92-3 overall record, including an awesome 136-22-0 mark over the last seven seasons. He is as close to wrestling royalty as it gets in Minnesota and has single-handedly turned the Gopher Wrestling program into one of the nation's elite. Robinson is a phenomenal motivator, an amazing recruiter and is considered as a true player's coach. One of the most modest people you will ever meet, Robinson attributes much of his success to his coaching staff of Marty Morgan, Mark Schwab and Joe Russell. Most importantly, however, Robinson is a winner and the numbers speak for themselves.

During his tenure at Minnesota, more than three dozen wrestlers have earned more than five dozen All-America honors. In addition, he has also coached seven NCAA individual titleists as well: Marty Morgan (1991), Tim Hartung (1998 & 1999), Brock Lesnar (2000), Luke Becker (2002), Jared Lawrence (2002), and Damion Hahn (2003 & 2004). Robinson has also coached more

than two dozen Big Ten Champions and has led his teams to top-six conference finishes in 17 of his 18 seasons, including five straight from 1999-2004.

Additionally, Robinson has coached at the national and international levels as well. In fact, he served as an assistant coach on four consecutive U.S. Olympic squads from 1976 to 1988, and then as the head coach for the U.S. at the 1983 Pan American Games. Among his many awards and honors, Robinson was named as the 1998 and 2001 Dan Gable National Coach of the Year, and the 2001 National Wrestling Coaches Association Coach of the Year. Furthermore, the five-time Big Ten Coach of the Year was awarded the 2001 Amateur Wrestling News Man of the Year award for his work and support of wrestling at all levels as well.

A brilliant tactician and teacher, Robinson's teams are consistently nationally ranked because he knows how to recruit and attract the top talent from around the world to his program. Since taking over Minnesota's wrestling program 18 years ago, he has built one of the strongest and most respected programs in the nation

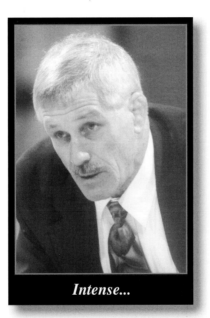

Intense...

and has emerged as one of the elite college coaches in the nation — for any sport. Presently, J and his wife Sue reside in Plymouth. J's son Jeb and daughter are students at the University of Iowa.

Known not only for his amazing coaching ability, but also for his passion to get others involved in the promotion and growth of the sport he so dearly loves, J is truly a living legend. So, who better to talk about the state-of-the-state of Minnesota wrestling than our very own J Robinson…

"I think overall it is good," said Robinson, of amateur wrestling in the Land of 10,000 Lakes. "It is growing at all levels and that is what is most important. We have very good organization at the high school level, which is key, and we also have outstanding grass-roots kids programs. There are a lot of programs for our young people here today and because of that they are learning the sport at an early age and then graduating on to participate at the junior high and high school levels. We are evolving too, from grass-roots volunteers, to full-time administrators and coaches, which is so important for long-term success. In fact, I think our youth programs can serve as a model for the nation, many of them are that well run. From pull-tab fundraising, to youth camps and tournaments, it is just really solid from top to bottom.

"I would say, however, that there are three areas where we need to get better. First, the one place where Minnesota has really lost a step is at the collegiate level. We have lost a lot of our Division II and III schools over the years, as well as junior college programs, and that has hurt. We need to try and make that up in order to continue giving kids opportunities to compete at the next level. We really need to do a better job of recruiting kids to get into the sport and then getting them to come to our colleges to compete at that next level. If the people of the state of Minnesota are not happy with the current system, they need to stand up and demand more out of their wrestling programs, as well as out of some of their coaches. I also think that we should reward the good coaches and weed out the mediocre ones. That is how we are going to get better.

"With regards to Title IX, I would say it has had a really big affect on college wrestling, maybe more so than any other sport, because schools can drop wrestling and in the process they can change their numbers dramatically for their proportionality. For a long time wrestling was kind of the weak sister and if you dropped it, you didn't have to drop any other sports because the numbers changed automatically. Title IX is a good law and it has been good for women's athletics, no question, but it is not very good for college wrestling, and that is unfortunate.

"Secondly, I would also say that sometimes wrestling people are their own worst enemy. And what I mean by that is that they are not demanding excellence out of their state universities with regards to their wrestling programs. We have allowed some of our programs to slip into where they have part-time coaches, with no teaching positions available for them in the physical education departments. As a result, we can't find enough qualified coaches. What happens is you get a spiraling down affect in that these individuals can't make enough money as a part-time coach, so they have to find another job to make ends meet — and programs suffer. Take it a step further and because that part-time coach is not a teacher, in school with those kids every day, he can't recruit kids to become wrestlers. As a result, your numbers go down, which hurts your program. The bottom line is that at the end of the day, wrestling can't grow because we aren't putting the resources into it at the state level.

"Take a program like Augsburg, which has taken it even further and has a couple full-time coaches who can focus on recruiting, coaching and marketing, without having to worry about teaching a class or working another job somewhere else. That is obviously the ideal situation, but one that is certainly unique. In the long run, those coaches are doing a tremendous service to their university by bringing in kids who will in turn pay tuition and room and board. So, when you look at it that way, it makes it very viable for the amount of money that they actually spend on the program. Then, when they have tremendous success, like they do, the alumni get behind them and make contributions to the school because they are proud of their alma maters. It all goes hand in hand.

"Thirdly, unfortunately there are also a lot of administrators who just don't get it. We talk about our programs being a business, yet we don't have administrations which understand how to generate income — like a successful business does. Their only thought is how to 'request' more money from the state. As a result, there is not enough income to go around with the increases in women's sports, which ultimately translates into budgets cuts. If they ran the numbers they could see pretty quickly that it works. For example, if a program brought in 30 wrestlers a year, who would each pay about $10-15K apiece in tuition, which would generate between $300K-$400K, and then hire a couple of coaches and create a program for a total of about $150-$200K — they might be looking at a profit of anywhere from $150K-$200K. Sure, it might take a little time to build up a program, but it is an investment. Instead of generating potential income, they are cutting income. It makes no sense. So, when you take all three of those factors playing together, it is hard on wrestling — no question about it.

"As for the big picture of wrestling in Minnesota, I think you have to look at it real long-term, like 10-15 years. Again, I think we have some great youth programs here and those kids are the future of the sport, no question. I am proud of the fact that we, at the University of Minnesota, have had so much success here as of late, because a lot of those little kids have been hanging around our practices and at our meets. Now, there is a whole generation of kids who want to be a part of this program the same way football, baseball, basketball and hockey have been for so long. We want

kids growing up dreaming about being Gophers, that is where it all begins and that is what it is all about.

"That also translates into the top kids staying home to go to college and wrestle, instead of going out of state. Again, the problem there is that we don't have enough programs to keep them all here. So, it is all intertwined together and once you start looking at it that way, you realize that we need to keep our college programs healthy and build them back up to create a solid feeder system. Could you imagine what would happen if all the assistant basketball coaches in the state were part-timers, like they are in wrestling? All of a sudden basketball would start suffering and you would see the same exact trickle down affect. It would never happen in basketball or football and we should not let it happen in wrestling.

"The big picture is all about teaching kids about values and morals, and one of the greatest facilitators of that is extracurricular activities, or sports. If you were to go out and ask people what it was in high school or college that had the biggest affect on them, they probably wouldn't say it was their algebra or biology classes, in all probability they would say it was being on the cross country team, or football team or wrestling team. I think that for young males, in particular, these are very important bonding issues and I don't think they are being used efficiently in our educational system.

"I think it is ironic that as we continue to have problems with the youth of America, as we are continuing to cut out high school athletics, which is perhaps one of the most important things that there is for them. I just read a statistic that said high school athletic budgets represent only about 1% of their schools' total budget. That is not much for what our society gets in return. That 1% investment that developments values, work ethic, sportsmanship and fair play is a very small investment for the return that our youth receive. So to cut that is a terrible decision and truly makes no sense to me.

"With regards to recruiting, I think we are right there with anybody on the national scale. In fact, over the last eight years, when you figure our placings, I think we have done better than any other school. We are on par with the elite teams such as Oklahoma, Oklahoma State, Iowa, and Iowa State. Two years ago we had the No. 1 recruiting class, so we get our share, no question. Now we are in that elite category of college wrestling schools and we are competing for all those same top kids. You have to be diligent. It just takes a lot of hard work, a lot of travel and a lot of dedication. Our formula has always been that if we can keep all the best kids from the state of Minnesota and then get half of the other top kids from around the nation, then we will be a perennial power.

"The flip side of that was the fact that we had two kids leave after only a semester at school last year, for personal reasons, and that was probably the difference in us not finishing in the top two or so nationally. We couldn't recruit replacements for those two weights in the short time frame and that hurt us down the road. It is a fragile thing, recruiting, and you have to make sure you are going after solid, stable kids. It always drives me crazy when people go into their spiel about how 18 year old kids 'have to do what is best for them,' and so on and so forth. I don't think we put nearly enough responsibility on these kids. I mean what if some 18 year old kid contracted to buy your car and then after a few months he said he couldn't afford it anymore and gave it back? What would the majority of Americans say? Tough. Well, when that same kid signs a scholarship it is completely different for some reason. So, it's about perspective they are plenty old to hold up there part of the bargain.

"You know, winning those two national championships

Tough...

definitely put us in the 'game,' and the legacy of that will be felt for years to come. As a coach, the first one sort of vindicates you and lets you know that you were doing the right things all along. The second one validates you in a different way in that it wasn't a fluke, and puts you at another level.. Both titles have been great for recruiting, great for fundraising and just great for our overall program. They have also been great for the University of Minnesota as well, which makes me very happy. I love knowing that people from around the state take pride in us and that we can bring some excitement and joy into their lives.

"As far as the state-of-the-state of Greco Roman and freestyle Olympic wrestling, we have been really strong there over the years. First and foremost, Alan Rice has single-handedly built up our Greco program and in the process has literally become synonymous with the sport. He is an amazing person and someone who doesn't get nearly enough credit for what he has done. From coaching to fund-raising to having a passion like no other, he has just done it all. As a result of all of his dedication, we have had at least one Minnesotan on the World or Olympic Greco team every year since 1970. From that, now you've got kids seeing success and wanting to participate in that sport and it is just a case of 'success-breeds-success.' Dan Chandler is another person who has just been tremendous for the sport. He is a three-time Olympian and as a coach is just phenomenal. Because of all that success we have a Greco training center here in Minnesota, which is a huge plus. The state is lucky to have people like that who are making a difference for our kids.

"For us, to have such strong Greco Roman and Freestyle programs, that is a tremendous recruiting tool. Our assistant, Joe Russell, is one of the coaches along with former All-American Gordy Morgan who coaches the Storm (our freestyle team), which is another avenue for kids. We can sell kids on the fact that they can come here to Minneapolis and instead of wrestling for four years, they can wrestle for eight or nine or ten, on U.S. National and World Teams. If kids attend college in a small town, and then want to continue on and compete internationally, it is tough to leave their friends and their support groups. Here, they don't have to. Minneapolis is a very livable city for them and their families to find work later on. So, these are some factors that come into play and it is all part of the process of recruiting.

Compassionate...

"Take that a step further and it even translates into the top wrestlers staying in Minnesota after college and going on to become coaches at the youth level, sharing their knowledge for the next crop of kids who want to learn the sport. That is what it is growing our wrestling popularity is all about. Conversely, if we go back to the lack of full-time wrestling coaches in the state, where are we going to get the next crop of coaches 20 years from now? If nobody wants to be a wrestling coach we are all going to have a big problems in the future. We need to develop incentives to bring more coaches into the sport

"I go back to an article that Patrick Reusse wrote one time about football, and hockey at their roots are fun to play. He said there is nothing fun about wrestling except winning. He's right. The only thing fun about wrestling is winning. Period. It is just really hard work. The journey is fun and that comes with time, but getting there takes a lot of sacrifice that most kids aren't willing to go through. Look at the sports people participate in when they are 40 years old: running, tennis, basketball, hockey, and so on. But not wrestling. Why? It is way too hard and way too demanding.

"It takes a unique person to be a wrestler, you have to have a certain mentality and you have to be tough. In comparing with other sports —for instance if you are not any good at basketball, a guy will shoot a lay-up over you; or in track, if you get beat by someone, you finish last. But in wrestling, if you are not any good — you get physically beat up for an hour. Trust me, it is not any fun having some guy crank on your head over and over again. So, what happens, the sport weeds out the guys who can't take the intensity. It takes a special person to wrestle, and it also takes a special coach to identify those kids and nurture that attitude.

"Wrestling requires so much more dedication because of cutting weight. It is really tough. Once you are hungry, you drastically increase your stress level in your body, which in turn requires people to function under duress. It literally makes you tougher and more focused. Take football or basketball players and cut them down to 5% body fat and then don't let them eat the day before a game and see how they do — probably not very good. Well, wrestlers have to learn how to do that and how to perform under stress, when they don't physically feel good. Eventually they learn that it is not how you feel, it's what you want to do that counts. In fact, that is the reason why so many Army Rangers and Navy SEALS are former wrestlers, because they are so disciplined. They have already learned how to compete and function at a very high level under pressure with no sleep, no food and in extreme physical exhaustion.

"Overall, I would say that the sport of wrestling is unique though because kids can be individualistic and shoot for individual goals, while also being on a team. Being on a team sport and competing as an individual are both different experiences. Wrestling also gives kids of all sizes an equal opportunity to shine. I mean a kid can grow up playing pee-wee football or basketball, but eventually, if he is only five-foot-four and 120 pounds, he is not going to get the chance to play at the high school level. Now, eight years after perfecting those football or basketball skills, they are limited in the athletic career because he is not tall enough or big enough. Wrestling doesn't exclude anybody, the 120 pounder is just as valuable as the heavyweight, because it is the ultimate team sport. And, it is equal. If you weigh 120 pounds, you compete against kids the same size, which is fair. Then it comes down to conditioning, strength, intelligence and heart. That is pretty cool.

"At the end of the day, I just think that we all need to do our part to grow the sport. Whether that means coaching, volunteering, coming out to meets, or working fund-raisers. It is a grass roots sport and it survives thanks to people who go above and beyond. I would also say to those parents who support the sport while their kids are in it, and follow them up the ladder, that we need is for you too to stick around after they graduate. Otherwise we lose those people as fans, as supporters and as boosters. We all need to do our parts to keep it going and to recruit others to get on board. This is a wonderful sport, our fans are so passionate, I just think it could be even bigger and better if we all tried a little bit harder. That is my challenge to everyone out there.

"Finally, to our supporters, I would just say thank you very much for being there and for caring, I appreciate it. I would also like to say thank you to all the people who stuck by me during the lean years and when things weren't going our way. I think loyalty is a huge issue and I am grateful to our fans who have believed in me and supported me through the years. When you do finally win the big one, it is so special to share that moment with all of those people who have been there for you. I was so proud to share those two wrestling titles with the state of Minnesota and with all of our wrestling fans. For two years they were able to say that they were the best and that was just a great feeling. Seeing their pride and happiness is special and I am so proud to be a part of that. It makes me want to win a lot more of them too."

196

BIBLIOGRAPHY

1. Ross Bernstein: Interviews from over 200 Minnesota sports personalities

2. "55 Years - 55 Heroes" A Celebration of Minnesota Sports, by Ross Bernstein

3. Minnesota State High School League Programs: 1937-2004

4. Kayfabememories.com (Various research articles by Jim Zordani, James Melby, Don Luce, George Lentz, Dave Meltzer, Royal Duncan, Gary Will, Dale Litwaki, Steve Yohe and Steve Slagle.)

5. "What's it all About?," by Max Nichols, Sports Editor, Minneapolis Star, MSHSL Program, 1972.

6. "Paul Wellstone Still Standing Tall After Taking Up Wrestling as Youth," by Bruce Brothers, 1993 State Tourney Program

7. 'Route 66' to Retirement Two Men With 66 Years of Head Coaching Experience on the Road to Retirement, BY Laurie Thieler & Jim Beshey, the editor and publisher of The Guillotine, 1999 State Tourney Program.

8. "Jean among wrestling legends at Albert Lea," By Patrick Reusse, Star Tribune, February 22, 1997.

9. "Apple Valley wrestling family helped coach Wellstone deal with grief," by John Millea, Star Tribune, February 27, 2003.

10. "Inside Out," by Ole Anderson

11. "Hollywood Hulk Hogan," by Hulk Hogan

12. "Wrestling's Bad Boy Tells All," by Bobby Heenan w/Steve Anderson

13. "Have a Nice Day!," by Mick Foley

14. "In the Pit with Piper," by Roddy Piper

15. "Listen You Pencil Neck Geeks," by Freddie Blassie

16. "Brock Lesnar: Lord of the Ring," By Doug Frattallone, Winter 2003

17. "Former Minnesota pro-wrestler finally makes Olympics," by Neal St. Anthony, Feb 19, 2002 Star Tribune.

18. "Grappling with his future," By Wayne Drehs,. June 28, 2004. ESPN.com

19. "Lesnar takes his shot at pro football," by Mark Craig, Star Tribune, May 30, 2004.

20. "Road Warrior Hawk, wrestler, dies at 46," by Richard Meryhew, Star Tribune, October 21, 2003

21. "Iron Man: The Legend of the Road Warriors," by Ervin Griffin Jr., Solie's Newsletter.

22. "Interview with Road Warrior Hawk," by Steve Gerweck, Gerweck.net, 8/1/02.

23. "Wrestling to Rasslin': Ancient Sport to American Spectacle," by George O'Brien.

24. "The Rise and Fall and Rise of the Minnesota Pro Wrestling Scene, by Ray Whebbe Jr.. Pulse of the Twin Cities

25. "Action figure," by Kay Miller, Minneapolis Star-Tribune, May 30, 2004.

26. http://www.baronvonraschke.com/history/

27. AWA History from kayfabememories.com, by Scott Keith

28. "The Champion's Name Is Bockwinkel," by George Schire

29. "The Case for the American Wrestling Association," by Pat Langer, Wrestling Monthly, October, 1971.

30. http://www.kayfabememories.com

31. http://www.canoe.ca/SlamWrestlingReviews/buzz_on_excerpt.html

32. http://www.1wrestlinglegends.com/memories/nwa/nwa79a.html

33. AWA History from kayfabememories.com, by Scott Keith

34. "Grappling for success," By Allen Powell, Pioneer Press, Jul. 28, 2004.

35. http://www.deathvalleydriver.com/Benaka/Sharkey.html

36. "Sharkey Mania," by Mike Mosedale, City Pages, Nov 15, 2000.

37. http://www.deathvalleydriver.com/Benaka/Sharkey.html

38. http://www.harleyrace.com/race_hennig.htm

39. "Paul Wellstone Still Standing Tall After Taking Up Wrestling as Youth," by Bruce Brothers, 1993 State Tourney Program

40. "Bread and Peace," by Will Van Overbeek as told to Vicki Stavig, January 14, 2004.

41. "Acorn to Mighty Oak," by John Matlon, University of Minnesota Dept. of Sport Information, 1969.

42. "Requiem for an Ex-Heavyweight," by Mike Mosedale, City Pages, August 27, 2003.

43. "Augsburg College Wrestling History, "By Don Stoner, Augsburg College Sports Information Coordinator, 2004.

44. "The Oldest Sport," By Bob Dellinger, National Wrestling Hall of Fame

45. "The Magnificent Scufflers," by Charles Morrow Wilson © 1959.

46. "A Pictorial History of Wrestling," by Graeme Kent © 1968.

47. "Wrestling In The USA," By Bob Dellinger, Director Emeritus, National Wrestling Hall of Fame

48. "Changing of the Guard," by Bob Dellinger, Director Emeritus, National Wrestling Hall of Fame

49. HickokSports.com Sports Glossaries, © 2002 Ralph Hickok.

50. "Glossary of Insider Terminology," compiled by Aaron Solomon

51. "Minnesota's wrestling girls fight prejudice to make their mark," by Michele St. Martin, Minnesota Women's Press, Inc. 2004.

52. "New Ulm teen a long shot at Olympics women's wrestling, despite national standing," Jay Weiner, Star Tribune May 21, 2004.

53. "Amateur Wrestling's 5 Styles," by Bruce Gabrielson, Southern Maryland Wrestling Club, www.smwc.org.

54. "Minn. Trivia," by Laurel Winter: Rutledge Hill Press, 1990

55. "NCAA Championships": The Official National Collegiate Championships Records

56. "Scoreboard," by Dunstan Tucker & Martin Schirber, St. John's Press, Collegeville, MN, 1979.

57. "Awesome Almanac Minn" by Jean Blashfield, B&B Publishing, Fontana, WI, 1993.

58. "The Encyclopedia of Sports," by Frank Menke, AC Barnes Pub, Cranbury, NJ, 1975.

59. "My lifetime in sports," by George Barton, Stan Carlson Pub., Minneapolis, 1957.

60. "The Encyclopedia of North American Sports History," by Ralph Hickock, 1992.

61. "Concordia Sports - The First 100 Years" by Finn Grinaker, Concordia Website.

62. "Sports Leagues & Teams," by Mark Pollak, McFarland and Co. Pub, 1996.

63. Minnesota Almanacs - various throughout 1970s

64. "The Husky Tradition: A History of Men's Athletics at St. Cloud State," by John Kasper.

65. "Carleton: the first century," by Leal Headley and Merrill Jarchow, Carelton, 1992.

66. University of Minnesota Men's Athletics Media Guides

67. NCC & NSIC Media Guides: Bemidji State, Moorhead State, UM-Duluth, UM-Morris, Winona State, Southwest State, MSU-Mankato, St. Cloud State

68. MIAC Media Guides: Augsburg, Concordia, St. John's, St. Olaf and St. Thomas

69. NSIC Web-Site & Corresponding Member Web-Pages

70. NCC Web-Site & Corresponding Member Web-Pages

71. MIAC Web-Site & Corresponding Member Web-Pages

72. "HickokSports.com," Web-Site

73. gophersports.com

74. mshsl.com

75. usoc.org

76. National Wrestling Hall of Fame

77. Obsesseswithwrestling.com

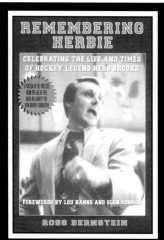

"BATTER-UP!"
CELEBRATING A CENTURY OF MINNESOTA BASEBALL

Minnesota's incredible baseball history comes to life in "Batter-Up! With a Foreword by Harmon Killebrew and an Afterword by Paul Molitor, the book is both entertaining as well as insightful. Featured in it are literally thousands of this past century's greatest professional, minor league, amateur, collegiate and high school teams, along with hundreds of biographies and stories of their star players. From the Twins to the Gophers, and from the Duluth Dukes to the Fargo-Moorhead Red Hawks — its all here. Learn about what it was like to play town team baseball in the old Southern Minny League of the 1950s; or how much fun it must have been to spend a holiday double-header at both Nicollet and Lexington Parks watching the St. Paul Saints and Minneapolis Millers do battle. Not only is there a complete history of the state high school tournament, there are even chapters on Minnesota's MIAC, NSIC and NCC college and university teams as well. In addition, there are also features on the evolution of the women's game, town-ball, the minor leagues, Negro Leagues, American Legion & VFW, Little League and more than 400 pictures to boot. Batter-Up! has captured the pure essence of just what the sport of baseball means to so many of us and pays homage to the countless men and women who have made the game what it is today. From Kent Hrbek to Harmon Killebrew and from Kirby Puckett to Paul Molitor, "Batter-Up!" truly celebrates one of our states greatest treasures — the sport, lifestyle and state-of-mind of baseball.

"HARDWOOD HEROES"
CELEBRATING A CENTURY OF MINNESOTA BASKETBALL

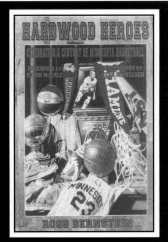

Minnesota's incredible basketball history comes to life in "Hardwood Heroes." With a Foreword by Kevin McHale and an Afterword by Vern Mikkelsen, the book includes more than 500 photos and is truly a blast. Featured in it are literally thousands of this past century's greatest professional, semi-pro, collegiate, and high school teams, along with hundreds of biographies and stories of their star players — all chronicled in one amazing package. From the Lakers to the Gophers, and from the Minnesota Muskies to the Hamline Pipers — its all here. Not only is there a complete history of high school basketball in Minnesota, there is also an exciting year-by-year account of the states vaunted annual high school tourney. There are even chapters on all of Minnesota's college and university teams, as well as on all of the states MIAC, NSIC and NCC schools. In addition, there are features on the evolution of the women's game, the CBA, IBA and so much more! Learn about the Minneapolis Lakers six world championships, Minnesota's two ABA franchises: the Pipers and Muskies, and even what it was like to be a part of the upstart Gophers back at the turn of the century. Hundreds of wonderful stories, along with countless personal memories from the stars themselves dot the canvas of this epic tale. From George Mikan to Whitey Skoog, and from Kevin Garnett to Kevin Lynch, "Hardwood Heroes" truly celebrates one of our states greatest treasures — the sport, lifestyle and state-of-mind of basketball.

"PIGSKIN PRIDE"
CELEBRATING A CENTURY OF MINNESOTA FOOTBALL

Minnesota's football history comes to life in "Pigskin Pride." With a Foreword by Paul Giel and an Afterword by Johnny Randle, the book includes more than 450 photos. Featured in it are literally thousands of this past century's greatest professional, semipro, collegiate, and high school teams, along with hundreds of biographies and stories of their star players — all chronicled in one amazing package. From the Vikings to the Gophers, and from the St. Thomas Tommies to the St. John's Johnnies — its all here. Not only is there a complete history of high school football in Minnesota, there is also an exciting year-by-year account of the states annual Prep Bowl as well. There are even chapters on all of Minnesota's college and university teams, as well as on all of the states MIAC, NSIC and NCC schools. In addition, there are features on the evolution of the women's game, semipro football, arena football and so much more! Learn about the six Gopher National Championships, the four Vikings Super Bowls, and even what it was like to be a part of the upstart NFL back in the 1920s with the old Minneapolis Red Jackets and Duluth Eskimos. Hundreds of wonderful stories, along with countless personal memories from the stars themselves dot the canvas of this epic tale. From Bernie Bierman to Bud Grant, and from Fran Tarkenton to Daunte Culpepper, "Pigskin Pride" truly celebrates one of our states greatest treasures — the sport, lifestyle and state-of-mind of football.

"FROZEN MEMORIES"
CELEBRATING A CENTURY OF MINNESOTA HOCKEY

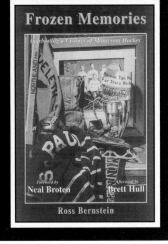

Minnesota's wonderful hockey history comes to life in "Frozen Memories." With a Foreword by Neal Broten and an Afterword by Brett Hull, the book includes more than 300 photos. Featured in it are literally hundreds of this past century's greatest professional, senior and amateur teams, along with countless biographies and stories of their star players. From Roseau to Rochester, and from Warroad to White Bear Lake, its all here. Not only is there a complete history of Minnesota's amazing High School Hockey Tournament, there are also feature chapters on the histories of the North Stars, Fighting Saints, Duluth Hornets, Eveleth Reds, Minneapolis Millers, St. Paul Athletic Club and Warroad Lakers, among others. There are also chapters on nearly all of Minnesota's college and university teams, including the Minnesota Gophers, UMD Bulldogs, St. Cloud State Huskies, Minnesota State, Mankato Mavericks, Bemidji State Beavers, and all of the MIAC schools. In addition, there are chapters on the evolution of the women's game, in-line skating, junior hockey, and so much more. Go back in time to relive the 1981 and 1991 Stanley Cup runs of the North Stars, or feel what it was like to be a part of a Gopher Hockey National Championship, it's all in there. From John Mariucci to Moose Goheen, and from Herbie Lewis to the Hanson Brothers, Frozen Memories truly celebrates one of Minnesota's greatest treasures — the sport and lifestyle of hockey.

ABOUT THE AUTHOR

Ross Bernstein

Best-selling sports author Ross Bernstein grew up in Fairmont, Minn., loving sports and went on to attend the University of Minnesota. It was there where he first got into writing through some rather unique circumstances. You see, after a failed attempt to make it as a walk-on to the University of Minnesota's Golden Gopher hockey team, Bernstein opted instead to become the team's mascot, "Goldy the Gopher." His humorous accounts as a mischievous rodent, back at old Mariucci Arena, then inspired the 1992 best-seller: *"Gopher Hockey by the Hockey Gopher."* And the rest, they say... is history!

After spending the next five years living in both Chicago and New York City with his wife, Sara, working as a marketing executive with a start-up children's entertainment company, Bernstein moved home in 1997 to begin writing full-time. As a full-time sports author Bernstein is truly having a ball and is now working on his 30th book. In addition to writing for local publishers Nodin Press and Lerner Publishing, Bernstein also writes for Triumph, out of Chicago, as well as Enslow and Barnes & Noble Press on the East Coast. Bernstein is also a contributing editor for *Minnesota Hockey Journal* Magazine as well.

Bernstein has been featured as a guest on hundreds of local and national television and radio programs over his career, including: CNN, ESPN, MSG, ESPN radio, FOX Sports Radio, Sporting News Radio and NPR. He has also been the subject of more than 1,000 written reviews in newspapers, magazines and on-line articles over the years too.

On deck for 2005 are several new books including *"The Code,"* which is fascinating behind-the-scenes look at the secret honor code of conduct which governs tough guys, fighting and the rules of retaliation in the National Hockey League. In addition, Minnesota golf, racing and yes, more hockey are all on the plate as well.

Ross, his wife Sara, their two year old daughter, Campbell, and their sock-snarfing Jack Russell Terrier, Herbie, presently reside in Eagan, Minn.

To order additional signed and personalized copies of any of these books, please send a check to the following address:

Ross Bernstein • P.O. Box #22151 • Eagan, MN 55122-0151

*Prices include tax and bubble-packed Fed-Ex Ground or U.S. Priority Mail shipping. Thank you!

SOME MORE OF BERNSTEIN'S BOOKS...

1.) *"Grappling Glory: Celebrating a Century of Minnesota Wrestling & Rassling"* — $35.00
2.) *"Remembering Herbie: Celebrating the Life & Times of Hockey Legend Herb Brooks"* — $25.00
3.) *"Legends & Legacies: Celebrating a Century of Minnesota Coaches"* — $35.00
4.) *"Batter-Up!: Celebrating a Century of Minnesota Baseball"* — $30.00
5.) *"Hardwood Heroes: Celebrating a Century of Minnesota Basketball"* — $30.00
6.) *"Pigskin Pride: Celebrating a Century of Minnesota Football"* — $30.00
7.) *"Frozen Memories: Celebrating a Century of Minnesota Hockey"* — $28.00
8.) *"Fifty Five Years • Fifty Five Heroes: A Celebration of Minnesota Sports"* — $25.00
9.) *"Gopher Hockey by the Hockey Gopher"* — $20.00
10.) *"The Hall: Celebrating the History and Heritage of the U.S. Hockey Hall of Fame"* (Class of 2004) — $20.00
11.) *"Randy Moss: Star Receiver"* [Kids Book — Junior High Reading Level] —$25.00
12.) *"Kevin Garnett: Star Forward"* [Kids Book — Junior High Reading Level] —$25.00
13.) *"Daunte Culpepper: Star Quarterback"* [Kids Book — Junior High Reading Level] — $25.00
14.) *"Barry Bonds: All-Star"* [Kids Book — Junior High Reading Level] — $25.00
15.) *"Gary Payton: Star Guard"* [Kids Book — Junior High Reading Level] — $25.00
16.) *"Shaquille O'Neal"* [Kids Book — 3rd Grade Reading Level] — $25.00

WWW.BERNSTEINBOOKS.COM

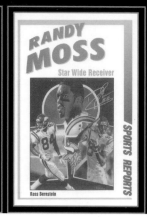
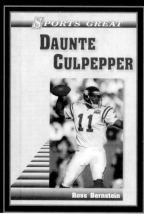
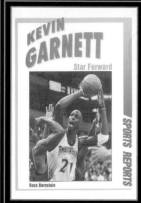